COMPUTER-BASED NUMERICAL & STATISTICAL TECHNIQUES

COMPUTER-BASED NUMERICAL & STATISTICAL TECHNIQUES

M. GOYAL

INFINITY SCIENCE PRESS
INFINITY SCIENCE PRESS LLC
Hingham (Boston), Massachusetts

FIREWALL MEDIA
(An Imprint of Laxmi Publications Pvt. Ltd.)
An ISO 9001:2008 Company
BENGALURU • CHENNAI • COCHIN • GUWAHATI • HYDERABAD
JALANDHAR • KOLKATA • LUCKNOW • MUMBAI • RANCHI • NEW DELHI
BOSTON (USA) • ACCRA (GHANA) • NAIROBI (KENYA)

COMPUTER-BASED NUMERICAL & STATISTICAL TECHNIQUES

Printed and bound in India
Edition : 2008, *Reprint* : 2014, 2016
ISBN : 978-81-318-0362-2

PUBLISHED IN INDIA BY

FIREWALL MEDIA

(An Imprint of Laxmi Publications Pvt. Ltd.)
An ISO 9001:2008 Company
113, GOLDEN HOUSE, DARYAGANJ, NEW DELHI-110002, INDIA
Telephone : 91-11-4353 2500, 4353 2501
Fax : 91-11-2325 2572, 4353 2528
www.laxmipublications.com info@laxmipublications.com

Branches

✆ Bengaluru	080-26 75 69 30
✆ Chennai	044-24 34 47 26
✆ Cochin	0484-237 70 04, 405 13 03
✆ Guwahati	0361-254 36 69, 251 38 81
✆ Hyderabad	040-27 55 53 83, 27 55 53 93
✆ Jalandhar	0181-222 12 72
✆ Kolkata	033-22 27 43 84
✆ Lucknow	0522-220 99 16
✆ Mumbai	022-24 91 54 15, 24 92 78 69
✆ Ranchi	0651-220 44 64

C—10683/015/08

Printed at : Sanjeev Offset Press, Delhi.

CONTENTS

PART 1

Chapter 1 Introduction **3–30**

1.1 Introduction to Computers 4
1.2 Definitions 4
1.3 Introduction to "C" Language 6
1.4 Advantages/Features of 'C' language 7
1.5 'C' Character Set 7
1.6 'C' Constants 8
1.7 "C" Variables 9
1.8 'C' Key Words 10
1.9 "C Instructions" 10
1.10 Hierarchy of Operations 11
1.11 Escape Sequences 12
1.12 Basic Structure of "C" Program 12
1.13 Decision Making Instructions in "C" 14
1.14 Loop Control Structure 17
1.15 Arrays and String 18
1.16 Pointers 19
1.17 Structure and Unions 20
1.18 Storage Classes in 'C' 21

Chapter 2 Errors **31–76**

2.1 Errors and Their Analysis 31
2.2 Accuracy of Numbers 32
2.3 Errors 34
2.4 A General Error Formula 42
2.5 Errors in Numerical Computations 43
2.6 Inverse Problems 46

2.7 Error in a Series Approximation 56
2.8 Mathematical Preliminaries 60
2.9 Floating Point Representation of Numbers 61
2.10 Arithmetic Operations with Normalized Floating Point Numbers 63
2.11 Machine Computation 71
2.12 Computer Software 72

Chapter 3 Algebraic and Transcendental Equations 77—196

3.1 Bisection (or Bolzano) Method 77
3.2 Algorithm 78
3.3 Flow-Chart 79
3.4 Program Writing 80
3.5 Order of Convergence of Iterative Methods 80
3.6 Order of Convergence of Bisection Method 80
3.7 Convergence of a Sequence 81
3.8 Prove that Bisection Method Always Converges 81
3.9 Program to Implement Bisection Method 84
3.10 Iteration Method—(Successive Approximation Method) 94
3.11 Sufficient Condition for Convergence of Iterations 95
3.12 Theorem 95
3.13 Convergence of Iteration Method 96
3.14 Algorithm for Iteration Method 96
3.15 Flow-Chart for Iteration Method 98
3.16 Computer Program 99
3.17 The Method of Iteration for System of Non-Linear Equations 111
3.18 Method of False Position or Regula-Falsi Method 113
3.19 Algorithm 114
3.20 Flow-Chart 116
3.21 Convergence of Regula-Falsi Method 130
3.22 Secant Method 132
3.23 Lin-Bairstow's Method or Method for Complex Root 135
3.24 Muller's Method 141
3.25 Algorithm of Muller's Method 142
3.26 Flow-Chart for Muller's Method 144
3.27 The Quotient-Difference Method 152
3.28 Horner's Method 156
3.29 Newton-Raphson Method 158
3.30 Convergence 159

3.31 Order of Convergence 159
3.32 Geometrical Interpretation 161
3.33 Algorithm of Newton-Raphson Method 161
3.34 Flow-Chart of Newton–Raphson Method 162
3.35 Newton's Iterative Formulae for Finding Inverse, Square Root 163
3.36 Rate of Convergence of Newton's Square Root Formula 164
3.37 Rate of Convergence of Newton's Inverse Formula 164
3.38 Definitions 182
3.39 Methods for Multiple Roots 182
3.40 Nearly Equal Roots 187
3.41 Comparison of Newton's Method with Regula-Falsi Method 189
3.42 Comparison of Iterative Methods 189
3.43 Graeffe's Root-Squaring Method 190
3.44 Ramanujan's Method 195

PART 2

Chapter 4 Interpolation 199–390

4.1 Introduction 199
4.2 Assumptions for Interpolation 200
4.3 Errors in Polynomial Interpolation 200
4.4 Finite Differences 202
4.5 Other Difference Operators 205
4.6 Relation Between Operators 205
4.7 Differences of a Polynomial 207
4.8 Factorial Notation 225
4.9 To Show that (*i*) $\Delta^n[x]^n = n\,!$ (*ii*) $\Delta^{n+1}\,[x]^n = 0$ 225
4.10 Reciprocal Factorial 226
4.11 Missing Term Technique 227
4.12 Method of Separation of Symbols 234
4.13 Detection of Errors by Use of Difference Tables 234
4.14 Newton's Formulae for Interpolation 243
4.15 Newton's Gregory Forward Interpolation Formula 243
4.16 Newton's Gregory Backward Interpolation Formula 262
4.17 Central Difference Interpolation Formulae 278
4.18 Gauss' Forward Difference Formula 278
4.19 Gauss' Backward Difference Formula 289
4.20 Stirling's Formula 301

4.21 Bessel's Interpolation Formula 312
4.22 Laplace-Everett's Formula 327
4.23 Interpolation by Unevenly Spaced Points 338
4.24 Lagrange's Interpolation Formula 339
4.25 Error in Lagrange's Interpolation Formula 357
4.26 Expression of Rational Function as a Sum of Partial Fractions 359
4.27 Inverse Interpolation 360
4.28 Divided Differences 361
4.29 Properties of Divided Differences 362
4.30 Newton's General Interpolation Formula or Newton's Divided Difference Interpolation Formula 363
4.31 Relation Between Divided Differences and Ordinary Differences 364
4.32 Merits and Demerits of Lagrange's Formula 365
4.33 Hermite's Interpolation Formula 381

PART 3

Chapter 5 Numerical Integration and Differentiation 393–476

5.1 Introduction 393
5.2 Numerical Differentiation 394
5.3 Formulae for Derivatives 394
5.4 Maxima and Minima of a Tabulated Function 402
5.5 Errors in Numerical Differentiation 422
5.6 Numerical Integration 423
5.7 Newton-cote's Quadrature Formula 423
5.8 Trapezoidal Rule ($n = 1$) 424
5.9 Simpson's One-third Rule ($n = 2$) 425
5.10 Simpson's Three-Eighth Rule ($n = 3$) 426
5.11 Boole's Rule 426
5.12 Weddle's Rule ($n = 6$) 427
5.13 Algorithm of Trapezoidal Rule 429
5.14 Flow-Chart for Trapezoidal Rule 430
5.15 Program to Implement Trapezoidal Method of Numerical Integration 431
5.16 Output 433
5.17 Algorithm of Simpson's 3/8th Rule 433
5.18 Flow-Chart of Simpson's 3/8th Rule 434

5.19 Program to Implement Simpson's 3/8th Method of Numerical Integration 435
5.20 Output 437
5.21 Algorithm of Simpson's 1/3rd Rule 437
5.22 Flow-Chart of Simpson's 1/3rd Rule 438
5.23 Program to Implement Simpson's 1/3rd Method of Numerical Integration 439
5.24 Output 441
5.25 Euler-Maclaurin's Formula 461
5.26 Gaussian Quadrature Formula 463
5.27 Numerical Evaluation of Singular Integrals 465
5.28 Evaluation of Principal Value Integrals 466

PART 4

Chapter 6 Numerical Solution of Ordinary Differential Equations 479—544

6.1 Introduction 479
6.2 Initial-Value and Boundary-Value Problems 480
6.3 Single Step and Multi-Step Methods 480
6.4 Comparison of Single-Step and Multi-Step Methods 480
6.5 Numerical Methods of Solution of O.D.E. 480
6.6 Picard's Method of Successive Approximations 481
6.7 Picard's Method for Simultaneous First Order Differential Equations 488
6.8 Euler's Method 492
6.9 Algorithm of Euler's Method 493
6.10 Flow-Chart of Euler's Method 494
6.11 Program of Euler's Method 495
6.12 Modified Euler's Method 496
6.13 Algorithm of Modified Euler's Method 497
6.14 Flow-Chart of Modified Euler's Method 498
6.15 Program of Modified Euler's Method 499
6.16 Taylor's Method 506
6.17 Taylor's Method for Simultaneous I Order Differential Equations 508
6.18 Runge-Kutta Methods 513
6.19 Fourth Order Runge-Kutta Method 515
6.20 Runge-Kutta Method for Simultaneous First Order Equations 519

6.21 Predictor-Corrector Methods 525
6.22 Milne's Method 525
6.23 Adams-Moulton (or Adams–Bashforth) Formula 537
6.24 Stability 541
6.25 Stability in the Solution of Ordinary Differential Equations 542
6.26 Stability of I Order Linear Differential Equation of Form $dy/dx = Ay$ with Initial Condition $y(x_0) = y_0$ 542

PART 5

Chapter 7 Statistical Computation 547–670

7.1 The Statistical Methods 547
7.2 Limitation of Statistical Methods 547
7.3 Frequency Charts 548
7.4 Graphical Representation of a Frequency Distribution 550
7.5 Types of Graphs and Diagrams 550
7.6 Histograms 551
7.7 Frequency Polygon 552
7.8 Frequency Curve 552
7.9 Cumulative Frequency Curve or the Ogive 553
7.10 Types of Frequency Curves 553
7.11 Diagrams 555
7.12 Curve Fitting 556
7.13 Principle of Least Squares 556
7.14 Fitting a Straight Line 558
7.15 Algorithm for Fitting a Straight Line of the Form $y = a + bx$ for a Given Set of Data Points 559
7.16 Flow-Chart for Fitting a Straight Line $y = a + bx$ for a Given Set of Data Points 560
7.17 Program to Implement Curve Fitting to Fit a Straight Line 561
7.18 Fitting of an Exponential Curve $y = ae^{bx}$ 569
7.19 Fitting of the Curve $y = ax^b$ 569
7.20 Fitting of the Curve $y = ab^x$ 569
7.21 Fitting of the Curve $pv^r = k$ 570
7.22 Fitting of the Curve of Type $xy = b + ax$ 570
7.23 Fitting of the Curve $y = ax^2 + b/x$ 570
7.24 Fitting of the Curve $y = ax + bx^2$ 571
7.25 Fitting of the Curve $y = ax + b/x$ 572

7.26 Fitting of the Curve $y = a + b/x + c/x^2$ 573
7.27 Fitting of the Curve $y = c_0/x + c_1\sqrt{x}$ 573
7.28 Fitting of the Curve $2^x = ax^2 + bx + c$ 574
7.29 Most Plausible Solution of a System of Linear Equations 586
7.30 Curve-Fitting by Sum of Exponentials 588
7.31 Spline Interpolation 594
7.32 Spline Function 594
7.33 Cubic Spline Interpolation 594
7.34 Steps to Obtain Cubic Spline for Given Data 597
7.35 Approximations 601
7.36 Legendre and Chebyshev Polynomials 601
7.37 Legendre Polynomials 601
7.38 Chebyshev Polynomials 602
7.39 Special Values of Chebyshev Polynomials 603
7.40 Orthogonal Properties 603
7.41 Recurrence Relations 603
7.42 Aliter to Find Chebyshev Polynomials 604
7.43 Expression of Powers of x in terms of Chebyshev Polynomials 604
7.44 Properties of Chebyshev Polynomials 605
7.45 Chebyshev Polynomial Approximation 605
7.46 Lanczos Economization of Power Series for a General Function 606
7.47 Regression Analysis 614
7.48 Curve of Regression and Regression Equation 614
7.49 Linear Regression 614
7.50 Lines of Regression 614
7.51 Derivation of Lines of Regression 615
7.52 Use of Regression Analysis 618
7.53 Comparison of Correlation and Regression Analysis 618
7.54 Properties of Regression Co-efficients 619
7.55 Angle between Two Lines of Regression 620
7.56 Algorithm for Linear Regression 621
7.57 Program to Implement Least Square Fit of a Regression Line of y on x 622
7.58 Program to Implement Least Square Fit of a Regression Line of x on y 623
7.59 Polynomial Fit: Non-linear Regression 639
7.60 Multiple Linear Regression 652
7.61 Statistical Quality Control 654

7.62 Advantages of Statistical Quality Control 656
7.63 Reasons for Variations in the Quality of a Product 657
7.64 Techniques of Statistical Quality Control 657
7.65 Control Chart 658
7.66 Objectives of Control Charts 658
7.67 Construction of Control Charts for Variables 659
7.68 Control Charts for Attributes 661

Chapter 8 Testing of Hypothesis 671—728

8.1 Population or Universe 671
8.2 Sampling 672
8.3 Parameters of Statistics 672
8.4 Standard Error 672
8.5 Test of Significance 673
8.6 Critical Region 674
8.7 Level of Significance 674
8.8 Errors in Sampling 674
8.9 Steps in Testing of Statistical Hypothesis 676
8.10 Test of Significance for Large Samples 676
8.11 Test of Significance of Small Samples 690
8.12 Student's *t*-Distribution 691
8.13 Test I: *t*-test of Significance of the Mean of a Random Sample 692
8.14 Test II: *t*-test for Difference of Means of Two Small Samples (From a Normal Population) 695
8.15 Snedecor's Variance Ratio Test or F-test 703
8.16 Chi-square (χ^2) Test 708
8.17 The χ^2 Distribution 710
8.18 χ^2 Test as a Test of Goodness of Fit 711
8.19 χ^2 Test as a Test of Independence 718

PART 6 APPENDICES

Appendix A (Answers to Selected Exercises) 731

Appendix B (Sample Examination) 743

Appendix C (About the CD-ROM) 747

Index 749

Part 1

- **Introduction**

  Numbers and Their Accuracy, Computer Arithmetic, Mathematical Preliminaries.

- **Errors**

  Errors and Their Computation, General Error Formula, Error in a Series Approximation.

- **Algebraic and Transcendental Equations**

  Bisection Method, Iteration Method, Method of False Position, Newton-Raphson Method, Methods of Finding Complex Roots, Muller's Method, Rate of Convergence of Iterative Methods, Polynomial Equations.

Chapter 1 INTRODUCTION

The limitations of analytical methods in practical applications have led mathematicians to evolve numerical methods.

We know that exact methods often fail in drawing plausible inferences from a given set of tabulated data or in finding roots of transcendental equations or in solving non-linear differential equations.

Even if analytical solutions are available, they are not amenable to direct numerical interpretation.

The aim of numerical analysis is, therefore, to provide constructive methods for obtaining answers to such problems in a numerical form. With the advent of high speed computers and increasing demand for numerical solutions to various problems, numerical techniques have become indispensible tools in the hands of engineers and scientists.

We can solve equations $x^2 - 5x + 6 = 0$, $ax^2 + bx + c = 0$, $y'' + 3y' + 2y = 0$ by analytical methods, but transcendental equations such as $a \cos^2 x + be^x = 0$ cannot be solved by analytical methods. Such equations are solved by numerical analysis.

Methods of numerical analysis are used to approximate the problem satisfactorily so that an approximate solution, amenable to precise analysis, within a desired degree of accuracy is obtained.

To attain a desired degree of accuracy, insight into the process and resulting error is essential.

Consequently, numerical analysis may be regarded as a process to develop and evaluate the methods for computing required mathematical numerical results from the given numerical data.

Three broad steps are incorporated in the process

(*i*) Given data, called input information

(*ii*) Algorithm

(*iii*) The results obtained, called output information.

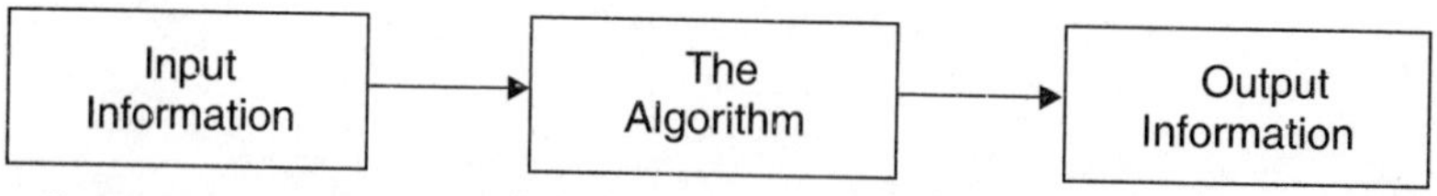

Computers have changed, almost revolutionized, the field of numerical methods as a whole as well as many individual methods. That development is continuing.

Much research is devoted to creating new methods, adapting existing methods to new computer generations, improving existing methods, and investigating stability and accuracy of methods. In large scale work, even small improvements bring large savings in time and storage space.

1.1 INTRODUCTION TO COMPUTERS

The computer is an information-processing and an information-accessing tool. It accepts information or data from the outside world and processes it to produce new information. It also retrieves the stored information efficiency.

Hence, "The computer is an electronic device capable of accepting information, applying prescribed processes to the information, and supplying the results of these processes."

A computer usually consists of input and output devices, storage, arithmetic and logical units, and a control unit.

1.2 DEFINITIONS

Cursor

A position indicator or blinking character employed in a display on a video terminal to indicate a character to be corrected or a position in which data is to be entered.

Algorithm

A finite, step-by-step procedure made up of mathematical and/or logical operations designed to solve a problem is called an algorithm.

Flow-chart

A pictorial or graphical representation of a specific sequence of steps to be used by a computer is called a flow-chart. It is, essentially, a convenient way of planning the order of operations involved in an algorithm and helps in writing a program.

A flow-chart contains certain symbols to represent the various operations . These symbols are connected by arrows to indicate the flow of information. The commonly used symbols with meanings are given below:

1. This oval shaped symbol is used to indicate **'Start'** or **'Stop/End'** of a program. It is also used to mark the end of a sub-program by writing **'Return'.**

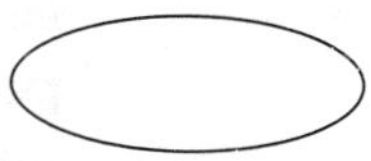

(Terminal point)

2. This parallelogram shaped symbol is used to indicate an input or output of data.

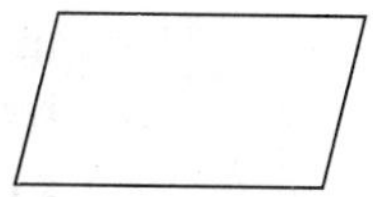

(Input/output)

3. This rectangle-shaped symbol is a processing symbol, *e.g.,* addition, subtraction, or movement of data to computer memory.

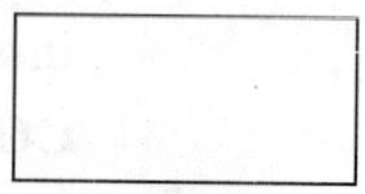

(Processing operation box)

4. This diamond shaped symbol is a decision-making symbol. A particular path is chosen depending on 'Yes' or 'No' answer.

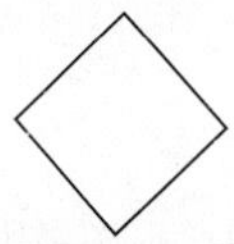

(Decision logic)

5. A small circle with any number or letter in it is used as a connector symbol. It connects various parts of a flow-chart which are far apart or spread over pages.

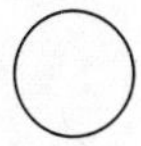

(Connector point)

(Subprocess symbol)

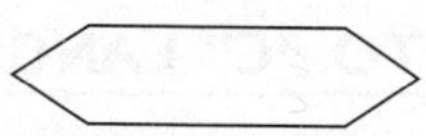

(Subroutine)

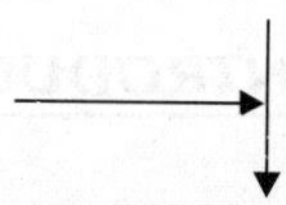

(Connector arrows)

A rectangle with double vertical sides is used to denote a subprocess which is given elsewhere as indicated by connector symbol.

When this box is encountered, the flow goes to the subroutine and it continues till a 'Return' statement is encountered. Then it goes back to main flow-chart and flow resumes onward processing.

The flow-chart can be translated into any computer language and can also be executed on the computer.

PROGRAM. A computer does not have the capability of reading and understanding instructions written in a natural language like English. Thus, it is necessary to express the algorithm in a language understood by the computer. An algorithm coded in a computer language is called a program and the language used for coding is called a programming language.

INSTRUCTION. A single operation to be executed by the computer is called an instruction.

LOGIC. The science that deals with the canons and criteria of validity in thought and demonstration, or the science of the formal principles of reasoning is called logic.

LOOP. A series of instructions or one instruction in a program that is repeated for a prescribed number of times, followed by a branch instruction that exits the program from the loop.

COMPILER. A program designed to translate high level language (source program into machine language object program) is called a compiler.

ASSEMBLER. A machine language program that converts all instructions into the binary format.

LOADER. A program required on practically all systems that loads the user's program along with required system routines into the central processor for execution.

SYNTAX. The set of grammatical rules defining the structure of a programming language is called syntax.

GARBAGE. An accumulation of unwanted, meaningless data after processing of any program is called Garbage.

1.3 INTRODUCTION TO "C" LANGUAGE

In 1960, a number of computer languages had come into existence, among them *COBOL* and *FORTRAN*. A drawback of these languages was that they were only suitable for specific purposes. There was a need for a single computer language that could cater to the needs of different applications uniformly and efficiently.

This led to the formation of an International Committee to develop such a language. The result was a language called *ALGOL 60*. It did not become popular as it was too abstract and too general. Successive refinements on *ALGOL 60* resulted in the birth of language CPL (combined programming language), BCPL, and 'B' language. These languages were again found to be either very big and exhaustive or less powerful. Finally, in 1972, *'Dennis Ritchie'* developed the 'C' language at AT and T Bell Laboratories, USA. He inherited the features of 'B' and BCPL languages and added some of his own in development of 'C' language.

Languages can be classified into two categories:

(*i*) **High level languages** (Problem Oriented Languages). *e.g.,*—FORTRAN, BASIC, PASCAL, etc.

(*ii*) **Low level languages** (Machine Oriented Languages). *e.g.,*—Assembly and machine language.

'C' language was designed to give both a relatively good programming efficiency and a relatively good machine efficiency. Hence 'C' is said to be a Middle level language as it stands between the above two categories.

1.4 ADVANTAGES/FEATURES OF 'C' LANGUAGE

Following are some advantages of 'C' language:

(*i*) Portability

(*ii*) Suitable for low level programming

(*iii*) Fewer Key words

(*iv*) 'C' is a structured language

(*v*) 'C' is a programmers language

1.5 'C' CHARACTER SET

"Character" denotes any alphabet, digit or special symbol used to represent information. The following table shows the valid alphabets, digits, and special symbols allowed in 'C';

Alphabets: A, B, C, ..., Y, Z.

a, b, c, ..., y, z.

Digits: 0, 1, 2, ..., 8, 9.
Special Symbols: ‘–’, ‘–’, + , = , /, \, {}, [ ], < >,?.

The alphabets, digits, and special symbol, when properly combined, form constants, variables, and keywords.

1.6 ‘C’ CONSTANTS

A constant is a quantity that doesn’t change. ‘C’ constants can be divided into two major categories:

(*i*) Primary constants (also called primary data types).

(*ii*) Secondary constants (also called secondary data types).

Primary constants can be of three types:

(*a*) Integer constant

(*b*) Real constant

(*c*) Character constant.

Secondary data types or constants are:

(*a*) Array (*b*) Pointer (*c*) Structure (*d*) Union (*e*) Enum.

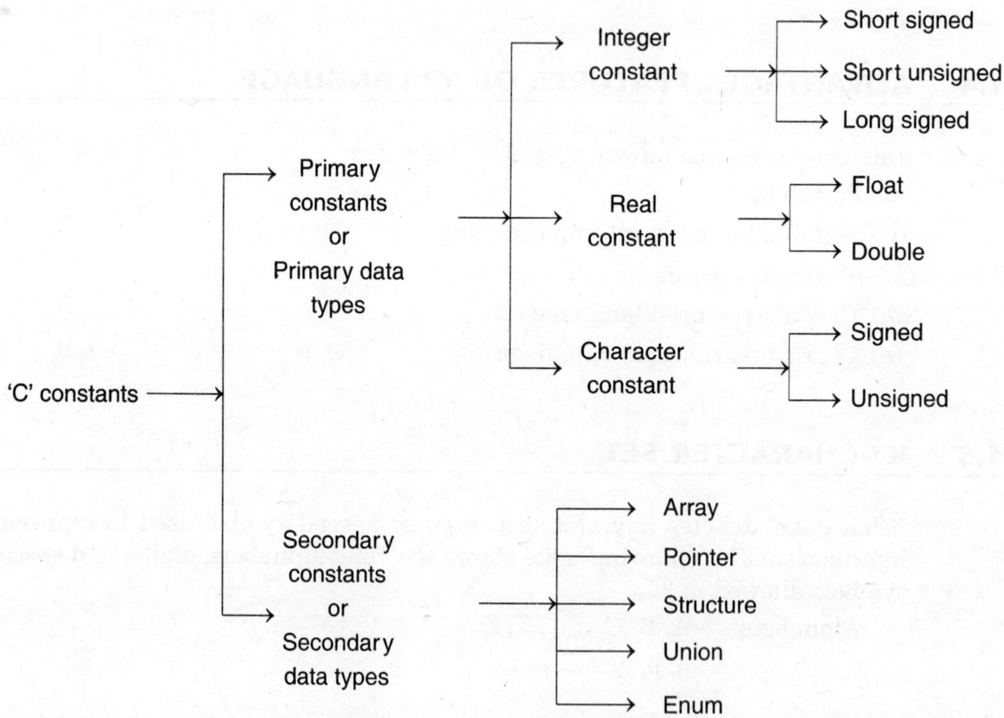

1.6.1 Primary Data Types

Data types	*Byte occupied*	*Range*	*Format*
(*i*) Signed character	One	– 128 to + 127	% C
(*ii*) Unsigned character	One	0 to 255	% C
(*iii*) Short signed integer	Two	– 32768 to + 32767	% *d*
(*iv*) Short unsigned integer	Two	0 to 65535	% *u*
(*v*) Long signed integer	Four	– 2147483648 to + 214748 3647	% *l*
(*vi*) Float	Four	± 3.4 *e* – 38 to ± 3.4 *e* + 38	% *f*
(*vii*) Double	Eight	± 1.7 *e* – 308 to ± 1.7 *e* + 308	% *lf*

1.7 "C" VARIABLES

Suppose we want to find the average of three numbers. The three numbers are the input and the average is the output.

Following are the tasks to be performed by the computer.

1. Read the three numbers.
2. Calculate the average.
3. Output the average.

The computer actually works as follows:

- Reads the three numbers and stores them in three locations of memory.
- Adds the contents of the three locations and divides the result by 3. The result is stored in a fourth location.
- The content of the fourth location is printed as output.

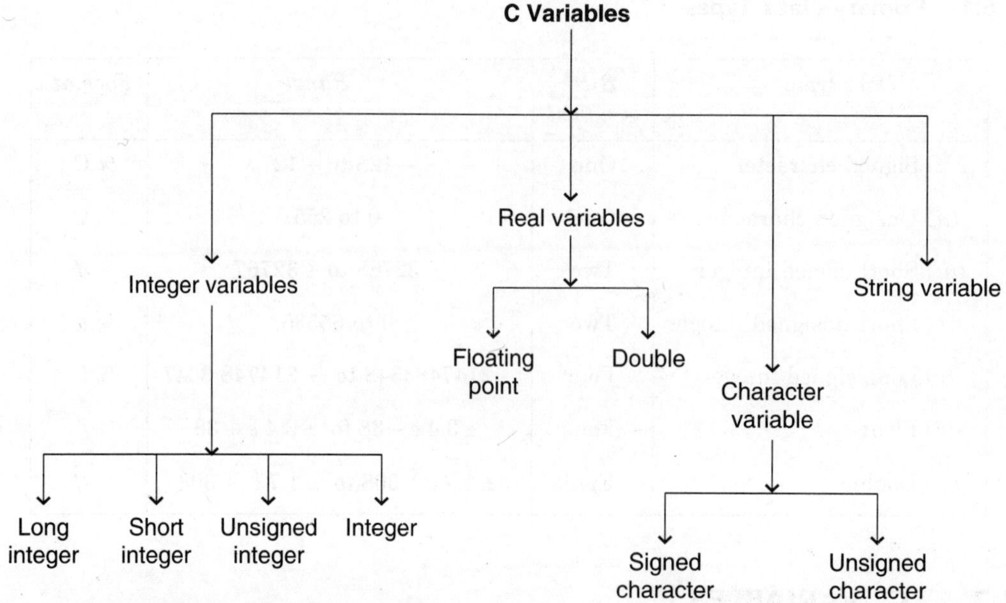

When numbers are stored in various locations of memory, it becomes necessary to name each of the memory locations. The name of the memory location is called **variable.**

Memory locations may contain integer, real, or character constants. Depending upon the data contained in the memory location, the variables are classified as integer, real, character, and string variables.

Secondary variables can be

(*a*) Array variables (*b*) Pointer variables (*c*) Structure variables

(*d*) Union variables (*e*) Enum variables.

1.8 'C' KEY WORDS

Key words (also called reserved words) are an integral part of a language. Their meanings are predefined and hence these words cannot be used as variable names. There are 32 key words in C language.

1.9 "C INSTRUCTIONS"

The constants, variables, and key words are combined to form instructions. Basically, there are four types of instructions in 'C':

(*a*) *Type declaration Instruction:*

e.g.:
```
int bas_sal;
float tot_sal;
char name;
```

(*b*) *Arithmetic Instruction:*

e.g.:
```
int a;
float b, C;
C = a * b;
```
└→ assignment operator.

(*c*) *Input / Output Instruction:*

e.g.:
```
printf (''<format string>'',<list of variables>);
```
<format string> could be

% f — for real values

% d — for integer values

% C — for character values

% S — for printing a string (sequence of character).

(*d*) *Control Instruction:*

Control Instructions specify the order in which the various instructions in a program are to be executed by the computer. They define the flow of control in a program.

There are four types of Control Instructions in 'C'

(*i*) Sequence Control Instruction

(*ii*) Selection or Decision Control Instruction

(*iii*) Repetition or Loop Control Instruction

(*iv*) Case Control Instruction

1.10 HIERARCHY OF OPERATIONS

The order or priority in which the arithmetic operations are performed in an arithmetic statement is called the hierarchy of operations. Hierarchy of operations is given below:

Priority	*Operators*
1.	Parentheses—All parentheses are evaluated first
2.	Multiplication and division
3.	Addition and Subtraction.

1.11 ESCAPE SEQUENCES

In 'C' the backslash symbol (\) is called an escape character.

\t — Tab

\n — New line character takes control to the next line

\b — Backspace character moves the cursor one position to the left of its current position.

\r — Carriage return character takes the cursor to the beginning of the line in which it is currently placed.

\a — Alert character alerts the user by sounding the speaker inside the computer.

1.12 BASIC STRUCTURE OF "C" PROGRAM

A program is defined as a valid set of instructions which perform a given task. Each instruction in C program is written as a separate statement. However big a problem or program is, the following rules are applicable to all 'C' Statements:

(*a*) Blank spaces may be inserted between two words to improve readability of the statement.

(*b*) All statements are usually entered in small case letters.

(*c*) C is free from language, *i.e.*, there is no restriction on position of statements within the program.

(*d*) A 'C' statement always ends with a semicolon (;).

Any 'C' program is a combination of functions. Main( ) is one such function. Empty parentheses after main is a must. The set of statements belonging to a function is enclosed within a pair of braces. For example,

```
main( )
{
      Statement 1;
      Statement 2;
      Statement 3;
}
```

Functions can be of two types:

(*i*) Library functions or Built-in functions or intrinsic functions

(*ii*) User defined functions.

Library functions are those which are available as a part of 'C' language (C Compiler). These can be used by the programmers (users) directly to do a specific task. For example, the input/output operations are performed by a group as functions which belong to a particular set. These sets are called header files in 'C'. The header file is denoted by the file extension *h*.

The following table shows some popular library functions.

S. No.	*Functions*	*Meaning*	*Argument*	*Value*
1.	sqrt (x)	$\sqrt{x}$	float	float
2.	log (x)	$\log_e x$	float	float
3.	abs (x)	$\| x \|$	integer	integer
4.	fabs (x)	$\| x \|$	float	float
5.	exp (x)	e^x	float	float
6.	pow (x, y)	x^y	float	float
7.	ceil (x)	Rounding x to next integer value	float	float
8.	f mod (x, y)	returns the remainder of x/y	float	float
9.	rand ( )	generates *a* (+) ve random integer	—	integer
10.	srand (v)	to initialize the random number generator	Unsigned	—
11.	sin (x)	sin x	float in radian measure	float
12.	cos (x)	cos x	"	"
13.	tan (x)	tan x	float in radian measure	float
14.	toascii (x)	returns integer value to particular character	character integer	integer
15.	tolower (x)	To convert character to lower case	"	character
16.	toupper (x)	To convert character to upper case	character	"

1.12.1. Simple 'C' Program

```
#include<stdio.h>
/*program for average of three numbers*/
main( )
      {
            int a, b, c, d;
            a = 2;
            b = 3;
```

```
        c = 6;
        d = (a + b + c)/3;
        Printf(''% d'', d);
    }
```

In the above C-program, the first line contains a reference to a *header file.* Since any standard program will have some i/o functions, the above statement appears as the first line in every C program.

Library functions of stdio.h are scanf , printf, getchr, putchr, putc, puts.

If we want to use certain mathematical functions then the header file **math.h** is included using statement

```
#include <math.h>
```

Library functions of math.h are cos, cosh, sin, sinh, tan, log, *a* cos, *a* sin, exp.

The second line of the above program is a *comment line.* It can be anywhere in the program and any number of comment lines are allowed. This comment line improves the readability and helps the programmer to understand the program.

The function name main( ) is written next. Function name is always followed by a set of parentheses. Arguments, if any, are placed within the parentheses. The opening brace and the closing brace indicate the beginning and end of the function.

Next the variables are declared as integers. The declaration part must be written as the first part of the function.

Next, a, b, c values are assigned and d is calculated.

In the next line, d is printed using printf function.

The basic rules for a program can be stated as follows:

1. Proper header file must be referred to.
2. There should be one and only one main function.
3. Contents of the function should be enclosed by opening and closing braces.
4. Variables must be declared first in the function.
5. Every C statement except the comment line headlines and function names in a function must end with a semicolon.

1.13 DECISION MAKING INSTRUCTIONS IN "C"

The ability to make decisions regarding execution of the instructions in a "C" program is accomplished using decision control instructions. C has three major decision-making instructions:

(*i*) The if statement;
(*ii*) The if-else statement; and
(*iii*) The switch statement.

(*i*) **The if statement.** The general form (syntax) of this statement is as follows:

if (this condition is true)
  execute this statement;

e.g.,:
```
if (exp > 5)
  {
     bonus = 3000;
     printf ("% d", bonus);
  }
```

(*ii*) **The if-else statement.** The if statement executes a single statement or a group of statements if the condition following if is true. The ability to execute a group of statements if the condition is true and to execute another group of statements if the condition is false is provided by if-else statement.

The general syntax of if-else is as follows:

```
if (condition)
      statement  1;
else
      statement  2;
          or
if (condition)
      {
            statement 1;
            statement 2;
      }
else
      {
            statement 1;
            statement 2;
      }
```

The group of statements after the if, up to and not including the else, is called as if block. Similarly, the statements after the else form the else block.

(*iii*) **Decision using switch.** The control structure which allows decisions to be made from a number of choices is called as switch or switch-case-default. These 3 keywords together make up the control structure.

Syntax is as follows:

```
Switch (integer expression)
      {
            case constant 1;
                  do this;
                  break;
            case constant 2:
                  do this;
                  break;
            default:
                  do this;
      }
```

The integer expression following the keyword switch in any C expression will yield an integer value. The keyword case is followed by an integer or a character constant.

Each constant in each case must be different from all others. The break statement helps in getting out of the control structure.

NOTE *There is no need for a break statement after the default, since the control automatically comes out of the control structure as it is last.*

e.g.,:

```
main( )
      {
            int i = 6;
            switch (i)
            {
            case 1:
                  printf (''This is case 1'');
                  break;
            case 2:
                  printf (''This is case 2'');
                  break;
                  default:
                  printf (''This is default'');
            }
}
```

Points to Remember. (*i*) The cases need not be arranged in any specific order.

(*ii*) It is allowed to use char values in case and switch.

(*iii*) There may be no statements in some of the cases in switch, but they can still be useful.

(*iv*) The switch statement is very useful while writing menu-driven programs.

1.14 LOOP CONTROL STRUCTURE

The process of repeating some portion of the program either a specified number of times or until a particular condition is satisfied is called *looping*.

Three methods of implementing a loop in "C" are:

(*a*) using a *for* statement

(*b*) using a *while* statement

(*c*) using a *do-while* statement.

(*a*) **The for statement.** It is the most popular loop control structure.

General form is as below:

for (initialize counter; test counter; increment counter).

This control structure allows us to specify 3 things about a loop in a single line.

(*i*) Setting a loop counter to an initial value.

(*ii*) Testing the loop counter to determine whether its value has reached the number of repetitions desired.

(*iii*) Increasing the value of the loop counter each time the program segment within the loop has been executed.

e.g.,:

```
for (i = 1; i < = 10; i = i + 1)
                              | i = i + 1 may be written as i++
  printf ("% d", i);
```

o/p = prints values from 1 to 10.

(*b*) **The while loop.** General form is:

```
initialize the loop counter;
while (test of loop counter using a condition)
{
    do this;                 |
    :                        |  Body of while loop
    increment loop counter;  |
}
```

NOTE

(*i*) *The statement within the loop keep on getting executed as long as the condition being tested remains true. As soon as it becomes false, the control passes to the first statement that follows the body of the while loop.*

(*ii*) *The condition being tested may use relational or logical operators.*

(*iii*) *Instead of incrementing the loop counter, it can be decremented also.*

e.g.:
```
int i = 4;
while (i > = 1)
{
        printf ("% d", i);
        i = i - 1;
}
```

(*iv*) *The loop counter need not be of int type, it can be of float type also.*

(*c*) **The do-while loop.** General form (syntax)

```
do
    {
        this;
        and this;
        and this;
    }   while (this condition is true);
```

The difference between while and do-while is that the do-while executes its statements at least once even if the condition fails for the first time itself. The while loop, however, does not execute the statements even once if the condition is false.

The break and continue keywords are usually associated with all three loops, *i.e.*, for, while, and do-while. A break keyword inside the loop takes the control out of the loop, bypassing the conditional test. A continue keyword, on the other hand, takes the control to the conditional test.

1.15 ARRAYS AND STRING

Arrays. An array is a collection of similar elements. These elements could all be ints, or all floats or all charcs, etc. However, there are situations in which it is required to store more than one value at a time in a single variable.

e.g.,: if it is required to arrange the scores obtained by 100 students in a particular subject, then the two following methods can be used.

(*a*) Construct 100 variables to store scores obtained by 100 students in a particular subject.

or

(*b*) Construct a single variable (called as a subscripted variable) capable of holding all 100 values of the students is a particular subject.

A subscripted variable is a collective name given to a group of similar quantities.

e.g.,: scores = {20, 50, 60, 80}

Array declaration. In order to use an array in the program, we need to declare it in order to tell the 'C' Compiler what type and size of array we want.

e.g.,: int scores [100];

An array can be of more than one dimension. The two dimensional array is also called a *Matrix.*

e.g.,: Scores [i] [J];

String. The character arrays are called strings. Character arrays or strings are the data types used by programming languages to manipulate text such as words or sentences. *e.g.*, :

Static character name [ ] = {'A', 'S', 'H', 'I', '\o'};

Static character name [ ] = "ASHISH";

NOTE

(*i*) *The length of the string entered while using scanf should not exceed the size of the character array.*

(*ii*) *Scanf is not capable of receiving multiword strings. Hence, names such as "Mansi Choubey" would be unacceptable. In order to get around this limitation of scanf function, gets ( ) and puts ( ) functions are used.*

```
Syntax: gets (Name);
puts ('' Hello ! ");
```

1.16 POINTERS

When a variable is declared in a program, the compiler does three things

(*i*) Reserves space in memory for this variable.

(*ii*) Associates the name of the variable with the memory location.

(*iii*) If some value is assigned to the variable, this value is stored at this location.

It is possible to find the memory address of a variable using an "address of" (&) operator. If the integer variable i is stored in memory as follows:

Memory location (address)	*Value*	*Location name*
1000	2	i

then its memory address can be printed using a *printf* statement as shown below:

```
printf (''Address of i = % d", and i);
```

Similarly, there is another operator called 'value at address' (*) operator which returns the value stored at a particular address.

```
printf ("value of i = % d", * (& i));
```

1.17 STRUCTURE AND UNIONS

Structures. A structure is a data type which facilitates storage of similar or dissimilar types of information about a particular entity.

all information regarding an employee.

```
struct employee
{
        char name [10];
        int code;
        char address [20];
        char sex;
};
```

The keyword *struct* is used to declare a structure data type.

Union. In 'C', a union is a memory location that is shared by two or more different variables, generally of different types, at different times.

Defining a union is similar to defining a structure.

Its general form is;

```
union union_name
{
type variable_name;
type variable_name;
   :
} union_variables;
```

Example:

```
union item
{
int i;
char ch;
};
```

Unions are useful when:

(*i*) It is required to produce portable (machine independent) code. This is, because the compiler keeps track of actual sizes of the variables that make up the union, so no machine dependecies are produced.

(*ii*) When type conversions are needed because we can refer to the data held in the union in different ways.

1.18 STORAGE CLASSES IN 'C'

In order to fully define a variable, two things are required:

(*i*) The type of the variable

(*ii*) The storage class of the variable.

There are four storage classes provided in 'C'

(*a*) Automatic storage classes (*b*) Register storage classes

(*c*) Static storage classes (*d*) Extern storage classes

EXAMPLES

Example 1. *Draw a flow-chart to find real roots of the equation*

$$ax^2 + bx + c = 0$$

Sol. We know that the roots of quadratic equation $ax^2 + bx + c = 0$ are given by

$$x_1 = \frac{-b + \sqrt{b^2 - 4ac}}{2a}$$

and
$$x_2 = \frac{-b - \sqrt{b^2 - 4ac}}{2a}$$

or
$$x_1 = \frac{-b + \sqrt{d}}{2a},$$

$$x_2 = \frac{-b - \sqrt{d}}{2a}, \text{ where } d = b^2 - 4ac.$$

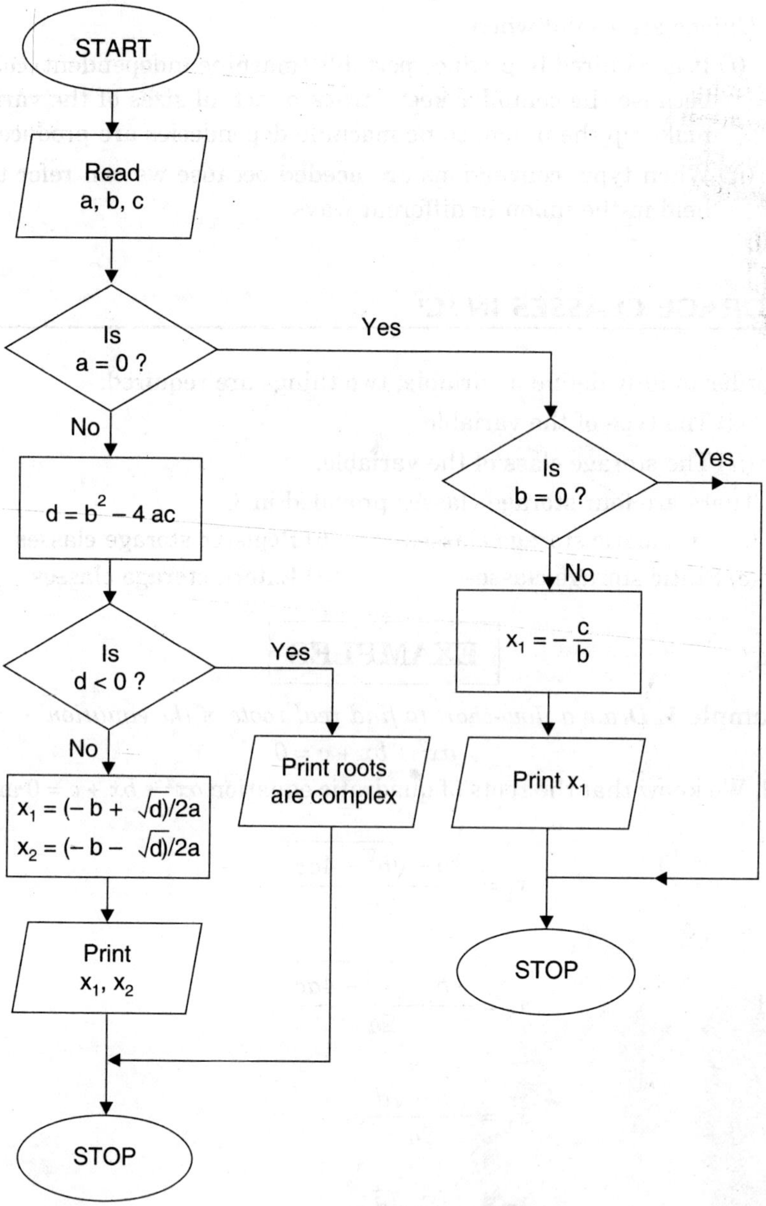
START
Read
a, b, c
Is
a = 0 ?
Yes
No
$d = b^2 - 4ac$
Is
b = 0 ?
Yes
No
$x_1 = -\frac{c}{b}$
Is
d < 0 ?
Yes
No
$x_1 = (-b + \sqrt{d})/2a$
$x_2 = (-b - \sqrt{d})/2a$
Print roots
are complex
Print x_1
Print
x_1, x_2
STOP
STOP

Flow-chart

Example 2. *Develop a flow-chart to select the largest number of a given set of 100 numbers.*

Sol.

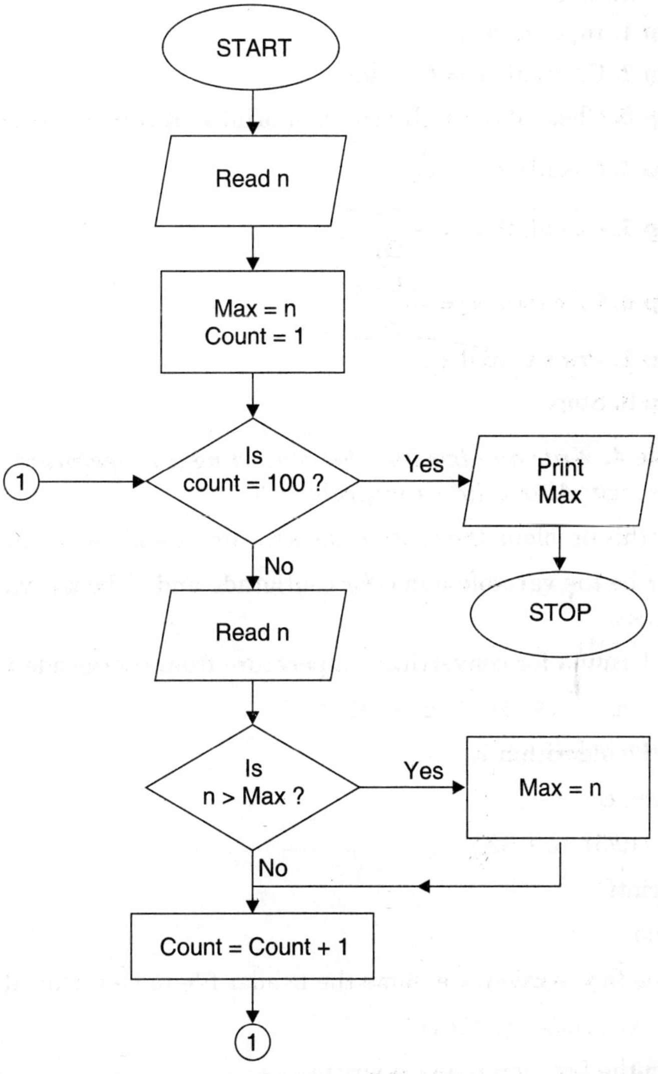

Example 3. *Write an algorithm to find the real roots of the equation* $ax^2 + bx + c = 0$; *a, b, c are real and* $a, b \neq 0$.

Sol. We know that the roots of the equation

$$ax^2 + bx + c = 0$$

are $$x_1 = \frac{-b+e}{2a}, \quad x_2 = \frac{-b-e}{2a}$$

where $e = \sqrt{b^2 - 4ac} = \sqrt{d}$

Algorithm is

Step 1. Input a, b, c.

Step 2. Calculate $d = b^2 - 4ac$.

Step 3. Check if $d < 0$. If yes, then print roots are complex, go to step 8.

Step 4. Calculate $e = \sqrt{d}$.

Step 5. Calculate $x_1 = \dfrac{-b+e}{2a}$.

Step 6. Calculate $x_2 = \dfrac{-b-e}{2a}$.

Step 7. Print x_1 and x_2.

Step 8. Stop.

Example 4. *Write an algorithm for converting a temperature from centigrade to Fahrenheit. Also write its program in 'C'.*

Sol. For this problem, the centigrade is the input and Fahrenheit is the output.

Let c be the variable name for centigrade and f be the variable name for Fahrenheit.

The formula for converting temperature from centigrade to Fahrenheit is

```
f = (9/5) * c + 32
```

So, the algorithm is

1. read c
2. f = (9/5) * c + 32
3. printf
4. end

In the first section, we name the header file to be included.

```
1. # include<stdio.h>
```

Then the function name is written as

```
main( )
```

In the second section, the variables c and f are declared as floating point variables.

2. `float c, f;`

In the third section, reading the values for c, calculating f and printing the value of f takes place.

3. `scanf ("% f ", & c);`

```
f = (9.0 /5.0) * c + 32.0;
printf ("Fahrenheit = % f", f);
```

The complete program is given below:

```
# include<stdio.h>
main( )
{
    float c, f;
    scanf  ("% f", & c);
    f = (9.0/5.0) * c + 32.0;
printf ("Fahrenheit = % f", f);
}
```

The sample output is shown below:

40.0

Fahrenheit = 104.00.

Example 5. *Write a C program to determine the area of a triangle using the formula*

$$area = \sqrt{s(s-a)(s-b)(s-c)}, \text{ where } s = \frac{a+b+c}{2}.$$

Sol. The algorithm is

1. read *a, b, c*
2. $s = \dfrac{a+b+c}{2}$
3. area = sqrt $(s * (s - a) * (s - b) * (s - c))$
4. print area
5. end.

The program is given below

```
# include<stdio.h>
# include<math.h>
main( )
```

```
{
      float a, b, c, s, area;
      printf ("Type the sides a, b, c");
      scanf ("%f  %f  %f", & a, & b, & c );
      s = (a + b + c) /2.0;
      area  = sqrt (s * (s - a) * (s - b) * (s - c));
      printf ("Area = % f ", area);
}
```

Following is a sample output

Type the sides a, b, c

2.0 3.0 4.0

Area = 2.905.

Example 6. *Write a flow-chart to evaluate the sum of the series*

$$1 + x + x^2 + x^3 + \ldots.. + x^n.$$

Sol.

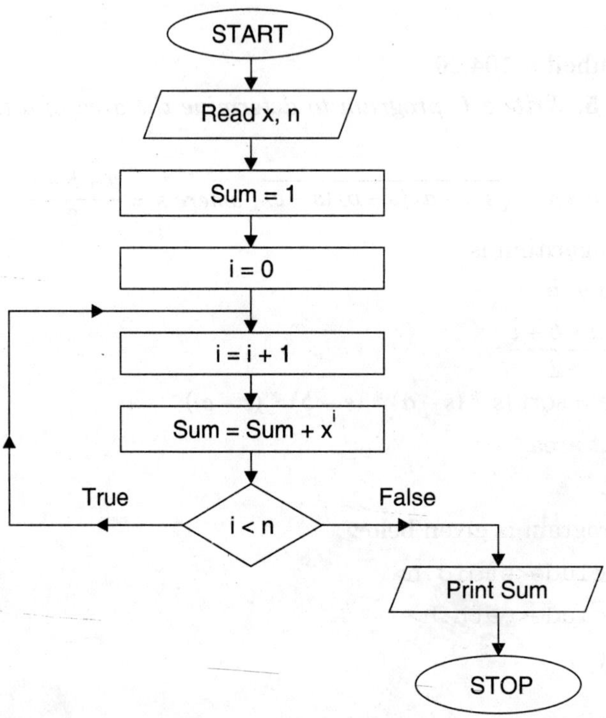

Example 7. *Write a C-program to print all the Fibonacci numbers less than 50.*

Sol. The following are the Fibonacci numbers.

0, 1, 1, 2, 3, 5, 8, 13, ...

The first Fibonacci number is 0. The second Fibonacci number is 1.

Any k^{th} Fibonacci number = $(k-1)^{th}$ Fibonacci number + $(k-2)^{th}$ Fibonacci number

The algorithm is

1. $n_0 = 0$
2. $n_1 = 1$
3. print n_0, n_1
4. $n = n_0 + n_1$
5. if n > = 50 stop
6. print n
7. $n_0 = n_1$
8. $n_1 = n$
9. goto step 4.

For this problem, there is no input.

The C–program is given below:

```
/* Program for Fibonacci Numbers */
# include<stdio.h>
main( )
{
int n, n0, n1;
n0 = 0;
n1 = 1;
printf (''% d \t %d", n0, n1);
step 1: n = n1 + n0;
     if (n > = 50)
     goto end;
else
     { print f ("\ t % d", n);
     n0 = n1;
     n1 = n;
          goto step 1;}
end: printf ("   ");
  }
```

The sample output is

0 1 1 2 3 5 8 13 21 34

Example 8. *Write a C-program to*

(*i*) *print integers from 1 to 10* (*ii*) *print odd numbers from 1 to 10.*

Sol. (*i*)
```
# include<stdio.h>
main( )
{
      int i;
      for (i = 1; i < = 10; i + +)
      printf (''% d\t'' , i);
}
```
The output will be

1 2 3 4 5 6 7 8 9 10

(*ii*)
```
# include<stdio.h>
main( )
{
      int i;
      for (i = 1; i < = 10; i + = 2)
      printf ("%d\t", i);
}
```
The output will be

1 3 5 7 9

ASSIGNMENT 1.1

1. Write a C-program to find the magnitude of a vector $\overline{a} = a_1 i + a_2 j + a_3 k$.
2. State whether the following statements are correct or not:
   (*i*) scanf ("Enter the value of A% d", a); (*ii*) scanf ("%d; %d, %d", & a, & b, & c);
3. Write a C program to solve a set of linear equations with two variables

$$a_1 x + b_1 y = c_1$$
$$a_2 x + b_2 y = c_2$$

$$\left[\textbf{Hint: } \text{Solution is } x = \frac{b_2 c_1 - b_1 c_2}{a_1 b_2 - a_2 b_1}, y = \frac{a_1 c_2 - a_2 c_1}{a_1 b_2 - a_2 b_1} \right].$$

4. Write a C-program to read the principal, rate of interest, and the number of years and find the simple interest using the formula

$$\text{Simple interest} = \frac{\text{PNR}}{100}$$

5. Write a printf statement to print "The given value is 22.23."
6. Give an algorithm and write a program in C to check whether a given number is prime or not.

7. What will be the value of x and the sum after the execution of the following program?

```
        x = 1;
        sum = 0;
    step 1: if (x < 10)
    {
        sum + = 1.0/x;
        x + = 1;
        goto step 1
    }
```

8. Write a program in C to determine whether a number is odd or even. Also, draw its flow-chart.
9. Given a circle $x^2 + y^2 = c$,
   Write a C-program to determine whether a point (x, y) lies inside the circle, on the circle, or outside the circle.
10. Draw a flow-chart for adding marks of 5 subjects for a student and print the total.
11. Write a C-program to print the message CRICKET WORLD CUP-2007 six times.
12. Give any five library functions in "C".
13. Write a program in C to print the following triangle of numbers

```
1
1   2
1   2   3
1   2   3   4
1   2   3   4   5
1   2   3   4   5   6
```

14. Write an algorithm for addition of two matrices of same order.
15. Write a C-program to find the multiplication of two square matrices each of order 2.
16. Write a C-program to find factorial of a given number.
17. Give a flow-chart for finding the determinant of a square non-singular matrix.
18. Write an algorithm for finding the inverse of a square non-singular matrix.
19. What is the maximum length allowed in defining a variable in "C"?
20. Write a C-program to find whether a year is leap year.
21. Develop a flow-chart to select the largest number of a given set of 500 numbers.

Chapter 2 ERRORS

2.1 ERRORS AND THEIR ANALYSIS

2.1.1 Sources of Errors

Following are the broad sources of errors in numerical analysis:

(1) **Input errors.** The input information is rarely exact since it comes from the experiments and any experiment can give results of only limited accuracy. Moreover, the quantity used can be represented in a computer for only a limited number of digits.

(2) **Algorithmic errors.** If direct algorithms based on a finite sequence of operations are used, errors due to limited steps don't amplify the existing errors, but if infinite algorithms are used, exact results are expected only after an infinite number of steps. As this cannot be done in practice, the algorithm has to be stopped after a finite number of steps and the results are not exact.

(3) **Computational errors.** Even when elementary operations such as multiplication and division are used, the number of digits increases greatly so that the results cannot be held fully in a register available in a given computer. In such cases, a certain number of digits must be discarded. Furthermore, the errors here accumulate

one after another from operation to operation, changing during the process and producing new errors.

The following diagram gives a schematic sequence for solving a problem using a digital computer pointing out the sources of errors.

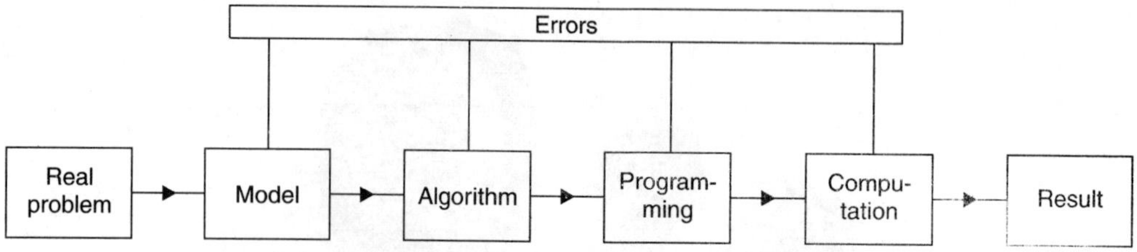

Our effort will be to minimize these errors so as to get the best possible results.

We begin by explaining the various kinds of errors and approximations that may occur in a problem and derive some results on error propagation in numerical calculations.

2.2 ACCURACY OF NUMBERS

(1) **Approximate numbers.** There are two types of numbers: exact and approximate. Exact numbers are 2, 4, 9, $\frac{7}{2}$, 6.45, ... etc. but there are numbers such that

$\frac{4}{3}$ (= 1.333 ......), $\sqrt{2}$ (= 1.414213 ...) and π (= 3.141592......) which cannot be expressed by a finite number of digits. These may be approximated by numbers 1.3333, 1.4141, and 3.1416, respectively.

Such numbers, which represent the given numbers to a certain degree of accuracy, are called approximate numbers.

(2) **Significant digits.** The digits used to express a number are called significant digits.

The digits 1, 2, 3, 4, 5, 6, 7, 8, 9 are significant digits. '0' is also a significant digit except when it is used to fix the decimal point or to fill the places of unknown or discarded digits.

For example, each of the numbers 7845, 3.589, and 0.4758 contains 4 significant figures while the numbers 0.00386, 0.000587, 0.0000296 contain only three significant figures (since zeros only help to fix the position of the decimal point).

Similarly, in the number 0.0003090, the first four '0' s' are not significant digits since they serve only to fix the position of the decimal point and indicate the place values of the other digits. The other two '0' s' are significant.

To be more clear, the number 3.0686 contains five significant digits.

A. The significant figure in a number **in positional notation** consists of

(*i*) All non-zero digits

(*ii*) Zero digits which

(*a*) lie between significant digits;

(*b*) lie to the right of decimal point and at the same time to the right of a non-zero digit;

(*c*) are specifically indicated to be significant.

B. The significant figure in a number written **in scientific notation** (*e.g.,* $M \times 10^k$) consists of all the digits explicitly in M.

NOTE *Significant digits are counted from left to right starting with the non-zero digit on the left.*

A list is provided to help students understand how to calculate significant digits in a given number:

Number	*Significant digits*	*Number of significant digits*
3969	3, 9, 6, 9	04
3060	3, 0, 6	03
3900	3, 9	02
39.69	3, 9, 6, 9	04
0.3969	3, 9, 6, 9	04
39.00	3, 9, 0, 0	04
0.00039	3, 9	02
0.00390	3, 9, 0	03
3.0069	3, 0, 0, 6, 9	05
3.9×10^6	3, 9	02
3.909×10^5	3, 9, 0, 9	04
6×10^{-2}	6	01

(3) **Rounding-off.** There are numbers with many digits, *e.g.*, $\frac{22}{7}$ = 3.142857143. In practice, it is desirable to limit such numbers to a manageable number of digits, such as 3.14 or 3.143. This process of dropping unwanted digits is called rounding-off.

Numbers are rounded-off according to the following rule:

To round-off a number to n significant digits, discard all digits to the right of the nth digit and if this discarded number is

(*i*) less than 5 in $(n + 1)^{th}$ place, leave the nth digit unaltered. *e.g.*, 7.893 to 7.89.

(*ii*) greater than 5 in $(n + 1)^{th}$ place, increase the nth digit by unity, *e.g.*, 6.3456 to 6.346.

(*iii*) exactly 5 in $(n + 1)^{th}$ place, increase the nth digit by unity if it is odd, otherwise leave it unchanged.

e.g., 12.675 ≃ 12.68

12.685 ≃ 12.68

The number thus rounded-off is said to be correct to n significant figures. A list is provided for explanatory proposes:

Number	*Rounded-off to*		
	Three digits	*Four digits*	*Five digits*
00.543241	00.543	00.5432	00.54324
39.5255	39.5	39.52	39.526
69.4155	69.4	69.42	69.416
00.667676	00.668	00.6677	00.66768

2.3 ERRORS

Machine epsilon

We know that a computer has a finite word length, so only a fixed number of digits is stored and used during computation. Hence, even in storing an exact decimal number in its converted form in the computer memory, an error is introduced. This error is machine dependant and is called machine epsilon.

Error = True value – Approximate value

In any numerical computation, we come across the following types of errors:

(1) **Inherent errors.** Errors which are already present in the statement of a problem before its solution are called inherent errors. Such errors arise either due to the fact that the given data is approximate or due to limitations of mathematical tables, calculators, or the digital computer. Inherent errors can be minimized by taking better data or by using high precision* computing aids. Accuracy refers to the number of significant digits in a value, for example, 53.965 is accurate to 5 significant digits. Precision refers to the number of decimal positions or order of magnitude of the last digit in the value. For example, in 53.965, precision is 10^{-3}.

Example. *Which of the following numbers has the greatest precision?*

4.3201, 4.32, 4.320106.

Sol. In 4.3201, precision is 10^{-4}

In 4.32, precision is 10^{-2}

In 4.320106, precision is 10^{-6}.

Hence, the number 4.320106 has the greatest precision.

(2) **Rounding errors.** Rounding errors arise from the process of rounding-off numbers during the computation. They are also called procedual errors or numerical errors. Such errors are unavoidable in most of the calculations due to limitations of computing aids.

These errors can be reduced, however, by

(*i*) changing the calculation procedure so as to avoid subtraction of nearly equal numbers or division by a small number

(*ii*) retaining at least one more significant digit at each step and rounding-off at the last step. Rounding-off may be executed in two ways:

(*a*) **Chopping.** In chopping, extra digits are dropped by truncation of number. Suppose we are using a computer with a fixed word length of four digits, then a number like 12.92364 will be stored as 12.92.

We can express the number 12.92364 in the floating print form as

$$\begin{aligned} \text{True} \quad x &= 12.92364 \\ &= 0.1292364 \times 10^2 = (0.1292 + 0.0000364) \times 10^2 \\ &= 0.1292 \times 10^2 + 0.364 \times 10^{-4+2} \\ &= f_x \cdot 10^{E} + g_x \cdot 10^{E-d} \\ &= \text{Approximate } x + \text{Error} \end{aligned}$$

*Concept of accuracy and precision are closely related to significant digits.

$\therefore$ Error $= g_x \cdot 10^{E-d}$, $0 \le g_x \le d$

Here, g_x is the mantissa, d is the length of mantissa and E is exponent

Since $0 \le g_x < 1$

$\therefore$ Absolute error $\le 10^{E-d}$

Case I. If $g_x < 0.5$ then approximate $x = f_x \cdot 10^E$

Case II. If $g_x \ge .5$ then approximate $x = f_x \cdot 10^E + 10^{E-d}$

$$\text{Error} = \text{True value} - \text{Approximate value}$$
$$= f_x \cdot 10^E + g_x \cdot 10^{E-d} - f_x \cdot 10^E - 10^{E-d}$$
$$= (g_x - 1) \cdot 10^{E-d}$$

absolute error $\le 0.5.(10)^{E-d}$.

(*b*) **Symmetric round-off.** In symmetric round-off, the last retained significant digit is rounded up by unity if the first discarded digit is ≥ 5, otherwise the last retained digit is unchanged.

(3) **Truncation errors**

Truncation errors are caused by using approximate results or by replacing an infinite process with a finite one.

If we are using a decimal computer having a fixed word length of 4 digits, rounding-off of 13.658 gives 13.66, whereas truncation gives 13.65.

e.g., If $S = \sum_{i=1}^{\infty} a_i x_i$ is replaced by or truncated to $S = \sum_{1}^{n} a_i x_i$, then the error developed is a truncation error.

A truncation error is a type of algorithm error. Also,

if $e^x = 1 + x + \frac{x^2}{2!} + \frac{x^3}{3!} + \frac{x^4}{4!} + \ldots\ldots \infty = X$ (say) is truncated to

$1 + x + \frac{x^2}{2!} + \frac{x^3}{3!} = X'$ (say), then truncation error $= X - X'$

Example. *Find the truncation error for* e^x *at* $x = \frac{1}{5}$ *if*

(*i*) *The first three terms are retained in expansion.*

(*ii*) *The first four terms are retained in expansion.*

Sol. (*i*) Error = True value – Approximate value

$$= \left(1 + x + \frac{x^2}{2!} + \frac{x^3}{3!} + \ldots\ldots\right) - \left(1 + x + \frac{x^2}{2!}\right) = \frac{x^3}{3!} + \frac{x^4}{4!} + \frac{x^5}{5!} + \ldots\ldots$$

Put $x = \frac{1}{5}$

$$\text{error} = \frac{.008}{6} + \frac{.0016}{24} + \frac{.00032}{120} + \ldots\ldots$$

$$= .0013333 + .0000666 + .0000026 + \ldots = .0014025$$

(*ii*) Similarly the error for case II may be found.

(4) **Absolute error.** Absolute error is the numerical difference between the true value of a quantity and its approximate value.

Thus, if X is the true value of a quantity and X′ is its approximate value, then | X – X′ | is called the absolute error e_a.

$$e_a = | X - X' | = | \text{Error} |$$

(5) **Relative error.**

The relative error e_r is defined by

$$e_r = \frac{|\text{Error}|}{\text{True value}} = \left|\frac{X - X'}{X}\right|$$

where X is true value and X – X′ is error.

(6) **Percentage error.** Percentage error e_p is defined as

$$e_p = 100\, e_r = 100 \left|\frac{X - X'}{X}\right|.$$

NOTE

1. *The relative and percentage errors are independent of units used while absolute error is expressed in terms of these units.*
2. *If a number is correct to n decimal places, then the error*

$$= \frac{1}{2}\,(10^{-n}).$$

e.g., if the number 3.1416 is correct to 4 decimal places, then the error

$$= \frac{1}{2}\,(10^{-4}) = .00005.$$

3. *If the first significant digit of a number is k and the number is correct to n significant digits, then the relative error* $< \frac{1}{(k \times 10^{n-1})}$.

EXAMPLES

Example 1. *Suppose 1.414 is used as an approximation to $\sqrt{2}$. Find the absolute and relative errors.*

Sol. True value $= \sqrt{2} = 1.41421356$

Approximate value $= 1.414$

$$\text{Error} = \text{True value} - \text{Approximate value}$$
$$= \sqrt{2} - 1.414 = 1.41421356 - 1.414$$
$$= 0.00021356$$

Absolute error $e_a = |\text{ Error }|$

$$= |\ 0.00021356\ | = 0.21356 \times 10^{-3}$$

Relative error $e_r = \dfrac{e_a}{\text{True value}} = \dfrac{0.21356 \times 10^{-3}}{\sqrt{2}}$

$$= 0.151 \times 10^{-3}.$$

Example 2. *If 0.333 is the approximate value of $\frac{1}{3}$, find the absolute, relative, and percentage errors.*

Sol. True value $(X) = \dfrac{1}{3}$

Approximate value $(X') = 0.333$

$\therefore$ Absolute error $e_a = |\ X - X'\ |$

$$= \left|\frac{1}{3} - 0.333\right| = |\,0.333333 - 0.333\,| = .000333$$

Relative error $e_r = \dfrac{e_a}{X} = \dfrac{.000333}{.333333} = .000999$

Percentage error $e_p = e_r \times 100 = .000999 \times 100 = .099\%.$

Example 3. *An approximate value of π is given by 3.1428571 and its true value is 3.1415926. Find the absolute and relative errors.*

Sol. True value $= 3.1415926$

Approximate value $= 3.1428571$

$$\text{Error} = \text{True value} - \text{Approximate value}$$
$$= 3.1415926 - 3.1428571$$
$$= -\,0.0012645$$

Absolute error e_a = | Error | = 0.0012645

Relative error $e_r = \dfrac{e_a}{\text{True value}} = \dfrac{0.0012645}{3.1415926}$

= 0.000402502.

Example 4. *Three approximate values of the number $\frac{1}{3}$ are given as 0.30, 0.33, and 0.34. Which of these three is the best approximation?*

Sol. The best approximation will be the one which has the least absolute error.

True value $= \dfrac{1}{3} = 0.33333.$

Case I. Approximate value = 0.30

Absolute error = | True value – Approximate value |

= | 0.33333 – 0.30 |

= 0.03333

Case II. Approximate value = 0.33

Absolute error = | True value – Approximate value |

= | 0.33333 – 0.33 |

= 0.00333.

Case III. Approximate value = 0.34

Absolute error = | True value – Approximate value |

= | 0.33333 – 0.34 |

= | – 0.00667 | = 0.00667

Since the absolute error is **least** in case II, 0.33 is the best approximation.

Example 5. *Find the relative error of the number 8.6 if both of its digits are correct.*

Sol. Here, $e_a = .05$ $\left(\because\ e_a = \dfrac{1}{2} \times 10^{-1}\right)$

$\therefore$ $e_r = \dfrac{.05}{8.6} = .0058.$

Example 6. *Find the relative error if $\frac{2}{3}$ is approximated to 0.667.*

Sol. True value $= \dfrac{2}{3} = 0.666666$

Approximate value = 0.667

Absolute error $e_a = |\text{ True value} - \text{approximate value }|$

$$= |\ .666666 - .667\ | = .000334$$

Relative error $e_r = \dfrac{.000334}{.666666} = .0005.$

Example 7. *Find the percentage error if 625.483 is approximated to three significant figures.*

Sol. $e_a = |\ 625.483 - 625\ | = 0.483$

$$e_r = \frac{e_a}{625.483} = \frac{.483}{625.483} = .000772$$

$\therefore$ $e_p = e_r \times 100 = .077\%.$

Example 8. *Round-off the numbers 865250 and 37.46235 to four significant figures and compute e_a, e_r, e_p in each case.*

Sol. (*i*) Number rounded-off to four significant digits = 865200

$$X = 865250$$

$$X' = 865200$$

$$\text{Error} = X - X' = 865250 - 865200 = 50$$

Absolute error $e_a = |\text{ error }| = 50$

Relative error $e_r = \dfrac{e_a}{X} = \dfrac{50}{865250} = 5.77 \times 10^{-5}$

Percentage error $e_p = e_r \times 100 = 5.77 \times 10^{-3}$

(*ii*) Number rounded-off to four significant digits = 37.46

$$X = 37.46235$$

$$X' = 37.46$$

$$\text{Error} = X - X' = 0.00235$$

Absolute error $e_a = |\text{ error }| = 0.00235$

Relative error $e_r = \dfrac{e_a}{X} = \dfrac{0.00235}{37.46235}$

$$= 6.2729 \times 10^{-5}$$

Percentage error $e_p = e_r \times 100 = 6.2729 \times 10^{-3}.$

Example 9. *Round-off the number 75462 to four significant digits and then calculate the absolute error and percentage error.*

Sol. Number rounded-off to four significant digits = 75460

Absolute error $e_a = |\ 75462 - 75460\ | = 2$

Relative error $e_r = \dfrac{e_a}{75462} = \dfrac{2}{75462} = .0000265$

Percentage error $e_p = e_r \times 100 = .00265.$

Example 10. *Find the absolute, relative, and percentage errors if x is rounded-off to three decimal digits. Given x = 0.005998.*

Sol. Number rounded-off to three decimal digits =.006

Error $= .005998 - .006 = - .000002$

Absolute error $e_a = |\ \text{error}\ | = .000002$

Relative error $e_r = \dfrac{e_a}{.005998} = \dfrac{.000002}{.005998} = .0033344$

Percentage error $e_p = e_r \times 100 = .33344.$

Example 11. *Evaluate the sum* $S = \sqrt{3} + \sqrt{5} + \sqrt{7}$ *to 4 significant digits and find its absolute and relative errors.*

Sol. $\sqrt{3} = 1.732, \quad \sqrt{5} = 2.236, \quad \sqrt{7} = 2.646$

Hence, $S = 6.614$

and $e_a = .0005 + .0005 + .0005 = .0015.$

The total absolute error shows that the sum is correct to 3 significant figures only.

$\therefore$ We take, $S = 6.61$

then, $e_r = \dfrac{.0015}{6.61} = 0.0002.$

Example 12. *It is necessary to obtain the roots of* $X^2 - 2X + \log_{10} 2 = 0$ *to four decimal places. To what accuracy should* $\log_{10} 2$ *be given?*

Sol. Roots of $X^2 - 2X + \log_{10} 2 = 0$ are given by

$$X = \frac{2 \pm \sqrt{4 - 4\log_{10} 2}}{2} = 1 \pm \sqrt{1 - \log_{10} 2}$$

$$\therefore \quad |\ \Delta X\ | = \frac{1}{2} \frac{\Delta(\log 2)}{\sqrt{1 - \log 2}} < 0.5 \times 10^{-4}$$

or $\Delta(\log 2) < 2 \times .5 \times 10^{-4} (1 - \log 2)^{1/2} < .83604 \times 10^{-4} \approx 8.3604 \times 10^{-5}.$

ASSIGNMENT 2.1

1. Round-off the following numbers correct to four significant digits:

3.26425, 35.46735, 4985561, 0.70035, 0.00032217, 1.6583, 30.0567, 0.859378, 3.14159.

2. The height of an observation tower was estimated to be 47 m. whereas its actual height was 45 m. Calculate the percentage of relative error in the measurement.

3. If the number p is correct to three decimal places, what will be the error?

4. If true value = $\frac{10}{3}$, approximate value = 3.33, find the absolute and relative errors.

5. Round-off the following numbers to two decimal places.

48.21416, 2.3742, 52.275, 2.375, 2.385, 81.255.

6. Calculate the value of $\sqrt{102} - \sqrt{101}$ correct to four significant digits.

7. If X = 2.536, find the absolute error and relative error when

(*i*) X is rounded-off

(*ii*) X is truncated to two decimal digits.

8. If $\pi = \frac{22}{7}$ is approximated as 3.14, find the absolute error, relative error, and percentage of relative error.

9. Given the solution of a problem as X′ = 35.25 with the relative error in the solution atmost 2%, find, to four decimal digits, the range of values within which the exact value of the solution must lie.

10. Given that:

$$a = 10.00 \pm 0.05,\ b = 0.0356 \pm 0.0002$$

$$c = 15300 \pm 100,\ d = 62000 \pm 500$$

Find the maximum value of the absolute error in

(*i*) $a + b + c + d$ (*ii*) $a + 5c - d$ (*iii*) d^3.

11. What do you understand by machine epsilon of a computer? Explain.

12. What do you mean by truncation error? Explain with examples.

2.4 A GENERAL ERROR FORMULA

Let $y = f(x_1, x_2)$ be a function of two variables x_1, x_2.

Let $\delta x_1, \delta x_2$ be the errors in x_1, x_2, then the error δy in y is given by

$$y + \delta y = f(x_1 + \delta x_1, x_2 + \delta x_2)$$

Expanding R.H.S. by Taylor's series, we get

$$y + \delta y = f(x_1, x_2) + \left(\frac{\partial f}{\partial x_1}\delta x_1 + \frac{\partial f}{\partial x_2}\delta x_2\right)$$

$$+ \text{ terms involving higher powers of } \delta x_1 \text{ and } \delta x_2 \qquad (1)$$

If the errors δx_1, δx_2 are so small that their squares and higher powers can be neglected, then (1) gives

$$\delta y = \frac{\partial f}{\partial x_1}\delta x_1 + \frac{\partial f}{\partial x_2}\delta x_2 \text{ approximately}$$

Hence, $$\delta y = \frac{\partial y}{\partial x_1}\delta x_1 + \frac{\partial y}{\partial x_2}\delta x_2$$

In general, the error δy in the function

$$y = f(x_1, x_2, \ldots\ldots, x_n)$$

corresponding to the errors δx_i in x_i $(i = 1, 2, \ldots\ldots, n)$ is given by

$$\delta y \approx \frac{\partial y}{\partial x_1}\delta x_1 + \frac{\partial y}{\partial x_2}\delta x_2 + \ldots\ldots + \frac{\partial y}{\partial x_n}\delta x_n$$

and the relative error in y is

$$e_r = \frac{\delta y}{y} = \frac{\partial y}{\partial x_1}\cdot\frac{\delta x_1}{y} + \frac{\partial y}{\partial x_2}\cdot\frac{\delta x_2}{y} + \ldots\ldots + \frac{\partial y}{\partial x_n}\cdot\frac{\delta x_n}{y}.$$

2.5 ERRORS IN NUMERICAL COMPUTATIONS

(1) **Error in addition of numbers**

Let $$X = x_1 + x_2 + \ldots\ldots + x_n$$

$$\therefore \quad X + \Delta X = (x_1 + \Delta x_1) + (x_2 + \Delta x_2) + \ldots\ldots + (x_n + \Delta x_n)$$

The absolute error is

$$\therefore \quad \Delta X = \Delta x_1 + \Delta x_2 + \ldots\ldots + \Delta x_n$$

$$\Rightarrow \quad \frac{\Delta X}{X} = \frac{\Delta x_1}{X} + \frac{\Delta x_2}{X} + \ldots\ldots + \frac{\Delta x_n}{X}$$

which is the relative error.

The maximum relative error is

$$\left|\frac{\Delta X}{X}\right| \le \left|\frac{\Delta x_1}{X}\right| + \left|\frac{\Delta x_2}{X}\right| + \ldots\ldots + \left|\frac{\Delta x_n}{X}\right|.$$

It is clear that if two numbers are added then the magnitude of absolute error in the result is the sum of the magnitudes of the absolute errors in the two numbers.

NOTE *While adding up several numbers of different absolute accuracies, the following procedure is adopted:*

(i) Isolate the number with the greatest absolute error.

(ii) Round-off all other numbers, retaining in them one digit more than in the isolated number.

(iii) Add up.

(iv) Round-off the sum by discarding one digit.

(2) **Error in subtraction of numbers**

Let $$X = x_1 - x_2$$

$\therefore$ $$X + \Delta X = (x_1 + \Delta x_1) - (x_2 + \Delta x_2)$$

$$= (x_1 - x_2) + (\Delta x_1 - \Delta x_2)$$

$\therefore$ $$\Delta X = \Delta x_1 - \Delta x_2 \text{ is the absolute error}$$

and $$\frac{\Delta X}{X} = \frac{\Delta x_1}{X} - \frac{\Delta x_2}{X} \text{ is the relative error.}$$

The maximum relative error $$= \left|\frac{\Delta X}{X}\right| \le \left|\frac{\Delta x_1}{X}\right| + \left|\frac{\Delta x_2}{X}\right|$$

and The maximum absolute error = $| \Delta X | \le | \Delta x_1 | + | \Delta x_2 |$.

(3) **Error in product of numbers**

Let $$X = x_1\, x_2 \,......,\, x_n$$

We know that if X is a function of $x_1, x_2, ..., x_n$

then, $$\Delta X = \frac{\partial X}{\partial x_1}\Delta x_1 + \frac{\partial X}{\partial x_2}\Delta x_2 + ... + \frac{\partial X}{\partial x_n}\Delta x_n$$

Now, $$\frac{\Delta X}{X} = \frac{1}{X}\frac{\partial X}{\partial x_1}\Delta x_1 + \frac{1}{X}\frac{\partial X}{\partial x_2}\Delta x_2 + ... + \frac{1}{X}\frac{\partial X}{\partial x_n}\Delta x_n$$

Now, $$\frac{1}{X}\frac{\partial X}{\partial x_1} = \frac{x_2 . x_3 \ldots\ldots x_n}{x_1 x_2 x_3 \ldots\ldots x_n} = \frac{1}{x_1}$$

$$\frac{1}{X}\frac{\partial X}{\partial x_2} = \frac{x_1 x_3 \ldots\ldots x_n}{x_1 x_2 x_3 \ldots\ldots x_n} = \frac{1}{x_2}$$

$$\vdots \qquad \vdots$$

$$\frac{1}{X}\frac{\partial X}{\partial x_n} = \frac{1}{x_n}$$

$\therefore$ $$\frac{\Delta X}{X} = \frac{\Delta x_1}{x_1} + \frac{\Delta x_2}{x_2} + \ldots\ldots + \frac{\Delta x_n}{x_n}.$$

$\therefore$ The relative and absolute errors are given by,

Maximum relative error $= \left|\frac{\Delta X}{X}\right| \le \left|\frac{\Delta x_1}{x_1}\right| + \left|\frac{\Delta x_2}{x_2}\right| + \ldots\ldots + \left|\frac{\Delta x_n}{x_n}\right|$

Maximum absolute error $= \left|\frac{\Delta X}{X}\right| X = \left|\frac{\Delta X}{X}\right| . (x_1 x_2 x_3 \ldots\ldots x_n)$

(4) **Error in division of numbers**

Let, $$X = \frac{x_1}{x_2}$$

$\therefore$ $$\frac{\Delta X}{X} = \frac{1}{X}\frac{\partial X}{\partial x_1}\Delta x_1 + \frac{1}{X} . \frac{\partial X}{\partial x_2} . \Delta x_2$$

$$= \frac{\Delta x_1}{\left(\frac{x_1}{x_2}\right)} . \frac{1}{x_2} + \frac{\Delta x_2}{\left(\frac{x_1}{x_2}\right)}\left(\frac{-x_1}{x_2^{\,2}}\right) = \frac{\Delta x_1}{x_1} - \frac{\Delta x_2}{x_2}$$

$\therefore$ $$\left|\frac{\Delta X}{X}\right| \le \left|\frac{\Delta x_1}{x_1}\right| + \left|\frac{\Delta x_2}{x_2}\right|$$ which is relative error.

Absolute error $= |\ \Delta X\ | \le \left|\frac{\Delta X}{X}\right| . X.$

(5) **Error in evaluating x^k**

$$X = x^k, \quad \text{where } k \text{ is an integer or fraction}$$

$$\Delta X = \frac{dX}{dx}\Delta x = kx^{k-1}.\Delta x$$

$$\frac{\Delta X}{X} = k.\frac{\Delta x}{x}$$

$$\therefore \quad \left|\frac{\Delta X}{X}\right| \le k.\frac{\Delta x}{x}$$

The relative error in evaluating $x^k = k.\left|\frac{\Delta x}{x}\right|$.

2.6 INVERSE PROBLEMS

Now we have to find errors in $x_1, x_2, ..., x_n$, where $X = f(x_1, x_2, ..., x_n)$, to have a desired accuracy.

We have $$\Delta X = \frac{\partial X}{\partial x_1}\Delta x_1 + \frac{\partial X}{\partial x_2}\Delta x_2 + ... + \frac{\partial X}{\partial x_n}\Delta x_n$$

According to the principle of equal effects,

$$\frac{\partial X}{\partial x_1}\Delta x_1 = \frac{\partial X}{\partial x_2}\Delta x_2 = ... = \frac{\partial X}{\partial x_n}\Delta x_n$$

$$\therefore \quad \Delta X = n\frac{\partial X}{\partial x_1}\Delta x_1$$

$$\therefore \quad \Delta x_1 = \frac{\Delta X}{n\left(\frac{\partial X}{\partial x_1}\right)}$$

Similarly, $$\Delta x_2 = \frac{\Delta X}{n\frac{\partial X}{\partial x_2}} \text{ and so on.}$$

NOTE *The above article is needed when we are to find errors in both independent variables involved and error in dependent variable is given.*

EXAMPLES

Example 1. *If* $u = \dfrac{4x^2y^3}{z^4}$ *and errors in x, y, z be 0.001, compute the relative maximum error in u when* $x = y = z = 1$.

Sol.
$$\delta u = \frac{\partial u}{\partial x}\delta x + \frac{\partial u}{\partial y}\delta y + \frac{\partial u}{\partial z}\delta z$$
$$= \frac{8x\,y^3}{z^4}\delta x + \frac{12x^2y^2}{z^4}\delta y - \frac{16x^2y^3}{z^5}\delta z$$

Since the errors δx, δy, δz may be (+) ve or (–) ve, we take the absolute values of terms on R.H.S. giving,

$$(\delta u)_{\text{max.}} = \left|\frac{8xy^3}{z^4}\delta x\right| + \left|\frac{12x^2y^2}{z^4}\delta y\right| + \left|\frac{16x^2y^3}{z^5}\delta z\right|$$
$$= 8(.001) + 12(.001) + 16(.001) = 0.036$$

$$\therefore \quad \text{Maximum relative error} = \frac{.036}{4} = .009.$$

Example 2. *Find the relative error in the function*

$$y = ax_1^{m_1}x_2^{m_2} \ldots\ldots x_n^{m_n}.$$

Sol. We have $\quad \log y = \log a + m_1 \log x_1 + m_2 \log x_2 + \ldots\ldots + m_n \log x_n$

$$\therefore \quad \frac{1}{y}\left(\frac{\partial y}{\partial x_1}\right) = \frac{m_1}{x_1} = \frac{1}{y}\frac{\partial y}{\partial x_2} = \frac{m_2}{x_2}, \ldots\ldots \text{etc.}$$

$$\therefore \quad e_r = \frac{\partial y}{\partial x_1}\cdot\frac{\delta x_1}{y} + \frac{\partial y}{\partial x_2}\cdot\frac{\delta x_2}{y} + \ldots\ldots + \frac{\partial y}{\partial x_n}\cdot\frac{\delta x_n}{y}$$
$$= m_1\frac{\delta x_1}{x_1} + \frac{m_2}{x_2}\delta x_2 + \ldots\ldots + m_n \cdot \frac{\delta x_n}{x_n}$$

Since errors δx_1, δx_2 may be (+) ve or (–) ve we take the absolute values of terms on R.H.S.

This gives,

$$(e_r)_{\text{max.}} \le m_1\left|\frac{\delta x_1}{x_1}\right| + m_2\left|\frac{\delta x_2}{x_2}\right| + \ldots\ldots + m_n\left|\frac{\delta x_n}{x_n}\right|.$$

Corollary. If $$y = x_1 x_2 \ldots\ldots, x_n$$

$$e_r \approx \frac{\delta x_1}{x_1} + \frac{\delta x_2}{x_2} + \ldots\ldots + \frac{\delta x_n}{x_n}$$

$\therefore$ The relative error of a product of n numbers is approximately equal to the algebraic sum of their relative errors.

Example 3. *Compute the percentage error in the time period* $T = 2\pi \sqrt{\frac{l}{g}}$ *for* $l = 1$ *m if the error in the measurement of* l *is 0.01.*

Sol. $$T = 2\pi \sqrt{\frac{l}{g}}$$

Taking log

$$\log T = \log 2\pi + \frac{1}{2} \log l - \frac{1}{2} \log g$$

$$\Rightarrow \qquad \frac{1}{T} \delta T = \frac{1}{2} \frac{\delta l}{l}$$

$$\frac{\delta T}{T} \times 100 = \frac{\delta l}{2l} \times 100 = \frac{.01}{2 \times 1} \times 100 = 0.5\% .$$

Example 4. *If* $u = 2\,V^6 - 5V$*, find the percentage error in u at* $V = 1$ *if error in V is .05.*

Sol. $$u = 2V^6 - 5V$$

$$\delta u = \frac{\partial u}{\partial V} \delta V = (12\,V^5 - 5)\,\delta V$$

$$\frac{\delta u}{u} \times 100 = \left(\frac{12V^5 - 5}{2V^6 - 5V}\right) . \delta V \times 100$$

$$= \frac{(12 - 5)}{(2 - 5)} \times (.05) \times 100 = -\frac{7}{3} \times 5 = -\,11.667\%$$

The maximum percentage error = 11.667%.

Example 5. *If* $r = 3h(h^6 - 2)$*, find the percentage error in r at* $h = 1$*, if the percentage error in h is 5.*

Sol. $$\delta r = \frac{\partial r}{\partial h} \delta h = (21h^6 - 6)\,\delta h$$

$$\frac{\delta r}{r} \times 100 = \left(\frac{21h^6 - 6}{3h^7 - 6h}\right) \delta h \times 100$$

$$= \left(\frac{21-6}{3-6}\right)\left(\frac{\delta h}{h} \times 100\right) = \frac{15}{(-3)} . 5\% = -25\%$$

Percentage error $= \left| \frac{\delta r}{r} \times 100 \right| = 25\%.$

Example 6. *The discharge Q over a notch for head H is calculated by the formula $Q = kH^{5/2}$, where k is a given constant. If the head is 75 cm and an error of 0.15 cm is possible in its measurement, estimate the percentage error in computing the discharge.*

Sol. $$Q = kH^{5/2}$$

$$\log Q = \log k + \frac{5}{2} \log H$$

Differentiating, $$\frac{\delta Q}{Q} = \frac{5}{2} . \frac{\delta H}{H}$$

$$\frac{\delta Q}{Q} \times 100 = \frac{5}{2} \times \frac{0.15}{75} \times 100 = \frac{1}{2} = 0.5 .$$

Example 7. *The error in the measurement of the area of a circle is not allowed to exceed 0.1%. How accurately should the diameter be measured?*

Sol. $$A = \pi \frac{d^2}{4}$$

$$\log A = \log \pi + 2 \log d - \log 4$$

$$\frac{\delta A}{A} \times 100 = \frac{2}{d} (\delta d \times 100)$$

$$\frac{\delta d}{d} \times 100 = \frac{0.1}{2} = .05 .$$

Example 8. (*i*) *Prove that the absolute error in the common logarithm of a number is less than half the relative error of the given number.*

(*ii*) *Prove that the error in the antilogarithm is many times the error in the logarithm.*

Sol. (*i*) $$N = \log_{10} x = .43429 \log_e x$$

Hence, $$\Delta N = 0.43429 \frac{\Delta x}{x} < \frac{1}{2}\left(\frac{\Delta x}{x}\right).$$

(*ii*) From (*i*), $\Delta x = \dfrac{x\,\Delta N}{0.43429} = 2.3026\,x(\Delta N).$

Example 9. *Find the smaller root of the equation $x^2 - 32x + 1 = 0$ correct to four significant figures.*

Sol. The roots of the equation $x^2 - 32x + 1 = 0$ are

$$\frac{32 - \sqrt{(32)^2 - 4}}{2} \quad \text{and} \quad \frac{32 + \sqrt{(32)^2 - 4}}{2}$$

The smaller root is $\dfrac{32 - \sqrt{1020}}{2} = 16 - \sqrt{255}$

I Algorithm. Smaller root $= 16 - \sqrt{255} = 16 - 15.97 = 0.03$

II Algorithm. Smaller root

$$= (16 - \sqrt{255})\,.\,\frac{16 + \sqrt{255}}{16 + \sqrt{255}} = \frac{1}{16 + 15.97} = \frac{1}{31.97} = 0.0313$$

The second algorithm is evidently a better one, as gives the result correct to 4 figures.

Example 10. *If $X = x + e$, prove that $\sqrt{X} - \sqrt{x} \approx \dfrac{e}{2\sqrt{X}}$.*

Sol. $\sqrt{X} - \sqrt{x} = \sqrt{X} - \sqrt{X - e} = \sqrt{X} - \sqrt{X}\left(1 - \dfrac{e}{X}\right)^{1/2} = \sqrt{X} - \sqrt{X}\left(1 - \dfrac{e}{2X}\right)$

$$= \sqrt{X} - \sqrt{X} + \frac{e}{2\sqrt{X}} \approx \frac{e}{2\sqrt{X}}.$$

Example 11. *In a ΔABC, $a = 6$ cm, $c = 15$ cm, $\angle B = 90°$. Find the possible error in the computed value of A if the errors in measurements of a and c are 1 mm and 2 mm respectively.*

Sol. Here, $\tan A = \dfrac{a}{c}$

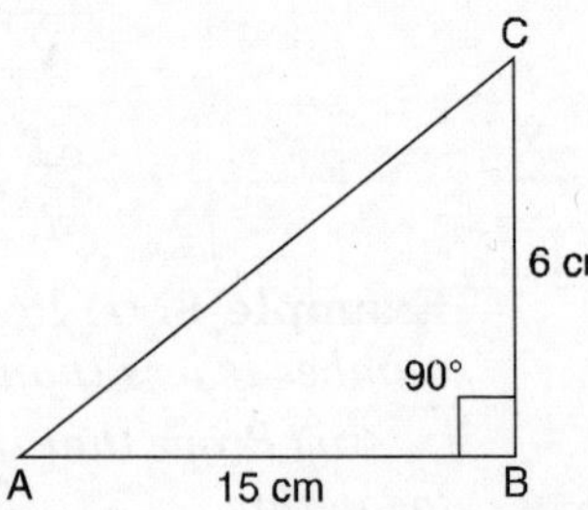

$\therefore$ $A = \tan^{-1}\left(\dfrac{a}{c}\right)$

$$\delta A = \frac{\partial A}{\partial a}\,\delta a + \frac{\partial A}{\partial c}\,\delta c$$

$$= \frac{c}{a^2 + c^2}\,\delta a - \frac{a}{a^2 + c^2}\,\delta c$$

or $$|\delta A| \le \left|\frac{c}{a^2 + c^2} \cdot \delta a\right| + \left|\frac{a}{a^2 + c^2} \cdot \delta c\right|$$

$$= \frac{15}{261} \cdot (0.1) + \frac{6}{261} \cdot (0.2) = .0103 \text{ radians}$$

$\therefore$ $\delta A \le .0103$ radians.

Example 12. *In a ΔABC, a = 30 cm, b = 80 cm, $\angle B = 90°$, find the maximum error in the computed value of A if possible errors in a and b are $\frac{1}{3}$% and $\frac{1}{4}$%, respectively.*

Sol. $\sin A = \frac{a}{b} \Rightarrow A = \sin^{-1}\left(\frac{a}{b}\right)$

$$|\delta A| < \left|\frac{\partial A}{\partial a}\delta a\right| + \left|\frac{\partial A}{\partial b}\delta b\right| \quad (2)$$

Here, $\frac{\delta a}{a} \times 100 = \frac{1}{3}$ $\therefore$ $\delta a = 0.1$

$\frac{\delta b}{b} \times 100 = \frac{1}{4}$ $\therefore$ $\delta b = 0.2$

$\therefore$ $\frac{\partial A}{\partial a} = \frac{1}{\sqrt{b^2 - a^2}}$, $\frac{\partial A}{\partial b} = \frac{-a}{b\sqrt{b^2 - a^2}}$

Substituting in (2), we get $\delta A < .00135 + .00100 < .00235$.

Example 13. *The approximate values of $\frac{1}{7}$ and $\frac{1}{11}$ correct to 4 decimal places are 0.1429 and 0.0909, respectively. Find the possible relative error and absolute error in the sum of .1429 and .0909.*

Sol. Numbers 0.1429 and 0.0909 are correct to four places of decimal. The maximum error in each case is $\frac{1}{2} \times .0001 = 0.00005$.

(*i*) **Relative error**

$$\frac{|\Delta X|}{|X|} < \frac{|\Delta x_1|}{|X|} + \frac{|\Delta x_2|}{|X|} < \frac{0.00005}{0.2338} + \frac{0.00005}{0.2338} \quad (\because X = x_1 + x_2)$$

$$\left|\frac{\Delta X}{X}\right| < \frac{0.0001}{0.2338} = .00043.$$

(*ii*) **Absolute error**

$$\Delta X = \Delta x_1 + \Delta x_2 = 0.00005 + 0.00005 = 0.0001.$$

Example 14. *The approximate values of* $\frac{1}{7}$ *and* $\frac{1}{15}$, *correct to four decimal places, are 0.1429 and 0.0667 respectively. Find the relative error for the sum of 0.1429 and 0.0667.*

Sol.
$$\left|\frac{\Delta X}{X}\right| < \frac{0.0001}{0.2096} = 0.000477.$$

Example 15. $\sqrt{29} = 5.385$ *and* $\sqrt{11} = 3.317$ *are correct to four significant figures. Find the relative error in their sum and difference.*

Sol. Numbers 5.385 and 3.317 are correct to four significant figures

$\therefore$ The maximum error in each case is $\frac{1}{2} \times 10^{-3} = 0.0005$

$$\therefore \quad \Delta x_1 = \Delta x_2 = 0.0005$$

The relative error in their sum is

$$\left|\frac{\Delta X}{X}\right| \leq \left|\frac{\Delta x_1}{X}\right| + \left|\frac{\Delta x_2}{X}\right| \qquad | \because \; X = x_1 + x_2 = 8.702$$

$$\leq \left|\frac{0.0005}{8.702}\right| + \left|\frac{0.0005}{8.702}\right| < 1.149 \times 10^{-4}$$

The relative error in their difference is

$$\left|\frac{\Delta X}{X}\right| \leq \left|\frac{\Delta x_1}{X}\right| + \left|\frac{\Delta x_2}{X}\right|, \text{ where } X = x_1 - x_2 = 2.068$$

$$\leq \left|\frac{0.0005}{2.068}\right| + \left|\frac{0.0005}{2.068}\right| < 4.835 \times 10^{-4}.$$

Example 16. *Sum the following numbers: 0.1532, 15.45, 0.000354, 305.1, 8.12, 143.3, 0.0212, 0.643, and 0.1734, where digits are correct.*

Sol. 305.1 and 143.3 have the greatest absolute error of .05 in each.

Rounding-off all other numbers to two decimal digits, we have 0.15, 15.45, 0.00, 8.12, 0.02, 0.64, and 0.17.

The sum S is given by

$$S = 305.1 + 143.3 + 0.15 + 15.45 + 0.00 + 8.12 + 0.02 + 0.64 + 0.17$$
$$= 472.59 = 472.6.$$

To determine the absolute error, we note that the first two numbers have absolute errors of 0.05 and the remaining seven numbers have absolute errors of 0.005 each.

$\therefore$ The absolute error in all 9 numbers

$$= 2(0.05) + 7(0.005) = 0.1 + 0.035 = 0.135 \approx 0.14.$$

In addition to the above absolute error, we have to take into account the rounding error, which is 0.01. Hence the total absolute error in

$$S = 0.14 + 0.01 = 0.15$$

Thus, $S = 472.6 \pm 0.15.$

Example 17. $\sqrt{5.5} = 2.345$ *and* $\sqrt{6.1} = 2.470$ *correct to four significant figures. Find the relative error in taking the difference of these numbers.*

Sol. The maximum error in each case $= \dfrac{1}{2} \times 0.001 = 0.0005$

$\therefore$ The relative error $< \left|\dfrac{\Delta x_1}{X}\right| + \left|\dfrac{\Delta x_2}{X}\right| = 2\left|\dfrac{\Delta x_1}{X}\right| = 2\left(\dfrac{0.0005}{0.125}\right) = 0.008.$

Example 18. $\sqrt{10} = 3.162$ *and* $e \simeq 2.718$ *correct to three decimal places. Find the percentage error in their difference.*

Sol. Relative error $= 2 \times \dfrac{0.0005}{(3.162 - 2.718)} = \dfrac{0.001}{.444}$

$\therefore$ Percentage error $= \dfrac{0.001}{.444} \times 100 \simeq 0.23$.

Example 19. *Find the product of 346.1 and 865.2. State how many figures of the result are trustworthy, given that the numbers are correct to four significant figures.*

Sol. $\Delta x_1 = 0.05, \Delta x_2 = 0.05$

$$X = 346.1 \times 865.2 = 299446 \text{ (correct to 6 digits)}$$

Maximum relative error $(e_r) \le \left|\dfrac{\Delta x_1}{x_1}\right| + \left|\dfrac{\Delta x_2}{x_2}\right|$

$$= \left|\frac{0.05}{346.1}\right| + \left|\frac{0.05}{865.2}\right|$$

$$= 0.000144 + 0.000058 = 0.000202$$

$\therefore$ Absolute error $= e_r \,.\, X = 0.000202 \times 299446 \simeq 60$

$\therefore$ The true value of the product of the numbers given lies between

$$299446 - 60 = 299386 \text{ and } 299446 + 60 = 299506.$$

The mean of these values is $\dfrac{299386 + 299506}{2} = 299446$

which is 299.4×10^3, correct to four significant digits. There is some uncertainty about the last digit.

Example 20. *Two numbers are given as 2.5 and 48.289, both of which are correct to the significant figures given. Find their product.*

Sol. 2.5 is the number with the greatest absolute error. Rounding-off the other number to three significant digits, we get 48.3.

Their product is given by,

$$P = 48.3 \times 2.5 = 120.75 = 1.2 \times 10^2$$

where, we have retained only two significant digits.

Example 21. *Find the relative error in calculation of* $\dfrac{7.342}{0.241}$. *Numbers are correct to three decimal places. Determine the smallest interval in which true result lies.*

Sol. $\Delta x_1 = \Delta x_2 = 0.0005$

Relative error $\leq \left|\dfrac{0.0005}{7.342}\right| + \left|\dfrac{0.0005}{0.241}\right|$

$$\leq 0.0005\left(\frac{1}{7.342} + \frac{1}{.241}\right) = 0.0021$$

Absolute error $= 0.0021 \times \dfrac{x_1}{x_2} = 0.0021 \times \dfrac{7.342}{0.241} = 0.0639$

Now, $\dfrac{x_1}{x_2} = \dfrac{7.342}{0.241} = 30.4647$

$\therefore$ The true value of x_1/x_2 lies between $30.4647 - 0.0639 = 30.4008$ and 30.5286.

Example 22. *Find the number of trustworthy figures in* $(0.491)^3$, *assuming that the number 0.491 is correct to the last figure.*

Sol. Relative error $e_r = k\,\dfrac{\Delta x}{x}$

$$= 3 \,.\, \frac{0.0005}{0.491} = 0.003054989$$

Absolute error $< e_r \,.\, X$

$= (0.003054989) \,.\, (0.491)^3$

$= 0.000361621$

The error affects the fourth decimal place, therefore X is correct to three decimal places.

Example 23. *If* $R = \dfrac{1}{2}\left(\dfrac{r^2}{h} + h\right)$ *and the error in R is at the most 0.4%, find the percentage error allowable in r and h when r = 5.1 cm and h = 5.8 cm.*

Sol. Percentage error in R $= \dfrac{\Delta R}{R} \times 100 = 0.4$

$$\therefore \qquad \Delta R = \frac{0.4}{100} \times R = \frac{0.4}{100} \times \frac{1}{2}\left[\frac{(5.1)^2}{5.8} + 5.8\right] = 0.0206$$

(*i*) Percentage error in $r = \dfrac{\Delta r}{r} \times 100$

$$= \frac{1}{r} \cdot \left(\frac{\Delta R}{2\dfrac{\partial R}{\partial r}}\right) \times 100 \qquad \left| \because \; 2\frac{\partial R}{\partial r} = \frac{2r}{h} \right.$$

$$= \frac{100}{r} \cdot \frac{\Delta R}{2\left(\dfrac{r}{h}\right)} = \frac{50\,h}{r^2}\,\Delta R$$

$$= \frac{50 \times 5.8}{(5.1)^2} \times 0.0206 = 0.22968\%$$

(*ii*) Percentage error in $h = \dfrac{\Delta h}{h} \times 100$

$$= \frac{100}{h} \times \frac{\Delta R}{\left(2\dfrac{\partial R}{\partial h}\right)} = \frac{100}{h} \cdot \frac{\Delta R}{2\left[-\dfrac{r^2}{2h^2} + \dfrac{1}{2}\right]}$$

$$= \frac{100}{h} \cdot \frac{\Delta R}{\left(-\dfrac{r^2}{h^2} + 1\right)} = \frac{100}{5.8} \times \frac{0.0206}{(-0.773186 + 1)}$$

$$= \frac{2.06}{5.8 \times 0.2268} = 1.5659\%.$$

Example 24. *Calculate the value of x – x cos θ correct to three significant figures if x = 10.2 cm, and θ = 5°. Find permissible errors also in x and θ.*

Sol.
$$\theta = 5° = \frac{5\pi}{180} = \frac{11}{126} \text{ radian}$$

$$1 - \cos\theta = 1 - \left[1 - \frac{\theta^2}{2!} + \frac{\theta^4}{4!} - \ldots\ldots\right]$$

$$= \frac{\theta^2}{2!} - \frac{\theta^4}{4!} + \ldots\ldots = \frac{1}{2}\left(\frac{11}{126}\right)^2 - \frac{1}{24}\left(\frac{11}{126}\right)^4 + \ldots\ldots$$

$$= 0.0038107 - 0.0000024$$

$$\simeq 0.0038083$$

$$\therefore \quad X = x(1 - \cos\theta)$$

$$= 10.2\ (0.0038083)$$

$$= 0.0388446 \simeq 0.0388$$

Further,
$$\Delta x = \frac{\Delta X}{2\left(\frac{\partial X}{\partial x}\right)} = \frac{0.0005}{2 \times 0.0038083} \simeq 0.0656$$

$$\Delta\theta = \frac{\Delta X}{2\left(\frac{\partial X}{\partial \theta}\right)} = \frac{0.0005}{2x \sin\theta} = \frac{0.0005}{2 \times 10.2 \times 0.0871907}$$

where
$$\sin\theta = \theta - \frac{\theta^3}{3!} + \ldots\ldots = \frac{11}{126} - \frac{1}{6}\left(\frac{11}{126}\right)^3 + \ldots\ldots = 0.0871907$$

$$\therefore \quad \Delta\theta = \frac{0.0005}{20.4 \times 0.0871907} \simeq 0.0002809 \simeq 0.00028.$$

2.7. ERROR IN A SERIES APPROXIMATION

The error committed in a series approximation can be evaluated by using the remainder after n terms.

Taylor's series for $f(x)$ at $x = a$ is given by

$$f(x) = f(a) + (x-a)f'(a) + \frac{(x-a)^2}{2!}f''(a) + \ldots\ldots + \frac{(x-a)^{n-1}}{(n-1)!}f^{(n-1)}(a) + R_n(x)$$

where
$$R_n(x) = \frac{(x-a)^n}{n!}f^{(n)}(\xi);\ a < \xi < x.$$

For a convergent series, $R_n(x) \to 0$ as $n \to \infty$. If we approximate $f(x)$ first by n terms of series, then by maximum error committed, we get $R_n(x)$.

If the accuracy required is specified in advance, it would be possible to find n, the number of terms such that the finite series yields the required accuracy.

EXAMPLES

Example 1. *Find the number of terms of the exponential series such that their sum gives the value of e^x correct to six decimal places at $x = 1$.*

Sol.
$$e^x = 1 + x + \frac{x^2}{2!} + \frac{x^3}{3!} + \ldots\ldots + \frac{x^{n-1}}{(n-1)!} + R_n(x) \quad (3)$$

where
$$R_n(x) = \frac{x^n}{n!}\, e^{\theta},\ 0 < \theta < x$$

Maximum absolute error (at $\theta = x$) $= \dfrac{x^n}{n!}\, e^x$

and Maximum relative error $= \dfrac{x^n}{n!}$

Hence, $(e_r)_{\text{max.}}$ at $x = 1$ is $= \dfrac{1}{n!}$

For a six decimal accuracy at $x = 1$, we have

$$\frac{1}{n!} < \frac{1}{2} \times 10^{-6} \quad i.e., \quad n! > 2 \times 10^6$$

which gives $n = 10$.

Hence we need 10 terms of series (3) to ensure that its sum is correct to 6 decimal places.

Example 2. *Use the series*

$$\log_e \left(\frac{1+x}{1-x} \right) = 2\left(x + \frac{x^3}{3} + \frac{x^5}{5} + \ldots\ldots \right)$$

to compute the value of log (1.2) correct to seven decimal places and find the number of terms retained.

Sol.
$$\log_e \left(\frac{1+x}{1-x} \right) = 2\left(x + \frac{x^3}{3} + \frac{x^5}{5} + \ldots + \frac{x^{2n-1}}{2n-1} \right) + R_n(x)$$

If we retain n terms, then

$$R_n(x) = \frac{2x^{2n+1}}{2n+1} \log_e \left(\frac{1+\xi}{1-\xi}\right); 0 < \xi < x$$

$$\text{Maximum absolute error (at } \xi = x) = \frac{2x^{2n+1}}{2n+1} \log_e \left(\frac{1+x}{1-x}\right)$$

and maximum relative error $= \dfrac{2}{2n+1} x^{2n+1}$

Let $\quad \dfrac{1+x}{1-x} = 1.2 \Rightarrow x = \dfrac{1}{11}$

Hence $(e_r)_{max.}$ at $x = \dfrac{1}{11}$ is $\dfrac{2}{2n+1}\left(\dfrac{1}{11}\right)^{2n+1}$.

For seven decimal accuracy,

$$\frac{2}{2n+1} \cdot \left(\frac{1}{11}\right)^{2n+1} < \frac{1}{2} \times 10^{-7}$$

$$(2n + 1)\,(11)^{2n+1} > 4 \times 10^7$$

which gives $n \geq 3$.

Hence, retaining the first three terms of the given series, we get

$$\log_e (1.2) = 2\left(x + \frac{x^3}{3} + \frac{x^5}{5}\right) \text{ at } \left(x = \frac{1}{11}\right) = 0.1823215 .$$

Example 3. *The function $f(x) = tan^{-1}x$ can be expanded as*

$$tan^{-1}x = x - \frac{x^3}{3} + \frac{x^5}{5} - ...... + (-1)^{n-1} . \frac{x^{2n-1}}{2n-1} + ...$$

Find n such that the series determines $tan^{-1}(1)$ correct to eight significant digits.

Sol. If we retain n terms, then $(n + 1)^{th}$ term $= (-1)^n . \dfrac{x^{2n+1}}{2n+1}$

For $x = 1$, $\quad (n + 1)^{th}$ term $= \dfrac{(-1)^n}{2n+1}$

For the determination of $\tan^{-1}(1)$ correct up to eight significant digit accuracy,

$$\left|\frac{(-1)^n}{2n+1}\right| < \frac{1}{2} \times 10^{-8}$$

$$\Rightarrow \qquad 2n + 1 > 2 \times 10^8$$

such as $n = 10^8 + 1$.

Example 4. *The function $f(x) = \cos x$ can be expanded as*

$$\cos x = 1 - \frac{x^2}{2!} + \frac{x^4}{4!} - \frac{x^6}{6!} + \ldots$$

Compute the number of terms required to estimate $\cos\left(\frac{\pi}{4}\right)$ so that the result is correct to at least two significant digits.

Sol. $$\cos x = 1 - \frac{x^2}{2!} + \frac{x^4}{4!} - \frac{x^6}{6!} + \ldots + R_n(x)$$

where $$R_n(x) = (-1)^n \frac{x^{2n}}{2n!} \cos \xi;\ 0 < \xi < x$$

$$\text{Maximum absolute error (at } \xi = x) = \left|(-1)^n \frac{x^{2n}}{(2n)!} \cos x\right| = \frac{x^{2n}}{(2n)!} \cos x$$

$$\text{Maximum relative error} = \frac{x^{2n}}{(2n)!}$$

At $x = \frac{\pi}{4}$, $$(e_r)_{\text{max.}} = \frac{(\pi/4)^{2n}}{(2n)!}$$

For two significant digit accuracy,

$$\frac{(\pi/4)^{2n}}{(2n)!} \le \frac{1}{2} \times 10^{-2}$$

i.e., $$\frac{(2n)!}{(\pi/4)^{2n}} \ge 200$$

$n = 3$ satisfies it.

ASSIGNMENT 2.2

1. If $R = 4xy^2z^{-3}$ and errors in x, y, z be 0.001, show that the maximum relative error at $x = y = z = 1$ is 0.006.
2. If $R = 10x^3y^2z^2$ and errors in x, y, z are 0.03, 0.01, 0.02 respectively at $x = 3, y = 1, z = 2$. Calculate the absolute error and percentage relative error in evaluating R.
3. If $R = 4x^2y^3z^{-4}$, find the maximum absolute error and maximum relative error in R when errors in $x = 1, y = 2, z = 3$, respectively, are equal to 0.001, 0.002, 0.003.
4. If $u = \dfrac{5xy^2}{z^3}$ and errors in x, y, z are 0.001 at $x = 1, y = 1, z = 1$, calculate the maximum relative error in evaluating u.
5. Find the number of terms of the exponential series such that their sum yields the value of e^x correct to 8 decimal places at $x = 1$.
6. Find the product of the numbers 56.54 and 12.4, both of which are correct to the significant digits given.
7. Find the quotient $q = \dfrac{x}{y}$, where $x = 4.536$ and $y = 1.32$; both x and y being correct to the digits given. Find also the relative error in the result.
8. Write a short note on error in a series approximation.
9. Explain the procedure of adding several numbers of different absolute accuracies.
10. Find the smaller root of the equation $x^2 - 30x + 1 = 0$ correct to three decimal places. State different algorithms. Which algorithm is better and why?
11. Write a short note on Errors in numerical computation.

2.8 MATHEMATICAL PRELIMINARIES

Following are certain mathematical results which would be useful in the sequel.

Theorem 1. If $f(x)$ is continuous in $a \le x \le b$ and if $f(a)$ and $f(b)$ are of opposite signs then $f(c) = 0$ for at least one number c such that $a < c < b$.

Theorem 2. Rolle's theorem.

If (*i*) $f(x)$ in continuous in $[a, b]$ (*ii*) $f'(x)$ exists in (a, b)

(*iii*) $f(a) = f(b) = 0$.

then $\exists$ at least one value of x, say c, such that

$$f'(c) = 0, a < c < b.$$

Theorem 3. Mean value theorem for derivatives.

If (*i*) $f(x)$ is continuous in $[a, b]$ (*ii*) $f'(x)$ exists in (a, b) then, $\exists$ at least one value of x, say c, between a and b such that

$$f'(c) = \frac{f(b) - f(a)}{b - a}, \; a < c < b.$$

Theorem 4. Taylor's series for a function of one variable. If $f(x)$ is continuous and possesses continuous derivatives of order n in an interval that includes $x = a$, then in that interval

$$f(x) = f(a) + (x - a) f'(a) + \frac{(x-a)^2}{2!} f''(a) + \ldots\ldots + \frac{(x-a)^{n-1}}{(n-1)!} f^{(n-1)}(a) + R_n(x)$$

where $R_n(x)$ is remainder term, can be expressed in the form

$$R_n(x) = \frac{(x-a)^n}{n!} f^n(c), \; a < c < x.$$

Theorem 5. Maclaurin's expansion.

$$f(x) = f(0) + x f'(0) + \frac{x^2}{2!} f''(0) + \ldots\ldots + \frac{x^n}{n!} f^{(n)}(0) + \ldots\ldots$$

Theorem 6. Taylor's series for a function of two variables.

$$f(x_1 + \Delta x_1, x_2 + \Delta x_2) = f(x_1, x_2) + \frac{\partial f}{\partial x_1} \Delta x_1 + \frac{\partial f}{\partial x_2} \Delta x_2$$

$$+ \frac{1}{2}\left[\frac{\partial^2 f}{\partial {x_1}^2}(\Delta x_1)^2 + 2\frac{\partial^2 f}{\partial x_1 \partial x_2}\Delta x_1 . \Delta x_2 + \frac{\partial^2 f}{\partial {x_2}^2}(\Delta x_2)^2\right] + \ldots\ldots$$

2.9 FLOATING POINT REPRESENTATION OF NUMBERS

There are two types of arithmetic operations available in a computer.

They are:

(*i*) Integer arithmetic (*ii*) Real or floating point arithmetic.

Integer arithmetic deals with integer operands and is used mainly in counting and as subscripts. Real arithmetic uses numbers with fractional parts as operands and is used in most computations. Computers are usually designed such that each location, called **word,** in memory stores only a finite number of digits. Consequently, all operands in arithmetic operations have only a finite number of digits.

Let us assume a hypothetical computer having memory in which each location can store 6 digits and having provision to store one or more signs. One method of representing real numbers in that computer would be to assume a fixed position for the decimal point and store all numbers after appropriate shifting if necessary with an assumed decimal point.

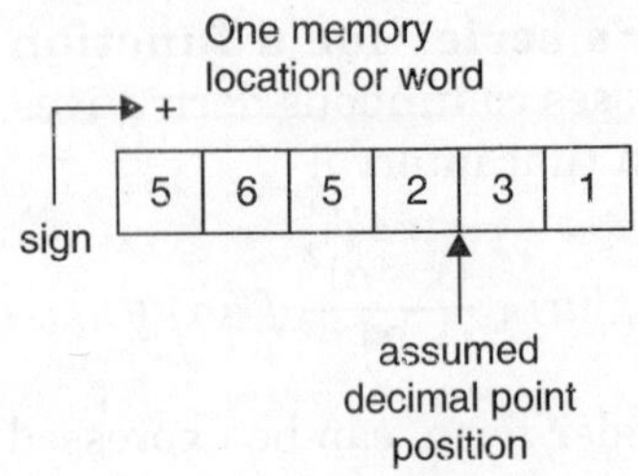

A memory location storing number 5652.31

In such a convention, the maximum and minimum possible numbers to be stored are 9999.99 and 0000.01, respectively, in magnitude. This range is quite inadequate in practice.

For this, a new convention is adopted that aims to preserve the maximum number of significant digits in a real number and also increase the range of values of real numbers stored. This representation is called the **normalized floating point** mode of representing and storing real numbers.

In this mode, a real number is expressed as a combination of a **mantissa** and an **exponent.** The mantissa is made less than 1 or $\geq .1$ and the exponent is the power of 10 which multiplies the mantissa.

For example, the number 43.76×10^6 is represented in this notation as .4376 E 8, where E 8 is used to represent 10^8. The mantissa is .4376 and the exponent is 8.

The number is stored in memory location as:

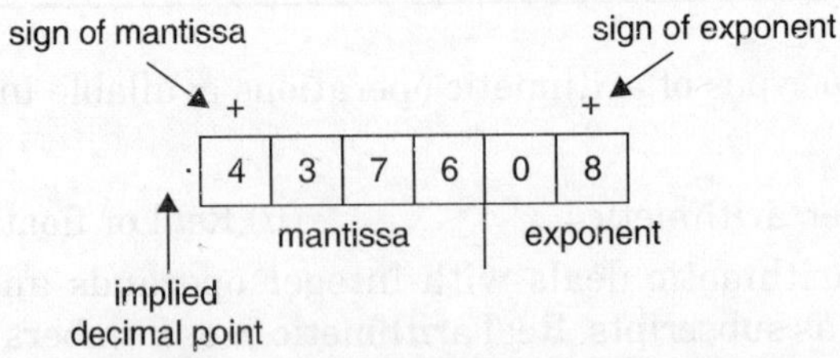

Moreover, the shifting of the mantissa to the left until its most significant digit is non-zero is called **normalization.**

For example, the number .006831 may be stored as .6831 E–2 because the leading zeros serve only to locate the decimal point.

The range of numbers that may be stored is $.9999 \times 10^{99}$ to $.1000 \times 10^{-99}$ in magnitude, which is obviously much larger than that used earlier in fixed decimal point notation.

This increment in range has been obtained by reducing the number of significant digits in a number by 2.

2.10 ARITHMETIC OPERATIONS WITH NORMALIZED FLOATING POINT NUMBERS

2.10.1 Addition and Subtraction

If two numbers represented in normalized floating point notation are to be added, the exponents of the two numbers must be made equal and the Mantissa shifted appropriately. The operation of subtraction is nothing but the addition of a negative number. Thus the principles are the same.

EXAMPLES

Example 1. *Add the following floating point numbers:*

(*i*) *.4546 E 5 and .5433 E 5*

(*ii*) *.4546 E 5 and .5433 E 7*

(*iii*) *.4546 E 3 and .5433 E 7*

(*iv*) *.6434 E 3 and .4845 E 3*

(*v*) *.6434 E 99 and .4845 E 99.*

Sol. (*i*) Here the exponents are equal ∴ Mantissas are added

∴ Sum = .9979 E 5

(*ii*) Here exponents are not equal. The operand with the larger exponent is kept as it is

$$\begin{array}{r} .5433 \text{ E } 7 \\ +\ .0045 \text{ E } 7 \\ \hline .5478 \text{ E } 7 \\ \hline \end{array} \qquad | \ .4546 \text{ E } 5 = .0045 \text{ E } 7$$

(*iii*) The addition will be as follows:

$$\begin{array}{r} .5433 \text{ E } 7 \\ +\ .0000 \text{ E } 7 \\ \hline .5433 \text{ E } 7 \\ \hline \end{array} \qquad | \because \ .4546 \text{ E } 3 = .0000 \text{ E } 7$$

(*iv*) The exponents are equal but when the mantissas are added, the sum is 1.1279 E 3. As the mantissa has 5 digits and is > 1, it is shifted right one place before it is stored.

Hence Sum = .1127 E 4

(*v*) Here, again the sum of the mantissas exceeds 1. The mantissa is shifted right and the exponent increased by 1, resulting in a value of 100 for the exponent. The exponent part cannot store more than two digits. This condition is called an **overflow** condition and the arithmetic unit will intimate an error condition.

Example 2. *Subtract the following floating point numbers:*

(*i*) *.9432 E – 4 from .5452 E – 3* (*ii*) *.5424 E 3 from .5452 E 3*

(*iii*) *.5424E – 99 from .5452 E – 99.*

Sol. (*i*)

$$\begin{array}{r} .5452\text{ E} - 3 \\ -\ .0943\text{ E} - 3 \\ \hline .4509\text{ E} - 3 \\ \hline \end{array}$$

(*ii*)

$$\begin{array}{r} .5452\text{ E } 3 \\ -\ .5424\text{ E } 3 \\ \hline .0028\text{ E } 3 \\ \hline \end{array}$$

In a normalized floating point, the mantissa is ≥ .1

Hence, the result is .28 E 1

(*iii*)

$$\begin{array}{r} .5452\text{ E} - 99 \\ -\ .5424\text{ E} - 99 \\ \hline .0028\text{ E} - 99 \\ \hline \end{array}$$

For normalization, the mantissa is shifted left and the exponent is reduced by 1. The exponent would thus become – 100 with the first left shift, which can not be accommodated in the exponent part of the number.

This condition is called an **underflow** condition and the arithmetic unit will signal an error condition.

NOTE *If the result of an arithmetic operation gives a number smaller than .1000 E – 99 then it is called an* ***underflow*** *condition. Similarly, any result greater than .9999 E 99 leads to an* ***overflow*** *condition.*

Example 3. *In normalized floating point mode, carry out the following mathematical operations:*

(*i*) (.4546 E 3) + (.5454 E 8) (*ii*) (.9432 E – 4) – (.6353 E – 5).

Sol. (*i*)

.5454 E 8
+ .0000 E 8 | ∵ .4546 E 3 = .0000 E 8

.5454 E 8

(*ii*)

.9432 E – 4
– .0635 E – 4 | ∵ .6353 E – 5 = .0635 E – 4

.8797 E – 4

2.10.2 Multiplication

Two numbers are multiplied in the normalized floating point mode by multiplying the mantissas and adding the exponents. After the multiplication of the mantissas, the resulting mantissa is normalized as in an addition or subtraction operation, and the exponent is appropriately adjusted.

EXAMPLES

Example 1. *Multiply the following floating point numbers:*

(*i*) .5543 E 12 and .4111 E – 15 (*ii*) .1111 E 10 and .1234 E 15

(*iii*) .1111 E 51 and .4444 E 50 (*iv*) .1234 E – 49 and .1111 E – 54.

Sol. (*i*) .5543 E 12 × .4111 E – 15 = .2278 E – 3

(*ii*) .1111 E 10 × .1234 E 15 = .1370 E 24

(*iii*) .1111 E 51 × .4444 E 50 = .4937 E 100

The result overflows.

(*iv*) .1234 E – 49 × .1111 E – 54 = .1370 E – 104

The result underflows.

Example 2. *Apply the procedure for the following multiplications:*

$$(.5334 \times 10^{9}) * (.1132 \times 10^{-25})$$

$$(.1111 \times 10^{74}) * (.2000 \times 10^{80})$$

Indicate if the result is overflow or underflow.

Sol. (*i*) .5334 E 9 × .1132 E – 25 = .6038 E – 17

(*ii*) .1111 E 74 × .2000 E 80 = .2222 E 153

Hence the above result overflows.

2.10.3 Division

In division, the mantissa of the numerator is divided by that of the denominator. The denominator exponent is subtracted from the numerator exponent. The quotient mantissa is normalized to make the most significant digit non-zero and the exponent is appropriately adjusted. The mantissa of the result is chopped down to 4 digits.

EXAMPLES

Example 1. *Perform the following operations:*

(i) .9998 E 1 ÷ .1000 E – 99 *(ii) .9998 E – 5 ÷ .1000 E 98*

(iii) .1000 E 5 ÷ .9999 E 3.

Sol. (*i*) .9998 E 1 ÷ .1000 E – 99 = .9998 E 101

Hence the result overflows.

(*ii*) .9998 E – 5 ÷ .1000 E 98 = .9998 E – 104

Hence the result underflows.

(*iii*) .1000 E 5 ÷ .9999 E 3 = .1000 E 2.

Example 2. *Evaluate, applying normalized floating point arithmetic, for the following:*

$$1 - \cos x \text{ at } x = .1396 \text{ radian}$$

Assume $\cos(.1396) = .9903$

Compare it when evaluated $2\sin^2 \frac{x}{2}$

Assume $\sin .0698 = .6974 \text{ E} - 1.$

Sol. $1 - \cos(.1396) = .1000 \text{ E } 1 - .9903 \text{ E } 0$

$$= .1000 \text{ E } 1 - .0990 \text{ E } 1 = .1000 \text{ E} - 1$$

Now, $\sin\frac{x}{2} = \sin(.0698) = .6974 \text{ E} - 1$

$$2\sin^2\frac{x}{2} = (.2000 \text{ E } 1) \times (.6974 \text{ E} - 1) \times (.6974 \text{ E} - 1)$$

$$= .9727 \text{ E} - 2$$

The value obtained by the alternate formula is closer to the true value .9728 E – 2.

Example 3. *For $x = .4845$ and $y = .4800$, calculate the value of $\frac{x^2 - y^2}{x + y}$ using normalized floating point arithmetic. Compare with the value of $(x - y)$. Indicate the error in the former.*

Sol.

$$x + y = .4845 \text{ E } 0 + .4800 \text{ E } 0 = .9645 \text{ E } 0$$

$$x^2 = (.4845 \text{ E } 0) \times (.4845 \text{ E } 0) = .2347 \text{ E } 0$$

$$y^2 = (.4800 \text{ E } 0) \times (.4800 \text{ E } 0) = .2304 \text{ E } 0$$

$$x^2 - y^2 = .2347 \text{ E } 0 - .2304 \text{ E } 0 = .0043 \text{ E } 0$$

Now, $$\frac{x^2 - y^2}{x + y} = .0043 \text{ E } 0 \div .9645 \text{ E } 0 = .4458 \text{ E} - 2$$

Also, $$x - y = .4845 \text{ E } 0 - .4800 \text{ E } 0 = .0045 \text{ E } 0 = .4500 \text{ E} - 2$$

Relative error $$= \frac{.4500 - 0.4458}{.4500} = .93\%.$$

Example 4. *For $e = 2.7183$, calculate the value of e^x when $x = .5250$ E 1. The expression for e^x is*

$$e^x = 1 + x + \frac{x^2}{2!} + \frac{x^3}{3!}.$$

Sol.

$$e^{.5250 \text{ E } 1} = e^5 * e^{.25}$$

$$e^5 = (.2718 \text{ E } 1) \times (.2718 \text{ E } 1) \times (.2718 \text{ E } 1) \times (.2718 \text{ E } 1) \times (.2718 \text{ E } 1)$$

$$= .1484 \text{ E } 3$$

Also, $$e^{.25} = 1 + (.25) + \frac{(.25)^2}{2!} + \frac{(.25)^3}{3!}$$

$$= 1.25 + .03125 + .002604 = .1284 \text{ E } 1$$

Now, $$e^{.5250 \text{ E } 1} = (.1484 \text{ E } 3) \times (.1284 \text{ E } 1) = .1905 \text{ E } 3.$$

Example 5. *Find the solution of the following equation using floating point arithmetic with a 4 digit mantissa*

$$x^2 - 1000x + 25 = 0$$

Give comments or the result so obtained.

Sol.

$$x^2 - 1000\,x + 25 = 0$$

$$\Rightarrow \qquad x = \frac{1000 \pm \sqrt{10^6 - 10^2}}{2}$$

Now, $10^6 = .1000\text{ E }7$ and $10^2 = .1000\text{ E }3$

$\therefore$ $10^6 - 10^2 = .1000\text{ E }7$

$\therefore$ $\sqrt{10^6 - 10^2} = .1000\text{ E }4$

$\therefore$ Roots are $\left(\dfrac{.1000\text{ E }4 + .1000\text{ E }4}{2}\right)$ and $\left(\dfrac{.1000\text{ E }4 - .1000\text{ E }4}{2}\right)$

which are .1000 E 4 and .0000 E 4 respectively. One of the roots becomes zero due to the limited precision allowed in calculation. Let us reformulate the problem and remember that in a quadratic equation $ax^2 + bx + c = 0$, the product of roots is given by $\dfrac{c}{a}$, so the smaller root may be obtained by dividing (c/a) by the larger root.

So, First root $= .1000\text{ E }4$

and Second root $= \dfrac{25}{.1000\text{ E }4} = \dfrac{.2500\text{ E }2}{.1000\text{ E }4} = .2500\text{ E} - 1$

Such a situation may be recognized in an algorithm by checking to see if

$$b^2 >> |\ 4\ ac\ |.$$

Example 6. *Find the smaller root of the equation $x^2 - 400\ x + 1 = 0$ using four digit arithmetic.*

Sol. Here $b^2 >> |\ 4ac\ |$ | See Example 5

The roots of the equation $ax^2 - bx + c = 0$ are

$$\frac{b + \sqrt{b^2 - 4ac}}{2a} \text{ and } \frac{b - \sqrt{b^2 - 4ac}}{2a}$$

The product of the roots is $\dfrac{c}{a}$.

$\therefore$ The smaller root is $\dfrac{c/a}{\left(\dfrac{b + \sqrt{b^2 - 4ac}}{2a}\right)}$ *i.e.*, $\dfrac{2c}{b + \sqrt{b^2 - 4ac}}$

Here $a = 1 = .1000\text{ E }1$, $b = 400 = .4000\text{ E }3$, $c = 1 = .1000\text{ E }1$

$b^2 - 4ac = .1600\text{ E }6 - .4000\text{ E }1 = .1600\text{ E }6$ (to four digit accuracy)

$\therefore$ $\sqrt{b^2 - 4ac} = .4000\text{ E }3$

$\therefore$ Smaller root $= \dfrac{2 \times (.1000\text{ E }1)}{.4000\text{ E }3 + .4000\text{ E }3} = \dfrac{.2000\text{ E }1}{.8000\text{ E }3} = .25\text{ E} - 2 = .0025.$

Example 7. *Compute the middle value of numbers a = 4.568 and b = 6.762 using four digit arithmetic and compare the result by taking* $c = a + \left(\frac{b-a}{2}\right)$.

Sol. $a = .4568 \text{ E } 1, b = .6762 \text{ E } 1$

Let c be the middle value of numbers, then

$$c = \frac{a+b}{2} = \frac{.4568 \text{ E } 1 + .6762 \text{ E } 1}{.2000 \text{ E } 1} = \frac{.1133 \text{ E } 2}{.2000 \text{ E } 1} = .5665 \text{ E } 1$$

However, if we use the formula

$$c = a + \left(\frac{b-a}{2}\right) = .4568 \text{ E } 1 + \left(\frac{.6762 \text{ E } 1 - .4568 \text{ E } 1}{.2000 \text{ E } 1}\right)$$

$$= .4568 \text{ E } 1 + .1097 \text{ E } 1 = .5665 \text{ E } 1$$

The results are the same.

Example 8. *Obtain a second degree polynomial approximation to* $f(x) = (1 + x)^{1/2}$, $x \in [0, 0.1]$ *using Taylor's series expansion about* $x = 0$. *Use the expansion to approximate* $f(0.05)$ *and bound the truncation error.*

Sol. $f(x) = (1 + x)^{1/2}, \qquad f(0) = 1$

$$f'(x) = \frac{1}{2}(1 + x)^{-1/2}, \qquad f'(0) = \frac{1}{2}$$

$$f''(x) = -\frac{1}{4}(1 + x)^{-3/2}, \quad f''(0) = -\frac{1}{4}$$

$$f'''(x) = \frac{3}{8}(1 + x)^{-5/2}$$

Taylor's series expansion with remainder term may be written as

$$(1 + x)^{1/2} = 1 + \frac{x}{2} - \frac{x^2}{8} + \frac{1}{16}\frac{x^3}{[(1+\xi)^{1/2}]^5}; \; 0 < \xi < 0.1$$

The truncation term is given by

$$T = (1 + x)^{1/2} - \left(1 + \frac{x}{2} - \frac{x^2}{8}\right) = \frac{1}{16} \cdot \frac{x^3}{[(1+\xi)^{1/2}]^5}$$

We have $f(0.05) = 1 + \frac{0.05}{2} - \frac{(0.05)^2}{8} = 0.10246875 \times 10^1$

Bound of the truncation error, for $x \in [0, 0.1]$ is

$$|\,T\,| \le \frac{(0.1)^3}{16\,[(1+\xi)^{1/2}]^5} \le \frac{(0.1)^3}{16} = 0.625 \times 10^{-4}.$$

Example 9. *In a case of normalized floating point representation, associative and distributive laws are not always valid. Give examples to prove this statement.*

Or

If the normalization on the floating point is carried out at each stage, prove the following:

(*i*) $a(b - c) \neq ab - ac$

where $a = .5555 \text{ E } 1$, $b = .4545 \text{ E } 1$, $c = .4535 \text{ E } 1$

(*ii*) $(a + b) - c \neq (a - c) + b$

where $a = .5665 \text{ E } 1$, $b = .5556 \text{ E} - 1$, $c = .5644 \text{ E } 1$.

Sol. This is a consequence of the normalized floating point representation that the associative and the distributive laws of arithmetic are not always valid.

The following examples are chosen intentionally to illustrate the inaccuracies that may build up due to shifting and truncation of numbers in arithmetic operations.

Non-distributivity of arithmetic

Let $a = .5555 \text{ E } 1$

$b = .4545 \text{ E } 1$

$c = .4535 \text{ E } 1$

$(b - c) = .0010 \text{ E } 1 = .1000 \text{ E} - 1$

$a(b - c) = (.5555 \text{ E } 1) \times (.1000 \text{ E} - 1)$

$= (.0555 \text{ E } 0) = .5550 \text{ E} - 1$

Also, $ab = (.5555 \text{ E } 1) \times (.4545 \text{ E } 1) = .2524 \text{ E } 2$

$ac = (.5555 \text{ E } 1) \times (.4535 \text{ E } 1) = .2519 \text{ E } 2$

$\therefore$ $ab - ac = .0005 \text{ E } 2 = .5000 \text{ E} - 1$

Thus, $a(b - c) \neq ab - ac$

which shows the non-distributivity of arithmetic.

Non-associativity of arithmetic

Let $a = .5665 \text{ E } 1$

$b = .5556 \text{ E} - 1$

$c = .5644 \text{ E } 1$

$$\therefore \qquad (a + b) = .5665 \text{ E } 1 + .5556 \text{ E} - 1$$

$$= .5665 \text{ E } 1 + .0055 \text{ E } 1 = .5720 \text{ E } 1$$

$$(a + b) - c = .5720 \text{ E } 1 - .5644 \text{ E } 1 = .0076 \text{ E } 1 = .7600 \text{ E} - 1$$

$$a - c = .5665 \text{ E } 1 - .5644 \text{ E } 1 = .0021 \text{ E } 1 = .2100 \text{ E} - 1$$

$$(a - c) + b = .2100 \text{ E} - 1 + .5556 \text{ E} - 1 = .7656 \text{ E} - 1$$

Thus, $(a + b) - c \neq (a - c) + b$

which proves the non-associativity of arithmetic.

2.11 MACHINE COMPUTATION

To obtain meaningful results for a given problem using computers, there are five distinct phases:

(*i*) Choice of a method
(*ii*) Designing the algorithm
(*iii*) Flow charting
(*iv*) Programming
(*v*) Computer execution

A method is defined as a mathematical formula for finding the solution of a given problem. There may be more than one method available to solve the same problem. We should choose the method which suits the given problem best. The inherent assumptions and limitations of the method must be studied carefully.

Once the method has been decided, we must describe a complete and unambiguous set of computational steps to be followed in a particular sequence to obtain the solution. This description is called an **algorithm.** It may be emphasized that the computer is concerned with the algorithm and not with the method. The algorithm tells the computer where to start, what information to use, what operations to be carried out and in which order, what information to be printed, and when to stop.

An algorithm has five important features:

(1) **finiteness:** an algorithm must terminate after a finite number of steps.

(2) **definiteness:** each step of an algorithm must be clearly defined or the action to be taken must be unambiguously specified.

(3) **inputs:** an algorithm must specify the quantities which must be read before the algorithm can begin.

(4) **outputs:** an algorithm must specify the quantities which are to be outputted and their proper place.

(5) **effectiveness:** an algorithm must be effective, which means that all operations are executable.

A **flow-chart** is a graphical representation of a specific sequence of steps (algorithm) to be followed by the computer to produce the solution of a given problem. It makes use of the flow chart symbols to represent the basic operations to be carried out. The various symbols are connected by arrows to indicate the flow of information and processing. While drawing a flow chart, any logical error in the formulation of the problem or application of the algorithm can be easily seen and corrected.

2.12 COMPUTER SOFTWARE

The purpose of computer software is to provide a useful computational tool for users. The writing of computer software requires a good understanding of numerical analysis and art of programming. Good computer software must satisfy certain criteria of **self-starting, accuracy** and **reliability, minimum number of levels, good documentation, ease of use,** and **portability.**

Computer software should be self-starting as far as possible. A numerical method very often involves parameters whose values are determined by the properties of the problem to be solved. For example, in finding the roots of an equation, one or more initial approximations to the root have to be given. The program will be more acceptable if it can be made automatic in the sense that the program will select the initial approximations itself rather than requiring the user to specify them.

Accuracy and reliability are measures of the performance of an algorithm on all similar problems. Once an error criterion is fixed, it should produce solutions of all similar problems to that accuracy. The program should be able to prevent and handle most of the exceptional conditions like division by zero, infinite loops, etc.

The structure of the program should avoid many levels. For example, many programs used to find roots of an equation have three levels:

Program calls zero-finder (parameters, function)

Zero-finder calls function

Function subprogram

The more number of levels in the program, the more time is wasted in interlinking and transfer of parameters.

Documentation that is accurate and easy to use is a very important criteria. The program must have some comment lines or comment paragraphs at various places giving explanation and clarification of the method used and steps involved. Accurate documentation should clarify what kind of problems can be solved using this software, what parameters are to be supplied, what accuracy can be achieved, which method has been used, and other relevant details.

The criterion of portability means that the software should be made independent of the computer being used as far as possible. Since most machines have different hardware configuration, complete independence from the machine may not be possible. However, the aim of writing the computer software should be that the same program should be able to run on any machine with minimum modifications. Machine-dependent constants, for example machine error EPS, must be avoided or automatically generated. A standard dialect of the programming language should be used rather than a local dialect.

Most of the numerical methods are available in the form of **software,** which is a package of thoroughly tested, portable, and self documented subprograms. The general purpose packages contain a number of subroutines for solving a variety of mathematical problems that commonly arise in scientific and engineering computation. The special purpose packages deal with specified problem areas. Many computer installations require one or both types of packages and make it available, on-line, to their users. Most of the software packages are available for PCs also.

General Purpose Packages

IMSL: (*International Mathematical and Statistical Library*). The IMSL is a general purpose library of over 900 subroutines written in ANSI Fortran for solving a large number of mathematical and statistical problems.

NAG: (*Numerical Algorithms Group*). This package covers the basic areas of mathematical and statistical computation. The package is available in any one of the three languages ANSI Fortran, Algol 60 or Algol 68.

Special Purpose Packages

All the following packages are distributed by IMSL.

BLAS: (*Basic Linear Algebra Subroutines*). BLAS contains 38 ANSI Fortran subroutines for the methods in numerical linear algebra. The objective is fast computer execution.

B-Splines: A package of subroutines for performing calculations with piece-wise polynomials.

DEPACK: (*Differential Equations Package*). DEPACK contains Fortran subprograms for the integration of initial value problems in ordinary differential equations. This package includes Runge-Kutta methods, variable step, variable order Adams type methods, and backward differentiation methods for stiff problems.

EISPACK: (*Matrix Eigensystem Routines*). EISPACK contains 51 Fortran subprograms for computing the eigenvalues and/or eigenvectors of a matrix.

ELLPACK: (*Elliptic Partial Differential Equations Solver*). ELLPACK contains over 30 numerical method modules for solving elliptic partial differential equations in two dimensions with general domains and in three dimensions with rectangular domains. The 5-point discretization is used and the resulting system of equations is solved by Gauss elimination for band matrices and by SOR iterations.

FISHPACK: (*Routines for the Helmholtz Problems in Two or Three Dimensions*). FISHPACK contains a set of Fortran programs for solving Helmholtz problems in two or three dimensions. There are separate programs for rectangular, polar, spherical and cylindrical coordinates.

FUNPACK: (*Special Function Subroutines*). The FUNPACK package contains Fortran and assembly language subroutines for evaluating important special functions like exponential integral, elliptic integrals of first and second kind, Bessel functions, Dawson integrals, etc.

ITPACK: (*Iterative Methods*). ITPACK contains Fortran subprograms for iterative methods for solving linear system of equations. The package is oriented towards the sparse matrices that arise in solving partial differential equations and in other applications.

LINPACK: (*Linear Algebra Package*). LINPACK contains Fortran subprograms for direct methods for general, symmetric, symmetric positive definite, triangular, and tridiagonal matrices. The package also includes programs for least-squares problems, along with the QR and singular value decompositions of rectangular matrices.

MINPACK: MINPACK is a package of subroutines for solving systems of nonlinear equations and nonlinear least-squares problems. The package also includes programs for minimization and optimization problems.

QUADPACK: QUADPACK contains subroutines for evaluating a definite integral.

Software packages for PCs are also available for most of the areas mentioned above.

ASSIGNMENT 2.3

1. Represent 44.85×10^6 in normalized floating point mode.

2. Subtract the following two floating point numbers as

(*i*) .36143448 E 7 – .36132346 E 7

(*ii*) (.9682 E – 7) – (.3862 E – 9).

3. Explain underflow and overflow conditions of error in floating point's addition and subtraction.

4. Find the solution of the following equation using floating point arithmetic with 4-digit mantissa.

$$x^2 - 7x + 4 = 0$$

Give comments on the results so obtained.

5. Discuss the consequences of normalized floating point representation of numbers.

6. Calculate the value of $x^2 + 2x - 2$ and $(2x - 2) + x^2$

   where $x = .7320$ E 0

   using normalized floating point arithmetic and prove that they are not the same. Compare with value of $(x^2 - 2) + 2x$.

7. Find the value of $(1 + x)^2$ and $(x^2 + 2x) + 1$

   when $x = .5999$ E – 2.

8. Find the value of

$$\sin x \simeq x - \frac{x^3}{3!} + \frac{x^5}{5!}$$

   with an absolute error smaller than .005 for $x = .2000$ E 0 using normalized floating point arithmetic with a 4 digit mantissa.

9. Write a short note on machine computation.

10. Prove the following consequence of the normalized floating point representation of numbers by taking $x = .6667$

$$6x \neq x + x + x + x + x + x.$$

11. Define normalized floating point representation of numbers and round off errors in representation. Find the sum of 0.123×10^3 and 0.456×10^2 and write the result in three digit mantissa form.

12. (*i*) Calculate the value of the polynomial

$$p_3(x) = 2.75x^3 - 2.95x^2 + 3.16x - 4.67$$

   for $x = 1.07$ using both chopping and rounding-off to three digits, proceeding through the polynomial term by term from left to right.

   (*ii*) Explain how floating point numbers are stored in computers. What factors affect their accuracy and range?

Chapter 3 ALGEBRAIC AND TRANSCENDENTAL EQUATIONS

Consider the equation of the form $f(x) = 0$.

If $f(x)$ is a quadratic, cubic, or biquadratic expression, then algebraic formulae are available for expressing the roots. But when $f(x)$ is a polynomial of higher degree or an expression involving transcendental functions, for example, $1 + \cos x - 5x$, $x \tan x - \cosh x$, $e^{-x} - \sin x$, etc., algebraic methods are not available.

In this unit, we shall describe some numerical methods for the solution of $f(x) = 0$, where $f(x)$ is algebraic or transcendental or both.

3.1 BISECTION (OR BOLZANO) METHOD

This method is based on the repeated application of intermediate value property.

Let the function $f(x)$ be continuous between a and b. For definiteness, let $f(a)$ be (–)ve and $f(b)$ be (+)ve. Then the first approximation to the root is $x_1 = \frac{1}{2}(a + b)$.

If $f(x_1) = 0$, then x_1 is a root of $f(x) = 0$, otherwise, the root lies between a and x_1 or x_1 and b according to $f(x_1)$ is (+)ve or (–)ve. Then we bisect the interval as before and continue the process until the root is found to the desired accuracy.

In the adjoining figure, $f(x_1)$ is (+)ve so that the root lies between a and x_1. The second approximation to the root is $x_2 = \frac{1}{2}(a + x_1)$. If $f(x_2)$ is (–)ve the root lies between x_1 and x_2. The third approximation to the root is $x_3 = \frac{1}{2}(x_1 + x_2)$, and so on.

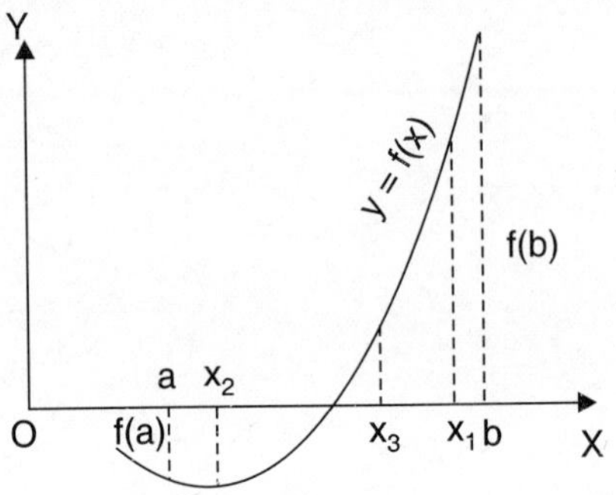

Once the method of calculation has been decided, we must describe clearly the computational steps to be followed in a particular sequence. These steps constitute the algorithm of method.

3.2 ALGORITHM

Step 01. Start of the program
Step 02. Input the variables x1, x2 for the task
Step 03. Check f(x1) *f(x2) < 0
Step 04. If yes, proceed
Step 05. If no exit and print error message
Step 06. Repeat 7-11 if conditions are not satisfied
Step 07. x0 = (x1 + x2)/2
Step 08. If f(x0) *f(x1) < 0
Step 09. x2 = x0.
Step 10. ELSE
Step 11. x1 = x0
Step 12. Condition:
Step 13. | (x1-x2)/x1 | < maximum possible error or f(x0) = 0
Step 14. Print output
Step 15. End of program.

3.3 FLOW-CHART

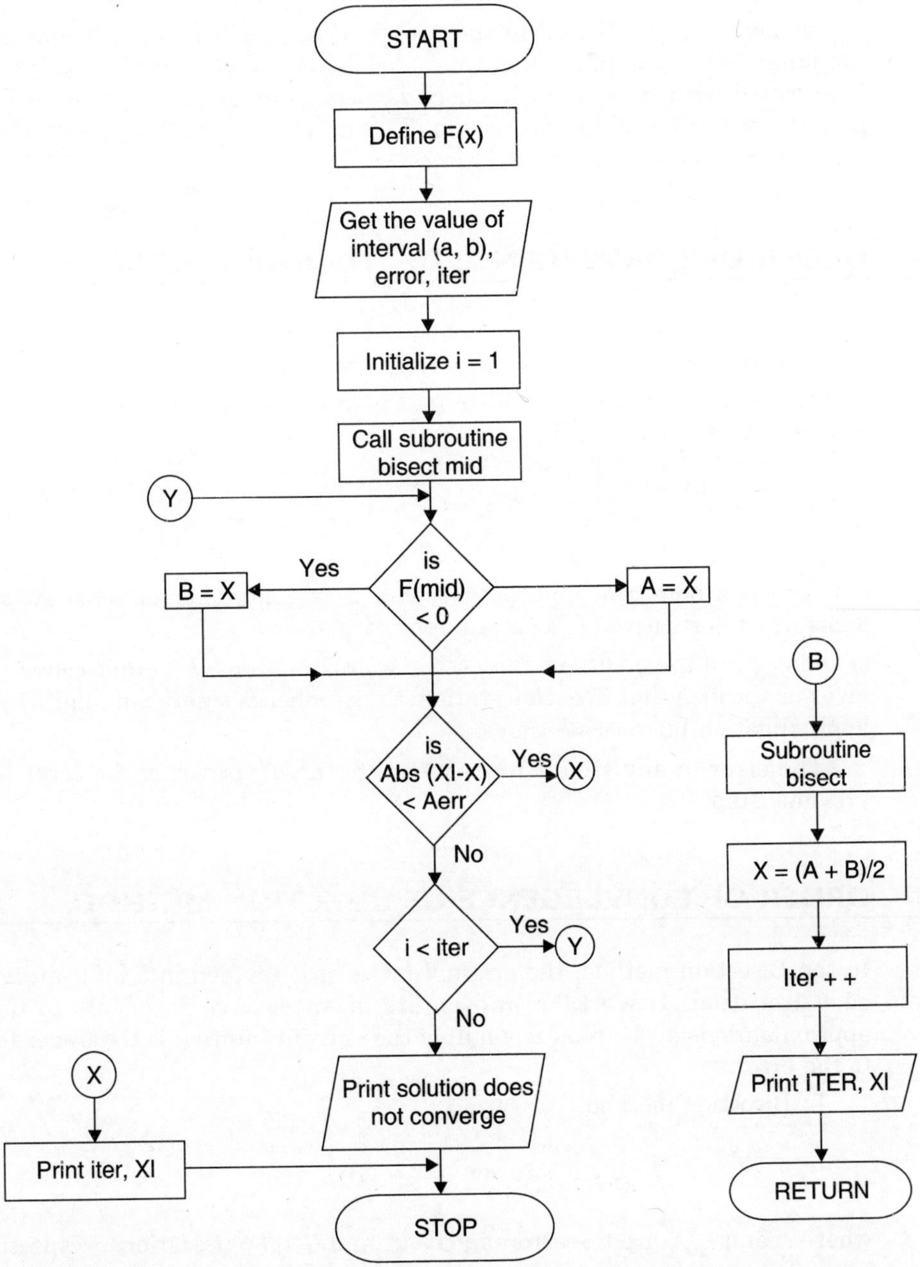

3.4 PROGRAM WRITING

Based on the flow-chart, we write the instructions in a code which the computer can understand. A series of such instructions is called a **program.**

If there are any errors in the program, they will be pointed out by the computer during compilation. After correcting compilation errors, the program is executed with input data to check for logical errors which may be due to misinterpretation of the algorithm. The process of finding the errors and correcting them is called **debugging.**

3.5 ORDER OF CONVERGENCE OF ITERATIVE METHODS

Convergence of an iterative method is judged by the order at which the error between successive approximations to the root decreases.

An iterative method is said to be k^{th} order convergent if k is the largest positive real number, such that

$$\lim_{i\to\infty}\left|\frac{e_{i+1}}{e_i^{\,k}}\right| \le \text{A}$$

where A is a non-zero finite number called asymptotic error constant and it depends on derivative of $f(x)$ at an approximate root x.

e_i and e_{i+1} are the errors in successive approximations. k^{th} order convergence gives us the idea that in each iteration, the number of significant digits in each approximation increases k times.

The error in any step is proportional to the kth power of the error in the previous step.

3.6 ORDER OF CONVERGENCE OF BISECTION METHOD

In the Bisection method, the original interval is divided into half interval in each iteration. If we take mid-points of successive intervals to be the approximations of the root, one half of the current interval is the upper bound to the error.

In Bisection method,

$$e_{i+1} = 0.5\, e_i \quad \text{or} \quad \frac{e_{i+1}}{e_i} = 0.5 \qquad (1)$$

where e_i and e_{i+1} are the errors in the ith and $(i+1)^{\text{th}}$ iterations, respectively.

Comparing (1) with

$$\lim_{i\to\infty}\left|\frac{e_{i+1}}{e_i^{\,k}}\right| \le A$$

we get $k = 1$ and $A = 0.5$

Thus the *Bisection method is I order convergent, or linearly convergent.*

3.7 CONVERGENCE OF A SEQUENCE

A sequence $< x_n >$ of successive approximations of a root $x = \alpha$ of the equation $f(x) = 0$ is said to converge to $x = \alpha$ with order $p \ge 1$ iff

$$| x_{n+1} - \alpha | \le c \,| x_n - \alpha |^p, \; n \ge 0$$

c being some constant greater than zero.

Particularly, if $| x_{n+1} - \alpha | = c \,| x_n - \alpha |, n \ge 0, 0 < c < 1$ then convergence is called **geometric.** Also, If $p = 1$ and $0 < c < 1$, then convergence is called **linear** or of first order. Constant c is called the **rate of linear convergence.** Convergence is rapid or slow depending on whether c is near 0 or 1.

Using induction, the condition for linear convergence can be simplified to the form

$$| x_n - \alpha | \le c^n \,| x_0 - \alpha |, \; n \ge 0, \; 0 < c < 1.$$

3.8 PROVE THAT BISECTION METHOD ALWAYS CONVERGES

Let $[p_n, q_n]$ be the interval at n^{th} step of bisection, having a root of the equation $f(x) = 0$. Let x_n be the nth approximation for the root. Then, initially, $p_1 = a$ and $q_1 = b$.

$\Rightarrow$ $$x_1 = \text{first approximation} = \left(\frac{p_1 + q_1}{2}\right)$$

$\Rightarrow$ $$p_1 < x_1 < q_1$$

Now either the root lies in $[a, x_1]$ or in $[x_1, b]$.

$\therefore$ either $[p_2, q_2] = [p_1, x_1]$ or $[p_2, q_2] = [x_1, q_1]$

$\Rightarrow$ either $p_2 = p_1, q_2 = x_1$ or $p_2 = x_1, q_2 = q_1$

$\Rightarrow$ $$p_1 \le p_2, \; q_2 \le q_1$$

Also, $$x_2 = \frac{p_2 + q_2}{2} \text{ so that } p_2 < x_2 < q_2$$

Continuing this way, we obtain that at n^{th} step,

$$x_n = \frac{p_n + q_n}{2}, p_n < x_n < q_n$$

and $$p_1 \le p_2 \le ...... \le p_n \text{ and } q_1 \ge q_2 \ge ...... \ge q_n$$

$\therefore$ $<p_1, p_2, ..., p_n, ...>$ is a bounded, non-decreasing sequence bounded by b and $< q_1, q_2, ..., q_n, ...>$ is a bounded, non-increasing sequence of numbers bounded by a.

Hence, both these sequences converge.

Let, $$\lim_{n \to \infty} p_n = p \text{ and } \lim_{n \to \infty} q_n = q.$$

Now, since the length of the interval is decreasing at every step, we get that

$$\lim_{n \to \infty} (q_n - p_n) = 0 \Rightarrow q = p$$

Also, $$p_n < x_n < q_n$$

$$\Rightarrow \lim p_n \le \lim x_n \le \lim q_n$$

$$\Rightarrow p \le \lim x_n \le q$$

$$\Rightarrow \lim x_n = p = q \quad (2)$$

Further, since a root lies in $[p_n, q_n]$, we shall have

$$f(p_n) . f(q_n) < 0$$

$$\Rightarrow 0 \ge \lim_{n \to \infty} [f(p_n) . f(q_n)]$$

$$\Rightarrow 0 \ge f(p) . f(q)$$

$$\Rightarrow 0 \ge [f(p)]^2$$

But, $[f(p)]^2 \ge 0$ being a square

$\therefore$ we get $f(p) = 0$

$\therefore$ p is a root of $f(x) = 0$ (3)

From (2) and (3), we see that $<x_n>$ converges *necessarily* to a root of equation $f(x) = 0$

The method is not rapidly converging, but it is useful in the sense that it converges surely.

EXAMPLES

Example 1. *Find the real root of the equation $x \log_{10} x = 1.2$ by Bisection method correct to four decimal places. Also write its program in C-language.*

Sol. $f(x) = x \log_{10} x - 1.2$

Since $f(2.74) = -.000563$ *i.e.,* (–)ve

and $f(2.75) = .0081649$ *i.e.,* (+)ve

Hence, the root lies between 2.74 and 2.75.

∴ First approximation to the root is

$$x_1 = \frac{2.74 + 2.75}{2} = 2.745$$

Now $f(x_1) = f(2.745) = .003798$ *i.e.,* (+)ve

Hence, the root lies between 2.74 and 2.745.

∴ Second approximation to the root is

$$x_2 = \frac{2.74 + 2.745}{2} = 2.7425$$

Now $f(x_2) = f(2.7425) = .001617$ *i.e.,* (+)ve

Hence, the root lies between 2.74 and 2.7425.

∴ Third approximation to the root is

$$x_3 = \frac{2.74 + 2.7425}{2} = 2.74125$$

Now $f(x_3) = f(2.74125) = .0005267$ *i.e.,* (+)ve

Hence, the root lies between 2.74 and 2.74125.

∴ Fourth approximation to the root is

$$x_4 = \frac{2.74 + 2.74125}{2} = 2.740625$$

Now $f(x_4) = f(2.740625) = -.00001839$ *i.e.,* (–)ve.

Hence, the root lies between 2.740625 and 2.74125.

∴ Fifth approximation to the root is

$$x_5 = \frac{2.740625 + 2.74125}{2} = 2.7409375$$

Now $f(x_5) - f(2.7409375) = .000254$ *i.e.,* (+)ve

Hence, the root lies between 2.740625 and 2.7409375.

∴ Sixth approximation to the root is

$$x_6 = \frac{2.740625 + 2.7409375}{2} = 2.74078125$$

Now $f(x_6) = f(2.74078125) = .0001178$ *i.e.,* (+)ve

Hence, the root lies between 2.740625 and 2.74078125.

∴ Seventh approximation to the root is

$$x_7 = \frac{2.740625 + 2.74078125}{2} = 2.740703125$$

Now $f(x_7) = f(2.740703125) = .00004973$ *i.e.,* (+)ve

Hence, the root lies between 2.740625 and 2.740703125

∴ Eighth approximation to the root is

$$x_8 = \frac{2.740625 + 2.740703125}{2} = 2.740664063$$

Now $f(x_8) = f(2.740664063) = .00001567$ *i.e.,* (+)ve

Hence, the root lies between 2.740625 and 2.740664063.

∴ Nineth approximation to the root is

$$x_9 = \frac{2.740625 + 2.740664063}{2} = 2.740644532$$

Since x_8 and x_9 are the same up to four decimal places, the approximate real root is **2.7406.** C-program for above problem is given below:

3.9 PROGRAM TO IMPLEMENT BISECTION METHOD

```
//...Included Header Files
#include<stdio.h>
#include<math.h>
#include<conio.h>
#include<process.h>
#include<string.h>
#define EPS      0.00000005
#define F(x)     (x)*log10(x)-1.2
```

```
//...Function Prototype Declaration
void Bisect();
//...Global Variable Declaration field
int count=1,n;
float root=1;
//... Main Function Implementation
void main()
     {
     clrscr();
     printf("\n Solution by BISECTION method \n");
     printf("\n Equation is ");
     printf("\n\t\t\t x*log(x) - 1.2 = 0\n\n");
     printf("Enter the number of iterations:");
     scanf("%d",&n);
     Bisect();
     getch();
     }
//... Function Declaration
void Bisect()
     {
     float x0,x1,x2;
     float f0,f1,f2;
     int i=0;
     /*Finding an Approximate ROOT of Given Equation, Having
+ve Value*/
     for(x2=1;;x2++)
          {
          f2=F(x2);
          if (f2>0)
               {
               break;
               }
          }
     /*Finding an Approximate ROOT of Given Equation, Having
-ve Value*/
```

```
        for(x1=x2-1;;x2--)
        {
        f1=F(x1);
        if(f1<0)
            {
            break;
            }
    }
    //...Printing Result
    printf("\t\t-----------------------------------------");
    printf("\n\t\t ITERATIONS\t\t      ROOTS\n");
    printf("\t\t-----------------------------------------");
    for(;count<=n;count++)
        {
        x0=(x1+x2)/2.0;
        f0=F(x0);
        if(f0==0)
                {
                root=x0;
                }
        if(f0*f1<0)
                {
                x2=x0;
                }
        else
                {
                x1=x0;
                f1=f0;
                }
        printf("\n\t\t ITERATION %d", count);
        printf("\t   :\t   %f",x0);
        if(fabs((x1-x2)/x1) < EPS)
           {
          printf("\n\t\t-----------------------------------");
              printf("\n\t\t        Root = %f",x0);
```

```
        printf("\n\t\t  Iterations = %d\n", count);
        printf("\t\t-----------------------------------");
        getch();
        exit(0);
        }
  }
printf("\n\t\t-----------------------------------------");
printf("\n\t\t\t Root = %7.4f",x0);
printf("\n\t\t\t Iterations = %d\n", count-1);
printf("\t\t-----------------------------------------");
getch();
}
```

OUTPUT

```
Solution by BISECTION method
Equation is
                x* log(x) - 1.2=0
Enter the number of iterations: 30
    ------------------------------------------
    ITERATIONS                          ROOTS
    ------------------------------------------
    ITERATION 1:                     2.500000
    ITERATION 2:                     2.750000
    ITERATION 3:                     2.625000
    ITERATION 4:                     2.687500
    ITERATION 5:                     2.718750
    ITERATION 10:                    2.741211
    ITERATION 11:                    2.740723
    ITERATION 12:                    2.740479
    ITERATION 13:                    2.740601
    ITERATION 14:                    2.740662
    ITERATION 15:                    2.740631
    ITERATION 16:                    2.740646
    ITERATION 17:                    2.740639
    ITERATION 18:                    2.740643
    ITERATION 19:                    2.740644
    ITERATION 20:                    2.740645
```

```
              ITERATION 21:                    2.740646
              ITERATION 22:                    2.740646
              ITERATION 23:                    2.740646
              ITERATION 24:                    2.740646
              ITERATION 25:                    2.740646
              ITERATION 26:                    2.740646
              ITERATION 27:                    2.740646
              ITERATION 28:                    2.740646
              ITERATION 29:                    2.740646
              ITERATION 30:                    2.740646
             ----------------------------------------------
                      Root = 2.7406
                Iterations = 30
             ----------------------------------------------
C:\tc\exe>
```

Example 2. *Find a root of the equation*

$$x^3 - 4x - 9 = 0$$

using Bisection method in four stages.

Sol. Let $$f(x) \equiv x^3 - 4x - 9$$

Since $$f(2.706) = -.009488 \quad i.e., (-)\text{ve}$$

and $$f(2.707) = .008487 \quad i.e., (+)\text{ve}$$

Hence, the root lies between 2.706 and 2.707.

$\therefore$ First approximation to the root is

$$x_1 = \frac{2.706 + 2.707}{2} = 2.7065$$

Now $$f(x_1) = -.0005025 \quad i.e., (-)\text{ve}$$

Hence, the root lies between 2.7065 and 2.707.

$\therefore$ Second approximation to the root is

$$x_2 = \frac{2.7065 + 2.707}{2} = 2.70675$$

Now $$f(x_2) = .003992 \quad i.e., (+)\text{ve}$$

Hence, the root lies between 2.7065 and 2.70675.

∴ Third approximation to the root is

$$x_3 = \frac{2.7065 + 2.70675}{2} = 2.706625$$

Now $f(x_3) = .001744$ *i.e.*, (+)ve

Hence, the root lies between 2.7065 and 2.706625.

∴ Fourth approximation to the root is

$$x_4 = \frac{2.7065 + 2.706625}{2} = 2.7065625$$

Hence, the root is **2.7065625,** correct to three decimal places.

Example 3. *Find a positive real root of $x - \cos x = 0$ by bisection method, correct up to 4 decimal places between 0 and 1.*

Sol. Let $f(x) = x - \cos x$

$$f(0.73) = (-)\text{ve} \quad \text{and} \quad f(0.74) = (+)\text{ve}$$

Hence, the root lies between 0.73 and 0.74. First approximation to the root is

$$x_1 = \frac{0.73 + 0.74}{2} = 0.735$$

Now $f(0.735) = (-)$ve

Hence, the root lies between 0.735 and 0.74. Second approximation to the root is

$$x_2 = \frac{0.73 + 0.74}{2} = 0.7375$$

Now $f(0.7375) = (-)$ve

Hence, the root lies between 0.7375 and 0.74. Third approximation to the root is

$$x_3 = \frac{0.7375 + 0.74}{2} = 0.73875$$

Now $f(0.73875) = (-)$ve

Hence, the root lies between 0.73875 and 0.74.

Fourth approximation to the root is

$$x_4 = \frac{1}{2}\,(0.73875 + 0.74) = 0.739375$$

Now $f(x_4) = f(0.739375) = (+)$ve

Hence, the root lies between 0.73875 and 0.739375.

Fifth approximation to the root is

$$x_5 = \frac{1}{2}(0.73875 + 0.739375) = 0.7390625$$

Now $\quad f(0.7390625) = (-)\text{ve}$

Hence, the root lies between 0.7390625 and 0.739375

Sixth approximation to the root is

$$x_6 = \frac{1}{2}(0.7390625 + 0.739375) = 0.73921875$$

Now $\quad f(0.73921875) = (+)\text{ve}$

Hence, the root lies between 0.7390625 and 0.73921875

Seventh approximation to the root is

$$x_7 = \frac{1}{2}(0.7390625 + 0.73921875) = 0.73914$$

Now $\quad f(0.73914) = (+)\text{ve}$

Hence, the root lies between 0.7390625 and 0.73914

Eighth approximate to the root is

$$x_8 = \frac{1}{2}(0.7390625 + 0.73914) = 0.73910$$

Hence, the approximate real root is 0.7391.

Example 4. *Perform five iterations of the bisection method to obtain the smallest positive root of equation*

$$f(x) \equiv x^3 - 5x + 1 = 0.$$

Sol. $\quad f(x) = x^3 - 5x + 1$

Since $\quad f(.2016) = .0001935 \quad$ *i.e.,* (+)ve

and $\quad f(.2017) = -\ .0002943 \quad$ *i.e.,* (–)ve

Hence, the root lies between .2016 and .2017.

First approximation to the root is

$$x_1 = \frac{.2016 + .2017}{2} = .20165$$

Now $\quad f(x_1) = -\ .00005036 \quad$ *i.e.,* (–)ve

Hence, the root lies between .2016 and .20165.

Second approximation to the root is

$$x_2 = \frac{.2016 + .20165}{2} = .201625$$

Now $f(x_2) = .00007159$ *i.e.*, (+)ve

Hence, the root lies between .201625 and .20165.

Third approximation to the root is

$$x_3 = \frac{.201625 + .20165}{2} = .2016375$$

Now $f(x_3) = .00001061$ *i.e.*, (+)ve

Hence, the root lies between .2016375 and .20165.

Fourth approximation to the root is

$$x_4 = \frac{.2016375 + .20165}{2} = .20164375$$

Now $f(x_4) = -\ .00001987$ *i.e.*, (–)ve

Hence, the root lies between .2016375 and .20164375.

∴ Fifth approximation to the root is

$$x_5 = \frac{.2016375 + .20164375}{2} = .201640625$$

Hence, after performing five iterations, the **smallest positive root** of the given equation is **.20164,** correct to **five decimal places.**

Example 5. *Find a real root of* $x^3 - x = 1$ *between 1 and 2 by bisection method. Compute five iterations.*

Sol. Here, $f(x) = x^3 - x - 1$

Since $f(1.324) = -\ .00306$ *i.e.*, (–)ve

and $f(1.325) = .00120$ *i.e.*, (+)ve

Hence, the root lies between 1.324 and 1.325.

∴ First approximation to the root is

$$x_1 = \frac{1.324 + 1.325}{2} = 1.3245$$

Now $f(x_1) = -\ .000929$ *i.e.*, (–)ve

Hence, the root lies between 1.3245 and 1.325

∴ Second approximation to the root is

$$x_2 = \frac{1.3245 + 1.325}{2} = 1.32475$$

Now $f(x_2) = .000136$ *i.e.*, (+)ve

Hence, the root lies between 1.3245 and 1.32475.

Third approximation to the root is

$$x_3 = \frac{1.3245 + 1.32475}{2} = 1.324625$$

Now $f(x_3) = -.000396$ *i.e.*, (–)ve

Hence, the root lies between 1.324625 and 1.32475.

∴ Fourth approximation to the root is

$$x_4 = \frac{1.324625 + 1.32475}{2} = 1.3246875$$

Now $f(x_4) = -.0001298$ *i.e.*, (–)ve

Hence, the root lies between 1.3246875 and 1.32475

∴ Fifth approximation to the root is

$$x_5 = \frac{1.3246875 + 1.32475}{2} = 1.32471875$$

Hence, the real root of the given equation is **1.324** correct to three decimal places after computing five iterations.

Example 6. *Use bisection method to find out the positive square root of 30 correct to 4 decimal places.*

Sol. Let $f(x) = x^2 - 30$

Since $f(5.477) = -.00247$ *i.e.*, (–)ve

and $f(5.478) = .00848$ *i.e.*, (+)ve

Hence, the root lies between 5.477 and 5.478

∴ First approximation to the root is

$$x_1 = \frac{5.477 + 5.478}{2} = 5.4775$$

Now $f(x_1) = .003$ *i.e.*, (+)ve

Hence, the root lies between 5.477 and 5.4775

∴ Second approximation to the root is

$$x_2 = \frac{5.477 + 5.4775}{2} = 5.47725$$

Now $f(x_2) = .00026$ *i.e.*, (+)ve

Hence, the root lies between 5.477 and 5.47725

$\therefore$ Third approximation to the root is

$$x_3 = \frac{5.477 + 5.47725}{2} = 5.477125$$

Now $f(x_3) = -\ .0011$ *i.e.*, (–)ve

Hence, the root lies between 5.477125 and 5.47725

$\therefore$ Fourth approximation to the root is

$$x_4 = \frac{5.477125 + 5.47725}{2} = 5.4771875$$

Since x_3 and x_4 are the same up to four decimal places, the positive square root of 30, correct to 4 decimal places, is **5.4771.**

ASSIGNMENT 3.1

1. (*i*) Transcendental equation is given as

$$f(x) = 2^x - x - 3$$

Calculate $f(x)$ for $x = -4, -3, -2, -1, 0, 1, 2, 3, 4$ and determine, between which integer the values roots are lying.

(*ii*) The equation $x^2 - 2x - 3\cos x = 0$ is given. Locate the smallest root in magnitude in an interval of length one unit.

2. Find a real root of $e^x = 3x$ by Bisection method.
3. Find the smallest positive root of $x^3 - 9x + 1 = 0$, using Bisection method correct to three decimal places.
4. Find the real root lying in interval (1, 2) up to four decimal places for the equation $x^6 - x^4 - x^3 - 1 = 0$ by bisection method.
5. Find the root of $\tan x + x = 0$ up to two decimal places which lies between 2 and 2.1 using Bisection method.
6. Compute the root of $\log x = \cos x$ correct to 2 decimal places using Bisection method.
7. Compute the root of $f(x) = \sin 10x + \cos 3x$ by computer using Bisection method. The initial approximations are 4 and 5.
8. Find the real root correct to three decimal places for the following equations:

(*i*) $x^3 - x - 4 = 0$ (*ii*) $x^3 - x^2 - 1 = 0$

(*iii*) $x^3 + x^2 - 1 = 0$ (*iv*) $x^3 - 3x - 5 = 0$.

9. Find a root of $x^3 - x - 11 = 0$ using Bisection method correct to 3 decimal places which lies between 2 and 3.
10. Find a real root of the equation $x^3 - 2x - 5 = 0$ using Bisection method.
11. Find a positive root of the equation $xe^x = 1$ which lies between 0 and 1.

12. Apply Bisection method to find a root of the equation $x^4 + 2x^3 - x - 1 = 0$ in the interval [0, 1].

13. Obtain a root correct to three decimal places for each of these equations using Bisection method.

(*i*) $x^3 + x^2 + x + 7 = 0$ (*ii*) $x^3 - 18 = 0$

(*iii*) $x^3 + x - 1 = 0$ (*iv*) $x^3 - 5x + 3 = 0$.

14. By displaying procedure in tabular form, use Bisection method to compute the root of 36.

15. Find a positive root of the equation $x^3 + 3x - 1 = 0$ by bisection method.

16. Find a real root of $x^3 - 2x - 1 = 0$ which lies between 1 and 2 by using Bisection method correct to 2 decimal places.

17. Find the approximate value of the root of the equation $3x - \sqrt{1 + \sin x} = 0$ by Bisection method.

18. (*i*) Explain the Bisection method to calculate the roots of an equation. Write an algorithm and implement it in 'C'.

(*ii*) Write computer program in a language of your choice which implements bisection method to compute the real root of the equation $3x + \sin x - e^x = 0$ in a given interval.

19. Solve $x^3 - 9x + 1 = 0$ for the root between $x = 2$ and $x = 4$ by the method of Bisection.

20. If a root of $f(x) = 0$ lies in the interval (a, b), then find the minimum number of iterations required when the permissible error is E.

21. The negative root of the smallest magnitude of the equation $f(x) = 3x^3 + 10x^2 + 10x + 7 = 0$ is to be obtained.

(*i*) Find an interval of unit length which contains this root.

(*ii*) Perform two iterations of the bisection method.

22. The smallest positive root of the equation

$$f(x) = x^4 - 3x^2 + x - 10 = 0$$

is to be obtained.

(*i*) Find an interval of unit length which contains this root.

(*ii*) Perform two iterations of the bisection method.

3.10 ITERATION METHOD—(Successive Approximation Method)

To find the roots of the equation $f(x) = 0$ by successive approximations, we write it in the form

$$x = \phi(x)$$

The roots of $f(x) = 0$ are the same as the points of intersection of the straight line $y = x$ and the curve representing

$$y = \phi(x).$$

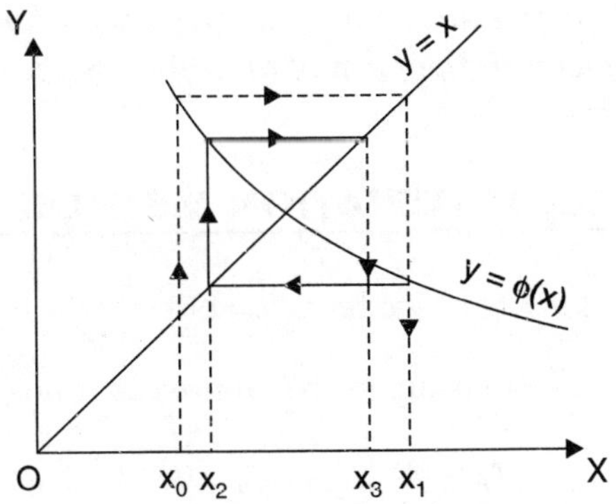

(Working of Iteration method)

Let $x = x_0$ be an initial approximation of the desired root α, then first approximation x_1 is given by

$$x_1 = \phi(x_0)$$

Now, treating x_1 as the initial value, the second approximation is

$$x_2 = \phi(x_1)$$

Proceeding in this way, the nth approximation is given by

$$x_n = \phi(x_{n-1}).$$

3.11 SUFFICIENT CONDITION FOR CONVERGENCE OF ITERATIONS

It is not definite that the sequence of approximations $x_1, x_2, ..., x_n$ always converges to the same number, which is a root of $f(x) = 0$.

As such, we have to choose the initial approximation x_0 suitably so that the successive approximations $x_1, x_2, ..., x_n$ converge to the root α. The following theorem helps in making the right choice of x_0.

3.12 THEOREM

If (*i*) α be a root of $f(x) = 0$ which is equivalent to $x = \phi(x)$*.

(*ii*) I be any interval containing $x = \alpha$.

(*iii*) $| \phi'(x) | < 1$ for all x in I, then the sequence of approximations $x_0, x_1, x_2, ..., x_n$ will converge to the root a provided the initial approximation x_0 is chosen in I.

*x is obtained interms of $\phi(x)$ such that $| \phi'(x) | < 1$.

NOTE *This method of iteration is particularly useful for finding the real roots of an equation given in the form of an infinite series.*

3.13 CONVERGENCE OF ITERATION METHOD

Since α is a root of $x = \phi(x)$, we have $\alpha = \phi(\alpha)$

If x_{n-1} and x_n are two successive approximations to α, we have

$$x_n = \phi(x_{n-1}), \quad x_n - \alpha = \phi(x_{n-1}) - \phi(\alpha) \tag{4}$$

By mean value theorem,

$$\frac{\phi(x_{n-1}) - \phi(\alpha)}{x_{n-1} - \alpha} = \phi'(\xi), \text{ where } x_{n-1} < \xi < \alpha$$

Hence (4) becomes $x_n - \alpha = (x_{n-1} - \alpha)\, \phi'(\xi)$

If $|\, \phi'(x_i) \,| \le k < 1$ for all i, then,

$$|\, x_n - \alpha \,| \le k \,|\, x_{n-1} - \alpha \,|, \; k < 1$$

Hence it is clear that the iteration method is linearly convergent.

NOTE **1.** *The smaller the value of $\phi'(x)$, the more rapid will be the convergence.*

2. *For rapid convergence, $f'(a) \approx 0$.*

3.14 ALGORITHM FOR ITERATION METHOD

3.14.1 Algorithm 1

1. Read x_0, e, n

NOTE *x_0 is the initial guess, e is the allowed error in root, n is total iterations to be allowed for convergence.*

2. $x_1 \leftarrow g(x_0)$

NOTE *Steps 4 to 6 are repeated until the procedure converges to a root or iterations reach n.*

3. For $i = 1$ to n in steps of 1 do

4. $x_0 \leftarrow x_1$

5. $x_1 \leftarrow g(x_0)$

6. If $\left|\dfrac{x_1 - x_0}{x_1}\right| \le e$ then, GO TO 9

   end for.

7. Write 'Does not converge to a root', x_0, x_1

8. Stop

9. Write 'converges to a root', i, x_1

10. Stop.

3.14.2 Algorithm 2 (Aliter)

1. Define function $f(x)$

2. Define function $df(x)$

3. Get the value of a, max_err.

4. Initialize j

5. If $df(a) < 1$ then $b = 1$, $a = f(a)$

6. Print root after j, iteration is $f(a)$

7. If $fabs(b - a) >$ max_err then

8. j++, goto (5)

   End if

   Else print root doesn't exist

9. End.

3.15 FLOW-CHART FOR ITERATION METHOD

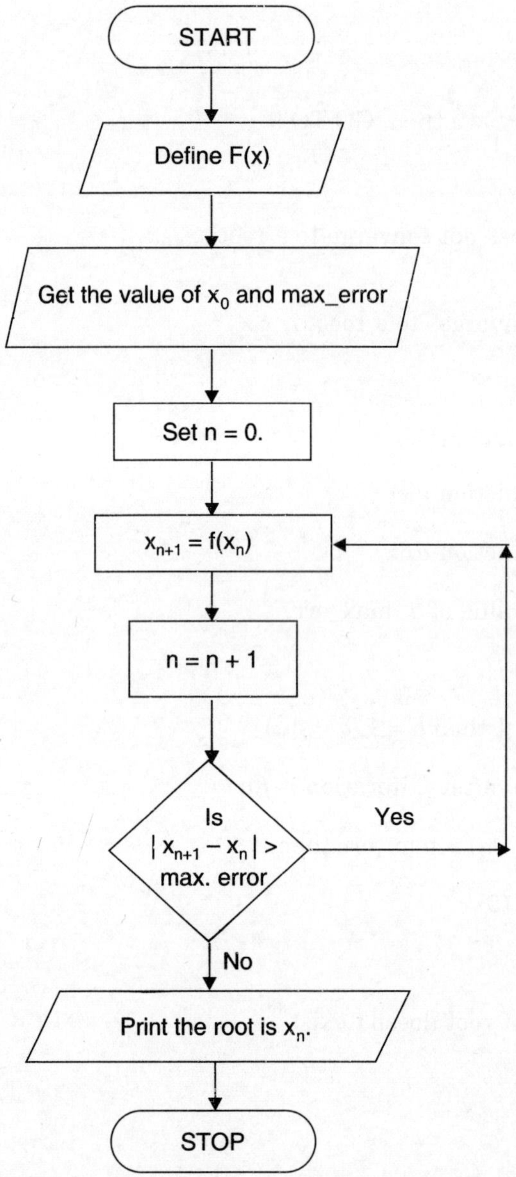

3.16 COMPUTER PROGRAM

```
//Program for Solution by ITERATION method
#include<stdio.h>
#include<math.h>
#include<conio.h>
#define EPS 0.00005
#define F(x)     (x*x*x + 1)/2
#define f(x)     x*x*x - 2*x + 1
void ITER();
void main ()
{
 clrscr();
 printf("\n\t Solution by ITERATION method \n");
 printf("\n\t Equation is ");
 printf("\n\t\t\t\t X*X*X - 2*X + 1 = 0\n\n");
 ITER();
 getch();
}
void ITER()
{
 float x1,x2,x0,f0,f1,f2,error;
 int i=0,n;
 for(x1=1;;x1++)
 {
      f1=F(x1);
      if (f1>0)
           break;
 }
 for(x0=x1-1;;x0--)
 {
 f0=f(x0);
 if(f0<0)
      break;
 }
```

```
x2=(x0+x1)/2;
printf("Enter the number of iterations:");
scanf("%d",&n);
printf("\n\n\t\t The 1 approximation to the root is: %f",x2);
for(;i<n-1;i++)
{
f2=F(x2);
printf("\n\n\t\t The %d approximation to the root is:
%f",i+2,f2);
        x2=F(x2);
        error=fabs(f2-f1);
        if(error<EPS)
            break;
        f1=f2;
}
    if(error>EPS)
        printf("\n\n\t NOTE:- The number of iterations
are not sufficient.");
    printf("\n\n\n\t\t\t-----------------------------");
    printf("\n\t\t\t The root is %.4f",f2);
        printf("\n\t\t\t-----------------------------");
}
```

3.16.1 Output

```
Solution by ITERATION method
Equation is
                x*x*x-2*x+1=0
Enter the number of iterations: 15
The 1 approximation to the root is: 0.000000
The 2 approximation to the root is: 0.500000
The 3 approximation to the root is: 0.562500
The 4 approximation to the root is: 0.588989
The 5 approximation to the root is: 0.602163
The 6 approximation to the root is: 0.609172
The 7 approximation to the root is: 0.613029
```

```
The 8 approximation to the root is: 0.615190
The 9 approximation to the root is: 0.616412
The 10 approximation to the root is:0.617107
The 11 approximation to the root is:0.617504
The 12 approximation to the root is:0.617730
The 13 approximation to the root is:0.617860
The 14 approximation to the root is:0.617934
The 15 approximation to the root is:0.617977
-----------------------------------------------------
The Root is 0.6179 (Correct to four decimal places)
-----------------------------------------------------
```

3.16.2 Insufficient Output

```
Solution by ITERATION method
Equation is
                x*x*x-2*x+1=0
Enter the number of Iterations:5
The 1 approximation to the root is: 0.000000
The 2 approximation to the root is: 0.500000
The 3 approximation to the root is: 0.562500
The 4 approximation to the root is: 0.588989
The 5 approximation to the root is: 0.602163
```

NOTE

```
The number of Iterations are not sufficient.
-----------------------------------------------------
              The Root is 0.6022
```

EXAMPLES

Example 1. *Use the method of iteration to find a positive root between 0 and 1 of the equation* $xe^x = 1$.

Sol. Writing the equation in the form $x = e^{-x}$

we find, $$\phi(x) = e^{-x} \text{ so } \phi'(x) = -e^{-x}$$

Hence, $|\phi'(x)| < 1$ for $x < 1$, which assures that iteration is convergent.

Starting with $x_0 = 1$, we find that successive iterates are given by

$$x_1 = \frac{1}{e} = 0.3678794$$

$$x = e^{-0.3678794} = 0.6922006$$

$$\vdots$$

$$x_{20} = 0.5671477.$$

Example 2. *Find a real root of the equation cos x = 3x – 1 correct to 3 decimal places using iteration method.*

Sol. We have $f(x) = \cos x - 3x + 1 = 0$

Now, $f(0) = 2$ and $f(\pi/2) = -\frac{3\pi}{2} + 1 = (-)\text{ve}$

$\therefore$ A root lies between 0 and $\pi/2$.

Rewriting the given equation as

$$x = \frac{1}{3}(\cos x + 1) = \phi(x)$$

We have $\phi'(x) = -\frac{\sin x}{3}$

and $|\phi'(x)| = \frac{1}{3}|\sin x| < 1$ in $(0, \pi/2)$

Hence the iteration method can be applied and we start with $x_0 = 0$. Then the successive approximations are

$$x_1 = \phi(x_0) = \frac{1}{3}(\cos 0 + 1) = 0.6667$$

$$x_2 = \phi(x_1) = \frac{1}{3}[\cos 0.6667 + 1] = 0.5953$$

$$x_3 = \phi(x_2) = \frac{1}{3}[\cos (0.5953) + 1] = 0.6093$$

$$x_4 = \phi(x_3) = 0.6067$$

$$x_5 = \phi(x_4) = 0.6072$$

$$x_6 = \phi(x_5) = 0.6071.$$

Since x_5 and x_6 are almost the same, the root is 0.607 correct to three decimal places.

Example 3. *Find a real root of $2x - \log_{10} x = 7$ correct to four decimal places using the iteration method.*

Sol. We have
$$f(x) = 2x - \log_{10} x - 7$$
$$f(3) = 6 - \log 3 - 7 = 6 - 0.4771 - 7 = -1.4471$$
$$f(4) = 0.398$$

$\therefore$ A root lies between 3 and 4.

Rewriting the given equation as

$$x = \frac{1}{2}(\log_{10} x + 7) = \phi(x),$$

we have
$$\phi'(x) = \frac{1}{2}\left(\frac{1}{x}\log_{10} e\right)$$

$\therefore$ $$|\phi'(x)| < 1 \text{ when } 3 < x < 4 \qquad (\because \log_{10} e = 0.4343)$$

Since $|f(4)| < |f(3)|$, the root is near 4.

Hence the iteration method can be applied.

The successive approximations of $x_0 = 3.6$ are

$$x_1 = \phi(x_0) = \frac{1}{2}(\log_{10} 3.6 + 7) = 3.77815$$

$$x_2 = \phi(x_1) = \frac{1}{2}(\log_{10} 3.77815 + 7) = 3.78863$$

$$x_3 = \phi(x_2) = 3.78924$$

$$x_4 = \phi(x_3) = 3.78927$$

Since x_3 and x_4 are almost equal, the root is 3.7892, correct to four decimal places.

Example 4. *Find the smallest root of the equation*

$$1 - x + \frac{x^2}{(2!)^2} - \frac{x^3}{(3!)^2} + \frac{x^4}{(4!)^2} - \frac{x^5}{(5!)^2} + \ldots\ldots = 0.$$

Sol. Writing the given equation as

$$x = 1 + \frac{x^2}{(2!)^2} - \frac{x^3}{(3!)^2} + \frac{x^4}{(4!)^2} - \frac{x^5}{(5!)^2} + \ldots\ldots = \phi(x)$$

and omitting x^2 and higher powers of x, we get $x = 1$ approximately.

Taking $x_0 = 1$, we obtain,

$$x_1 = \phi(x_0) = 1 + \frac{1}{(2!)^2} - \frac{1}{(3!)^2} + \frac{1}{(4!)^2} - \frac{1}{(5!)^2} + \ldots\ldots = 1.2239$$

$$x_2 = \phi(x_1) = 1 + \frac{(1.2239)^2}{(2!)^2} - \frac{(1.2239)^3}{(3!)^2} + \frac{(1.2239)^4}{(4!)^2} - \frac{(1.2239)^5}{(5!)^2} + \ldots\ldots$$

$$= 1.3263$$

Similarly, $x_3 = \phi(x_2) = 1.38$

$$x_4 = 1.409, \quad x_5 = 1.425, \quad x_6 = 1.434, \quad x_7 = 1.439, \quad x_8 = 1.442$$

Values of x_7 and x_8 indicate that the root is 1.44, correct to two decimal places.

Example 5. *If* α, β *are the roots of* $x^2 + ax + b = 0$, *show that the iteration* $x_{n+1} = -\left(\frac{ax_n + b}{x_n}\right)$ *will converge near* $x = \alpha$ *if* $|\alpha| > |\beta|$ *and the iteration*

$x_{n+1} = \frac{-b}{x_n + a}$ *will converge near* $x = \alpha$ *if* $|\alpha| < |\beta|$.

Sol. Since α, β are the roots of $x^2 + ax + b = 0$,

we have $\alpha + \beta = -a$ and $\alpha\beta = b$

The formula $x_{n+1} = -\left(\frac{ax_n + b}{x_n}\right)$, which is of the form $x_{n+1} = f(x_n)$, will converge to $x = \alpha$ if

$$\left| \frac{d}{dx}\left\{\frac{-(ax+b)}{x}\right\}_{x = x_n} \right| < 1 \qquad \left|\ \text{Using condition of iteration method}\right.$$

$$\Rightarrow \quad \left|\frac{b}{x_n^2}\right| < 1$$

$$\Rightarrow \quad |x_n^2| > |b| \quad \text{or} \quad x_n^2 > |b|$$

or $$|\alpha|^2 > |b| \quad \text{as} \quad x_n \to \alpha$$

or $$|\alpha|^2 > |\alpha|\,|\beta| \qquad (\because \alpha\beta = b)$$

or $$|\alpha| > |\beta|$$

Similarly, $x_{n+1} = \dfrac{-b}{x_n + a}$ will converge to $x = \alpha$ if

$$\left| \left[\frac{d}{dx} \left(\frac{-b}{x+a} \right) \right]_{x = x_n} \right| < 1$$

or
$$\left| \frac{b}{(x_n + a)^2} \right| < 1$$

or
$$(x_n + a)^2 > | b | \quad \text{or} \quad (\alpha + a)^2 > | b | \quad \text{as } x_n \to \alpha$$

or
$$\beta^2 > | b | \qquad (\because \ \alpha + a = -\beta)$$

or
$$| \beta |^2 > | \alpha | \, | \beta |$$

or
$$| \beta | > | \alpha | \quad \text{or} \quad | \alpha | < | \beta |.$$

Example 6. *Show that the following rearrangement of equation $x^3 + 6x^2 + 10x - 20 = 0$ does not yield a convergent sequence of successive approximations by iteration method near $x = 1$,*

$$x = (20 - 6x^2 - x^3)/10.$$

Sol. Here,
$$x = \frac{20 - 6x^2 - x^3}{10} = f(x)$$

Hence,
$$f'(x) = \frac{-12x - 3x^2}{10}$$

Clearly, $f'(x) < -1$ in neighborhood of $x = 1$. Hence $| f'(x) | > 1$, and neither the method nor the sequence $<x_n>$ converge.

Example 7. *Suggest a value of constant k, so that the iteration formula $x = x + k(x^2 - 3)$ may converge at a good rate, given that $x = \sqrt{3}$ is a root.*

Sol. Formula $x = f(x)$ where $f(x) = x + k(x^2 - 3)$

will converge if

$$| f'(x) | < 1 \quad \text{or} \quad -1 < f'(x) < 1$$

i.e., if
$$-1 < 1 + 2kx < 1$$

Moreover, the convergence will be rapid if $f'(a) \simeq 0$

i.e., if
$$1 + 2ka \simeq 0$$

i.e.,
$$1 + 2k\sqrt{3} \simeq 0 \;\Rightarrow\; k = -\frac{1}{2\sqrt{3}}$$

We may take $k = -\frac{1}{4}$ to insure a rapid convergence by this formula.

Example 8. *If F(x) is sufficiently differentiable and the iteration $x_{n+1} = F(x_n)$ converges, prove that the order of convergence is a positive integer.*

Sol. Let $x = a$ be a root of the equation $x = F(x)$ then, $a = F(a)$

Let, for some p(positive integer)

$$F'(a) = 0, \quad F''(a) = 0, \; ......, \; F^{(p-1)}(a) = 0 \text{ and } F^{(p)}(a) \neq 0$$

then expanding $F(x_n)$ about a, we get

$$x_{n+1} = F(x_n) = F(a + x_n - a)$$

$$= F(a) + (x_n - a) F'(a) + ... + \frac{(x_n - a)^{p-1}}{(p-1)!} F^{(p-1)}(a) + \frac{(x_n - a)^p}{p!} F^{(p)}(\xi)$$

where ξ is some point between $x = x_n$ and $x = a$.

$$\Rightarrow \qquad x_{n+1} = a + \frac{(x_n - a)^p}{p!} F^{(p)}(\xi)$$

$$\Rightarrow \qquad x_{n+1} - a = (x_n - a)^p \cdot \frac{F^{(p)}(\xi)}{p!}$$

$\therefore$ The order of convergence is p, a positive integer.

Example 9. *The equation $\sin x = 5x - 2$ can be written as $x = \sin^{-1}(5x - 2)$ and also as $x = \frac{1}{5}(\sin x + 2)$, suggesting two iterating procedures for its solution. Which of these, if either, would succeed, and which would fail to give a root in the neighborhood of 0.5?*

Sol. In case I, $\phi(x) = \sin^{-1}(5x - 2)$

$$\therefore \qquad \phi'(x) = \frac{5}{\sqrt{1-(5x-2)^2}}$$

Hence, $|\phi'(x)| > 1$ for all x for which $(5x - 2)^2 < 1$ or $x < 3/5$ or $x < 0.6$ in neighborhood of 0.5. Thus the method would not give a convergent sequence.

In case II, $\phi(x) = \frac{1}{5}(\sin x + 2)$

$$\therefore \qquad \phi'(x) = \frac{1}{5} \cos x$$

Hence $| \phi'(x) | \le \frac{1}{5}$ for all x because $| \cos x | \le 1$

$\therefore$ $\phi(x)$ will succeed.

Hence, taking $x = \phi(x) = \frac{1}{5}(\sin x + 2)$ and the initial value $x_0 = 0.5$, we have the first approximation x_1 given by

$$x_1 = \frac{1}{5}(\sin 0.5 + 2) = 0.4017$$

$$x_2 = \frac{1}{5}[\sin(0.4017) + 2] = 0.4014$$

$$x_3 = \frac{1}{5}[\sin(0.4014) + 2] = 0.4014$$

Hence, up to four decimal places, the value of the required root is 0.4014.

Example 10. *Starting with $x = 0.12$, solve $x = 0.21 \sin(0.5 + x)$ by using the iteration method.*

Sol. Here, $x = 0.21 \sin(0.5 + x)$

$\therefore$ First approximation of x is given by

$$x^{(1)} = 0.21 \sin(0.5 + 0.12) = 0.122$$

$$x^{(2)} = 0.21 \sin(0.5 + 0.122) = 0.1224$$

Similarly, $x^{(3)} = 0.12242,\ x^{(4)} = 0.12242$

Obviously, $x^{(3)} = x^{(4)}$

Hence the required root is 0.12242.

Example 11. *Find a real root of the equation $f(x) = x^3 + x^2 - 1 = 0$ by using the iteration method.*

Sol. Here, $f(0) = -1$ and $f(1) = 1$ so a root lies between 0 and 1. Now, $x = \frac{1}{\sqrt{1+x}}$

so that,

$$\phi(x) = \frac{1}{\sqrt{1+x}}$$

$$\therefore \quad \phi'(x) = -\frac{1}{2(1+x)^{3/2}}$$

We have, $|\phi'(x)| < 1$ for $x < 1$

Hence the iterative method can be applied.

Take $x_0 = 0.5$, we get

$$x_1 = \phi(x_0) = \frac{1}{\sqrt{1.5}} = 0.81649$$

$$x_2 = \phi(x_1) = \frac{1}{\sqrt{1.81649}} = 0.74196$$

$$\vdots$$

$$x_8 = 0.75487.$$

Example 12. *Find the reciprocal of 41 correct to 4 decimal places by iterative formula*

$$x_{i+1} = x_i(2 - 41x_i).$$

Sol. Iterative formula is $x_{i+1} = x_i\,(2 - 41\,x_i)$ (5)

Putting $i = 0,\ x_1 = x_0(2 - 41\,x_0)$

Let $x_0 = 0.02$

$$x_1 = (0.02)\,(2 - 0.82) = 0.024$$

Put $i = 1$ in (5),

$$x_2 = (0.024)\,\{2 - (41 \times 0.024)\} = 0.0244$$

Put $i = 2$, $x_3 = 0.02439$

$\therefore$ Reciprocal of 41 is 0.0244.

Example 13. *Find the square root of 20 correct to 3 decimal places by using recursion formula*

$$x_{i+1} = \frac{1}{2}\left(x_i + \frac{20}{x_i}\right).$$

Sol. Put $i = 0$, $x_1 = \frac{1}{2}\left(x_0 + \frac{20}{x_0}\right)$

Let $x_0 = 4.5$

$$\therefore \quad x_1 = \frac{1}{2}\left(4.5 + \frac{20}{4.5}\right) = 4.47$$

Put $i = 1,\ x_1 = 4.47$, $x_2 = \frac{1}{2}\left(4.47 + \frac{20}{4.47}\right) = 4.472$

Put $i = 2, x_2 = 4.472, \quad x_3 = 4.4721$

$\therefore \quad \sqrt{20} \simeq 4.472$ correct to three decimal places.

Example 14. *Find the cube root of 15 correct to four significant figures by iterative method.*

Sol. Let $\qquad x = (15)^{1/3} \quad \therefore \quad x^3 - 15 = 0$

The real root of the above equation lies in (2, 3). The equation may be written as

$$x = \frac{15 + 20x - x^3}{20} = \phi(x)$$

Now, $\qquad \phi'(x) = 1 - \frac{3x^2}{20} \quad \therefore \quad |\, \phi'(x) \,| < 1 \text{ (for } x \approx 2.5)$

Iterative formula is $x_{i+1} = \dfrac{15 + 20x_i - x_i^3}{20}$ (6)

Put $i = 0, x_0 = 2.5$, we get $x_1 = 2.47$

Put $i = 1$ in (6), $\qquad x_2 = 2.466 \qquad$ (where $x_1 = 2.47$)

Similarly, $\qquad x_3 = 2.4661$

$\therefore \quad \sqrt[3]{15}$ correct to 3 decimal places is 2.466.

Example 15. *The equation $x^4 + x = e$ where e is a small number has a root close to e. Computation of this root is done by the expression $\alpha = e - e^4 + 4e^7$.*

(*i*) *Find an iterative formula $x_{n+1} = F(x_n)$, $x_0 = 0$ for the computation. Show that we get the above expression after three iterations when neglecting terms of higher order.*

(*ii*) *Give a good estimate (of the form Ne^k, where N and k are integers) of the maximum error when the root is estimated by the above expression.*

Sol. $x^4 + x = e$ may be written as

$$x = \frac{e}{x^3 + 1}$$

Consider the formula

$$x_{n+1} = \frac{e}{x_n^3 + 1}$$

Starting with $x_0 = 0$, we get

$$x_1 = e$$

$$x_2 = \frac{e}{1+e^3} = e(1+e^3)^{-1}$$

$$= e(1 - e^3 + e^6 - ...)$$

$$= e - e^4 + e^7 \quad \text{(neglecting higher powers of } e\text{)}$$

$$x_3 = \frac{e}{1+(e-e^4+e^7)^3}$$

$$= e - e^4 + 4e^7 \quad \text{(neglecting higher powers of } e\text{)}$$

Taking $\alpha = e - e^4 + 4e^7$, we find that

$$\text{error} = \alpha^4 + \alpha - e$$

$$= (e - e^4 + 4e^7)^4 + (e - e^4 + 4e^7) - e$$

$$= 22e^{10} + \text{higher powers of } e.$$

ASSIGNMENT 3.2

1. Apply iteration method to solve $e^{-x} = 10x$.

   $\left[\textbf{Hint: } |\phi'(x)| = \frac{1}{10}\left|\frac{1}{e^x}\right| < 1 \text{ if } x \geq 0.\right]$

2. Find by iterative method, the real root of the equation $3x - \log_{10} x = 6$ correct to four significant figures.
3. Solve by iteration method:

   (*i*) $1 + \log x = \frac{x}{2}$ (*ii*) $\sin x = \frac{x+1}{x-1}$

   (*iii*) $x^3 = x^2 + x + 1$ near 2 (use 5 iterations)

   (*iv*) $x^3 + x + 1 = 0$ (*v*) $x^3 - 2x^2 - 5 = 0$ (*vi*) $x^3 - 2x^2 - 4 = 0$.
4. Use the iterative method to find, correct to four significant figures, a real root of each of the following equations:

   (*i*) $x = \frac{1}{(x+1)^2}$ (*ii*) $x = (5-x)^{1/3}$ (*iii*) $\sin x = 10(x - 1)$

   (*iv*) $x \sin x = 1$ (*v*) $e^x = \cot x$ (*vi*) $1 + x^2 - x^3 = 0$

   (*vii*) $x^2 - 1 = \sin^2 x$ (*viii*) $5x^3 - 20x + 3 = 0$.
5. By iteration method, find $\sqrt{30}$.
6. The root of the equation $x = \frac{1}{2} + \sin x$ by using the iteration method

$$x_{n+1} = \frac{1}{2} + \sin x_n,\ x_0 = 1$$

$x = 1.497300$ is correct to 6 decimal places. Determine the number of iteration steps required to reach the root by the linear iteration.

7. The equation $f(x) = 0$, where

$$f(x) = 0.1 - x + \frac{x^2}{(2\,!)^2} - \frac{x^3}{(3\,!)^2} + \frac{x^4}{(4\,!)^2} - \ldots$$

has one root in the interval (0, 1). Calculate this root correct to 5 decimal places.

8. Find a catenary $y = c \cosh\left(\frac{x-a}{c}\right)$ passing through the points (1, 1) and (2, 3).

[**Hint:** Eliminate a from $c \cosh\left(\frac{1-a}{c}\right) = 1$ and $c \cosh\left(\frac{2-a}{c}\right) = 3$ to get

$$c = \frac{1 + c \cosh^{-1}\left(\frac{1}{c}\right)}{\cosh^{-1}\left(\frac{3}{c}\right)} = \phi(c)]$$

9. The equation $x^2 + ax + b = 0$ has two real roots, α and β. Show that the iteration method

$$x_{n+1} = -\left(\frac{x_n^{\,2} + b}{a}\right)$$

is convergent near $x = \alpha$ if $2 \mid \alpha \mid < \mid \alpha + \beta \mid$.

10. The equation $x^3 - 5x^2 + 4x - 3 = 0$ has one root near $x = 4$ which is to be computed by the iteration

$$x_{n+1} = \frac{3 + (k-4)x_n + 5x_n^{\,2} - x_n^{\,3}}{k}, \; k \text{ integer; } x_0 = 4$$

(*i*) Determine which value of k will give the fastest convergence.

(*ii*) Using this value of k, iterate three times and estimate the error in x_3.

[**Hint:** Put $x_n = \alpha + e_n$, $\alpha = 4 + \delta$, where α is the exact root. Find the error eqn. $ke_{n+1} = (k - 12)\, e_n + O(\delta e_n)$]

3.17 THE METHOD OF ITERATION FOR SYSTEM OF NON-LINEAR EQUATIONS

Let the equation be $f(x, y) = 0$, $g(x, y) = 0$ whose real roots are required within a specified accuracy.

We assume, $\quad x = F(x, y)$ and $y = G(x, y)$

where functions F and G satisfy conditions

$$\left|\frac{\partial F}{\partial x}\right| + \left|\frac{\partial F}{\partial y}\right| < 1 \quad \text{and} \quad \left|\frac{\partial G}{\partial x}\right| + \left|\frac{\partial G}{\partial y}\right| < 1 \text{ in neighborhood of root.}$$

Let (x_0, y_0) be the initial approximation to a root (α, β) of the system. We then construct successive approximations as

$$x_1 = F(x_0, y_0), \qquad y_1 = G(x_0, y_0)$$

$$x_2 = F(x_1, y_1), \qquad y_2 = G(x_1, y_1)$$

$$x_3 = F(x_2, y_2), \qquad y_3 = G(x_2, y_2)$$

....

$$x_{n+1} = F(x_n, y_n), \qquad y_{n+1} = G(x_n, y_n)$$

If the iteration process converges, we get

$$\alpha = F(\alpha, \beta)$$

$$\beta = G(\alpha, \beta) \text{ in the limit.}$$

Thus α, β are the roots of the system.

Example. *Find a real root of the equations by the iteration method.*

$$x = 0.2x^2 + 0.8, \quad y = 0.3xy^2 + 0.7.$$

Sol. We have $F(x, y) = 0.2x^2 + 0.8$

$$G(x, y) = 0.3xy^2 + 0.7$$

$$\frac{\partial F}{\partial x} = 0.4x \qquad \frac{\partial G}{\partial x} = 0.3y^2$$

$$\frac{\partial F}{\partial y} = 0 \qquad \frac{\partial G}{\partial y} = 0.6xy$$

It is easy to see that $x = 1$ and $y = 1$ are the roots of the system.

Choosing $x_0 = \frac{1}{2}$, $y_0 = \frac{1}{2}$, we find that

$$\left|\frac{\partial F}{\partial x}\right|_{(x_0, y_0)} + \left|\frac{\partial F}{\partial y}\right|_{(x_0, y_0)} = 0.2 < 1$$

and

$$\left|\frac{\partial G}{\partial x}\right|_{(x_0, y_0)} + \left|\frac{\partial G}{\partial y}\right|_{(x_0, y_0)} = 0.225 < 1$$

∴ Conditions are satisfied. Hence,

$$x_1 = F(x_0, y_0) = \frac{0.2}{4} + 0.8 = 0.85$$

and $$y_1 = G(x_0, y_0) = \frac{0.3}{8} + 0.7 = 0.74^*$$

For approximation II, we obtain

$$x_2 = F(x_1, y_1) = 0.2(0.85)^2 + 0.8 = 0.9445$$

and $$y_2 = G(x_1, y_1) = 0.3(0.85) \times (0.74)^2 + 0.7 = 0.81$$

Convergence to the root (1, 1) is obvious.

3.18 METHOD OF FALSE POSITION *Or* REGULA-FALSI METHOD

The bisection method guarantees that the iterative process will converge. It is, however, slow. Thus, attempts have been made to speed up** the bisection method retaining its guaranteed convergence. A method of doing this is called the **method of false position.**

It is sometimes known as the **method of linear interpolation.**

This is the oldest method for finding the real roots of a numerical equation and closely resembles the bisection method.

In this method, we choose two points x_0 and x_1 such that $f(x_0)$ and $f(x_1)$ are of opposite signs. Since the graph of $y = f(x)$ crosses the X-axis between these two points, a root must lie in between these points.

Consequently, $f(x_0)\, f(x_1) < 0$

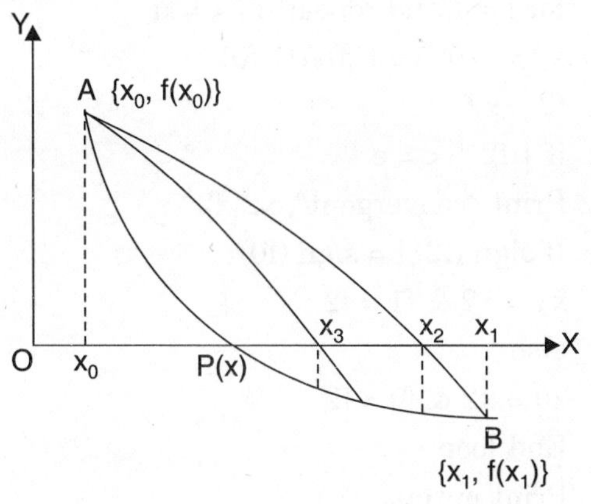

*y_1 can also be obtained more accurately by assigning the value of $x_1 = 0.85$.

**Order of convergence greater than 1.

The equation of the chord joining points $\{x_0, f(x_0)\}$ and $\{x_1, f(x_1)\}$ is

$$y - f(x_0) = \frac{f(x_1) - f(x_0)}{x_1 - x_0}(x - x_0)$$

The method consists in replacing the curve AB by means of the chord AB and taking the point of intersection of the chord with the X-axis as an approximation to the root.

So the abscissa of the point where the chord cuts $y = 0$ is given by

$$x_2 = x_0 - \frac{x_1 - x_0}{f(x_1) - f(x_0)} f(x_0) \qquad (7)$$

which is an approximation to the root.

If $f(x_0)$ and $f(x_2)$ are now of opposite signs, then the root lies between x_0 and x_2. So replacing x_1 with x_2 in (7), we obtain the next approximation, x_3. However, the root could also lie between x_1 and x_2 and then we find x_3 accordingly.

This procedure is repeated until the root is found to the desired accuracy.

NOTE *The order of convergence of the Regula Falsi method is 1.618.*

3.19 ALGORITHM

Step 01. Start of the program.
Step 02. Input the variables x0, x1, e, n for the task.
Step 03. f0 = f(x0)
Step 04. f1 = f(x1)
Step 05. for i = 1 and repeat if i < = n
Step 06. x2 = (x0 f1-x1 f0)/(f1-f0)
Step 07. f2 = x2
Step 08. if | f2 | < = e
Step 09. Print "convergent", x2, f2
Step 10. If sign (f2) ! = sign (f0)
Step 11. x1 = x2 & f1 = f2
Step 12. else
Step 13. x0 = x2 & f0 = f2
Step 14. End loop
Step 15. Print output
Step 16. End of program.

3.19.1 Aliter Algorithm: Method of False Position

1. Read x_0, x_1, e, n

NOTE *x_0 and x_1 are two initial guesses to the root such that sign $f(x_0) \neq$ sign $f(x_1)$. The prescribed precision is e and n is maximum number of iterations. Steps 2 and 3 are initialization steps.*

2. $f_0 \leftarrow f(x_0)$

3. $f_1 \leftarrow f(x_1)$

4. For $i = 1$ to n in steps of 1 do

5. $x_2 \leftarrow (x_0 f_1 - x_1 f_0)/(f_1 - f_0)$

6. $f_2 \leftarrow f(x_2)$

7. If $| f_2 | \leq e$ then

8. Begin write 'convergent solution', x_2, f_2

9. Stop end

10. If sign $(f_2) \neq$ sign (f_0)

11. Then begin $x_1 \leftarrow x_2$

12. $f_1 \leftarrow f_2$ end

13. Else begin $x_0 \leftarrow x_2$

14. $f_0 \leftarrow f_2$ end

end for

15. Write 'Does not converge in n iterations'

16. Write x_2, f_2

17. Stop.

3.20 FLOW-CHART

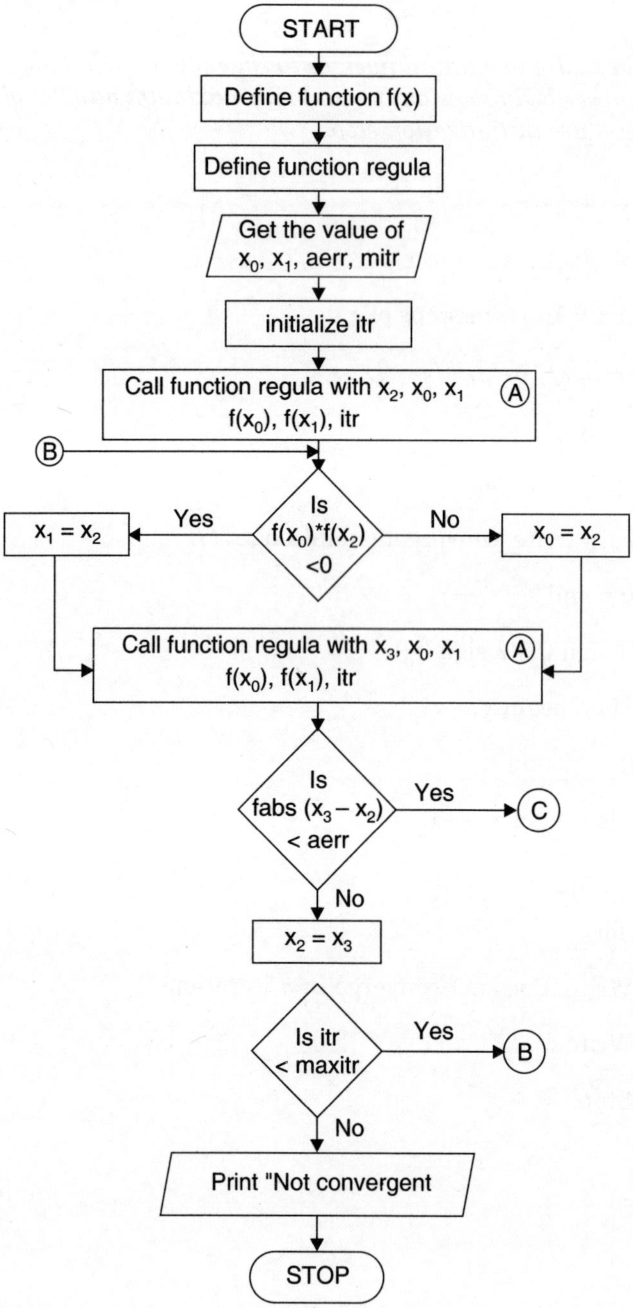

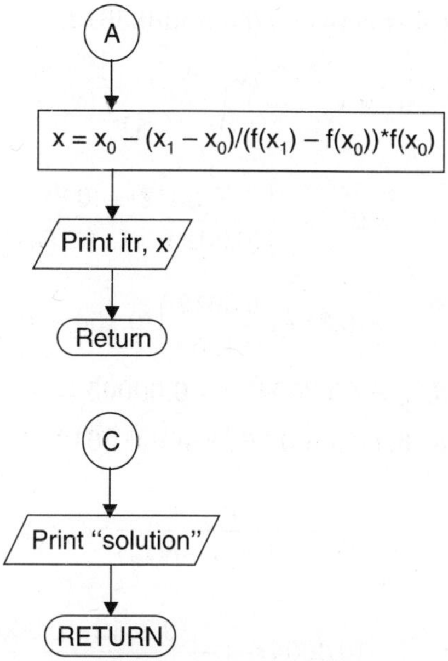

EXAMPLES

Example 1. *Find a real root of the equation $3x + \sin x - e^x = 0$ by the method of false position correct to four decimal places.*

Also write its program in 'C' language.

Sol. Let $f(x) \equiv 3x + \sin x - e^x = 0$

$$f(0.3) = -\,0.154 \quad i.e., \quad (-)\text{ve}$$

and $f(0.4) = 0.0975 \quad i.e., \quad (+)\text{ve}$

$\therefore$ The root lies between 0.3 and 0.4.

Using Regula Falsi method,

$$x_2 = x_0 - \frac{x_1 - x_0}{f(x_1) - f(x_0)}\, f(x_0)$$

$$= (0.3) - \frac{(0.4) - (0.3)}{(0.0975) - (-\,0.154)}(-\,0.154)$$

$$| \because \quad x_0 = 0.3 \text{ and } x_1 = 0.4 \text{ (let)}$$

$$= (0.3) + \left(\frac{0.1 \times 0.154}{0.2515}\right) = 0.3612$$

Now $f(x_2) = f(0.3612) = 0.0019 = (+)\text{ve}$

Hence, the root lies between 0.3 and 0.3612.

Now again, $$x_3 = x_0 - \frac{(x_2 - x_0)}{f(x_2) - f(x_0)} f(x_0) \qquad \text{| Replacing } x_1 \text{ by } x_2$$

$$= (0.3) - \left\{\frac{(0.3612) - (0.3)}{(0.0019) - (-0.154)}\right\}(-0.154)$$

$$= (0.3) + \left(\frac{0.0612}{0.1559}\right)(0.154) = 0.3604$$

Now $f(x_3) = f(0.3604) = -0.00005 = (-)$ve

∴ The root lies between 0.3604 and 0.3612.

Now again, $$x_4 = x_3 - \left\{\frac{x_2 - x_3}{f(x_2) - f(x_3)}\right\} f(x_3) \qquad \text{| Replacing } x_0 \text{ by } x_3$$

$$= (0.3604) - \left[\frac{(0.3612 - 0.3604)}{(0.0019) - (-0.00005)}\right](-0.00005)$$

$$= 0.3604 + \left(\frac{0.0008}{0.00195}\right)(0.00005) = 0.36042$$

Since x_3 and x_4 are approximately the same, the required real root is **0.3604,** correct to four decimal places.

```
/* ***********************************************************
Program to Implement the Method of Regula Falsi (False
Position)
*********************************************************** */
// ... Included Header files
#include<stdio.h>
#include<math.h>
#include<conio.h>
#include<string.h>
#include<process.h>

//...Formulae declaration
#define EPS              0.00005
#define f(x)             3*x+sin(x)-exp(x)
```

```
//...Function Declaration Prototype
void FAL_POS();

//...Main Execution Thread
void main()
 {
 clrscr();
 printf("\n Solution by FALSE POSITION method\n");
 printf("\n Equation is ");
 printf("\n\t\t\t 3*x + sin(x)-exp(x)=0\n\n");
 FAL_POS();
 }
//...Function Definition
void FAL_POS()
 {
 float f0,f1,f2;
 float x0,x1,x2;
 int itr;
 int i;
 printf("Enter the number of iteration:");
 scanf("%d",&itr);
 for(x1=0.0;;)
      {
      f1=f(x1);
      if(f1>0)
           {
           break;
           {
      else
           {
           x1=x1+0.1;
           }
 }
 x0=x1-0.1;
 f0=f(x0);
```

```
printf("\n\t\t-----------------------------------------------");
printf("\n\t\t     ITERATION\t x2\t\t F(x)\n");
printf("\t\t-----------------------------------------------");
for(i=0;i<itr;i++)
     {
     x2=x0-((x1-x0)/(f1-f0))*f0;
     f2=f(x2);
     if(f0*f2>0)
          {
          x1=x2;
          f1=f2;
          }
     else
          {
          x0=x2;
          f0=f2;
          }
     if(fabs(f(2))>EPS)
          {
          printf("\n\t\t%d\t%f\t%f\n",i+1,x2,f2);
          }
     }
printf("\t\t-----------------------------------------------");
printf("\n\t\t\t\tRoot=%f\n",x2);
printf("\t\t-----------------------------------------------");
getch();
}
```

OUTPUT

```
Solution by FALSE POSITION method
Equation is
                    3*x+sin(x)-exp(x)=0
Enter the number of iteration: 11
```

```
------------------------------------------------------------
ITERATION              X2                     F(x)
------------------------------------------------------------
    1               0.361262               0.002101
    2               0.360409              -0.000031
    3               0.360422               0.000000
    4               0.360422              -0.000000
    5               0.360422               0.000000
    6               0.360422               0.000000
    7               0.360422               0.000000
    8               0.360422               0.000000
    9               0.360422               0.000000
   10               0.360422               0.000000
   11               0.360422               0.000000
------------------------------------------------------------
                    Root=0.360422
------------------------------------------------------------
```

Example 2. *Find the root of the equation $xe^x = \cos x$ in the interval (0, 1) using Regula-Falsi method correct to four decimal places. Write its computer programme in 'C' language.*

Sol. Let $f(x) = \cos x - xe^x = 0$ so that

$$f(0) = 1, f(1) = \cos 1 - e = -2.17798$$

i.e., the root lies between 0 and 1.

By Regula-Falsi method,

$$x_2 = x_0 - \frac{(x_1 - x_0)}{f(x_1) - f(x_0)} f(x_0)$$

$$= 0 - \frac{1-0}{-3.17798}(1) = 0.31467$$

Now $f(x_2) = f(0.31467) = 0.51987$

i.e., the root lies between 0.31487 and 1.

Again $$x_3 = 0.31487 - \frac{(1-0.31487)}{(-2.17798 - 0.51987)}(0.51987)$$

$$= 0.44673$$

Now $f(x_3) = 0.20356$

$\therefore$ The root lies between 0.44673 and 1. Repeating this process, $x_{10} = 0.51775$, corrected as 0.5177 up to 4 decimal places.

COMPUTER PROGRAMME

```
\\METHOD OF FALSE POSITION
#include<stdio.h>
#include<conio.h>
#include<math.h>
float f(float x)
{
return cos(x)-x*exp(x);
}
void regula (float *x, float x0,float x1, float fx0, float
fx1,int*itr)
{
*x=x0-((x1-x0)/(fx1-fx0))*fx0;
++(*itr);
printf("Iteration no.%3d x=%7.5f\n",*itr,*x);
}
main()
{
 int itr=0,maxitr;
 float x0,x1,x2,x3,aerr;
 printf("Enter the values for x0,x1, allowed error,
max.iteration\n");
 scanf("%f%f%f%d",&x0,&x1,&aerr,&maxitr);
 regula(&x2,x0,x1,f(x0),f(x1),&itr);
 do
 {          if(f(x0)*f(x2)<0)
                 x1=x2;
            else
                 x0=x2;
            regula(&x3,x0,x1,f(x0),f(x1),&itr);
            if(fabs(x3-x2)<aerr)
```

```
        {
                printf("After %d iterations,
                        root=%6.4f\n",itr,x3);
                getch();
                return (0);
        }
        x2=x3;
}while (itr<maxitr);
printf("Solution does not converge, iterations not
                                        sufficient\n");
getch();
return(1);
```

OUTPUT

```
Enter the values for x0,x1, allowed error, max.iteration
0
1
.00005
20
Iteration number   1 x = 0.31467
Iteration number   2 x = 0.44673
Iteration number   3 x = 0.49402
Iteration number   4 x = 0.50995
Iteration number   5 x = 0.51520
Iteration number   6 x = 0.51692
Iteration number   7 x = 0.51748
Iteration number   8 x = 0.51767
Iteration number   9 x = 0.51773
Iteration number   10 x = 0.51775
After 10 iterations, root = 0.5177
```

Example 3. *Find a real root of the equation $x^3 - 2x - 5 = 0$ by the method of false position correct to three decimal places.*

Sol. Let $f(x) = x^3 - 2x - 5$ so that $f(2) = -1$ and $f(3) = 16$

i.e., A root lies between 2 and 3. Using Regula-Falsi method,

$$x_2 = x_0 - \frac{(x_1 - x_0)}{f(x_1) - f(x_0)} f(x_0)$$

$$= 2 - \frac{(3-2)}{(16+1)}(-1) = 2.0588$$

Now $f(x_2) = f(2.0588) = -0.3908$

i.e., The root lies between 2.0588 and 3.

Now again, $x_3 = 2.0588 - \left(\frac{3 - 2.0588}{16 + 0.3908}\right)(-0.3908) = 2.0813$

Repeating this process, the successive approximations are

$$x_4 = 2.0862 \;......\; x_8 = 2.0943 \text{ etc.}$$

Hence, the root is 2.094, correct to three decimal places.

Example 4. *Find the root of the equation tan x + tanh x = 0 which lies in the interval (1.6, 3.0) correct to four significant digits using the method of false position.*

Sol. Let $f(x) \equiv \tan x + \tanh x = 0$

Since $f(2.35) = -0.03$

and $f(2.37) = 0.009$

Hence, the root lies between 2.35 and 2.37.

Using Regula-Falsi method,

$$x_2 = x_0 - \left\{\frac{x_1 - x_0}{f(x_1) - f(x_0)}\right\} f(x_0)$$

$$= 2.35 - \left(\frac{2.37 - 2.35}{0.009 + 0.03}\right)(-0.03)$$

| Let $x_0 = 2.35$ and $x_1 = 2.37$

$$= 2.35 + \left(\frac{0.02}{0.039}\right)(0.03) = 2.365$$

Now $f(x_2) = -0.00004$ (–)ve

Hence, the root lies between 2.365 and 2.37.

Using Regula-Falsi method,

$$x_3 = x_2 - \left\{\frac{x_1 - x_2}{f(x_1) - f(x_2)}\right\} f(x_2)$$

| Replacing x_0 by x_2

$$= 2.365 - \left(\frac{2.37 - 2.365}{0.009 + 0.00004}\right)(-0.00004)$$

$$= 2.365 + \left(\frac{0.005}{0.00904}\right)(0.00004) = 2.365$$

Hence, the required root is **2.365,** correct to four significant digits.

Example 5. *Using the method of false position, find the root of the equation* $x^6 - x^4 - x^3 - 1 = 0$ *up to four decimal places.*

Sol. Let $f(x) = x^6 - x^4 - x^3 - 1$

$$f(1.4) = -0.056$$

$$f(1.41) = 0.102$$

Hence, the root lies between 1.4 and 1.41.

Using the method of false position,

$$x_2 = x_0 - \left\{\frac{x_1 - x_0}{f(x_1) - f(x_0)}\right\} f(x_0)$$

$$= 1.4 - \left(\frac{1.41 - 1.4}{0.102 + 0.056}\right)(-0.056) \qquad \text{Let, } x_0 = 1.4 \text{ and } x_1 = 1.41$$

$$= 1.4 + \left(\frac{0.01}{0.158}\right)(0.056) = 1.4035$$

Now $f(x_2) = -0.0016$ (–)ve

Hence, the root lies between 1.4035 and 1.41.

Using the method of false position,

$$x_3 = x_2 - \left\{\frac{x_1 - x_2}{f(x_1) - f(x_2)}\right\} f(x_2) \qquad \text{Replacing } x_0 \text{ by } x_2$$

$$= 1.4035 - \left(\frac{1.41 - 1.4035}{0.102 + 0.0016}\right)(-0.0016)$$

$$= 1.4035 + \left(\frac{0.0065}{0.1036}\right)(0.0016) = 1.4036$$

Now $f(x_3) = -0.00003$ (–)ve

Hence, the root lies between 1.4036 and 1.41.

Using the method of false position,

$$x_4 = x_3 - \left\{\frac{x_1 - x_3}{f(x_1) - f(x_3)}\right\} f(x_3)$$

$$= 1.4036 + \left(\frac{1.41 - 1.4036}{0.102 + 0.00003}\right)(0.00003)$$

$$= 1.4036 + \left(\frac{0.0064}{0.10203}\right)(0.00003) = 1.4036$$

Since x_3 and x_4 are approximately the same up to four decimal places, the required root of the given equation is **1.4036.**

Example 6. *Find a real root of the equation x $\log_{10}$ x = 1.2 by Regula-Falsi method correct to four decimal places.*

Sol. Let $f(x) = x \log_{10} x - 1.2$

Since $f(2.74) = -.0005634$

and $f(2.741) = .0003087$

Hence, the root lies between 2.74 and 2.741.

Using the method of False position,

$$x_2 = x_0 - \left\{\frac{x_1 - x_0}{f(x_1) - f(x_0)}\right\} f(x_0)$$ | Let $x_0 = 2.74$ and $x_1 = 2.741$

$$= 2.74 - \left\{\frac{2.741 - 2.74}{.0003087 - (-.0005634)}\right\}(-.0005634)$$

$$= 2.74 + \left(\frac{.001}{.0008721}\right)(.0005634)$$

$$= 2.740646027$$

Now $f(x_2) = -.00000006016$ *i.e.*, (–)ve

Hence, the root lies between 2.740646027 and 2.741.

Using the method of false position,

$$x_3 = x_2 - \left\{\frac{x_1 - x_2}{f(x_1) - f(x_2)}\right\} f(x_2)$$ | Replacing x_0 by x_2

$$= 2.740646027 - \left(\frac{2.741 - 2.740646027}{.0003087 + .00000006016}\right)(-.00000006016)$$

$$= 2.740646096$$

Since x_2 and x_3 agree up to seven decimal places, the required root, correct to four decimal places, is **2.7406.**

Example 7. (*i*) *Apply False-position method to find the smallest positive root of the equation*

$$x - e^{-x} = 0$$

correct to three decimal places.

(*ii*) *Find a positive root of* $xe^x = 2$ *by the method of false position.*

Sol. (*i*) Let $f(x) = x - e^{-x}$

Since $f(.56) = -\ .01121$

and $f(.58) = .0201$

Hence, the root lies between .56 and .58.

Let $x_0 = .56$ and $x_1 = .58$

Using the method of false position,

$$x_2 = x_0 - \left\{\frac{x_1 - x_0}{f(x_1) - f(x_0)}\right\} f(x_0)$$

$$= .56 - \left(\frac{.58 - .56}{.0201 + .01121}\right)(-\ .01121)$$

$$= .56716$$

Now $f(x_2) = .00002619$ *i.e.,* (+)ve

Hence, the root lies between .56 and .56716.

Using the method of false position,

$$x_3 = x_0 - \left\{\frac{x_2 - x_0}{f(x_2) - f(x_0)}\right\} f(x_0) \qquad | \text{ Replacing } x_1 \text{ by } x_2$$

$$= .56 - \left(\frac{.56716 - .56}{.00002619 + .01121}\right)(-\ .01121)$$

$$= .567143$$

Since x_2 and x_3 agree up to four decimal places, the required root correct to three decimal places is **0.567.**

(*ii*) Let $f(x) = xe^x - 2$

Since $f(.852) = -\ .00263$

and $f(.853) = .001715$

The root lies between .852 and .853.

Let $x_0 = .852$ and $x_1 = .853$

Using the method of false position,

$$x_2 = x_0 - \left\{\frac{x_1 - x_0}{f(x_1) - f(x_0)}\right\} f(x_0)$$

$$= .852 - \left\{\frac{.853 - .852}{.001715 - (-.00263)}\right\}(-.00263)$$

$$= .852605293$$

Now $\qquad f(x_2) = -.00000090833$

Hence, the root lies between .852605293 and .853

Using the method of false position,

$$x_3 = x_2 - \left\{\frac{x_1 - x_2}{f(x_1) - f(x_2)}\right\} f(x_2) \qquad | \text{ Replacing } x_0 \text{ by } x_2$$

$$= (.852605293) - \left\{\frac{.853 - 852605293}{.001715 - (-.00000090833)}\right\}(-.00000090833)$$

$$= 0.852605501$$

Since x_2 and x_3 agree up to 6 decimal places, the required root correct to 6 decimal places is **0.852605.**

Example 8. (*i*) *Solve $x^3 - 5x + 3 = 0$ by using Regula-Falsi method.*

(*ii*) *Use the method of false position to solve $x^3 - x - 4 = 0$.*

Sol. (*i*) Let $\qquad f(x) = x^3 - 5x + 3$

Since $\qquad f(.65) = .024625$

and $\qquad f(.66) = -.012504$

The root lies between .65 and .66.

Let $\qquad x_0 = .65$ and $x_1 = .66$

Using the method of false position,

$$x_2 = x_0 - \left\{\frac{x_1 - x_0}{f(x_1) - f(x_0)}\right\} f(x_0)$$

$$= .65 - \left(\frac{.66 - .65}{-.012504 - .024625}\right)(.024625)$$

$$= .656632282$$

Now $\qquad f(x_2) = -.00004392$

Hence, the root lies between .65 and .656632282.

Using the method of false position,

$$x_3 = x_0 - \left\{\frac{x_2 - x_0}{f(x_2) - f(x_0)}\right\} f(x_0) \qquad \left| \begin{array}{l}\text{Replacing} \\ x_1 \text{ by } x_2\end{array}\right.$$

$$= .65 - \left(\frac{.656632282 - .65}{-.00004392 - .024625} \right) (.024625)$$

$$= .656620474.$$

Since x_2 and x_3 agree up to 4 decimal places, the required root is **.6566,** correct up to four decimal places. Similarly, the other roots of this equation are 1.8342 and – 2.4909.

(*ii*) Let $f(x) = x^3 - x - 4$

Since $f(1.79) = -.054661$

and $f(1.80) = .032$

The root lies between 1.79 and 1.80

Let $x_0 = 1.79$ and $x_1 = 1.80$

Using the method of false position,

$$x_2 = x_0 - \left\{ \frac{x_1 - x_0}{f(x_1) - f(x_0)} \right\} f(x_0)$$

$$= 1.79 - \left\{ \frac{1.80 - 1.79}{.032 - (-.054661)} \right\} (-.054661)$$

$$= 1.796307$$

Now, $f(x_2) = -.00012936$

Hence, the root lies between 1.796307 and 1.80.

Using the method of false position,

$$x_3 = x_2 - \left\{ \frac{x_1 - x_2}{f(x_1) - f(x_2)} \right\} f(x_2)$$

$$= 1.796307 - \left\{ \frac{1.8 - 1.796307}{.032 - (-.00012936)} \right\} (-.00012936)$$

$$= 1.796321.$$

Since x_2 and x_3 are the same up to four decimal places, the required root is **1.7963,** correct up to four decimal places.

3.21 CONVERGENCE OF REGULA-FALSI METHOD

If $< x_n >$ is the sequence of approximations obtained from

$$x_{n+1} = x_n - \frac{(x_n - x_{n-1})}{f(x_n) - f(x_{n-1})} f(x_n) \tag{8}$$

and α is the exact value of the root of the equation $f(x) = 0$, then

Let
$$x_n = \alpha + e_n$$
$$x_{n+1} = \alpha + e_{n+1}$$

where e_n, e_{n+1} are the errors involved in n^{th} and $(n + 1)^{\text{th}}$ approximations, respectively.

Clearly, $f(\alpha) = 0$. Hence, (8) gives

$$\alpha + e_{n+1} = \alpha + e_n - \frac{(e_n - e_{n-1})}{f(\alpha + e_n) - f(\alpha + e_{n-1})} . f(\alpha + e_n)$$

or
$$e_{n+1} = \frac{e_{n-1} f(\alpha + e_n) - e_n f(\alpha + e_{n-1})}{f(\alpha + e_n) - f(\alpha + e_{n-1})}$$

$$= \frac{e_{n-1}\left[f(\alpha) + e_n f'(\alpha) + \frac{e_n^2}{2!} f''(\alpha) + \ldots\ldots\right] - e_n\left[f(\alpha) + e_{n-1} f'(\alpha) + \frac{e_{n-1}^2}{2!} f''(\alpha) + \ldots\ldots\right]}{\left[f(\alpha) + e_n f'(\alpha) + \frac{e_n^2}{2!} f''(\alpha) + \ldots\ldots\right] - \left[f(\alpha) + e_{n-1} f'(\alpha) + \frac{e_{n-1}^2}{2!} f''(\alpha) + \ldots\ldots\right]}$$

$$= \frac{(e_{n-1} - e_n) f(\alpha) + \frac{e_{n-1} e_n}{2!}(e_n - e_{n-1}) f''(\alpha) + \ldots\ldots}{(e_n - e_{n-1}) f'(\alpha) + \frac{(e_n - e_{n-1})(e_n + e_{n-1})}{2!} f''(\alpha) + \ldots\ldots}$$

$$= \frac{\frac{e_{n-1} e_n}{2} f''(\alpha) + \ldots\ldots}{f'(\alpha) + \left(\frac{e_n + e_{n-1}}{2}\right) f''(\alpha) + \ldots\ldots} \qquad | \because \; f(\alpha) = 0$$

or $$e_{n+1} \approx \frac{e_n\, e_{n-1}}{2!} \frac{f''(\alpha)}{f'(\alpha)} \tag{9}$$

(neglecting high powers of e_n, e_{n-1})

Let $e_{n+1} = c\, e_n^{\ k}$, where c is a constant and $k > 0$.

$\therefore$ $$e_n = c\, e_{n-1}^k$$

or $$e_{n-1} = c^{-1/k}\, e_n^{\ 1/k}$$

$\therefore$ From (9), $$c\, e_n^{\ k} \approx \frac{e_n\, c^{-1/k}}{2!}\, e_n^{\ 1/k} \cdot \frac{f''(\alpha)}{f'(\alpha)} = \frac{c^{-1/k}}{2!}\, e_n^{\ 1+1/k} \cdot \frac{f''(\alpha)}{f'(\alpha)}$$

Comparing the two sides, we get

$$k = 1 + \frac{1}{k} \quad \text{and} \quad c = \frac{c^{-1/k}}{2!} \frac{f''(\alpha)}{f'(\alpha)}$$

Now, $$k = 1 + \frac{1}{k} \Rightarrow k^2 - k - 1 = 0 \Rightarrow k = 1.618$$

Also, $$c = c^{-1/k} \cdot \frac{1}{2!} \frac{f''(\alpha)}{f'(\alpha)}$$

$$c^{1+\frac{1}{k}} = c^{1.618} = \frac{1}{2} \frac{f''(\alpha)}{f'(\alpha)}$$

or $$c = \left[\frac{f''(\alpha)}{2f'(\alpha)}\right]^{0.618}$$

This gives the rate of convergence and $k = 1.618$ gives the order of convergence.

ASSIGNMENT 3.3

1. Solve $x^3 - 9x + 1 = 0$ for the root lying between 2 and 4 by the method of false position.
2. Find real cube root of 18 by Regula-Falsi method.
3. Find the smallest positive root correct to three decimal places of the equation $\cosh x \cos x = -1$.
4. Determine the real roots of $f(x) = x^3 - 98$ using False position method within $E_s = 0.1\%$.
5. Write a short note on Regula-Falsi method.
6. Using the False-position method, find x when $x^2 - 9 = 0$. Give computer program using 'C'.

7. Find the real root of the equations

(i) $x^3 - 4x + 1 = 0$ (ii) $x^3 - x^2 - 2 = 0$

(iii) $x^3 + x - 3 = 0$ (iv) $x^3 - 5x - 7 = 0$

by using the method of false-position.

8. Find the real root of the equations

(i) $x^4 - x^3 - 2x^2 - 6x - 4 = 0$ (ii) $x^6 - x^4 - x^3 - 3 = 0$

(iii) $xe^x = 3$ (iv) $x^2 - \log_e x - 12 = 0$

(v) $x = \tan x$ (vi) $3x = \cos x + 1$

by using the method of false position.

9. (i) Explain Regula-Falsi method by stating at least one advantage over the bisection method.

(ii) Discuss the method of false position.

10. Solve the following equations by Regula-Falsi method.

(i) $(5 - x) e^x = 5$ near $x = 5$ (ii) $x^3 + x - 1 = 0$ near $x = 1$

(iii) $2x - \log_{10} x = 7$ lying b/w 3.5 and 4 (iv) $x^3 + x^2 - 3x - 3 = 0$ lying b/w 1 and 2

(v) $x^3 - 3x + 4 = 0$ b/w – 2 and – 3 (vi) $x^4 + x^3 - 7x^2 - x + 5 = 0$ lying b/w 2 and 3.

11. Find the rate of convergence for Regula-Falsi method.

12. Illustrate the false position method by plotting the function on a graph and discuss the speed of convergence to the root. Develop the algorithm for computing the roots using the false-position technique.

13. Find all the roots of $\cos x - x^2 - x = 0$ to 5 decimal places.

14. A root of the equation $f(x) = x - \phi(x) = 0$ can often be determined by combining the iteration method with Regula-Falsi.

(i) With a given approximate value x_0, we compute

$$x_1 = \phi(x_0),\ x_2 = \phi(x_1)$$

(ii) Observing that $f(x_0) = x_0 - x_1$ and $f(x_1) = x_1 - x_2$, we find a better approximation x' using Regula-Falsi on the points $(x_0, x_0 - x_1)$ and $(x_1, x_1 - x_2)$.

(iii) This last x' is taken as a new x_0 and we start from (i) all over again.

Compute the smallest root of the equation $x - 5 \log_e x = 0$ with an error less than 0.5×10^{-4} starting with $x_0 = 1.3$.

3.22 SECANT METHOD

This method is quite similar to that of the Regula-Falsi method except for the condition $f(x_1) . f(x_2) < 0$. Here the graph of the function $y = f(x)$ in the neighborhood of the root is approximated by a secant line or chords. Further, the interval at each iteration may not contain the root.

Let the limits of interval initially be x_0 and x_1.

Then the first approximation is given by:

$$x_2 = x_1 - \left[\frac{x_1 - x_0}{f(x_1) - f(x_0)}\right] f(x_1)$$

Again, the formula for successive approximation in general form is

$$x_{n+1} = x_n - \left[\frac{x_n - x_{n-1}}{f(x_n) - f(x_{n-1})}\right] f(x_n)$$

If at any stage $f(x_n) = f(x_{n-1})$, this method will fail.

Hence this method does not always converge while the Regula-Falsi method will always converge. The only advantage in this method lies in the fact that if it converges, it will converge more rapidly than the Regula-Falsi method.

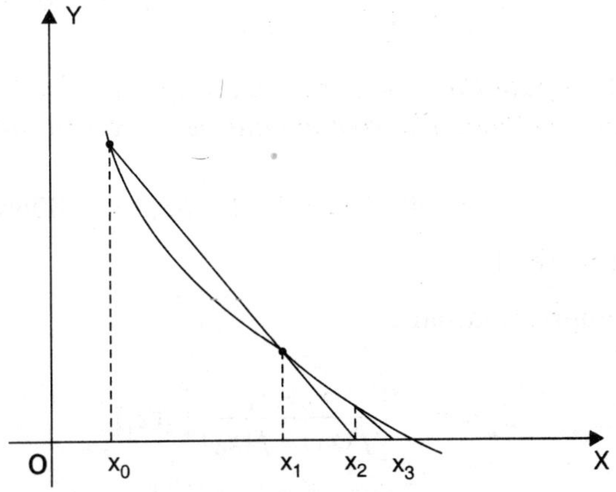

Secant Method

EXAMPLES

Example 1. *A real root of the equation $f(x) = x^3 - 5x + 1 = 0$ lies in the interval (0, 1). Perform four iterations of the secant method.*

Sol. We have, $x_0 = 0$, $x_1 = 1$, $f(x_0) = 1$, $f(x_1) = -3$

By Secant Method,

The first approximation is

$$x_2 = x_1 - \left[\frac{x_1 - x_0}{f(x_1) - f(x_0)}\right] f(x_1) = 0.25$$

$$f(x_2) = -0.234375.$$

The second approximation is

$$x_3 = x_2 - \left[\frac{x_2 - x_1}{f(x_2) - f(x_1)}\right] f(x_2) = 0.186441$$

$f(x_3) = 0.074276$

The third approximation is

$$x_4 = x_3 - \left[\frac{x_3 - x_2}{f(x_3) - f(x_2)}\right] f(x_3) = 0.201736$$

$f(x_4) = -0.000470$

The fourth approximation is

$$x_5 = x_4 - \left[\frac{x_4 - x_3}{f(x_4) - f(x_3)}\right] f(x_4) = 0.201640.$$

Example 2. *Compute the root of the equation $x^2e^{-x/2} = 1$ in the interval [0, 2] using the secant method. The root should be correct to three decimal places.*

Sol. We have,

$$x_0 = 1.42, \quad x_1 = 1.43, \quad f(x_0) = -.0086, \quad f(x_1) = .00034.$$

By secant method,

The first approximation is

$$x_2 = x_1 - \left[\frac{x_1 - x_0}{f(x_1) - f(x_0)}\right] f(x_1)$$

$$= 1.43 - \left(\frac{1.43 - 1.42}{.00034 + .0086}\right)(.00034) = 1.4296$$

$f(x_2) = -.000011$

The second approximation is

$$x_3 = x_2 - \left[\frac{x_2 - x_1}{f(x_2) - f(x_1)}\right] f(x_2)$$

$$= 1.4296 - \left(\frac{1.4296 - 1.42}{-.000011 - .00034}\right)(-.000011) = 1.4292$$

Since x_2 and x_3 agree up to three decimal places, the required root is **1.429.**

ASSIGNMENT 3.4

1. Write the procedure of the secant method to find a root of a polynomial equation to implement it in 'C'.
2. The equation $x^2 - 2x - 3\cos x = 0$ is given
   (*i*) Locate the smallest root in magnitude in an interval of length one unit.
   (*ii*) Hence, find this root correct to 3 decimal points using the secant method.
3. Use the secant method to determine the root of the equation $\cos x - xe^x = 0$.

Now we proceed to discuss some methods useful for obtaining the **complex roots** of polynomial equations $f(x) = 0$.

3.23 LIN-BAIRSTOW'S METHOD *OR* METHOD FOR COMPLEX ROOT

This method is applied to obtain complex roots of an algebraic equation with real coefficients. The complex roots of such an equation occur in pairs $a \pm ib$. Each such pair corresponds to a quadratic factor

$$\{x - (a + ib)\}\{x - (a - ib)\} = x^2 - 2ax + a^2 + b^2 = x^2 + px + q$$

where coefficients p and q are real.

Let $$f(x) = x^n + a_1 x^{n-1} + \ldots\ldots + a_{n-1} x + a_n$$

If we divide $f(x)$ by $x^2 + px + q$, we obtain a quotient

$$Q_{n-2} = x^{n-2} + b_1 x^{n-3} + \ldots\ldots + b_{n-2}$$

and a remainder $$R_n = Rx + S$$

Thus, $$f(x) = (x^2 + px + q)(x^{n-2} + b_1 x^{n-3} + \ldots\ldots + b_{n-2}) + Rx + S \tag{10}$$

If $x^2 + px + q$ divides $f(x)$ completely, the remainder $Rx + S = 0$ *i.e.*, $R = 0$, $S = 0$. Therefore, R and S depend upon p and q.

Our problem is to find p and q such that

$$R(p, q) = 0, \quad S(p, q) = 0 \tag{11}$$

Let $p + \Delta p$, $q + \Delta q$ be the actual values of p and q which satisfy (11), then,

$$R(p + \Delta p, q + \Delta q) = 0; \quad S(p + \Delta p, q + \Delta q) = 0$$

To find the corrections Δp, Δq, we have the following equations:

$$c_{n-2}\,\Delta p + c_{n-3}\,\Delta q = b_{n-1}$$

$$(c_{n-1} - b_{n-1})\,\Delta p + c_{n-2}\,\Delta q = b_n$$

After finding the values of b_i' s and c_i' s by synthetic division scheme, we obtain approximate values of Δp and Δq, say Δp_0 and Δq_0.

If p_0, q_0 are the initial approximations, then their improved values are

$$p_1 = p_0 + \Delta p_0, \; q_1 = q_0 + \Delta q_0.$$

Now, taking p_1 and q_1 as the initial values and repeating the process, we can get better values of p and q.

NOTE

1. *Synthetic division scheme is as follows*

$a_0 (= 1)$	a_1	a_2	$a_3 \ldots\ldots a_{n-2}$	a_{n-1}	a_n	
	$-pb_0$	$-pb_1$	$-pb_2 \ldots\ldots -pb_{n-3}$	$-pb_{n-2}$	$-pb_{n-1}$	$-p$
		$-qb_0$	$-qb_1 \ldots\ldots -qb_{n-4}$	$-qb_{n-3}$	$-qb_{n-2}$	$-q$
$b_0 (= 1)$	b_1	b_2	$b_3 \ldots\ldots b_{n-2}$	b_{n-1}	b_n	
	$-pc_0$	$-pc_1$	$-pc_2 \ldots\ldots -pc_{n-3}$	$-pc_{n-2}$		$-p$
		$-qc_0$	$-qc_1 \ldots\ldots -qc_{n-4}$	$-qc_{n-3}$		$-q$
$c_0 (= 1)$	c_1	c_2	$c_3 \ldots\ldots c_{n-2}$	c_{n-1}		

2. *Values of p_0 and q_0 should be given, otherwise we pick values of p and q which make R and S both zero.*

3. *Bairstow's method works well only if the starting trial values of p and q are close to the correct values. In this case the convergence is quite rapid. If the starting values are arbitrarily chosen, then the method does not converge but very often diverges.*

4. *Δp, Δq provide new guesses. The process is repeated until the approximate error falls below the prespecified tolerance.*

$$|\epsilon_p| = \left|\frac{\Delta p_i}{p_{i+1}}\right| \times 100\%$$

and

$$|\epsilon_q| = \left|\frac{\Delta q_i}{q_{i+1}}\right| \times 100\%.$$

EXAMPLES

Example 1. *Solve $x^4 - 5x^3 + 20x^2 - 40x + 60 = 0$ given that all the roots of $f(x) = 0$ are complex, by using Lin-Bairstow method. Take the values as $p_0 = -4$, $q_0 = 8$.*

Sol. Starting with the values $p_0 = -4$, $q_0 = 8$, we have

1	– 5	20	– 40	60	
–	4	– 4	32	0	4
		– 8	8	– 64	– 8
1	– 1	8	$0(= b_{n-1})$	$-4(= b_n)$	
	4	12	48		4
		– 8	– 24		– 8
1	$3(= c_{n-3})$	$12(= c_{n-2})$	$24(= c_{n-1})$		

$$\therefore \qquad c_{n-1} - b_{n-1} = 24 - 0 = 24 \tag{12}$$

Corrections Δp_0 and Δq_0 are given by

$$c_{n-2}\,\Delta p_0 + c_{n-3}\,\Delta q_0 = b_{n-1} \quad \Rightarrow \quad 12\,\Delta p_0 + 3\,\Delta q_0 = 0 \tag{13}$$

and $$(c_{n-1} - b_{n-1})\,\Delta p_0 + c_{n-2}\,\Delta q_0 = b_n$$

$$\Rightarrow \qquad 24\,\Delta p_0 + 12\,\Delta q_0 = -4 \tag{14}$$

Solving (13) and (14), we get

$$\Delta p_0 = 0.1667, \quad \Delta q_0 = -0.6667$$

$$\therefore \qquad p_1 = p_0 + \Delta p_0 = -3.8333$$

$$q_1 = q_0 + \Delta q_0 = 7.3333$$

Also, $$|\epsilon_p| = \left|\frac{\Delta p_0}{p_1}\right| \times 100\%$$

$$= \left|\frac{0.1667}{-3.8333}\right| \times 100\% = 4.3487\%$$

and $$|\epsilon_q| = \left|\frac{\Delta q_0}{q_1}\right| \times 100\%$$

$$= \left|\frac{-.6667}{7.3333}\right| \times 100\% = 9.0914\%$$

Now, repeating the same process, *i.e.*, dividing $f(x)$ by $x^2 - 3.8333x + 7.3333$, we get

1	– 5	20	– 40	60	
	3.8333	– 4.4723	31.4116	– 0.125	3.8333
		– 7.3333	8.5558	– 60.092	– 7.3333
1	– 1.1667	8.1944	– 0.0326	– 0.217	
			$\begin{pmatrix} \Vert \\ b_{n-1} \end{pmatrix}$	$\begin{pmatrix} \Vert \\ b_n \end{pmatrix}$	
	3.8333	10.2219	42.4845		3.8333
		– 7.3333	– 19.555		– 7.3333
1	2.6666	11.083	22.8969		
	$(= c_{n-3})$	$(= c_{n-2})$	$(= c_{n-1})$		

$$\therefore \qquad c_{n-1} - b_{n-1} = 22.8969 - (-0.0326) = 22.9295$$

Corrections Δp_1 and Δq_1 are given by

$$11.083\ \Delta p_1 + 2.6666\ \Delta q_1 = -0.0326$$

$$22.9295\ \Delta p_1 + 11.083\ \Delta q_1 = -0.217$$

Solving, we get $\Delta p_1 = 0.0033$

$$\Delta q_1 = -0.0269$$

$$\therefore \qquad p_2 = p_1 + \Delta p_1 = -3.83$$

$$q_2 = q_1 + \Delta q_1 = 7.3064$$

Also,
$$| \epsilon_p | = \left| \frac{\Delta p_1}{p_2} \right| \times 100\%$$

$$= \left| \frac{0.0033}{-3.83} \right| \times 100\% = .08616\%$$

and
$$| \epsilon_q | = \left| \frac{\Delta q_1}{q_2} \right| \times 100\%$$

$$= \left| \frac{-0.0269}{7.3064} \right| \times 100\% = .3682\%$$

So, one of the quadratic factors of $f(x)$ is

$$x^2 - 3.83x + 7.3064 \qquad (15)$$

If $\alpha \pm i\beta$ are its roots, then,

$$2\alpha = 3.83, \quad \alpha^2 + \beta^2 = 7.3064$$

giving, $\alpha = 1.9149, \quad \beta = 1.9077$

Hence, the pair of roots is $1.9149 \pm 1.9077i$

To find the remaining two roots of $f(x) = 0$, we divide $f(x)$ by (15) as follows

1	– 5	20	– 40	60	
	3.83	– 4.4811	31.4539		3.83
		– 7.3064	8.5485	– 60.0038	– 7.3064
1	– 1.17	8.2125	0.0024	– .0038	
			≈ 0	≈ 0	

The other quadratic factor is $x^2 - 1.17x + 8.2125$

If $\gamma \pm i\delta$ are its roots, then $2\delta = 1.17, \quad \gamma^2 + \delta^2 = 8.2125$

giving, $\gamma = 0.585, \quad \delta = 2.8054$

Hence, the pair of roots is $0.585 \pm 2.8054\, i$.

Example 2. *Find a quadratic factor of the polynomial*

$$x^4 + 5x^3 + 3x^2 - 5x - 9 = 0$$

starting with $p_0 = 3$, $q_0 = -5$ by using Bairstow's method.

Sol. We have

1	5	3	– 5	– 9	
	– 3	– 6	– 6	3	– 3
		5	10	10	5
1	2	2	– 1(= b_{n-1})	4(= b_n)	
	– 3	3	– 30		– 3
		5	– 5		5
1	– 1	10	– 36		
	↓	↓	↓		
	c_{n-3}	c_{n-2}	c_{n-1}		

$$\therefore \quad c_{n-1} - b_{n-1} = -36 + 1 = -35$$

Corrections Δp_0 and Δq_0 are given by

$$c_{n-2}\,\Delta p_0 + c_{n-3}\,\Delta q_0 = b_{n-1} \quad \Rightarrow \quad 10\,\Delta p_0 - \Delta q_0 = -1 \qquad (16)$$

and $(c_{n-1} - b_{n-1})\,\Delta p_0 + c_{n-2}\,\Delta q_0 = b_n \quad \Rightarrow \quad -35\,\Delta p_0 + 10\,\Delta q_0 = 4 \qquad (17)$

Solving (16) and (17), we get

$$\Delta p_0 = -0.09, \quad \Delta q_0 = 0.08$$

Thus p_1, q_1, the first approximations of p and q are given by

$$p_1 = p_0 + \Delta p_0 = 2.91$$

$$q_1 = q_0 + \Delta q_0 = -4.92$$

$$|\epsilon_p| = \left|\frac{\Delta p_0}{p_1}\right| \times 100\%$$

$$= \left|\frac{-0.09}{2.91}\right| \times 100\% = 3.0927\%$$

$$|\epsilon_q| = \left|\frac{\Delta q_0}{q_1}\right| \times 100\%$$

$$= \left|\frac{0.08}{-4.92}\right| \times 100\% = 1.6260\%.$$

Repeating the same process, *i.e.*, dividing $f(x)$ by $x^2 + 2.91x - 4.92$, we get

1	5	3	– 5	– 9	
	– 2.91	– 6.08	– 5.35	0.20	– 2.91
		4.92	10.28	9.05	4.92
1	2.09	1.84	– 0.07	0.25	
	– 2.91	2.37	– 26.57		– 2.91
		4.92	– 4.03		4.92
1	– 0.82	9.13	– 30.67		

At this step, the corrections Δp_1 and Δq_1 are given by

$$9.13\, \Delta p_1 - 0.82\, \Delta q_1 = -0.07$$

$$-30.60\, \Delta p_1 + 9.13\, \Delta q_1 = 0.25$$

$$\Rightarrow \quad \Delta p_1 = -0.00745$$

$$\Delta q_1 = 0.00241$$

Hence, the second approximations of p and q are given by

$$p_2 = p_1 + \Delta p_1 = 2.91 - 0.00745 = 2.90255$$

$$q_2 = q_1 + \Delta q_1 = -4.92 + 0.00241 = -4.91759$$

$$| \in_p | = \left| \frac{\Delta p_1}{p_2} \right| \times 100\%$$

$$= \left| \frac{-0.00745}{2.90255} \right| \times 100\% = .2566\%$$

$$| \in_q | = \left| \frac{\Delta q_1}{q_2} \right| \times 100\%$$

$$= \left| \frac{0.00241}{-4.91759} \right| \times 100\% = .04901\%.$$

Thus, a quadratic factor is

$$x^2 + 2.90255\, x - 4.91759$$

Dividing the given equation by this factor, we can obtain the other quadratic factor.

ASSIGNMENT 3.5

1. Find the quadratic factor of $x^3 - 3.7x^2 + 6.25x - 4.069$ after two iterations. Use $p_0 = -2.5$, $q_0 = 0$.
2. Solve the equation $x^4 - 8x^3 + 39x^2 - 62x + 50 = 0$ starting with $p = q = 0$.
3. Find the quadratic factor of $x^4 - 3x^3 + 20x^2 + 44x + 54 = 0$ close to $x^2 + 2x + 2$.
   [**Hint:** Take $p_0 = 2$, $q_0 = 2$]

3.24 MULLER'S METHOD

In this method, $f(x)$ is approximated by a second degree curve in the vicinity of a root. The roots of the quadratic are then assumed to be the approximations to the roots of the equation $f(x) = 0$.

The method is iterative, converges almost quadratically, and can be used to obtain complex roots.

Let x_{i-2}, x_{i-1}, x_i be the three distinct approximations to a root of $f(x) = 0$ and let y_{i-2}, y_{i-1}, y_i be the corresponding values of $y = f(x)$.

Assuming that $P(x) = A(x - x_i)^2 + B(x - x_i) + y_i$ is the parabola passing through the points (x_{i-2}, y_{i-2}), (x_{i-1}, y_{i-1}) and (x_i, y_i), we have

$$y_{i-1} = A(x_{i-1} - x_i)^2 + B(x_{i-1} - x_i) + y_i \qquad (18)$$

and

$$y_{i-2} = A(x_{i-2} - x_i)^2 + B(x_{i-2} - x_i) + y_i \qquad (19)$$

From equations (18) and (19), we get

$$y_{i-1} - y_i = A(x_{i-1} - x_i)^2 + B(x_{i-1} - x_i) \quad (20)$$

and

$$y_{i-2} - y_i = A(x_{i-2} - x_i)^2 + B(x_{i-2} - x_i) \quad (21)$$

Solution of equations (20) and (21) gives,

$$A = \frac{(x_{i-2} - x_i)(y_{i-1} - y_i) - (x_{i-1} - x_i)(y_{i-2} - y_i)}{(x_{i-1} - x_{i-2})(x_{i-1} - x_i)(x_{i-2} - x_i)} \quad (22)$$

and

$$B = \frac{(x_{i-2} - x_i)^2 (y_{i-1} - y_i) - (x_{i-1} - x_i)^2 (y_{i-2} - y_i)}{(x_{i-2} - x_{i-1})(x_{i-1} - x_i)(x_{i-2} - x_i)} \quad (23)$$

with the values of A and B given in (22) and (23), the quadratic equation now gives next approximation x_{i+1}.

$$\therefore \quad x_{i+1} - x_i = \frac{-B \pm \sqrt{B^2 - 4Ay_i}}{2A} \quad (24)$$

A direct solution from (24) leads to inaccurate results and therefore it is usually written in the form,

$$x_{i+1} - x_i = -\frac{2y_i}{B \pm \sqrt{B^2 - 4Ay_i}} \quad (25)$$

In (25), sign in denominator should be chosen so that the denominator will be largest in magnitude. With this choice, equation (25) gives the next approximation to the root.

3.25 ALGORITHM OF MULLER'S METHOD

Step 01. Start of the program.
Step 02. Input the variables xi, xi1, xi2
Step 03. Input absolute error-aerr
Step 04. Repeat Steps 5-12 until |Xn-Xi| < aerr
Step 05. Yi = y(Xi)
Step 06. Yil = y(Xi1)
Step 07. Yi2 = y(Xi2)
Step 08. a = A(Xi, Xi1, Xi2, Yi, Yi1, Yi2)
Step 09. b = B(Xi, Xi1, Xi2, Yi, Yi1, Yi2);

Step 10. Xn = approx (Xi, Yi, a, b);

Step 11. Check loop condition

Step 12. if no

Step 13. exit loop

Step 14. if yes

Step 15. Xi = Xn

Step 16. increment i

Step 17. End loop

Step 18. Print output

Step 19. End of program

Step 20. Start of section A

Step 21. take Xa, Xb, Xc, Ya, Yb, Yc

Step 22. x = ((Yb-Ya)*(Xc-Xa)-(Yc-Ya)*(Xb-Xa))/((Xb-Xa)*(Xc-Xa)*(Xb-Xc))

Step 23. Return x

Step 24. End of section A

Step 25. Start of section B

Step 26. Take Xa, Xb, Xc, Ya, Yb, Yc

Step 27. c = (((Yc-Ya)*pow((Xb-Xa),2))-((Yb-Ya)*pow((Xc-Xa),2)))/((Xb-Xa)*(Xc-Xa)*(Xb-Xc))

Step 28. Return c

Step 29. End of section B

Step 30. Start of section approx

Step 31. Take x, y, a, b

Step 32. c = sqrt(b*b-4*a*y)

Step 33. If (b + c) > (b-c): t = x-((2*y)/(b + c))

Step 34. Else: t = (x-((2*y)/(b-c)))

Step 35. Return t

Step 36. End of section approx

3.26 FLOW-CHART FOR MULLER'S METHOD

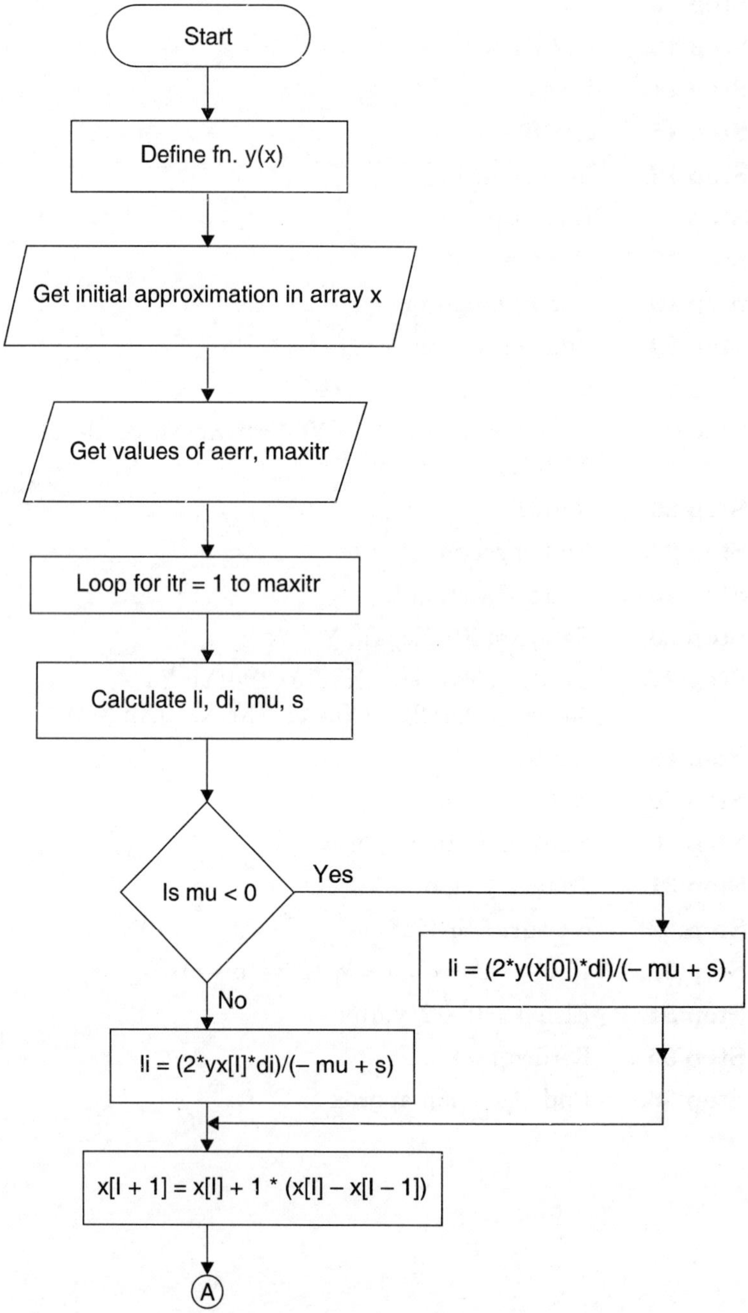

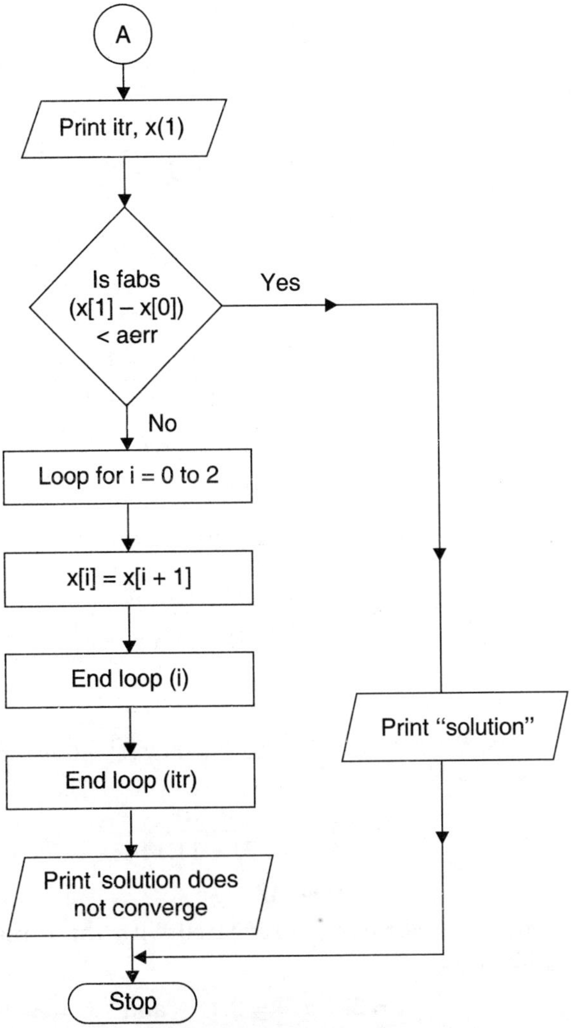

EXAMPLE

Example. *Using Muller's method, find the root of the equation*

$$y(x) = x^3 - 2x - 5 = 0$$

which lies between 2 and 3. Write its program in 'C' language.

Sol. Let $x_{i-2} = 1.9, \quad x_{i-1} = 2, \quad x_i = 2.1$

then $y_{i-2} = -1.941, \quad y_{i-1} = -1, \quad y_i = .061$

$$A = \frac{(x_{i-2} - x_i)(y_{i-1} - y_i) - (x_{i-1} - x_i)(y_{i-2} - y_i)}{(x_{i-1} - x_{i-2})(x_{i-1} - x_i)(x_{i-2} - x_i)}$$

$$= \frac{(-.2)(-1.061) - (-.1)(-2.002)}{(.1)(-.1)(-.2)} = \frac{.2122 - .2002}{.002} = 6$$

$$B = \frac{(x_{i-2} - x_i)^2 (y_{i-1} - y_i) - (x_{i-1} - x_i)^2 (y_{i-2} - y_i)}{(x_{i-2} - x_{i-1})(x_{i-1} - x_i)(x_{i-2} - x_i)}$$

$$= \frac{(-.2)^2 (-1.061) - (-.1)^2 (-2.002)}{(-.1)(-.1)(-.2)}$$

$$= \frac{-.04244 + 0.02002}{-.002} = 11.21$$

The next approximation to the desired root is

$$x_{i+1} = x_i - \frac{2y_i}{B \pm \sqrt{B^2 - 4Ay_i}}$$

$$= 2.1 - \frac{2(.061)}{11.21 \pm \sqrt{(11.21)^2 - (24 \times .061)}}$$

$$= 2.1 - \frac{0.122}{11.21 + 11.1445}$$ | Taking (+)ve sign

$$= 2.094542$$

The procedure can now be repeated with the three approximations as 2, 2.1, and 2.094542.

Let $x_{i-2} = 2,\ \ x_{i-1} = 2.1$ and $x_i = 2.094542$

then $y_{i-2} = -1,\ y_{i-1} = .061$ and $y_i = -.0001058$

$$A = \frac{(x_{i-2} - x_i)(y_{i-1} - y_i) - (x_{i-1} - x_i)(y_{i-2} - y_i)}{(x_{i-1} - x_{i-2})(x_{i-1} - x_i)(x_{i-2} - x_i)}$$

$$= \frac{(2 - 2.094542)(.061 + .0001058) - (2.1 - 2.094542)(-1 + .0001058)}{(2.1 - 2)(2.1 - 2.094542)(2 - 2.094542)}$$

$$= \frac{(-.094542)(.0611058) - (.005458)(-.9998942)}{(.1)(.005458)(-.094542)}$$

$$= \frac{-.005777064 + .005457422}{-.000051601}$$

$$= \frac{-.000319642}{-.000051601} = 6.194492$$

$$B = \frac{(x_{i-2} - x_i)^2 (y_{i-1} - y_i) - (x_{i-1} - x_i)^2 (y_{i-2} - y_i)}{(x_{i-2} - x_{i-1})(x_{i-1} - x_i)(x_{i-2} - x_i)}$$

$$= \frac{(-.094542)^2 (.0611058) - (.005458)^2 (-.9998942)}{(-.1)(.005458)(-.094542)}$$

$$= \frac{(.008938189)(.0611058) + (.000029789)(.9998942)}{.000051601}$$

$$= \frac{.000546175 + .000029785}{.000051601} = 11.161799$$

The next approximation to the desired root is

$$x_{i+1} = x_i - \frac{2y_i}{B \pm \sqrt{B^2 - 4Ay_i}}$$

$$= 2.094542 - \frac{2(-.0001058)}{11.161799 \pm \sqrt{(11.161799)^2 - 4(6.194492)(-.0001058)}}$$

$$= 2.094542 + \frac{.0002116}{11.161799 + 11.161916} = 2.094551$$

Hence, the required root is 2.0945 correct up to 4 decimal places.

The procedure can be repeated with the three approximations as 2.1, 2.094542, and 2.094551.

```
/*  ******************************************************
 PROGRAM TO IMPLEMENT MULLER'S METHOD OF FINDING ROOTS
****************************************************** */


//...HEADER FILES DECLARATION
#include <stdio.h>
#include <string.h>
#include <conio.h>
```

```
#include <math.h>
#include <process.h>
#include <dos.h>
//... Function Prototype Declaration
float y(float);
float A(float,float,float,float,float,float);
float B(float,float,float,float,float,float);
float approx(float,float,float,float);

void main()

 {
 //... Variable Declaration Field
 //... Floating Type
 float a,b;
 float Xi,Xi1,Xi2;
 float Yi,Yi1, Yi2;
 float Xn;
 float aerr;
 //... Integer Type
 int i=1;
 int loop=0;

 //... Invoke Function Clear Screen
 clrscr();
 //...Input Section
 printf("\n\n ");
 printf("Enter the values of X(i),X(i-1),X(i-2), absolute
error\n");
 printf("\n\n Enter the value of X(i)          - ");
 scanf("%f",&Xi);
 printf("\n\n Enter the value of X(i-1)        - ");
 scanf("%f",&Xi1);
 printf("\n\n Enter the value of X(i-2)        - ");
 scanf("%f",&Xi2);
```

```
printf("\n\n Enter the value of Absolute Error - ");
scanf("%f",&aerr);
printf("\n\n Processing ");
for(loop=0; loop<10;loop++)
     {
     delay(200);
     printf("...");
     }
printf("\n\n\n");
//...Calculation And Processing Section
while(1)
     {
     Yi=y(Xi);
     Yi1=y(Xi1);
     Yi2=y(Xi2);
     a=A(Xi,Xi1,Xi2,Yi,Yi1,Yi2);
     b=B(Xi,Xi1,Xi2,Yi,Yi1,Yi2);
     Xn=approx(Xi,Yi,a,b);
     printf("\n\n After Iteration %d value of x-%f",i,Xn);
     if(fabs(Xn-Xi)<aerr)
          {
          goto jmp;
          }
     Xi=Xn;
     i++;
     }
jmp:
//...Output Section
printf("\n\n After %d iterations root is-%6.6f\n",i+1,Xn);
//...Invoke User Watch Halt Function
printf("\n\n\n Press Enter to Exit");
getch();
}

//...Termination Of Main Execution Thread
```

```
//...Function y body
float y(float x)
 {
 float t;
 t=(x*x*x)-(2*x)-5;
 return(t);
 }
//...Termination of Function y

//...Function A body
float A(float Xa;float Xb,float Xc,float Ya,float Yb,
                                             float Yc)
 {
 float x;
 x=((Yb-Ya)*(Xc-Xa)-(Yc-Ya)*(Xb-Xa))/((Xb-Xa)*(Xc-Xa)
                                          *(Xb-Xc));
 return(x);
 }
//...Termination of function A

//...Function B body
float B(float Xa,float Xb,float Xc,float Ya,float Yb,
                                             float Yc)
 {
 float c;
 c=(((Yc-Ya)*pow((Xb-Xa),2))-((Yb-Ya)*pow((Xc-Xa),2)))
        /((Xb-Xa)*(Xc-Xa)*(Xb-Xc));
 return(c);
 }
//...Termination of Function B
//...Function approx body
float approx(float x,float y,float a,float b)
 {
 int c;
 float t;
```

```
c=sqrt(b*b-4*a*y);
if((b+c)>(b-c))
    {
    t=x-((2*y)/(b+c));
    }
else
    {
    t=(x-((2*y)/(b-c)));
    }
return (t);
}
//...Termination of Function approx
```

OUTPUT

```
Enter the values of X(i),X(i-1),X(i-2), absolute error
Enter the value of X(i)                    - 3
Enter the value of X(i-1)                  - 2
Enter the value of X(i-2)                  - 1
Enter the value of Absolute Error          - 0.000001
Processing ................................
After Iteration 1 value of x - 2.085714
After Iteration 2 value of x - 2.094654
After Iteration 3 value of x - 2.094550
After Iteration 4 value of x - 2.094552
After Iteration 5 value of x - 2.094552
After 6 iteration root is - 2.094552
Press Enter to Exit
```

ASSIGNMENT 3.6

1. Use Muller's method to find a root of the equations:
   (*i*) $x^3 - x - 1 = 0$ (*ii*) $x^3 - x^2 - x - 1 = 0$
   which lie between 1 and 2.
2. Apply Muller's method to find the root of the equation $\cos x = xe^x$ which lies between 0 and 1.
3. Using Muller's method, find a root of the equations:
   (*i*) $x^3 - 3x - 5 = 0$ which lie between 2 and 3 (*ii*) $\log x = x - 3$ taking $x_0 = 0.25$, $x_1 = 0.5$ and $x_2 = 1$

(*iii*) $x^3 - \frac{1}{2} = 0$ take $x_0 = 0$, $x_1 = 1$ and $x_2 = \frac{1}{2}$.

4. Solve by Muller's method: $x^3 + 2x^2 + 10x - 20 = 0$ by taking $x = 0$, $x = 1$, $x = 2$ as initial approximations.

3.27 THE QUOTIENT-DIFFERENCE METHOD

This is a general method to obtain the approximate roots of polynomial equations. Let the given cubic equation be

$$f(x) \equiv a_0x^3 + a_1x^2 + a_2x + a_3 = 0 \tag{26}$$

and let x_1, x_2, and x_3 be its roots such that $0 < | x_1 | < | x_2 | < | x_3 |$.

The roots can be obtained, directly by considering the transformed equation

$$a_3x^3 + a_2x^2 + a_1x + a_0 = 0 \tag{27}$$

whose roots are the reciprocals of those of (26).

We then have $$\frac{1}{a_3x^3 + a_2x^2 + a_1x + a_0} = \sum_{i=0}^{\infty} \alpha_i \, x_i$$

so that, $$(a_3 x^3 + a_2 x^2 + a_1x + a_0)(\alpha_0 + \alpha_1x + \alpha_2x^2 + ...) = 1 \tag{28}$$

Comparing the coefficients of like powers of x on both sides of (28), we get

$$\alpha_0 = \frac{1}{a_0}, \quad \alpha_1 = -\frac{a_1}{a_0^2}, \quad \alpha_2 = \frac{-a_2}{a_0^2} + \frac{a_1^2}{a_0^3}$$

Hence, $$q_1^{(1)} = \frac{\alpha_1}{\alpha_0} = -\frac{a_1}{a_0}$$

$$q_1^{(2)} = \frac{\alpha_2}{\alpha_1} = \frac{a_2\, a_0 - a_1^2}{a_0\, a_1}$$

and so, $$\Delta_1^{(1)} = q_1^{(2)} - q_1^{(1)} = \frac{a_2}{a_1}, \quad \Delta_2^{(0)} = \frac{a_3}{a_2}$$

In general, $$\Delta_m^{(m)} = \frac{a_{m+1}}{a_m}, \quad m = 1, 2, 3, ..., (n-1)$$

$$q_m^{(1-m)} = 0, \quad m = 2, 3, \ldots\ldots, n$$

(*i.e.*, $q_1^{(0)}, q_2^{(-1)}, q_3^{(-2)}, \ldots\ldots$, top q's are 0)

We also set $\Delta_0^{(k)} = \Delta_n^{(k)} = 0$, for all k

[*i.e.*, First and last columns of Q-d table are zero].

Following is the Quotient-difference table for a cubic equation

	$q_1^{(0)}$		$q_2^{(-1)}$		$q_3^{(-2)}$	
$\Delta_0^{(1)}$		$\Delta_1^{(0)}$		$\Delta_2^{(-1)}$		$\Delta_3^{(-2)}$
	$q_1^{(1)}$		$q_2^{(0)}$		$q_3^{(-1)}$	
$\Delta_0^{(2)}$		$\Delta_1^{(1)}$		$\Delta_2^{(0)}$		$\Delta_3^{(-1)}$
	$q_1^{(2)}$		$q_2^{(1)}$		$q_3^{(0)}$	
$\Delta_0^{(3)}$		$\Delta_1^{(2)}$		$\Delta_2^{(1)}$		$\Delta_3^{(0)}$

(*i*) If a Δ-element is at the top of a rhombus, then the product of one pair is equal to that of the other pair.

For example, in rhombus

	$\Delta_1^{(1)}$	
$q_1^{(2)}$		$q_2^{(1)}$
	$\Delta_1^{(2)}$	

we have $\Delta_1^{(1)} \cdot q_2^{(1)} = \Delta_1^{(2)} \cdot q_1^{(2)}$

from which $\Delta_1^{(2)}$ can be computed, since other quantities are known.

(*ii*) If a q-element is at the top, then the sum of one pair is equal to that of the other pair.

In the rhombus,

	$q_2^{(0)}$	
$\Delta_1^{(1)}$		$\Delta_2^{(0)}$
	$q_2^{(1)}$	

we have $q_2^{(0)} + \Delta_2^{(0)} = q_2^{(1)} + \Delta_1^{(1)}$

from which $q_2^{(1)}$ can be computed when $q_2^{(0)}, \Delta_1^{(1)}, \Delta_2^{(0)}$ are known.

As the building up of the table proceeds, the quantities $q_1^{(i)}, q_2^{(i)}, q_3^{(i)}$ tend to roots of cubic equations.

The disadvantage of this method is that additional computation is also necessary. This method can be applied to find the complex roots and multiple roots of polynomials and also for determining the eigen values of a matrix.

An important feature of this method is that it gives approximate values of all the roots simultaneously, enabling one to use this method to obtain the first approximation of all the roots and then apply a rapidly convergent method such as the generalized Newton method.

EXAMPLE

Example. *Find the real roots of the equation $x^3 - 6x^2 + 11x - 6 = 0$ using the Quotient-difference method.*

Sol. Here, $a_0 = 1, \quad a_1 = -6, \quad a_2 = 11, \quad a_3 = -6$

Now,
$$q_1^{(1)} = -\frac{a_1}{a_0} = 6$$

$$q_1^{(2)} = \frac{a_2 a_0 - a_1^2}{a_0 a_1} = \frac{11-36}{-6} = 4.167$$

$$\Delta_1^{(1)} = q_1^{(2)} - q_1^{(1)} = \frac{a_2}{a_1} = -1.833$$

Also,
$$q_2^{(0)} = 0, \quad q_3^{(-1)} = 0$$

$$\Delta_2^{(0)} = \frac{a_3}{a_2} = -\frac{6}{11} = -0.5454.$$

The first two rows containing starting values of

	$q_1^{(1)}$		$q_2^{(0)}$		$q_3^{(-1)}$		
$\Delta_0^{(2)}$		$\Delta_1^{(1)}$		$\Delta_2^{(0)}$		$\Delta_3^{(-1)}$	

i.e.,

	6		0		0	
0		– 1.833		– 0.5454		0

The succeeding rows can be constructed as below:

Δ_0	q_1	Δ_1	q_2	Δ_2	q_3	Δ_3
	6		0		0	
0		– 1.833		– 0.5454		0
	4.167		1.288		0.5454	
0		– 0.5666		– 0.2310		0
	3.600		1.624		0.7764	
0		– 0.2556		– 0.1105		0
	3.344		1.770		0.8869	
0		– 0.1353		– 0.0553		0
	3.209		1.8550		0.9422	
0		– 0.0782		– 0.0281		0
	3.131		1.9051		0.9703	
0		– .0476		– .0143		0
	3.083		1.9384		0.9846	
0		– .0299		– .0073		0
	3.053		1.961		.9919	
0		– .0192		– .0037		0
	3.0338		1.976		.9956	
0		– .0125		– .0019		0
	3.0213		1.987		.9975	

It is evident that q_1, q_2, q_3 are gradually converging to the roots 3, 2, and 1, respectively.

ASSIGNMENT 3.7

1. Apply the quotient-difference method to obtain the approximate roots of the equation

$$f(x) \equiv x^3 - 7x^2 + 10x - 2 = 0.$$

3.28 HORNER'S METHOD

This is the best method of finding the real root of a numerical polynomial equation. The method works as follows.

Let a positive root of $f(x) = 0$ lie in between α and $\alpha + 1$, where α is an integer. Then the value of the root is $\alpha . d_1d_2d_3$ ...... where α is the integral part and d_1, d_2, d_3, ... are the digits in the decimal part.

Finding d_1. First diminish the roots of $f(x) = 0$ by α so that the roots of the transformed equation lie between 0 and 1. *i.e.*, the root of the transformed equation is $0 . d_1d_2d_3$ ......

Now multiply the roots of the transformed equation by 10 so that the root of the new equation is $d_1 . d_2d_3$ .... Thus the first figure after the decimal place is d_1.

Again, diminish the root by d_1 and multiply the roots of the resulting equation by 10 so that the root is $d_2 . d_3$ ...... *i.e.*, the second figure after the decimal place is d_2.

Continue the process to obtain the root to any desired degree of accuracy digit by digit.

EXAMPLE

Example. *Using Horner's method, find the root of* $x^3 + 9x^2 - 18 = 0$, *correct to two decimal places.*

Sol. Let $f(x) = x^3 + 9x^2 - 18$

Then $f(1) = 1 + 9 - 18 = -$ ve

and $f(2) = 8 + 36 - 18 = +$ ve

i.e., $f(1)$ and $f(2)$ are of opposite signs. Hence $f(x) = 0$ has a root between 1 and 2.

$\therefore$ The integral part of the root of $f(x) = 0$ is 1.

Now diminish the roots of the equation by 1.

1	1	9	0	– 18
	0	1	10	10
1	1	10	10	– 8
	0	1	11	
1	1	11	21	
	0	1		
	1	12		

∴ The transformed equation is $x^3 + 12x^2 + 21x - 8 = 0$.

This equation has a root between 0 and 1.

Multiply the roots of this equation by 10.

∴ The new equation is $f_1(x) = x^3 + 120x^2 + 2100x - 8000 = 0$

We can see that $f_1(3) < 0$ and $f_1(4) > 0$

∴ The root of $f_1(x) = 0$ lies in between 3 and 4.

Hence the first figure after the decimal place is 3.

Now, diminish the roots of $f_1(x) = 0$ by 3.

3	1	120	2100	– 8000
	0	3	369	7407
3	1	123	2469	– 593
	0	3	378	
3	1	126	2847	
	0	3		
	3	129		

The transformed equation is $3x^3 + 129x^2 + 2847x - 593 = 0$, whose root lies between 0 and 1.

Multiplying the roots of this equation by 10, we get the new equation:

$$f_2(x) = 3x^3 + 1290x^2 + 284700x - 593000 = 0$$

We can easily see that root of $f_2(x)$ lies between 2 and 3, since $f_2(2) < 0$ and $f_3(3) > 0$.

∴ The second figure after the decimal place is 2.

Diminish the roots of $f_2(x) = 0$ by 2

2	3	1290	284700	– 593000
	0	6	2592	574584
2	3	1296	287292	– 18416
	0	6	2604	
2	3	1302	289896	
	0	6		
	3	1308		

The transformed equation is $3x^3 + 1308x^2 + 289896x - 18416 = 0$ whose root lies between 0 and 1.

Multiplying the roots of this equation by 10, we get the new equation as

$$f_3(x) = 3x^3 + 13080x^2 + 28989600x - 18416000 = 0$$

We can easily see that $f_3(0) < 0$ and $f_3(1) > 0$, *i.e.*, the root of $f_3(x) = 0$ lies between 0 and 1.

∴ The third figure after the decimal is zero. We can stop here as the case requires that the root be correct to 2 decimals. Hence the root is 1.32.

ASSIGNMENT 3.8

1. Find a root of the following equations correct to three decimal places using Horner's method.

(*i*) $x^3 + 3x^2 - 12x - 11 = 0$ (*ii*) $x^4 + x^3 - 4x^2 - 16 = 0$

(*iii*) $x^3 - 30 = 0$.

2. Find the positive root of the equation $x^3 + x^2 + x - 100 = 0$, correct to four decimal places using Horner's method.

3.29 NEWTON-RAPHSON METHOD

This method is generally used to improve the result obtained by one of the previous methods. Let x_0 be an approximate root of $f(x) = 0$ and let $x_1 = x_0 + h$ be the correct root so that $f(x_1) = 0$.

Expanding $f(x_0 + h)$ by Taylor's series, we get

$$f(x_0) + hf'(x_0) + \frac{h^2}{2!} f''(x_0) + \ldots\ldots = 0$$

Since h is small, neglecting h^2 and higher powers of h, we get

$$f(x_0) + hf'(x_0) = 0 \quad \text{or} \quad h = -\frac{f(x_0)}{f'(x_0)} \qquad (29)$$

A better approximation than x_0 is therefore given by x_1, where

$$x_1 = x_0 - \frac{f(x_0)}{f'(x_0)}$$

Successive approximations are given by $x_2, x_3, \ldots\ldots, x_{n+1}$, where

$$x_{n+1} = x_n - \frac{f(x_n)}{f'(x_n)} \qquad (30) \quad (n = 0, 1, \ldots\ldots)$$

which is the Newton-Raphson formula.

NOTE

1. *This method is useful in cases of large values of $f'(x)$, i.e., when the graph of $f(x)$ while crossing the x-axis is nearly vertical.*
2. *If $f'(x)$ is zero or nearly 0, the method fails.*
3. *Newton's formula converges provided the initial approximation x_0 is chosen sufficiently close to the root.*

   In the beginning, we guess two numbers b and c such that f(b) and f(c) are of opposite signs. Then the first approximate root a lies between b and c.
4. *This method is also used to obtain complex roots.*

3.30 CONVERGENCE

Comparing (30) with $x_{n+1} = \phi(x_n)$ of the iteration method, we get

$$\phi(x_n) = x_{n+1} = x_n - \frac{f(x_n)}{f'(x_n)}$$

In general, $$\phi(x) = x - \frac{f(x)}{f'(x_n)}$$

which gives $$\phi'(x) = \frac{f(x)\, f''(x)}{[f'(x)]^2}$$

Since the iteration method converges if $|\phi'(x)| < 1$

$\therefore$ Newton's method converges if

$$|f(x) f''(x)| < [f'(x)]^2$$

in the interval considered.

Assuming $f(x)$, $f'(x)$, and $f''(x)$ to be continuous, we can select a small interval in the vicinity of the root α in which the above condition is satisfied.

The rate at which the iteration method converges if the initial approximation to the root is sufficiently close to the desired root is called the **rate of convergence.**

3.31 ORDER OF CONVERGENCE

Suppose x_n differs from the root α by a small quantity e_n so that

$$x_n = \alpha + e_n \quad \text{and} \quad x_{n+1} = \alpha + e_{n+1}$$

Then (30) becomes, $e_{n+1} = e_n - \dfrac{f(\alpha + e_n)}{f'(\alpha + e_n)}$

$$= e_n - \frac{f(\alpha) + e_n f'(\alpha) + \frac{e_n^2}{2!} f''(\alpha) + ...}{f'(\alpha) + e_n f''(\alpha) + ...} \quad \text{(By Taylor's expansion)}$$

$$= e_n - \frac{e_n f'(\alpha) + \frac{e_n^2}{2} f''(\alpha) + ...}{f'(\alpha) + e_n f''(\alpha) + ...} \quad | \because f(\alpha) = 0$$

$$= \frac{e_n^2 f''(\alpha)}{2[f'(\alpha) + e_n f''(\alpha)]} \quad | \text{ Neglect high powers of } e_n$$

$$= \frac{e_n^2}{2} \frac{f''(\alpha)}{f'(\alpha)\left\{1 + e_n \frac{f''(\alpha)}{f'(\alpha)}\right\}}$$

$$= \frac{e_n^2}{2} \cdot \frac{f''(\alpha)}{f'(\alpha)} \left\{1 + e_n \frac{f''(\alpha)}{f'(\alpha)}\right\}^{-1}$$

$$= \frac{e_n^2}{2} \frac{f''(\alpha)}{f'(\alpha)} \left\{1 - e_n \frac{f''(\alpha)}{f'(\alpha)} + ...\right\}$$

$$= \frac{e_n^2}{2} \frac{f''(\alpha)}{f'(\alpha)} - \frac{e_n^3}{2} \left\{\frac{f''(\alpha)}{f'(\alpha)}\right\}^2 + ...$$

or $$\frac{e_{n+1}}{e_n^2} = \frac{1}{2} \frac{f''(\alpha)}{f'(\alpha)} - \frac{e_n}{2} \left\{\frac{f''(\alpha)}{f'(\alpha)}\right\}^2 + ...$$

$$\approx \frac{f''(\alpha)}{2f'(\alpha)} \quad \text{(Neglecting terms containing powers of } e_n\text{)}$$

Hence by definition, the order of convergence of Newton-Raphson method is 2, *i.e.*, Newton-Raphson method is **quadratic convergent**.

This also shows that subsequent error at each step is proportional to the square of the previous error and as such the *convergence is quadratic.*

Hence, if at the first iteration we have an answer correct to one decimal place, then it should be correct to two places at the second iteration, and to four places at the third iteration.

This means that the number of correct decimal places at each iteration is almost doubled.

∴ Method converges very rapidly.

Due to its quadratic convergence, the formula (30) is also termed as a **second order formula.**

3.32 GEOMETRICAL INTERPRETATION

Let x_0 be a point near the root α of equation $f(x) = 0$, then tangent at A$\{x_0, f(x_0)\}$ is

$$y - f(x_0) = f'(x_0)(x - x_0)$$

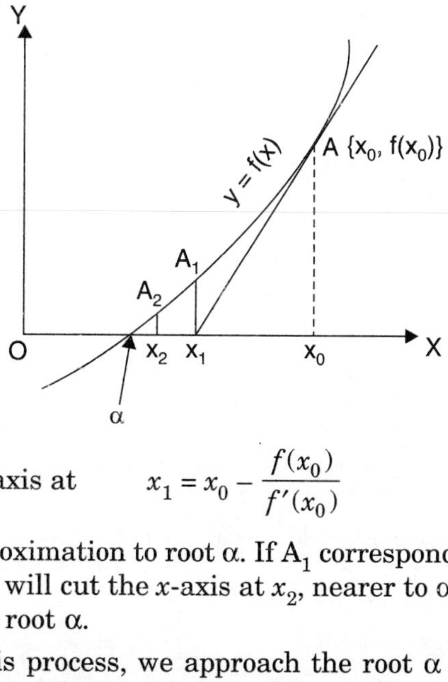

It cuts the x-axis at $\quad x_1 = x_0 - \dfrac{f(x_0)}{f'(x_0)}$

which is one approximation to root α. If A_1 corresponds to x_1 on the curve, then the tangent at A_1 will cut the x-axis at x_2, nearer to α and is therefore another approximation to root α.

Repeating this process, we approach the root α quite rapidly. Hence the method consists of replacing the part of the curve between A and the x-axis by the means of the tangent to the curve at A_0.

3.33 ALGORITHM OF NEWTON-RAPHSON METHOD

Step 01. Start of the program

Step 02. Input the variables x0, n for the task

Step 03. Input Epsilon & delta

Step 04. for i = 1 and repeat if i <= n

Step 05. f0 = f(x0)

Step 06. df0 = df(x1)

Step 07. if |df0| <= delta

a. Print Slope too small

b. Print x0, f0, df0, i

c. End of Program

Step 08. x1 = x0-(f0/df0)

Step 09. if |(x1-x0)/x1| <epsilon

a. Print convergent

b. Print x1, f(x1), i

c. End of Program

Step 10. x0 = x1

Step 11. End Loop

3.34 FLOW-CHART OF NEWTON–RAPHSON METHOD

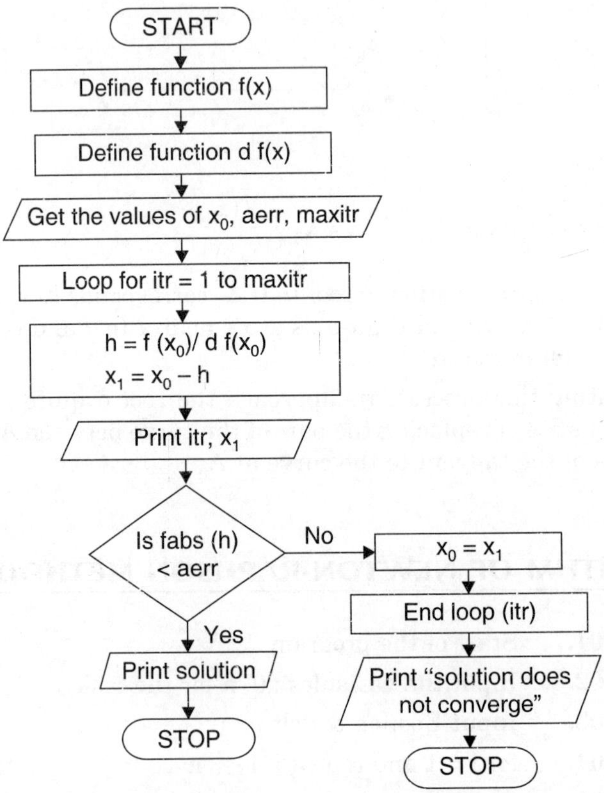

3.35 NEWTON'S ITERATIVE FORMULAE FOR FINDING INVERSE, SQUARE ROOT

1. Inverse. The reciprocal or inverse of a number 'a' can be considered as a root of the equation $\frac{1}{x} - a = 0$, which can be solved by Newton's method.

Since $$f(x) = \frac{1}{x} - a,\ f'(x) = -\frac{1}{x^2}$$

$\therefore$ Newton's formula gives

$$x_{n+1} = x_n + \frac{\left(\frac{1}{x_n} - a\right)}{\left(\frac{1}{x_n^2}\right)}$$

$$\boxed{x_{n+1} = x_n (2 - ax_n)}$$

2. Square root. The square root of 'a' can be considered a root of the equation $x^2 - a = 0$, solvable by Newton's method.

Since $$f(x) = x^2 - a, \quad f'(x) = 2x$$

$$x_{n+1} = x_n - \frac{x_n^2 - a}{2x_n}$$

$$\boxed{x_{n+1} = \frac{1}{2}\left(x_n + \frac{a}{x_n}\right)}$$

3. Inverse square root. Equation is $\frac{1}{x^2} - a = 0$

Iterative formula is

$$\boxed{x_{n+1} = \frac{1}{2} x_n (3 - a\, x_n^2)}$$

4. General formula for pth root. The pth root of a can be considered a root of the equation $x^p - a = 0$. To solve this by Newton's method, we have

$$f(x) = x^p - a \quad \text{and hence,} \quad f'(x) = px^{p-1}$$

$\therefore$ The iterative formula is $x_{n+1} = x_n - \dfrac{(x_n{}^p - a)}{p x_n{}^{p-1}}$

$$\boxed{x_{n+1} = \frac{(p-1)\, x_n{}^p + a}{p x_n{}^{p-1}}}$$

Also, the general formula for the reciprocal of pth root of a is

$$x_{n+1} = x_n \left(\frac{p + 1 - a x_n{}^p}{p} \right).$$

3.36 RATE OF CONVERGENCE OF NEWTON'S SQUARE ROOT FORMULA

Let $\sqrt{a} = \alpha$ so that $a = \alpha^2$. If we write

$$x_n = \alpha \left(\frac{1 + e_n}{1 - e_n} \right)$$

then, $$x_{n+1} = \alpha \left(\frac{1 + e_{n+1}}{1 - e_{n+1}} \right) \qquad (31)$$

Also, by formula, $x_{n+1} = \dfrac{1}{2}\left(x_n + \dfrac{a}{x_n} \right)$, we get

$$x_{n+1} = \frac{1}{2}\left[\alpha \left(\frac{1 + e_n}{1 - e_n} \right) + \frac{a}{\alpha} \left(\frac{1 - e_n}{1 + e_n} \right) \right]$$

$$= \alpha \left(\frac{1 + e_n{}^2}{1 - e_n{}^2} \right) \qquad (32) \quad (\because \ a = \alpha^2)$$

Comparing (31) and (32), we get $e_{n+1} = e_n{}^2$
confirming quadratic convergence of Newton's method.

3.37 RATE OF CONVERGENCE OF NEWTON'S INVERSE FORMULA

Let $\alpha = \dfrac{1}{a}$ *i.e.,* $a = \dfrac{1}{\alpha}$. If we write $x_n = \alpha(1 - e_n)$

then, $x_{n+1} = \alpha\,(1 - e_{n+1})$

By formula, $x_{n+1} = x_n (2 - ax_n)$, we get

$$x_{n+1} = \alpha(1-e_n)\,[2 - a\alpha\,(1-e_n)] = \alpha(1-e_n^2) \qquad |\ \because\ a\alpha = 1$$

Comparing, we get $e_{n+1} = e_n^2$, hence, convergence is quadratic.

EXAMPLES

Example 1. *Using Newton-Raphson method, find the real root of the equation $3x = \cos x + 1$ correct to four decimal places. Give computer program using 'C'.*

Sol. Let $f(x) = 3x - \cos x - 1$

Since $f(0) = -2 = (-)\text{ve}$;

$f(1) = 1.4597 = (+)\text{ve}$

$\therefore$ A root of $f(x) = 0$ lies between 0 and 1. It is nearer to 1. Let us take $x_0 = 0.6$.

Also, $f'(x) = 3 + \sin x$

Newton's iteration formula gives,

$$x_{n+1} = x_n - \frac{f(x_n)}{f'(x_n)}$$

$$= x_n - \frac{3x_n - \cos x_n - 1}{3 + \sin x_n} = \frac{x_n \sin x_n + \cos x_n + 1}{3 + \sin x_n}$$

If $n = 0$, the first approximation x_1 is given by,

$$x_1 = \frac{x_0 \sin x_0 + \cos x_0 + 1}{3 + \sin x_0}$$

$$= \frac{0.6 \sin 6 + \cos 0.6 + 1}{3 + \sin 0.6} = .6071$$

If $n = 1$,
the second approximation is

$$x_2 = \frac{x_1 \sin x_1 + \cos x_1 + 1}{3 + \sin x_1}$$

$$= \frac{.6071 \sin(.6071) + \cos(.6071) + 1}{3 + \sin(.6071)} = 0.6071$$

Clearly $x_1 = x_2$. Hence the desired root is **0.6071,** correct to 4 decimal places.

```
/* ********************************************************
     Program made for NEWTON RAPHSON to solve the equation
******************************************************* *\

//....including source header files
# include <stdio.h>
# include <conio.h>
# include <math.h>
# include <process.h>
# include <string.h>

//....defining formulae
# define f(x)       3*x -cos(x)-1
# define df(x) 3+sin(x)
//...Function Declaration prototype
void NEW_RAP();

//... Main Execution Thread
void main()
 {
 clrscr();
 printf ("\n Solution by NEWTON RAPHSON method \n");
 printf ("\n Equation is: ");
 printf ("\n\t\t\t 3*X - COS X - 1=0 \n\n ");
 NEW_RAP();
 getch();
 }
//...Function Declaration
void NEW_RAP()
 {
 //...Internal Declaration Field
 long float x1,x0;
 long float f0,f1;
 long float df0;
 int i=1;
 int itr;
```

```
float EPS;
float error;
/*Finding an Approximate ROOT of Given Equation, Having
+ve Value*/
for(x1=0;;x1 +=0.01)
     {
     f1=f(x1);
     if (f1 > 0)
          {
          break;
          }
     }
/*Finding an Approximate ROOT of Given Equation, Having
-ve value*/
x0=x1-0.01;
f0=f(x0);
printf(" Enter the number of iterations: ");
scanf(" %d",&itr);
printf(" Enter the maximum possible error: ");
scanf("%f",&EPS);
if (fabs(f0) > f1)
     {
     printf("\n\t\t The root is near to %.4f\n",x1);
     }
If (f1 > fabs(f(x0)))
     {
     printf("\n\t\t The root is near to %.4f\n",x0);
     }
x0=(x0+x1)/2;
for(;i<=itr;i++)
     {
     f0=f(x0);
     df0=df(x0);
     x1=x0 - (f0/df0);
     printf("\n\t\t The %d approximation to the root is:
%f",i,x1);
```

```
        error=fabs(x1-x0);
        if(error<EPS)
            {
            break;
            }
        x0 = x1;
    }
    if(error>EPS)
        {
        prinf("\n\n\t NOTE:- ");
        printf("The number of iterations are not sufficient.");
        }
    printf("\n\n\n\t\t\t ------------------------------");
    printf("\n\t\t\t       The root is %.4f ",x1);
    printf("\n\t\t\t ------------------------------");
    }
```

OUTPUT

```
Solution by NEWTON RAPHSON method
Equation is:
                3*X - cos X - 1=0
Enter the number of iterations: 10
Enter the maximum possible error: .0000001
The root is near to 0.6100
The 1 approximation to the root is:0.607102
The 2 approximation to the root is:0.607102
The 3 approximation to the root is:0.607102
    --------------------------------
            The root is 0.6071
    --------------------------------
```

Example 2. *Using Newton's iterative method, find the real root of* $x \log_{10} x = 1.2$, *correct to five decimal places.*

Sol.
$$f(x) = x \log_{10} x - 1.2$$

$\because$
$$f(1) = -1.2 = (-)\text{ve}$$
$$f(3) = 3 \log_{10} 3 - 1.2 = (+)\text{ve}$$

So a root of $f(x) = 0$ lies between 1 and 3.

Let us take $x_0 = 2.$

and $f'(x) = \log_{10} x + \log_{10} e = \log_{10} x + 0.43429$

Newton's iteration formula gives,

$$x_{n+1} = x_n - \frac{f(x_n)}{f'(x_n)}$$

$$= x_n - \frac{x_n \log_{10} x_n - 1.2}{\log_{10} x_n + .43429} = \frac{.43429 x_n + 1.2}{\log_{10} x_n + .43429} \quad (33)$$

Given $n = 0$, the first approximation is

$$x_1 = \frac{.43429\, x_0 + 1.2}{\log_{10} 2 + .43429} = 2.81 \qquad (\because \; x_0 = 2)$$

Similarly, given $n = 1, 2, 3, 4$ in (33), we get

$$x_2 = 2.741,\ x_3 = 2.74064,\ x_4 = 2.74065,\quad x_5 = 2.74065$$

Clearly, $x_4 = x_5$

Hence the required root is **2.74065,** correct to five decimal places.

Example 3. *Evaluate* $\sqrt{12}$ *to four decimal places by Newton's iterative method.*

Sol. Let $x = \sqrt{12}$ so that $x^2 - 12 = 0$ (34)

Take $f(x) = x^2 - 12$, Newton's iteration formula gives,

$$x_{n+1} = x_n - \frac{f(x_n)}{f'(x_n)} = x_n - \frac{x_n^2 - 12}{2x_n} = \frac{1}{2}\left(x_n + \frac{12}{x_n}\right) \quad (35)$$

Now, since $f(3) = -3$ (–)ve

$f(4) = 4$ (+)ve

∴ The root of (34) lies between 3 and 4.

Given $x_0 = 3.5$, (35) gives,

$$x_1 = \frac{1}{2}\left(x_0 + \frac{12}{x_0}\right) = \frac{1}{2}\left(3.5 + \frac{12}{3.5}\right) = 3.4643$$

$$x_2 = \frac{1}{2}\left(x_1 + \frac{12}{x_1}\right) = 3.4641$$

$$x_3 = 3.4641$$

Since $x_2 = x_3$ up to 4 decimal places,

we have $\sqrt{12}$ **= 3.4641.**

Example 4. *Using Newton's iterative method, find the real root of x sin x + cos x = 0 which is near x = π, correct to 3 decimal places.*

Sol. We have

$$f(x) = x \sin x + \cos x \quad \text{and} \quad f'(x) = x \cos x$$

The iteration formula is

$$x_{n+1} = x_n - \frac{x_n \sin x_n + \cos x_n}{x_n \cos x_n}$$

with $x_0 = \pi$, $$x_1 = x_0 - \frac{x_0 \sin x_0 + \cos x_0}{x_0 \cos x_0} = \pi - \frac{\pi \sin \pi + \cos \pi}{\pi \cos \pi} = 2.8233$$

Successive iteratives are

$$x_2 = 2.7986, \quad x_3 = 2.7984, \quad x_4 = 2.7984$$

Since $x_3 = x_4$, the required root is **2.798,** correct to three decimal places.

Example 5. *Find a real root of the equation* $x = e^{-x}$ *using the Newton-Raphson method.*

Sol. We have $f(x) = xe^x - 1$

then, $f'(x) = (1 + x)\, e^x$

Let $x_0 = 1$

then, $$x_1 = 1 - \left(\frac{e-1}{2e}\right) = \frac{1}{2}\left(1 + \frac{1}{e}\right) = 0.6839397$$

Now, $f(x_1) = 0.3553424$ and $f'(x_1) = 3.337012$

so that, $$x_2 = 0.6839397 - \frac{0.3553424}{3.337012} = 0.5774545$$

Proceeding in this way, we obtain

$$x_3 = 0.5672297, \quad x_4 = 0.5671433$$

Hence the required root is **0.5671,** correct to 4 decimal places.

Example 6. *Find to four decimal places, the smallest root of the equation* $e^{-x} = \sin x$.

Sol. The given equation is

$$f(x) \equiv e^{-x} - \sin x = 0$$

so that,
$$x_{n+1} = x_n + \frac{e^{-x_n} - \sin x_n}{e^{-x_n} + \cos x_n}$$

Take $x_0 = .6$ then,
$$x_1 = .58848, \quad x_2 = .588559$$

Hence, the desired value of the root is 0.5885.

Example 7. (*i*) *Find a positive value of* $(17)^{1/3}$, *correct to four decimal places, by the Newton-Raphson method.*

(*ii*) *Find the cube root of 10.*

Sol. (*i*) The iterative formula is
$$x_{n+1} = \frac{1}{3}\left(2x_n + \frac{a}{x_n^2}\right) \tag{36}$$

Here $a = 17$

Take $x_0 = 2.5$ $\quad \left|\because \sqrt[3]{8} = 2 \text{ and } \sqrt[3]{27} = 3\right.$

Putting $n = 0$ in (36), we get
$$x_1 = \frac{1}{3}\left(2x_0 + \frac{17}{x_0^2}\right) = \frac{1}{3}\left(5 + \frac{17}{6.25}\right) = 2.5733$$

Putting $n = 1$ in (36), we get
$$x_2 = \frac{1}{3}\left(2x_1 + \frac{17}{x_1^2}\right) = \frac{1}{3}\left(5.1466 + \frac{17}{6.6220}\right) = 2.5713$$

Again putting $n = 2$ in (36), we get
$$x_3 = \frac{1}{3}\left(2x_2 + \frac{17}{x_2^2}\right) = \frac{1}{3}\left(5.1426 + \frac{17}{6.61158}\right) = 2.57128$$

Putting $n = 3$ in (36), we get
$$x_4 = \frac{1}{3}\left(2x_3 + \frac{17}{x_3^2}\right) = \frac{1}{3}\left(5.14256 + \frac{17}{6.61148}\right) = 2.57128$$

Since x_3 and x_4 agree to four decimal places, the required root is **2.5713,** correct to four decimal places.

(*ii*)
$$x_{n+1} = \frac{2x_n^3 + a}{3x_n^2} = \frac{1}{3}\left(2x_n + \frac{a}{x_n^2}\right)$$

Take $x_0 = 2.5$ $(\because\ \sqrt[3]{8} = 2 \text{ and } \sqrt[3]{27} = 3)$

$\therefore$ $x_1 = 2.2$ $(n = 0)$

$x_2 = 2.155$ $(n = 1)$

$x_3 = 2.15466$ $(n = 2)$

$\therefore$ $\sqrt[3]{10} \approx 2.15466.$

Example 8. *Show that the following two sequences both have convergence of the second order with the same limit* $\sqrt{a}$.

$$x_{n+1} = \frac{1}{2}x_n\left(1 + \frac{a}{x_n^2}\right) \text{ and, } x_{n+1} = \frac{1}{2}x_n\left(3 - \frac{x_n^2}{a}\right).$$

Sol. Since, $x_{n+1} = \frac{1}{2}x_n\left(1 + \frac{a}{x_n^2}\right)$, we have

$$x_{n+1} - \sqrt{a} = \frac{1}{2}x_n\left(1 + \frac{a}{x_n^2}\right) - \sqrt{a} = \frac{1}{2}\left(x_n + \frac{a}{x_n} - 2\sqrt{a}\right)$$

$$= \frac{1}{2}\left(\sqrt{x_n} - \frac{\sqrt{a}}{\sqrt{x_n}}\right)^2 = \frac{1}{2x_n}(x_n - \sqrt{a})^2$$

Thus, $$e_{n+1} = \frac{1}{2x_n}e_n^2 \tag{37}$$

which shows the quadratic convergence. Similarly for the second,

$$x_{n+1} - \sqrt{a} = \frac{1}{2}x_n\left(3 - \frac{x_n^2}{a}\right) - \sqrt{a}$$

$$= \frac{1}{2}x_n\left(1 - \frac{x_n^2}{a}\right) + (x_n - \sqrt{a})$$

$$= \frac{x_n}{2a}(a - x_n^2) + (x_n - \sqrt{a}) = (x_n - \sqrt{a})\left[1 - \frac{x_n}{2a}(x_n + \sqrt{a})\right]$$

$$e_{n+1} = \frac{x_n - \sqrt{a}}{2a}[2a - x_n^2 - x_n\sqrt{a}]$$

$$= \frac{x_n - \sqrt{a}}{2a}[(a - x_n^2) + (a - x_n\sqrt{a})]$$

$$= -\left(\frac{x_n - \sqrt{a}}{2a}\right)(x_n - \sqrt{a})(x_n + 2\sqrt{a})$$

$$e_{n+1} = -\frac{(x_n - \sqrt{a})^2}{2a}(x_n + 2\sqrt{a}) = -\frac{(x_n + 2\sqrt{a})}{2a} \cdot e_n^2 \qquad (38)$$

which shows the quadratic convergence.

Example 9. *If x_n is a suitably close approximation to $\sqrt{a}$, show that the error in the formula*

$$x_{n+1} = \frac{1}{2}x_n\left(1 + \frac{a}{x_n^{2}}\right) \text{ is about } \frac{1}{3}\text{rd that in the formula,}$$

$$x_{n+1} = \frac{1}{2}x_n\left(3 - \frac{x_n^2}{a}\right), \text{ and deduce that the formula}$$

$$x_{n+1} = \frac{x_n}{8}\left(6 + \frac{3a}{x_n^2} - \frac{x_n^2}{a}\right) \text{ gives a sequence with third order convergence.}$$

Sol. Since x_n is very close to $\sqrt{a}$

$$e_{n+1} \simeq -\left(\frac{x_n + 2x_n}{2x_n^2}\right)e_n^2 \qquad | \text{ From (38)}$$

$$= 3 \cdot \frac{1}{2x_n} e_n^2 \qquad (39)$$

A simple observation shows that from (37) (see Ex. 8) and (39), the error in the first formula for e_{n+1} is about $\frac{1}{3}$rd of that in the second formula.

To find the rate of convergence of the given formula, we have

$$x_{n+1} - \sqrt{a} = \frac{x_n}{8}\left(6 + \frac{3a}{x_n^2} - \frac{x_n^2}{a}\right) - \sqrt{a} = \frac{x_n(6x_n^2 a + 3a^2 - x_n^4)}{8\,ax_n^2} - \sqrt{a}$$

$$= \frac{6\,x_n^2 a + 3a^2 - x_n^4 - 8\,x_n\,a\sqrt{a}}{8\,x_n a} = \frac{-(x_n + 3\sqrt{a})(x_n - \sqrt{a})^3}{8x_n a}$$

$$\therefore \quad e_{n+1} = -\left(\frac{x_n + 3\sqrt{a}}{8x_n a}\right)e_n^3$$

It shows that above formula has a convergence of third order.

Exmaple 10. *Apply Newton's formula to find the values of $(30)^{1/5}$.*

Sol. To find the pth root of a, we have

$$x_{n+1} = \frac{(p-1)\,x_n{}^p + a}{p\,x_n{}^{p-1}}$$

Here, $a = 30$, $p = 5$, the first approximation is

$$x_1 = \frac{4x_0{}^5 + 30}{5x_0{}^4}$$

Take $\quad x_0 = 1.9, \quad$ we get $x_1 = 1.98$

Again, $\quad x_2 = 1.973$

$\therefore$ Value = 1.973 (correct to 3 decimal places).

Example 11. *Using the starting value 2(1 + i), solve $x^4 - 5x^3 + 20x^2 - 40x + 60 = 0$ by Newton-Raphson method, given that all the roots of the given equation are complex.*

Sol. Let $\quad f(x) = x^4 - 5x^3 + 20x^2 - 40x + 60$

so that, $\quad f'(x) = 4x^3 - 15x^2 + 40x - 40$

$\therefore$ Newton-Raphson method gives,

$$x_{n+1} = x_n - \frac{f(x_n)}{f'(x_n)}$$

$$= x_n - \frac{x_n{}^4 - 5x_n{}^3 + 20x_n{}^2 - 40x_n + 60}{4x_n{}^3 - 15x_n{}^2 + 40x_n - 40}$$

$$= \frac{3x_n{}^4 - 10x_n{}^3 + 20x_n{}^2 - 60}{4x_n{}^3 - 15x_n{}^2 + 40x_n - 40}$$

Put $n = 0$, take $x_0 = 2(1 + i)$ by trial, we get

$$x_1 = 1.92\,(1 + i)$$

Again, $\quad x_2 = 1.915 + 1.908\,i$

Since imaginary roots occur in conjugate pairs roots are $1.915 \pm 1.908\,i$ up to 3 decimal places. Assuming the other pairs of roots to be $\alpha \pm i\beta$, then

$$\text{Sum} = \begin{pmatrix} \alpha + i\beta + \alpha - i\beta \\ +1.915 + 1.908\,i \\ +1.915 - 1.908\,i \end{pmatrix} = 2\alpha + 3.83 = 5$$

$\Rightarrow \quad \alpha = 0.585$

Also, the product of the roots $= (\alpha^2 + \beta^2)$ $[(1.915)^2 + (1.908)^2] = 60$

$\Rightarrow$ $\beta = 2.805$

Hence, the other two roots are $0.585 \pm 2.805\, i$.

Example 12. *Obtain Newton-Raphson's extended formula*

$$x_1 = x_0 - \frac{f(x_0)}{f'(x_0)} - \frac{1}{2}\cdot\frac{\{f(x_0)\}^2 \,.\, f''(x_0)}{\{f'(x_0)\}^3}$$

for the root of the equation $f(x) = 0$, also known as Chebyshev formula of third order.

Sol. Expanding $f(x)$ by Taylor's series in the neighborhood of x_0, we get

$$f(x) = 0 \Rightarrow f(x_0) + (x - x_0)\, f'(x_0) = 0$$

$$\Rightarrow \qquad x = x_0 - \frac{f(x_0)}{f'(x_0)}$$

This is I approximation to the root.

$$\therefore \qquad x_1 = x_0 - \frac{f(x_0)}{f'(x_0)}$$

Again By Taylor's series, we have

$$f(x) = f(x_0) + (x - x_0)\, f'(x_0) + \frac{(x - x_0)^2}{2}\, f''(x_0)$$

$$\therefore \qquad f(x_1) = f(x_0) + (x_1 - x_0)\, f'(x_0) + \frac{(x_1 - x_0)^2}{2} f''(x_0)$$

But $f(x_1) = 0$ as x_1 is an approximation to the root.

$$\therefore \qquad f(x_0) + (x_1 - x_0)\, f'(x_0) + \frac{1}{2}\, (x_1 - x_0)^2\, f''(x_0) = 0$$

or

$$f(x_0) + (x_1 - x_0)\, f'(x_0) + \frac{1}{2}\, \frac{\{f(x_0)\}^2\, f''(x_0)}{f'(x_0)^2} = 0$$

$$\Rightarrow \qquad x_1 = x_0 - \frac{f(x_0)}{f'(x_0)} - \frac{1}{2}\, \frac{\{f(x_0)\}^2\, f''(x_0)}{\{f'(x_0)\}^3}$$

This formula can be used iteratively.

Example 13. *The graph of $y = 2 \sin x$ and $y = \log x + c$ touch each other in the neighborhood of point $x = 8$. Find c and the coordinates of point of contact.*

Sol. The graphs will touch each other if the values of dy/dx at their point of contact is same.

For $\quad y = 2 \sin x, \quad \frac{dy}{dx} = 2 \cos x$

For $\quad y = \log x + c \quad \frac{dy}{dx} = \frac{1}{x}$

$\therefore \quad 2 \cos x = \frac{1}{x} \Rightarrow x \cos x - .5 = 0$

Let $\quad f(x) = x \cos x - .5$

$\therefore \quad f'(x) = \cos x - x \sin x$

$\therefore$ Newton's iterative formula is

$$x_{n+1} = x_n - \frac{x_n \cos x_n - 0.5}{\cos x_n - x_n \sin x_n}$$

For $n = 0$, $x_0 = 8$, first app. $\quad x_1 = 7.793$

Second approximation, $\quad x_2 = 7.789 \approx 7.79$

Now, $\quad y = 2 \sin 7.79 = 1.9960$

$\therefore$ Point of contact $\rightarrow (7.79, 1.996)$

Now, $\quad y = \log x + c$

$\Rightarrow \quad 1.996 = \log 7.79 + c \Rightarrow c = -0.054.$

Example 14. *Using the starting value $x_0 = i$, find a zero of*

$$x^4 + x^3 + 5x^2 + 4x + 4 = 0.$$

Sol. By Newton's method

$$x_1 = i - \frac{f(i)}{f'(i)} = i - \frac{3i}{1+6i} = .486 + .919\, i$$

Now, $$x_2 = .486 + .919\, i - \frac{f(.486 + .919i)}{f'(.486 + .919i)}$$

$$= .486 + .919\, i - \left(\frac{-.292 + .174\, i}{1.78 + 6.005\, i}\right) = -.499 + 0.866i$$

The actual root is $x = \frac{-1 + i\sqrt{3}}{2}$.

Example 15. *Show that the square root of $N = AB$ is given by*

$$\sqrt{N} \simeq \frac{S}{4} + \frac{N}{S}, \text{ where } S = A + B.$$

Sol. Let $x = \sqrt{N}$

$\Rightarrow \quad x^2 - N = 0$

Let $f(x) = x^2 - N$

$\therefore \quad f'(x) = 2x$

By Newton-Raphson formula,

$$x_{n+1} = x_n - \frac{f(x_n)}{f'(x_n)} = x_n - \frac{x_n^2 - N}{2x_n} = \frac{x_n}{2} + \frac{N}{2x_n}$$

Let $x_n = \dfrac{A+B}{2}$

then, $x_{n+1} = \dfrac{A+B}{4} + \dfrac{N}{A+B} \simeq \dfrac{S}{4} + \dfrac{N}{S}$ | Since S = A + B

Example 16. *Determine the value of p and q so that the rate of convergence of the iterative method*

$$x_{n+1} = px_n + q\frac{N}{x_n^2}$$

for computing $N^{1/3}$ becomes as high as possible.

Sol. We have $x^3 = N$

$\therefore \quad f(x) = x^3 - N$

Letting α be the exact root, we have

$$\alpha^3 = N$$

Substituting $x_n = \alpha + e_n$, $x_{n+1} = \alpha + e_{n+1}$, $N = \alpha^3$ in $x_{n+1} = px_n + q\dfrac{N}{x_n^2}$, we get

$$\alpha + e_{n+1} = p(\alpha + e_n) + q\frac{\alpha^3}{(\alpha + e_n)^2}$$

$$= p(\alpha + e_n) + q\frac{\alpha^3}{\alpha^2\left(1 + \frac{e_n}{\alpha}\right)^2}$$

$$= p(\alpha + e_n) + q\alpha\left(1 + \frac{e_n}{\alpha}\right)^{-2}$$

$$= p(\alpha + e_n) + q\alpha\left\{1 - 2\frac{e_n}{\alpha} + 3\left(\frac{e_n}{\alpha}\right)^2 - \ldots\ldots\right\}$$

$$= p(\alpha + e_n) + q\alpha - 2qe_n + 3q\frac{e_n^2}{\alpha} - ....$$

$$\Rightarrow \qquad e_{n+1} = (p + q - 1)\alpha + (p - 2q)e_n + 0(e_n^{\,2}) + ...$$

Now for the method to become of the highest order as possible, *i.e.*, of order 2, we must have

$$p + q = 1 \quad \text{and} \quad p - 2q = 0$$

so that, $$p = \frac{2}{3} \quad \text{and} \quad q = \frac{1}{3}.$$

Example 17. *How should the constant* α *be chosen to ensure the fastest possible convergence with the iteration formula?*

$$x_{n+1} = \frac{\alpha x_n + x_n^{-2} + 1}{\alpha + 1}.$$

Sol. Since $\lim\limits_{n\to\infty} x_n = \lim\limits_{n\to\infty} x_{n+1} = \xi$, we have

$$\xi = \left(\frac{\alpha\xi + \dfrac{1}{\xi^2} + 1}{\alpha + 1}\right)$$

$$\Rightarrow \qquad (\alpha + 1)\xi^3 = \alpha\xi^3 + \xi^2 + 1$$

$$\Rightarrow \qquad \xi^3 - \xi^2 - 1 = 0$$

ξ can be obtained by finding a root of the equation $x^3 - x^2 - 1 = 0$.

We have $\qquad f(x) = x^3 - x^2 - 1$

$$f'(x) = 3x^2 - 2x$$

Since $f(1.45) = (-)$ve and $f(1.47) = (+)$ve

$\therefore$ Root lies between 1.45 and 1.47.

Let $\qquad x_0 = 1.46$

By Newton-Raphson method,

First approximation is

$$x_1 = x_0 - \frac{f(x_0)}{f'(x_0)} = x_0 - \left(\frac{x_0^{\,3} - x_0^{\,2} - 1}{3x_0^{\,2} - 2x_0}\right) = 1.465601.$$

Second approximation is

$$x_2 = x_1 - \frac{f(x_1)}{f'(x_1)} = x_1 - \left(\frac{x_1^{\,3} - x_1^{\,2} - 1}{3x_1^{\,2} - 2x_1}\right) = 1.46557$$

Hence $\xi = 1.465$ correct to three decimal places.

Now, we have

$$x_{n+1} = \frac{\alpha x_n + x_n^{-2} + 1}{\alpha + 1} \qquad (40)$$

Putting $x_n = \xi + e_n$ and $x_{n+1} = \xi + e_{n+1}$ in (40), we get

$$(\alpha + 1)(\xi + e_{n+1}) = \alpha(\xi + e_n) + \frac{1}{(\xi + e_n)^2} + 1$$

$$= \alpha(\xi + e_n) + \frac{1}{\xi^2}\left(1 + \frac{e_n}{\xi}\right)^{-2} + 1$$

which gives,

$$(1 + \alpha)e_{n+1} = \left(\alpha - \frac{2}{\xi^3}\right) e_n + O(e_n^2)$$

For fastest convergence, we must have $\alpha = \frac{2}{\xi^3}$

$$\therefore \qquad \alpha = \frac{2}{(1.465)^3} = 0.636.$$

Example 18. *Newton-Raphson's method for solving the equation $f(x) = c$, where c is a real valued constant, is applied to the function*

$$f(x) = \begin{cases} \cos x, & \text{when } |x| \leq 1 \\ \cos x + (x^2 - 1)^2, & \text{when } |x| \geq 1 \end{cases}$$

For which c is $x_n = (-1)^n$, when $x_0 = 1$ and the calculations are carried out with no errors? Even in high precision arithmetic, the convergence is troublesome. Explain.

Sol. $\qquad f(x) - c = 0 \qquad (41)$

Applying the Newton-Raphson method to eqn. (41), we get

$$x_{n+1} = x_n - \left[\frac{f(x_n) - c}{f'(x_n)}\right]$$

For $n = 0$, we have

$$x_1 = x_0 - \left[\frac{f(x_0) - c}{f'(x_0)}\right]$$

$$= 1 - \left[\frac{\cos 1 - c}{-\sin 1}\right] \qquad | \because \; x_0 = 1$$

$$-1 = 1 + \left[\frac{\cos 1 - c}{\sin 1}\right] \qquad | \because \; x_1 = (-1)^1 = -1$$

Hence $\quad -2 \sin 1 = \cos 1 - c$

$\Rightarrow \qquad c = \cos 1 + 2 \sin 1$

with this value of c, we get

$$x_2 = 1, \quad x_3 = -1, \ldots, x_n = (-1)^n$$

Since $f'(x) = 0$ between x_0 and the roots and also at $x = 0$, the convergence is troublesome inspite of high precision arithmetic.

ASSIGNMENT 3.9

1. By using Newton-Raphson's method, find the root of $x^4 - x - 10 = 0$ which is near to $x = 2$, correct to three decimal places.
2. Compute one positive root of $2x - \log_{10} x = 7$ by the Newton-Raphson method correct to four decimal places.
3. (*i*) Use the Newton-Raphson method to find a root of the equation $x^3 - 2x - 5 = 0$.

   (*ii*) Use Newton-Raphson method to find a root of the equation $x^3 - 3x - 5 = 0$.
4. Find the real root of the equations

   (*i*) $\log x = \cos x$ (*ii*) $x^2 + 4 \sin x = 0$

   by Newton-Raphson method, correct to three decimal places.
5. Use Newton-Raphson method to obtain a root correct to three decimal places of the following equations:

   (*i*) $\sin x = 1 - x$ (*ii*) $x^3 - 5x + 3 = 0$ (*iii*) $x^4 + x^2 - 80 = 0$

   (*iv*) $x^3 + 3x^2 - 3 = 0$ (*v*) $4(x - \sin x) = 1$ (*vi*) $x - \cos x = 0$

   (*vii*) $\sin x = \frac{x}{2}$ (*viii*) $x + \log x = 2$ (*ix*) $\tan x = x$.
6. Explain the method of Newton-Raphson for computing roots. Apply it for finding x from $x^2 - 25 = 0$. Write a program using 'C'.
7. Write a computer program in 'C' for finding out a real root of eqn. $f(x) = 0$ by the Newton-Raphson method.
8. Using the Newton-Raphson method, obtain the formula for $\sqrt{N}$ and find $\sqrt{20}$ correct to 2 decimal places.
9. Obtain the cube root of 120 using the Newton-Raphson method, starting with $x_0 = 4.5$.
10. Develop an algorithm using the Newton-Raphson method to find the fourth root of a positive number N, and find $\sqrt[4]{32}$.

11. Find the cube root of 3 correct to three decimal places by Newton's iterative method.

12. Prove the recurrence formula

$$x_{i+1} = \frac{1}{3}\left(2x_i + \frac{N}{x_i^2}\right)$$

for finding the cube root of N. Find the cube root of 63.

13. Use Newton's formula to prove that the square root of N can be obtained by the recursion formula,

$$x_{i+1} = x_i\left(1 - \frac{x_i^2 - N}{2N}\right)$$

Find the square root of

(*a*) 26 (*b*) 29 (*c*) 35.

14. Show that the iterative formula for finding the reciprocal of n is $x_{i+1} = x_i(2 - nx_i)$, and find the value of $\frac{1}{31}$.

15. Determine p, q, and r so that the order of the iterative method

$$x_{n+1} = px_n + \frac{qa}{x_n^2} + \frac{ra^2}{x_n^5}$$

for $a^{1/3}$ becomes as high as possible.

[**Hint:** $p + q + r = 1, p - 2q - 5r = 0, 3q + 15r = 0.$]

16. Derive the expression for the Newton-Raphson method to find a root of an equation. Find the order of the convergence of this method.

17. Find all positive roots of the equation

$$10\int_0^x e^{-x^2}\,dt - 1 = 0 \text{ with six correct decimals.}$$

18. The equation

$$2e^{-x} = \frac{1}{x+2} + \frac{1}{x+1}$$

has two roots greater than – 1.

Calculate these roots correct to five decimal places.

19. The equation $x = 0.2 + 0.4 \sin\left(\frac{x}{b}\right)$ where b is a parameter, has one solution near $x = 0.3$.

The parameter is known only with some uncertainty: $b = 1.2 \pm 0.05$.

Calculate the root with an accuracy reasonable with respect to the uncertainty of b.

20. Find the positive root of the equation

$$e^x = 1 + x + \frac{x^2}{2} + \frac{x^3}{6}e^{0.3x}$$

correct to 6 decimal places.

21. Show that the equation

$$f(x) = \cos\left\{\frac{\pi(x+1)}{8}\right\} + 0.148x - 0.9062 = 0$$

has one root in the interval (– 1, 0) and one in (0, 1). Calculate the negative root correct to 4 decimals.

3.38 DEFINITIONS

1. A number α is a solution of $f(x) = 0$ if $f(\alpha) = 0$. Such a solution α is a root or a zero of $f(x) = 0$. Geometrically, a root of the eqn. $f(x) = 0$ is the value of x at which the graph of $y = f(x)$ intersects x-axis.
2. If we can write $f(x) = 0$ as

$$f(x) = (x - \alpha)^m\, g(x) = 0$$

where $g(x)$ is bounded and $g(\alpha) \neq 0$ then α is called a **multiple root** of multiplicity m. In this case,

$$\mathbf{f(\alpha) = f'(\alpha) = \ldots\ldots\ldots = f^{(m-1)}(\alpha) = 0,\ f^{(m)}(\alpha) \neq 0}$$

For $m = 1$, the number α is said to be a simple root.

3.39 METHODS FOR MULTIPLE ROOTS

If α is a multiple root of multiplicity m of the eqn. $f(x) = 0$, then we have

$$f(\alpha) = f'(\alpha) = \ldots\ldots = f^{(m-1)}(\alpha) = 0 \quad \text{and} \quad f^{(m)}(\alpha) \neq 0$$

It can easily be verified that all the iteration methods discussed so far have only a linear rate of convergence when $m > 1$.

For example, in the Newton-Raphson method, we have

$$f(x_k) = f(\alpha + e_k) = \frac{e_k^m}{m!} f^{(m)}(\alpha) + \frac{e_k^{m+1}}{(m+1)!} f^{(m+1)}(\alpha)$$

$$+ \frac{e_k^{m+2}}{(m+2)!} f^{(m+2)}(\alpha) + \ldots\ldots$$

$$f'(x_k) = f'(\alpha + e_k) = \frac{e_k^{m-1}}{(m-1)!} f^{(m)}(\alpha) + \frac{e_k^m}{m!} f^{(m+1)}(\alpha) + \ldots\ldots$$

The error equation for the Newton-Raphson method becomes,

$$e_{k+1} = \left(1 - \frac{1}{m}\right) e_k + \frac{1}{m^2 (m \mid 1)} \frac{f^{(m+1)}(\alpha)}{f^{(m)}(\alpha)} e_k^2 + \text{O}(e_k^3)$$

If $m \neq 1$, we obtain,

$$e_{k+1} = \left(1 - \frac{1}{m}\right) e_k + \text{O}(e_k^2) \tag{42}$$

which shows that the method has **only linear rate of convergence.**

However, if the multiplicity of the root is known in advance, we can modify the methods by introducing parameters dependent on the multiplicity of the root to increase their order of convergence.

For example, consider the Newton-Raphson method in the form

$$x_{k+1} = x_k - \beta \frac{f_k}{f_k'} \tag{43}$$

where β is an arbitrary parameter to be determined.

If α is a multiple root of multiplicity m, we obtain from (43), the error equation

$$e_{k+1} = \left(1 - \frac{\beta}{m}\right) e_k + \frac{\beta}{m^2 (m+1)} \frac{f^{(m+1)}(\alpha)}{f^{(m)}(\alpha)} e_k^2 + 0\,(e_k^3)$$

If the method (43) is to have the quadratic rate of convergence, then the coefficient of e_k must vanish, which gives

$$1 - \frac{\beta}{m} = 0 \quad \text{or} \quad \beta = m$$

Thus the method

$$\boxed{x_{k+1} = x_k - m \frac{f_k}{f_k'}}$$

has a quadratic rate of convergence for determining a multiple root of multiplicity m.

If the multiplicity of the root is not known in advance, then we use the following procedure.

It is known that if $f(x) = 0$ has a root α of multiplicity m, then $f'(x) = 0$ has the same root α of multiplicity $m - 1$.

Hence, $g(x) = \dfrac{f(x)}{f'(x)}$ has a simple root α and we can now use the Newton-Raphson method

$$x_{k+1} = x_k - \frac{g(x_k)}{g'(x_k)}$$

to find the approximate value of the multiple root α.

Simplifying, we have

$$x_{k+1} = x_k - \frac{f_k f_k'}{f_k'^2 - f_k f_k''}$$

which has a quadratic rate of convergence for multiple roots.

NOTE *If initial approximation x_0 is sufficiently close to the root, then the expressions*

$$x_0 - m\frac{f(x_0)}{f'(x_0)},\ x_0 - (m-1)\frac{f'(x_0)}{f''(x_0)},\ x_0 - (m-2)\frac{f''(x_0)}{f'''(x_0)}$$ *will have same value.*

EXAMPLES

Example 1. *Show that the modified Newton-Raphson's method*

$$x_{n+1} = x_n - \frac{2f(x_n)}{f'(x_n)}$$

gives a quadratic convergence when $f(x) = 0$ has a pair of double roots in the neighborhood of $x = x_n$.

Sol. $e_{n+1} = e_n - \dfrac{2f(a+e_n)}{f'(a+e_n)}$, where a, e_n, and e_{n+1} have their usual meanings.

Expanding in powers of e_n and using $f(a) = 0$, $f'(a) = 0$ since $x = a$ is a double root near $x = x_n$, we get

$$e_{n+1} = e_n - \frac{2\left[\frac{e_n^2}{2!} f''(a) + ...\right]}{\left[e_n f''(a) + \frac{e_n^2}{2!} f'''(a) + ...\right]}$$

$$= e_n - \frac{2e_n^2\left[\frac{1}{2!} f''(a) + \frac{1}{3!} f'''(a) + ...\right]}{e_n\left[f''(a) + \frac{e_n}{2!} f'''(a) + ...\right]}$$

$$\simeq e_n - \frac{2e_n\left[\frac{1}{2!}f''(a)+\frac{1}{3!}f'''(a)\right]}{f''(a)+\frac{e_n}{2!}f'''(a)}$$

$$e_{n+1} \simeq \frac{1}{6}e_n^{\ 2}\cdot\frac{f'''(a)}{\left[f''(a)+\frac{e_n}{2!}f'''(a)\right]}$$

$\therefore$ $$e_{n+1} \approx \frac{1}{6}e_n^{\ 2}\frac{f'''(a)}{f''(a)}$$

$\Rightarrow$ $$e_{n+1} \propto e_n^{\ 2}$$

and hence the convergence is quadratic.

Example 2. *Find the double root of the equation*

$$x^3 - x^2 - x + 1 = 0.$$

Sol. Let $$f(x) = x^3 - x^2 - x + 1$$

so that $$f'(x) = 3x^2 - 2x - 1$$

$$f''(x) = 6x - 2$$

Starting with $x_0 = 0.9$, we have

$$x_0 - 2\frac{f(x_0)}{f'(x_0)} = .9 - \frac{2\times .019}{(-.37)} = 1.003$$

and $$x_0 - (2-1)\frac{f'(x_0)}{f''(x_0)} = .9 - \frac{(-.37)}{3.4} = 1.009$$

The closeness of these values implies that there is a double root near $x = 1$.

Choosing $x_1 = 1.01$ for the next approximation, we get

$$x_1 - 2\frac{f(x_1)}{f'(x_1)} = 1.01 - 2\times\frac{0.0002}{0.0403} = 1.0001$$

and $$x_1 - (2-1)\frac{f'(x_1)}{f''(x_1)} = 1.01 - \frac{.0403}{4.06} = 1.0001$$

This shows that there is a double root at $x = 1.0001$ which is quite near the actual root $x = 1$.

Example 3. *The equation*

$$f(x) = x^3 - 7x^2 + 16x - 12 = 0$$

has a double root at $x = 2$. Starting with the initial approximation $x_0 = 1$, find the root correct to 3 decimal places using the modified Newton-Raphson method with $m = 2$.

Sol. The modified Newton-Raphson method with $m = 2$ becomes,

$$x_{n+1} = x_n - 2\left[\frac{x_n^3 - 7x_n^2 + 16x_n - 12}{3x_n^2 - 14x_n + 16}\right], n = 0, 1, ...$$

Starting with $x_0 = 1$, we get

$$x_1 = 1.8$$

$$x_2 = 1.984615385$$

$$x_3 = 1.999884332$$

$$x_4 = 2.000000161$$

$$x_5 = 2.000000161$$

$\therefore$ The root correct to 3 decimal places is 2.000.

Example 4. *Show that the equation*

$$f(x) = 1 - xe^{1-x} = 0$$

has a double root at $x = 1$. The root is obtained by using the modified Newton-Raphson method with $m = 2$ starting with $x_0 = 0$.

Sol. Since $f(1) = f'(1) = 0$ and $f''(1) \neq 0$, the root $x = 1$ is a double root.

$$x_{n+1} = x_n - 2\left[\frac{1 - x_n e^{1-x_n}}{(x_n - 1)e^{1-x_n}}\right]; n = 0, 1, ...$$

Starting with $x_0 = 0$, we get

$$x_1 = .735758882$$

$$x_2 = .978185253$$

$$x_3 = .999842233$$

$$x_4 = 1.000000061$$

$$x_5 = 1.000000061$$

Hence the root correct to six decimal places is 1.000000.

3.40 NEARLY EQUAL ROOTS

So far, Newton's method is applicable when $f'(x) \neq 0$ in the neighborhood of actual root $x = a$, *i.e.*, in the interval $(a - h, a + h)$.

If the quantity h is very very small, it will not satisfy the above restriction. The application of Newton's method will not be practical in that case. This condition occurs when the roots are very close to one another.

We know that in case of the double root $x = a$, $f(x)$ and $f'(x)$ both vanish at $x = a$. Thus, while applying Newton's method, if x_i is simultaneously near zeros of $f(x)$ and $f'(x)$, *i.e.*, $f(x_i)$ and $f'(x_i)$ are both very small, then it is usually practical to depart from the standard sequence and proceed to obtain two new starting values for the two nearly equal roots.

To obtain these values, we first apply Newton's method to the equation $f'(x) = 0$, *i.e.*, we use the iteration formula

$$x_{i+1} = x_i - \frac{f'(x_i)}{f''(x_i)} \tag{44}$$

with the last available iterate as the initial value x_0 for (44).

Suppose $x = c$ is the solution obtained by (44).

Now, by Taylor's series, we have

$$f(x) = f(c) + (x - c) f'(c) + \frac{1}{2}(x - c)^2 f''(c) + \ldots\ldots.$$

But $\quad f'(c) = 0$

$$f(x) = f(c) + \frac{1}{2}(x - c)^2 f''(c) + \text{R}$$

Assuming R to be small, we conclude that the zero's of $f(x)$ near $x = c$ are approximately given by

$$f(c) + \frac{1}{2}(x - c)^2 f''(c) = 0$$

$$\Rightarrow \qquad x = c \pm \sqrt{\frac{-2f(c)}{f''(c)}} \tag{45}$$

Using these values as starting values, we can use the original iteration formula to get two close roots of $f(x) = 0$.

EXAMPLE

Example. *Use synthetic division to solve* $f(x) \equiv x^3 - x^2 - 1.0001\,x + 0.9999 = 0$ *in the neighborhood of* $x = 1$.

Sol. To find $f(1)$ and $f'(1)$,

1	−1	−1.0001	0.9999	1
	1	0	− 1.0001	
1	0	− 1.0001	− 0.0002 = $f(1)$	
	1	1		
1	1	− .0001 = $f'(1)$		
	1			
1	$2 = \frac{1}{2} f''(1)$			

From the above synthetic division, we observe that $f(1)$ and $f'(1)$ are small. Hence there exists two nearly equal roots. Taking $x_0 = 1$, we will use

$x_{i+1} = x_i - \dfrac{f'(x_i)}{f''(x_i)}$ to modify the root. For this, we require $f''(1)$.

From the above synthetic division, we have

$$\frac{1}{2} f''(1) = 2 \;\Rightarrow\; f''(1) = 4$$

$\therefore$ First approximation $x_1 = 1 - \dfrac{f'(1)}{f''(1)} = 1 - \dfrac{(-.0001)}{4} = 1.000025$

Now we again calculate $f(x_1)$ and $f''(x_1)$ by synthetic division.

1	−1	− 1.000100	0.999900	1.000025
	1.000025	0.000025	− 1.000095	
1	. 000025	− 1.00075	− 0.000 195 = $f(x_1)$	
	1.000025	1.000075		
1	1.000050	0 = $f'(x_1)$		
	1.000025			
1	$2.000075 = \frac{1}{2} f''(x_1)$			

$$\therefore \quad f(1.000025) = -0.000195 \quad \text{and} \quad f''(1.000025) = 4.000150$$

Now, For nearly equal roots,

$$x = c \pm \sqrt{\frac{-2f(c)}{f''(c)}}, \quad \text{where } c = 1.000025$$

$$= 1.000025 \pm \sqrt{\frac{-2(-.000195)}{4.000150}} = 1.009899, 0.990151.$$

3.41 COMPARISON OF NEWTON'S METHOD WITH REGULA-FALSI METHOD

Regula-Falsi is surely convergent while Newton's method is conditionally convergent. But once Newton's method converges, it converges faster.

In the Falsi method, we calculate only one more value of the function at each step *i.e.*, $f(x^{(n)})$ while in Newton's method, we require two calculations $f(x_n)$ and $f'(x_n)$ at each step.

∴ Newton's method generally requires fewer iterations but also requires more time for computation at each iteration.

When $f'(x)$ is large near the root the correction to be applied is smaller in the case of Newton's method which is then preferred. If $f'(x)$ is small near the root, the correction to be applied is large and the curve becomes parallel to the x-axis.

In this case the Regula-Falsi method should be applied.

3.42 COMPARISON OF ITERATIVE METHODS

1. Convergence in the case of the Bisection method is slow but steady. It is the simplest method and never fails.
2. The method of false position is slow and it is I order convergent. Convergence is guaranteed.
3. Newton's method has the fastest rate of convergence. This method is quite sensitive to starting value. It may diverge if $f'(x) \approx 0$ during iterative cycle.
4. For locating complex roots, the bisection method cannot be applied. Newton's and Muller's methods are effective.
5. If all the roots of a given equation are required, Lin-Bairstow's method is recommended. After a quadratic factor has been found, this method must be applied on the reduced polynomial.

If the location of some roots is known, first find these roots to a desired accuracy and then apply this method on the reduced polynomial.

ASSIGNMENT 3.10

1. The equation $f(x) = (x - 1)^2 (x - 3)^2$ has roots at $x = 1$ and $x = 3$. Which of the following methods can be applied to find all the roots?
   (*i*) Bisection method
   (*ii*) False-position method
   (*iii*) Newton-Raphson method
   Justify your answer.
2. A sphere of wood, 2 m in diameter, floating in water sinks to a depth d given by
   $$d^3 - 3d^2 + 2.5 = 0$$
   find d correct to 2 decimal places.
3. Discuss the working of modified Newton-Raphson method.
4. Find the root of the equation
   $$f(x) \equiv \sin x - \frac{x+1}{x-1} = 0 \quad \text{near } x = -.4$$
5. Give a comparative study of iterative methods.
6. Under what conditions does the Newton-Raphson method become linearly convergent? Explain.

3.43 GRAEFFE'S ROOT-SQUARING METHOD

This method has a great advantage over the other methods in that it does not require prior information about the approximate values, etc., of the roots. It is applicable to polynomial equations only and is capable of giving all the roots. Here below we discuss the case of the polynomial equation having real and distinct roots.

Consider the polynomial equation

$$f(x) = x^n + a_1 x^{n-1} + a_2 x^{n-2} + \ldots\ldots + a_{n-1} x + a_n = 0 \quad (46)$$

Separating the even and odd powers of x and squaring, we get

$$(x^n + a_2 x^{n-2} + a_4 x^{n-4} + \ldots\ldots)^2 = (a_1 x^{n-1} + a_3 x^{n-3} + a_5 x^{n-5} + \ldots\ldots)^2$$

Putting $x^2 = y$ and simplifying, the new equation becomes

$$y^n + b_1 y^{n-1} + b_2 y^{n-2} + \ldots\ldots + b_{n-1} y + b_n = 0 \quad (47)$$

where $b_1 = a_1^2 + 2a_2$; $b_2 = a_2^2 - 2a_1a_3 + 2a_4 \ldots\ldots b_n = (-1)^n an^2$ (48)

If $p_1, p_2, ..., p_n$ are the roots of (46), then the roots of (47) are $p_1^2, p_2^2, ..., p_n^2$.

Let us suppose that after m squarings, the new transformed equation is

$$z^n + \lambda_1 z^{n-1} + ... + \lambda_{n-1} z + \lambda_n = 0 \tag{49}$$

whose roots are $q_1, q_2, ..., q_n$ such that $q_i = p_i^{2m}$, $i = 1, 2, ..., n$.

Assuming the order of magnitude of the roots as

$|p_1| > |p_2| > ...... > |p_n|$, we have

$|q_1| >> |q_2| >> ...... >> |q_n|$ where >> stands for 'much greater than'.

Thus $$\frac{|q_2|}{|q_1|} = \frac{q_2}{q_1}, ..., \frac{|q_n|}{|q_{n-1}|} = \frac{q_n}{q_{n-1}} \tag{50}$$

Also q_i being an even power of p_i, is always positive.
Now, from (49), we have

$$\Sigma q_1 = -\lambda_1 \quad \Rightarrow \quad \lambda_1 = -q_1\left(1 + \frac{q_2}{q_1} + \frac{q_3}{q_1} + ...\right)$$

$$\Sigma q_1 q_2 = \lambda_2 \quad \Rightarrow \quad \lambda_2 = q_1 q_2\left(1 + \frac{q_3}{q_1} + ...\right)$$

$$\Sigma q_1 q_2 q_3 = -\lambda_3 \quad \Rightarrow \quad \lambda_3 = q_1 q_2 q_3\left(1 + \frac{q_4}{q_1} + ...\right)$$

....

$$q_1 q_2 q_3 ...... q_n = (-1)^n \lambda_n \quad \Rightarrow \quad \lambda_n = (-1)^n q_1 q_2 q_3 ...... q_n.$$

Hence by (50), we find $q_1 \approx -\lambda_1$; $q_2 \approx -\dfrac{\lambda_2}{\lambda_1}$, $q_3 \approx -\dfrac{\lambda_3}{\lambda_2}$, ..., $q_n \approx -\dfrac{\lambda_n}{\lambda_{n-1}}$

But $$q_i = p_i^{2m}$$

$$\therefore \quad p_i = (q_i)^{1/2m} = \left(-\frac{\lambda_i}{\lambda_{i-1}}\right)^{1/2m} \tag{51}$$

We can thus determine $p_1, p_2, ..., p_n$ the roots of the equation (46).

Case 1. Double root. If the magnitude of λ_i is half the square of the magnitude of the corresponding coefficient in the previous equation after a few squarings, then it implies that p_i is a double root of (46). We determine it as follows:

$$q_i = -\frac{\lambda_i}{\lambda_{i-1}} \quad \text{and} \quad q_{i+1} = -\frac{\lambda_{i+1}}{\lambda_i}$$

$$\therefore \qquad q_i q_{i+1} \approx q_i^{\,2} \approx \left|\frac{\lambda_{i+1}}{\lambda_{i-1}}\right| \quad \textit{i.e.,} \quad p_i^{\,2m} = q_i^{\,2} = \left|\frac{\lambda_{i+1}}{\lambda_{i-1}}\right| \qquad (52)$$

which gives the magnitude of the double root and substituting in (46), we can find the sign.

Case 2. Complex roots. If p_r and p_{r+1} form the complex pair $P_r e^{\pm i\phi_r}$, then the co-efficient of x^{n-r} in successive squarings would vary both in magnitude and sign by an amount $2P_r^{\,m} \cos m\phi_r$. For sufficiently large P_r and ϕ_r can be determined by

$$P_r^{\,2(2^m)} \approx \frac{\lambda_{r+1}}{\lambda_{r-1}}; \; 2P_r^{\,2^m} \cos 2^m \phi_r = -\frac{\lambda_r}{\lambda_{r-1}} \qquad (53)$$

If there is only one pair of complex roots, say

$P_r e^{\pm i\phi_r} = \xi_r + i\eta_r$ then ξ_r is given by

$$p_1 + p_2 + \ldots\ldots + p_{r-1} + 2\xi_r + p_{r+2} + \ldots\ldots + p_n = -a_1 \qquad (54)$$

and
$$\eta_r = \sqrt{P_r^{\,2} - \xi_r^{\,2}} \qquad (55)$$

If there are two pairs of complex roots, say

$$P_r e^{\pm i\phi_r} = \xi_r \pm i\eta_r \quad \text{and} \quad P_s e^{\pm i\phi_s} = \xi_s \pm i\eta_s$$

where $p_1 + p_2 + \ldots\ldots + p_{r-1} + 2\xi_r + P_{r+2} + \ldots\ldots + p_{s-1} + 2\xi_s + p_{s+2} + \ldots\ldots + p_n = -a_1$ (56)

$$2\left(\frac{\xi_r}{P_r^{\,2}} + \frac{\xi_s}{P_s^{\,2}}\right) = -\left[\frac{a_{n-1}}{n} + \frac{1}{a_1} + \ldots\ldots + \frac{1}{a_n}\right] \qquad (57)$$

and
$$\eta_r = \sqrt{P_r^{\,2} - \xi_r^{\,2}}\,;\; \eta_s = \sqrt{P_s^{\,2} - \xi_s^{\,2}} \qquad (58)$$

EXAMPLES

Example 1. *Apply Graeffe's root squaring method to solve the equation*

$$x^3 - 8x^2 + 17x - 10 = 0.$$

Sol. Here $\quad f(x) = x^3 - 8x^2 + 17x - 10 = 0$ (59)

Clearly $f(x)$ has three changes *i.e.*, from + to –, – to + and + to –. Hence from Descartes rule of signs $f(x)$ may have three positive roots.

Rewriting (59) as $\quad x(x^2 + 17) = (8x^2 + 10)$ (60)

Squaring on both sides and putting $x^2 = y$, we get

$$y(y + 17)^2 = (8y + 10)^2$$

or $$y^3 + 34y^2 + 289y = 64y^2 + 160y + 100$$

or $$y(y^2 + 129) = (30y^2 + 100) \qquad (61)$$

Squaring again and putting $y^2 = z$, we get

$$z(z + 129)^2 = (30z + 100)^2$$

or $$z^3 + 258z^2 + 16641z = 900z^2 + 6000z + 10000$$

or $$z(z^2 + 10641) = (642z^2 + 10000) \qquad (62)$$

Squaring again and putting $z^2 = u$, we get

$$u(u + 10641)^2 = (642u + 10000)^2$$

or $$u^3 + 21282u^2 + 113230881u = 412164u^2 + 12840000u + 10^8$$

or $$u^3 - 390882u^2 + 100390881u - 10^8 = 0 \qquad (63)$$

If the roots of (59) are p_1, p_2, p_3 and those of (63) are q_1, q_2, q_3, then

$$p_1 = (q_1)^{1/8} = (-\lambda_1)^{1/8} = (390882)^{1/8} = 5.000411082 \cong 5$$

$$p_2 = (q_2)^{1/8} = (-\lambda_2/\lambda_1)^{1/8} = \left[\frac{100390881}{378882}\right]^{1/8} = 2.000811036 \cong 2$$

$$p_3 = (q_3)^{1/8} = (-\lambda_3/\lambda_2)^{1/8} = \left[\frac{10^8}{100390881}\right] = 0.99951247 \cong 1$$

Now $f(5) = f(1) = f(2) = 0.$

Hence the roots are 5, 2, and 1.

Example 2. *Find all the roots of the equation $x^4 - 3x + 1 = 0$ by Graeffe's method.*

Sol. Here $$f(x) = x^4 - 3x + 1 = 0 \qquad (64)$$

Now $f(x)$ has two changes in sign *i.e.*, + to – and – to +. Therefore it may have two positive real roots.

Again $f(-x) = x^4 + 3x + 1$. Since no change in sign of $f(-x)$ there is no negative root. But $f(x)$, being of degree four, will have four roots of which two are real positive and the remaining two are complex.

Rewriting (64) as $x^4 + 1 = 3x$.

Squaring and putting $x^2 = y$, we have

$$(y^2 + 1)^2 = 9y$$

Squaring again and putting, $y^2 = z$

$$(z + 1)^4 = 81z$$

i.e., $z^4 + 4z^3 + 6z^2 - 77z + 1 = 0$ (65)

or $$z^4 + 6z^2 + 1 = -z(4z^2 - 77)$$

Squaring once again and putting $z^2 = u$, we get

$$(u^2 + 6u + 1)^2 = u(4u - 77)^2$$

or $u^4 - 4u^3 + 654u^2 - 5917u + 1 = 0$ (66)

If p_1, p_2, p_3, p_4 are the roots of (64) and q_1, q_2, q_3, q_4 are the roots of (66), then

$$p_1 = (q_1)^{1/8} = (-\lambda_1)^{1/8} = (4)^{1/8} = 1.1892071$$

$$p_2 = (q_2)^{1/8} = \left[-\frac{\lambda_2}{\lambda_1}\right]^{1/8} = \left[\frac{654}{4}\right]^{1/8} = 1.8909921$$

$$p_3 = (q_3)^{1/8} = \left[-\frac{\lambda_3}{\lambda_1}\right]^{1/8} = \left[\frac{5917}{654}\right]^{1/8} = 1.3169384$$

$$p_4 = (q_4)^{1/8} = \left[-\frac{\lambda_4}{\lambda_3}\right]^{1/8} = \left[\frac{1}{5917}\right]^{1/8} = 0.3376659$$

From (65) and (66), we observe that the magnitudes of the co-efficients λ_1 and λ_4 have become constant.

$\Rightarrow$ p, p_4 are the real roots and p_2, p_3 are complex roots. Let these complex roots be

$\rho_2 e^{\pm i\phi_2} = \xi_2 \pm i\eta_2$. From (66), its magnitude is given by

$$\rho_2^{2(2^3)} \approx \frac{\lambda_3}{\lambda_1} = \frac{5917}{4} \qquad \therefore \quad \rho_2 = 1.5780749$$

also from (64) the sum of the roots = 0, *i.e.,* $p_1 + 2\xi_2 + p_4 = 0$

$$\therefore \qquad \xi_2 = -\frac{1}{2}(p_1 + p_4) = -0.7634365$$

and $$\eta_2 = \sqrt{\rho_2^2 - \xi_2^2} = \sqrt{1.9074851} = 1.3811173$$

Hence, the four roots are 1.1892071, 0.3376659, $-0.7634365 \pm 1.3811173i$.

ASSIGNMENT 3.11

1. Find all the roots of the following equations by Graeffe's method squaring thrice:
   (*i*) $x^3 - 4x^2 + 5x - 2 = 0$ (*ii*) $x^3 - 2x^2 + 5x + 6 = 0$
   (*iii*) $x^3 - x - 1 = 0$.

3.44 RAMANUJAN'S METHOD

S. Ramanujan (1887 – 1920) proposed an iterative method which can be used to determine the smallest root of the equation $f(x) = 0$
where $f(x)$ is of the form

$$f(x) = 1 - (a_1x + a_2x^2 + a_3x^3 + ...)$$

For smaller values of x, we can write,

$$[1 - (a_1x + a_2x^2 + a_3x^3 + ...)]^{-1} = b_1 + b_2x + b_3x^2 + ...$$

$$\Rightarrow \quad 1 + (a_1x + a_2x^2 + a_3x^3 + ...) + (a_1x + a_2x^2 + a_3x^3 + ...)^2 + ...$$

$$= b_1 + b_2x + b_3x^2 + ... \quad \Bigg| \begin{array}{l}\text{Expanding L.H.S. by}\\ \text{Binomial theorem}\end{array}$$

Comparing the coefficient of like powers of x on both sides, we get

$$\left.\begin{array}{l} b_1 = 1 \\ b_2 = a_1 = a_1b_1 \\ b_3 = a_1{}^2 + a_2 = a_1b_2 + a_2b_1 \\ \vdots \qquad \vdots \qquad \vdots \qquad \vdots \\ b_n = a_1b_{n-1} + a_2b_{n-2} + ... + a_{n-1}b_1 \\ \quad n = 2, 3, ... \end{array}\right\}$$

Ramanujan stated that the successive convergents *viz.* $\dfrac{b_n}{b_{n+1}}$ approach a root of the equation $f(x) = 0$.

EXAMPLE

Example. *Find the smallest root of the equation*

$x^3 - 6x^2 + 11x - 6 = 0$ using Ramanujan's method.

Sol. We have

$$\left[1 - \left(\frac{11x - 6x^2 + x^3}{6}\right)\right]^{-1} = b_1 + b_2x + b_3x^2 + ...$$

Here, $\quad a_1 = \dfrac{11}{6}, \quad a_2 = -1, \quad a_3 = \dfrac{1}{6}, \quad a_4 = a_5 = a_6 = ... = 0$

Hence

$$b_1 = 1$$

$$b_2 = a_1 = \frac{11}{6} \qquad \therefore \quad \frac{b_1}{b_2} = \frac{6}{11} = .54545$$

$$b_3 = a_1 b_2 + a_2 b_1$$

$$= \frac{121}{36} - 1 = \frac{85}{36}; \qquad \frac{b_2}{b_3} = \frac{66}{85} = .7764705$$

$$b_4 = a_1 b_3 + a_2 b_2 + a_3 b_1$$

$$= \frac{575}{216}; \qquad \frac{b_3}{b_4} = \frac{102}{115} = .8869565$$

$$b_5 = a_1 b_4 + a_2 b_3 + a_3 b_2 + a_4 b_1$$

$$= \frac{3661}{1296}; \qquad \frac{b_4}{b_5} = \frac{3450}{3661} = .9423654$$

$$b_6 = a_1 b_5 + a_2 b_4 + a_3 b_3 + a_4 b_2 + a_5 b_1$$

$$= \frac{22631}{7776}; \qquad \frac{b_5}{b_6} = \frac{3138}{3233} = .9706155$$

The smallest root of the given equation is 1 and the successive convergents approach this root.

ASSIGNMENT 3.12

1. Find a root of the equation $xe^x = 1$ using Ramanujan's method.
2. Find a root of the equation $\sin x = 1 - x$ using Ramanujan's method.
3. Using Ramanujan's method, obtain the first eight convergents of the equation $x + x^3 = 1$.

Part 2

■ **Interpolation**

Finite Differences, Difference Tables, Errors in Polynomial Interpolation, Newton's Forward and Backward Formula, Gauss's Forward and Backward Formula, Stirling's, Bessel's, Everett's Formula, Lagrange's Interpolation, Newton's Divided Difference Formula, Hermite's Interpolation.

Part 2

Interpolation:

Finite Differences, Difference Tables, Errors in Polynomial Interpolation, Newton's Forward and Backward Formula, Gauss's Forward and Backward Formula, Stirling's, Bessel's, Everett's Formula, Lagrange's Interpolation, Newton's Divided Difference Formula, Hermite's Interpolation.

Chapter 4

INTERPOLATION

4.1 INTRODUCTION

According to Theile, *'Interpolation is the art of reading between the lines of the table'.*

It also means insertion or filling up intermediate terms of the series. Suppose we are given the following values of $y = f(x)$ for a set of values of x:

x: x_0	x_1	x_2	......	x_n
y: y_0	y_1	y_2	......	y_n

Thus the process of finding the value of y corresponding to any value of $x = x_i$ between x_0 and x_n is called **interpolation.**

Hence interpolation is the technique of estimating the value of a function for any intermediate value of the independent variable, while the process of computing the value of the function outside the given range is called **extrapolation.**

4.2 ASSUMPTIONS FOR INTERPOLATION

1. There are no sudden jumps or falls in the values during the period under consideration.
2. The rise and fall in the values should be uniform.

   For example, if we are given data regarding deaths in various years in a particular town and some of the observations are for the years in which epidemic or war overtook the town, then interpolation methods are not applicable.
3. When we apply calculus of finite differences, we assume that the given set of observations is capable of being expressed in a polynomial form.

   If the function $f(x)$ is known explicitly, the value of y corresponding to any value of x can be found easily.

   If the function $f(x)$ is not known, it is necessary to find a simpler function, say $\phi(x)$, such that $f(x)$ and $\phi(x)$ agree at the set of tabulated points. This process is called interpolation. If $\phi(x)$ is a polynomial, then the process is called polynomial interpolation and $\phi(x)$ is called the interpolating polynomial.

4.3 ERRORS IN POLYNOMIAL INTERPOLATION

Let the function $y(x)$ defined by $(n + 1)$ points (x_i, y_i) $i = 0, 1, 2, \ldots\ldots, n$ be continuous and differentiable $(n + 1)$ times and let $y(x)$ be approximated by a polynomial $\phi_n(x)$ of degree not exceeding n such that

$$\phi_n(x_i) = y_i;\ i = 0, 1, 2, \ldots\ldots, n \tag{1}$$

The problem lies in finding the accuracy of this approximation if we use $\phi_n(x)$ to obtain approximate values of $y(x)$ at some points other than those defined above.

Since the expression $y(x) - \phi_n(x)$ vanishes for $x = x_0, x_1, \ldots\ldots, x_n$, we put

$$y(x) - \phi_n(x) = \text{L}\, \Pi_{n+1}(x) \tag{2}$$

where $$\Pi_{n+1}(x) = (x - x_0)(x - x_1) \ldots\ldots (x - x_n) \tag{3}$$

and L is to be determined such that equation (2) holds for any intermediate value of x say x' where $x_0 < x' < x_n$.

Clearly, $$\text{L} = \frac{y(x') - \phi_n(x')}{\Pi_{n+1}(x')} \tag{4}$$

Construct a function, $$\text{F}(x) = y(x) - \phi_n(x) - \text{L}\, \Pi_{n+1}(x) \tag{5}$$

where L is given by (4).

It is clear that, $F(x_0) = F(x_1) = \ldots\ldots = F(x_n) = F(x') = 0$
i.e., $F(x)$ vanishes $(n + 2)$ times in interval $[x_0, x_n]$ consequently, by repeated application of Rolle's theorem, $F'(x)$ must vanish $(n + 1)$ times, $F''(x)$ must vanish n times in the interval $[x_0, x_n]$

Particularly, $F^{(n+1)}(x)$ must vanish once in $[x_0, x_n]$.

Let this point be $x = \xi;\ x_0 < \xi < x_n$.

Differentiating (5) $(n + 1)$ times with respect to x and put $x = \xi$, we get

$$0 = (y)^{(n+1)}(\xi) - L\,(n+1)! \qquad \left|\ \frac{d^{n+1}}{dx^{n+1}}(x^{n+1}) = (n+1)!\right.$$

so that,
$$L = \frac{y^{(n+1)}(\xi)}{(n+1)!} \tag{6}$$

Comparison of (4) and (6) give

$$y(x') - \phi_n(x') = \frac{y^{(n+1)}(\xi)}{(n+1)!}\,\Pi_{n+1}(x')$$

Hence, the required expression of error is

$$y(x) - \phi_n(x) = \frac{\Pi_{n+1}(x)}{(n+1)!}\,y^{n+1}(\xi),\ x_0 < \xi < x_n \tag{7}$$

Since $y(x)$ is generally unknown, and we do not have any information concerning $y^{(n+1)}(x)$, equation (7) is useless in practical computations.

We will use it to determine errors in Newton's interpolating formulae.

The various methods of interpolation are as follows:

(1) The method of graph

(2) The method of curve fitting

(3) Use of calculus of finite difference formulae.

The merits of the last method over the others are

(*i*) It does not assume the form of function to be known.

(*ii*) It is less approximate than the method of graphs.

(*iii*) The calculations remain simple even if some additional observations are included in the given data.

The demerit is there is no definite way to verify whether the assumptions for the application of finite difference calculus are valid for the given set of observations.

4.4 FINITE DIFFERENCES

The calculus of finite differences deals with the changes that take place in the value of the function (dependent variable) due to finite changes in the independent variable.

Suppose we are given a set of values (x_i, y_i); $i = 1, 2, 3, ..., n$ of any function $y = f(x)$. A value of the independent variable x is called **argument** and the corresponding value of the dependent variable y is called **entry.**

Suppose that the function $y = f(x)$ is tabulated for the equally spaced values $x = x_0, x_0 + h, x_0 + 2h, ..., x_0 + nh$, giving $y = y_0, y_1, y_2, ..., y_n$. To determine the values of $f(x)$ or $f'(x)$ for some intermediate values of x, the following three types of differences are useful:

1. **Forward differences.** The differences $y_1 - y_0, y_2 - y_1, y_3 - y_2, ..., y_n - y_{n-1}$ when denoted by $\Delta y_0, \Delta y_1, \Delta y_2, ..., \Delta y_{n-1}$ are respectively, called the first forward differences where D is the forward difference operator.

   Thus the first forward differences are

$$\Delta y_r = y_{r+1} - y_r$$

   Similarly, the second forward differences are defined by

$$\Delta^2 y_r = \Delta y_{r+1} - \Delta y_r$$

   Particularly, $\Delta^2 y_0 = \Delta y_1 - \Delta y_0 = y_2 - y_1 - (y_1 - y_0) = y_2 - 2y_1 + y_0$

   Similarly, $\Delta^3 y_0 = y_3 - 3y_2 + 3y_1 - y_0$

$$\Delta^4 y_0 = y_4 - 4y_3 + 6y_2 - 4y_1 + y_0.$$

   Clearly, any higher order difference can easily be expressed in terms of ordinates since the coefficients occurring on R.H.S. are the binomial coefficients*. In general, $\Delta^p y_r = \Delta^{p-1} y_{r+1} - \Delta^{p-1} y_r$ defines the pth forward differences.

---

* $\Delta^n(y_0) = y_n - {}^nC_1\, y_{n-1} + {}^nC_2 y_{n-2} + ... + (-1)^n y_0$

The following table shows how the forward differences of all orders can be formed.

Forward difference table

x	y	Δy	$\Delta^2 y$	$\Delta^3 y$	$\Delta^4 y$	$\Delta^5 y$
x_0	y_0					
		Δy_0				
x_1	y_1		$\Delta^2 y_0$			
$(= x_0 + h)$		Δy_1		$\Delta^3 y_0$		
x_2	y_2		$\Delta^2 y_1$		$\Delta^4 y_0$	
$(= x_0 + 2h)$		Δy_2		$\Delta^3 y_1$		$\Delta^5 y_0$
x_3	y_3		$\Delta^2 y_2$		$\Delta^4 y_1$	
$= (x_0 + 3h)$		Δy_3		$\Delta^3 y_2$		
x_4	y_4		$\Delta^2 y_3$			
$= (x_0 + 4h)$		Δy_4				
x_5	y_5					
$= (x_0 + 5h)$						

Here the first entry, y_0, is called the leading term and Δy_0, $\Delta^2 y_0$, ... are called leading differences.

NOTE *Δ obeys distributive, commutative and index laws:*

1. *$\Delta [f(x) \pm \phi(x)] = \Delta f(x) \pm \Delta \phi (x)$*

2. *$\Delta [c\, f(x)] = c\, \Delta f(x)$; c is constant*

3. *$\Delta^m \Delta^n f(x) = \Delta^{m+n} f(x)$, m, n being (+)ve integers.*

But, $\Delta [f(x) \,.\, \phi(x)] \neq f(x) \,.\, \Delta \phi(x)$.

2. **Backward differences.** The differences $y_1 - y_0, y_2 - y_1, ..., y_n - y_{n-1}$ when denoted by $\nabla y_1, \nabla y_2, ..., \nabla y_n$, respectively, are called first backward differences where ∇ is the backward difference operator.

Similarly, we define higher order backward differences as,

$$\nabla y_r = y_r - y_{r-1}$$

$$\nabla^2 y_r = \nabla y_r - \nabla y_{r-1}$$

$$\nabla^3 y_r = \nabla^2 y_r - \nabla^2 y_{r-1} \text{ etc.}$$

Particularly, $\nabla^2 y_2 = \nabla y_2 - \nabla y_1$

$$= y_2 - y_1 - (y_1 - y_0) = y_2 - 2y_1 + y_0$$

$$\nabla^3 y_3 = \nabla^2 y_3 - \nabla^2 y_2 = y_3 - 3y_2 + 3y_1 - y_0 \text{ etc.}$$

Backward difference table

x	y	∇y	$\nabla^2 y$	$\nabla^3 y$	$\nabla^4 y$	$\nabla^5 y$
x_0	y_0					
		∇y_1				
x_1	y_1		$\nabla^2 y_2$			
$(= x_0 + h)$		∇y_2		$\nabla^3 y_3$		
x_2	y_2		$\nabla^2 y_3$		$\nabla^4 y_4$	
$(= x_0 + 2h)$		∇y_3		$\nabla^3 y_4$		$\nabla^5 y_5$
x_3	y_3		$\nabla^2 y_4$		$\nabla^4 y_5$	
$(= x_0 + 3h)$		∇y_4		$\nabla^3 y_5$		
x_4	y_4		$\nabla^2 y_5$			
$(= x_0 + 4h)$		∇y_5				
x_5	y_5					
$(= x_0 + 5h)$						

3. **Central differences.** The central difference operator d is defined by the relations

$$y_1 - y_0 = \delta y_{1/2}, y_2 - y_1 = \delta y_{3/2}, \ldots\ldots, y_n - y_{n-1} = \delta y_{n-\frac{1}{2}}.$$

Similarly, high order central differences are defined as

$$\delta y_{3/2} - \delta y_{1/2} = \delta^2 y_1, \quad \delta y_{5/2} - \delta y_{3/2} = \delta^2 y_2$$

and so on.

These differences are shown as follows:

Central difference table

x	y	δy	$\delta^2 y$	$\delta^3 y$	$\delta^4 y$	$\delta^5 y$
x_0	y_0					
		$\delta y_{1/2}$				
x_1	y_1		$\delta^2 y_1$			
		$\delta y_{3/2}$		$\delta^3 y_{3/2}$		
x_2	y_2		$\delta^2 y_2$		$\delta^4 y_2$	
		$\delta y_{5/2}$		$\delta^3 y_{5/2}$		$\delta^5 y_{5/2}$
x_3	y_3		$\delta^2 y_3$		$\delta^4 y_3$	
		$\delta y_{7/2}$		$\delta^3 y_{7/2}$		
x_4	y_4		$\delta^2 y_4$			
		$\delta y_{9/2}$				
x_5	y_5					

NOTE 1. *The central differences on the same horizontal line have the same suffix.*
2. *It is only the notation that changes, not the differences.*

e.g., $$y_1 - y_0 = \Delta y_0 = \nabla y_1 = \delta y_{1/2}.$$

4.5 OTHER DIFFERENCE OPERATORS

1. Shift operator E.

Shift operator E is the operation of increasing the argument x by h so that

$$Ef(x) = f(x + h)$$
$$E^2 f(x) = f(x + 2h) \text{ and so on.}$$

The inverse operator, E^{-1}, is defined by

$$E^{-1}f(x) = f(x - h).$$

Also $$E^n y_x = y_{x+nh}.$$

2. Averaging operator μ.

The averaging operator is defined by

$$\mu y_x = \frac{1}{2}\left[y_{x+\frac{1}{2}h} + y_{x-\frac{1}{2}h}\right]$$

In difference calculus, E is the fundamental operator and ∇, Δ, δ, μ can be expressed in terms of E.

4.6 RELATION BETWEEN OPERATORS

1. $$\boxed{\Delta = E - 1 \quad \text{or} \quad E = 1 + \Delta.}$$

Proof. We know that,

$$\Delta y_x = y_{x+h} - y_x = Ey_x - y_x = (E - 1)y_x$$

⇒ $$\Delta = E - 1$$

or $$E = 1 + \Delta$$

2. $$\boxed{\nabla = 1 - E^{-1}}$$

Proof. $$\nabla y_x = y_x - y_{x-h} = y_x - E^{-1}y_x$$

∴ $$\nabla = 1 - E^{-1}$$

3. $$\boxed{\delta = E^{1/2} - E^{-1/2}}$$

Proof. $\delta y_x = y_{x+\frac{h}{2}} - y_{x-\frac{h}{2}}$

$= E^{1/2} y_x - E^{-1/2} y_x$

$= (E^{1/2} - E^{-1/2})\, y_x$

$\therefore \quad \delta = E^{1/2} - E^{-1/2}$

4. $$\boxed{\mu = \frac{1}{2}(E^{1/2} + E^{-1/2})}$$

Proof. $\mu y_x = \frac{1}{2}\left(y_{x+\frac{h}{2}} + y_{x-\frac{h}{2}}\right) = \frac{1}{2}(E^{1/2} + E^{-1/2})\, y_x$

$\Rightarrow \quad \mu = \frac{1}{2}(E^{1/2} + E^{-1/2})$

5. $$\boxed{\Delta = E\nabla = \nabla E = \delta E^{1/2}}$$

Proof. $E(\nabla y_x) = E(y_x - y_{x-h}) = y_{x+h} - y_x = \Delta y_x$

$\Rightarrow \quad E\nabla = \Delta$

$\nabla(E\, y_x) = \nabla\, y_{x+h} = y_{x+h} - y_x = \Delta y_x$

$\Rightarrow \quad \nabla E = \Delta$

$\delta E^{1/2}\, y_x = \delta y_{x+\frac{h}{2}} = y_{x+h} - y_x = \Delta y_x$

$\Rightarrow \quad \delta E^{1/2} = \Delta$

6. $$\boxed{E = e^{hD}}$$

Proof. $Ef(x) = f(x + h)$

$= f(x) + h\, f'(x) + \frac{h^2}{2!} f''(x) + \ldots..$ (By Taylor series)

$= f(x) + hDf(x) + \frac{h^2}{2!} D^2 f(x) + \ldots...$

$= \left[1 + hD + \frac{(hD)^2}{2!} + \ldots...\right] f(x) = e^{hD} f(x)$

$\therefore \quad E = e^{hD} \quad \text{or} \quad \Delta = e^{hD} - 1.$

4.7 DIFFERENCES OF A POLYNOMIAL

The nth differences of a polynomial of nth degree are constant and all higher order differences are zero when the values of the independent variable are at equal intervals.

Let $\quad f(x) = ax^n + bx^{n-1} + cx^{n-2} + \ldots\ldots + kx + l$

$$\therefore \quad \Delta f(x) = f(x + h) - f(x)$$
$$= a[(x + h)^n - x^n] + b\,[(x + h)^{n-1} - x^{n-1}] + \ldots\ldots + kh$$
$$= anhx^{n-1} + b'x^{n-2} + c'x^{n-3} + \ldots\ldots + k'x + l' \quad (8)$$

where $b', c', \ldots\ldots l'$ are new constant coefficients.

$\therefore$ First differences of a polynomial of nth degree is a polynomial of degree $(n - 1)$.

Similarly,

$$\Delta^2 f(x) = \Delta f(x + h) - \Delta f(x)$$
$$= anh\,[(x + h)^{n-1} - x^{n-1}] + b'[(x + h)^{n-2} - x^{n-2}] + \ldots\ldots + k'h$$
$$= an(n - 1)\,h^2 x^{n-2} + b''x^{n-3} + \ldots\ldots + k'' \quad (9)$$

$\therefore$ Second differences represent a polynomial of degree $(n - 2)$.

Continuing this process, for n^{th} differences, we get a polynomial of degree zero, *i.e.*,

$$\Delta^n f(x) = an(n - 1)\,(n - 2) \ldots\ldots 1\, h^n = a\; n!\; h^n$$

which is a constant. Hence the $(n + 1)^{th}$ and higher differences of a polynomial of nth degree will be zero. The converse of this theorem is also true.

EXAMPLES

Example 1. *Construct the forward difference table, given that*

x:	*5*	*10*	*15*	*20*	*25*	*30*
y:	*9962*	*9848*	*9659*	*9397*	*9063*	*8660*

and point out the values of $\Delta^2 y_{10}, \Delta^4 y_5$.

Sol. Forward difference table is as follows:

x	y	Δy	$\Delta^2 y$	$\Delta^3 y$	$\Delta^4 y$
5	9962				
		– 114			
10	9848		– 75		
		– 189		2	
15	9659		– 73		– 1
		– 262		1	
20	9397		– 72		2
		– 334		3	
25	9063		– 69		
		– 403			
30	8660				

From the table, $\Delta^2 y_{10} = -73$ and $\Delta^4 y_5 = -1$.

Example 2. *If $y = x^3 + x^2 - 2x + 1$, calculate values of y for $x = 0, 1, 2, 3, 4, 5$ and form the difference table. Find the value of y at $x = 6$ by extending the table and verify that the same value is obtained by substitution.*

Sol. For $x = 0$, $y = 1$;

$x = 1$, $y = 1$;

$x = 2$, $y = 9$;

$x = 3$, $y = 31$;

$x = 4$, $y = 73$;

$x = 5$, $y = 141$

Difference table is as follows:

x	y	Δy	$\Delta^2 y$	$\Delta^3 y$
0	1			
		0		
1	1		8	
		8		6
2	9		14	
		22		6
3	31		20	
		42		6
4	73		26	
		68		6
5	141		32	
		100		
6	241			

$\because$ Third differences are constant.

$\therefore \quad \Delta^3 y_3 = 6 \quad \Rightarrow \quad \Delta^2 y_4 - \Delta^2 y_3 = 6$

$\Rightarrow \quad \Delta^2 y_4 - 26 = 6 \quad \Rightarrow \quad \Delta^2 y_4 = 32$

Now, $\quad \Delta^2 y_4 = 42 \quad \Rightarrow \quad \Delta y_5 - \Delta y_4 = 32$

$\Rightarrow \quad \Delta y_5 - 68 = 32 \quad \Rightarrow \quad \Delta y_5 = 100$

Further, $\quad \Delta y_5 = 100$

$$y_6 - y_5 = 100$$

$$\Rightarrow \quad y_6 - 141 = 100$$

$$y_6 = 241$$

Verification. $y(6) = (6)^3 + (6)^2 - 2(6) + 1 = 241$. Hence verified.

Example 3. *Construct a backward difference table for y = log x given that*

x:	*10*	*20*	*30*	*40*	*50*
y:	*1*	*1.3010*	*1.4771*	*1.6021*	*1.6990*

and find values of ∇^3 *log 40 and* ∇^4 *log 50.*

Sol. Backward difference table is:

x	y	∇y	$\nabla^2 y$	$\nabla^3 y$	$\nabla^4 y$
10	1				
		0.3010			
20	1.3010		– 0.1249		
		0.1761		0.0738	
30	1.4771		– 0.0511		– 0.0508
		0.1250		0.0230	
40	1.6021		– 0.0281		
		0.0969			
50	1.6990				

From the table, ∇^3 log 40 = 0.0738 and ∇^4 log 50 = – 0.0508.

Example 4. *Construct a backward difference table from the data:*

sin 30° = 0.5, sin 35° = 0.5736, sin 40° = 0.6428 sin 45° = 0.7071

Assuming third differences to be constant, find the value of sin 25°.

Sol. Backward difference table is:

x	y	∇y	$\nabla^2 y$	$\nabla^3 y$
25	.4225			
		.0775		
30	0.5000		– .0039	
		0.0736		– .0005
35	0.5736		– .0044	
		0.0692		– .0005
40	0.6428		– .0049	
		0.0643		
45	0.7071			

Since third differences are constant

$\therefore \quad \nabla^3 y_{40} = -.0005$

$\Rightarrow \quad \nabla^2 y_{40} - \nabla^2 y_{35} = -.0005$

$\Rightarrow \quad -.0044 - \nabla^2 y_{35} = -.0005$

$\Rightarrow \quad \nabla^2 y_{35} = -.0039$

Again $\quad \nabla y_{35} - \nabla y_{30} = -.0039$

$\Rightarrow \quad .0736 - \nabla y_{30} = -.0039$

$\Rightarrow \quad \nabla y_{30} = .0775$

Again $\quad y_{30} - y_{25} = .0775$

$\Rightarrow \quad 0.5 - y_{25} = .0775$

$\Rightarrow \quad y_{25} = 0.4225$

$\therefore \quad \sin 25° = .4225.$

Example 5. *Evaluate:*

(i) $\Delta \tan^{-1} x$ *(ii)* $\Delta^2 \cos 2x$

where h is the interval of differencing.

Sol. *(i)* $\Delta \tan^{-1} x = \tan^{-1} (x + h) - \tan^{-1} x$

$$= \tan^{-1} \left\{ \frac{x + h - x}{1 + x(x + h)} \right\} = \tan^{-1} \left(\frac{h}{1 + hx + x^2} \right)$$

(ii) $\Delta^2 \cos 2x = \Delta[\cos 2(x + h) - \cos 2x]$

$$= [\cos 2(x + 2h) - \cos 2(x + h)] - [\cos 2(x + h) - \cos 2x]$$

$$= -2\sin(2x+3h)\sin h + 2\sin(2x+h)\sin h$$

$$= -2\sin h\,[2\cos(2x+2h)\sin h] = -4\sin^2 h\cos 2(x+h).$$

Example 6. *Evaluate*:

$$\Delta^2\left(\frac{5x+12}{x^2+5x+6}\right); \text{ the interval of differencing being unity.}$$

Sol. $\Delta^2\left\{\frac{5x+12}{(x+2)(x+3)}\right\}$

$$= \Delta^2\left(\frac{2}{x+2}+\frac{3}{x+3}\right) = \Delta\left[\Delta\left(\frac{2}{x+2}\right)+\Delta\left(\frac{3}{x+3}\right)\right]$$

$$= \Delta\left[2\left(\frac{1}{x+3}-\frac{1}{x+2}\right)+3\left(\frac{1}{x+4}-\frac{1}{x+3}\right)\right]$$

$$= -2\Delta\left\{\frac{1}{(x+2)(x+3)}\right\}-3\Delta\left\{\frac{1}{(x+3)(x+4)}\right\}$$

$$= -2\left[\frac{1}{(x+3)(x+4)}-\frac{1}{(x+2)(x+3)}\right]$$

$$-3\left[\frac{1}{(x+4)(x+5)}-\frac{1}{(x+3)(x+4)}\right]$$

$$= \frac{4}{(x+2)(x+3)(x+4)}+\frac{6}{(x+3)(x+4)(x+5)}$$

$$= \frac{2(5x+16)}{(x+2)(x+3)(x+4)(x+5)}.$$

Example 7. *If $f(x) = \exp(ax)$, evaluate $\Delta^n f(x)$.*

Sol. $\Delta e^{ax} = e^{a(x+h)} - e^{ax} = (e^{ah}-1)e^{ax}$

$$\Delta^2 e^{ax} = \Delta(\Delta e^{ax}) = \Delta[(e^{ah}-1)e^{ax}]$$

$$= (e^{ah}-1)(e^{ah}-1)e^{ax} = (e^{ah}-1)^2 e^{ax}$$

Similarly $\Delta^3 e^{ax} = (e^{ah}-1)^3 e^{ax}$

$\vdots \quad \vdots \quad \vdots$

$$\Delta^n e^{ax} = (e^{ah}-1)^n e^{ax}.$$

Example 8. *With usual notations, prove that*

$$\Delta^n\left(\frac{1}{x}\right) = (-1)^n \cdot \frac{n!\,h^n}{x(x+h)\ldots\ldots(x+nh)}.$$

Sol. $$\Delta^n\left(\frac{1}{x}\right) = \Delta^{n-1}\,\Delta\left(\frac{1}{x}\right) = \Delta^{n-1}\left[\frac{1}{x+h} - \frac{1}{x}\right]$$

$$= \Delta^{n-1}\left\{\frac{-h}{x(x+h)}\right\}$$

$$= (-h)\,\Delta^{n-2}\,\Delta\left\{\frac{1}{x(x+h)}\right\}$$

$$= (-1)\,\Delta^{n-2}\left[\Delta\left(\frac{1}{x} - \frac{1}{x+h}\right)\right]$$

$$= (-1)\,\Delta^{n-2}\left[\left(\frac{1}{x+h} - \frac{1}{x}\right) - \left(\frac{1}{x+2h} - \frac{1}{x+h}\right)\right]$$

$$= (-1)\,\Delta^{n-2}\left[\frac{2}{x+h} - \frac{1}{x} - \frac{1}{x+2h}\right]$$

$$= (-1)\,\Delta^{n-2}\left[\frac{-2h^2}{x(x+h)(x+2h)}\right]$$

$$= (-1)^2\,\Delta^{n-2}\left[\frac{2!\,h^2}{x(x+h)(x+2h)}\right]$$

$$= (-1)^3\,\Delta^{n-3}\left[\frac{3!\,h^3}{x(x+h)(x+2h)(x+3h)}\right]$$

$$\vdots$$

$$= (-1)^n\,\frac{n!\,h^n}{x(x+h)\ldots\ldots(x+nh)}.$$

Example 9. *Assuming that the following values of y belong to a polynomial of degree 4, compute the next three values:*

x:	*0*	*1*	*2*	*3*	*4*	5	6	7
y:	*1*	*– 1*	*1*	*– 1*	*1*	–	–	–

Sol. Difference table is:

x	y	Δy	$\Delta^2 y$	$\Delta^3 y$	$\Delta^4 y$
0	1				
		– 2			
1	– 1		4		
		2		– 8	
2	1		– 4		16
		– 2		8	
3	– 1		4		16
		2		$\Delta^3 y_2$	
4	1		$\Delta^2 y_3$		16
		Δy_4		$\Delta^3 y_3$	
5	y_5		$\Delta^2 y_4$		16
		Δy_5		$\Delta^3 y_4$	
6	y_6		$\Delta^2 y_5$		
		Δy_6			
7	y_7				

Since values of y belong to a polynomial of degree 4, the fourth differences must be constant.

But $\Delta^4 y_0 = 16$

$\therefore$ Other fourth order differences will be 16.

Thus, $\Delta^4 y_1 = 16$

$\therefore$ $\Delta^3 y_2 - \Delta^3 y_1 = 16$

$\Rightarrow$ $\Delta^3 y_2 = 24$

$\therefore$ $\Delta^2 y_3 - \Delta^2 y_2 = 24$

$\Rightarrow$ $\Delta^2 y_3 = 28$

$\Delta y_4 - \Delta y_3 = 28$

$\Rightarrow$ $\Delta y_4 = 30$

$y_5 - y_4 = 30$

$\Rightarrow$ $y_5 = 31$

Again, $\Delta^4 y_2 = 16$ and solving, we get $y_6 = 129$

and $\Delta^4 y_3 = 16$ gives $y_7 = 351$.

Example 10. *Prove that*

$$\Delta \log f(x) = \log \left[1 + \frac{\Delta f(x)}{f(x)}\right].$$

Sol. L.H.S. $= \log f(x+h) - \log f(x)$

$= \log [f(x) + \Delta f(x)] - \log f(x)$ $\quad | \because \Delta f(x) = f(x+h) - f(x)$

$$= \log \left[\frac{f(x) + \Delta f(x)}{f(x)}\right] = \log \left[1 + \frac{\Delta f(x)}{f(x)}\right] = \text{R.H.S.}$$

Example 11. *Prove that*

$$e^x = \left(\frac{\Delta^2}{E}\right) e^x \cdot \frac{Ee^x}{\Delta^2 e^x}.$$

Sol. $\left(\frac{\Delta^2}{E}\right) e^x = \Delta^2 E^{-1} e^x = \Delta^2 e^{x-h} = e^{-h} \Delta^2 e^x$

$$\text{R.H.S.} = e^{-h} \cdot \Delta^2 e^x \cdot \frac{E\, e^x}{\Delta^2 e^x} = e^{-h} \cdot E\, e^x = e^{-h} e^{x+h} = e^x.$$

Example 12. *Prove that* $hD = -\log (1 - \nabla) = \sin h^{-1} (\mu\delta)$.

Sol. $hD = \log E = -\log (E^{-1}) = -\log (1 - \nabla)$ $\quad | \because E^{-1} = 1 - \nabla$

Also, $\mu = \frac{1}{2} (E^{1/2} + E^{-1/2})$

$\delta = E^{1/2} - E^{-1/2}$

$\therefore$ $\mu\delta = \frac{1}{2} (E - E^{-1}) = \frac{1}{2} (e^{hD} - e^{-hD}) = \sin h\,(hD)$

or $hD = \sin h^{-1} (\mu\delta)$.

Example 13. *Prove that*

(*i*) $(E^{1/2} + E^{-1/2})(1 + \Delta)^{1/2} = 2 + \Delta$ $\quad$ (*ii*) $\Delta = \frac{1}{2}\delta^2 + \delta\sqrt{1 + \delta^2/4}$

(*iii*) $\Delta^3 y_2 = \nabla^3 y_5$.

Sol. (*i*) $(E^{1/2} + E^{-1/2}) E^{1/2} = E + 1 = 1 + \Delta + 1 = \Delta + 2$

(*ii*) $$\frac{1}{2}\delta^2 + \delta\sqrt{1 + \frac{\delta^2}{4}} = \frac{1}{2}(E^{1/2} - E^{-1/2})^2 + (E^{1/2} - E^{-1/2})\sqrt{1 + \frac{1}{4}(E^{1/2} - E^{-1/2})^2}$$

$$= \frac{1}{2}(E + E^{-1} - 2) + (E^{1/2} - E^{-1/2})\left(\frac{E^{1/2} + E^{-1/2}}{2}\right)$$

$$= \frac{1}{2}(2E - 2) = E - 1 = \Delta$$

(*iii*) $$\Delta^3 y_2 = (E-1)^3 y_2$$
$$= (E^3 - 3E^2 + 3E - 1)\, y_2 = y_5 - 3y_4 + 3y_3 - y_2$$
$$\nabla^3 y_5 = (1 - E^{-1})\, y_5$$
$$= (1 - 3E^{-1} + 3E^{-2} - E^{-3})\, y_5 = y_5 - 3y_4 + 3y_3 - y_2.$$

Example 14. *Prove that*

(*i*) $\Delta + \nabla = \dfrac{\Delta}{\nabla} - \dfrac{\nabla}{\Delta}$

where Δ *and* ∇ *are forward difference and backward difference operators respectively.*

(*ii*) $\sum_{r=0}^{n-1} \Delta^2 y_r = \Delta y_n - \Delta y_0$ (*iii*) $\Delta^r y_k = \nabla^r y_{k+r}.$

Sol. (*i*) $$\left(\frac{\Delta}{\nabla} - \frac{\nabla}{\Delta}\right) y_x = \left(\frac{E-1}{1-E^{-1}} - \frac{1-E^{-1}}{E-1}\right) y_x$$
$$= \left\{\frac{E-1}{\left(\frac{E-1}{E}\right)} - \frac{\left(\frac{E-1}{E}\right)}{E-1}\right\} y_x = \left(E - \frac{1}{E}\right) y_x = (E - E^{-1}) y_x$$
$$= \{(1+\Delta) - (1-\nabla)\} y_x = (\Delta + \nabla) y_x$$

Hence, $$\frac{\Delta}{\nabla} - \frac{\nabla}{\Delta} = \Delta + \nabla$$

(*ii*) $$\sum_{r=0}^{n-1} \Delta^2 y_r = \sum_{r=0}^{n-1} (\Delta y_{r+1} - \Delta y_r)$$
$$= \Delta y_1 - \Delta y_0 + \Delta y_2 - \Delta y_1 + \ldots\ldots + \Delta y_n - \Delta y_{n-1}$$
$$= \Delta y_n - \Delta y_0.$$

(*iii*) $$\nabla^r y_{k+r} = (1 - E^{-1})^r y_{k+r} = \left(\frac{E-1}{E}\right)^r y_{k+r}$$
$$= (E-1)^r E^{-r} y_{k+r} = \Delta^r y_k.$$

Example 15. *Denoting* $\binom{x}{n} = \dfrac{x(x-1)\ldots\ldots(x-n+1)}{n!}$, *prove that for any polynomial* $\phi(x)$ *of degree k*

$$\phi(x) = \sum_{i=0}^{k} \binom{x}{i} \Delta^i \phi(0).$$

Sol. We have

$$E^n f(a) = f(a + nh) = f(a) + {}^nC_1 \Delta f(a) + {}^nC_2 \Delta^2 f(a) + \ldots\ldots + {}^nC_n \Delta^n f(a)$$

Put $a = 0, n = x$, we get for $h = 1$

$$f(x) = f(0) + {}^xC_1 \Delta f(0) + {}^xC_2 \Delta^2 f(0) + \ldots\ldots + {}^xC_x \Delta^x f(0)$$

Again, $f(x) = \phi(x)$ is the given polynomial of degree k

$\therefore$ $\Delta^k \phi(x)$ = constant and higher order differences will be zero.

$$\therefore \quad \phi(x) = \phi(0) + {}^xC_1 \Delta \phi(0) + \ldots\ldots + {}^xC_k \Delta^k \phi(0) = \sum_{i=1}^{k} \binom{x}{i} \Delta^i \phi(0).$$

Example 16. *Obtain the first term of the series whose second and subsequent terms are 8, 3, 0, – 1, 0.*

Sol. $f(1) = E^{-1} f(2) = (1 + \Delta)^{-1} f(2)$

$$= (1 - \Delta + \Delta^2 - \Delta^3 + \ldots\ldots) f(2)$$

Since five observations are given

$\therefore$ $\Delta^4 f(x)$ = constant and $\Delta^5 f(x) = 0$

We construct the table as:

x	$f(x)$	$\Delta f(x)$	$\Delta^2 f(x)$
2	8		
		– 5	
3	3		2
		– 3	
4	0		2
		– 1	
5	– 1		2
		1	
6	0		

Hence, $f(1) = f(2) - \Delta f(2) + \Delta^2 f(2) = 8 - (-5) + 2 = 15.$

Example 17. *Given u_0, u_1, u_2, u_3, u_4, and u_5, and assuming the fifth order differences to be constant, prove that*

$$u_{2\frac{1}{2}} = \frac{1}{2}c + \frac{25(c-b) + 3(a-c)}{256}$$

where $a = u_0 + u_5, b = u_1 + u_4, c = u_2 + u_3$.

Sol. $u_{2\frac{1}{2}} = E^{5/2} u_0 = (1 + \Delta)^{5/2} u_0$

$$= \left[1 + \frac{5}{2}\Delta + \frac{\frac{5}{2}\left(\frac{5}{2}-1\right)}{2!}\Delta^2 + ... + \frac{\frac{5}{2}\left(\frac{5}{2}-1\right)\left(\frac{5}{2}-2\right)\left(\frac{5}{2}-3\right)\left(\frac{5}{2}-4\right)}{5!}\Delta^5\right] u_0$$

$$= u_0 + \frac{5}{2}\Delta u_0 + \frac{15}{8}\Delta^2 u_0 + \frac{5}{16}\Delta^3 u_0 - \frac{5}{128}\Delta^4 u_0 + \frac{3}{256}\Delta^5 u_0$$

$$= u_0 + \frac{5}{2}(u_1 - u_0) + \frac{15}{8}(u_2 - 2u_1 + u_0) + \frac{5}{16}(u_3 - 3u_2 + 3u_1 - u_0) + ...$$

$$+ \frac{3}{256}(u_5 - 5u_4 + 10u_3 - 10u_2 + 5u_1 - u_0)$$

$$= \frac{3}{256}(u_0 + u_5) - \frac{25}{256}(u_1 + u_4) + \frac{75}{128}(u_2 + u_3) = \frac{3a}{256} - \frac{25}{256}b + \frac{75}{128}c$$

$$= \frac{3a}{256} - \frac{25b}{256} + \left(\frac{1}{2} + \frac{11}{128}\right)c = \frac{c}{2} + \frac{3(a-c) + 25(c-b)}{256}.$$

Example 18. (*i*) *Prove the relation:* $(1 + \Delta)(1 - \nabla) \equiv 1$

(*ii*) *Find the function whose first difference is* e^x.

(*iii*) *If* $\Delta^3 u_x = 0$ *prove that:*

$$u_{x+\frac{1}{2}} = \frac{1}{2}(u_x + u_{x+1}) - \frac{1}{16}(\Delta^2 u_x + \Delta^2 u_{x+1}).$$

Sol. (*i*) $(1 + \Delta)(1 - \nabla) f(x) = (1 + \Delta)[f(x) - \nabla f(x)]$

$$= (1 + \Delta)[f(x) - \{f(x) - f(x-h)\}] = (1 + \Delta)[f(x-h)]$$

$$= \text{E} f(x-h) = 1 . f(x)$$

$$(1 + \Delta)(1 - \nabla) \equiv 1.$$

(*ii*) $$\Delta e^x = e^{x+h} - e^x = (e^h - 1) e^x$$

$\Rightarrow$ $$e^x = \frac{\Delta e^x}{e^h - 1}$$

Hence, $$\Delta\left(\frac{e^x}{e^h - 1}\right) = e^x \quad \text{or} \quad f(x) = \frac{e^x}{e^h - 1}.$$

(*iii*) $$u_{x+\frac{1}{2}} = \text{E}^{1/2} u_x = (1 + \Delta)^{1/2} u_x$$

$$= \left(1 + \frac{1}{2}\Delta - \frac{1}{8}\Delta^2\right) u_x \qquad (10) \quad | \because \ \Delta^3 u_x = 0$$

Now, $\Delta^3 u_x = 0$

$\Rightarrow \Delta^2 u_{x+1} - \Delta^2 u_x = 0$

$\Rightarrow \Delta^2 u_{x+1} = \Delta^2 u_x$ and $\Delta u_x = u_{x+1} - u_x$

$\therefore$ From (10),

$$u_{x+\frac{1}{2}} = u_x + \frac{1}{2}(u_{x+1} - u_x) - \frac{1}{8}\left(\frac{\Delta^2 u_x}{2} + \frac{\Delta^2 u_{x+1}}{2}\right)$$

$$= \frac{1}{2}(u_x + u_{x+1}) - \frac{1}{16}(\Delta^2 u_x + \Delta^2 u_{x+1}).$$

Example 19. (*i*) *Find f(6) given f(0) = – 3, f(1) = 6, f(2) = 8, f(3) = 12; third difference being constant.*

(*ii*) *Find* $\Delta^{10}(1 - ax)(1 - bx^2)(1 - cx^3)(1 - dx^4)$.

(*iii*) *Evaluate* $\Delta^n(ax^n + bx^{n-1})$.

Sol. (*i*) The difference table is:

x	$f(x)$	$\Delta f(x)$	$\Delta^2 f(x)$	$\Delta^3 f(x)$
0	– 3			
		9		
1	6		– 7	
		2		9
2	8		2	
		4		
3	12			

$$f(0 + 6) = E^6 f(0) = (1 + \Delta)^6 f(0) = (1 + 6\Delta + 15\Delta^2 + 20\Delta^3)\, f(0)$$

$$= -3 + 6\,(9) + 15\,(-7) + 20\,(9) = -3 + 54 - 105 + 180 = 126.$$

(*ii*) Maximum power of x in the polynomial will be 10 and the coefficient of x^{10} will be $abcd$.

Here $k = abcd,\ h = 1,\ n = 10$

$\therefore$ Expression $= k\, h^n\, n\,! = abcd\ 10\,!$.

(*iii*) $\Delta^n(ax^n + bx^{n-1}) = a\,\Delta^n(x^n) + b\,\Delta^n(x^{n-1}) = a(n)\,! + b(0) = a(n)\,!$.

Example 20. (*i*) *Prove that if m is a (+)ve integer, then*

$$\frac{(x+1)^{(m)}}{m\,!} = \frac{x^{(m)}}{m\,!} + \frac{x^{(m-1)}}{(m-1)\,!}$$

(*ii*) *Given* $u_0 + u_8 = 1.9243, \quad u_1 + u_7 = 1.9590$

$u_2 + u_6 = 1.9823, \quad u_3 + u_5 = 1.9956$. *Find* u_4.

Sol. (*i*) $\text{R.H.S.} = \dfrac{x(x-1)\ldots\ldots(x-m+1)}{m!} + \dfrac{x(x-1)\ldots\ldots(x-m+2)}{(m-1)!}$

$$= \frac{x(x-1)(x-2)\ldots\ldots(x-m+2)}{m!}\,[(x-m+1)+m]$$

$$= \frac{(x+1)\,x(x-1)(x-2)\ldots\ldots(x-m+2)}{m!} = \frac{(x+1)^{(m)}}{m!} = \text{L.H.S.}$$

(*ii*) Taking $\Delta^8 u_0 = 0$

$\Rightarrow \quad (E-1)^8 u_0 = 0$

$\Rightarrow \quad u_8 - 8c_1u_7 + 8c_2u_6 - 8c_3u_5 + 8c_4u_4 - 8c_5u_3 + 8c_6u_2 - 8c_7u_1 + 8c_8u_0 = 0$

$\Rightarrow \quad (u_0+u_8) - 8(u_1+u_7) + 28(u_2+u_6) - 56(u_3+u_5) + 70\,u_4 = 0$

$\Rightarrow \quad u_4 = 0.99996.$ (After giving the values)

Example 21. *Prove that*

(*i*) $\delta[f(x)\,g(x)] = \mu f(x)\,\delta g(x) + \mu g(x)\,\delta f(x)$

(*ii*) $\delta\left[\dfrac{f(x)}{g(x)}\right] = \dfrac{\mu g(x)\,\delta f(x) - \mu f(x)\,\delta g(x)}{g(x-\frac{1}{2})\,g(x+\frac{1}{2})}$

(*iii*) $\mu\left[\dfrac{f(x)}{g(x)}\right] = \dfrac{\mu f(x)\,\mu g(x) - \frac{1}{4}\delta f(x)\,\delta g(x)}{g(x-\frac{1}{2})\,g(x+\frac{1}{2})}$

The interval of difference is said to be unity.

Sol. (*i*) **R.H.S.** $= \mu \mathbf{f(x)}\,\delta \mathbf{g(x)} + \mu \mathbf{g(x)}\,\delta \mathbf{f(x)}$

$$= \frac{E^{1/2}+E^{-1/2}}{2} f(x)\,.\,(E^{1/2}-E^{-1/2})\,g(x) + \frac{E^{1/2}+E^{-1/2}}{2} g(x)\,(E^{1/2}-E^{-1/2})\,f(x)$$

$$= \tfrac{1}{2}[\{f(x+\tfrac{1}{2}) + f(x-\tfrac{1}{2})\}\{g(x+\tfrac{1}{2}) - g(x-\tfrac{1}{2})\}$$
$$+ \{g(x+\tfrac{1}{2}) + g(x-\tfrac{1}{2})\}\,\{f(x+\tfrac{1}{2}) - f(x-\tfrac{1}{2})\}]$$

$$= \tfrac{1}{2}[\{f(x+\tfrac{1}{2})g(x+\tfrac{1}{2}) - f(x+\tfrac{1}{2})\,g(x-\tfrac{1}{2}) + f(x-\tfrac{1}{2})\,g(x+\tfrac{1}{2})$$
$$- f(x-\tfrac{1}{2})\,g(x-\tfrac{1}{2})\} + \{f(x+\tfrac{1}{2})\,g(x+\tfrac{1}{2})$$
$$+ f(x+\tfrac{1}{2})\,g(x-\tfrac{1}{2}) - f(x-\tfrac{1}{2})\,g(x+\tfrac{1}{2}) - f(x-\tfrac{1}{2})\,g(x-\tfrac{1}{2})\}]$$

$= \frac{1}{4} f(x + \frac{1}{2})\, g(x + \frac{1}{2}) - f(x - \frac{1}{2})\, g(x - \frac{1}{2})$

$= E^{1/2} f(x)\, g(x) - E^{-1/2} f(x)\, g(x) = (E^{1/2} - E^{-1/2}) f(x)\, g(x) = \delta f(x)\, g(x).$

(*ii*) **R.H.S.** $= \dfrac{\mu g(x)\, \delta f(x) - \mu f(x)\, \delta g(x)}{g(x - \frac{1}{2})\, g(x + \frac{1}{2})}$

Numerator of R.H.S.

$$= \frac{E^{1/2} + E^{-1/2}}{2}\, g(x)\, (E^{1/2} - E^{-1/2})\, f(x) - \frac{E^{1/2} + E^{-1/2}}{2}\, f(x)\, (E^{1/2} - E^{-1/2})\, g(x)$$

$$= \frac{1}{2} [\{g(x + \tfrac{1}{2}) + g(x - \tfrac{1}{2})\}\{f(x + \tfrac{1}{2}) - f(x - \tfrac{1}{2})\} - \{f(x + \tfrac{1}{2}) + f(x - \tfrac{1}{2})\}\{g(x + \tfrac{1}{2}) - g(x - \tfrac{1}{2})\}]$$

$$= \frac{1}{2} [f(x + \tfrac{1}{2})\; g(x + \tfrac{1}{2}) + f(x + \tfrac{1}{2})\, g(x - \tfrac{1}{2}) - f(x - \tfrac{1}{2})\; g(x + \tfrac{1}{2}) - f(x - \tfrac{1}{2})\, g(x - \tfrac{1}{2})] - \frac{1}{2} [f(x + \tfrac{1}{2})\, g(x + \tfrac{1}{2}) - f(x + \tfrac{1}{2}) g(x - \tfrac{1}{2}) + f(x - \tfrac{1}{2})\, g(x + \tfrac{1}{2}) - f(x - \tfrac{1}{2})\, g(x - \tfrac{1}{2})]$$

$$= f(x + \tfrac{1}{2})\, g(x - \tfrac{1}{2}) - f(x - \tfrac{1}{2})\, g(x + \tfrac{1}{2})$$

$\therefore$ R.H.S. $= \dfrac{f(x + \frac{1}{2})\, g(x - \frac{1}{2}) - f(x - \frac{1}{2})\, g(x + \frac{1}{2})}{g(x - \frac{1}{2})\, g(x + \frac{1}{2})}$

$$= \frac{f(x + \frac{1}{2})}{g(x + \frac{1}{2})} - \frac{f(x - \frac{1}{2})}{g(x - \frac{1}{2})} = E^{1/2} \left[\frac{f(x)}{g(x)}\right] - E^{1/2} \left[\frac{f(x)}{g(x)}\right]$$

$$= (E^{1/2} - E^{-1/2}) \left(\frac{f(x)}{g(x)}\right) = \delta \left[\frac{f(x)}{g(x)}\right].$$

(*iii*) **R.H.S.** $= \dfrac{\mu f(x)\;\, \mu g(x) - \frac{1}{4}\, \delta f(x)\, \delta g(x)}{g(x - \frac{1}{2})\, g(x + \frac{1}{2})}$

Numerator of R.H.S.

$$= \frac{1}{2} [E^{1/2} + E^{-1/2}]\, f(x)\, .\, \frac{1}{2} (E^{1/2} + E^{-1/2})\, g(x) - \frac{1}{4} (E^{1/2} - E^{-1/2})\, f(x)\, (E^{1/2} - E^{-1/2})\, g(x)$$

$$= \frac{1}{4} [f(x + \tfrac{1}{2}) + f(x - \tfrac{1}{2})][g(x + \tfrac{1}{2}) + g(x - \tfrac{1}{2})] - \frac{1}{4} [f(x + \tfrac{1}{2}) - f(x - \tfrac{1}{2})][g(x + \tfrac{1}{2}) - g(x - \tfrac{1}{2})]$$

$$= \tfrac{1}{4}[f(x+\tfrac{1}{2})\,g(x+\tfrac{1}{2}) + f(x+\tfrac{1}{2})\,g(x-\tfrac{1}{2}) + f(x-\tfrac{1}{2})\,g(x+\tfrac{1}{2})$$

$$+ f(x-\tfrac{1}{2})\,g(x-\tfrac{1}{2}) - \tfrac{1}{4}[f(x+\tfrac{1}{2})\,g(x+\tfrac{1}{2}) - f(x+\tfrac{1}{2})\,g(x-\tfrac{1}{2})$$

$$- f(x-\tfrac{1}{2})\,g(x+\tfrac{1}{2}) + f(x-\tfrac{1}{2})\,g(x-\tfrac{1}{2})$$

$$= \tfrac{1}{2}[f(x+\tfrac{1}{2})\,g(x-\tfrac{1}{2}) + f(x-\tfrac{1}{2})\,g(x+\tfrac{1}{2})]$$

$$\therefore \quad \text{R.H.S.} = \frac{\tfrac{1}{2}[f(x+\tfrac{1}{2})\,g(x-\tfrac{1}{2}) + f(x-\tfrac{1}{2})\,g(x+\tfrac{1}{2})]}{g(x-\tfrac{1}{2})\,g(x+\tfrac{1}{2})}$$

$$= \frac{1}{2}\left[\frac{f(x+\tfrac{1}{2})}{g(x+\tfrac{1}{2})} + \frac{f(x-\tfrac{1}{2})}{g(x-\tfrac{1}{2})}\right] = \frac{\mathrm{E}^{1/2} + \mathrm{E}^{-1/2}}{2}\left[\frac{f(x)}{g(x)}\right] = \mu\left[\frac{f(x)}{g(x)}\right].$$

Example 22. *Evaluate:*

(*i*) $\Delta(e^{ax} \log bx)$ (*ii*) $\Delta\left(\dfrac{2^x}{(x+1)!}\right)$; $h = 1$.

Sol. (*i*) Let $f(x) = e^{ax}$, $g(x) = \log bx$

$$\Delta f(x) = e^{a(x+h)} - e^{ax} = e^{ax}(e^{ah} - 1)$$

Also, $\Delta g(x) = \log b(x+h) - \log bx = \log\left(1 + \dfrac{h}{x}\right)$

We know that,

$$\Delta f(x)\,g(x) = f(x+h)\,\Delta g(x) + g(x)\,\Delta f(x)$$

$$\therefore \quad \Delta(e^{ax}\log bx) = e^{a(x+h)}\log\left(1+\frac{h}{x}\right) + (\log bx)\,e^{ax}(e^{ah} - 1)$$

$$= e^{ax}\left[e^{ah}\log\left(1+\frac{h}{x}\right) + (e^{ah} - 1)\log bx\right].$$

(*ii*) Let $f(x) = 2^x$, $g(x) = (x+1)!$

$$\therefore \quad \Delta f(x) = 2^{x+1} - 2^x = 2^x$$

and $\Delta g(x) = (x+1+1)! - (x+1)! = (x+1)(x+1)!$

We know that,

$$\Delta\left[\frac{f(x)}{g(x)}\right] = \frac{g(x)\,\Delta f(x) - f(x)\,\Delta g(x)}{g(x+h)\,g(x)}$$

$$= \frac{(x+1)!\,.\,2^x - 2^x\,.\,(x+1)(x+1)!}{(x+1+1)!\,(x+1)!} \qquad (\because \; h = 1)$$

$$= \frac{2^x\,(x+1)!\,(1-x-1)}{(x+2)!\,(x+1)!} = -\frac{x}{(x+2)!}\,2^x.$$

Example 23. *Evaluate:*

(i) Δ^n [*sin (ax + b)*] *(ii)* Δ^n [*cos (ax + b)*].

Sol. *(i)* $\Delta \sin (ax + b)$

$$= \sin [a (x + h) + b] - \sin (ax + b)$$

$$= 2 \sin \frac{ah}{2} \cos \left[a\left(x+\frac{h}{2}\right)+b\right]$$

$$= 2 \sin \frac{ah}{2} \sin \left(ax+b+\frac{ah+\pi}{2}\right)$$

$\therefore$ $\Delta^2 \sin (ax + b)$

$$= \Delta \left[2 \sin \frac{ah}{2} \sin \left(ax+b+\frac{ah+\pi}{2}\right)\right]$$

$$= \left(2 \sin \frac{ah}{2}\right)\left(2 \sin \frac{ah}{2}\right) \sin \left[ax+b+\frac{ah+\pi}{2}+\frac{ah+\pi}{2}\right]$$

$$= \left(2 \sin \frac{ah}{2}\right)^2 \sin \left[ax+b+2\left(\frac{ah+\pi}{2}\right)\right]$$

Proceeding in the same manner, we get

$$\Delta^3 \sin (ax + b) = \left(2 \sin \frac{ah}{2}\right)^3 \sin \left[ax+b+\frac{3(ah+\pi)}{2}\right]$$

$$\vdots \qquad \vdots$$

$$\Delta^n \sin (ax + b) = \left(2 \sin \frac{ah}{2}\right)^n \sin \left[ax+b+\frac{n(ah+\pi)}{2}\right]$$

Similarly,

$$(ii)\ \Delta^n \cos (ax + b) = \left(2 \sin \frac{ah}{2}\right)^n \cos \left[ax+b+n\left(\frac{ah+\pi}{2}\right)\right].$$

Example 24. *Prove that*

(i) $\mu\delta = \frac{1}{2} (\Delta + \nabla)$ *(ii)* $1 + \left(\frac{\delta^2}{2}\right) = \sqrt{1+\delta^2\mu^2}$

(iii) $\nabla^2 = h^2D^2 - h^3D^3 + \frac{7}{12} h^4D^4$. ...... *(iv)* $\nabla - \Delta = - \nabla\Delta$

Sol. *(i)* $\mu\delta y_x = \mu(E^{1/2} - E^{-1/2})y_x$

$$= \mu(y_{x+\frac{h}{2}} - y_{x-\frac{h}{2}}) = \mu(y_{x+\frac{h}{2}}) - \mu(y_{x-\frac{h}{2}})$$

$$= \frac{1}{2}(E^{1/2} + E^{-1/2})(y_{x+\frac{h}{2}}) - \frac{1}{2}(E^{1/2} + E^{-1/2})(y_{x-\frac{h}{2}})$$

$$= \frac{1}{2}(y_{x+h} + y_x) - \frac{1}{2}(y_x + y_{x-h}) = \frac{1}{2}(y_{x+h} - y_x) + \frac{1}{2}(y_x - y_{x-h})$$

$$= \frac{1}{2}(\Delta y_x) + \frac{1}{2}(\nabla y_x) = \frac{1}{2}(\Delta + \nabla)y_x$$

Hence, $\mu\delta = \frac{1}{2}(\Delta + \nabla)$

(*ii*) $$\text{L.H.S.} = \left\{1 + \left(\frac{\delta^2}{2}\right)\right\} y_x = \left\{1 + \frac{(E^{1/2} - E^{-1/2})^2}{2}\right\} y_x$$

$$= \left\{1 + \left(\frac{E + E^{-1} - 2}{2}\right)\right\} y_x = \frac{1}{2}(E + E^{-1})y_x$$

$$\text{R.H.S.} = (\sqrt{1 + \delta^2\mu^2})y_x$$

$$= \left[1 + \left\{(E^{1/2} - E^{-1/2})^2 \cdot \frac{1}{4}(E^{1/2} + E^{-1/2})^2\right\}\right]^{1/2} y_x$$

$$= \left\{1 + \left(\frac{(E - E^{-1})^2}{4}\right)\right\}^{1/2} y_x$$

$$= \left(\frac{E^2 + E^{-2} + 2}{4}\right)^{1/2} y_x = \left(\frac{E + E^{-1}}{2}\right) y_x$$

Hence L.H.S. = R.H.S.

(*iii*) $E = e^{hD}$ and $\nabla = 1 - E^{-1}$

$\therefore$ $\nabla^2 = (1 - E^{-hD})^2$

$$= \left[1 - \left\{1 - hD + \frac{(hD)^2}{2!} - \frac{(hD)^3}{3!} + \frac{(hD)^4}{4!} - \ldots\right\}\right]^2$$

$$= \left\{hD - \frac{(hD)^2}{2!} + \frac{(hD)^3}{3!} - \frac{(hD)^4}{4!} + \ldots\right\}^2$$

$$= h^2D^2\left[1 - \left\{\frac{hD}{2} - \frac{(hD)^2}{6} + \ldots\right\}\right]^2$$

$$= h^2D^2 \left[1 + \left\{ \frac{hD}{2} - \frac{(hD)^2}{6} + ... \right\}^2 - 2\left\{ \frac{hD}{2} - \frac{(hD)^2}{6} + ... \right\} \right]$$

$$= h^2D^2 \left[1 - hD + \left(\frac{1}{4} + \frac{1}{3} \right) (hD)^2 - ... \right]$$

$$= h^2D^2 \left(1 - hD + \frac{7}{12} h^2D^2 - ... \right) = h^2D^2 - h^3D^3 + \frac{7}{12} h^4D^4 - ...$$

(*iv*) $\nabla - \Delta = (1 - E^{-1}) - (E - 1) = \left(\frac{E-1}{E} \right) - (E - 1) = (E - 1)(E^{-1} - 1)$

$$= -(E - 1)(1 - E^{-1}) = -\nabla\Delta$$

ASSIGNMENT 4.1

1. Form a table of differences for the function:

$f(x) = x^3 + 5x - 7$ for $x = -1, 0, 1, 2, 3, 4, 5$

Continue the table to obtain $f(6)$ and $f(7)$.

2. Given the set of values

x:	10	15	20	25	30	35
y:	19.97	21.51	22.47	23.52	24.65	25.89.

Form the difference table and find the values of $\Delta^2 y_{10}$, Δy_{20}, $\Delta^3 y_{15}$, and $\Delta^5 y_{10}$.

3. Write the forward difference table for

x:	10	20	30	40
y:	1.1	2.0	4.4	7.9.

4. Construct the table of differences for the data below:

x:	0	1	2	3	4
$f(x)$:	1.0	1.5	2.2	3.1	4.6

Evaluate $\Delta^3 f(2)$.

5. Prove that:

(*i*) $\nabla = \Delta E^{-1} = E^{-1}\Delta = 1 - E^{-1}$

(*ii*) $E^{1/2} = \mu + \frac{1}{2}\delta$

(*iii*) $\delta = \Delta E^{-1/2} = \nabla E^{1/2}$

(*iv*) $\delta(E^{1/2} + E^{-1/2}) = \Delta E^{-1} + \Delta$

(*v*) $\Delta\nabla = \nabla\Delta = \delta^2$

(*vi*) $\delta = \Delta(1 + \Delta)^{-1/2} = \nabla(1 - \nabla)^{-1/2}$

(*vii*) $E = (1 - \Delta)^{-1}$.

6. u_x is a function of x for which fifth differences are constant and

$$u_1 + u_7 = -786, \qquad u_2 + u_6 = 686, \qquad u_3 + u_5 = 1088. \quad \text{Find } u_4.$$

7. Prove that:

(i) $u_4 = u_3 + \Delta u_2 + \Delta^2 u_1 + \Delta^3 u_1$ (ii) $u_4 = u_0 + 4\Delta u_0 + 6\,\Delta^2 u_{-1} + 10\,\Delta^3 u_{-1}$.

8. Prove that:

$$\Delta \sin^{-1} x = \sin^{-1} [(x+1)\sqrt{1-x^2} - x\sqrt{1-(x+1)^2}\,].$$

9. Evaluate:

(i) $(E^{-1}\,\Delta)\, x^3$ (ii) $\left(\frac{\Delta^2}{E}\right) x^3$; $h = 1$.

10. Evaluate:

(i) $\Delta\left(\frac{e^x}{e^x + e^{-x}}\right)$ (ii) $\Delta \cos a^x$

the interval of difference being h.

4.8 FACTORIAL NOTATION

A product of the form $x(x-1)(x-2)\ ......\ (x-r+1)$ is denoted by $[x]^r$ and is called a factorial.

Particularly, $[x] = x$; $[x]^2 = x(x-1)$; $[x]^3 = x\,(x-1)(x-2)$, etc.

In case the interval of difference is h, then

$$[x]^n = x(x-h)\,(x-2h)\ ......\ (x - \overline{n-1}\,h)$$

Factorial notation helps in finding the successive differences of a polynomial directly by the simple rule of differentiation.

4.9 TO SHOW THAT (i) $\Delta^n[x]^n = n\,!$ (ii) $\Delta^{n+1}\,[x]^n = 0$

$$\begin{aligned}\Delta[x]^n &= [(x+h)]^n - [x]^n \\ &= (x+h)(x+h-h)\,(x+h-2h)\ ......\ (x+h-\overline{n-1}\,h) \\ &\qquad - x(x-h)\,(x-2h)\ ......\ (x-\overline{n-1}\,h) \\ &= x(x-h)\ ......\ (x-\overline{n-2}\,h)\,[x+h-(x-nh+h)] = nh\,[x]^{n-1}\end{aligned}$$

Similarly, $\Delta^2[x]^n = \Delta[nh\ [x]^{n-1}] = nh\ \Delta[x]^{n-1} = n(n-1)\ h^2\ [x]^{n-2}$

$$\vdots$$

$$\Delta^n [x]^n = n(n-1) \ldots\ldots 2\ .\ 1\ .\ h^{n-1} (x + h - x) = n\ !\ h^n$$

Also, $\Delta^{n+1}[x]^n = n\ !\ h^n - n\ !\ h^n = 0$

when $h = 1$, $\Delta[x]^n = n[x]^{n-1}$ and $\Delta^n[x]^n = n\ !$

Hence the result of difference $[x]^r$ is analogous to that of difference x^r when $h = 1$.

4.10 RECIPROCAL FACTORIAL

$x^{(-n)} = \dfrac{1}{(x+n)^{(n)}}$, the interval of difference being unity.

By definition of $x^{(n)}$, we have

$$x^{(n)} = (x - \overline{n-1}\ h)\ x^{(n-1)} \tag{11}$$

when the interval of difference is h.

$\therefore$ When $n = 0$, we have $x^{(0)} = (x + h)\ x^{(-1)}$ (12)

Since, $\Delta x^{(n)} = nhx^{(n-1)}$ (13)

when $n = 1$, $\Delta x^{(1)} = hx^{(0)}$.

$$\Rightarrow \quad \Delta x = h\ x^{(0)} \quad \Rightarrow \quad h = hx^{(0)} \quad \Rightarrow \quad x^{(0)} = 1$$

From (12), $x^{(-1)} = \dfrac{1}{(x+h)}$ (14)

when $n = -1$, from (11),

$$x^{(-1)} = (x + 2h)\ x^{(-2)}$$

$$\Rightarrow \quad \frac{1}{x+h} = (x + 2h)\ x^{(-2)} \quad \Rightarrow \quad x^{(-2)} = \frac{1}{(x+h)(x+2h)}$$

In general, $x^{(-n)} = \dfrac{1}{(x+h)(x+2h) \ldots\ldots (x+nh)}$ (15)

$$x^{(-n)} = \frac{1}{(x+nh)^{(n)}}$$

Here $x^{(-n)}$ is called the reciprocal factorial where n is a (+)ve integer.

Particular case. When $h = 1$, $x^{(-n)} = \dfrac{1}{(x+n)^{(n)}}$.

4.11 MISSING TERM TECHNIQUE

Suppose n values out of $(n + 1)$ values of $y = f(x)$ are given, the values of x being equidistant.

Let the unknown value be N. We construct the difference table.

Since only n values of y are known, we can assume $y = f(x)$ to be a polynomial of degree $(n - 1)$ in x.

Equating to zero the nth difference, we can get the value of N.

EXAMPLES

Example 1. *Express* $y = 2x^3 - 3x^2 + 3x - 10$ *in factorial notation and hence show that* $\Delta^3 y = 12$.

Sol. Let $$y = A[x]^3 + B[x]^2 + c[x] + D$$

Using the method of synthetic division, we divide by x, $x - 1$, $x - 2$ etc. successively, then

1	2	− 3	3	− 10 = D
		2	− 1	
2	2	− 1	2 = C	
		4		
3	2	3 = B		
	2 = A			

Hence, $$y = 2[x]^3 + 3[x]^2 + 2[x] - 10$$

$\therefore$ $$\Delta y = 6[x]^2 + 6[x] + 2$$

$$\Delta^2 y = 12[x] + 6$$

$$\Delta^3 y = 12$$

which shows that the third differences of y are constant.

Example 2. *Express* $f(x) = x^4 - 12x^3 + 24x^2 - 30x + 9$ *and its successive differences in factorial notation. Hence show that* $\Delta^5 f(x) = 0$.

Sol. Let

$$f(x) = A[x]^4 + B[x]^3 + C[x]^2 + D[x] + E$$

Using the method of synthetic division, we divide by x, $x - 1$, $x - 2$, $x - 3$, etc. successively, then

1	1	– 12	24	– 30	9 = E
		1	– 11	13	
2	1	– 11	13	– 17 = D	
		2	– 18		
3	1	– 9	– 5 = C		
		3			
4	1	– 6 = B			
	1 = A				

Hence, $f(x) = [x]^4 - 6[x]^3 - 5[x]^2 - 17[x] + 9$

$\therefore$ $\Delta f(x) = 4[x]^3 - 18[x]^2 - 10[x] - 17$

$\Delta^2 f(x) = 12[x]^2 - 36[x] - 10$

$\Delta^3 f(x) = 24[x] - 36$

$\Delta^4 f(x) = 24$

and $\Delta^5 f(x) = 0.$

Example 3. *Obtain the function whose first difference is* $9x^2 + 11x + 5$.

Sol. Let $f(x)$ be the required function so that

$$\Delta f(x) = 9x^2 + 11x + 5$$

Let $9x^2 + 11x + 5 = 9[x]^2 + A[x] + B = 9x(x-1) + Ax + B$

Putting $x = 0, \quad B = 5$

$x = 1, \quad A = 20$

$\therefore$ $\Delta f(x) = 9[x]^2 + 20[x] + 5$

Integrating, we get

$$f(x) = 9\frac{[x]^3}{3} + 20\frac{[x]^2}{2} + 5[x] + c$$

$$= 3x(x-1)(x-2) + 10x(x-1) + 5x + c = 3x^3 + x^2 + x + c$$

where c is the constant of integration.

Example 4. *Find the missing values in the table:*

x:	45	50	55	60	65
y:	3	–	2	–	– 2.4.

Sol. The difference table is as follows:

x	y	Δy	$\Delta^2 y$	$\Delta^3 y$
45	3			
		$y_1 - 3$		
50	y_1		$5 - 2y_1$	
		$2 - y_1$		$3y_1 + y_3 - 9$
55	2		$y_1 + y_3 - 4$	
		$y_3 - 2$		$3.6 - y_1 - 3y_3$
60	y_3		$-0.4 - 2y_3$	
		$-2.4 - y_3$		
65	-2.4			

As only three entries y_0, y_2, y_4 are given, the function y can be represented by a second degree polynomial.

$$\therefore \qquad \Delta^3 y_0 = 0 \quad \text{and} \quad \Delta^3 y_1 = 0$$

$$\Rightarrow \qquad 3y_1 + y_3 = 9 \quad \text{and} \quad y_1 + 3y_3 = 3.6$$

Solving these, we get

$$y_1 = 2.925, \quad y_2 = 0.225.$$

Example 5. *Express* $f(x) = \dfrac{x-1}{(x+1)(x+3)}$ *in terms of negative factorial polynomials.*

Sol.
$$f(x) = \frac{x-1}{(x+1)(x+3)} = \frac{(x-1)(x+2)}{(x+1)(x+2)(x+3)}$$

$$= \frac{1}{x+1} - \frac{4}{(x+1)(x+2)} + \frac{4}{(x+1)(x+2)(x+3)}$$

$$= x^{(-1)} - 4x^{(-2)} + 4x^{(-3)}.$$

Example 6. *Find the relation between* α, β, *and* γ *in order that* $\alpha + \beta x + \gamma x^2$ *may be expressible in one term in the factorial notation.*

Sol. Let $\qquad f(x) = \alpha + \beta x + \gamma x^2 = (a + bx)^{(2)}$

where a and b are certain unknown constants.

Now, $(a + bx)^{(2)} = (a + bx)\,[a + b(x - 1)]$

$$= (a + bx)\,(a - b + bx) = (a + bx)^2 - ab - b^2 x$$

$$= (a^2 - ab) + (2ab - b^2)x + b^2 x^2 = \alpha + \beta x + \gamma x^2$$

Comparing the coefficients of various powers of x, we get

$$\alpha = a^2 - ab,\ \beta = 2ab - b^2,\ \gamma = b^2$$

Eliminating a and b from the above equations,

we get $$\gamma^2 + 4\alpha\gamma = \beta^2$$

which is the required relation.

Example 7. *Given, log 100 = 2, log 101 = 2.0043, log 103 = 2.0128, log 104 = 2.0170. Find log 102.*

Sol. Since four values are given, $\Delta^4 f(x) = 0$.

Let the missing value be y_2.

x	y	Δy	$\Delta^2 y$	$\Delta^3 y$	$\Delta^4 y$
100	2				
		.0043			
101	2.0043		$y_2 - 2.0086$		
		$y_2 - 2.0043$		$6.0257 - 3y_2$	
102	y_2		$4.0171 - 2y_2$		$6y_2 - 12.0514$
		$2.0128 - y_2$		$3y_2 - 6.0257$	
103	2.0128		$y_2 - 2.0086$		
		.0042			
104	2.0170				

Since $\Delta^4 y = 0$

$\therefore\ 6y_2 - 12.0514 = 0 \ \Rightarrow\ y_2 = 2.0086.$

Example 8. *Estimate the missing term in the following table:*

x:	*0*	*1*	*2*	*3*	*4*
y = f(x):	*1*	*3*	*9*	*?*	*81.*

Sol. We are given 4 values

$$\therefore\quad \Delta^4 f(x) = 0\ \ \forall\, x \ \Rightarrow\ (E - 1)^4 f(x) = 0\ \ \forall\, x$$

$$\Rightarrow\quad (E^4 - 4E^3 + 6E^2 - 4E + 1)\, f(x) = 0\ \ \forall\, x$$

$$\Rightarrow\quad f(x + 4) - 4f(x + 3) + 6f(x + 2) - 4f(x + 1) + f(x) = 0\ \ \forall\, x$$

where the interval of difference is 1.

Now given $x = 0$, we obtain

$$f(4) - 4f(3) + 6f(2) - 4f(1) + f(0) = 0$$

$$\Rightarrow \qquad 81 - 4f(3) + 54 - 12 + 1 = 0 \qquad \text{(From table)}$$

$$\Rightarrow \qquad 4f(3) = 124 \Rightarrow f(3) = 31.$$

Example 9. *A second degree polynomial passes through (0, 1), (1, 3), (2, 7), (3, 13). Find the polynomial.*

Sol. Let $f(x) = Ax^2 + Bx + C$

The difference table is:

x	$f(x)$	$\Delta f(x)$	$\Delta^2 f(x)$
0	1		
		2	
1	3		2
		4	
2	7		2
		6	
3	13		

$$\Delta f(x) = A\,\Delta x^2 + B\Delta x + \Delta C$$

$$= A\,\{(x+1)^2 - x^2\} + B(x + 1 - x) + 0 = A(2x + 1) + B$$

Put $x = 0$,

$$\Delta f(0) = A + B \quad \Rightarrow \quad A + B = 2$$

Also, $\Delta^2 f(x) = 2A \quad \Rightarrow \quad \Delta^2 f(0) = 2 = 2A \quad \Rightarrow \quad A = 1$

Also, $B = 1$

$\therefore$ Polynomial is $f(x) = x^2 + x + 1$.

Example 10. *Estimate the production for 1964 and 1966 from the following data:*

Year:	*1961*	*1962*	*1963*	*1964*	*1965*	*1966*	*1967*
Production:	*200*	*220*	*260*	—	*350*	—	*430*

Sol. Since five figures are known, assume all the fifth order differences as zero. Since two figures are unknown, we need two equations to determine them.

Hence $\quad \Delta^5 y_0 = 0 \quad \text{and} \quad \Delta^5 y_1 = 0$

$$\Rightarrow \quad (E - 1)^5 y_0 = 0 \quad \text{and} \quad (E - 1)^5 y_1 = 0$$

$$\Rightarrow \quad y_5 - 5y_4 + 10y_3 - 10y_2 + 5y_1 - y_0 = 0$$

and $\quad y_6 - 5y_5 + 10y_4 - 10y_3 + 5y_2 - y_1 = 0$

Substituting the known values, we get

$$y_5 - 1750 + 10y_3 - 2600 + 1100 - 200 = 0$$

and $\quad 430 - 5y_5 + 3500 - 10y_3 + 1300 - 220 = 0$

$$\Rightarrow \quad y_5 + 10y_3 = 3450 \tag{16}$$

$$\text{and} \quad -5y_5 - 10y_3 = -5010 \tag{17}$$

Adding (16) and (17), we get

$$-4y_5 = -1560$$

$$\Rightarrow \quad y_5 = 390$$

From (16), $\quad 390 + 10y_3 = 3450$

$$\Rightarrow \quad 10y_3 = 3060$$

$$\Rightarrow \quad y_3 = 306$$

Hence, production for year 1964 = 306

and production for year 1966 = 390.

Example 11. *Find the missing figures in the following table:*

x:	*2*	*2.1*	*2.2*	*2.3*	*2.4*	*2.5*	*2.6*
y:	*0.135*	—	*0.111*	*0.100*	—	*0.082*	*0.074.*

Sol. Here five values are given.

$\therefore$ It is assumed that fifth differences are zero and hence both $\Delta^5 y_{2.0}$ and $\Delta^5 y_{2.1}$ are zero.

$$\Delta^5 y_{2.0} = (E - 1)^5 y_{2.0}$$

$$= (E^5 - 5E^4 + 10E^3 - 10E^2 + 5E - 1)y_{2.0}$$

$$= y_{2.5} - 5y_{2.4} + 10y_{2.3} - 10y_{2.2} + 5y_{2.1} - y_{2.0} \qquad | \because h = 0.1$$

$$= .082 - 5y_{2.4} + 1 - 1.11 + 5y_{2.1} - .135$$

$$= -5y_{2.4} + 5y_{2.1} - .163$$

Since $\quad \Delta^5 y_{2.0} = 0$

$$\therefore \quad -5y_{2.4} + 5y_{2.1} - .163 = 0 \tag{18}$$

Further,

$$\Delta^5 y_{2.1} = (E - 1)^5 y_{2.1}$$

$$= (E^5 - 5E^4 + 10E^3 - 10E^2 + 5E - 1)y_{2.1}$$

$$= y_{2.6} - 5y_{2.5} + 10y_{2.4} - 10y_{2.3} + 5y_{2.2.} - y_{2.1}$$

$$= .074 - (5 \times .082) + 10y_{2.4} - 1 + .555 - y_{2.1}$$

$$= .074 - .41 + 10y_{2.4} - 1 + .555 - y_{2.1}$$

$$= 10y_{2.4} - y_{2.1} - .781$$

Since $\Delta^5 y_{2.1} = 0$

$\therefore$ $10y_{2.4} - y_{2.1} - .781 = 0$ (19)

Solving (18) and (19), we get

$$y_{2.1} = .123 \quad \text{and} \quad y_{2.4} = .0904.$$

Example 12. *Find the missing value of the following data:*

x:	*1*	*2*	*3*	*4*	*5*
f(x):	*7*	☒	*13*	*21*	*37.*

Sol. Since four values are known, assume all the fourth order differences are zero.

Since one value is unknown

we assume $\Delta^4 y_1 = 0$

$\Rightarrow$ $(E - 1)^4 y_1 = 0$

$\Rightarrow$ $(E^4 - 4E^3 + 6E^2 - 4E + 1)y_1 = 0$

$\Rightarrow$ $y_5 - 4y_4 + 6y_3 - 4y_2 + y_1 = 0$ $\quad | \because h = 1$

$\Rightarrow$ $37 - 4(21) + 6(13) - 4y_2 + 7 = 0$

$\Rightarrow$ $38 - 4y_2 = 0$

$\Rightarrow$ $y_2 = 9.5$

Hence the required missing value is **9.5.**

ASSIGNMENT 4.2

1. Estimate the missing term in the following:

x:	1	2	3	4	5	6	7
y:	2	4	8	—	32	64	128

Explain why the result differs from 16?

2. Estimate the production of cotton in the year 1935 from the data given below:

Year x:	1931	1932	1933	1934	1935	1936	1937
Production f(x): (*in millions*)	17.1	13	14	9.6	—	12.4	18.2

3. From the following data, find the value of U_{47}:

$$U_{46} = 0.2884, \quad U_{48} = 0.5356, \quad U_{49} = 0.6513, \quad U_{50} = 0.7620.$$

[**Hint:** $\Delta^4 U_x = 0 \Rightarrow (E - 1)^4 U_x = 0.$]

4. Find by constructing the difference table, the tenth term of the series

$$3, 14, 39, 84, 155, 258, \ldots\ldots$$

[**Hint:** $f(10) = E^9 f(1) = (1 + \Delta)^9 f(1)$]

5. Find the missing terms in the following table:

x:	1	2	3	4	5	6	7	8
$f(x)$:	1	8	?	64	?	216	343	512

6. Represent the following polynomials:

(*i*) $11x^4 + 5x^3 + x - 15$ (*ii*) $2x^3 - 3x^2 + 3x + 10$

and its successive differences in factorial notation.

4.12 METHOD OF SEPARATION OF SYMBOLS

The relationship $E = 1 + \Delta$ can be used to prove a number of useful identities. The method is known as separation of symbols.

4.13 DETECTION OF ERRORS BY USE OF DIFFERENCE TABLES

Difference tables can be used to check errors in tabular values. Let $f(x_1), f(x_2), \ldots\ldots, f(x_n)$ be the true values of $f(x)$ at $x = x_1, x_2, \ldots\ldots, x_n$. If $f(x)$ at $x = x_i$ is incorrect, we have to determine the error in such cases and correct the functional value.

In particular, let the functional value at $x = x_5$ be $f(x_5) + e$ and let other true functional values $f(x_1), f(x_2), \ldots\ldots, f(x_4), f(x_6), \ldots\ldots, f(x_9)$ be known.

x	$f(x)$	$\Delta f(x)$	$\Delta^2 f(x)$	$\Delta^3 f(x)$	$\Delta^4 f(x)$
x_1	$f(x_1)$				
		$\Delta f(x_1)$			
x_2	$f(x_2)$		$\Delta^2 f(x_1)$		
		$\Delta f(x_2)$		$\Delta^3 f(x_1)$	
x_3	$f(x_3)$		$\Delta^2 f(x_2)$		$\Delta^4 f(x_1) + e$
		$\Delta f(x_3)$		$\Delta^3 f(x_2) + e$	
x_4	$f(x_4)$		$\Delta^2 f(x_3) + e$		$\Delta^4 f(x_2) - 4e$
		$\Delta f(x_4) + e$		$\Delta^3 f(x_3) - 3e$	
x_5	$f(x_5)$	$\longrightarrow$	$\Delta^2 f(x_4) - 2e$	$\longrightarrow$	$\Delta^4 f(x_3) + 6e$
		$\Delta f(x_5) - e$		$\Delta^3 f(x_4) + 3e$	
x_6	$f(x_6)$		$\Delta^2 f(x_5) + e$		$\Delta^4 f(x_4) - 4e$
		$\Delta f(x_6)$		$\Delta^3 f(x_5) - e$	
x_7	$f(x_7)$		$\Delta^2 f(x_6)$		$\Delta^4 f(x_5) + e$
		$\Delta f(x_7)$		$\Delta^3 f(x_6)$	
x_8	$f(x_8)$		$\Delta^2 f(x_7)$		
		$\Delta f(x_8)$			
x_9	$f(x_9)$				

From the table, we observe that,

(*i*) Error spreads in triangular form.

(*ii*) Coefficient of e's are binomial coefficient with alternate signs + , –, ...

(*iii*) Algebraic sum of errors in each column is 0.

(*iv*) In even differences columns, the maximum error occurs in a horizontal line in which incorrect y lies.

(*v*) In odd differences columns, the incorrect value of y lies between two middle terms.

(*vi*) If n^{th} differences are constant, $(n + 1)^{\text{th}}$ differences vanish. The sum of all the values in $(n + 1)^{\text{th}}$ differences column is zero or the sum is very small as compared to the functional values

These observations help us in finding out the error, and hence the required correct value of y can be found.

EXAMPLES

Example 1. *Find the error and correct the wrong figure in the following functional values:*

2, 5, 10, 18, 26, 37, 50.

Sol.

x	y	Δy	$\Delta^2 y$	$\Delta^3 y$
1	2			
		3		
2	5		2	
		5		1
3	10		3	
		8		– 3
4	18 ←		0	
		8		3
5	26		3	
		11		– 1
6	37		2	
		13		
7	50			

Sum of all the third differences is zero.

Adjacent values – 3, 3 are equal in magnitude. The horizontal line between – 3 and 3 points out the incorrect functional value 18.

The coefficient of the first middle term on expansion of $(1-p)^3 = -3$

$$\Rightarrow \qquad -3e = -3 \quad \Rightarrow \quad e = 1$$

$\therefore$ The correct functional value = 18 – 1 = 17.

Example 2. *Locate the error in the following entries and correct it:*

1.203, 1.424, 1.681, 1.992, 2.379, 2.848, 3.429, and 4.136.

Sol. Difference table is as follows:

$10^3 y$	$10^3 \Delta y$	$10^3 \Delta^2 y$	$10^3 \Delta^3 y$	$10^3 \Delta^4 y$
1203				
	221			
1424		36		
	257		18	
1681		54		4
	311		22	
1992		76		– 16
	387		6	
2379 ←		82		24
	469		30	
2848		112		– 16
	581		14	
3429		126		
	707			
4136				

The sum of all values in the column of fourth difference is – .004, which is very small as compared to the sum of values in other columns.

$\therefore \qquad \Delta^4 y = 0$

The errors in this column are e, – $4e$, $6e$, – $4e$, and e.

The term of maximum value = 24 $\Rightarrow$ $6e = 24$ $\Rightarrow$ $e = 4$

The error lies in 2379.

Hence, the required correct entry = 2379 – 4 = 2375

Hence, the correct value = 2.375.

Example 3. *Using the method of separation of symbols, show that*

$$u_0 - u_1 + u_2 - u_3 + \ldots = \frac{1}{2} u_0 - \frac{1}{4} \Delta u_0 + \frac{1}{8} \Delta^2 u_0 - \ldots\ldots .$$

Sol. $\text{R.H.S.} = \frac{1}{2}\left[1 - \frac{1}{2}\Delta + \left(\frac{1}{2}\Delta\right)^2 - \left(\frac{1}{2}\Delta\right)^3 + \ldots\ldots\right] u_0$

$$= \frac{1}{2} \cdot \frac{1}{\left(1 + \frac{1}{2}\Delta\right)} u_0 = \frac{1}{2}\left(1 + \frac{1}{2}\Delta\right)^{-1} u_0 = (2 + \Delta)^{-1} u_0 = (1 + \text{E})^{-1} u_0$$

$$= (1 - \text{E} + \text{E}^2 - \text{E}^3 + \ldots) u_0 = u_0 - u_1 + u_2 - u_3 + \ldots\ldots = \text{L.H.S.}$$

Example 4. *Using the method of separation of symbols, show that:*

$$\Delta^n u_{x-n} = u_x - n u_{x-1} + \frac{n(n-1)}{2} u_{x-2} + \ldots\ldots + (-1)^n u_{x-n}.$$

Sol. $\text{R.H.S.} = u_x - n\text{E}^{-1} u_x + \frac{n(n-1)}{2} \text{E}^{-2} u_x + \ldots\ldots + (-1)^n \text{E}^{-n} u_x$

$$= \left[1 - n\text{E}^{-1} + \frac{n(n-1)}{2}\text{E}^{-2} + \ldots\ldots + (-1)^n \text{E}^{-n}\right] u_x$$

$$= (1 - \text{E}^{-1})^n u_x$$

$$= \left(1 - \frac{1}{\text{E}}\right)^n u_x$$

$$= \left(\frac{\text{E} - 1}{\text{E}}\right)^n u_x = \frac{\Delta^n}{\text{E}^n} u_x$$

$$= \Delta^n \text{E}^{-n} u_x$$

$$= \Delta^n u_{x-n}$$

$$= \text{L.H.S.}$$

Example 5. *Show that:*

$$e^x\left(u_0 + x\,\Delta\, u_0 + \frac{x^2}{2!}\Delta^2\, u_0 + \ldots\ldots\right) = u_0 + u_1 x + u_2\,\frac{x^2}{2!} + \ldots\ldots .$$

Sol. $$\text{L.H.S.} = e^x\left(1 + x\Delta + \frac{x^2\Delta^2}{2!} + \ldots\ldots\right) u_0 = e^x \,.\, e^{x\Delta}\, u_0 = e^{x(1+\Delta)}\, u_0 = e^{x\text{E}}\, u_0$$

$$= \left(1 + x\text{E} + \frac{x^2\text{E}^2}{2!} + \ldots\ldots\right) u_0 = \left(u_0 + xu_1 + \frac{x^2}{2!}u_2 + \ldots\ldots\right) = \text{R.H.S.}$$

Example 6. *Prove the following identity:*

$$u_1 x + u_2 x^2 + u_3 x^3 + \ldots\ldots = \frac{x}{1-x}\,u_1 + \frac{x^2}{(1-x)^2}\,\Delta u_1 + \ldots..$$

Sol. $$\text{L.H.S.} = xu_1 + x^2\,\text{E}\,u_1 + x^3\,\text{E}^2 u_1 + \ldots\ldots = x\,(1 + x\text{E} + x^2\text{E}^2 + \ldots\ldots)\,u_1$$

$$= x\,.\,\frac{1}{(1-x\text{E})}\,u_1 = x\,.\,\frac{1}{[1-x(1+\Delta)]}\,u_1$$

$$= x\left[\frac{1}{1-x-x\,\Delta}\right]u_1 = \frac{x}{1-x}\left[\frac{1}{1-\dfrac{x\Delta}{1-x}}\right]u_1$$

$$= \frac{x}{1-x}\left[1-\frac{x\Delta}{1-x}\right]^{-1}(u_1) = \frac{x}{1-x}\left[1+\frac{x\Delta}{1-x}+\frac{x^2\Delta^2}{(1-x)^2}+\ldots\ldots\right]u_1$$

$$= \frac{x}{1-x}\,u_1 + \frac{x^2}{(1-x)^2}\,\Delta u_1 + \frac{x^3}{(1-x)^3}\,\Delta^2 u_1 + \ldots\ldots = \text{R.H.S.}$$

Example 7. *Prove that:* $u_x = u_{x-1} + \Delta u_{x-2} + \Delta^2 u_{x-3} + \ldots\ldots + \Delta^{n-1}\, u_{x-n} + \Delta^n u_{x-n}$

Hence, or otherwise, prove that:

$$u_3 = u_2 + \Delta u_1 + \Delta^2 u_0 + \Delta^3 u_0.$$

Sol. $u_x - \Delta^n\, u_{x-n} = (1 - \Delta^n\,\text{E}^{-n})u_x$

$$= \left[1-\left(\frac{\Delta}{\text{E}}\right)^n\right]u_x = \frac{1}{\text{E}^n}\,(\text{E}^n - \Delta^n)\,u_x = \frac{1}{\text{E}^n}\left(\frac{\text{E}^n - \Delta^n}{\text{E}-\Delta}\right)u_x$$

$| \because\ 1 + \Delta = \text{E}$

$$= \frac{1}{\text{E}^n}\,[\text{E}^{n-1} + \Delta\text{E}^{n-2} + \Delta^2\text{E}^{n-3} + \ldots\ldots + \Delta^{n-1}]\,u_x$$

$$= (\text{E}^{-1} + \Delta\text{E}^{-2} + \Delta^2\text{E}^{-3} + \ldots\ldots + \Delta^{n-1}\,\text{E}^{-n})\,u_x$$

$$= u_{x-1} + \Delta u_{x-2} + \Delta^2 u_{x-3} + \ldots\ldots + \Delta^{n-1} u_{x-n}$$

To prove the second result, put $x = 3$ and $n = 3$.

Example 8. *Prove that:*

$$\Delta x^n - \frac{1}{2}\Delta^2 x^n + \frac{1.3}{2.4}\Delta^3 x^n - \frac{1.3.5}{2.4.6}\Delta^4 x^n + \ldots\ldots \; n \text{ terms}$$

$$= \left(x + \frac{1}{2}\right)^n - \left(x - \frac{1}{2}\right)^n$$

Sol.

$$\text{L.H.S.} = \Delta\left[1 - \frac{1}{2}\Delta + \frac{\left(-\frac{1}{2}\right)\left(-\frac{3}{2}\right)}{1.2}.\Delta^2 + \ldots\ldots\infty\right]x^n$$

$$= \Delta(1 + \Delta)^{-1/2} x^n = \Delta\,E^{-1/2} x^n = \Delta\left(x - \frac{1}{2}\right)^n$$

$$= \left(x + 1 - \frac{1}{2}\right)^n - \left(x - \frac{1}{2}\right)^n = \left(x + \frac{1}{2}\right)^n - \left(x - \frac{1}{2}\right)^n = \text{R.H.S.}$$

Example 9. *Prove that:*

$$u_x - \frac{1}{8}\Delta^2 u_{x-1} + \frac{1.3}{8.16}\Delta^4 u_{x-2} - \frac{1.3.5}{8.16.24}\Delta^6 u_{x-3} + \ldots\ldots$$

$$= u_{x+\frac{1}{2}} - \frac{1}{2}\Delta u_{x+\frac{1}{2}} + \frac{1}{4}\Delta^2 u_{x+\frac{1}{2}} - \frac{1}{8}\Delta^3 u_{x+\frac{1}{2}} + \ldots.$$

Sol.

$$\text{L.H.S.} = u_x - \frac{1}{8}\Delta^2 E^{-1} u_x + \frac{1.3}{8.16}\Delta^4 E^{-2} u_x - \frac{1.3.5}{8.16.24}\Delta^6 E^{-3} u_x + \ldots\ldots$$

$$= u_x - \frac{1}{2}\left(\frac{\Delta^2}{4E}\right)u_x + \frac{\left(-\frac{1}{2}\right)\left(-\frac{1}{2}-1\right)}{1.2}\left(\frac{\Delta^2}{4E}\right)^2 u_x$$

$$+ \frac{\left(-\frac{1}{2}\right)\left(-\frac{1}{2}-1\right)\left(-\frac{1}{2}-2\right)}{1.2.3}\left(\frac{\Delta^2}{4E}\right)^3 u_x + \ldots\ldots$$

$$= \left[1 + \left(-\frac{1}{2}\right)\left(\frac{\Delta^2}{4E}\right) + \frac{\left(-\frac{1}{2}\right)\left(-\frac{1}{2}-1\right)}{2!}\left(\frac{\Delta^2}{4E}\right)^2 + \ldots\ldots\right]u_x$$

$$= \left(1+\frac{\Delta^2}{4E}\right)^{-1/2} u_x = \left(\frac{4E+\Delta^2}{4E}\right)^{-1/2} u_x$$

$$= \left[\frac{4(1+\Delta)+\Delta^2}{4E}\right]^{-1/2} u_x = \left[\frac{(2+\Delta)^2}{4E}\right]^{-1/2} u_x$$

$$= \left[\frac{4E}{(2+\Delta)^2}\right]^{1/2} u_x = 2\,E^{1/2}\left(\frac{1}{2+\Delta}\right) u_x = E^{1/2}\left(1+\frac{\Delta}{2}\right)^{-1} u_x$$

$$= E^{1/2}\left(1-\frac{\Delta}{2}+\frac{\Delta^2}{2^2}-......\right) u_x$$

$$= u_{x+\frac{1}{2}} - \frac{1}{2}\Delta u_{x+\frac{1}{2}} + \frac{1}{4}\Delta^2 u_{x+\frac{1}{2}} - ...... = \text{R.H.S.}$$

Example 10. *Use the method of separation of symbols to prove the following identities:*

(*i*) $u_x + {}^xC_1\,\Delta^2 u_{x-1} + {}^xC_2\Delta^4 u_{x-2} + ... = u_0 + {}^xC_1\,\Delta u_1 + {}^xC_2\Delta^2 u_2 + ...$

(*ii*) $u_{x+n} = u_n + {}^xC_1\,\Delta u_{n-1} + {}^{x+1}C_2\,\Delta^2 u_{n-2} + {}^{x+2}C_3\,\Delta^3 u_{n-3} + ...$

(*iii*) $u_0 + u_1 + u_2 + ... + u_n = {}^{n+1}C_1\,u_0 + {}^{n+1}C_2\,\Delta u_0 + {}^{n+1}C_3\,\Delta^2 u_0 + ... + \Delta^n u_0.$

Sol. (*i*) L.H.S. $= (1 + {}^xC_1\,\Delta^2E^{-1} + {}^xC_2\,\Delta^4\,E^{-2} + ...)\,u_x$

$$= (1+\Delta^2E^{-1})^x\,u_x = \left(\frac{E+\Delta^2}{E}\right)^x u_x = \left(\frac{E^2-E+1}{E}\right)^x u_x$$

$$= \frac{1}{E^x}\,[1+E\,(E-1)]^x\,u_x = E^{-x}\,(1+\Delta E)^x\,u_x = (1+\Delta E)^x\,u_0$$

$$= (1 + {}^xC_1\,\Delta E + {}^xC_2\,\Delta^2E^2 + ...)\,u_0$$

$$= u_0 + {}^xC_1\,\Delta u_1 + {}^xC_2\,\Delta^2 u_2 + ... = \text{R.H.S.}$$

(*ii*) R.H.S. $= u_n + {}^xC_1\,\Delta E^{-1}\,u_n + {}^{x+1}C_2\,\Delta^2E^{-2}\,u_n + {}^{x+2}C_3\,\Delta^3E^{-3}u_n + ...$

$$= (1 + {}^xC_1\,\Delta E^{-1} + {}^{x+1}C_2\,\Delta^2E^{-2} + ...)\,u_n = (1-\Delta E^{-1})^{-x}\,u_n$$

$$= \left(1-\frac{\Delta}{E}\right)^{-x} u_n = \left(\frac{E-\Delta}{E}\right)^{-x} u_n$$

$$= \left(\frac{1}{E}\right)^{-x} u_n = E^x u_n = u_{n+x} = \text{L.H.S.}$$

(*iii*) L.H.S. $= u_0 + Eu_0 + E^2 u_0 + ... + E^n u_0 = (1 + E + E^2 + ... + E^n) u_0$

$$= \left(\frac{E^{n+1} - 1}{E - 1}\right) u_0 = \left[\frac{(1+\Delta)^{n+1} - 1}{\Delta}\right] u_0$$

$$= \frac{1}{\Delta} [(1 + {}^{n+1}C_1 \Delta + {}^{n+1}C_2 \Delta^2 + {}^{n+1}C_3 \Delta^3 + ... + \Delta^{n+1}) - 1] u_0$$

$$= {}^{n+1}C_1 u_0 + {}^{n+1}C_2 \Delta u_0 + {}^{n+1}C_3 \Delta^2 u_0 + ... + \Delta^n u_0 = \text{R.H.S.}$$

Example 11. *Sum the following series*

$$1^3 + 2^3 + 3^3 + ... + n^3$$

using the calculus of finite differences.

Sol. Let us denote $1^3, 2^3, 3^3$, ... by u_0, u_1, u_2, ..., respectively, we get

$$S = u_0 + u_1 + u_2 + ... + u_{n-1} = (1 + E + E^2 + ... + E^{n-1}) u_0$$

$$= \left(\frac{E^n - 1}{E - 1}\right) u_0 = \left[\frac{(1+\Delta)^n - 1}{\Delta}\right] u_0$$

$$= \frac{1}{\Delta}\left[1 + n\Delta + \frac{n(n-1)}{2!}\Delta^2 + \frac{n(n-1)(n-2)}{3!}\Delta^3 + ... + \Delta^n - 1\right] u_0$$

$$= n + \frac{n(n-1)}{2!}\Delta u_0 + \frac{n(n-1)(n-2)}{3!}\Delta^2 u_0 + ...$$

Now, $\Delta u_0 = u_1 - u_0 = 2^3 - 1^3 = 7$

and $\Delta^2 u_0 = u_2 - 2u_1 + u_0 = 3^3 - 2(2)^3 + (1)^3 = 12$

Similarly, $\Delta^3 u_0 = u_3 - 3u_2 + 3u_1 - u_0 = (4)^3 - 3(3)^3 + 3(2)^3 - (1)^3 = 6$

and $\Delta^4 u_0$, $\Delta^5 u_0$, ...are all zero as $u_r = r^3$ is a polynomial of the third degree.

$$\therefore \quad S = n + \frac{n(n-1)}{2!}(7) + \frac{n(n-1)(n-2)}{6}(12) + \frac{n(n-1)(n-2)(n-3)}{24}(6)$$

$$= \frac{n^2}{4}(n^2 + 2n + 1) = \left[\frac{n(n+1)}{2}\right]^2.$$

Example 12. *Sum to n terms, the series*

$$1.2\Delta x^n - 2.3\Delta^2 x^n + 3.4\Delta^3 x^n - 4.5\Delta^4 x^n + ...$$

Sol. Since $\Delta^{n+m} x^n = 0$ for $m \geq 1$, the sum of the above series to n terms is the same up to infinity.

Let, $S = 1.2\Delta x^n - 2.3\Delta^2 x^n + 3.4\Delta^3 x^n - ...$

$$\Delta S = 1.2\Delta^2 x^n - 2.3\Delta^3 x^n + 3.4\Delta^4 x^n - ...$$

Hence, $(\Delta + 1)S = 1.2\Delta x^n - 2.2\Delta^2 x^n + 2.3\Delta^3 x^n - 2.4\Delta^4 x^n + ...$

$$= 2\Delta(1 - 2\Delta + 3\Delta^2 - ...)x^n = 2\Delta(1 + \Delta)^{-2} x^n$$

or

$$S = 2\Delta(1 + \Delta)^{-3} x^n = 2\Delta E^{-3} x^n = 2\Delta(x - 3)^n$$

$$= 2(E - 1)(x - 3)^n = 2[E(x - 3)^n - (x - 3)^n]$$

$$= 2[(x - 2)^n - (x - 3)^n].$$

ASSIGNMENT 4.3

1. The values of a polynomial of degree 5 are tabulated below:
If $f(3)$ is known to be in error, find its correct value.

x:	0	1	2	3	4	5	6
$f(x)$:	1	2	33	254	1025	3126	7777.

2. If $y = f(x)$ is a polynomial of degree 3 and the following table gives the values of x and y, locate and correct the wrong values of y

x:	0	1	2	3	4	5	6
y:	4	10	30	75	160	294	490.

3. Prove the identities:

(*i*) $u_x - \Delta^2 u_x + \Delta^3 u_x - \Delta^5 u_x + \Delta^6 u_x - \Delta^8 u_x + ...$

$$= u_x - \Delta^2 u_{x-1} + \Delta^4 u_{x-2} - \Delta^6 u_{x-3} + \Delta^8 u_{x-4} - ......$$

(*ii*) $\sum_{x=0}^{\infty} u_{2x} = \frac{1}{2}\sum_{x=0}^{\infty} u_x + \frac{1}{4}\left(1 - \frac{\Delta}{2} + \frac{\Delta^2}{4} - ......\right) u_0.$

4. Prove that:

$$x^2 + \frac{1}{2}(1 + x)^2 + \frac{1}{2^2}(2 + x)^2 + \frac{1}{2^3}(3 + x)^2 + ... = 2(x^2 + 2x + 3)$$

using the calculus of finite differences and taking the interval of difference unity.
[**Hint:** $(1 + x)^2 = Ex^2$, $(2 + x)^2 = E^2x^2$, $(3 + x)^2 = E^3x^3$, ...]

5. If $f(E)$ is a polynomial in E such that $f(E) = a_0E^n + a_1 E^{n-1} + a_2 E^{n-2} + ... + a_n$
Prove that $f(E)\, e^x = e^x f(e)$, taking the interval of differencing unity.

We now proceed to study the use of finite difference calculus for the purpose of interpolation. This we shall do in three cases as follows:

(*i*) The value of the argument in the given data varies by an equal interval. The technique is called an **interpolation with equal intervals.**

(*ii*) The values of argument are not at equal intervals. This is known as **interpolation with unequal intervals.**

(*iii*) The technique of **central differences.**

4.14 NEWTON'S FORMULAE FOR INTERPOLATION

Newton's formula is used for constructing the interpolation polynomial. It makes use of divided differences. This result was first discovered by the Scottish mathematician James Gregory (1638–1675) a contemporary of Newton.

Gregory and Newton did extensive work on methods of interpolation but now the formula is referred to as Newton's interpolation formula. Newton has derived general forward and backward difference interpolation formulae.

4.15 NEWTON'S GREGORY FORWARD INTERPOLATION FORMULA

Let $y = f(x)$ be a function of x which assumes the values $f(a)$, $f(a + h)$, $f(a + 2h)$, ..., $f(a + nh)$ for $(n + 1)$ equidistant values a, $a + h$, $a + 2h$, ..., $a + nh$ of the independent variable x. Let $f(x)$ be a polynomial of nth degree.

$$\text{Let } f(x) = A_0 + A_1 (x - a) + A_2 (x - a)(x - a - h)$$

$$+ A_3 (x - a)(x - a - h)(x - a - 2h) + ...$$

$$+ A_n (x - a) ...... (x - a - \overline{n - 1}h) \quad (20)$$

where A_0, A_1, A_2, ..., A_n are to be determined.

Put $x = a, a + h, a + 2h$, ..., $a + nh$ in (20) successively.

For $x = a$, $\quad f(a) = A_0 \quad (21)$

For $x = a + h$, $\quad f(a + h) = A_0 + A_1 h$

$\Rightarrow \quad f(a + h) = f(a) + A_1 h \quad$ | By (21)

$$\Rightarrow \quad A_1 = \frac{\Delta f(a)}{h} \quad (22)$$

For $x = a + 2h$,

$$f(a + 2h) = A_0 + A_1 (2h) + A_2 (2h) h$$

$$= f(a) + 2h \left\{\frac{\Delta f(a)}{h}\right\} + 2h^2 A_2$$

$$\Rightarrow \quad 2h^2 A_2 = f(a + 2h) - 2f(a + h) + f(a) = \Delta^2 f(a)$$

$$\Rightarrow \quad A_2 = \frac{\Delta^2 f(a)}{2!\,h^2}$$

Similarly, $\quad A_3 = \dfrac{\Delta^3 f(a)}{3!\,h^3}$ and so on.

Thus, $\quad A_n = \dfrac{\Delta^n f(a)}{n!\,h^n}$.

From (20), $$f(x) = f(a) + (x-a)\frac{\Delta f(a)}{h} + (x-a)(x-a-h)\frac{\Delta^2 f(a)}{2!\,h^2} + \ldots\ldots + (x-a)\ldots\ldots(x-a-\overline{n-1}\,h)\frac{\Delta^n f(a)}{n!\,h^n}$$

Put $x = a + hu \Rightarrow u = \dfrac{x-a}{h}$, we have

$$f(a+hu) = f(a) + hu\frac{\Delta f(a)}{h} + \frac{(hu)(hu-h)}{2!\,h^2}\Delta^2 f(a) + \ldots\ldots + \frac{(hu)(hu-h)(hu-2h)\ldots\ldots(hu-\overline{n-1}\,h)}{n!\,h^n}\Delta^n f(a)$$

$$\Rightarrow \boxed{f(a+hu) = f(a) + u\Delta f(a) + \frac{u(u-1)}{2!}\Delta^2 f(a) + \ldots + \frac{u(u-1)(u-2)\ldots(u-n+1)}{n!}\Delta^n f(a)}$$

which is the required formula.

This formula is particularly useful for interpolating the values of $f(x)$ near the beginning of the set of values given. h is called the interval of difference, while Δ is forward difference operator.

4.15.1 Algorithm for Newton's Forward Difference Formula

Step 01. Start of the program
Step 02. Input number of terms n
Step 03. Input the array ax
Step 04. Input the array ay
Step 05. h=ax[1] – ax[0]
Step 06. for i=0; i<n-1; i++
Step 07. diff[i] [1]=ay[i + 1] – ay[i]
Step 08. End Loop i
Step 09. for j=2; j<=4; j++
Step 10. for i = 0; i <n – j; i++
Step 11. diff[i][j]=diff [i + 1] [j – 1]-diff [i][j – 1]
Step 12. End Loop i
Step 13. End Loop j
Step 14. i=0
Step 15. Repeat Step 16 until ax[i]<x
Step 16. i=i + 1
Step 17. i=i – 1;

Step 18. p=(x – ax [i])/h
Step 19. y1=p*diff[i – 1][1]
Step 20. y2=p*(p+1)*diff [i – 1][2]/2
Step 21. y3=(p+1)*p*(p-1)*diff[i –2][3]/6
Step 22. y4=(p+2)*(p+1)*p*(p – 1)*diff[i – 3][4]/24
Step 23. y=ay[i]+y1+y2+y3+y4
Step 24. Print output x, y
Step 25. End of program.

4.15.2 Flow-chart

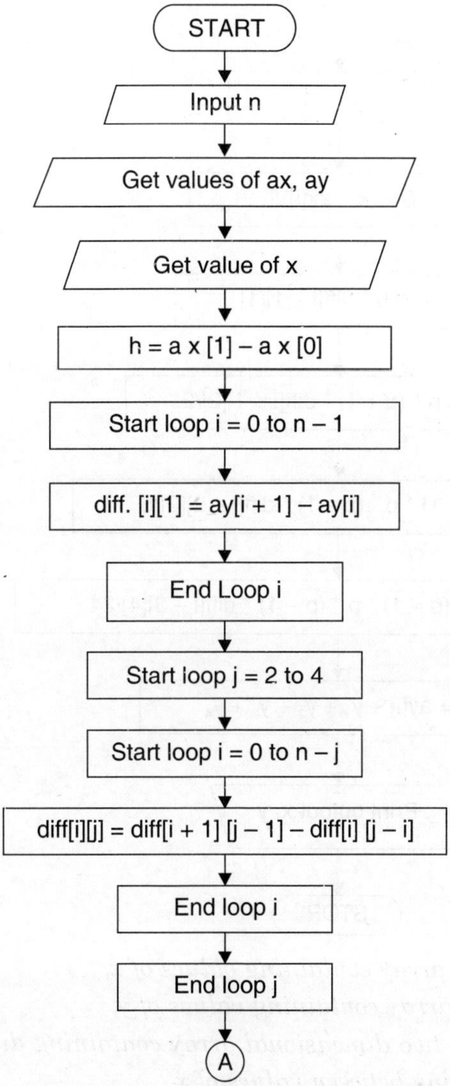

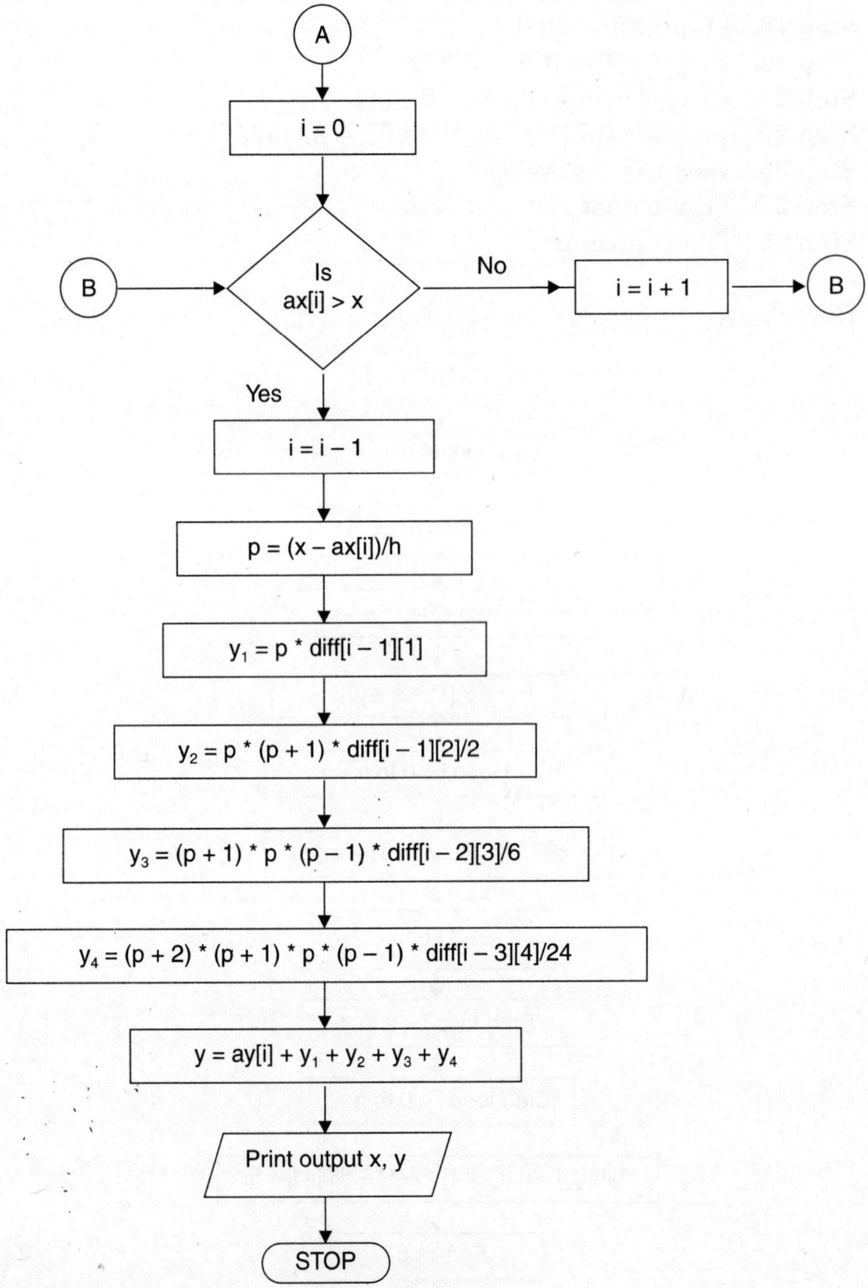

NOTE *ax is an array containing values of x,*
ay is an array containing values of y,
Diff. is a two dimensional array containing difference table,
h is spacing between values of x

* **

4.15.3 Program to Implement Newton's Forward Method of Interpolation

** */

```
//... HEADER FILES DECLARATION
# include <stdio.h>
# include <conio.h>
# include <math.h>
# include <process.h>
# include <string.h>

//... MAIN EXECUTION THREAD
void main()
 {
 //... Variable declaration Field
 //... Integer Type
 int n;                        //... Number of terms
 int i,j;                      //... Loop Variables

 //...Floating Type
 float ax[10];                 //... array limit 9
 float ay[10];                 //... array limit 9
 float x;                      //... User Querry
 float y = 0;                  //... Initial value 0
 float h;                      //... Calc. section
 float p;                      //... Calc. section
 float diff[20][20];           //... array limit 19,19
 float y1,y2,y3,y4;            //... Formulae variables

 //... Invoke Function Clear Screen
 clrscr();
 //... Input Section
 printf("\n Enter the number of terms - ");
 scanf("%d",&n);
 //... Input Sequel for array X
```

```
Printf ("\n\n Enter the value in the form of x - ");
//... Input Loop for X
for (i=0;i<n;i++)
         {
         printf("\n\n Enter the value of x%d - ",i+1);
         scanf("%f",&ax[i]);
         }

//... Input Sequel for array Y
printf("\n\n Enter the value in the form of y - ");
//... Input Loop for Y
for (i=0;i<n;i++)
     {
     printf ("\n\n Enter the value of y%d - ", i+1);
     scanf ("%f",&ay [i]);
     }

//... Inputting the required value quarry
printf("\nEnter the value of x for");
printf("\nwhich you want the value of y - ");
scanf("%f",&x);
//... Calculation and Processing Section
h=ax[1]-ax[0];
for(i=0;i<n-1;i++)
     {
     diff[i][1]=ay[i+1]-ay[i];
     }
for(j=2;j<=4;j++)
     {
     for(i=0;i<n-j;i++)
             {
             diff[i][j]=diff[i+1][j-1]-diff[i][j-1];
             }
     }
```

```
    i=0;
    do   {
         i++;
         }while(ax[i]<x);
    i--;
    p=(x-ax[i])/h;
    y1=p*diff[i-1][1];
    y2=p*(p+1)*diff[i-1][2]/2;
    y3=(p+1)*p*(p-1)*diff[i-2][3]/6;
    y4=(p+2)*(p+1)*p*(p-1)*diff[i-3][4]/24;
    //... Taking Sum
    y=ay[i]+y1+y2+y3+y4;

    //... Output Section
    printf("\nwhen x=%6.4f, y=%6.8f ",x,y);
    //... Invoke User Watch Halt Function
    Printf("\n\n\n Press Enter to Exit");
    getch();
    }
//... Termination of Main Execution Thread
```

4.15.4 Output

```
Enter the number of terms - 7
Enter the value in the form of x -
Enter the value of x1 - 100
Enter the value of x2 - 150
Enter the value of x3 - 200
Enter the value of x4 - 250
Enter the value of x5 - 300
Enter the value of x6 - 350
Enter the value of x7 - 400
Enter the value in the form of y -
Enter the value of y1 - 10.63
Enter the value of y2 - 13.03
Enter the value of y3 - 15.04
```

```
Enter the value of y4 - 16.81
Enter the value of y5 - 18.42
Enter the value of y6 - 19.9
Enter the value of y7 - 21.27
Enter the value of x for which you want the value of y-218
When X=218.0000, Y=15.69701481
Press Enter to Exit
```

EXAMPLES

Example 1. *Find the value of sin 52° from the given table:*

θ°	45°	50°	55°	60°
sin θ	0.7071	0.7660	0.8192	0.8660

Sol. $a = 45°, h = 5, x = 52$

$$\therefore \quad u = \frac{x-a}{h} = \frac{7}{5} = 1.4$$

Difference table is:

$x°$	$10^4 y$	$10^4 \Delta y$	$10^4 \Delta^2 y$	$10^4 \Delta^3 y$
		Differences		
45°	7071			
		589		
50°	7660		– 57	
		532		– 7
55°	8192		– 64	
		468		
60°	8660			

By forward difference formula,

$$f(a + hu) = f(a) + u\,\Delta f(a) + \frac{u(u-1)}{2!}\Delta^2 f(a) + \frac{u(u-1)(u-2)}{3!}\Delta^3 f(a)$$

$$\Rightarrow \quad 10^4 f(x) = 10^4 f(a) + 10^4\, u\,\Delta f(a) + 10^4 \frac{u(u-1)}{2!}\Delta^2 f(a)$$

$$+ 10^4 \frac{u(u-1)(u-2)}{3!}\Delta^3 f(a)$$

$$\Rightarrow \quad 10^4 f(52) = 10^4 f(45) + (1.4)\, 10^4 \Delta f(45) + \frac{(1.4)(1.4-1)}{2!} 10^4 \Delta^2 f(45)$$

$$+ \frac{(1.4)(1.4-1)(1.4-2)}{3!} 10^4 \Delta^3 f(45)$$

$$= 7071 + (1.4)(589) + \frac{(1.4)(.4)}{2}(-57) + \frac{(1.4)(.4)(-.6)}{6}(-7)$$

$$= 7880$$

$\therefore \quad f(52) = .7880$. Hence, $\sin 52° = 0.7880$.

Example 2. *The population of a town in the decimal census was as given below. Estimate the population for the year 1895.*

Year x:	*1891*	*1901*	*1911*	*1921*	*1931*
Population y: (in thousands)	*46*	*66*	*81*	*93*	*101*

Sol. Here $a = 1891,\ h = 10,\quad a + hu = 1895$

$$\Rightarrow \quad 1891 + 10\,u = 1895 \quad \Rightarrow \quad u = 0.4$$

The difference table is as under:

x	y	Δy	$\Delta^2 y$	$\Delta^3 y$	$\Delta^4 y$
1891	46				
		20			
1901	66		– 5		
		15		2	
1911	81		– 3		– 3
		12		– 1	
1921	93		– 4		
		8			
1931	101				

Applying Newton's forward difference formula,

$$y(1895) = y(1891) + u\, \Delta y(1891) + \frac{u(u-1)}{2!} \Delta^2 y(1891)$$

$$+ \frac{u(u-1)(u-2)}{3!} \Delta^3 y(1891)$$

$$+ \frac{u(u-1)(u-2)(u-3)}{4!} \Delta^4 y(1891)$$

$$\Rightarrow \quad y(1895) = 46 + (.4)(20) + \frac{(.4)(.4-1)}{2}(-5)$$

$$+ \frac{(.4)(.4-1)(.4-2)}{6}(2) + \frac{(.4)(.4-1)(.4-2)(.4-3)}{24}(-3)$$

$$\Rightarrow \quad y(1895) = 54.8528 \text{ thousands}$$

Hence the population for the year 1895 is **54.8528 thousands** approximately.

Example 3. *The values of f(x) for x = 0, 1, 2, ..., 6 are given by*

x:	*0*	*1*	*2*	*3*	*4*	*5*	*6*
f(x):	*2*	*4*	*10*	*16*	*20*	*24*	*38*

Estimate the value of f(3.2) using only four of the given values. Choose the four values that you think will give the best approximation.

Sol. Last four values of $f(x)$ for $x = 3, 4, 5, 6$ are taken into consideration so that 3.2 occurs in the beginning of the table.

Here $a = 3$, $h = 1, x = 3.2 \quad \therefore \quad a + h\,u = 3.2$

i.e., $3 + 1 \times u = 3.2$ or $u = 0.2$

The difference table is:

x	$f(x)$	$\Delta f(x)$	$\Delta^2 f(x)$	$\Delta^3 f(x)$
3	16			
		4		
4	20		0	
		4		10
5	24		10	
		14		
6	38			

Applying Newton's forward difference formula,

$$f(3.2) = f(3) + u\,\Delta f(3) + \frac{u(u-1)}{2!}\Delta^2 f(3) + \frac{u(u-1)(u-2)}{3!}\Delta^3 f(3)$$

$$= 16 + (.2)(4) + \frac{(.2)(.2-1)}{2}(0) + \frac{(.2)(.2-1)(.2-2)}{6}(10) = 17.28.$$

Example 4. *From the following table, find the value of* $e^{0.24}$

x: *0.1*

0.2

0.3

Sol. The difference table is:

x	10^5y	$10^5\Delta y$	$10^5\Delta^2 y$	$10^5\ \Delta^3 y$	$10^4\Delta^4 y$
0.1	110517				
		11623			
0.2	122140		1223		
		12846		127	
0.3	134986		1350		17
		14196		144	
0.4	149182		1494		
		15690			
0.5	164872				

Here $h = 0.1$. $\therefore$ $0.24 = 0.1 + 0.1 \times u$ or $u = 1.4$

Newton-Gregory forward formula is

$$y(.24) = y(.1) + u\,\Delta\, y(.1) + \frac{u(u-1)}{2!}\Delta^2\, y(.1) + \frac{u(u-1)(u-2)}{3!}\Delta^3 y(.1) + \frac{u(u-1)(u-2)(u-3)}{4!}\Delta^4\, y(.1)$$

$$\Rightarrow\ 10^5\, y(.24) = 10^5\, y(.1) + u\ 10^5\ \Delta y(.1) + \frac{u(u-1)}{2!}\ 10^5\ \Delta^2 y(.1) + \frac{u(u-1)(u-2)}{3!}\ 10^5\ \Delta^3 y(.1) + \frac{u(u-1)(u-2)(u-3)}{4!}\ 10^5\ \Delta^4 y(.1)$$

$$\Rightarrow\ 10^5\, y(.24) = 110517 + (1.4)(11623) + \frac{(1.4)(1.4-1)}{2}(1223) + \frac{(1.4)(1.4-1)(1.4-2)}{3!}(127) + \frac{(1.4)(1.4-1)(1.4-2)(1.4-3)}{4!}(17)$$

$$= 127124.9088$$

$\therefore$ $y(.24) = 1.271249088$

Hence, $e^{.24} = 1.271249088$.

Example 5. *From the following table of half-yearly premiums for policies maturing at different ages, estimate the premium for policies maturing at age of 46.*

Age	*45*	*50*	*55*	*60*	*65*
Premium (in dollars)	*114.84*	*96.16*	*83.32*	*74.48*	*68.48*

Sol. The difference table is:

Age *(x)*	*Premium* *(in dollars)* *(y)*	Δy	$\Delta^2 y$	$\Delta^3 y$	$\Delta^4 y$
45	114.84				
		– 18.68			
50	96.16		5.84		
		– 12.84		– 1.84	
55	83.32		4		.68
		– 8.84		– 1.16	
60	74.48		2.84		
		– 6			
65	68.48				

Here $h = 5, a = 45, a + hu = 46$

$\therefore \quad 45 + 5u = 46 \Rightarrow u = .2$

By Newton's forward difference formula,

$$y_{46} = y_{45} + u\,\Delta y_{45} + \frac{u(u-1)}{2!}\Delta^2 y_{45} + \frac{u(u-1)(u-2)}{3!}\Delta^3 y_{45} + \frac{u(u-1)(u-2)(u-3)}{4!}\Delta^4 y_{45}$$

$$= 114.84 + (.2)(-18.68) + \frac{(.2)(.2-1)}{2!}(5.84) + \frac{(.2)(.2-1)(.2-2)}{3!}(-1.84) + \frac{(.2)(.2-1)(.2-2)(.2-3)}{4!}(.68)$$

$$= 110.525632$$

Hence the premium for policies maturing at the age of 46 is **\$ 110.52.**

Example 6. *From the table, estimate the number of students who obtained scores between 40 and 45.*

Scores:	*30—40*	*40—50*	*50—60*	*60—70*	*70—80*
Number of students:	*31*	*42*	*51*	*35*	*31.*

Sol. The difference table is:

Scores less than (*x*)	*y*	Δy	$\Delta^2 y$	$\Delta^3 y$	$\Delta^4 y$
40	31				
		42			
50	73		9		
		51		– 25	
60	124		– 16		37
		35		12	
70	159		– 4		
		31			
80	190				

We shall find y_{45}, number of students with scores less than 45.

$$a = 40, h = 10, a + hu = 45.$$

$$\therefore \quad 40 + 10u = 45 \Rightarrow u = .5$$

By Newton's forward difference formula,

$$y(45) = y(40) + u\,\Delta y(40) + \frac{u(u-1)}{2!}\Delta^2 y(40) + \frac{u(u-1)(u-2)}{3!}\Delta^3 y(40) + \frac{u(u-1)(u-2)(u-3)}{4!}\Delta^4 y(40)$$

$$= 31 + (.5)(42) + \frac{(.5)(.5-1)}{2}(9) + \frac{(.5)(.5-1)(.5-2)}{6}(-25) + \frac{(.5)(.5-1)(.5-2)(.5-3)}{24}(37)$$

$$= 47.8672 \approx 48$$

Hence, the number of students getting scores less than 45 = 48

By the number of students getting scores less than 40 = 31

Hence, the number of students getting scores between 40 and 45 = 48 – 31 = 17.

Example 7. *Find the cubic polynomial which takes the following values:*

x:	*0*	*1*	*2*	*3*
f(x):	*1*	*2*	*1*	*10.*

Sol. Let us form the difference table:

x	y	Δy	$\Delta^2 y$	$\Delta^3 y$
0	1			
		1		
1	2		−2	
		−1		12
2	1		10	
		9		
3	10			

Here, $h = 1$. Hence, using the formula,

$$x = a + hu$$

and choosing $a = 0$, we get $x = u$

∴ By Newton's forward difference formula,

$$y = y_0 + x\,\Delta y_0 + \frac{x(x-1)}{2!}\Delta^2 y_0 + \frac{x(x-1)(x-2)}{3!}\Delta^3 y_0$$

$$= 1 + x(1) + \frac{x(x-1)}{2!}(-2) + \frac{x(x-1)(x-2)}{3!}(12)$$

$$= 2x^3 - 7x^2 + 6x + 1$$

Hence, the required cubic polynomial is

$$y = f(x) = 2x^3 - 7x^2 + 6x + 1.$$

Example 8. *The following table gives the scores secured by100 students in the Numerical Analysis subject:*

Range of scores:	*30—40*	*40—50*	*50—60*	*60—70*	*70—80*
Number of students:	*25*	*35*	*22*	*11*	*7*

Use Newton's forward difference interpolation formula to find.

(i) the number of students who got scores more than 55.

(ii) the number of students who secured scores in the range between 36 and 45.

Sol. The given table is re-arranged as follows:

Scores obtained	*Number of students*
Less than 40	25
Less than 50	60
Less than 60	82
Less than 70	93
Less than 80	100

(*i*) Here, $a = 40$, $h = 10$, $a + hu = 55$

$\therefore \quad 40 + 10u = 55 \quad \Rightarrow \quad u = 1.5$

First, we find the number of students who got scores less than 55.

The difference table follows:

Scores obtained less than	*Number of students = y*	Δy	$\Delta^2 y$	$\Delta^3 y$	$\Delta^4 y$
40	**25**				
		35			
50	60		**– 13**		
		22		**2**	
60	82		– 11		**5**
		11		7	
70	93		– 4		
		7			
80	100				

Applying Newton's forward difference formula,

$$y_{55} = y_{40} + u\,\Delta y_{40} + \frac{u(u-1)}{2!}\Delta^2 y_{40} + \frac{u(u-1)(u-2)}{3!}\Delta^3 y_{40} + \frac{u(u-1)(u-2)(u-3)}{4!}\Delta^4 y_{40}$$

$$= 25 + (1.5)(35) + \frac{(1.5)(.5)}{2!}(-13) + \frac{(1.5)(.5)(-.5)}{3!}(2) + \frac{(1.5)(.5)(-.5)(-1.5)}{4!}(5)$$

$$= 71.6171875 \approx 72$$

There are 72 students who got scores less than 55.

$\therefore$ Number of students who got scores more than 55 = 100 – 72 = 28

(*ii*) To calculate the number of students securing scores between 36 and 45, take the difference of y_{45} and y_{36}.

$$u = \frac{x-a}{h} = \frac{36-40}{10} = -.4$$

Also,

$$u = \frac{45-40}{10} = .5$$

Newton's forward difference formula:

$$y_{36} = y_{40} + u\,\Delta y_{40} + \frac{u(u-1)}{2!}\Delta^2 y_{40} + \frac{u(u-1)(u-2)}{3!}\Delta^3 y_{40} + \frac{u(u-1)(u-2)(u-3)}{4!}\Delta^4 y_{40}$$

$$= 25 + (-.4)(35) + \frac{(-.4)(-1.4)}{2!}(-13) + \frac{(-.4)(-1.4)(-2.4)}{3!}(2) + \frac{(-.4)(-1.4)(-2.4)(-3.4)}{4!}(5) = 7.864 \approx 8$$

Also, $$y_{45} = y_{40} + u\,\Delta y_{40} + \frac{u(u-1)}{2!}\Delta^2 y_{40} + \frac{u(u-1)(u-2)}{3!}\Delta^3 y_{40} + \frac{u(u-1)(u-2)(u-3)}{4!}\Delta^4 y_{40}$$

$$= 25 + (.5)(35) + \frac{(.5)(-.5)}{2}(-13) + \frac{(.5)(-.5)(-1.5)}{6}(2) + \frac{(.5)(-.5)(-1.5)(-2.5)}{24}(5)$$

$$= 44.0546 \approx 44.$$

Hence, the number of students who secured scores between 36 and 45 is $y_{45} - y_{36} = 44 - 8 = 36$.

Example 9. *The following are the numbers of deaths in four successive ten year age groups. Find the number of deaths at 45—50 and 50—55.*

Age group:	*25—35*	*35—45*	*45—55*	*55—65*
Deaths:	*13229*	*18139*	*24225*	*31496.*

Sol. Difference table of cumulative frequencies:

Age upto x	*Number of deaths f(x)*	*Δf(x)*	*Δ²f(x)*	*Δ³f(x)*
35	13229			
		18139		
45	31368		6086	
		24225		1185
55	55593		7271	
		31496		
65	87089			

Here, $h = 10, a = 35, a + hu = 50$

$\therefore \quad 35 + 10u = 50 \quad \Rightarrow \quad u = 1.5$

By Newton's forward difference formula,

$$y_{50} = y_{35} + u\,\Delta y_{35} + \frac{u(u-1)}{2!}\Delta^2 y_{35} + \frac{u(u-1)(u-2)}{3!}\Delta^3 y_{35}$$

$$= 13229 + (1.5)(18139) + \frac{(1.5)(.5)}{2}(6086) + \frac{(1.5)(.5)(-.5)}{6}(1185)$$

$$= 42645.6875 \approx 42646$$

$\therefore$ Deaths at ages beween 45 – 50 are 42646 – 31368 = 11278

and Deaths at ages between 50 – 55 are 55593 – 42646 = 12947.

Example 10. *If p, q, r, s are the successive entries corresponding to equidistant arguments in a table, show that when the third differences are taken into account, the entry corresponding to the argument half way between the arguments at q and r is* $A + \left(\frac{B}{24}\right)$*, where A is the arithmetic mean of q and r and B is arithmetic mean of* $3q - 2p - s$ *and* $3r - 2s - p$.

Sol. $A = \frac{q+r}{2} \quad \Rightarrow \quad q + r = 2A$

$$B = \frac{(3q - 2p - s) + (3r - 2s - p)}{2} = \frac{3q + 3r - 3p - 3s}{2}$$

$$= \frac{3(q+r)}{2} - \frac{3(p+s)}{2}$$

Let the entries $p, q, r,$ and s correspond to $x = a, a + h, a + 2h,$ and $a + 3h$, respectively. Then the value of the argument lying half way between $a + h$ and $a + 2h$ will be $a + h + \left(\frac{h}{2}\right)$ *i.e.,* $a + \frac{3h}{2}$.

Hence $\quad a + mh = a + \frac{3}{2}h \quad \Rightarrow \quad m = \frac{3}{2}$

Let us now construct the difference table:

x	$f(x)$	$\Delta f(x)$	$\Delta^2 f(x)$	$\Delta^3 f(x)$
a	p			
		$q - p$		
$a + h$	q		$r - 2q + p$	
		$r - q$		$s - 3r + 3q - p$
$a + 2h$	r		$s - 2r + q$	
		$s - r$		
$a + 3h$	s			

Using Newton's Gregory Interpolation formula up to third difference only and taking $m = 3/2$, we get

$$f\left(a+\frac{3}{2}h\right) = f(a) + \frac{3}{2}\Delta f(a) + \frac{\frac{3}{2}\left(\frac{3}{2}-1\right)}{2}\Delta^2 f(a) + \frac{\frac{3}{2}\left(\frac{3}{2}-1\right)\left(\frac{3}{2}-2\right)}{6}\Delta^3 f(a)$$

$$= p + \frac{3}{2}(q-p) + \frac{3}{8}(r-2q+p) - \frac{1}{16}(s-3r+3q-p)$$

$$= \frac{(16p - 24q - 24p + 6r - 12q + 6p - s + 3r - 3q + p)}{16}$$

$$= \frac{1}{16}(-p + 9q + 9r - s) = \frac{9}{16}(q+r) - \left(\frac{p+s}{16}\right)$$

$$= \frac{9}{16}(2A) - \frac{2}{3}\left(\frac{3A - B}{16}\right)$$

$$= \frac{9}{8}A - \frac{1}{8}A + \frac{B}{24} = A + \frac{B}{24}.$$

ASSIGNMENT 4.4

1. The following table gives the distance in nautical miles of the visible horizon for the given heights in feet above the earth's surface.

x:	100	150	200	250	300	350	400
y:	10.63	13.03	15.04	16.81	18.42	19.9	21.27

Use Newton's forward formula to find y when $x = 218$ ft.

2. If l_x represents the number of persons living at age x in a life table, find, as accurately as the data will permit, l_x for values of $x = 35$, 42 and 47. Given

$$l_{20} = 512,\ l_{30} = 390,\ l_{40} = 360,\ l_{50} = 243.$$

3. The values of $f(x)$ for $x = 0, 1, 2, ..., 6$ are given by

x:	0	1	2	3	4	5	6
$f(x)$:	1	3	11	31	69	131	223

Estimate the value of $f(3.4)$, using only four of the given values.

4. Given that:

x:	1	2	3	4	5	6
$y(x)$:	0	1	8	27	64	125

Find the value of $f(2.5)$.

5. Ordinates $f(x)$ of a normal curve in terms of standard deviation x are given as

x:	1.00	1.02	1.04	1.06	1.08
$f(x)$:	0.2420	0.2371	0.2323	0.2275	0.2227

Find the ordinate for standard deviation $x = 1.025$.

6. Using Newton's formula for interpolation, estimate the population for the year 1905 from the table:

Year	*Population*
1891	98,752
1901	132,285
1911	168,076
1921	195,690
1931	246,050

7. Find the number of students from the following data who secured scores not more than 45

Scores range:	30—40	40—50	50—60	60—70	70—80
Number of students:	35	48	70	40	22

8. Find the number of men getting wages between \$ 10 and \$ 15 from the following table:

Wages (in \$):	0—10	10—20	20—30	30—40
Frequency:	9	30	35	42

9. Following are the scores obtained by 492 candidates in a certain examination

Scores	*Number of candidates*
0—40	210
40—45	43
45—50	54
50—55	74
55—60	32
60—65	79

Find out the number of candidates
(*a*) who secured scores more than 48 but not more than 50;
(*b*) who secured scores less than 48 but not less than 45.

10. Use Newton's forward difference formula to obtain the interpolating polynomial $f(x)$, satisfying the following data:

x:	1	2	3	4
$f(x)$:	26	18	4	1

If another point $x = 5$, $f(x) = 26$ is added to the above data, will the interpolating polynomial be the same as before or different. Explain why.

11. The table below gives value of tan x for $.10 \le x \le .30$.

x:	.10	.15	.20	.25	.30
tan x:	.1003	.1511	.2027	.2553	.3093

Evaluate tan 0.12 using Newton's forward difference formula

12. (*i*) Estimate the value of $f(22)$ from the following available data:

x:	20	25	30	35	40	45
$f(x)$:	354	332	291	260	231	204

(*ii*) Find the cubic polynomial which takes the following values:

$$y(0) = 1, \quad y(1) = 0, \quad y(2) = 1 \text{ and } y(3) = 10$$

Hence or otherwise obtain $y(4)$.

(*iii*) Use Newton's method to find a polynomial $p(x)$ of lowest possible degree such that $p(n) = 2^n$ for $n = 0, 1, 2, 3, 4$.

4.16 NEWTON'S GREGORY BACKWARD INTERPOLATION FORMULA

Let $y = f(x)$ be a function of x which assumes the values $f(a)$, $f(a + h)$, $f(a + 2h)$, ..., $f(a + nh)$ for $(n + 1)$ equidistant values $a, a + h, a + 2h, ..., a + nh$ of the independent variable x.

Let $f(x)$ be a polynomial of the nth degree.

Let, $$f(x) = A_0 + A_1(x - a - nh) + A_2 (x - a - nh)(x - a - \overline{n-1}\, h) + ...$$
$$+ A_n (x - a - nh)(x - a - \overline{n-1}\, h) ...... (x - a - h)$$

where $A_0, A_1, A_2, A_3, ..., A_n$ are to be determined. (23)

Put $x = a + nh, a + \overline{n-1}\, h, ..., a$ in (23) respectively.

Put $x = a + nh$, then $f(a + nh) = A_0$ (24)

Put $x = a + (n - 1)h$, then

$$f(a + \overline{n-1}\, h) = A_0 - h A_1 = f(a + nh) - h A_1 \qquad | \text{ By (24)}$$

$$\Rightarrow \qquad A_1 = \frac{\nabla f(a + nh)}{h} \tag{25}$$

Put $x = a + (n - 2)h$, then

$$f(a + \overline{n-2}\, h) = A_0 - 2hA_1 + (-2h)(-h) A_2$$

$$\Rightarrow \qquad 2\,!\,h^2 A_2 = f(a + \overline{n-2}\,h) - f(a + nh) + 2\nabla f(a + nh) - \nabla^2 f(a + nh)$$

$$A_2 = \frac{\nabla^2 f(a+nh)}{2\,!\,h^2} \tag{26}$$

Proceeding, we get

$$A_n = \frac{\nabla^n f(a+nh)}{n\,!\,h^n} \tag{27}$$

Substituting the values in (24), we get

$$f(x) = f(a + nh) + (x - a - nh)\frac{\nabla f(a+nh)}{h} + \ldots\ldots + (x - a - nh)(x - a - \overline{n-1}\,h) \ldots\ldots (x - a - h)\frac{\nabla^n f(a+nh)}{n\,!\,h^n} \tag{28}$$

Put $x = a + nh + uh$, then

$$x - a - nh = uh$$

and $\quad x - a - (n - 1)h = (u + 1)h$

$$\vdots$$

$$x - a - h = (u + \overline{n-1})\,h$$

$\therefore$ (28) becomes,

$$f(x) = f(a + nh) + u\,\nabla f(a + nh) + \frac{u(u+1)}{2\,!}\nabla^2 f(a + nh) + \ldots\ldots + uh\,.\,(u + 1)h \ldots\ldots (u + \overline{n-1})(h)\frac{\nabla^n f(a+nh)}{n\,!\,h^n}$$

or

$$\boxed{f(a + nh + uh) = f(a + nh) + u\,\nabla f(a + nh) + \frac{u(u+1)}{2\,!}\nabla^2 f(a + nh) + \ldots\ldots + \frac{u(u+1)\ldots\ldots(u+\overline{n-1})}{n\,!}\nabla^n f(a + nh)}$$

which is the required formula.

This formula is useful when the value of $f(x)$ is required near the end of the table.

4.16.1 Algorithm for Newton's Backward Difference formula

Step 01. Start of the program.

Step 02. Input number of terms n

Step 03. Input the array ax

Step 04. Input the array ay

Step 05. h=ax[1]-ax[0]

Step 06. for i=0; i<n–1; i++

Step 07. diff[i][1]=ay[i+1]–ay[i]

Step 08. End Loop i

Step 09. for j = 2; j < = 4; j + +

Step 10. for i=0; i<n–j; i++

Step 11. diff[i][j]=diff[i+1][j–1]–diff [i][j–1]

Step 12. End Loop i

Step 13. End Loop j

Step 14. i=0

Step 15. Repeat Step 16 until (!ax[i]<x)

Step 16. i=i+1

Step 17. x0=mx[i]

Step 18. sum=0

Step 19. y0=my[i]

Step 20. fun=1

Step 21. p=(x–x0)/h

Step 22. sum=y0

Step 23. for k=1; k<=4; k++

Step 24. fun=(fun*(p–(k–1)))/k

Step 25. sum=sum+fun*diff[i][k]

Step 26. End loop k

Step 27. Print Output x,sum

Step 28. End of Program

4.16.2 Flow-chart

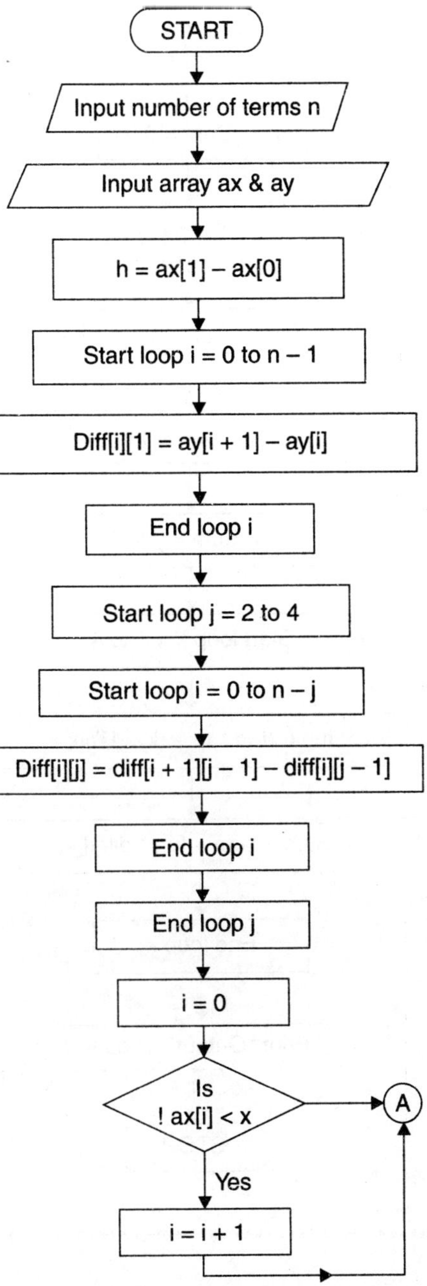

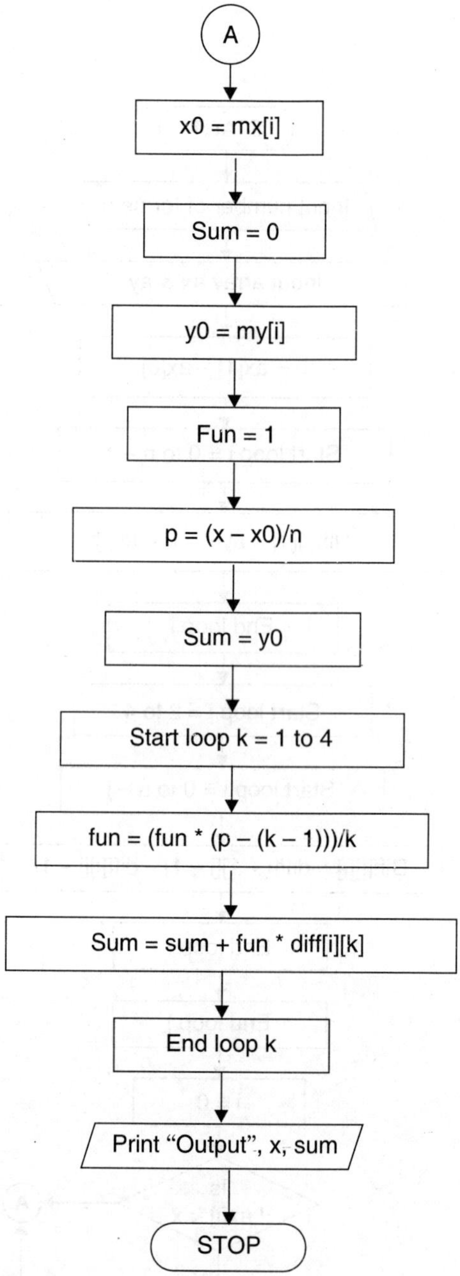
A
x0 = mx[i]
Sum = 0
y0 = my[i]
Fun = 1
p = (x – x0)/n
Sum = y0
Start loop k = 1 to 4
fun = (fun * (p – (k – 1)))/k
Sum = sum + fun * diff[i][k]
End loop k
Print "Output", x, sum
STOP

* **

4.16.3 Program to Implement Newton's Backward Method of Interpolation

```
* ******************************************************************************** */

    //...HEADER FILES DECLARATION
    # include <stdio.h>
    # include <conio.h>
    # include <math.h>
    # include <process.h>
    # include <string.h>

    //... MAIN EXECUTION THREAD
    void main()
     {
     //...Variable declaration Field
     //...Integer Type
     int n;                              //...Number of terms
     int i,j,k;                          //...Loop Variables

     //...Floating Type
     float my[10];                       //... array limit 9
     float my[10];                       //... array limit 9
     float x;                            //... User Querry
     float x0 = 0;                       //... Initial value 0
     float y0;                           //... Calc. Section
     float sum;                          //... Calc. Section
     float h;                            //... Calc. Section
     float fun;                          //... Calc. Section
     float p;                            //... Calc. Section
     float diff[20][20];                 //... array limit 19,19
     float y1, y2, y3, y4;               //... Formulae variables

     //...Invoke Function Clear Screen
     clrscr();

     //...Input Section
```

```
printf("\n Enter the number of terms - ");
scanf("%d",&n);
//...Input Sequel for array X
printf("\n\n Enter the value in the form of x - ");
//...Input Loop for X
for (i=0;i<n;i++)
    {
    printf("\n\n Enter the value of x%d - ",i+1);
    scanf ("%f",&mx[i]);
    }
//...Input Sequel for array Y
printf ("\n\n Enter the value in the form of y -");
//...Input Loop for Y
for (i=0;i<n;i++)
    {
    printf ("\n\n Enter the value of y%d - ",i+1);
    scanf ("%f",&my[i]);
    }
//...Inputting the required value query
printf ("\nEnter the value of x for");
printf("\nwhich you want the value of y - ");
scanf("%f",&x);
//...Calculation and Processing Section
h=mx[1]-mx[0];
for(i=0;i<n-1;i++)
    {
    diff[i][1]=my[i+1]-my[i];
    }
for (j=2;j<=4;j++)
    {
    for (i=0;i<n-j;i++)
        {
        diff[i][j]=diff[i+1][j-1]-diff[i][j-1];
        }
    }
```

```
i=0;
while(!mx[i]>x)
      {
      i++;
      }
x0=mx[i];
sum=0;
y0=my[i];
fun=1;
p=(x-x0)/h;
sum=y0;
for (k=1;k<=4;k++)
      {
      fun=(fun*(p-(k-1)))/k;
      sum=sum+fun*diff[i][k];
      }

//...Output Section
printf ("\nwhen x=%6.4f,y=%6.8f",x,sum);
//...Invoke User Watch Halt Function
printf("\n\n\n Press Enter to Exit");
getch( );
}
//...Termination of Main Execution Thread
```

4.16.4 Output

```
Enter the number of terms-7
Enter the value in the form of x-
Enter the value of x1 - 100
Enter the value of x2 - 150
Enter the value of x3 - 200
Enter the value of x4 - 250
Enter the value of x5 - 300
Enter the value of x6 - 350
Enter the value of x7 - 400
```

```
Enter the value in the form of y -
Enter the value of y1 - 10.63
Enter the value of y2 - 13.03
Enter the value of y3 - 15.04
Enter the value of y4 - 16.81
Enter the value of y5 - 18.42
Enter the value of y6 - 19.90
Enter the value of y7 - 21.27
Enter the value of x for which you want the value of y - 410
When x = 410.0000, y = 21.34462738
Press Enter to Exit
```

EXAMPLES

Example 1. *The population of a town was as given. Estimate the population for the year 1925.*

Year (x):	*1891*	*1901*	*1911*	*1921*	*1931*
Population (y): (in thousands)	*46*	*66*	*81*	*93*	*101*

Sol. Here, $a + nh = 1931, h = 10, \quad a + nh + uh = 1925$

$$\therefore \qquad u = \frac{1925 - 1931}{10} = -0.6$$

The difference table is:

x	y	∇y	$\nabla^2 y$	$\nabla^3 y$	$\nabla^4 y$
1891	46				
		20			
1901	66		– 5		
		15		2	
1911	81		– 3		– 3
		12		– 1	
1921	93		– 4		
		8			
1931	101				

Applying Newton's Backward difference formula, we get

$$y_{1925} = y_{1931} + u\nabla y_{1931} + \frac{u(u+1)}{2!}\nabla^2 y_{1931}$$

$$+ \frac{u(u+1)(u+2)}{3!}\nabla^3 y_{1931} + \frac{u(u+1)(u+2)(u+3)}{4!}\nabla^4 y_{1931}$$

$$= 101 + (-.6)(8) + \frac{(-.6)(.4)}{2!}(-4) + \frac{(-.6)(.4)(1.4)}{3!}(-1)$$

$$+ \frac{(-.6)(.4)(1.4)(2.4)}{4!}(-3)$$

$$= 96.8368 \text{ thousands.}$$

Hence the population for the year 1925 = 96836.8 ≈ 96837.

Example 2. *The population of a town is as follows:*

Year:	*1921*	*1931*	*1941*	*1951*	*1961*	*1971*
Population: (in Lakhs)	*20*	*24*	*29*	*36*	*46*	*51*

Estimate the increase in population during the period 1955 to 1961.

Sol. Here, $a + nh = 1971$, $h = 10$, $a + nh + uh = 1955$

$\therefore$ $1971 + 10u = 1955 \Rightarrow u = -1.6$

The difference table is:

x	y	∇y	$\nabla^2 y$	$\nabla^3 y$	$\nabla^4 y$	$\nabla^5 y$
1921	20					
		4				
1931	24		1			
		5		1		
1941	29		2		0	
		7		1		−9
1951	36		3		−9	
		10		−8		
1961	46		−5			
		5				
1971	51					

Applying Newton's backward difference formula, we get

$$y_{1955} = y_{1971} + u\nabla y_{1971} + \frac{u(u+1)}{2!}\nabla^2 y_{1971} + \frac{u(u+1)(u+2)}{3!}\nabla^3 y_{1971}$$

$$+ \frac{u(u+1)(u+2)(u+3)}{4!}\nabla^4 y_{1971} + \frac{u(u+1)(u+2)(u+3)(u+4)}{5!}\nabla^5 y_{1971}$$

$$= 51 + (-1.6)(5) + \frac{(-1.6)(-0.6)}{2!}(-5) + \frac{(-1.6)(-0.6)(0.4)}{6}(-8)$$

$$+ \frac{(-1.6)(-0.6)(.4)(1.4)}{24}(-9) + \frac{(-1.6)(-0.6)(0.4)(1.4)(2.4)}{120}(-9)$$

$$= 39.789632$$

$\therefore$ Increase in population during period 1955 to 1961 is

$$= 46 - 39.789632 = 6.210368 \text{ Lakhs}$$

$$= 621036.8 \text{ Lakhs.}$$

Example 3. *In the following table, values of y are consecutive terms of a series of which 23.6 is the 6th term. Find the first and tenth terms of the series.*

x:	*3*	*4*	*5*	*6*	*7*	*8*	*9*
y:	*4.8*	*8.4*	*14.5*	*23.6*	*36.2*	*52.8*	*73.9.*

Sol. The difference table is:

x	y	Δy	$\Delta^2 y$	$\Delta^3 y$	$\Delta^4 y$
3	4.8				
		3.6			
4	8.4		2.5		
		6.1		0.5	
5	14.5		3		0
		9.1		0.5	
6	23.6		3.5		0
		12.6		0.5	
7	36.2		4		0
		16.6		0.5	
8	52.8		4.5		
		21.1			
9	73.9				

To find the first term, we use Newton's forward interpolation formula.

Here, $a = 3, \quad h = 1, \quad x = 1 \quad \therefore \quad u = \dfrac{x-a}{h} = -2$

We have $y_1 = y_3 + u\Delta y_3 + \dfrac{u(u-1)}{2!}\Delta^2 y_3 + \dfrac{u(u-1)(u-2)}{3!}\Delta^3 y_3$

$$= 4.8 + (-2) \times 3.6 + \frac{(-2)(-3)}{2}(2.5) + \frac{(-2)(-3)(-4)}{6}(0.5)$$

$$= 3.1$$

To obtain the tenth term, we use Newton's Backward interpolation formula

$$a + nh = 9, h = 1, a + nh + uh = 10$$

$\therefore \quad 10 = 9 + u \Rightarrow u = 1$

$\therefore \quad y_{10} = y_9 + u\nabla y_9 + \dfrac{u(u+1)}{2!}\nabla^2 y_9 + \dfrac{u(u+1)(u+2)}{3!}\nabla^3 y_9$

$$= 73.9 + 21.1 + 4.5 + .5 = 100.$$

Example 4. *Given log x for x = 40, 45, 50, 55, 60 and 65 according to the following table:*

x:	*40*	*45*	*50*	*55*	*60*	*65*
log x:	*1.60206*	*1.65321*	*1.69897*	*1.74036*	*1.77815*	*1.81291*

Find the value of log 5875.

Sol. The difference table is:

x	$10^5 \log x = 10^5 y_x$	$10^5 \nabla y_x$	$10^5 \nabla^2 y_x$	$10^5 \nabla^3 y_x$	$10^5 \nabla^4 y_x$	$10^5 \nabla^5 y_x$
40	160206					
		5115				
45	165321		– 539			
		4576		102		
50	169897		– 437		– 25	
		4139		77		5
55	174036		– 360		– 20	
		3779		57		
60	177815		– 303			
		3476				
65	181291					

Newton's Backward difference formula is

$$f(a + nh + uh) = f(a + nh) + u\nabla f(a + nh) + \frac{u(u+1)}{2!}\nabla^2 f(a + nh)$$

$$+ \frac{u(u+1)(u+2)}{3!}\nabla^3 f(a + nh) + \frac{u(u+1)(u+2)(u+3)}{4!}\nabla^4 f(a + nh)$$

$$+ \frac{u(u+1)(u+2)(u+3)(u+4)}{5!}\nabla^5 f(a + nh) \qquad (29)$$

First we shall find the value of log(58.75).

Here, $a + nh = 65,\ h = 5,\ a + nh + uh = 58.75$

$\therefore$ $65 + 5u = 58.75 \Rightarrow u = -1.25$

From (29),

$$10^5 f(58.75) = 181291 + (-1.25)(3476) + \frac{(-1.25)(-.25)}{2!}(-303)$$

$$+ \frac{(-1.25)(-.25)(.75)}{3!}(57) + \frac{(-1.25)(-.25)(.75)(1.75)}{4!}(-20)$$

$$+ \frac{(-1.25)(-.25)(.75)(1.75)(2.75)}{5!}(5)$$

$\Rightarrow$ $10^5 f(58.75) = 176900.588$

$\therefore$ $f(58.75) = \log 58.75 = 176900.588 \times 10^{-5} = 1.76900588$

Hence,

log 5875 = 3.76900588 | $\because$ Mantissa remain the same

Example 5. *Calculate the value of tan 48° 15′ from the following table:*

x°:	*45*	*46*	*47*	*48*	*49*	*50*
tan x°:	*1.00000*	*1.03053*	*1.07237*	*1.11061*	*1.15037*	*1.19175*

Sol. Here $a + nh = 50,\ h = 1,\ a + nh + uh = 48°\ 15' = 48.25°$

$\therefore$ $50 + u(1) = 48.25 \Rightarrow u = -1.75$

The difference table is:

$x°$	10^5y	$10^5\nabla y$	$10^5\nabla^2y$	$10^5\nabla^3y$	$10^5\nabla^4y$	$10^5\nabla^5y$
45	100000					
		3553				
46	103553		131			
		3648		9		
47	107237		140		3	
		3824		12		– 5
48	111061		152		– 2	
		3976		10		
49	115037		162			
		4138				
50	119175					

$$y_{a+nh+uh} = y_{a+nh} + u\nabla y_{a+nh} + \frac{u(u+1)}{2}\nabla^2 y_{a+nh} + \frac{u(u+1)(u+2)}{3!}\nabla^3 y_{a+nh}$$

$$+ \frac{u(u+1)(u+2)(u+3)}{4!}\nabla^4 y_{a+nh} + \frac{u(u+1)(u+2)(u+3)(u+4)}{5!}\nabla^5 y_{a+nh}$$

$$\therefore\ 10^5 y_{48.25} = 119175 + (-1.75)\times 4138 + \frac{(-1.75)\times(-0.75)}{2}\times 162$$

$$+ \frac{(-1.75)(-0.75)(0.25)}{3!}\times 10 + \frac{(-1.75)(-.75)(.25)(1.25)}{4!}(-2)$$

$$+ \frac{(-1.75)(-.75)(.25)(1.25)(2.25)}{5!}(-5)$$

$$\Rightarrow \quad 10^5 y_{48.25} = 112040.2867$$

$$\therefore \quad y_{48.25} = \tan 48°15' = 1.120402867.$$

Example 6. *From the following table of half-yearly premium for policies maturing at different ages, estimate the premium for a policy maturing at the age of 63:*

Age:	*45*	*50*	*55*	*60*	*65*
Premium: (in dollars)	*114.84*	*96.16*	*83.32*	*74.48*	*68.48*

Sol. The difference table is:

Age (*x*)	*Premium* (*in dollars*) (*y*)	∇y	$\nabla^2 y$	$\nabla^3 y$	$\nabla^4 y$
45	114.84				
		– 18.68			
50	96.16		5.84		
		– 12.84		– 1.84	
55	83.32		4		.68
		– 8.84		– 1.16	
60	74.48		2.84		
		– 6			
65	68.48				

Here $\quad a + nh = 65, \quad h = 5, a + nh + uh = 63$

$\therefore \quad 65 + 5u = 63 \quad \Rightarrow \quad u = -.4$

By Newton's backward difference formula,

$$y(63) = y(65) + u\nabla y(65) + \frac{u(u+1)}{2!}\nabla^2 y(65) + \frac{u(u+1)(u+2)}{3!}\nabla^3 y(65) + \frac{u(u+1)(u+2)(u+3)}{4!}\nabla^4 y(65)$$

$$= 68.48 + (-.4)(-6) + \frac{(-.4)(.6)}{2}(2.84) + \frac{(-.4)(.6)(1.6)}{6}(-1.16) + \frac{(-.4)(.6)(1.6)(2.6)}{24}(.68)$$

$$= 70.585152$$

ASSIGNMENT 4.5

1. From the following table find the value of tan 17°

$\theta°$:	0	4	8	12	16	20	24
tan $\theta°$:	0	0.0699	0.1405	0.2126	0.2867	0.3640	0.4402

2. Find the value of an annuity at $5\frac{3}{8}\%$, given the following table:

Rate:	4	$4\frac{1}{2}$	5	$5\frac{1}{2}$	6
Annuity value:	172.2903	162.8889	153.7245	145.3375	137.6483

3. The values of annuities are given for the following ages. Find the value of annuity at the age of $27\frac{1}{2}$.

Age:	25	26	27	28	29
Annuity:	16.195	15.919	15.630	15.326	15.006

4. The table below gives the value of tan x for $0.10 \le x \le 0.30$.

x:	0.10	0.15	0.20	0.25	0.30
$y = tan\ x$:	0.1003	0.1511	0.2027	0.2553	0.3093

Find: (*i*) tan 0.50 (*ii*) tan 0.26 (*iii*) tan 0.40.

5. Given:

x:	1	2	3	4	5	6	7	8
$f(x)$:	1	8	27	64	125	216	343	512

Find $f(7.5)$ using Newton's Backward difference formula.

6. From the following table of values of x and $f(x)$, determine

(*i*) $f(0.23)$ (*ii*) $f(0.29)$

x:	0.20	0.22	0.24	0.26	0.28	0.30
$f(x)$:	1.6596	1.6698	1.6804	1.6912	1.7024	1.7139

7. The probability integral

$$P = \sqrt{\frac{2}{\pi}} \int_0^x e^{-\frac{1}{2}t^2}\, dt \text{ has following values:}$$

x:	1.00	1.05	1.10	1.15	1.20	1.25
P:	0.682689	0.706282	0.728668	0.749856	0.769861	0.788700

Calculate P for $x = 1.235$.

8. In an examination, the number of candidates who obtained scores between certain limits are as follows:

Scores	*Number of candidates*
0—19	41
20—39	62
40—59	65
60—79	50
80—99	17

Estimate the number of candidates who obtained fewer than 70 scores.

9. Estimate the value of $f(42)$ from the following available data:

x:	20	25	30	35	40	45
$f(x)$:	354	332	291	260	231	204

10. The area A of a circle of diameter d is given for the following values:

d:	80	85	90	95	100
A:	5026	5674	6362	7088	7854

Calculate the area of a cricle of diameter 105.

11. From the following table, find y, when $x = 1.84$ and 2.4 by Newton's interpolation formula:

x:	1.7	1.8	1.9	2.0	2.1	2.2	2.3
$y = e^x$:	5.474	6.050	6.686	7.389	8.166	9.025	9.974

12. Using Newton's backward difference formula, find the value of $e^{-1.9}$ from the following table of values of e^{-x}:

x:	1	1.25	1.50	1.75	2.00
e^{-x}:	0.3679	0.2865	0.2231	0.1738	0.1353

4.17 CENTRAL DIFFERENCE INTERPOLATION FORMULAE

We shall study now the central difference formulae most suited for interpolation near the middle of a tabulated set.

4.18 GAUSS' FORWARD DIFFERENCE FORMULA

Newton's Gregory forward difference formula is

$$f(a + hu) = f(a) + u\Delta f(a) + \frac{u(u-1)}{2!}\Delta^2 f(a) + \frac{u(u-1)(u-2)}{3!}\Delta^3 f(a) + \frac{u(u-1)(u-2)(u-3)}{4!}\Delta^4 f(a) + \ldots\ldots \quad (30)$$

Given $a = 0$, $h = 1$, we get

$$f(u) = f(0) + u\Delta f(0) + \frac{u(u-1)}{2!}\Delta^2 f(0) + \frac{u(u-1)(u-2)}{3!}\Delta^3 f(0) + \frac{u(u-1)(u-2)(u-3)}{4!}\Delta^4 f(0) + \ldots\ldots \quad (31)$$

Now, $\Delta^3 f(-1) = \Delta^2 f(0) - \Delta^2 f(-1) \Rightarrow \Delta^2 f(0) = \Delta^3 f(-1) + \Delta^2 f(-1)$

Also, $\Delta^4 f(-1) = \Delta^3 f(0) - \Delta^3 f(-1) \Rightarrow \Delta^3 f(0) = \Delta^4 f(-1) + \Delta^3 f(-1)$

and $\Delta^5 f(-1) = \Delta^4 f(0) - \Delta^4 f(-1) \Rightarrow \Delta^4 f(0) = \Delta^5 f(-1) + \Delta^4 f(-1)$ and so on.

$\therefore$ From (31),

$$f(u) = f(0) + u\Delta f(0) + \frac{u(u-1)}{2!}\{\Delta^2 f(-1) + \Delta^3 f(-1)\}$$

$$+ \frac{u(u-1)(u-2)}{3!}\{\Delta^3 f(-1) + \Delta^4 f(-1)\}$$

$$+ \frac{u(u-1)(u-2)(u-3)}{4!}\{\Delta^4 f(-1) + \Delta^5 f(-1)\} + \ldots\ldots$$

$$= f(0) + u\Delta f(0) + \frac{u(u-1)}{2!}\Delta^2 f(-1) + \frac{u(u-1)}{2}\left\{1 + \frac{u-2}{3}\right\}\Delta^3 f(-1)$$

$$+ \frac{u(u-1)(u-2)}{6}\left\{1 + \frac{u-3}{4}\right\}\Delta^4 f(-1) + \frac{u(u-1)(u-2)(u-3)}{4!}\Delta^5 f(-1) + \ldots\ldots$$

$$= f(0) + u\Delta f(0) + \frac{u(u-1)}{2!}\Delta^2 f(-1) + \frac{(u+1)u(u-1)}{3!}\Delta^3 f(-1)$$

$$+ \frac{(u+1)u(u-1)(u-2)}{4!}\Delta^4 f(-1) + \frac{u(u-1)(u-2)(u-3)}{4!}\Delta^5 f(-1) + \ldots\ldots \quad (32)$$

But, $\Delta^5 f(-2) = \Delta^4 f(-1) - \Delta^4 f(-2)$

$\therefore$ $\Delta^4 f(-1) = \Delta^4 f(-2) + \Delta^5 f(-2)$

then (32) becomes,

$$f(u) = f(0) + u\Delta f(0) + \frac{u(u-1)}{2!}\Delta^2 f(-1) + \frac{(u+1)u(u-1)}{3!}\Delta^3 f(-1)$$

$$+ \frac{(u+1)u(u-1)(u-2)}{4!}\{\Delta^4 f(-2) + \Delta^5 f(-2)\}$$

$$+ \frac{u(u-1)(u-2)(u-3)}{4!}\Delta^5 f(-1) + \ldots\ldots$$

$$f(u) = f(0) + u\Delta f(0) + \frac{u(u-1)}{2!}\Delta^2 f(-1) + \frac{(u+1)\,u\,(u-1)}{3!}\Delta^3 f(-1) + \frac{(u+1)\,u\,(u-1)(u-2)}{4!}\Delta^4 f(-2) + \ldots\ldots$$

This is called **Gauss' forward difference formula.**

NOTE *This formula is applicable when u lies between 0 and* $\frac{1}{2}$.

4.18.1 Algorithm

Step 01. Start of the program.

Step 02. Input number of terms n

Step 03. Input the array ax

Step 04. Input the array ay

Step 05. h=ax[1]-ax[0]

Step 06. for i=0;i<n–1;i++

Step 07. diff[i][1]=ay[i+1]-ay[i]

Step 08. End Loop i

Step 09. for j=2;j<=4;j++

Step 10. for i=0;i<n–j;i++

Step 11. diff[i][j]=diff[i+1][j–1]–diff[i][j–1]

Step 12. End Loop i

Step 13. End Loop j

Step 14. i=0

Step 15. Repeat Step 16 until ax[i]<x

Step 16. i=i+1

Step 17. i=i–1;

Step 18. p=(x–ax[i])/h

Step 19. y1=p*diff[i][1]

Step 20. y2=p*(p–1)*diff[i–1][2]/2

Step 21. y3=(p+1)*p*(p-1)*diff[i–2][3]/6

Step 22. y4=(p+1)*p*(p–1)*(p–2)*diff[i–3][4]/24

Step 23. y=ay[i]+y1+y2+y3+y4

Step 24. Print Output x,y

Step 25. End of Program

4.18.2 Flow-chart

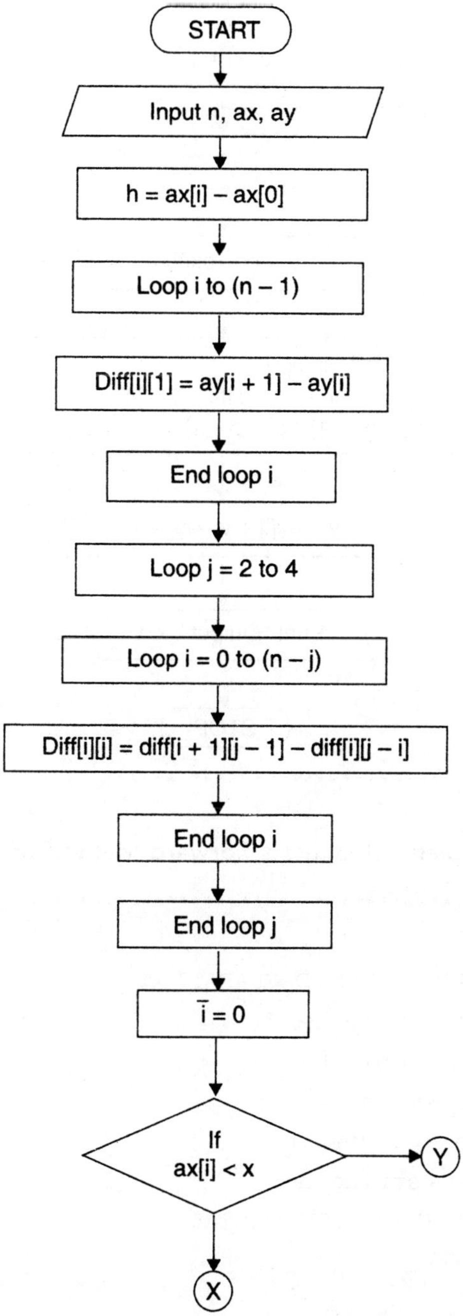

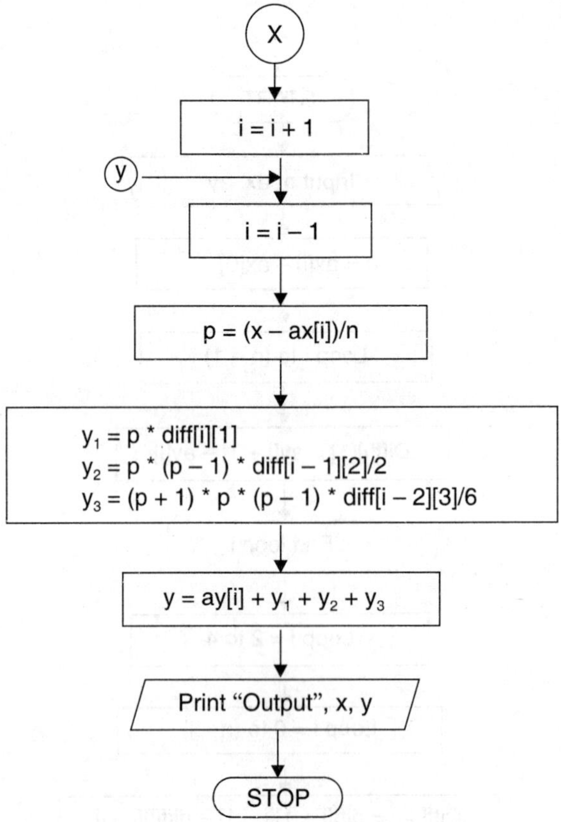

/* **

4.18.3 Program to Implement Gauss's Forward Method of Interpolation

** */

```
//...HEADER FILES DECLARATION
# include <stdio.h>
# include <conio.h>
# include <math.h>
# include <process.h>
# include <string.h>
//...MAIN EXECUTION THREAD
void main()
 {
 //...Variable declaration Field
```

```
//...Integer Type
int n;
int i,j;
//...Floating Type
float ax[10];                          //...array limit 9
float ax[10];                          //...array limit 9
float x;
float nr,dr;
float y=0;                             //...Initial value 0
float h;
float p;
float diff[20][20];                    //...array limit 19,19
float y1,y2,y3,y4;

//...Invoke Function Clear Screen
clrscr();

//...Input Section
printf("\n Enter the number of terms - ");
scanf("%d",&n);
//...Input Sequel for array X
printf("\n\n Enter the value in the form of x - ");
//...Input loop for Array X
for (i=0;i<n;i++)
    {
    printf("\n\n Enter the value of x%d - ",i+i);
    scanf("%f",&ax[i]);
    }
printf("\n\n Enter the value in the form of y - ");
//...Input Loop for Array Y
for(i=0;i<n;i++)
    {
    printf("\n\n Enter the value of y%d-",i+1);
    scanf("%f",&ay[i]);
    }
```

```
//...Inputting the required value query
printf("\nEnter the value of x for");
printf("\nwhich you want the value of y-");
scanf ("%f",&x);
//... Calculation and Processing Section
h=ax[1]-ax[0];
for(i=0;i<n-1;i++)
     {
     diff[i][1]=ay[i+1]-ay[i];
     }
for(j=2;j<=4;j++)
     {
     for(i=0;i<n-j;i++)
          {
          diff[i][j]=diff[i+1][j-1]-diff[i][j-1];
          }
     }
i=0;
do   {
     i++;
     }while(ax[i]<x);
i--;
p=(x-ax[i])/h;
y1=p*diff[i][1];
y2=p*(p-1)*diff[i-1][2]/2;
y3=(p+1)*p*(p-1)*diff[i-2][3]/6;
y4=(p+1)*p*(p-1)*(p-2)*diff[i-3][4]/24;
//...Taking Sum
y=ay[i]+y1+y2+y3+y4;
//...Output Section
printf("\nwhen x=%6.4f,y=%6.8f ",x,y);
//... Invoke User Watch Halt Function
printf("\n\n\n Press Enter to Exit");
getch();
}
//...Termination of Main Execution Thread
```

4.18.4 Output

```
Enter the number of terms - 7
Enter the value in the form of x -
Enter the value of x1 - 1.00
Enter the value of x2 - 1.05
Enter the value of x3 - 1.10
Enter the value of x4 - 1.15
Enter the value of x5 - 1.20
Enter the value of x6 - 1.25
Enter the value of x7 - 1.30
Enter the value in the form of y -
Enter the value of y1 - 2.7183
Enter the value of y2 - 2.8577
Enter the value of y3 - 3.0042
Enter the value of y4 - 3.1582
Enter the value of y5 - 3.3201
Enter the value of y6 - 3.4903
Enter the value of y7 - 3.6693
Enter the value of x for
which you want the value of y - 1.17
When x = 1.17, y = 3.2221
Press Enter to Exit
```

EXAMPLES

Example 1. *Apply a central difference formula to obtain f(32) given that:*

$$f(25) = 0.2707 \qquad f(35) = 0.3386$$

$$f(30) = 0.3027 \qquad f(40) = 0.3794.$$

Sol. Here $a + hu = 32$ and $h = 5$

Take origin at 30 $\therefore$ $a = 30$ then $u = 0.4$

The forward difference table is:

u	x	$f(x)$	$\Delta f(x)$	$\Delta^2 f(x)$	$\Delta^3 f(x)$
– 1	25	.2707			
			.032		
0	30	.3027		.0039	
			.0359		.0010
1	35	.3386		.0049	
			.0408		
2	40	.3794			

Applying Gauss' forward difference formula, we have

$$f(u) = f(0) + u\Delta f(0) + \frac{u(u-1)}{2!}\Delta^2 f(-1) + \frac{(u+1)\,u(u-1)}{3!}\Delta^3 f(-1)$$

$$\therefore \quad f(.4) = .3027 + (.4)(.0359) + \frac{(.4)(.4-1)}{2!}(.0039) + \frac{(1.4)(.4)(.4-1)}{3!}(.0010)$$

$$= 0.316536.$$

Example 2. *Use Gauss' forward formula to find a polynomial of degree four which takes the following values of the function f(x):*

x:	*1*	*2*	*3*	*4*	*5*
f(x):	*1*	*– 1*	*1*	*– 1*	*1*

Sol. Taking origin at 3 and $h = 1$

$$a + hu = x$$

$$\Rightarrow \quad 3 + u = x \Rightarrow u = x - 3$$

The difference table is:

u	x	$f(x)$	$\Delta f(x)$	$\Delta^2 f(x)$	$\Delta^3 f(x)$	$\Delta^4 f(x)$
– 2	1	1				
			– 2			
– 1	2	– 1		4		
			2		– 8	
0	3	1		– 4		16
			– 2		8	
1	4	– 1		4		
			2			
2	5	1				

Gauss' forward difference formula is

$$f(u) = f(0) + u\Delta f(0) + \frac{u(u-1)}{2!}\Delta^2 f(-1) + \frac{(u+1)\,u\,(u-1)}{3!}\Delta^3 f(-1) + \frac{(u+1)\,u\,(u-1)(u-2)}{4!}\Delta^4 f(-2)$$

$$= 1 + (x-3)(-2) + \frac{(x-3)(x-4)}{2}(-4) + \frac{(x-2)(x-3)(x-4)}{6}(8) + \frac{(x-2)(x-3)(x-4)(x-5)}{24}(16)$$

$$= 1 - 2x + 6 - 2x^2 + 14x - 24 + \frac{4}{3}(x^3 - 9x^2 + 26x - 24) + \frac{2}{3}(x^4 - 14x^3 + 71x^2 - 154x + 120)$$

$$\therefore \quad \boxed{F(x) = \frac{2}{3}x^4 - 8x^3 + \frac{100}{3}x^2 - 56x + 31}$$

Example 3. *The values of e^{-x} at $x = 1.72$ to $x = 1.76$ are given in the following table:*

x:	1.72	1.73	1.74	1.75	1.76
e^{-x}:	0.17907	0.17728	0.17552	0.17377	0.17204

Find the value of $e^{-1.7425}$ using Gauss' forward difference formula.

Sol. Here taking the origin at 1.74 and $h = 0.01$.

$$\therefore \quad x = a + uh$$

$$\Rightarrow \quad u = \frac{x-a}{h} = \frac{1.7425 - 1.7400}{0.01} = 0.25$$

The difference table is as follows:

u	x	$10^5 f(x)$	$10^5 \Delta f(x)$	$10^5 \Delta^2 f(x)$	$10^5 \Delta^3 f(x)$	$10^5 \Delta^4 f(x)$
−2	1.72	17907				
			−179			
−1	1.73	17728		3		
			−176		−2	
0	1.74	17552		1		3
			−175			
1	1.75	17377		2	1	
			−173			
2	1.76	17204				

Gauss's forward formula is

$$f(u) = f(0) + u\Delta f(0) + \frac{u(u-1)}{2!}\Delta^2 f(-1) + \frac{(u+1)u(u-1)}{3!}\Delta^3 f(-1)$$

$$+ \frac{(u+1)u(u-1)(u-2)}{4!}\Delta^4 f(-2)$$

$$\therefore\quad 10^5 f(.25) = 17552 + (.25)(-175) + \frac{(.25)(-.75)}{2}(1) + \frac{(1.25)(.25)(-.75)}{6}(1)$$

$$+ \frac{(1.25)(.25)(-.75)(-1.75)}{24}(3)$$

$$= 17508.16846$$

$$\therefore\quad f(0.25) = e^{-1.7425} = 0.1750816846.$$

Example 4. *Apply Gauss's forward formula to find the value of* u_9, *if* $u_0 = 14$, $u_4 = 24$, $u_8 = 32$, $u_{12} = 35$, $u_{16} = 40$.

Sol. The difference table is (taking origin at 8):

u	x	$f(x)$	$\Delta f(x)$	$\Delta^2 f(x)$	$\Delta^3 f(u)$	$\Delta^4 f(x)$
− 2	0	14				
			10			
− 1	4	24		− 2		
			8		− 3	
0	8	32		− 5		10
			3		7	
1	12	35		2		
			5			
2	16	40				

Here $\quad a = 8,\ h = 4,\quad a + hu = 9$

$\therefore\quad 8 + 4u = 9 \Rightarrow u = .25$

Gauss' forward difference formula is

$$f(.25) = f(0) + u\Delta f(0) + \frac{u(u-1)}{2!}\Delta^2 f(-1) + \frac{(u+1)u(u-1)}{3!}\Delta^3 f(-1)$$

$$+ \frac{(u+1)u(u-1)(u-2)}{4!}\Delta^4 f(-2)$$

$$= 32 + (.25)(3) + \frac{(.25)(-.75)}{2}(-5) + \frac{(1.25)(.25)(-.75)}{6}(7)$$

$$+ \frac{(1.25)(.25)(-.75)(-1.75)}{24}(10)$$

$= 33.11621094$

Hence $u_9 = 33.11621094.$

ASSIGNMENT 4.6

1. Apply Gauss's forward formula to find the value of $f(x)$ at $x = 3.75$ from the table:

x:	2.5	3.0	3.5	4.0	4.5	5.0
$f(x)$:	24.145	22.043	20.225	18.644	17.262	16.047.

2. Given that

x:	25	30	35	40	45
log x:	1.39794	1.47712	1.54407	1.60206	1.65321

Find the value of log 3.7, using Gauss's forward formula.

3. Find the value of $f(41)$ by applying Gauss's forward formula from the following data:

x:	30	35	40	45	50
$f(x)$:	3678.2	2995.1	2400.1	1876.2	1416.3

4. From the following table, find the value of $e^{1.17}$ using Gauss forward formula:

x:	1	1.05	1.10	1.15	1.20	1.25	1.30
e^x:	2.7183	2.8577	3.0042	3.1582	3.3201	3.4903	3.6693

5. From the following table find y when $x = 1.45$

x:	1.0	1.2	1.4	1.6	1.8	2.0
y:	0.0	– .112	– .016	.336	.992	2.0

4.19 GAUSS'S BACKWARD DIFFERENCE FORMULA

Newton's Gregory forward difference formula is

$$f(a + hu) = f(a) + u\Delta f(a) + \frac{u(u-1)}{2!}\Delta^2 f(a) + \frac{u(u-1)(u-2)}{3!}\Delta^3 f(a) + \ldots\ldots \quad (33)$$

Put $a = 0,\ \ h = 1$, we get

$$f(u) = f(0) + u\Delta f(0) + \frac{u(u-1)}{2!}\Delta^2 f(0) + \frac{u(u-1)(u-2)}{3!}\Delta^3 f(0)$$

$$+ \frac{u(u-1)(u-2)(u-3)}{4!}\Delta^4 f(0) + \ldots\ldots \quad (34)$$

Now, $\Delta f(0) = \Delta f(-1) + \Delta^2 f(-1)$

$\Delta^2 f(0) = \Delta^2 f(-1) + \Delta^3 f(-1)$

$\Delta^3 f(0) = \Delta^3 f(-1) + \Delta^4 f(-1)$

$\Delta^4 f(0) = \Delta^4 f(-1) + \Delta^5 f(-1)$ and so on.

∴ From (34),

$$f(u) = f(0) + u\,[\Delta f(-1) + \Delta^2 f(-1)] + \frac{u(u-1)}{2!}\,[\Delta^2 f(-1) + \Delta^3 f(-1)]$$

$$+ \frac{u(u-1)(u-2)}{3!}\,[\Delta^3 f(-1) + \Delta^4 f(-1)]$$

$$+ \frac{u(u-1)(u-2)(u-3)}{4!}\,[\Delta^4 f(-1) + \Delta^5 f(-1)] + \ldots\ldots \quad (35)$$

$$= f(0) + u\Delta f(-1) + u\left(1 + \frac{u-1}{2}\right)\Delta^2 f(-1)$$

$$+ \frac{u(u-1)}{2}\left(1 + \frac{u-2}{3}\right)\Delta^3 f(-1)$$

$$+ \frac{u(u-1)(u-2)}{6}\left\{1 + \frac{u-3}{4}\right\}\Delta^4 f(-1) + \frac{u(u-1)(u-2)(u-3)}{4!}\Delta^5 f(-1) + \ldots\ldots$$

$$= f(0) + u\Delta f(-1) + \frac{(u+1)u}{2!}\Delta^2 f(-1) + \frac{(u+1)\,u(u-1)}{3!}\Delta^3 f(-1)$$

$$+ \frac{(u+1)\,u(u-1)(u-2)}{4!}\Delta^4 f(-1) + \ldots\ldots \quad (36)$$

Again, $\Delta^3 f(-1) = \Delta^3 f(-2) + \Delta^4 f(-2)$

and $\Delta^4 f(-1) = \Delta^4 f(-2) + \Delta^5 f(-2)$ and so on

∴ (36) gives

$$f(u) = f(0) + u\Delta f(-1) + \frac{(u+1)u}{2!}\Delta^2 f(-1) + \frac{(u+1)u(u-1)}{3!}\{\Delta^3 f(-2) + \Delta^4 f(-2)\}$$

$$+ \frac{(u+1)u(u-1)(u-2)}{4!}\{\Delta^4 f(-2) + \Delta^5 f(-2)\} + \ldots\ldots$$

$$f(u) = f(0) + u\Delta f(-1) + \frac{(u+1)u}{2!}\Delta^2 f(-1) + \frac{(u+1)u(u-1)}{3!}\Delta^3 f(-2) + \frac{(u+2)(u+1)u(u-1)}{4!}\Delta^4 f(-2) + \ldots\ldots \quad (37)$$

This is known as **Gauss' backward difference formula.**

This formula is useful when u lies between $-\frac{1}{2}$ and 0.

4.19.1 Algorithm of Gauss's Backward Formula

Step 01. Start of the program.
Step 02. Input number of terms n
Step 03. Input the array ax
Step 04. Input the array ay
Step 05. h=ax[1]-ax[0]
Step 06. for i=0;i<n-l;i++
Step 07. diff[i][1]=ay[i+1]-ay[i]
Step 08. End Loop i
Step 09. for j=2;j<=4;j++
Step 10. for i=0;i<n–j;i++
Step 11. diff[i][j]=diff[i+1][j–1]–diff[i][j–1]
Step 12. End Loop i
Step 13. End Loop j
Step 14. i=0
Step 15. Repeat Step 16 until ax[i]<x
Step 16. i=i+1
Step 17. i=i–1;
Step 18. p=(x–ax[i])/h
Step 19. y1=p*diff[i-1][1]
Step 20. y2=p*(p+1)*diff[i–1][2]/2
Step 21. y3=(p+1)*p*(p-1)*diff[i–2][3]/6
Step 22. y4=(p+2)*(p+1)*p*(p–1)*diff[i–3][4]/24
Step 23. y=ay[i]+y1+y2+y3+y4
Step 24. Print Output x,y
Step 25. End of Program

4.19.2 Flow-chart

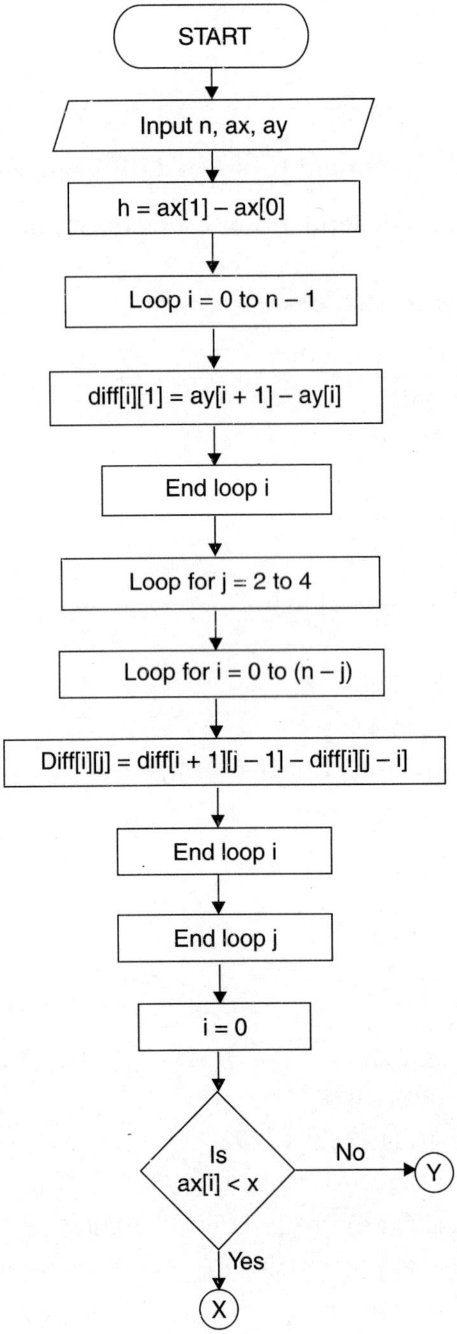

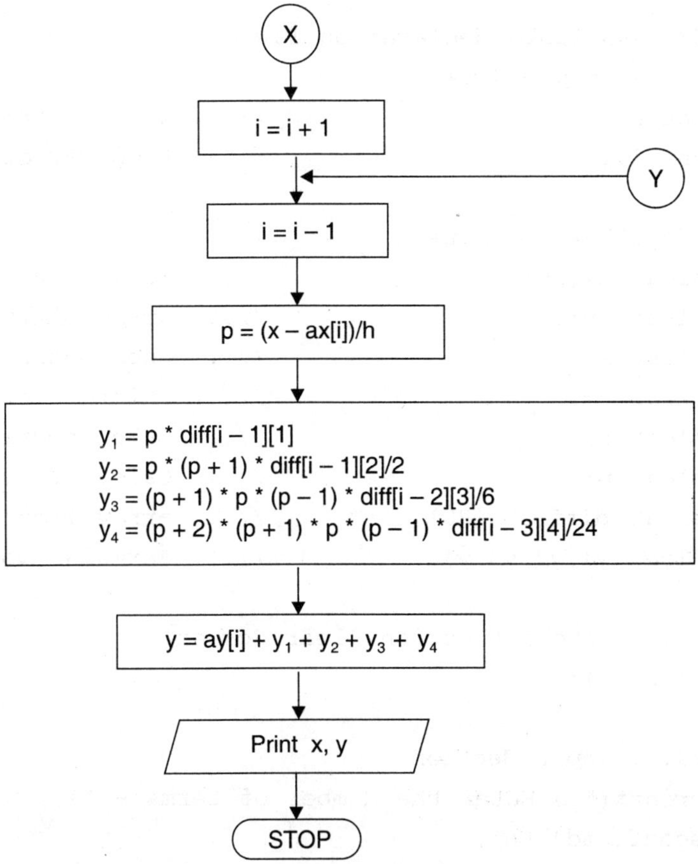


```
/* *******************************************************************
```

4.19.3 Program to Implement Gauss's Backward Method of Interpolation

```
*******************************************************************/*
   //...HEADER FILES DECLARATION
   # include <stdio.h>
   # include <conio.h>
   # include <math.h>
   # include <process.h>
   # include <string.h>

   //...MAIN EXECUTION THREAD

   void main()
```

```
{
//...Variable declaration Field
//...Integer Type
int n;                          //... No. of terms
int i,j;                        //... Loop Variables

//...Floating Type
float ax[10];                   //... array limit 9
float ay[10];                   //... array limit 9
float x;                        //... User Querry
float y=0;                      //... Initial value 0
float h;                        //... Calc. section
float p;                        //... Calc. section
float diff[20][20];             //... array limit 19, 19
float y1,y2,y3,y4;              //... Formulae variables

//... Invoke Function Clear Screen
clrscr();

//... Input Section
printf("\n Enter the number of terms - ");
scanf("%d",&n);
//... Input Sequel for array X
printf("\n\n Enter the value in the form of x - ");
//... Input loop for X
for (i=0;i<n;i++)
    {
    printf("\n\n Enter the value of x%d-",i+1);
    scanf("%f",&ax[i]);
    }
//...Input Sequel for array Y
printf("\n\n Enter the value in the form of y-");
//...Input Loop for Y
for(i=0;i<n;i++)
    {
    printf("\n\n Enter the value of y%d-",i+1);
```

```
     scanf("%f",&ay[i]);
     }

//... Inputting the required value query
printf("\nEnter the value of x for");
printf("\nwhich you want the value of y - ");
scanf("%f",&x);
//... Calculation and Processing Section
h=ax[1]-ax[0];
for(i=0;i<n-1;i++)
     {
     diff[i][1]=ay[i+1]-ay[i];
     }
for(j=2;j<=4;j++)
     {
     for(i=0;i<n-j;i++)
          {
          diff[i][j]=diff[i+1][j-1]-diff[i][j-1];
          }
     }
i=0;
do        {
          i++;
          }while (ax[i]<x);
i--;
p=(x-ax[i])/h;
y1=p*diff[i-1][1];
y2=p*(p+1)*diff[i-1][2]/2;
y3=(p+1)*p*(p-1)*diff[i-2][3]/6;
y4=(p+2)*(p+1)*p*(p-1)*diff[i-3][4]/24;
//... Taking Sum
y=ay[i]+y1+y2+y3+y4;
//... Output Section
printf("\nwhen x=%6.1f,y=%6.4f ",x,y);
//... Invoke User Watch Halt Function
printf("\n\n\n Press Enter to Exit");
```

```
getch();
}
//... Termination of Main Execution Thread
```

4.19.4 Output

```
Enter the number of terms - 7
Enter the value in the form of x -
Enter the value of x1 - 1.00
Enter the value of x2 - 1.05
Enter the value of x3 - 1.10
Enter the value of x4 - 1.15
Enter the value of x5 - 1.20
Enter the value of x6 - 1.25
Enter the value of x7 - 1.30
Enter the value in the form of y -
Enter the value of y1 - 2.1783
Enter the value of y2 - 2.8577
Enter the value of y3 - 3.0042
Enter the value of y4 - 3.1582
Enter the value of y5 - 3.3201
Enter the value of y6 - 3.4903
Enter the value of y7 - 3.6693
Enter the value of x for
which you want the value of y - 1.35
When x = 1.35, y=3.8483
Press Enter to Exit
```

EXAMPLES

Example 1. *Given that*

$$\sqrt{12500} = 111.803399, \sqrt{12510} = 111.848111$$

$$\sqrt{12520} = 111.892806, \sqrt{12530} = 111.937483$$

Show by Gauss's backward formula that $\sqrt{12516} = 111.8749301$.

Sol. Taking the origin at 12520

$$\therefore \qquad u = \frac{x-a}{h} = \frac{12516 - 12520}{10} = -\frac{4}{10} = -0.4$$

Gauss's backward formula is

$$f(u) = f(0) + u\Delta f(-1) + \frac{(u+1)\,u}{2!}\,\Delta^2 f(-1)$$

$$+ \frac{(u+1)\,u(u-1)}{3!}\,\Delta^3 f(-2) + \ldots\ldots \quad (38)$$

The difference table is:

u	x	$10^6 f(x)$	$10^6\Delta f(x)$	$10^6 \Delta^2 f(x)$	$10^6 \Delta^3 f(x)$
– 2	12500	111803399			
			44712		
– 1	12510	111848111		– 17	
			44695		– 1
0	12520	111892806		– 18	
			44677		
1	12530	111937483			

From (38),

$$10^6 f(-.4) = 111892806 + (-.4)(44695)$$

$$+ \frac{(.6)(-.4)}{2!}(-18) + \frac{(.6)(-.4)(-1.4)}{3!}(-1)$$

$$= 111874930.1$$

$$\therefore \quad f(-.4) = 111.8749301$$

Hence, $\sqrt{12516} = 111.8749301.$

Example 2. *Find the value of cos 51° 42′ by Gauss's backward formula. Given that*

x:	*50°*	*51°*	*52°*	*53°*	*54°*
cos x:	*0.6428*	*0.6293*	*0.6157*	*0.6018*	*0.5878.*

Sol. Taking the origin at 52° and $h = 1$

$$\therefore \quad u = (x - a) = 51°\,42' - 52° = -\,18' = -\,0.3°$$

Gauss's backward formula is

$$f(u) = f(0) + u\Delta f(-1) + \frac{(u+1)u}{2!}\,\Delta^2 f(-1) + \frac{(u+1)u(u-1)}{3!}\,\Delta^3 f(-2)$$

$$+ \frac{(u+2)(u+1)u(u-1)}{4!}\,\Delta^4 f(-2) \quad (39)$$

The difference table is as below:

u	x	$10^4 f(x)$	$10^4 \Delta f(x)$	$10^4 \Delta^2 f(x)$	$10^4 \Delta^3 f(x)$	$10^4 \Delta^4 f(x)$
– 2	50°	6428				
			– 135			
– 1	51°	6293		– 1		
			– 136		– 2	
0	52°	6157		– 3		4
			– 139		2	
1	53°	6018		– 1		
			– 140			
2	54°	5878				

From (39),

$$10^4 f(-.3) = 6157 + (-.3)(-136) + \frac{(.7)(-.3)}{2!}(-3) + \frac{(.7)(-.3)(-1.3)}{3!}(-2)$$

$$+ \frac{(1.7)(.7)(-.3)(-1.3)}{4!}(4)$$

$$= 6198.10135$$

$\therefore$ $f(-.3) = .619810135$

Hence $\cos 51°42' = 0.619810135.$

Example 3. *Using Gauss's backward interpolation formula, find the population for the year 1936 given that*

Year:	*1901*	*1911*	*1921*	*1931*	*1941*	*1951*
Population: (in thousands)	*12*	*15*	*20*	*27*	*39*	*52*

Sol. Taking the origin at 1941 and $h = 10$,

$$x = a + uh \quad \therefore \quad u = \frac{x-a}{h} = \frac{1936-1941}{10} = -0.5$$

Gauss's backward formula is

$$f(u) = f(0) + u\Delta f(-1) + \frac{(u+1)u}{2!}\Delta^2 f(-1) + \frac{(u+1)u(u-1)}{3!}\Delta^3 f(-2)$$

$$+ \frac{(u+2)(u+1)u(u-1)}{4!}\Delta^4 f(-2) + \frac{(u+2)(u+1)u(u-1)(u-2)}{5!}\Delta^5 f(-3) \quad (40)$$

The difference table is:

u	$f(u)$	$\Delta f(u)$	$\Delta^2 f(u)$	$\Delta^3 f(u)$	$\Delta^4 f(u)$	$\Delta^5 f(u)$
– 4	12					
		3				
– 3	15		2			
		5		0		
– 2	20		2		3	
		7		3		– 10
– 1	27		5		– 7	
		12		– 4		
0	39		1			
		13				
1	52					

From (40),

$$f(-.5) = 39 + (-.5)(12) + \frac{(.5)(-.5)}{2}(1) + \frac{(.5)(-.5)(-1.5)}{6}(-4)$$

$$= 32.625 \text{ thousands}$$

Hence, the population for the year 1936 = 32625

Example 4. *$f(x)$ is a polynomial of degree four and given that*

$$f(4) = 270,\ f(5) = 648,\ \Delta f(5) = 682,\ \Delta^3 f(4) = 132.$$

Find the value of $f(5.8)$ using Gauss's backward formula.

Sol. $\Delta f(5) = f(6) - f(5)$

$\therefore$ $f(6) = f(5) + \Delta f(5) = 648 + 682 = 1330$

$\Delta^3 f(4) = (E-1)^3 f(4) = f(7) - 3f(6) + 3f(5) - f(4) = 132$

$\therefore$ $f(7) = 3f(6) - 3f(5) + f(4) + 132$

$= 3 \times 1330 - 3 \times 648 + 270 + 132 = 2448.$

The difference table is (Taking origin at 6):

u	x	$f(x)$	$\Delta f(x)$	$\Delta^2 f(x)$	$\Delta^3 f(x)$
– 2	4	270			
			378		
– 1	5	648		304	
			682		132
0	6	1330		436	
			1118		
1	7	2448			

Here, $a = 6, \quad h = 1, \quad a + hu = 5.8$

$\therefore \quad 6 + u = 5.8 \Rightarrow u = -.2$

Gauss's backward formula is

$$f(-.2) = f(0) + u\Delta f(-1) + \frac{(u+1)u}{2!}\Delta^2 f(-1) + \frac{(u+1)u(u-1)}{3!}\Delta^3 f(-2)$$

$$= 1330 + (-.2)(682) + \frac{(.8)(-.2)}{2}(436) + \frac{(.8)(-.2)(-1.2)}{6}(132)$$

$$= 1162.944$$

$\therefore \quad f(5.8) = 1162.944.$

ASSIGNMENT 4.7

1. The population of a town in the years 1931, ..., 1971 are as follows:

Year:	1931	1941	1951	1961	1971
Population: *(in thousands)*	15	20	27	39	52

Find the population of the town in 1946 by applying Gauss's backward formula.

2. Apply Gauss's backward formula to find the value of $(1.06)^{19}$ if $(1.06)^{10} = 1.79085$, $(1.06)^{15} = 2.39656$, $(1.06)^{20} = 3.20714$, $(1.06)^{25} = 4.29187$ and $(1.06)^{30} = 5.74349$.

3. Given that

x:	50	51	52	53	54
$\tan x$:	1.1918	1.2349	1.2799	1.3270	1.3764

Using Gauss's backward formula, find the value of tan 51° 42′.

4. Interpolate by means of Gauss's backward formula, the population of a town for the year 1974 given that:

Year:	1939	1949	1959	1969	1979	1989
Population: *(in thousands)*	12	15	20	27	39	52

5. Apply Gauss's backward formula to find sin 45° from the following table:

θ°:	20	30	40	50	60	70	80
sin θ:	0.34202	0.502	0.64279	0.76604	0.86603	0.93969	0.98481

6. Using Gauss's backward formula, estimate the number of persons earning wages between $ 60 and $ 70 from the following data:

Wages ($):	Below 40	40—60	60—80	80—100	100—120
Number of people: *(in thousands)*	250	120	100	70	50

4.20 STIRLING'S FORMULA

Gauss's forward formula is

$$f(u) = f(0) + u\Delta f(0) + \frac{u(u-1)}{2!}\Delta^2 f(-1) + \frac{(u+1)u(u-1)}{3!}\Delta^3 f(-1)$$

$$+ \frac{(u+1)u(u-1)(u-2)}{4!}\Delta^4 f(-2) + \ldots\ldots \quad (41)$$

Gauss's backward formula is

$$f(u) = f(0) + u\Delta f(-1) + \frac{(u+1)u}{2!}\Delta^2 f(-1) + \frac{(u+1)u(u-1)}{3!}\Delta^3 f(-2)$$

$$+ \frac{(u+2)(u+1)u(u-1)}{4!}\Delta^4 f(-2) + \ldots\ldots \quad (42)$$

Take the mean of (41) and (42),

$$f(u) = f(0) + u\left\{\frac{\Delta f(0) + \Delta f(-1)}{2}\right\} + \frac{u^2}{2!}\Delta^2 f(-1)$$

$$+ \frac{(u+1)u(u-1)}{3!}\left\{\frac{\Delta^3 f(-1) + \Delta^3 f(-2)}{2}\right\}$$

$$+ \frac{u^2(u^2-1)}{4!}\Delta^4 f(-2) + \ldots\ldots \quad (43)$$

This is called Stirling's formula. It is useful when $|u| < \frac{1}{2}$ or $-\frac{1}{2} < u < \frac{1}{2}$. It gives the best estimate when $-\frac{1}{4} < u < \frac{1}{4}$.

4.20.1 Algorithm of Stirling's Formula

Step 01. Start of the program.

Step 02. Input number of terms n

Step 03. Input the array ax

Step 04. Input the array ay

Step 05. h = ax[1]-ax[0]

Step 06. for i = 1;i < n-1; i++

Step 07. diff [i][1] = ay[i + 1]-ay[i]

Step 08. End loop i

Step 09. for j = 2; j < = 4; j++

Step 10. for i = 0; i < n-j; i++

Step 11. diff[i][j] = diff[i + 1][j-1]-diff[i][j-1]

Step 12. End loop i

Step 13. End loop j

Step 14. i = 0

Step 15. Repeat step 16 until ax[i] < x

Step 16. i = i + 1

Step 17. i = i-1;

Step 18. p = (x-ax[i])/h

Step 19. y1= p*(diff[i][1] + diff[i-1][1])/2

Step 20. y2 = p*p*diff[i-1][2]/2

Step 21. y3 = p*(p*p-1)*(diff[i-1][3]+diff[i-2][3])/6

Step 22. y4 = p*p*(p*p-1)*diff[i-2][4]/24

Step 23. y = ay[i]+y1 + y2 + y3 + y4

Step 24. Print output

Step 25. End of program

4.20.2 Flow-chart

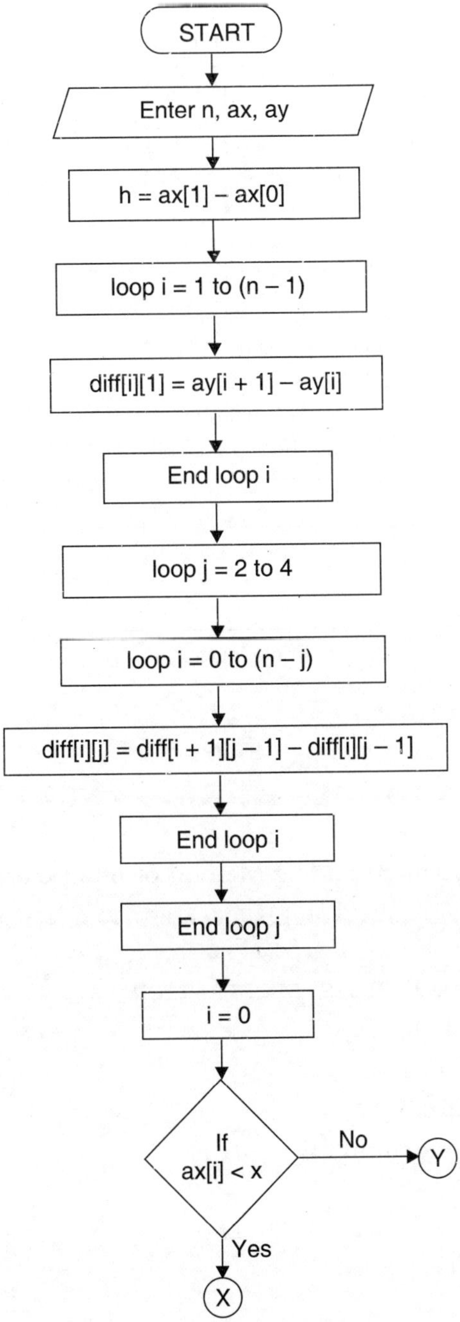

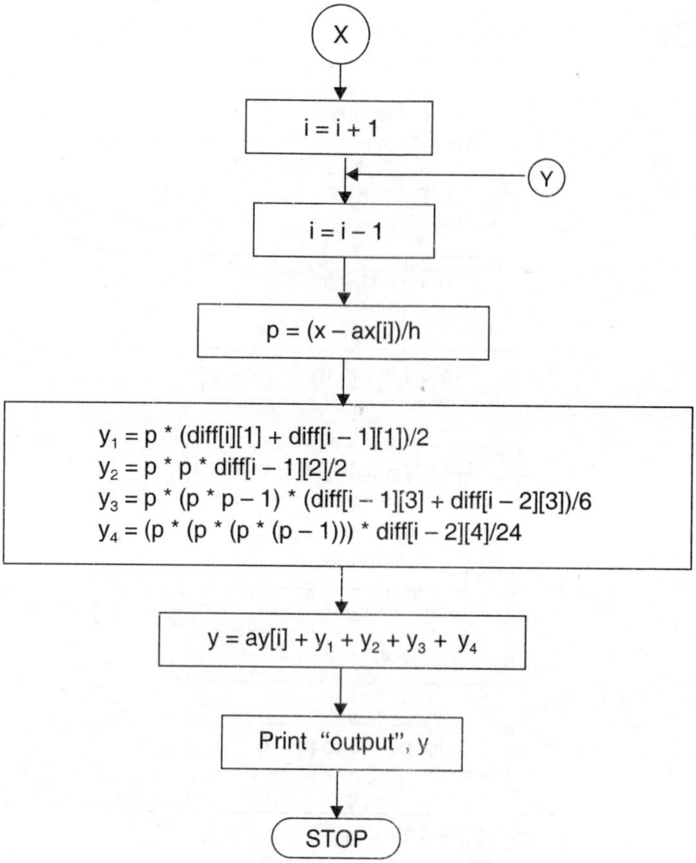


```
*/ ***********************************************************************
```

4.20.3 Program to Implement Stirling Method of Interpolation

```
*********************************************************************** /*

//... HEADER FILES DECLARATION
#include<stdio.h>
#include<conio.h>
#include<math.h>
#include<process.h>

//...MAIN EXECUTION THREAD
void main()
```

```
{
//...Variable declaration Field
//...Integer Type
int n;
int i,j;
//...Floating Type
float ax[10];                    //... array-limit 9
float ax[10];                    //... array-limit 9
float h;
float p;
float diff[20][20];              //...array 2d-limit 19,19
float x,y;
float y1,y2,y3,y4;
clrscr();                        //... Clear Screen
//... Input Section
printf("\n Enter the value of terms");
scanf("%d",%n);
//... Input Section Array X
printf("\n Enter the values for x \n");
//...Input Section Loop for X
for(i=0;i<n;i++)
    {
    printf("\n Enter the value for x%d-",i+1);
    scanf("%f",&ax[i]);
    }
//... Input Section for Y
printf("\n Enter the values for y \n");
//... Input Section Loop for Y
for(i=0;i<n;i++)
    {
    printf("\n Enter the value for y%d-",i+1);
    scanf("%f",&ay[i]);
    }
//... Input Section Loop for Value of X for Y
printf("\n Enter the value of x for");
```

```
printf("\n which you want the value of y");
scanf("%f",&x);

//...Calculation and Processing Section
h=ax[1]-ax[0];
for(i=0;i<n-1;i++)
    {
    diff[i][1]=ay[i+1]-ay[i];
    }
for(j=2;j<=4;j++)
    {
    for(i=0;i<n-j;i++)
        {
        diff[i][j]=diff[i+1][j-1]-diff[i][j-1];
        }
    }
i=0;
do  {
    i++;
    }while(ax[i]<x);
i--;
p=(x-ax[i])/h;
y1=p*(diff[i][1]+diff[i-1][1])/2;
y2=p*p*diff[i-1][2]/2;
y3=p*(p*p-1)*(diff[i-1][3]+diff[i-2][3])/6;
y4=p*p*(p*p-1)*diff[i-2][4]/24;
y=ay[i]+y1+y2+y3+y4;
//...Output Section
printf("\n\n When x=%6.2f, y=%6.8f",x,y);
//... Producing User Watch Halt Function
getch();
}
```

4.20.4 Output

```
Enter the value of terms-7
Enter the values for x
```

```
Enter the value for x1 - .61
Enter the value for x2 - .62
Enter the value for x3 - .63
Enter the value for x4 - .64
Enter the value for x5 - .65
Enter the value for x6 - .66
Enter the value for x7 - .67
Enter the values for y
Enter the value for y1 - 1.840431
Enter the value for y2 - 1.858928
Enter the value for y3 - 1.877610
Enter the value for y4 - 1.896481
Enter the value for y5 - 1.915541
Enter the value for y6 - 1.934792
Enter the value for y7 - 1.954237
Enter the value of x for
which you want the value of y - 0.6440
When x=0.6440,y=1.90408230
Press Enter to Continue
```

EXAMPLES

Example 1. *Given:*

θ:	$0°$	$5°$	$10°$	$15°$	$20°$	$25°$	$30°$
$\tan\theta$:	0	0.0875	0.1763	0.2679	0.364	0.4663	0.5774

Find the value of tan 16° using Stirling formula.

Sol. Take origin at 15°

$$\therefore \quad a = 15°, h = 5$$

$$a + hu = 16$$

$$\Rightarrow \quad 15 + 5u = 16 \quad \Rightarrow \quad u = .2$$

The difference table is:

u	θ	$10^4 f(\theta)$	$10^4 \Delta f(\theta)$	$10^4 \Delta^2 f(\theta)$	$10^4 \Delta^3 f(\theta)$	$10^4 \Delta^4 f(\theta)$	$10^4 \Delta^5 f(\theta)$	$10^4 \Delta^6 f(\theta)$
– 3	0	0						
			875					
– 2	5	875		13				
			888		15			
– 1	10	1763		28		2		
			916		17		– 2	
0	15	2679		45		0		11
			961		17		9	
1	20	3640		62		9		
			1023		26			
2	25	4663		88				
			1111					
3	30	5774						

Using Stirling's formula,

$$10^4 f(.2) = 2679 + (.2)\left(\frac{961+916}{2}\right) + \frac{(.2)^2}{2!}(45) + \frac{(1.2)(.2)(-.8)}{3!}\left(\frac{17+17}{2}\right)$$

$$+ \frac{(.2)^2\left\{(.2)^2-1\right\}}{4!}(0) + \frac{(2.2)(1.2)(.2)(-.8)(-1.8)}{5!}\left\{\frac{9+(-2)}{2}\right\}$$

$$+ \frac{(.2)^2\{(.2)^2-1\}\{(.2)^2-4\}}{6!}(11)$$

$$= 2866.980499$$

$$\therefore \quad f(.2) = .2866980499$$

Hence $\tan 16° = 0.2866980499.$

Example 2. *Apply Stirling's formula to find the value of f(1.22) from the following table which gives the values of* $f(x) = \frac{1}{\sqrt{2\pi}}\int_0^x e^{-\frac{x^2}{2}}\,dx$, *at intervals of* $x = 0.5$ *from* $x = 0$ *to 2.*

x:	*0*	*0.5*	*1.0*	*1.5*	*2.0*
f(x):	*0*	*0.191*	*0.341*	*0.433*	*0.477.*

Sol. Let the origin be at 1 and $h = 0.5$

$$\therefore \qquad x = a + hu,\ u = \frac{x-a}{h} = \frac{1.22 - 1.00}{0.5} = 0.44$$

Applying Stirling's formula

$$f(u) = f(0) + u \cdot \frac{1}{2}[\Delta f(0) + \Delta f(-1)] + \frac{u^2}{2!}\Delta^2 f(-1)$$

$$+ \frac{u(u^2-1)}{3!} \cdot \frac{1}{2}[\Delta^3 f(-1) + \Delta^3 f(-2)] + \frac{u^2(u^2-1)}{4!} \cdot \Delta^4 f(-2) + \ldots\ldots$$

$$\therefore \qquad f(0.44) = f(0) + (0.44)\,\frac{1}{2}[\Delta f(0) + \Delta f(-1)] + \frac{(0.44)^2}{2}\Delta^2 f(-1)$$

$$+ \frac{(0.44)[(0.44)^2 - 1]}{6} \cdot \frac{1}{2}[\Delta^3 f(-1) + \Delta^3 f(-2)] + \frac{(0.44)^2[(0.44)^2 - 1]}{24}\Delta^4 f(-2)$$

$$\simeq f(0) + (0.22)[\Delta f(0) + \Delta f(-1)] + 0.0968\,\Delta^2 f(-1)$$

$$- 0.029568\,[\Delta^3 f(-1) + \Delta^3 f(-2)] - 0.06505\,\Delta^4 f(-2) + \ldots\ldots$$

The difference table is as follows:

u	x	$10^3 f(x)$	$10^3\,\Delta f(x)$	$10^3\Delta^2 f(x)$	$10^3\Delta^3 f(x)$	$10^3\Delta^4 f(x)$
– 2	0	0				
			191			
– 1	.5	191		– 41		
			150		– 17	
0	1	341	...	– 58		27
			92		10	
1	1.5	433				
			44	– 48		
2	2	477				

$f(0)$ and the differences are being multiplied by 10^3

$$\therefore \qquad 10^3 f(0.44) \simeq 341 + 0.22 \times (150 + 92) + 0.0968 \times (-58)$$

$$- 0.029568 \times [-17 + 10] - 0.006505 \times 27$$

$$\simeq 341 + 0.22 \times 242 - 0.0968 \times 58 + 0.029568 \times 7 - 0.006505 \times 27$$

$$\simeq 341 + 53.24 - 5.6144 + 0.206276 - 0.175635 \simeq 388.66$$

$$\therefore \qquad f(0.44) = 0.389$$

Hence the required value of $f(x)$ at $x = 1.22$ is 0.389.

Example 3. *Use Stirling's formula to find* y_{28}, *given*

$$y_{20} = 49225, \quad y_{25} = 48316, \quad y_{30} = 47236,$$

$$y_{35} = 45926, \quad y_{40} = 44306.$$

Sol. Let the origin be at 30 and $h = 5$

$$a + hu = 28$$

$$\Rightarrow \qquad 30 + 5u = 28 \Rightarrow u = -.4$$

The difference table is as follows:

u	x	y	Δy	$\Delta^2 y$	$\Delta^3 y$	$\Delta^4 y$
– 2	20	49225				
			– 909			
– 1	25	48316		– 171		
			– 1080		– 59	
0	30	47236		– 230		– 21
			– 1310		– 80	
1	35	45926		– 310		
			– 1620			
2	40	44306				

By Stirling's formula,

$$f(-.4) = 47236 + (-.4)\left(\frac{-1080-1310}{2}\right) + \frac{(-.4)^2}{2!}(-230)$$

$$+ \frac{(.6)(-.4)(-1.4)}{3!}\left(\frac{-59-80}{2}\right) + \frac{(-.4)^2\{(-.4)^2-1\}}{4!}(-21)$$

$$= 47691.8256$$

Hence $\quad y_{28} = 47691.8256.$

Example 4. *Use Stirling's formula to find* y_{35}, *given* $y_{20} = 512, y_{30} = 439, y_{40} = 346$ *and* $y_{50} = 243$.

Sol. Let the origin be at 30 and $h = 10$

$$a + hu = 35$$

$$30 + 10u = 35 \Rightarrow u = .5$$

The difference table is as follows:

u	x	y	Δy	$\Delta^2 y$	$\Delta^3 y$
– 1	20	512			
			– 73		
0	30	439		– 20	
			– 93		10
1	40	346		– 10	
			– 103		
2	50	243			

By Stirling's formula,

$$f(.5) = 439 + (.5)\left(\frac{-93-73}{2}\right) + \frac{(.5)^2}{2!}(-20) + \frac{(1.5)(.5)(-.5)}{3!}\left(\frac{10}{2}\right)$$

$$= 394.6875$$

Hence, $y_{35} = 394.6875$.

ASSIGNMENT 4.8

1. Use Stirling's formula to find the value of $f(1.22)$ from the table.

x	$f(x)$
1.0	0.84147
1.1	0.89121
1.2	0.93204
1.3	0.96356
1.4	0.98545
1.5	0.99749
1.6	0.99957
1.7	0.99385
1.8	0.97385

2. Find $f(0.41)$ using Stirling's formula, if

$$f(0.30) = 0.1179,\ f(0.35) = 0.1368,\ f(0.40) = 0.1554$$
$$f(0.45) = 0.1736,\ f(0.50) = 0.1915.$$

3. Evaluate sin (0.197) from the data given below:

x:	0.15	0.17	0.19	0.21	0.23
sin x:	0.14944	0.16918	0.18886	0.20846	0.22798

4. Use Stirling's formula to find u_{32} from the following table:

$$u_{20} = 14.035 \quad u_{30} = 13.257$$
$$u_{40} = 12.089 \quad u_{25} = 13.674$$
$$u_{35} = 12.734 \quad u_{45} = 11.309.$$

5. Employ Stirling's formula to evaluate $y_{12.2}$ from the following table ($y_x = 1 + \log_{10} \sin x$):

$x°$:	10	11	12	13	14
$10^5\, y_x$:	23967	28060	31788	35209	38368.

6. The following table gives the values of e^x for certain equidistant values of x. Find the value of e^x when $x = 0.644$ using Stirling's method.

x:	0.61	0.62	0.63	0.64	0.65	0.66	0.67
$y = e^x$:	1.840431	1.858928	1.877610	1.896481	1.915541	1.934792	1.954237

4.21 BESSEL'S INTERPOLATION FORMULA

Gauss's forward formula is

$$f(u) = f(0) + u\Delta f(0) + \frac{u(u-1)}{2!}\Delta^2 f(-1) + \frac{(u+1)u(u-1)}{3!}\Delta^3 f(-1) + \frac{(u+1)u(u-1)(u-2)}{4!}\Delta^4 f(-2) \ldots.. \quad (44)$$

Gauss's backward formula is

$$f(u) = f(0) + u\Delta f(-1) + \frac{(u+1)u}{2!}\Delta^2 f(-1) + \frac{(u+1)u(u-1)}{3!}\Delta^3 f(-2) + \frac{(u+2)(u+1)u(u-1)}{4!}\Delta^4 f(-2) + \ldots.. \quad (45)$$

In eqn. (45), shift the origin to 1 by replacing u by $u - 1$ and adding 1 to each argument 0, – 1, – 2, ..., we get

$$f(u) = f(1) + (u-1)\,\Delta f(0) + \frac{u(u-1)}{2!}\Delta^2 f(0) + \frac{u(u-1)(u-2)}{3!}\Delta^3 f(-1) + \frac{(u+1)u(u-1)(u-2)}{4!}\Delta^4 f(-1) + \ldots.. \quad (46)$$

Taking mean of (44) and (46), we get

$$f(u) = \left\{\frac{f(0)+f(1)}{2}\right\} + \left\{\frac{u+(u-1)}{2}\right\}\Delta f(0) + \frac{u(u-1)}{2!}\left\{\frac{\Delta^2 f(-1)+\Delta^2 f(0)}{2}\right\} + \frac{u(u-1)}{3!}(u+1+u-2)\frac{\Delta^3 f(-1)}{2} + \frac{(u+1)u(u-1)(u-2)}{4!}\left\{\frac{\Delta^4 f(-2)+\Delta^4 f(-1)}{2}\right\} + \ldots..$$

Finally, we get

$$f(u) = \left\{\frac{f(0)+f(1)}{2}\right\} + \left(u-\frac{1}{2}\right)\Delta f(0) + \frac{u(u-1)}{2!}\left\{\frac{\Delta^2 f(-1)+\Delta^2 f(0)}{2}\right\} + \frac{(u-1)\left(u-\frac{1}{2}\right)u}{3!}\Delta^3 f(-1) + \frac{(u+1)u(u-1)(u-2)}{4!}\left\{\frac{\Delta^4 f(-2)+\Delta^4 f(-1)}{2}\right\} + \ldots... \quad (47)$$

This is called **Bessel's formula.**

It is very useful when $u = \frac{1}{2}$. It gives a better estimate when $\frac{1}{4} < \mathbf{u} < \frac{3}{4}$.

It is used mainly to compute entry against any argument between 0 and 1.

4.21.1 Algorithm of Bessel's Formula

Step 01. Start of the program.

Step 02. Input number of terms n

Step 03. Input the array ax

Step 04. Input the array ay

Step 05. h=ax[1]-ax[0]

Step 06. for i=1;i<n-l;i++

Step 07. diff[i][1]=ay[i+1]-ay[i]

Step 08. End Loop i

Step 09. for j=2;j<=4;j++

Step 10. for i=0;i<n–j;i++

Step 11. diff[i][j]=diff[i+1][j–1]–diff[i][j–1]

Step 12. End Loop i

Step 13. End Loop j

Step 14. i=0

Step 15. Repeat Step 16 until ax[i]<x

Step 16. i=i+1

Step 17. i=i–1;

Step 18. p=(x–ax[i])/h

Step 19. y1=p*(diff[i][1])

Step 20. y2=p*(p-1)*(diff[i][2]+diff[i–1][2])/4

Step 21. y3=p*(p-1)*(p-0.5)*(diff[i–1][3])/6

Step 22. y4=(p+1)*p*(p–1)*(p–2)*(diff[i–2][4]+diff[i–1][4])/48

Step 23. y=ay[i]+y1+y2+y3+y4

Step 24. Print Output

Step 25. End of Program

4.21.2 Flow-chart

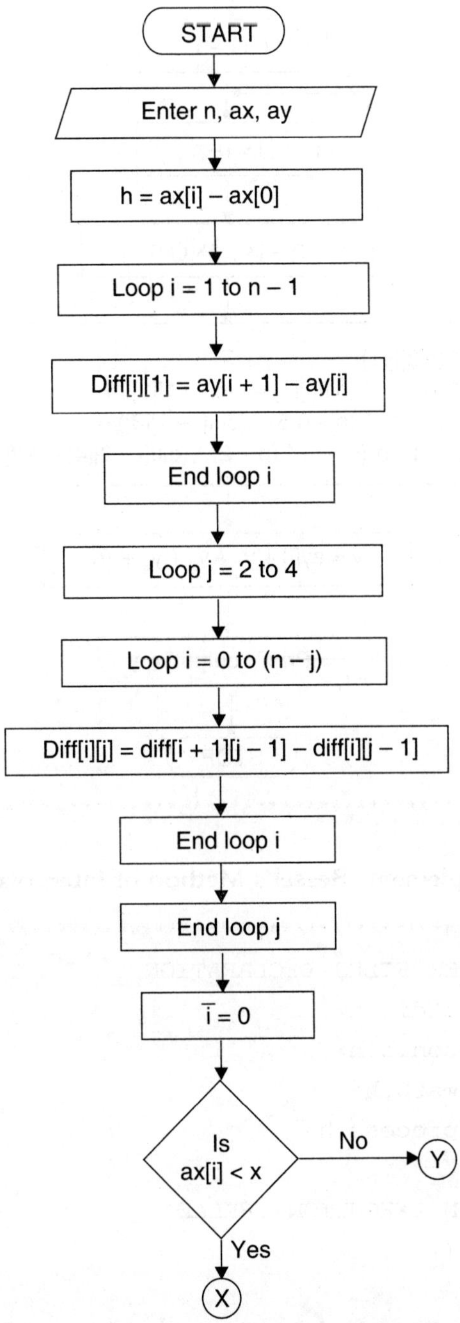

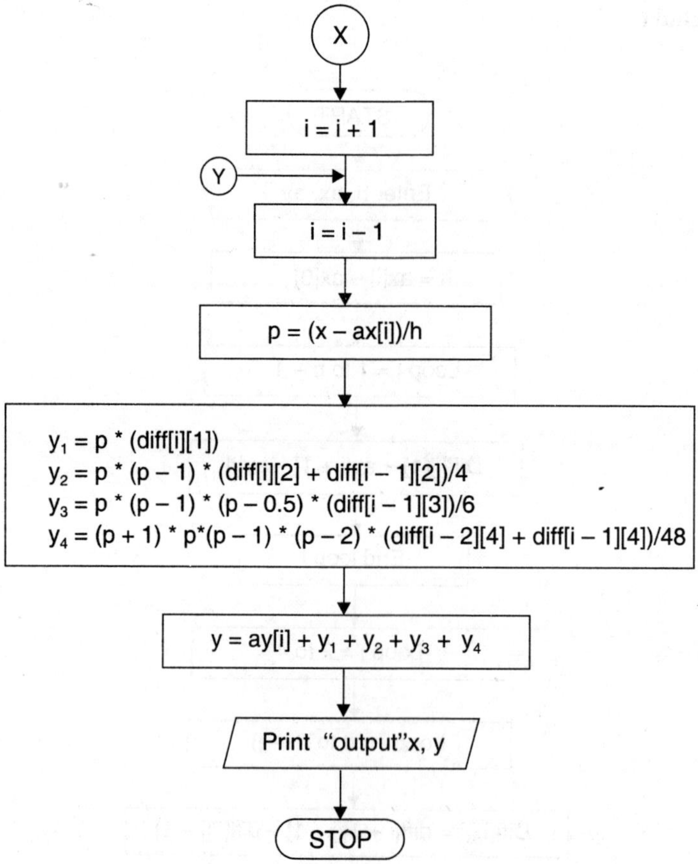

/* ***

4.21.3 Program to Implement Bessel's Method of Interpolation

*** */

```
//...HEADER FILES DECLARATION
#include<stdio.h>
#include<conio.h>
#include<math.h>
#include<process.h>

//... MAIN EXECUTION THREAD
void main()
{
//...Variable declaration Field
```

```
//...Integer Type
int n;
int i,j;
//...Floating Type
float ax[10];                    //...array - limit 9
float ay[10];                    //...array - limit 9
float h;
float p;
float diff[20][20];              //... array 2d - limit
19, 19
float x,y;
float y1,y2,y3,y4,
//...Invoke Clear Screen Function
clrscr();                        //... Clear Screen
//... Input Section
printf("\n Enter the number of terms");
scanf("%d",&n);
//... Input Section Array X
printf("\n Enter the values for x \n");
//... Input Section Loop for X
for(i=0;i<n;i++)
    {
    printf("\n Enter the value for x%d-",i+1);
    scanf("%f,&ax[i]);
    }
//... Input Section for Array Y
printf("\n Enter the values for y\n");
//...Input Section Loop for Y
for(i=0;i<n;i++)
{
    printf("\n Enter the value for y%d-",i+1);
    scanf("%f",&ay[i]);
    }
//...Input Section Loop for Value Of X for Y
printf("\n Enter the value of x for     ");
printf("\n which you want the value of y ");
```

```
scanf ("%f",&x);                         //...Input X
//...Calculation and Processing Section
h=ax[1]-ax[0];
for(i=0;i<n-1;i++)
     {
     diff[i][1]=ay[i+1]-ay[i];
     }
for(j=2;j<=4;j++)
     {
     for(i=0;i<n-j;i++)
          {
          diff[i][j]=diff[i+1][j-1]-diff[i][j-1];
          }
     }
i=0;
do   {
     i++;
     }while (ax[i]<x);
i--;

//... Bessel formulae Calculation
p=(x-ax[i])/h;
y1=p*(diff[i][1]);
y2=p*(p-1)*diff[i][2]+diff[i-1][2])/4;
y3=p*(p-1)*(p-0.5)*(diff[i-1][3])/6;
y4=(p+1)*p*(p-1)*(p-2)*(diff[i-2][4]+diff[i-1][4])/48;
//...Taking Sum
y=ay[i]+y1+y2+y3+y4;
//...Output Section
printf("\nwhen x=%6.2f,y=%6.8f ",x,y);
//...Invoke User Watch Halt Function
printf("\n\n Press Enter to Exit \t");
getch();
}

*End of Main Execution Thread */
```

4.21.4 Output

```
Enter the number of terms - 7
Enter the values of x
Enter the value of x1 - .61
Enter the value of x2 - .62
Enter the value of x3 - .63
Enter the value of x4 - .64
Enter the value of x5 - .65
Enter the value of x6 - .66
Enter the value of x7 - .67
Enter the values of y
Enter the value of y1 - 1.840431
Enter the value of y2 - 1.858928
Enter the value of y3 - 1.877610
Enter the value of y4 - 1.896481
Enter the value of y5 - 1.915541
Enter the value of y6 - 1.934792
Enter the value of y7 - 1.954237
Enter the value of x for
which you want the value of y - .644
When x = 0.644, y=1.90408230
Press Enter to Exit
```

EXAMPLES

Example 1. *Given* $y_{20} = 24$, $y_{24} = 32$, $y_{28} = 35$ *and* $y_{32} = 40$ *find* y_{25} *by Bessel's interpolation formula.*

Sol. Take origin at 24.

Here, $a = 24, \quad h = 4, \quad a + hu = 25$

$\therefore \quad 24 + 4u = 25 \quad \Rightarrow \quad u = .25$

The difference table is:

u	x	y	Δy	$\Delta^2 y$	$\Delta^3 y$
−1	20	24			
			8		
0	24	32		−5	
			3		7
1	28	35		2	
			5		
2	32	40			

Using Bessel's formula,

$$f(u) = \left\{\frac{f(0) + f(1)}{2}\right\} + \left(u - \frac{1}{2}\right) \Delta f(0)$$

$$+ \frac{u(u-1)}{2}\left\{\frac{\Delta^2 f(-1) + \Delta^2 f(0)}{2}\right\}$$

$$+ \frac{(u-1)\left(u - \frac{1}{2}\right)u}{3!} \Delta^3 f(-1)$$

$$\Rightarrow \quad f(.25) = \left(\frac{32+35}{2}\right) + (.25 - .5)(3) + \frac{(.25)(.25-1)}{2}\left\{\frac{-5+2}{2}\right\}$$

$$+ \frac{(.25-1)(.25-.5)(.25)}{3!}(7)$$

$$= 32.9453125$$

Hence $y_{25} = 32.9453125$.

Example 2. *Apply Bessel's formula to find the value of f(27.4) from the table:*

x:	*25*	*26*	*27*	*28*	*29*	*30*
f(x):	*4.000*	*3.846*	*3.704*	*3.571*	*3.448*	*3.333.*

Sol. Taking origin at 27 and $h = 1$

$$x = a + uh \quad \Rightarrow \quad 27.4 = 27 + u \times 1$$

$$\therefore \quad u = 0.4$$

The difference table is as follows:

u	$10^3 f(u)$	$10^3\, \Delta f(u)$	$10^3\, \Delta^2 f(u)$	$10^3\, \Delta^3 f(u)$	$10^3\, \Delta^4 f(u)$	$10^3\, \Delta^5 f(u)$
– 2	4000					
		– 154				
– 1	3847		12			
		– 142		– 3		
0	3704		9		4	
		– 133		1		– 7
1	3571		10		– 3	
		– 123		– 2		
2	3448		8			
		– 115				
3	3333					

Bessel's formula is

$$f(u) = \left\{\frac{f(0)+f(1)}{2}\right\} + \left(u - \frac{1}{2}\right)\Delta f(0) + \frac{u(u-1)}{2!}\left\{\frac{\Delta^2 f(0) + \Delta^2 f(-1)}{2}\right\}$$

$$+ \frac{(u-1)\left(u-\frac{1}{2}\right)u}{3!}\Delta^3 f(-1)$$

$$+ \frac{(u+1)u(u-1)(u-2)}{4!}\left\{\frac{\Delta^4 f(-1) + \Delta^4 f(-2)}{2}\right\}$$

$$+ \frac{(u-2)(u-1)\left(u-\frac{1}{2}\right)u(u+1)}{5!}\Delta^5 f(-2)$$

$$\therefore \quad 10^3 f(0.4) = \left\{\frac{3704+3571}{2}\right\} + (.4-.5)(-133) + \frac{(.4)(.4-1)}{2!}\left(\frac{10+9}{2}\right)$$

$$+ \frac{(.4-1)(.4-.5)(.4)}{3!}(1) + \frac{(.4+1)(.4)(.4-1)(.4-2)}{4!}\left(\frac{-3+4}{2}\right)$$

$$+ \frac{(.4-2)(.4-1)(.4-.5)(.4)(.4+1)}{5!}(-7)$$

$$= 3649.678336$$

$$\Rightarrow \quad f(.4) = 3.649678336$$

Hence $f(27.4) = 3.649678336$.

Example 3. *Probability distribution function values of a normal distribution are given as follows:*

x:	*0.2*	*0.6*	*1.0*	*1.4*	*1.8*
p(x):	*0.39104*	*0.33322*	*0.24197*	*0.14973*	*0.07895*

Find the value of p(x) for x = 1.2.

Sol. Taking the origin at 1.0 and $h = 0.4$

$$x = a + uh \quad \Rightarrow \quad 1.2 = 1.0 + u \times 0.4$$

$$\therefore \qquad u = \frac{1.2 - 1.0}{0.4} = \frac{1}{2}$$

The difference table is:

u	$10^5 f(u)$	$10^5\,\Delta f(u)$	$10^5\,\Delta^2 f(u)$	$10^5\,\Delta^3 f(u)$	$10^5\,\Delta^4 f(u)$
– 2	39104				
		– 5782			
– 1	33332		– 3343		
		– 9125		3244	
0	24197		– 99		– 999
		– 9224		2245	
1	14973		2146		
		– 7078			
2	7895				

Bessel's formula is

$$f(u) = \left\{\frac{f(0) + f(1)}{2}\right\} + \left(u - \frac{1}{2}\right)\Delta f(0) + \frac{u(u-1)}{2!}\left\{\frac{\Delta^2 f(0) + \Delta^2 f(-1)}{2}\right\} + \frac{(u-1)\left(u - \frac{1}{2}\right)(u)}{3!}\Delta^3 f(-1)$$

$$10^5 f(.5) = \left(\frac{24197 + 14973}{2}\right) + 0 + \frac{\left(\frac{1}{2}\right)\left(\frac{1}{2} - 1\right)}{2!}\left(\frac{2146 - 99}{2}\right) + 0$$

$$= 19457.0625$$

$\therefore \qquad f(.5) = 0.194570625$

Hence $\quad p(1.2) = 0.194570625.$

Example 4. *Given that*

x:	*4*	*6*	*8*	*10*	*12*	*14*
f(x):	*3.5460*	*5.0753*	*6.4632*	*7.7217*	*8.8633*	*9.8986*

Apply Bessel's formula to find the value of f(9).

Sol. Taking the origin at 8, $h = 2$,

$$9 = 8 + 2u \quad \text{or} \quad u = \frac{1}{2}$$

The difference table is:

u	$10^4 y_u$	$10^4 \Delta^2 y_u$	$10^4 \Delta^2 y_u$	$10^4 \Delta^3 y_u$	$10^4 \Delta^4 y_u$	$10^5 \Delta^5 y_u$
– 2	35460					
		15293				
– 1	50753		– 1414			
		13879		120		
0	64632		– 1294		5	
		1258		125		– 24
1	77217		– 1169		– 19	
		11416		106		
2	88633		– 1063			
		10353				
3	98986					

Bessel's formula is

$$y_u = \frac{1}{2}(y_1 + y_0) + \left(u - \frac{1}{2}\right)\Delta y_0 + \frac{u(u-1)}{2!}\frac{1}{2}(\Delta^2 y_0 + \Delta^2 y_{-1})$$

$$+ \frac{\left(u - \frac{1}{2}\right)u(u-1)}{3!}\Delta^3 y_{-1}$$

$$+ \frac{(u+1)\,u(u-1)(u-2)}{4!} \times \frac{1}{2}(\Delta^4 y_{-3} + \Delta^4 y_{-2})$$

$$+ \frac{(u-2)\,(u-1)\left(u - \frac{1}{2}\right)u\,(u+1)}{5!}\Delta^5\, y_{-2}$$

$$10^4 y_{1/2} = \frac{1}{2}(77217 + 64632) + 0 + \frac{\frac{1}{2}\left(-\frac{1}{2}\right)}{2} \cdot \frac{1}{2}(-1169 - 1294)$$

$$+ 0 + \frac{\frac{3}{2}\cdot\frac{1}{2}\cdot\left(-\frac{1}{2}\right)\left(-\frac{3}{2}\right)}{24} \cdot \frac{1}{2}(-19 + 5) + 0$$

$\Rightarrow \quad 10^4 y_{1/2} = 71078.27344$

$\therefore \quad y_{1/2} = 7.107827344$

Hence, $\quad f(9) = 7.107827344.$

Example 5. *Given $y_0, y_1, y_2, y_3, y_4, y_5$ (fifth differences constant), prove that*

$$y_{2\frac{1}{2}} = \frac{1}{2}c + \frac{25(c-b) + 3(a-c)}{256}$$

where $\quad a = y_0 + y_5, b = y_1 + y_4, c = y_2 + y_3.$

Sol. Put $\quad u = \frac{1}{2}$ in Bessel's formula, we get

$$y_{1/2} = \frac{1}{2}(y_0 + y_1) - \frac{1}{16}(\Delta^2 y_0 + \Delta^2 y_{-1}) + \frac{3}{256}(\Delta^4 y_{-1} + \Delta^4 y_{-2})$$

Shifting the origin to 2, we have

$$y_{2\frac{1}{2}} = \frac{1}{2}(y_2 + y_3) - \frac{1}{16}(\Delta^2 y_2 + \Delta^2 y_1) + \frac{3}{256}(\Delta^4 y_1 + \Delta^4 y_0)$$

$$= \frac{c}{2} - \frac{1}{16}(y_3 - 2y_2 + y_1 + y_4 - 2y_3 + y_2)$$

$$+ \frac{3}{256}(y_5 - 3y_4 + 2y_3 + 2y_2 - 3y_1 + y_0)$$

$$y_{2\frac{1}{2}} = \frac{c}{2} - \frac{1}{16}(y_4 - y_3 - y_2 + y_1) + \frac{3}{256}(a - 3b + 2c)$$

$$= \frac{c}{2} - \frac{1}{16}(b - c) + \frac{3}{256}(a - 3b + 2c)$$

$$y_{2\frac{1}{2}} = \frac{c}{2} + \frac{1}{256}[25(c-b) + 3(a-c)].$$

Example 6. *If third differences are constant, prove that*

$$y_{x+\frac{1}{2}} = \frac{1}{2}(y_x + y_{x+1}) - \frac{1}{16}(\Delta^2 y_{x-1} + \Delta^2 y_x).$$

Sol. Putting $u = \frac{1}{2}$ in Bessel's formula, we get

$$y_{1/2} = \frac{1}{2}(y_0 + y_1) - \frac{1}{16}(\Delta^2 y_0 + \Delta^2 y_{-1})$$

Shifting the origin to x,

$$y_{x+\frac{1}{2}} = \frac{1}{2}(y_x + y_{x+1}) - \frac{1}{16}(\Delta^2 y_x + \Delta^2 y_{x-1}).$$

Example 7. *Find the value of* y_{15}*, using Bessel's formula, if*

$$y_{10} = 2854, \quad y_{14} = 3162, \quad y_{18} = 3544, \quad y_{22} = 3992.$$

Sol. Taking the origin at 14, $h = 4$

$$\therefore \qquad 15 = 14 + 4 \,.\, u \quad \therefore \quad u = \frac{1}{4}$$

The difference table is:

u	x	$f(x)$	$\Delta f(x)$	$\Delta^2 f(x)$	$\Delta^3 f(x)$
−1	10	2854			
			308		
0	14	3162		74	
			382		−8
1	18	3544		66	
			448		
2	22	3992			

Bessel's formula is

$$f(u) = \left\{\frac{f(0) + f(1)}{2}\right\} + \left(u - \frac{1}{2}\right)\Delta f(0) + \frac{u(u-1)}{2!}\left\{\frac{\Delta^2 f(-1) + \Delta^2 f(0)}{2}\right\}$$

$$+ \frac{(u-1)\left(u - \frac{1}{2}\right)u}{3!}\Delta^3 f(-1)$$

$$\therefore \quad f(.25) = \left(\frac{3162 + 3544}{2}\right) + (.25 - .5)\,(382) + \frac{(.25)\,(.25 - 1)}{2}\left(\frac{74 + 66}{2}\right)$$

$$+ \frac{(.25 - 1)\,(.25 - .5)\,(.25)}{6}\,(-8)$$

$$= 3250.875$$

Hence $y_{15} = 3250.875.$

ASSIGNMENT 4.9

1. Apply Bessel's formula to find the value of $y_{2.73}$ given that

$y_{2.5} = 0.4938,\quad y_{2.6} = 0.4953,\quad y_{2.7} = 0.4965$

$y_{2.8} = 0.4974,\quad y_{2.9} = 0.4981,\quad y_{3.0} = 0.4987.$

2. Find the value of y if $x = 3.75$, given that

x:	2.5	3.0	3.5	4.0	4.5	5.0
y:	24.145	22.043	20.225	18.644	17.262	16.047.

Using Bessel's formula.

3. Apply Bessel's formula to find $u_{62.5}$ from the following data:

x:	60	61	62	63	64	65
u_x:	7782	7853	7924	7993	8062	8129.

4. Apply Bessel's formula to find the value of $f(12.2)$ from the following table:

x:	0	5	10	15	20	25	30
$f(x)$:	0	0.19146	0.34634	0.43319	0.47725	0.49379	0.49865

5. The following table gives the values of e^x for certain equidistant values of x. Find the value of e^x when $x = 0.644$ using Bessel's formula:

x:	.61	.62	.63	.64	.65	.66	.67
e^x:	1.840431	1.858928	1.877610	1.896481	1.915541	1.934792	1.954237

6. Find $y(0.543)$ from the following values of x and y:

x:	0.1	0.2	0.3	0.4	0.5	0.6	0.7
$y(x)$:	2.631	3.328	4.097	4.944	5.875	6.896	8.013

7. Apply Bessel's formula to obtain y_{25} given $y_{20} = 2854$, $y_{24} = 3162$, $y_{28} = 3544$, $y_{32} = 3992$.

8. The pressure p of wind corresponding to velocity v is given by following data. Estimate p when $v = 25$.

v:	10	20	30	40
p:	1.1	2	4.4	7.9

4.22 LAPLACE-EVERETT'S FORMULA

Gauss' forward formula is

$$f(u) = f(0) + u\Delta f(0) + \frac{u(u-1)}{2!}\Delta^2 f(-1) + \frac{(u+1)u(u-1)}{3!}\Delta^3 f(-1)$$

$$+ \frac{(u+1)u(u-1)(u-2)}{4!}\Delta^4 f(-2)$$

$$+ \frac{(u+2)(u+1)u(u-1)(u-2)}{5!}\Delta^5 f(-2) + ... \qquad (48)$$

We have,

$$\Delta f(0) = f(1) - f(0)$$

$$\Delta^3 f(-1) = \Delta^2 f(0) - \Delta^2 f(-1)$$

$$\Delta^5 f(-2) = \Delta^4 f(-1) - \Delta^4 f(-2)$$

$\therefore$ From (48),

$$f(u) = f(0) + u\{f(1) - f(0)\} + \frac{u(u-1)}{2!}\Delta^2 f(-1)$$

$$+ \frac{(u+1)u(u-1)}{3!}\{\Delta^2 f(0) - \Delta^2 f(-1)\}$$

$$+ \frac{(u+1)u(u-1)(u-2)}{4!}\Delta^4 f(-2)$$

$$+ \frac{(u+2)(u+1)u(u-1)(u-2)}{5!}\{\Delta^4 f(-1) - \Delta^4 f(-2)\} + ...$$

$$= (1-u) f(0) + uf(1) + \frac{(u+1)u(u-1)}{3!}\Delta^2 f(0)$$

$$- \frac{u(u-1)(u-2)}{3!}\Delta^2 f(-1)$$

$$+ \frac{(u+2)(u+1)u(u-1)(u-2)}{5!}\Delta^4 f(-1)$$

$$- \frac{(u+1)u(u-1)(u-2)(u-3)}{5!}\Delta^4 f(-2) + ...$$

$$= \left\{ u\,f(1) + \frac{(u+1)\,u\,(u-1)}{3!}\,\Delta^2 f(0) + \frac{(u+2)\,(u+1)\,u\,(u-1)\,(u-2)}{5!}\,\Delta^4 f(-1) + \ldots\ldots \right\}$$

$$+ \left\{ (1-u)\,f(0) + \frac{(1-u+1)\,(1-u)\,(1-u-1)}{3!}\,\Delta^2 f(-1) + \frac{(1-u+2)\,(1-u+1)\,(1-u)\,(1-u-1)\,(1-u-2)}{5!}\,\Delta^4 f(-2) + \ldots\ldots \right\}$$

$$\boxed{f(u) = \left\{ uf(1) + \frac{(u+1)\,u\,(u-1)}{3!}\,\Delta^2 f(0) + \frac{(u+2)\,(u+1)\,u\,(u-1)\,(u-2)}{5!}\,\Delta^4 f(-1) + \ldots\ldots \right\} + \left\{ wf(0) + \frac{(w+1)\,w\,(w-1)}{3!}\,\Delta^2 f(-1) + \frac{(w+2)\,(w+1)\,w\,(w-1)\,(w-2)}{5!}\,\Delta^4 f(-2) + \ldots\ldots \right\}} \tag{49}$$

where $w = 1 - u$

This is called **Laplace–Everett's formula.**

It gives the best estimate when $u > \frac{1}{2}$. It is used to compute any entry against any argument between 0 and 1. It is useful when intervening values in successive intervals are required.

4.22.1 Algorithm of Laplace' Everett Formula

Step 01. Start of the program.

Step 02. Input number of terms n

Step 03. Input the array ax

Step 04. Input the array ay

Step 05. h=ax[1]-ax[0]

Step 06. for i=0; i<n-l; i++

Step 07. diff[i][1]=ay[i+1]-ay[i]

Step 08. End Loop i

Step 09. for j=2; j<=4; j++

Step 10. for i=0; i<n–j; i++

Step 11. diff[i][j]=diff[i+1][j–1]–diff[i][j–1]

Step 12. End Loop i

Step 13. End Loop j

Step 14. i=0

Step 15. Repeat Step 16 until ax[i]<x

Step 16. i=i+1

Step 17. i=i–1;

Step 18. p=(x–ax[i])/h

Step 19. q=1–p

Step 20. y1=q*(ay[i])

Step 21. y2=q*(q*q–1)*diff[i–1][2]/6

Step 22. y3=q*(q*q–1)*(q*q–4)*(diff[i–2][4])/120

Step 23. py1=p*ay[i+1]

Step 24. py2=p*(p*p–1)*diff[i][2]/6

Step 25. py3=p*(p*p–1)*(p*p–4)*(diff[i–1][4])/120

Step 26. y=y1+y2+y3+y4+py1+py2+py3

Step 27. Print Output x, y

Step 28. End of Program

4.22.2 Flow-chart

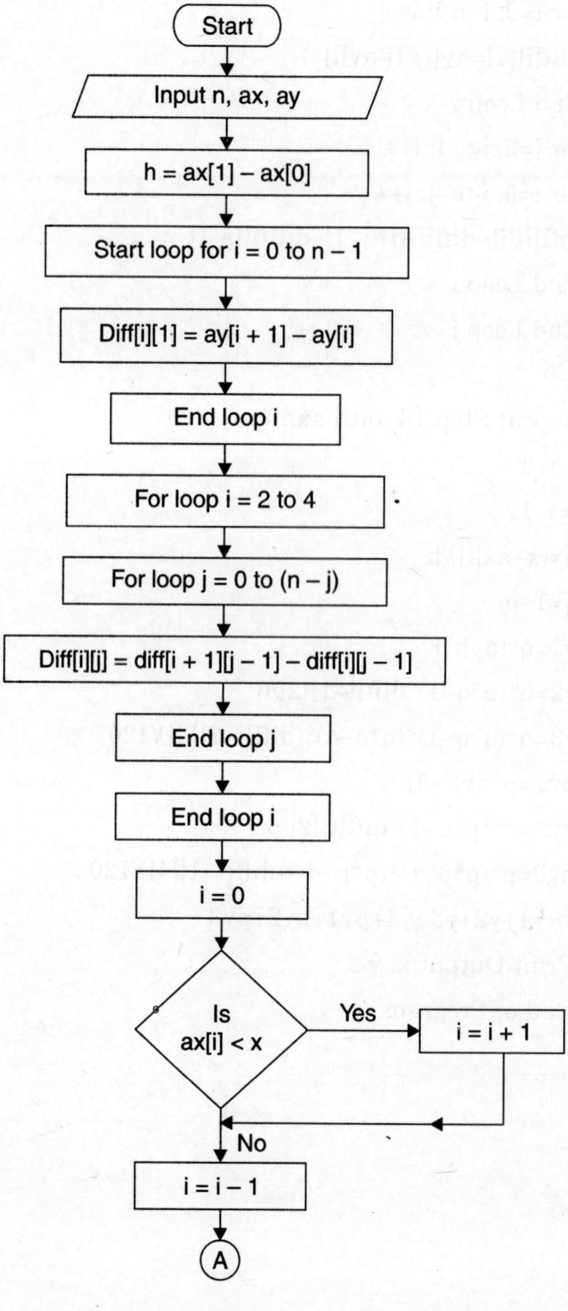

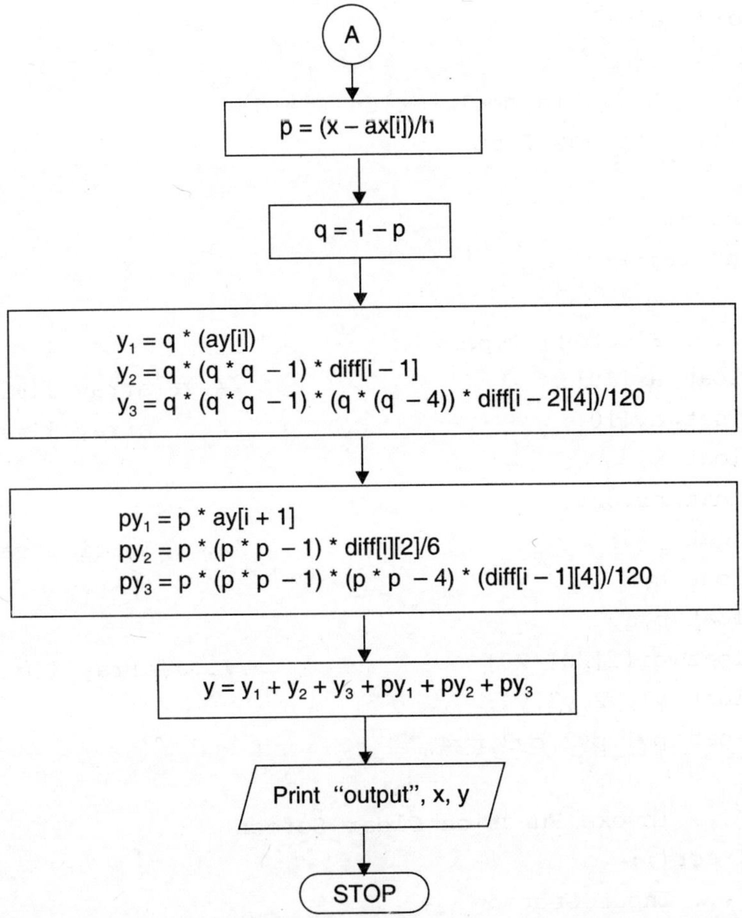

/* ***

4.22.3 Program to Implement Laplace Everett's Method of Interpolation

*** */

```
//... HEADER FILES DECLARATION
# include <stdio.h>
# include <conio.h>
# include <math.h>
# include <process.h>
# include <string.h>

//... MAIN EXECUTION THREAD
```

```
void main()
 {
 //... Variable declaration Field
 //... Integer Type

 int n;
 int i,j;

 //... Floating Type
 float ax[10];                         //... array limit 9
 float ay[10];                         //... array limit 9
 float x;
 float nr,dr;
 float y=0;                            //... Initial value 0
 float h;
 float p,q;
 float diff[20][20];                   //... array limit 19,19
 float y1,y2,y3,y4;
 float py1,py2,py3,py4;

 //... Invoke Function Clear Screen
 clrscr();
 //... Input Section
 printf ("\n Enter the number of terms - ");
 scanf("%d",&n);
 //... Input Sequel for array X
 printf("\n\n Enter the value in the form of x - ");
 //... Input Loop for Array X
 for (i=0;i<n;i++)
      {
      Printf("\n\n Enter the value of x%d - ",i+1);
      scanf("%f",&ax[i]);
      }
 //... Input Sequel for Array X
 printf ("\n\n Enter the value in the form of y - ");
```

```
//... Input Loop Array Y
for (i=0;i<n;i++)
     {
     printf ("\n\n Enter the value of y%d - ",i+1);
     scanf("%f",&ay[i]);
     }
//... Inputting the required value query
printf("\nEnter the value of x for ");
printf("\nwhich you want the value of y - ");
scanf("%f",&x);

//... Calculation and Processing Section
h=ax[1]-ax[0];
for(i=0;i<n-1;i++)
     {
     diff[i][1]=ay[i+1]-ay[i];
     }
for(j=2;j<=4;j++)
     {
     for(i=0;i<n-j;i++)
          {
          diff[i][j]=diff[i+1][j-1]-diff[i][j-1];
          }
     }
i=0;
do   {
     i++;
     }while(ax[i]<x);
i--;
p=(x-ax[i])/h;
q=1-p;
y1=q*(ay[i]);
y2=q*(q*q-1)*diff[i-1][2]/6;
y3=q*(q*q-1)*(q*q-4)*(diff[i-2][4])/120;
py1=p*ay[i+1];
```

```
py2=p*(p*p-1)*diff[i][2]/6;
py3=p*(p*p-1)*(p*p-4)*(diff[i-1][4])/120;
//... Taking sum
y=y1+y2+y3+y4+py1+py2+py3;
//... Output Section
printf("\n when x=%6.2f,y=%6.8f  ",x,y);
//... Invoke User Watch Halt Function
printf("\n\n\n Press Enter to Exit ");
getch();
}
//... Termination of Main Execution Thread
```

4.22.4 Output

```
Enter the number of terms - 7
Enter the value in the form of x -
Enter the value of x1 - 1.72
Enter the value of x2 - 1.73
Enter the value of x3 - 1.74
Enter the value of x4 - 1.75
Enter the value of x5 - 1.76
Enter the value of x6 - 1.77
Enter the value of x7 - 1.78
Enter the value in the form of y -
Enter the value of y1 - .1790661479
Enter the value of y2 - .1772844100
Enter the value of y3 - .1755204006
Enter the value of y4 - .1737739435
Enter the value of y5 - .1720448638
Enter the value of y6 - .1703329888
Enter the value of y7 - .1686381473
Enter the value of x for
which you want the value of y - 1.7475
When x = 1.7475, y = 0.17420892
Press Enter to Exit
```

EXAMPLES

Example 1. *Using Everett's formula, evaluate f(30) if*

$f(20) = 2854,\quad f(28) = 3162$

$f(36) = 7088,\quad f(44) = 7984.$

Sol. Take origin at 28.

$$\therefore \quad a = 28,\ h = 8$$

$$a + hu = 30$$

$$\Rightarrow \quad 28 + 8u = 30 \quad \Rightarrow \quad u = .25$$

Also, $w = 1 - u = 1 - .25 = .75$

The difference table is:

u	$f(u)$	$\Delta f(u)$	$\Delta^2 f(u)$	$\Delta^3 f(u)$
– 1	2854			
		308		
0	3162		3618	
		3926		– 6648
1	7088		– 3030	
		896		
2	7984			

By Everett's formula,

$$\therefore \quad f(.25) = \left\{(.25)(7088) + \frac{(1.25)(.25)(-.75)}{3!}(-3030) + ...\right\}$$

$$+ \left\{(.75)(3162) + \frac{(1.75)(.75)(-.25)}{3!}(3618) + ...\right\}$$

$$= 4064$$

Hence $f(30) = 4064$.

Example 2. *Find the value of f(27.4) from the following table:*

x:	*25*	*26*	*27*	*28*	*29*	*30*
f(x):	*4.000*	*3.846*	*3.704*	*3.571*	*3.448*	*3.333.*

Sol. Here $u = \dfrac{27.4 - 27.0}{1} = 0.4 \because$ origin is at 27.0, $h = 1$

Also, $w = 1 - u = 0.6$

The difference table is:

u	$10^3 f(u)$	$10^3 \Delta f(u)$	$10^3 \Delta^2 f(u)$	$10^3 \Delta^3 f(u)$	$10^3 \Delta^4 f(u)$
– 2	4000				
		– 154			
– 1	3846		12		
		– 142		– 3	
0	3704		9		4
		– 133		1	
1	3571		10		– 3
		– 123		– 2	
2	3448		8		
		– 115			
3	3333				

By Laplace Everett's formula,

$$f(.4) = \left\{(.4)(3571) + \frac{(1.4)(.4)(-.6)}{3!}(10) + \frac{(2.4)(1.4)(.4)(-.6)(-1.6)}{5!}(-3) + \ldots\right\}$$

$$+ \left\{(.6)(3704) + \frac{(1.6)(.6)(-.4)}{3!}(9) + \frac{(2.6)(1.6)(.6)(-.4)(-1.4)}{5!}(4)\right\}$$

$$= 3649.678336.$$

Hence $f(27.4) = 3649.678336$.

ASSIGNMENT 4.10

1. Given the table

x:	21	22	23	24	25	26
$log\ x$:	1.3222	1.3424	1.3617	1.3802	1.3979	1.4150

Apply Laplace-Everett's formula to find the value of log 2375.

2. From the following present value annuity a_n table:

x:	20	25	30	35	40
a_n:	11.4699	12.7834	13.7648	14.4982	15.0463

find the present value of the annuity a_{31}, a_{32}, a_{33}, a_{34}.

3. Find the value of $f(31)$, $f(32)$, $f(33)$, $f(34)$. Given that

$$f(20) = 3010, f(25) = 3979, f(30) = 4771$$

$$f(35) = 5441, f(40) = 6021 \text{ and } f(45) = 6532.$$

4. Find y_{12} if $y_0 = 0$, $y_{10} = 43214$, $y_{20} = 86002$ and $y_{30} = 128372$.

5. Obtain the values of y_{25}, given that

$$y_{20} = 2854, \qquad y_{24} = 3162$$

$$y_{28} = 3544 \text{ and } y_{32} = 3992$$

6. Find the value of e^{-x} when $x = 1.748$ from the following:

x:	1.72	1.73	1.74	1.75	1.76	1.77
e^{-x}:	0.1790	0.1773	0.1755	0.1738	0.1720	0.1703

7. Use Everett's formula to find the present value of the annuity for $n = 36$ from the table:

x:	25	30	35	40	45	50
a_x:	12.7834	13.7648	14.4982	15.0463	15.4558	15.7619.

8. Apply Everett's formula to find the value of $f(26)$ and $f(27)$ from the table:

x:	15	20	25	30	35	40
$f(x)$:	12.849	16.351	19.524	22.396	24.999	27.356.

9. Find the compound interest on the sum of Rs. 10,000 at 7% for the period 16 and 17 years if:

x:	5	10	15	20	25	30
$(1.07)^n$:	1.40255	1.96715	2.75903	3.86968	5.42743	7.61236.

10. Apply Everett's formula to find the values of e^{-x} for $x = 3.2, 3.4, 3.6, 3.8$, if

x:	1	2	3	4	5	6
e^{-x}:	0.36788	0.13534	0.04979	0.01832	0.00674	0.00248.

11. Given that

x:	40	45	50	55	60	65
$x^{1/3}$:	3.4200	3.3569	3.6840	3.8030	3.9149	4.0207

Find the values of $x^{1/3}$ when $x = 51$ to 54.

12. Prove that if third differences are assumed to be constant,

$$y_x = xy_1 + \frac{x(x^2-1)}{3!}\Delta^2 y_0 + uy_0 + \frac{u(u^2-1)}{3!}\Delta^2 y_{-1}$$

where $u = 1 - x$.

Apply this formula to find the value of y_{11} and y_{16}, given that

$$y_0 = 3010, y_5 = 2710, y_{10} = 2285, y_{15} = 1860, y_{20} = 1560, y_{25} = 1510, y_{30} = 1835.$$

13. The following table gives the values of e^x for certain equidistant values of x. Find the value of e^x when $x = 0.644$ using Everett's formula

x:	0.61	0.62	0.63	0.64	0.65	0.66	0.67
$y = e^x$:	1.840431	1.858928	1.877610	1.896481	1.915541	1.934792	1.954237.

14. The values of the elliptic integral,

$$k(m) = \int_0^{\pi/2} (1 - m\sin^2\theta)^{-\frac{1}{2}}\, d\theta$$

for certain equidistant values of m are given below. Use Everett's or Bessel's formula to determine $k(0.25)$.

m:	0.20	0.22	0.24	0.26	0.28	0.30
$k(m)$:	1.659624	1.669850	1.680373	1.691208	1.702374	1.713889.

15. From the following table of values of x and $y = e^x$, interpolate the value of y when $x = 1.91$

x:	1.7	1.8	1.9	2.0	2.1	2.2
$y = e^x$:	5.4739	6.0496	6.6859	7.3891	8.1662	9.0250.

16. Given the table:

x:	310	320	330	340	350	360
$\log x$:	2.49136	2.50515	2.51851	2.53148	2.54407	2.55630.

Find the value of log 337.5 by Laplace Everett's formula.

4.23 INTERPOLATION BY UNEVENLY SPACED POINTS

The interpolation formulae derived sofar possess the disadvantage of being applicable only to equally spaced values of the argument. It is then desirable to develop interpolation formulae for unequally spaced values of x. We shall study two such formulae:

(1) Lagrange's interpolation formula

(2) Newton's general interpolation formula with divided differences.

4.24 LAGRANGE'S INTERPOLATION FORMULA

Let $f(x_0)$, $f(x_1)$,......, $f(x_n)$ be $(n + 1)$ entries of a function $y = f(x)$, where $f(x)$ is assumed to be a polynomial corresponding to the arguments $x_0, x_1, x_2, ..., x_n$.

The polynomial $f(x)$ may be written as

$$f(x) = A_0 (x - x_1)(x - x_2) ...... (x - x_n)$$
$$+ A_1(x - x_0)(x - x_2) ...... (x - x_n)$$
$$+ ...... + A_n (x - x_0)(x - x_1) ...... (x - x_{n-1}) \quad (50)$$

where $A_0, A_1, ..., A_n$ are constants to be determined.

Putting $x = x_0, x_1, ..., x_n$ in (50), we get

$$f(x_0) = A_0 (x_0 - x_1)(x_0 - x_2) .... (x_0 - x_n)$$

$$\therefore \quad A_0 = \frac{f(x_0)}{(x_0 - x_1)(x_0 - x_2)......(x_0 - x_n)} \quad (51)$$

$$f(x_1) = A_1 (x_1 - x_0)(x_1 - x_2) ...... (x_1 - x_n)$$

$$\therefore \quad A_1 = \frac{f(x_1)}{(x_1 - x_0)(x_1 - x_2)......(x_1 - x_n)} \quad (52)$$

$$\vdots \qquad \vdots \qquad \vdots$$

$$\text{Similarly, } A_n = \frac{f(x_n)}{(x_n - x_0)(x_n - x_1)......(x_n - x_{n-1})} \quad (53)$$

Substituting the values of $A_0, A_1, ..., A_n$ in equation (50), we get

$$f(x) = \frac{(x - x_1)(x - x_2)......(x - x_n)}{(x_0 - x_1)(x_0 - x_2)......(x_0 - x_n)} f(x_0)$$
$$+ \frac{(x - x_0)(x - x_2)......(x - x_n)}{(x_1 - x_0)(x_1 - x_2)......(x_1 - x_n)} f(x_1)$$
$$+ ...... + \frac{(x - x_0)(x - x_1)......(x - x_{n-1})}{(x_n - x_0)(x_n - x_1)......(x_n - x_{n-1})} f(x_n) \quad (54)$$

This is called **Lagrange's Interpolation Formula.** In eqn. (54), dividing both sides by $(x - x_0)(x - x_1) ..... (x - x_n)$, Lagrange's formula may also be written as

$$\frac{f(x)}{(x-x_0)(x-x_1)......(x-x_n)} = \frac{f(x_0)}{(x_0-x_1)(x_0-x_2)......(x_0-x_n)} \cdot \frac{1}{(x-x_0)}$$

$$+ \frac{f(x_1)}{(x_1-x_0)(x_1-x_2)......(x_1-x_n)} \cdot \frac{1}{(x-x_1)} + ...$$

$$+ \frac{f(x_n)}{(x_n-x_0)(x_n-x_1)......(x_n-x_{n-1})} \cdot \frac{1}{(x-x_n)}. \quad (55)$$

4.24.1 Another form of Lagrange's Formula

§ **Prove that** the Lagrange's formula can be put in the form

$$\boxed{P_n(x) = \sum_{r=0}^{n} \frac{\phi(x) f(x_r)}{(x-x_r)\phi'(x_r)}}$$

where $$\phi(x) = \prod_{r=0}^{n} (x-x_r)$$

and $$\phi'(x_r) = \left[\frac{d}{dx}\{\phi(x)\}\right]_{x=x_r}$$

We have the Lagrange's formula,

$$P_n(x) = \sum_{r=0}^{n} \frac{(x-x_0)(x-x_1)\ldots(x-x_{r-1})(x-x_{r+1})\ldots(x-x_n)}{(x_r-x_0)(x_r-x_1)\ldots(x_r-x_{r-1})(x_r-x_{r+1})\ldots(x_r-x_n)} f(x_r)$$

$$= \sum_{r=0}^{n} \left\{\frac{\phi(x)}{x-x_r}\right\}\left\{\frac{f(x_r)}{(x_r-x_0)(x_r-x_1)\ldots(x_r-x_{r-1})(x_r-x_{r+1})\ldots(x_r-x_n)}\right\} \quad (56)$$

Now,

$$\phi(x) = \prod_{r=0}^{n} (x-x_r)$$

$$= (x-x_0)(x-x_1) ..... (x-x_{r-1})(x-x_r)(x-x_{r+1}) ..... (x-x_n)$$

$$\therefore \quad \phi'(x) = (x-x_1)(x-x_2) ..... (x-x_r) ..... (x-x_n)$$

$$+ (x-x_0)(x-x_2) ..... (x-x_r) ..... (x-x_n) + ...$$

$$+ (x-x_0)(x-x_1) ..... (x-x_{r-1})(x-x_{r+1}) ..... (x-x_n) + ...$$

$$+ (x-x_0)(x-x_1) ..... (x-x_r) ..... (x-x_{n-1})$$

$$\Rightarrow \quad \phi'(x_r) = [\phi'(x)]_{x = x_r}$$

$$= (x_r - x_0)(x_r - x_1) \ldots\ldots (x_r - x_{r-1})(x_r - x_{r+1}) \ldots\ldots (x_r - x_n) \qquad (57)$$

Hence from (56),

$$P_n(x) = \sum_{r=0}^{n} \frac{\phi(x) f(x_r)}{(x - x_r)\,\phi'(x_r)} \qquad \text{| using (57)}$$

4.24.2 Algorithm

Step 01. Start of the program

Step 02. Input number of terms n

Step 03. Input the array ax

Step 04. Input the array ay

Step 05. for i=0; i<n; i++

Step 06. nr=1

Step 07. dr=1

Step 08. for j=0; j<n; j++

Step 09. if j !=i

a. nr=nr*(x-ax[j])

b.dr*(ax[i]-ax[j])

Step 10. End Loop j

Step 11. y+=(nr/dr)*ay[i]

Step 12. End Loop i

Step 13. Print Output x, y

Step 14. End of Program

4.24.3 Flow-chart

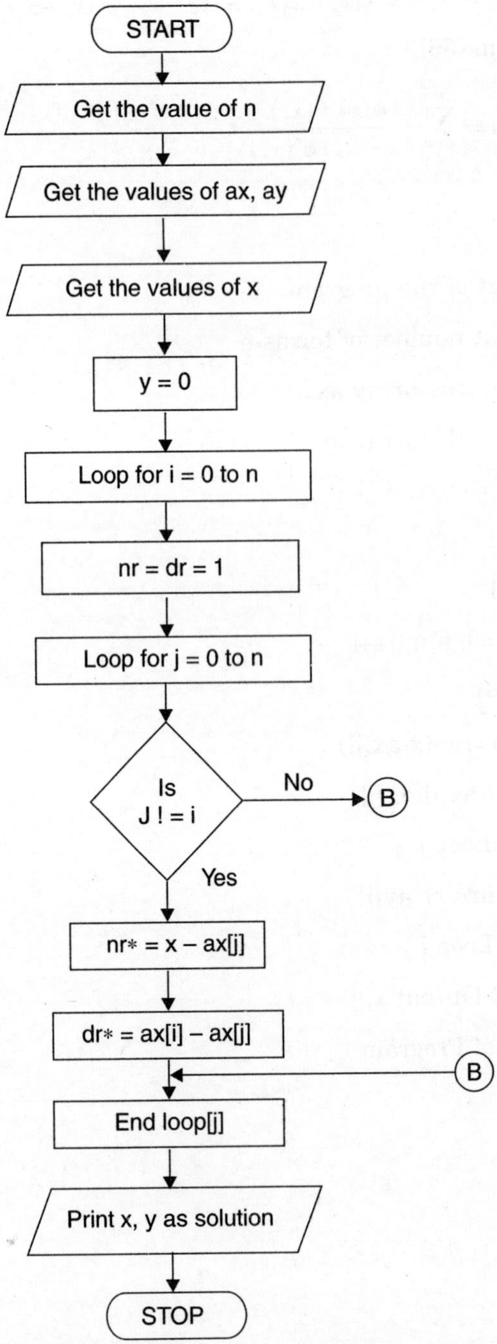

```
/* ********************************************************************
```

4.24.4 Program to Implement Lagrange's Method of Interpolation

```
******************************************************************** */

//... HEADER FILES DECLARATION
# include <stdio.h>
# include <conio.h>
# include <math.h>
# include <process.h>
# include <string.h>

//... MAIN EXECUTION THREAD
void main()
{
//... Variable declaration Field
//... Integer Type
int n;                              //... Number of terms
int i,j;                            //... Loop Variables
//... Floating Type
float ax[100];                      //... array limit 99
float ay[100];                      //... array limit 99
float x=0;                          //... User Querry
float y=0;                          //... Initial value 0
float nr;                           //... Calc. section
float dr;                           //... Calc. section

//... Invoke Function Clear Screen

clrscr();

//... Input Section
printf("\n Enter the number of terms - ");
scanf("%d",&n);
//... Input Sequel for array X
```

```
printf("\n\n Enter the value in the form of  x - ");
//... Input Loop for X
for (i=0;i<n;i++)
    {
    printf ("\n\n Enter the value of  x%d - ", i+1);
    scanf("%f",&ax[i]);
    }
//... Input Sequel for array Y
printf("\n\n Enter the value in the form of y - ");
//... Input Loop for Y
for (i=0;i<n;i++)
    {
    printf("\n\n Enter the value of y%d - ", i+1);
    scanf  ("%f",&ay[i]);
    }

//... Inputting the required value query
printf("\n Enter the value of x for ");
printf("\n which you want the value of y - ");
scanf("%f",&x);
//... Calculation & Processing Section
for(i=0;i<n;i++)
    {
    nr=1;
    dr=1;
    for(j=0;j<n;j++)
    {
        if(j!=i)
            {
            nr=nr*(x-ax[j]);
            dr=dr*(ax[i]-ax[j]);
            }
        y+=(nr/dr)*ay[i];
        }

}
```

```
//... Output Section
printf("\n\n When x=%5.2f,y=%5.2f ",x,y);
//... Invoke User Watch Halt Function
printf("\n\n\n Press Enter to Exit");
getch();
}
//... Termination of Main Execution Thread
```

4.24.5 Output

```
Enter the number of terms - 5
Enter the value in the form of x -
Enter the value of x1- 5
Enter the value of x2 - 7
Enter the value of x3 - 11
Enter the value of x4 - 13
Enter the value of x5 - 17
Enter the value in the form of y -
Enter the value of y1 - 150
Enter the value of y2 - 392
Enter the value of y3 - 1452
Enter the value of y4 - 2366
Enter the value of y5 - 5202
Enter the value of x for
Which you want the value of y - 9.0
When x = 9.00, y = 810.00
Press Enter to Exit
```

EXAMPLES

Example 1. *Using Lagrange's interpolation formula, find y(10) from the following table:*

x	5	6	9	11
y	12	13	14	16

Sol. Here $x_0 = 5$, $x_1 = 6$, $x_2 = 9$, $x_3 = 11$

$f(x_0) = 12$, $f(x_1) = 13$, $f(x_2) = 14$, $f(x_3) = 16$

Lagrange's formula is

$$f(x) = \frac{(x - x_1)(x - x_2)(x - x_3)}{(x_0 - x_1)(x_0 - x_2)(x_0 - x_3)} f(x_0) + \frac{(x - x_0)(x - x_2)(x - x_3)}{(x_1 - x_0)(x_1 - x_2)(x_1 - x_3)} f(x_1) + \frac{(x - x_0)(x - x_1)(x - x_3)}{(x_2 - x_0)(x_2 - x_1)(x_2 - x_3)} f(x_2) + \frac{(x - x_0)(x - x_1)(x - x_2)}{(x_3 - x_0)(x_3 - x_1)(x_3 - x_2)} f(x_3)$$

$$f(x) = \frac{(x-6)(x-9)(x-11)}{(5-6)(5-9)(5-11)}(12) + \frac{(x-5)(x-9)(x-11)}{(6-5)(6-9)(6-11)}(13) + \frac{(x-5)(x-6)(x-11)}{(9-5)(9-6)(9-11)}(14) + \frac{(x-5)(x-6)(x-9)}{(11-5)(11-6)(11-9)}(16)$$

$$= -\frac{1}{2}(x-6)(x-9)(x-11) + \frac{13}{15}(x-5)(x-9)(x-11) - \frac{7}{12}(x-5)(x-6)(x-11) + \frac{4}{15}(x-5)(x-6)(x-9)$$

Putting $x = 10$, we get

$$f(10) = -\frac{1}{2}(10-6)(10-9)(10-11) + \frac{13}{15}(10-5)(10-9)(10-11) - \frac{7}{12}(10-5)(10-6)(10-11) + \frac{4}{15}(10-5)(10-6)(10-9)$$

$$= 14.66666667$$

Hence,

$$y(10) = 14.66666667.$$

Example 2. *Compute the value of f(x) for x = 2.5 from the following table:*

x:	*1*	*2*	*3*	*4*
f(x):	*1*	*8*	*27*	*64*

using Lagrange's interpolation method.

Sol. Here $x_0 = 1, \quad x_1 = 2, \quad x_2 = 3, \quad x_3 = 4$

$f(x_0) = 1, \quad f(x_1) = 8, \quad f(x_2) = 27, \quad f(x_3) = 64$

Lagrange's formula is

$$f(x) = \frac{(x - x_1)(x - x_2)(x - x_3)}{(x_0 - x_1)(x_0 - x_2)(x_0 - x_3)} f(x_0)$$

$$+ \frac{(x - x_0)(x - x_2)(x - x_3)}{(x_1 - x_0)(x_1 - x_2)(x_1 - x_3)} f(x_1)$$

$$+ \frac{(x - x_0)(x - x_1)(x - x_3)}{(x_2 - x_0)(x_2 - x_1)(x_2 - x_3)} f(x_2)$$

$$+ \frac{(x - x_0)(x - x_1)(x - x_2)}{(x_3 - x_0)(x_3 - x_1)(x_3 - x_2)} f(x_3)$$

$$= \frac{(x-2)(x-3)(x-4)}{(1-2)(1-3)(1-4)}(1) + \frac{(x-1)(x-3)(x-4)}{(2-1)(2-3)(2-4)}(8)$$

$$+ \frac{(x-1)(x-2)(x-4)}{(3-1)(3-2)(3-4)}(27)$$

$$+ \frac{(x-1)(x-2)(x-3)}{(4-1)(4-2)(4-3)}(64)$$

$$= -\frac{1}{6}(x-2)(x-3)(x-4) + 4(x-1)(x-3)(x-4)$$

$$- \frac{27}{2}(x-1)(x-2)(x-4)$$

$$+ \frac{32}{3}(x-1)(x-2)(x-3)$$

Given $x = 2.5$, we get

$$f(2.5) = -\frac{1}{6}(2.5-2)(2.5-3)(2.5-4)$$

$$+ 4(2.5-1)(2.5-3)(2.5-4)$$

$$-\frac{27}{2}(2.5-1)(2.5-2)(2.5-4)$$

$$+\frac{32}{3}(2.5-1)(2.5-2)(2.5-3)$$

$$= 15.625$$

Hence, $f(2.5) = 15.625$.

Example 3. *Find the cubic Lagrange's interpolating polynomial from the following data:*

x:	*0*	*1*	*2*	*5*
f(x):	*2*	*3*	*12*	*147.*

Sol. Here $x_0 = 0,\quad x_1 = 1,\quad x_2 = 2,\quad x_3 = 5$

$f(x_0) = 2,\ f(x_1) = 3,\ f(x_2) = 12,\ f(x_3) = 147$

Lagrange's formula is

$$f(x) = \frac{(x-x_1)(x-x_2)(x-x_3)}{(x_0-x_1)(x_0-x_2)(x_0-x_3)} f(x_0)$$

$$+\frac{(x-x_0)(x-x_2)(x-x_3)}{(x_1-x_0)(x_1-x_2)(x_1-x_3)} f(x_1)$$

$$+\frac{(x-x_0)(x-x_1)(x-x_3)}{(x_2-x_0)(x_2-x_1)(x_2-x_3)} f(x_2)$$

$$+\frac{(x-x_0)(x-x_1)(x-x_2)}{(x_3-x_0)(x_3-x_1)(x_3-x_2)} f(x_3)$$

$$= \frac{(x-1)(x-2)(x-5)}{(0-1)(0-2)(0-5)}(2) + \frac{(x-0)(x-2)(x-5)}{(1-0)(1-2)(1-5)}(3)$$

$$+\frac{(x-0)(x-1)(x-5)}{(2-0)(2-1)(2-5)}(12)$$

$$+\frac{(x-0)(x-1)(x-2)}{(5-0)(5-1)(5-2)}(147)$$

$$= -\frac{1}{5}(x-1)(x-2) + \frac{3}{4}x(x-2)(x-5) - 2x(x-1)(x-5)$$

$$+\frac{49}{20}x(x-1)(x-2)$$

$$= -\frac{1}{5}(x^3 - 8x^2 + 17x - 10) + \frac{3}{4}(x^3 - 7x^2 + 10x) - 2(x^3 - 6x^2 + 5x)$$

$$+ \frac{49}{20}(x^3 - 3x^2 + 2x)$$

$$\Rightarrow \quad f(x) = x^3 + x^2 - x + 2$$

which is the required Lagrange's interpolating polynomial.

Example 4. *Find the unique polynomial P(x) of degree 2 such that:*

$$P(1) = 1, \qquad P(3) = 27, \qquad P(4) = 64$$

Use the Lagrange method of interpolation.

Sol. Here, $x_0 = 1, \qquad x_1 = 3, \qquad x_2 = 4$

$$f(x_0) = 1, \qquad f(x_1) = 27, \qquad f(x_2) = 64$$

Lagrange's interpolation formula is

$$P(x) = \frac{(x - x_1)(x - x_2)}{(x_0 - x_1)(x_0 - x_2)} f(x_0) + \frac{(x - x_0)(x - x_2)}{(x_1 - x_0)(x_1 - x_2)} f(x_1)$$

$$+ \frac{(x - x_0)(x - x_1)}{(x_2 - x_0)(x_2 - x_1)} f(x_2)$$

$$= \frac{(x-3)(x-4)}{(1-3)(1-4)}(1) + \frac{(x-1)(x-4)}{(3-1)(3-4)}(27) + \frac{(x-1)(x-3)}{(4-1)(4-3)}(64)$$

$$= \frac{1}{6}(x^2 - 7x + 12) - \frac{27}{2}(x^2 - 5x + 4) + \frac{64}{3}(x^2 - 4x + 3)$$

$$= 8x^2 - 19x + 12$$

Hence the required unique polynomial is

$$P(x) = 8x^2 - 19x + 12.$$

Example 5. *The function $y = f(x)$ is given at the points (7, 3), (8, 1), (9, 1) and (10, 9). Find the value of y for x = 9.5 using Lagrange's interpolation formula.*

Sol. We are given

x:	7	8	9	10
$f(x)$:	3	1	1	9

Here, $x_0 = 7, \quad x_1 = 8, \quad x_2 = 9, \quad x_3 = 10$

$$f(x_0) = 3, \quad f(x_1) = 1, \quad f(x_2) = 1, \quad f(x_3) = 9$$

Lagrange's interpolation formula is

$$f(x) = \frac{(x - x_1)(x - x_2)(x - x_3)}{(x_0 - x_1)(x_0 - x_2)(x_0 - x_3)} f(x_0)$$

$$+ \frac{(x - x_0)(x - x_2)(x - x_3)}{(x_1 - x_0)(x_1 - x_2)(x_1 - x_3)} f(x_1)$$

$$+ \frac{(x - x_0)(x - x_1)(x - x_3)}{(x_2 - x_0)(x_2 - x_1)(x_2 - x_3)} f(x_2)$$

$$+ \frac{(x - x_0)(x - x_1)(x - x_2)}{(x_3 - x_0)(x_3 - x_1)(x_3 - x_2)} f(x_3)$$

$$= \frac{(x-8)(x-9)(x-10)}{(7-8)(7-9)(7-10)}(3) + \frac{(x-7)(x-9)(x-10)}{(8-7)(8-9)(8-10)}(1)$$

$$+ \frac{(x-7)(x-8)(x-10)}{(9-7)(9-8)(9-10)}(1)$$

$$+ \frac{(x-7)(x-8)(x-9)}{(10-7)(10-8)(10-9)}(9)$$

$$= -\frac{1}{2}(x-8)(x-9)(x-10) + \frac{1}{2}(x-7)(x-9)(x-10)$$

$$-\frac{1}{2}(x-7)(x-8)(x-10)$$

$$+\frac{3}{2}(x-7)(x-8)(x-9) \qquad (58)$$

Given $x = 9.5$ in eqn. (58), we get

$$f(9.5) = -\frac{1}{2}(9.5-8)(9.5-9)(9.5-10) + \frac{1}{2}(9.5-7)(9.5-9)(9.5-10)$$

$$-\frac{1}{2}(9.5-7)(9.5-8)(9.5-10) + \frac{3}{2}(9.5-7)(9.5-8)(9.5-9)$$

$$= 3.625.$$

Example 6. *Use Lagrange's interpolation formula to fit a polynomial to the data:*

x:	-1	0	2	3
u_x:	-8	3	1	12

Hence or otherwise find the value of u_1.

Sol. Here,

$$x_0 = -1, \quad x_1 = 0, \quad x_2 = 2, \quad x_3 = 3$$

$$f(x_0) = -8, \quad f(x_1) = 3, \quad f(x_2) = 1, \quad f(x_3) = 12$$

Lagrange's interpolation formula is

$$f(x) = \frac{(x - x_1)(x - x_2)(x - x_3)}{(x_0 - x_1)(x_0 - x_2)(x_0 - x_3)} f(x_0)$$

$$+ \frac{(x - x_0)(x - x_2)(x - x_3)}{(x_1 - x_0)(x_1 - x_2)(x_1 - x_3)} f(x_1)$$

$$+ \frac{(x - x_0)(x - x_1)(x - x_3)}{(x_2 - x_0)(x_2 - x_1)(x_2 - x_3)} f(x_2)$$

$$+ \frac{(x - x_0)(x - x_1)(x - x_2)}{(x_3 - x_0)(x_3 - x_1)(x_3 - x_2)} f(x_3)$$

$$= \frac{(x-0)(x-2)(x-3)}{(-1-0)(-1-2)(-1-3)}(-8) + \frac{(x+1)(x-2)(x-3)}{(0+1)(0-2)(0-3)}(3)$$

$$+ \frac{(x+1)(x-0)(x-3)}{(2+1)(2-0)(2-3)}(1)$$

$$+ \frac{(x+1)(x-0)(x-2)}{(3+1)(3-0)(3-2)}(12)$$

$$= \frac{2}{3} x(x-2)(x-3) + \frac{1}{2}(x+1)(x-2)(x-3)$$

$$- \frac{1}{6}(x+1)x(x-3) + (x+1)x(x-2)$$

$$= \frac{2}{3}(x^3 - 5x^2 + 6x) + \frac{1}{2}(x^3 - 4x^2 + x + 6)$$

$$- \frac{1}{6}(x^3 - 2x^2 - 3x) + (x^3 - x^2 - 2x)$$

$$\Rightarrow \quad f(x) = 2x^3 - 6x^2 + 3x + 3$$

Hence, $u_x = 2x^3 - 6x^2 + 3x + 3$ (59)

Given $x = 1$ in (59), we get

$$u_1 = 2(1)^3 - 6(1)^2 + 3(1) + 3 = 2.$$

Example 7. *By means of Lagrange's formula, prove that*

$$(i)\ y_0 = \frac{1}{2}(y_1 + y_{-1}) - \frac{1}{8}\left[\frac{1}{2}(y_3 - y_1) - \frac{1}{2}(y_{-1} - y_{-3})\right]$$

$$(ii)\ y_3 = 0.05\,(y_0 + y_6) - 0.3\,(y_1 + y_5) + 0.75\,(y_2 + y_4)$$

$$(iii)\ y_1 = y_3 - 0.3\,(y_5 - y_{-3}) + 0.2\,(y_{-3} - y_{-5}).$$

Sol. (*i*) For the arguments – 3, – 1, 1, 3, the Lagrange's formula is

$$y_x = \frac{(x+1)(x-1)(x-3)}{(-3+1)(-3-1)(-3-3)} y_{-3} + \frac{(x+3)(x-1)(x-3)}{(-1+3)(-1-1)(-1-3)} y_{-1}$$

$$+ \frac{(x+3)(x+1)(x-3)}{(1+3)(1+1)(1-3)} y_1$$

$$+ \frac{(x+3)(x+1)(x-1)}{(3+3)(3+1)(3-1)} y_3$$

$$= \frac{(x+1)(x-1)(x-3)}{(-48)} y_{-3} + \frac{(x+3)(x-1)(x-3)}{16} y_{-1}$$

$$+ \frac{(x+3)(x+1)(x-3)}{(-16)} y_1$$

$$+ \frac{(x+3)(x+1)(x-1)}{48} y_3 \qquad (60)$$

Given $x = 0$ in (60), we get

$$y_0 = -\frac{1}{16} y_{-3} + \frac{9}{16} y_{-1} + \frac{9}{16} y_1 - \frac{1}{16} y_3$$

$$= \frac{1}{2}(y_1 + y_{-1}) - \frac{1}{8}\left[\frac{1}{2}(y_3 - y_1) - \frac{1}{2}(y_{-1} - y_{-3})\right]$$

(*ii*) For the arguments 0, 1, 2, 4, 5, 6, the Lagrange's formula is

$$y_x = \frac{(x-1)(x-2)(x-4)(x-5)(x-6)}{(0-1)(0-2)(0-4)(0-5)(0-6)} y_0$$

$$+ \frac{(x-0)(x-2)(x-4)(x-5)(x-6)}{(1-0)(1-2)(1-4)(1-5)(1-6)} y_1$$

$$+ \frac{(x-0)(x-1)(x-4)(x-5)(x-6)}{(2-0)(2-1)(2-4)(2-5)(2-6)} y_2$$

$$+\frac{(x-0)(x-1)(x-2)(x-5)(x-6)}{(4-0)(4-1)(4-2)(4-5)(4-6)}y_4$$

$$+\frac{(x-0)(x-1)(x-2)(x-4)(x-6)}{(5-0)(5-1)(5-2)(5-4)(5-6)}y_5$$

$$+\frac{(x-0)(x-1)(x-2)(x-4)(x-5)}{(6-0)(6-1)(6-2)(6-4)(6-5)}y_6 \quad (61)$$

Given $x = 3$ in (61), we get

$$y_3 = 0.05\,y_0 - 0.3\,y_1 + 0.75\,y_2 + 0.75\,y_4 - 0.3\,y_5 + 0.05\,y_6$$
$$= 0.05\,(y_0 + y_6) - 0.3(y_1 + y_5) + 0.75\,(y_2 + y_4).$$

(*iii*) For the arguments – 5, – 3, 3, 5, the Lagrange's formula is

$$y_x = \frac{(x+3)(x-3)(x-5)}{(-5+3)(-5-3)(-5-5)}y_{-5} + \frac{(x+5)(x-3)(x-5)}{(-3+5)(-3-3)(-3-5)}y_{-3}$$

$$+\frac{(x+5)(x+3)(x-5)}{(3+5)(3+3)(3-5)}y_3 + \frac{(x+5)(x+3)(x-3)}{(5+5)(5+3)(5-3)}y_5 \quad (62)$$

Given $x = 1$ in eqn. (62), we get

$$y_1 = -0.2\,y_{-5} + 0.5y_{-3} + y_3 - 0.3\,y_5$$
$$= y_3 - 0.3\,(y_5 - y_{-3}) + 0.2\,(y_{-3} - y_{-5}).$$

Example 8. *If four equidistant values u_{-1}, u_0, u_1, and u_2 are given, a value is interpolated by Lagrange's formula, show that it may be written in the form*

$$u_x = yu_0 + xu_1 + \frac{y(y^2-1)}{3!}\Delta^2 u_{-1} + \frac{x(x^2-1)}{3!}\Delta^2 u_0 \quad \text{where } x + y = 1.$$

Sol. $\Delta^2 u_1 = (E-1)^2 u_{-1} = (E^2 - 2E + 1)\,u_{-1} = u_1 - 2u_0 + u_{-1}$

$\Delta^2 u_0 = (E_2 - 2E + 1)\,u_0 = u_2 - 2u_1 + u_0$

$$\text{R.H.S.} = (1-x)\,u_0 + xu_1 + \frac{(1-x)\{(1-x)^2-1\}}{3!}(u_1 - 2u_0 + u_{-1})$$

$$+\frac{x(x^2-1)}{3!}(u_2 - 2u_1 + u_0) \qquad |\text{where } y = 1 - x$$

$$= -\frac{x(x-1)(x-2)}{6}u_{-1} + \frac{(x-2)(x-1)(x+1)}{2}u_0 - \frac{(x+1)x(x-2)}{2}u_1$$

$$+\frac{(x+1)x(x-1)}{6}u_2 \quad (63)$$

Applying Lagrange's formula for the arguments – 1, 0 , 1 and 2.

$$u_x = \frac{x(x-1)(x-2)}{(-1)(-2)(-3)} u_{-1} + \frac{(x+1)(x-1)(x-2)}{(1)(-1)(-2)} u_0 + \frac{(x+1)x(x-2)}{(2)(1)(-1)} u_1 + \frac{(x+1)x(x-1)}{(3)(2)(1)} u_2$$

$$= -\frac{x(x-1)(x-2)}{6} u_{-1} + \frac{(x-2)(x-1)(x+1)}{2} u_0 - \frac{(x+1)x(x-2)}{2} u_1 + \frac{(x+1)x(x-1)}{6} u_2 \qquad (64)$$

From (63) and (64), we observe that

R.H.S. = L.H.S.

Hence the result.

Example 9. *Prove that Lagrange's formula can be expressed in the form*

$$\begin{vmatrix} P_n(x) & 1 & x & x^2 & \dots & \dots & x^n \\ f(x_0) & 1 & x_0 & x_0^2 & \dots & \dots & x_0^n \\ f(x_1) & 1 & x_1 & x_1^2 & \dots & \dots & x_1^n \\ \dots & \dots & \dots & \dots & \dots & \dots & \dots \\ f(x_n) & 1 & x_n & x_n^2 & \dots & \dots & x_n^n \end{vmatrix} = 0 \quad \textit{where } P_n(x) = f(x).$$

Sol. Let $P_n(x) = a_0 + a_1x + a_2x^2 + \dots + a_nx^n$

Given $x = x_0, x_1, \dots, x_n,$ and $P_n(x_i) = f(x_i), i = 0, 1, 2, \dots, n$

$$f(x_0) = a_0 + a_1x_0 + a_2x_0^2 + \dots + a_nx_0^n$$

$$f(x_1) = a_0 + a_1x_1 + a_2x_1^2 + \dots + a_nx_1^n$$

$$\dots \quad \dots \quad \dots \quad \dots \quad \dots \quad \dots$$

$$f(x_n) = a_0 + a_1x_n + a_2x_n^2 + \dots + a_nx_n^n \quad \dots (n+2)$$

Eliminating $a_0, a_1, a_2, \dots\dots, a_n$ from these equations, we get

$$\begin{vmatrix} -P_n(x) & 1 & x & x^2 & \dots & \dots & x^n \\ -f(x_0) & 1 & x_0 & x_0^2 & \dots & \dots & x_0^n \\ -f(x_1) & 1 & x_1 & x_1^2 & \dots & \dots & x_1^n \\ \dots & \dots & \dots & \dots & \dots & \dots & \dots \\ -f(x_n) & 1 & x_n & x_n^2 & \dots & \dots & x_n^n \end{vmatrix} = 0$$

or $$\begin{vmatrix} P_n(x) & 1 & x & x^2 & \dots & \dots & x^n \\ f(x_0) & 1 & x_0 & x_0^2 & \dots & \dots & x_0^n \\ f(x_1) & 1 & x_1 & x_1^2 & \dots & \dots & x_1^n \\ \dots & \dots & \dots & \dots & \dots & \dots & \dots \\ f(x_n) & 1 & x_n & x_n^2 & \dots & \dots & x_n^n \end{vmatrix} = 0$$

ASSIGNMENT 4.11

1. Apply Lagrange's formula to find $f(5)$ and $f(6)$ given that

$$f(2) = 4, f(1) = 2, f(3) = 8, f(7) = 128$$

Explain why the result differs from those obtained by completing the series of powers of 2?

2. Values of $f(x)$ for values of x are given as

$$f(1) = 4, f(2) = 5, f(7) = 5, f(8) = 4$$

Find $f(6)$ and also the value of x for which $f(x)$ is maximum or minimum.

3. Find by Lagrange's formula, the value of

(*i*) u_5 if $u_0 = 1, u_3 = 19, u_4 = 49, u_6 = 181$

(*ii*) u_4 if $u_3 = 16, u_5 = 36, u_7 = 64, u_8 = 81$ and $u_9 = 100$.

4. Using Lagrange's formula, find the values of

(*i*) y_5 if $y_1 = 4, y_3 = 120, y_4 = 340, y_5 = 2544$

(*ii*) y_0 if $y_{-30} = 30, y_{-12} = 34, y_3 = 38, y_{18} = 42$.

5. Find the value of tan 33° by Lagrange's formula if

tan 30° = 0.5774, tan 32° = 0.6249,

tan 35° = 0.7002, tan 38° = 0.7813.

6. Use Lagrange's formula to find $f(6)$ from the following table:

x:	2	5	7	10	12
$f(x)$:	18	180	448	1210	2028.

7. Apply Lagrange's formula to find $f(15)$, if

x:	10	12	14	16	18	20
$f(x)$:	2420	1942	1497	1109	790	540.

8. If $y_0, y_1, \dots, y_9$ are consecutive terms of a series, prove that

$$y_5 = \frac{1}{70}[56(y_4 + y_6) - 28(y_3 + y_7) + 8(y_2 + y_8) - (y_1 + y_9)]$$

9. Using the following table, find $f(x)$ as a polynomial in x:

x:	– 1	0	3	6	7
$f(x)$:	3	– 6	39	822	1611.

10. If $y(1) = -3$, $y(3) = 9$, $y(4) = 30$, and $y(6) = 132$, find the four-point Lagrange interpolation polynomial that takes the same values as the function y at the given points.

11. Given the table of values

x:	150	152	154	156
$y = \sqrt{x}$:	12.247	12.329	12.410	12.490

Evaluate $\sqrt{155}$ using Lagrange's interpolation formula.

12. Applying Lagrange's formula, find a cubic polynomial which approximates the following data:

x:	– 2	– 1	2	3
$y(x)$:	– 12	– 8	3	5.

13. Given the table of values

x:	50	52	54	56
$\sqrt[3]{x}$:	3.684	3.732	3.779	3.825

Use Lagrange's formula to find x when $\sqrt[3]{x} = 3.756$.

14. Find the equation of the cubic curve that passes through the points (4, – 43), (7, 83), (9, 327) and (12, 1053).

15. Values of $f(x)$ are given at a, b, and c. Show that the maximum is obtained by

$$x = \frac{f(a)(b^2 - c^2) + f(b)(c^2 - a^2) + f(c)(a^2 - b^2)}{f(a)(b - c) + f(b)(c - a) + f(c)(a - b)}.$$

16. The following table gives the viscosity of an oil as a function of temperature. Use Lagrange's formula to find the viscosity of oil at a temperature of 140°.

Temp°:	110	130	160	190
Viscosity:	10.8	8.1	5.5	4.8

17. Certain corresponding values of x and $\log_{10}x$ are given below:

x:	300	304	305	307
$\log_{10} x$:	2.4771	2.4829	2.4843	2.4871

Find $\log_{10} 310$ by Lagrange's formula.

18. The following table gives the normal weights of babies during the first 12 months of life:

Age in months:	0	2	5	8	10	12
Weight in lbs:	7.5	10.25	15	16	18	21

19. Given $f(0) = -18$, $f(1) = 0$, $f(3) = 0$, $f(5) = -248$, $f(6) = 0$, $f(9) = 13104$; find $f(x)$.

20. (*i*) Determine by Lagrange's formula, the percentage number of criminals under 35 years:

Age	*% number of criminals*
under 25 years	52
under 30 years	67.3
under 40 years	84.1
under 50 years	94.4

(*ii*) Find a Lagrange's interpolating polynomial for the data given below:

$$x_0 = 1, \quad x_1 = 2.5, \quad x_2 = 4 \quad \text{and} \quad x_3 = 5.5$$

$$f(x_0) = 4, \quad f(x_1) = 7.5, \quad f(x_2) = 13 \quad \text{and} \quad f(x_3) = 17.5$$

Also, find the value of $f(5)$.

4.25 ERROR IN LAGRANGE'S INTERPOLATION FORMULA

Remainder,

$$y(x) - L_n(x) = R_n(x) = \frac{\Pi_{n+1}(x)}{(n+1)!} y^{(n+1)}(\xi), \; a < \xi < b$$

where Lagrange's formula is for the class of functions having continuous derivatives of order upto $(n + 1)$ on $[a, b]$.

Quantity $E_L = \max_{[a,b]} | R_n(x) |$ may be taken as an estimate of error.

Let us assume

$$| y^{(n+1)}(\xi) | \le M_{n+1}, \; a \le \xi \le b$$

then,

$$E_L \le \frac{M_{n+1}}{(n+1)!} \max_{[a,b]} | \Pi_{n+1}(x) |.$$

EXAMPLES

Example 1. *Show that the truncation error of quadratic interpolation in an equidistant table is bounded by* $\frac{h^3}{9\sqrt{3}}$ *max* $| f'''(\xi) |$ *where h is the step size and f is the tabulated function.*

Sol. Let x_{i-1}, x_i, x_{i+1} denote three consecutive equispaced points with step size h.

The truncation error of the quadratic Lagrange interpolation is bounded by

$$| E_2(f; x) | \le \frac{M_3}{6} \max | (x - x_{i-1})(x - x_i)(x - x_{i+1}) |$$

where $x_{i-1} \le x \le x_{i+1}$ and $M_3 = \max_{a \le x \le b} | f'''(x) |$

Substitute $t = \frac{x - x_i}{h}$ then,

$$x - x_{i-1} = x - (x_i - h) = x - x_i + h = th + h = (t + 1)h$$

$$x - x_{i+1} = x - (x_i + h) = x - x_i - h = th - h = (t - 1)h$$

and $(x - x_{i-1})(x - x_i)(x - x_{i+1}) = (t + 1)\, t(t - 1)h^3 = t(t^2 - 1)h^3 = g(t)$

Setting $g'(t) = 0$, we get

$$3t^2 - 1 = 0 \;\Rightarrow\; t = \pm \frac{1}{\sqrt{3}}.$$

For both these values of t, we obtain

$$\max | (x - x_{i-1})(x - x_i)(x - x_{i+1}) | = h^3 \max_{-1 \le t \le 1} | t(t^2 - 1) | = \frac{2h^3}{3\sqrt{3}}$$

Hence, the truncation error of the quadratic interpolation is bounded by

$$| E_2(f; x) | \le \frac{h^3}{9\sqrt{3}} M_3$$

or,
$$| E_2(f; x) | \le \frac{h^3}{9\sqrt{3}} \max | f'''(\xi) |.$$

Example 2. *Determine the step size that can be used in the tabulation of $f(x) = \sin x$ in the interval $\left[0, \frac{\pi}{4}\right]$ at equally spaced nodal points so that the truncation error of the quadratic interpolation is less than 5×10^{-8}.*

Sol. From Example 1, we have

$$| E_2(f; x) | \le \frac{h^3}{9\sqrt{3}} M_3$$

For $f(x) = \sin x$, we get $f'''(x) = -\cos x$

and
$$M_3 = \max_{0 \le x \le \pi/4} |\cos x| = 1$$

Hence the step size h is given by

$$\frac{h^3}{9\sqrt{3}} \leq 5 \times 10^{-8} \quad \text{or} \quad h \approx 0.009$$

Example 3. *Using Lagrange's interpolation formula, find the value of sin* $\left(\frac{\pi}{6}\right)$ *from the following data:*

x:	*0*	*π/4*	*π/2*
y = sin x:	*0*	*0.70711*	*1.0*

Also estimate the error in the solution.

Sol.

$$\sin\left(\frac{\pi}{6}\right) = \frac{\left(\frac{\pi}{6}-0\right)\left(\frac{\pi}{6}-\frac{\pi}{2}\right)}{\left(\frac{\pi}{4}-0\right)\left(\frac{\pi}{4}-\frac{\pi}{2}\right)}(0.70711) + \frac{\left(\frac{\pi}{6}-0\right)\left(\frac{\pi}{6}-\frac{\pi}{4}\right)}{\left(\frac{\pi}{2}-0\right)\left(\frac{\pi}{2}-\frac{\pi}{4}\right)}(1)$$

$$= \frac{8}{9}(0.70711) - \frac{1}{9} = \frac{4.65688}{9} = 0.51743$$

Now, $\quad y(x) = \sin x, \quad y'(x) = \cos x, \quad y''(x) = -\sin x, \quad y'''(x) = -\cos x$

Hence, $\quad |\, y'''(\xi)\,| < 1$

when $x = \pi/6$.

$$|\, R_n(x)\,| \leq \left| \frac{\left(\frac{\pi}{6}-0\right)\left(\frac{\pi}{6}-\frac{\pi}{4}\right)\left(\frac{\pi}{6}-\frac{\pi}{2}\right)}{3!} \right| = 0.02392$$

which agrees with the actual error in problem.

4.26 EXPRESSION OF RATIONAL FUNCTION AS A SUM OF PARTIAL FRACTIONS

Let

$$f(x) = \frac{3x^2 + x + 1}{(x-1)(x-2)(x-3)}$$

Consider $\phi(x) = 3x^2 + x + 1$ and tabulate its values for $x = 1, 2, 3$, we get

x:	1	2	3
$3x^2 + x + 1$:	5	15	31

Using Lagrange's interpolation formula, we get

$$f(x) = \frac{(x-2)(x-3)}{(1-2)(1-3)}(5) + \frac{(x-1)(x-3)}{-1}(15) + \frac{(x-1)(x-2)}{2}(31)$$

$$= \frac{5}{2}(x-2)(x-3) - 15(x-1)(x-3) + \frac{31}{2}(x-1)(x-2)$$

$$= \frac{5}{2(x-1)} - \frac{15}{x-2} + \frac{31}{2(x-3)}.$$

4.27 INVERSE INTERPOLATION

The process of estimating the value of x for the value of y not in the table is called *inverse interpolation.*

When values of x are unevenly spaced, Lagrange's method is used by interchanging x and y.

EXAMPLES

Example 1. *Values of elliptic integral* $F(\theta) = \sqrt{2}\int_0^{\theta} \frac{d\theta}{\sqrt{1+\cos^2\theta}}$ *are given below:*

θ:	*21°*	*23°*	*25°*
F(θ):	*0.3706*	*0.4068*	*0.4433*

Find θ for which F(θ) = 0.3887.

Sol. By inverse interpolation formula

$$\theta = \frac{(F-F_1)(F-F_2)}{(F_0-F_1)(F_0-F_2)}\theta_0 + \frac{(F-F_0)(F-F_2)}{(F_1-F_0)(F_1-F_2)}\theta_1 + \frac{(F-F_0)(F-F_1)}{(F_2-F_0)(F_2-F_1)}\theta_2$$

$$= \frac{(0.3887-0.4068)(0.3887-0.4433)}{(0.3706-0.4068)(0.3706-0.4433)}(.3706) + \ldots + \ldots$$

$$= 7.884 + 17.20 - 3.087 = 22°.$$

Example 2. *From the given table:*

x:	*20*	*25*	*30*	*35*
y(x):	*0.342*	*0.423*	*0.5*	*0.65*

Find the value of x for y(x) = 0.390.

Sol. By inverse interpolation formula,

$$x = \frac{(y-y_1)(y-y_2)(y-y_3)}{(y_0-y_1)(y_0-y_2)(y_0-y_3)} x_0 + \frac{(y-y_0)(y-y_2)(y-y_3)}{(y_1-y_0)(y_1-y_2)(y_1-y_3)} x_1$$

$$+ \frac{(y-y_0)(y-y_1)(y-y_3)}{(y_2-y_0)(y_2-y_1)(y_2-y_3)} x_2 + \frac{(y-y_0)(y-y_1)(y-y_2)}{(y_3-y_0)(y_3-y_1)(y_3-y_2)} x_3$$

$$= \frac{(.39-.423)(.39-.5)(.39-.65)}{(.342-.423)(.342-.5)(.342-.65)}(20)$$

$$+ \frac{(.39-.342)(.39-.5)(.39-.65)}{(.423-.342))(.423-.5)(.423-.65)}(25)$$

$$+ \frac{(.39-.342)(.39-.423)(.39-.65)}{(.5-.342)(.5-.423)(.5-.65)}(30)$$

$$+ \frac{(.39-.342)(.39-.423)(.39-.5)}{(.65-.342)(.65-.423)(.65-.5)}(35)$$

$$= 22.84057797.$$

4.28 DIVIDED DIFFERENCES

Lagrange's interpolation formula has the disadvantage that if another interpolation point were added, the interpolation coefficient will have to be recomputed.

We therefore seek an interpolation polynomial which has the property that a polynomial of higher degree may be derived from it by simply adding new terms.

Newton's general interpolation formula is one such formula and it employs divided differences.

If (x_0, y_0), (x_1, y_1), (x_2, y_2) ...... be given points then the first divided difference for the arguments x_0, x_1 is defined by

$$\underset{x_1}{\Delta} y_0 = [x_0, x_1] = \frac{y_1 - y_0}{x_1 - x_0}$$

Similarly, $\quad [x_1, x_2] = \dfrac{y_2 - y_1}{x_2 - x_1}$ and so on.

The second divided difference for x_0, x_1, x_2 is defined as

$$\underset{x_1, x_2}{\Delta^2} y_0 = [x_0, x_1, x_2] = \frac{[x_1, x_2] - [x_0, x_1]}{x_2 - x_0}$$

Third divided difference for x_0, x_1, x_2, x_3 is defined as

$$[x_0,\ x_1, x_2, x_3] = \frac{[x_1, x_2, x_3] - [x_0, x_1, x_2]}{x_3 - x_0} \text{ and so on.}$$

4.29 PROPERTIES OF DIVIDED DIFFERENCES

1. **The divided differences are symmetrical in their arguments,** *i.e.*, independent of the order of arguments.

$$[x_0, x_1] = \frac{y_1}{x_1 - x_0} + \frac{y_0}{x_0 - x_1} = [x_1, x_0]$$

Also, $[x_0, x_1, x_2] = \dfrac{y_0}{(x_0 - x_1)(x_0 - x_2)} + \dfrac{y_1}{(x_1 - x_0)(x_1 - x_2)} + \dfrac{y_2}{(x_2 - x_0)(x_2 - x_1)}$

$$= [x_2, x_0, x_1] \text{ or } [x_1, x_2, x_0]$$

2. **The nth divided differences of a polynomial of nth degree are constant.**

Let the arguments be equally spaced so that

$$x_1 - x_0 = x_2 - x_1 = ... = x_n - x_{n-1} = h$$

then, $$[x_0, x_1] = \frac{y_1 - y_0}{x_1 - x_0} = \frac{\Delta y_0}{h}$$

$$[x_0, x_1, x_2] = \frac{[x_1, x_2] - [x_0, x_1]}{(x_2 - x_0)}$$

$$= \frac{1}{2h}\left(\frac{\Delta y_1}{h} - \frac{\Delta y_0}{h}\right) = \frac{1}{2!} \cdot \frac{1}{h^2} (\Delta^2 y_0)$$

In general,

$$[x_0, x_1, x_2, ..., x_n] = \frac{1}{n\,!} \cdot \frac{1}{h^n} \Delta^n y_0$$

If tabulated function is a nth degree polynomial. $\therefore$ $\Delta^n y_0$ = constant

$\therefore$ n^{th} divided differences will also be constant.

4.30 NEWTON'S GENERAL INTERPOLATION FORMULA OR NEWTON'S DIVIDED DIFFERENCE INTERPOLATION FORMULA

Let $y_0, y_1, \ldots\ldots, y_n$ be the values of $y = f(x)$ corresponding to the arguments $x_0, x_1, \ldots\ldots, x_n$ then from the definition of divided differences, we have

$$[x, x_0] = \frac{y - y_0}{x - x_0}$$

so that,

$$y = y_0 + (x - x_0)\,[x, x_0] \tag{65}$$

Again,

$$[x, x_0, x_1] = \frac{[x, x_0] - [x_0, x_1]}{x - x_1}$$

which gives,

$$[x, x_0] = [x_0, x_1] + (x - x_1)\,[x, x_0, x_1] \tag{66}$$

From (65) and (66),

$$y = y_0 + (x - x_0)\,[x_0, x_1] + (x - x_0)(x - x_1)\,[x, x_0, x_1] \tag{67}$$

Also

$$[x, x_0, x_1, x_2] = \frac{[x, x_0, x_1] - [x_0, x_1, x_2]}{x - x_2}$$

which gives

$$[x, x_0, x_1] = [x_0, x_1, x_2] + (x - x_2)\,[x, x_0, x_1, x_2] \tag{68}$$

From (67) and (68),

$$y = y_0 + (x - x_0)\,[x_0, x_1] + (x - x_0)(x - x_1)\,[x_0, x_1, x_2] + (x - x_0)(x - x_1)(x - x_2)\,[x, x_0, x_1, x_2]$$

Proceeding in this manner, we get

$$\begin{aligned} y = f(x) = y_0 &+ (x - x_0)\,[x_0, x_1] + (x - x_0)(x - x_1)\,[x_0, x_1, x_2] \\ &+ (x - x_0)(x - x_1)(x - x_2)\,[x_0, x_1, x_2, x_3] \\ &+ \ldots\ldots + (x - x_0)(x - x_1)(x - x_2) \\ &\quad \ldots\ldots (x - x_{n-1})\,[x_0, x_1, x_2, x_3, \ldots\ldots, x_n] \\ &+ (x - x_0)(x - x_1)(x - x_2) \\ &\quad \ldots\ldots (x - x_n)\,[x, x_0, x_1, x_2, \ldots\ldots, x_n] \end{aligned}$$

which is called Newton's general interpolation formula with divided differences, the last term being the remainder term after $(n + 1)$ terms.

Newton's divided difference formula can also be written as

$$y = y_0 + (x - x_0) \underset{}{\Delta} y_0 + (x - x_0)(x - x_1) \Delta^2 y_0 + (x - x_0)(x - x_1)(x - x_2) \Delta^3 y_0 + (x - x_0)(x - x_1)(x - x_2)(x - x_3) \Delta^4 y_0 + \ldots + (x - x_0)(x - x_1) \ldots (x - x_{n-1}) \Delta^n y_0$$

4.31 RELATION BETWEEN DIVIDED DIFFERENCES AND ORDINARY DIFFERENCES

Let the arguments $x_0, x_1, x_2, \ldots, x_n$ be equally spaced such that

$$x_1 - x_0 = x_2 - x_1 = \ldots = x_n - x_{n-1} = h$$

$$\therefore \quad x_1 = x_0 + h$$

$$x_2 = x_0 + 2h$$

$$\ldots\ldots\ldots$$

$$x_n = x_0 + nh$$

Now
$$\underset{x_1}{\Delta} f(x_0) = \frac{f(x_1) - f(x_0)}{x_1 - x_0} = \frac{f(x_0 + h) - f(x_0)}{h} = \frac{\Delta f(x_0)}{h} \tag{69}$$

$$\underset{x_1 x_2}{\Delta^2} f(x_0) = \frac{1}{x_2 - x_0} [f(x_1, x_2) - f(x_0, x_1)]$$

$$= \frac{1}{x_2 - x_0}\left[\frac{f(x_2) - f(x_1)}{x_2 - x_1} - \frac{f(x_1) - f(x_0)}{x_1 - x_0}\right]$$

$$= \frac{1}{2h}\left[\frac{f(x_0 + 2h) - f(x_0 + h)}{h} - \frac{f(x_0 + h) - f(x_0)}{h}\right]$$

$$= \frac{1}{2h^2}[f(x_0 + 2h) - 2f(x_0 + h) + f(x_0)]$$

$$= \frac{\Delta^2 f(x_0)}{2!\,.\,h^2} \tag{70}$$

$$\underset{x_1, x_2, x_3}{\Delta^3} f(x_0) = \frac{1}{x_2 - x_0} [f(x_1, x_2, x_3) - f(x_0, x_1, x_2)]$$

$$= \frac{1}{3h}\left[\frac{\Delta^2 f(x_1)}{2h^2} - \frac{\Delta^2 f(x_0)}{2h^2}\right] = \frac{\Delta^2 f(x_1) - \Delta^2 f(x_0)}{6h^3}$$

[From (69)]

$$= \frac{\Delta^3 f(x_0)}{3!\,h^3}$$

... ...

$$\underset{x_1, \ldots\ldots, x_n}{\Delta^n} f(x_0) = \frac{\Delta^n f(x_0)}{n!\,h^n}.$$

4.32 MERITS AND DEMERITS OF LAGRANGE'S FORMULA

1. The formula is simple and easy to remember.
2. There is no need to construct the divided difference table and we can directly interpolate the unknown value with the help of given observations.
3. The calculations in the formula are more complicated than in the divided difference formula.
4. The application of the formula is not speedy
5. There is always a chance of commiting some error due to a number of (+)ve and (–)ve sign in the denominator and numerator of each term.
6. The calculations provide no check whether the functional values used are taken correctly or not, whereas the differences used in a difference formula provide a check on the functional values.

EXAMPLES

Example 1. *Construct a divided difference table for the following:*

x:	*1*	*2*	*4*	*7*	*12*
f(x):	*22*	*30*	*82*	*106*	*216.*

Sol.

x	$f(x)$	$\Delta f(x)$	$\Delta^2 f(x)$	$\Delta^3 f(x)$	$\Delta^4 f(x)$
1	22				
		$\dfrac{30-22}{2-1} = 8$			
2	30		$\dfrac{26-8}{4-1} = 6$		
		$\dfrac{82-30}{4-2} = 26$		$\dfrac{-3.6-6}{7-1} = -1.6$	
4	82		$\dfrac{8-26}{7-2} = -3.6$		$\dfrac{0.535+1.6}{12-1} = 0.194$
		$\dfrac{106-82}{7-4} = 8$		$\dfrac{1.75+3.6}{12-2} = 0.535$	
7	106		$\dfrac{22-8}{12-4} = 1.75$		
		$\dfrac{216-106}{5} = 22$			
12	216				

Example 2. *(i) Find the third divided difference with arguments 2, 4, 9, 10 of the function* $f(x) = x^3 - 2x$.

(ii) If $f(x) = \dfrac{1}{x^2}$, *find the first divided differences* $f(a, b)$, $f(a, b, c)$, $f(a, b, c, d)$.

(iii) If $f(x) = g(x)\, h(x)$, *prove that*

$$f(x_1, x_2) = g(x_1)\, h(x_1, x_2) + g(x_1, x_2)\, h(x_2).$$

Sol. (*i*)

x	$f(x)$	$\Delta f(x)$	$\Delta^2 f(x)$	$\Delta^3 f(x)$
2	4			
		$\dfrac{56-4}{4-2} = 26$		
4	56		$\dfrac{131-26}{9-2} = 15$	
		$\dfrac{711-56}{9-4} = 131$		$\dfrac{23-15}{10-2} = 1$
9	711		$\dfrac{269-131}{10-4} = 23$	
		$\dfrac{980-711}{10-9} = 269$		
10	980			

Hence, the third divided difference is 1.

(*ii*)

x	$f(x) = \dfrac{1}{x^2}$	$\underset{}{\Delta} f(x)$	$\Delta^2 f(x)$	$\Delta^3 f(x)$
a	$\dfrac{1}{a^2}$			
		$\dfrac{\left(\dfrac{1}{b^2}-\dfrac{1}{a^2}\right)}{b-a} = -\left(\dfrac{a+b}{a^2b^2}\right)$		
b	$\dfrac{1}{b^2}$		$\dfrac{ab+bc+ca}{a^2b^2c^2}$	
		$-\left(\dfrac{b+c}{b^2c^2}\right)$		$-\left(\dfrac{abc+acd+abd+bcd}{a^2b^2c^2d^2}\right)$
c	$\dfrac{1}{c^2}$		$\dfrac{bc+cd+db}{b^2c^2d^2}$	
		$-\left(\dfrac{c+d}{c^2d^2}\right)$		
d	$\dfrac{1}{d^2}$			

From the above divided difference table, we observe that the first divided differences,

$$f(a, b) = -\left(\frac{a+b}{a^2b^2}\right)$$

$$f(a, b, c) = \frac{ab+bc+ca}{a^2b^2c^2}$$

and $$f(a, b, c, d) = -\left(\frac{abc+acd+abd+bcd}{a^2b^2c^2d^2}\right)$$

(*iii*) $$\text{R.H.S.} = g(x_1)\frac{h(x_2)-h(x_1)}{x_2-x_1} + \frac{g(x_2)-g(x_1)}{x_2-x_1}h(x_2)$$

$$= \frac{1}{x_2-x_1}\,[\{g(x_1)\,h(x_2) - g(x_1)h(x_1)\} + \{g(x_2)\,h(x_2) - g(x_1)\,h(x_2)\}]$$

$$= \frac{g(x_2)\,h(x_2) - g(x_1)\,h(x_1)}{x_2-x_1}$$

$$= \underset{x_2}{\Delta}\, g(x_1)\,h(x_1) = \underset{x_2}{\Delta}\, f(x_1) = f(x_1, x_2) = \text{L.H.S.}$$

Hence the result.

Example 3. (*i*) *Prove that*

$$\underset{bcd}{\Delta^3}\left(\frac{1}{a}\right) = -\frac{1}{abcd}$$

(*ii*) *Show that the* n^{th} *divided differences*

$$[x_0, x_1, ..., x_n] \text{ for } u_x = \frac{1}{x} \text{ is } \left[\frac{(-1)^n}{x_0\, x_1\, ...\, x_n}\right].$$

Sol. (*i*)

x	$f(x)$	$\Delta f(x)$	$\Delta^2 f(x)$	$\Delta^3 f(x)$
a	$\frac{1}{a}$			
		$\frac{\frac{1}{b}-\frac{1}{a}}{b-a} = -\frac{1}{ba}$		
b	$\frac{1}{b}$		$(-1)^2 \frac{1}{abc}$	
		$\frac{\frac{1}{c}-\frac{1}{b}}{c-b} = -\frac{1}{bc}$		$(-1)^3 \frac{1}{abcd}$
c	$\frac{1}{c}$		$(-1)^2 \frac{1}{bdc}$	
		$\frac{\frac{1}{d}-\frac{1}{c}}{d-c} = -\frac{1}{dc}$		
d	$\frac{1}{d}$			

From the table, we observe that

$$\underset{bcd}{\Delta^3}\left(\frac{1}{a}\right) = -\frac{1}{abcd}. \qquad (71)$$

(*ii*) From (71), we see that

$$\underset{bcd}{\Delta^3}\left(\frac{1}{a}\right) = -\frac{1}{abcd} = (-1)^3 f(a, b, c, d)$$

∴ In general,

$$\underset{x_0, x_1, ..., x_n}{\Delta^n}\left(\frac{1}{x_0}\right) = (-1)^n f(x_0, x_1, x_2, ..., x_n) = \left[\frac{(-1)^n}{x_0\, x_1\, x_2 .....\, x_n}\right].$$

Example 4. *Using Newton's divided difference formula, find a polynomial function satisfying the following data:*

x:	*– 4*	*– 1*	*0*	*2*	*5*
f(x):	*1245*	*33*	*5*	*9*	*1335*

Hence find f(1).

Sol. The divided difference table is:

x	$f(x)$	$\Delta f(x)$	$\Delta^2 f(x)$	$\Delta^3 f(x)$	$\Delta^4 f(x)$
– 4	1245				
		– 404			
– 1	33		94		
		– 28		– 14	
0	5		10		3
		2		13	
2	9		88		
		442			
5	1335				

Applying Newton's divided difference formula

$$f(x) = 1245 + (x + 4)(-404) + (x + 4)(x + 1)\,94$$
$$+ (x + 4)(x + 1)(x - 0)(-14) + (x + 4)(x + 1)x(x - 2)(3)$$
$$= 3x^4 - 5x^3 + 6x^2 - 14x + 5$$

Hence, $f(1) = 3 - 5 + 6 - 14 + 5 = -5$.

Example 5. *By means of Newton's divided difference formula, find the values of f(8) and f(15) from the following table:*

x:	*4*	*5*	*7*	*10*	*11*	*13*
f(x):	*48*	*100*	*294*	*900*	*1210*	*2028.*

Sol. Newton's divided difference formula, using the arguments 4, 5, 7, 10, 11, and 13 is

$$f(x) = f(4) + (x - 4)\underset{5}{\Delta} f(4) + (x - 4)(x - 5)\underset{5,7}{\Delta} f(4)$$
$$+ (x - 4)(x - 5)(x - 7)\underset{5,7,10}{\Delta^3} f(4)$$
$$+ (x - 4)(x - 5)(x - 7)(x - 10)\underset{5,7,10,11}{\Delta^4} f(4)$$
$$+ (x - 4)(x - 5)(x - 7)(x - 10)(x - 11)\underset{5,7,10,11,13}{\Delta^4} f(4) \qquad (72)$$

The divided difference table is as follows:

x	$f(x)$	$\Delta f(x)$	$\Delta^2 f(x)$	$\Delta^3 f(x)$	$\Delta^4 f(x)$
4	$\boxed{48}$				
		$\dfrac{100-48}{5-4} = \boxed{52}$			
5	100		$\dfrac{97-52}{7-4} = \boxed{15}$		
		$\dfrac{294-100}{7-5} = 97$		$\dfrac{21-15}{10-4} = \boxed{1}$	
7	294		$\dfrac{202-97}{10-5} = 21$		0
		$\dfrac{900-294}{10-7} = 202$		$\dfrac{27-21}{11-5} = 1$	
10	900		$\dfrac{310-202}{11-7} = 27$		0
		$\dfrac{1210-900}{11-10} = 310$		$\dfrac{33-27}{13-7} = 1$	
11	1210		$\dfrac{409-310}{13-10} = 33$		
		$\dfrac{2028-1210}{13-11} = 409$			
13	2028				

Substituting the values of the divided differences in (72),

$$f(x) = 48 + (x-4) \times 52 + (x-4)(x-5) \times 15 + (x-5)(x-4)(x-7) \times 1$$

$$= 48 + 52(x-4) + 15(x-4)(x-5) + (x-4)(x-5)(x-7)$$

Putting $x = 8$ and 15

$$f(8) = 48 + 52 \times 4 + 15 \times 4 \times 3 + 4 \times 3 \times 1$$

$$= 48 + 208 + 180 + 12 = 448$$

$$f(15) = 48 + 52 \times 11 + 15 \times 11 \times 10 + 11 \times 10 \times 8$$

$$= 48 + 572 + 1650 + 880 = 3150.$$

Example 6. *Given the following table, find f(x) as a polynomial in powers of (x – 5)*

x:	*0*	*2*	*3*	*4*	*7*	*9*
f(x):	*4*	*26*	*58*	*112*	*466*	*922.*

Sol. The divided difference table is:

x	$f(x)$	$\Delta f(x)$	$\Delta^2 f(x)$	$\Delta^3 f(x)$
0	$\boxed{4}$			
		$\boxed{11}$		
2	26		$\boxed{7}$	
		32		$\boxed{1}$
3	58		11	
		54		1
4	112		16	
		118		1
7	466		22	
		228		
9	922			

By Newton's divided difference formula, we get

$$f(x) = 4 + (x - 0)(11) + (x - 0)(x - 2)7 + (x - 0)(x - 2)(x - 3)\,1$$
$$= x^3 + 2x^2 + 3x + 4$$

In order to express it in power of $(x - 5)$, we use synthetic division, as

5	1	2	3	4
		5	35	190
5	1	7	38	194
		5	60	
5	1	12	98	
		5		
	1	17		

$$\therefore \qquad 2x^2 + x^3 + 3x + 4 = (x - 5)^3 + 17(x - 5)^2 + 98\,(x - 5) + 194.$$

Example 7. *Given*

$\log_{10} 654 = 2.8156$, $\log_{10} 658 = 2.8182$, $\log_{10} 659 = 2.8189$ and $\log_{10} 661 = 2.8202$, find by the divided difference formula the value of $\log_{10} 656$.

Sol. For the arguments 654, 658, 659, and 661, the divided difference formula is

$$f(x) = f(654) + (x - 654) \underset{658}{\Delta} f(654)$$
$$+ (x - 655)\,(x - 658) \underset{658,\,659}{\Delta^2} f(654)$$
$$+ (x - 654)\,(x - 658)\,(x - 659) \underset{658,\,659,\,661}{\Delta^3} f(654) \qquad (73)$$

The divided difference table is as follows:

x	$10^5 f(x)$	$10^5 \Delta f(x)$	$10^5 \Delta^2 f(x)$	$10^5 \Delta^3 f(x)$
654	$\boxed{281560}$			
		$\frac{260}{4} = \boxed{65}$		
658	281820		$\frac{70-65}{5} = \boxed{1}$	
		$\frac{70}{1} = 70$		$\frac{-1.66-1}{7} = \boxed{-0.38}$
659	281890		$\frac{65-70}{3} = -1.66$	
		$\frac{130}{2} = 65$		
661	282020			

From (73),

$$10^5 f(x) = 281560 + (x-654)(65) + (x-654)(x-658)(1)$$
$$+ (x-654)(x-658)(x-659)(0.38)$$

Putting $x = 656$, we get

$$10^5 f(656) = 281560 + (2)(65) + (2)(-2)(1)$$
$$+ (2)(-2)(-3)(.38)$$
$$= 281690.56$$

$\therefore$ $f(656) = 2.8169056$

Hence, $\log_{10} 656 = 2.8169056.$

Example 8. *Find f '(10) from the following data:*

x:	*3*	*5*	*11*	*27*	*34*
f(x):	*– 13*	*23*	*899*	*17315*	*35606.*

Sol. The divided difference table is:

x	$f(x)$	$\Delta f(x)$	$\Delta^2 f(x)$	$\Delta^3 f(x)$	$\Delta^4 f(x)$
3	**– 13**				
		18			
5	23		**16**		
		146		**1**	
11	899		40		0
		1026		1	
27	17315		69		
		2613			
34	35606				

By Newton's divided difference formula,

$$f(x) = -13 + (x-3)\,18 + (x-3)(x-5)16 + (x-3)(x-5)(x-11)1$$

$$\therefore \quad f'(x) = 3x^2 - 6x - 7$$

Put $\quad x = 10, \quad f'(10) = 3(10)^2 - 6(10) - 7 = 233.$

Example 9. *Given that*

$$log_{10} 2 = 0.3010,\ log_{10} 3 = 0.4771,\ log_{10} 7 = 0.8451,$$

find the value of log_{10} *33.*

Sol. $\log 30 = 1.4771,$

$\log 32 = 5 \log 2 = 5 \times 0.3010 = 1.5050$

$\log 36 = 2 (\log 2 + \log 3) = 2 \times (0.3010 + 0.4771) = 1.5562$

$$\log 35 = \log \frac{70}{2} = \log 70 - \log 2 = 1.8451 - 0.3010 = 1.5441.$$

The divided difference table is as follows:

x	$10^4 \log_{10} x$	$10^4 \Delta \log_{10} x$	$10^4 \Delta^2 \log_{10} x$	$10^4 \Delta^3 \log_{10} x$
30	**14771**			
		$\frac{279}{2} =$ **139.5**		
32	15050		$-\frac{9.2}{5} =$ **– 1.84**	
		$\frac{391}{3} = 130.3$		$-\frac{0.48}{6} =$ **– 0.08**
35	15441		$-\frac{9.3}{7} = -2.32$	
		$\frac{121}{1} = 121$		
36	15562			

Applying Newton's divided difference formula, we get

$$10^4 \log_{10} x = 14771 + (x - 30)\,(139.5) + (x - 30)(x - 32)\,(-1.84) + (x - 30)(x - 32)(x - 35)(-0.08)$$

Putting $x = 33$

$$10^4 \log_{10} 33 = 14771 + 3 \times 139.5 + 3 \times 1 \times (-1.84) + 3 \times 1 \times (-2)(-0.08)$$

$$= 14771 + 418.5 - 5.52 + 0.48 = 15184.46$$

$$\therefore \quad \log_{10} 33 = 1.5184.$$

Example 10. *Find approximately the real root of the equation $x^3 - 2x - 5 = 0$.*

Sol. Let $f(x) = x^3 - 2x - 5$.

The real root of $f(x) = 0$ lies between 2 and 2.1.

$\therefore$ Values of $f(x)$ at $x = 1.9, 2, 2.1, 2.2$ are -1.941, -1.000, 0.061, 1.248, respectively.

Let

x:	– 1.941	– 1.000	0.061	1.248
u_x:	1.9	2.0	2.1	2.2

We have to find u_x at $u = 0$.

The divided difference table is:

x	u_x	Δu_x	$\Delta^2 u_x$	$\Delta^3 u_x$
– 1.941	1.9			
		0.1062699		
– 1.000	2.0		– 0.0060035	
		0.0942507		0.0004869
0.061	2.1		– 0.0044505	
		0.0842459		
1.248	2.2			

Applying the Newton-divided difference formula,

$$u_x = 1.9 + (x + 1.941) \times 0.1062699 + (x + 1.941)(x + 1)(-0.0060035) + (x + 1.941)(x + 1)(x - 0.061) \times 0.0004869.$$

Given $x = 0$

$$u_0 = 1.9 + 0.2062698 - 0.0116527 - 0.0000576 = 2.0945595$$

$\therefore$ The required root is 2.0945595.

Example 11. *The mode of a certain frequency curve $y = f(x)$ is very near to $x = 9$ and the values of frequency density $f(x)$ for $x = 8.9$, 9.0 and 9.3 are respectively equal to 0.30, 0.35, and 0.25. Calculate the approximate value of mode.*

Sol. The divided difference table is as follows:

x	$100\, f(x)$	$100\, \Delta f(x)$	$100\, \Delta^2 f(x)$
8.9	$\boxed{30}$		
		$\frac{5}{0.9} = \boxed{\frac{50}{9}}$	
9.0	35		$-\frac{350}{9 \times 0.4} = \boxed{-\frac{3500}{36}}$
		$-\frac{10}{0.3} = -\frac{100}{3}$	
9.3	25		

Applying Newton's divided difference formula

$$100\, f(x) = 30 + (x - 8.9) \times \frac{50}{9} + (x - 8.9)(x - 9)\left(-\frac{3500}{36}\right)$$

$$= -\,97.222\, x^2 + 1745.833x - 1759.7217.$$

$$\therefore \quad f(x) = -\,.9722x^2 + 17.45833x - 17.597217$$

$$f'(x) = -\,1.9444\, x + 17.45833$$

Given $f'(x) = 0$, we get

$$x = \frac{17.45833}{1.9444} = 8.9788$$

Also,

$$f''(x) = -\,1.9444 \text{ i.e., } (-)\text{ve}$$

$\therefore$ $f(x)$ is maximum at $x = 8.9788$

Hence, the mode is 8.9788.

Example 12. *The following are the mean temperatures (°F) on three days, 30 days apart during summer and winter. Estimate the approximate dates and values of maximum and minimum temperature.*

	Summer		*Winter*	
Day	*Date*	*Temp.*	*Date*	*Temp.*
0	*15 June*	*58.8*	*16 Dec.*	*40.7*
30	*15 July*	*63.4*	*15 Jan.*	*38.1*
60	*14 August*	*62.5*	*14 Feb.*	*39.3*

Sol. The divided difference table for summer is:

x	$f(x)$	$\Delta f(x)$	$\Delta^2 f(x)$
0	**58.8**		
		4.6	
1	63.4		**– 2.75**
		– 0.9	
2	62.5		

$$\therefore \quad f(x) = 58.8 + (x - 0)(4.6) + (x - 0)(x - 1)(-2.75)$$

$$= -2.75\,x^2 + 7.35\,x + 58.8$$

For maximum and minimum of $f(x)$, we have

$$f'(x) = 0$$

$$\Rightarrow \quad -5.5\,x + 7.35 = 0 \quad \Rightarrow \quad x = 1.342$$

Again, $\quad f''(x) = -5.5 < 0$

$\therefore$ $f(x)$ is maximum at $x = 1.342$

Since unit $1 \equiv 30$ days

$\therefore \quad 1.342 \equiv 30 \times 1.342 = 40.26$ days

$\therefore$ The maximum temperature was on 15 June + 40 days, *i.e.*, on 25 July, and the value of the maximum temperature is

$$[f(x)]_{\text{max.}} = [f(x)]_{1.342} = 63.711°\text{F. approximately.}$$

The divided difference table for winter is as follows:

x	$f(x)$	$\Delta f(x)$	$\Delta^2 f(x)$
0	**40.7**		
		– 2.6	
1	38.1		**1.9**
		1.2	
2	39.3		

$$\therefore \qquad f(x) = 40.7 + (x - 0)(-2.6) + x(x - 1)(1.9)$$

$$= 1.9x^2 - 4.5x + 40.7$$

For $f(x)$ to be maximum or minimum, we have $f'(x) = 0$

$$3.8x - 4.5 = 0 \quad \Rightarrow \quad x = 1.184$$

Again, $\qquad f''(x) = 3.8 > 0$

$\therefore$ $f(x)$ is minimum at $x = 1.184$

Again, unit $1 \equiv 30$ days

$$\therefore \qquad 1.184 \equiv 30 \times 1.184 = 35.52 \text{ days}$$

$\therefore$ The minimum temperature was on 16 Dec. + 35.5 days, *i.e.*, at midnight on the 20th of January and its value can be obtained similarly.

$$[f(x)]_{\text{min.}} = [f(x)]_{1.184} = 63.647°\text{F approximately.}$$

Example 13. *Using Newton's divided difference formula, calculate the value of f(6) from the following data:*

x:	*1*	*2*	*7*	*8*
f(x):	*1*	*5*	*5*	*4.*

Sol. The divided difference table is:

x	$f(x)$	$\Delta f(x)$	$\Delta^2 f(x)$	$\Delta^3 f(x)$
1	1			
		4		
2	5		$-\frac{2}{3}$	
		0		$\frac{1}{14}$
7	5		$-\frac{1}{6}$	
		-1		
8	4			

Applying Newton's divided difference formula,

$$f(x) = 1 + (x - 1)(4) + (x - 1)(x - 2)\left(-\frac{2}{3}\right)$$

$$+ (x - 1)(x - 2)(x - 7)\left(\frac{1}{14}\right)$$

$$\therefore \qquad f(6) = 1 + 20 + (5)\,(4)\left(-\frac{2}{3}\right) + (5)\,(4)\,(-1)\left(\frac{1}{14}\right)$$

$$= 6.2381.$$

Example 14. *Referring to the following table, find the value of f(x) at point x = 4:*

x:	*1.5*	*3*	*6*
f(x):	*– 0.25*	*2*	*20.*

Sol. The divided difference table is:

x	$f(x)$	$\Delta f(x)$	$\Delta^2 f(x)$
1.5	– 0.25		
		1.5	
3	2		1
		6	
6	20		

Applying Newton's divided difference formula,

$$f(x) = -0.25 + (x - 1.5)\,(1.5) + (x - 1.5)\,(x - 3)\,(1)$$

Putting $x = 4$, we get

$$f(4) = 6.$$

Example 15. *Using Newton's divided difference formula, prove that*

$$f(x) = f(0) + x\Delta f(-1) + \frac{(x+1)x}{2\,!}\,\Delta^2 f(-1) + \frac{(x+1)x(x-1)}{3\,!}\,\Delta^3 f(-2) + \ldots\ldots$$

Sol. Taking the arguments, 0, – 1, 1, – 2, ... the divided Newton's difference formula is

$$f(x) = f(0) + x \underset{-1}{\Delta} f(0) + x(x+1) \underset{-1,\,1}{\Delta^2} f(0) + x(x+1)(x-1) \underset{-1,\,1,\,-2}{\Delta^3} f(0) + \ldots \qquad (74)$$

$$= f(0) + x \underset{0}{\Delta} f(-1) + x(x+1) \underset{0,\,1}{\Delta^2} f(-1) + (x+1)x(x-1) \underset{-1,\,0,\,1}{\Delta^3} f(-2) + \ldots.$$

Now $\underset{0}{\Delta} f(-1) = \dfrac{f(0) - f(-1)}{0 - (-1)} = \Delta f(-1)$

$$\underset{0,1}{\Delta}^2 f(-1) = \frac{1}{1-(-1)} [\underset{1}{\Delta} f(0) - \underset{0}{\Delta} f(-1)]$$

$$= \tfrac{1}{2} [\Delta f(0) - \Delta f(-1)] = \tfrac{1}{2} \Delta^2 f(-1)$$

$$\underset{-1,0,1}{\Delta}^3 f(-2) = \frac{1}{1-(-2)} [\underset{0,1}{\Delta}^2 f(-1) - \underset{-1,0}{\Delta}^2 f(-2)]$$

$$= \frac{1}{3}\left[\frac{\Delta^2 f(-1)}{2} - \frac{\Delta^2 f(-2)}{2}\right]$$

$$= \frac{\Delta^3 f(-2)}{3.2} = \frac{\Delta^3 f(-2)}{3!} \quad \text{and so on.}$$

Substituting these values in (74)

$$f(x) = f(0) + x\Delta f(-1) + \frac{(x+1)x}{2!} \Delta^2 f(-1)$$

$$+ \frac{(x+1)x(x-1)}{3!} \Delta^3 f(-2) + \ldots\ldots$$

ASSIGNMENT 4.12

1. Given the values:

x:	5	7	11	13	17
$f(x)$:	150	392	1452	2366	5202

Evaluate $f(9)$ using Newton's divided difference formula.

2. The observed values of a function are, respectively, 168, 120, 72, and 63 at the four positions 3, 7, 9, and 20 of the independent variable. What is the best estimate you can give for value of the function at the position 6 of the independent variable?

3. Apply Newton's divided difference formula to find the value of $f(8)$ if

$$f(1) = 3, f(3) = 31, f(6) = 223, f(10) = 1011, f(11) = 1343.$$

4. Given that

x:	1	3	4	6	7
y_x:	1	27	81	729	2187

Find y_5. Why does it differ from 3^5?

5. Use Newton's divided difference formula to find $f(7)$ if $f(3) = 24$, $f(5) = 120$, $f(8) = 504$, $f(9) = 720$, and $f(12) = 1716$.

6. The following table is given:

x:	0	1	2	5
$f(x)$:	2	3	12	147

What is the form of the function?

7. Find the function u_x in powers of $x - 1$, given that $u_0 = 8$, $u_1 = 11$, $u_4 = 68$, $u_5 = 123$.

8. Find u_x in powers of $x - 4$ where $u_0 = 8$, $u_1 = 11$, $u_4 = 68$, $u_5 = 125$.

9. Using Lagrange's interpolation formula express the function

$$\frac{x^2 + x - 3}{x^3 - 2x^2 - x + 2}$$

as sums of portial fractions

10. Express the function

$$\frac{x^2 + 6x - 1}{(x^2 - 1)(x - 4)(x - 6)}$$

as a sum of partial fractions.

11. Certain corresponding values of x and $\log_{10} x$ are given below:

x:	300	304	305	307
$\log_{10} x$:	2.4771	2.4829	2.4843	2.4871

Find $\log_{10} 310$ by Newton's divided difference formula.

12. (*i*) The following table gives the values of x and y:

x:	1.2	2.1	2.8	4.1	4.9	6.2
y:	4.2	6.8	9.8	13.4	15.5	19.6

Find the value of x corresponding to $y = 12$ using Lagrange's technique of inverse interpolation.

(*ii*) Obtain the value of t when A = 85 from the following table using Lagrange's method

t:	2	5	8	14
A:	94.8	87.9	81.3	68.7

13. Using Newton's divided difference method, compute $f(3)$ from the following table

x:	0	1	2	4	5	6
$f(x)$:	1	14	15	5	6	19

14. Find the Newton's divided difference interpolation polynomial for:

x:	0.5	1.5	3.0	5.0	6.5	8.0
$f(x)$:	1.625	5.875	31.0	131.0	282.125	521.0

15. If $f(x) = U(x)V(x)$, find the divided difference $f(x_0, x_1)$ in terms of $U(x_0)$, $V(x_1)$ and the divided differences $U(x_0, x_1)$, $V(x_0, x_1)$. Write a code in C to implement.

16. Write an algorithm to compute the value of a function using Lagrange's interpolation.

4.33 HERMITE'S INTERPOLATION FORMULA

So far we have considered the interpolation formulae which make use only of a certain number of function values. We now derive an interpolation formula in which both the function and its first derivative are to be assigned at each point of interpolation. This is called **Hermite's interpolation formula** or **osculating interpolation formula.**

Let the set of data points (x_i, y_i, y_i'), $0 \le i \le n$ be given. A polynomial of the least degree say $H(x)$ is to be determined such that

$$H(x_i) = y_i \quad \text{and} \quad H'(x_i) = y_i';\ i = 0, 1, 2, \dots n \tag{75}$$

$H(x)$ is called Hermite's interpolating polynomial.

Since there are $2n + 2$ conditions to be satisfied, $H(x)$ must be a polynomial of degree $\le 2n + 1$.

The required polynomial may be written as

$$H(x) = \sum_{i=0}^{n} u_i(x)\, y_i + \sum_{i=0}^{n} v_i(x)\, y_i' \tag{76}$$

where $u_i(x)$ and $v_i(x)$ are polynomials in x of degree $\le (2n + 1)$ and satisfy

$$(i)\ u_i(x_j) = \begin{Bmatrix} 0, & i \ne j \\ 1, & i = j \end{Bmatrix} \tag{77 (i)}$$

$$(ii)\ v_i(x_j) = 0 \quad \forall\, i, j \tag{77 (ii)}$$

$$(iii)\ u_i'(x_j) = 0 \quad \forall\, i, j \tag{77 (iii)}$$

$$(iv)\ v_i'(x_j) = \begin{Bmatrix} 0, & i \ne j \\ 1, & i = j \end{Bmatrix} \tag{77 (iv)}$$

Using the Lagrange fundamental polynomials $L_i(x)$, we choose

$$\left.\begin{aligned} u_i(x) &= A_i(x)\, [L_i(x)]^2 \\ \text{and} \qquad v_i(x) &= B_i(x)\, [L_i(x)]^2 \end{aligned}\right\} \tag{78}$$

where $L_i(x)$ is defined as

$$L_i(x) = \frac{(x - x_0)(x - x_1) \dots (x - x_{i-1})(x - x_{i+1}) \dots (x - x_n)}{(x_i - x_0)(x_i - x_1) \dots (x_i - x_{i-1})(x_i - x_{i+1}) \dots (x_i - x_n)}$$

Since $L_i^2(x)$ is a polynomial of degree $2n$, $A_i(x)$ and $B_i(x)$ must be linear polynomials.

Let $$A_i(x) = a_i x + b_i$$

and $$B_i(x) = c_i x + d_i \quad \text{so that from (78),}$$

$$\left.\begin{aligned} u_i(x) &= (a_i x + b_i)\,[L_i(x)]^2 \\ v_i(x) &= (c_i x + d_i)\,[L_i(x)]^2 \end{aligned}\right\} \tag{79}$$

using conditions (77(*i*)) and (77(*ii*)) in (79), we get

$$a_i x + b_i = 1 \qquad (80\ (i))$$

and $$c_i x + d_i = 0 \qquad (80\ (ii)) \quad \mid \text{since } [L_i(x_i)]^2 = 1$$

Again, using conditions (77(*iii*)) and (77(*iv*)) in (79), we get

$$a_i + 2L_i'(x_i) = 0 \tag{80 (iii)}$$

and $$c_i = 1 \tag{80 (iv)}$$

From equations (80(*i*)), (80(*ii*)), (80(*iii*)) and (80(*iv*)), we deduce

$$\left.\begin{aligned} a_i &= -\,2L_i'(x_i) \\ b_i &= 1 + 2x_i L_i'(x_i) \\ c_i &= 1 \\ \text{and} \quad d_i &= -\,x_i \end{aligned}\right\} \tag{81}$$

Hence, from (79),

$$\begin{aligned} u_i(x) &= [-\,2x\,L_i'(x_i) + 1 + 2x_i L_i'(x_i)]\,[L_i(x)]^2 \\ &= [1 - 2(x - x_i)\,L_i'(x_i)]\,[L_i(x)]^2 \end{aligned}$$

and $$v_i(x) = (x - x_i)\,[L_i(x)]^2$$

Therefore from (76),

$$\boxed{H(x) = \sum_{i=0}^{n} [1 - 2(x - x_i)\,L_i'(x_i)]\,[L_i(x)]^2\,y_i + \sum_{i=0}^{n} (x - x_i)\,[L_i(x)]^2\,y_i'}$$

which is the required *Hermite's interpolation formula*.

EXAMPLES

Example 1. *Apply Hermite's interpolation formula to find a cubic polynomial which meets the following specifications.*

x_i	y_i	y_i'
0	0	0
1	1	1

Sol. Hermite interpolation formula is

$$H(x) = \sum_{i=0}^{1} [1-2(x-x_i)\,L_i'(x_i)]\,[L_i(x)]^2\, y_i + \sum_{i=0}^{1} (x-x_i)\,[L_i(x)]^2\, y_i'$$

$$= [1-2\,(x-x_0)\,L_0'(x_0)]\,[L_0(x)]^2 y_0$$

$$+ [1-2(x-x_1)\,L_1'(x_1)]\,[L_1(x)]^2 y_1$$

$$+ (x-x_0)\,[L_0(x)]^2 y_0' + (x-x_1)\,[L_1(x)]^2 y_1' \qquad (82)$$

Now, $$L_0(x) = \frac{x-x_1}{x_0-x_1} = \frac{x-1}{0-1} = 1-x$$

$$L_1(x) = \frac{x-x_0}{x_1-x_0} = \frac{x-0}{1-0} = x$$

$\therefore$ $L_0'(x) = -1$

and $L_1'(x) = 1$

Hence, $L_0'(x_0) = -1$ and $L_1'(x_1) = 1$

$\therefore$ From (82),

$$H(x) = [1-2\,(x-0)\,(-1)\,[\,(1-x)^2\,(0)$$

$$+ [1-2\,(x-1)\,(1)\,]\,x^2\,(1)$$

$$+ (x-0)\,(1-x)^2\,(0) + (x-1)\,x^2\,(1)$$

$$= x^2 - 2x^2(x-1) + x^2\,(x-1)$$

$$= x^2 - x^2\,(x-1) = x^2(2-x)$$

$$= 2x^2 - x^3.$$

Example 2. *Apply Hermite's formula to find a polynomial which meets these specifications*

x_k	y_k	y_k'
0	0	0
1	1	0
2	0	0

Sol. Hermite's interpolation formula is

$$H(x) = \sum_{i=0}^{2} [1-2(x-x_i)\,L_i'(x_i)]\,[L_i(x)]^2\, y_i + \sum_{i=0}^{2} (x-x_i)\,[L_i(x)]^2\, y_i'$$

$$= [1 - 2(x - x_0)\, L_0'(x_0)]\, [L_0(x)]^2\, y_0 + [1 - 2(x - x_1)\, L_1'(x_1)]\, [L_1(x)]^2 y_1$$
$$+ [1 - 2\,(x - x_2)\, L_2'(x_2)]\, [L_2(x)]^2\, y_2 + (x - x_0)\, [L_0(x)]^2\, y_0'$$
$$+ (x - x_1)\, [L_1(x)]^2\, y_1' + (x - x_2)\, [L_2(x)]^2\, y_2' \qquad (83)$$

Now, $$L_0(x) = \frac{(x-x_1)(x-x_2)}{(x_0-x_1)(x_0-x_2)} = \frac{(x-1)(x-2)}{(0-1)(0-2)} = \frac{1}{2}(x^2 - 3x + 2)$$

$$L_1(x) = \frac{(x-x_0)(x-x_2)}{(x_1-x_0)(x_1-x_2)} = \frac{(x-0)(x-2)}{(1-0)(1-2)} = 2x - x^2$$

$$L_2(x) = \frac{(x-x_0)(x-x_1)}{(x_2-x_0)(x_2-x_1)} = \frac{(x-0)(x-1)}{(2-0)(2-1)} = \frac{1}{2}(x^2 - x)$$

$\therefore$ $$L_0'(x) = \frac{2x-3}{2}, \qquad L_1'(x) = 2 - 2x, \qquad L_2'(x) = \frac{2x-1}{2}$$

Hence, $$L_0'(x_0) = -\frac{3}{2}, \qquad L_1'(x_1) = 0, \qquad L_2'(x_2) = \frac{3}{2}$$

$\therefore$ From (83),

$$H(x) = \left[1 - 2(x-0)\left(-\frac{3}{2}\right)\right]\frac{1}{4}(x^2 - 3x + 2)^2\,(0)$$
$$+ [1 - 2(x - 1)\,(0)]\,(2x - x^2)^2\,(1)$$
$$+ \left[1 - 2(x-2)\left(\frac{3}{2}\right)\right]\frac{1}{4}\,(x^2 - x)^2\,(0)$$
$$+ (x - 0)\,\frac{1}{4}\,(x^2 - 3x + 2)^2\,(0)$$
$$+ (x - 1)\,(2x - x^2)^2\,(0) + (x - 2)\,\frac{1}{4}\,(x^2 - x)^2\,(0)$$
$$= (2x - x^2)^2 = x^4 - 4x^3 + 4x^2.$$

Example 3. *A switching path between parallel railroad tracks is to be a cubic polynomial joining positions (0, 0) and (4, 2) and tangent to the lines y = 0 and y = 2 as shown in the figure. Apply Hermite's interpolation formula to obtain this polynomial.*

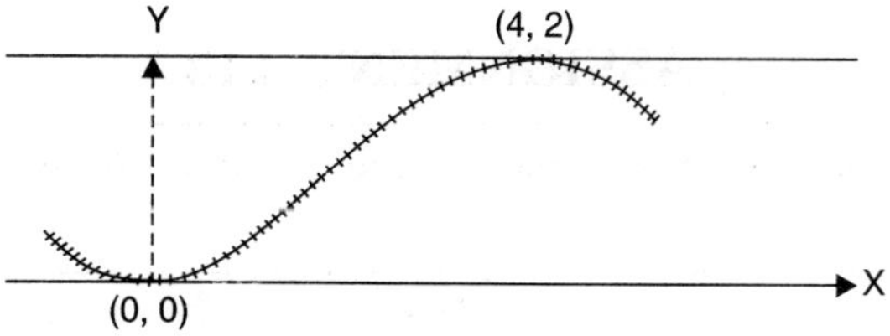

Sol. Since tangents are parallel to X-axis,
$y' = 0$ in both the cases.

∴ We have the table of values,

x	y	y'
0	0	0
4	2	0

The hermite interpolation formula is

$$H(x) = \sum_{i=0}^{1} [1 - 2(x - x_i)\, L_i'(x_i)]\, [L_i(x)]^2\, y_i + \sum_{i=0}^{1} (x - x_i)\, [L_i(x)]^2\, y_i' \qquad (84)$$

Now,
$$L_0(x) = \frac{x - x_1}{x_0 - x_1} = \frac{x - 4}{0 - 4} = 1 - \frac{x}{4}$$

$$L_1(x) = \frac{x - x_0}{x_1 - x_0} = \frac{x - 0}{4 - 0} = \frac{x}{4}$$

∴
$$L_0'(x) = -\frac{1}{4} \quad \text{and} \quad L_1'(x) = \frac{1}{4}$$

Hence,
$$L_0'(x_0) = -\frac{1}{4} \quad \text{and} \quad L_1'(x_1) = \frac{1}{4}$$

∴ From (84),
$$H(x) = \left[1 - 2(x - 0)\left(-\frac{1}{4}\right)\right]\left(1 - \frac{x}{4}\right)^2 (0)$$

$$+ \left[1 - 2(x - 4)\left(\frac{1}{4}\right)\right]\left(\frac{x}{4}\right)^2 (2)$$

$$+ (x - 0)\left(1 - \frac{x}{4}\right)^2 (0) + (x - 4)\left(\frac{x}{4}\right)^2 (0)$$

$$= \left[1 - \left(\frac{x - 4}{2}\right)\right]\frac{x^2}{8} = \frac{(6 - x)x^2}{16} = \frac{1}{16}(6x^2 - x^3).$$

ASSIGNMENT 4.13

1. Apply Hermite's interpolation formula to find $f(x)$ at $x = 0.5$ which meets the following requirement:

x_i	$f(x_i)$	$f'(x_i)$
−1	1	−5
0	1	1
1	3	7

Also find $f(-0.5)$.

2. Apply Hermite's interpolating formula to obtain a polynomial of degree 4 for the following data:

x_i	y_i	y_i'
0	1	0
1	0	0
2	9	24

3. Apply Hermite's formula to find a polynomial which meets the following specifications:

x_i	y_i	y_i'
−1	−1	0
0	0	0
1	1	0

4. Apply osculating interpolation formula to find a polynomial which meets the following requirements:

x_i	y_i	y_i'
0	1	0
1	0	0
2	9	0

5. Apply Hermite's formula to interpolate for sin 1.05 from the following data:

x	$\sin x$	$\cos x$
1.00	0.84147	0.54030
1.10	0.89121	0.45360

6. Find $y = f(x)$ by Hermite's interpolation from the table:

x_i	y_i	y_i'
– 1	1	– 5
0	1	1
1	3	7

Compute y_2 and y_2'.

7. Compute $\sqrt{e}$ by Hermite's formula for the function $f(x) = e^x$ at the points 0 and 1. Compare the value with the value obtained by using Lagrange's interpolation.

8. Show that

$$f\left(\frac{a+b}{2}\right) = \frac{f(a)+f(b)}{2} + \frac{(b-a)\,[f'(a)-f'(b)]}{8}$$

by Hermite's interpolation.

9. Apply Hermite's interpolation to find $f(1.05)$ given:

x	f	f'
1	1.0	0.5
1.1	1.04881	0.47673

10. Apply Hermite's interpolation to find log 2.05 given that

x	$\log x$	$\frac{1}{x}$
2.0	0.69315	0.5
2.1	0.74194	0.47619

11. Determine the Hermite polynomial of degree 5 which fits the following data and hence find an approximate value of $\log_e 2.7$.

x	$y = \log_e x$	$y' = \frac{1}{x}$
2.0	0.69315	0.5
2.5	0.91629	0.4
3.0	1.09861	0.33333

12. Using Hermite's interpolation formula, estimate the value of l_n (3.2) from the following table:

x	3	3.5	4.0
$y = l_n (x)$	1.09861	1.25276	1.38629
$y' = \frac{1}{x}$	0.33333	0.28571	0.25000

13. (*i*) Construct the Hermite interpolation polynomial that fits the data:

x	$f(x)$	$f'(x)$
1	7.389	14.778
2	54.598	109.196

Estimate the value of $f(1.5)$.

(*ii*) Consider the cubic polynomial

$$P(x) = c_0 + c_1 x + c_2 x^2 + c_3 x^3.$$

Fit the data in problem 13(*i*) and find P(x). Are these polynomials different? Comment.

14. (*i*) Construct the Hermite interpolation polynomial that fits the data:

x	$f(x)$	$f'(x)$
2	29	50
3	105	105

Interpolate $f(x)$ at $x = 2.5$.

(*ii*) Fit the cubic polynomial $P(x) = c_0 + c_1 x + c_2 x^2 + c_3 x^3$ to the data given in problem 14(*i*). Are these polynomials same?

15. (*i*) Construct the Hermite interpolation polynomial that fits the data:

x	$f(x)$	$f'(x)$
0	0	1
0.5	0.4794	0.8776
1.0	0.8415	0.5403

Estimate the value of $f(0.75)$.

(*ii*) Construct the Hermite interpolation polynomial that fits the data:

x	$y(x)$	$y'(x)$
0	4	– 5
1	– 6	– 14
2	– 22	– 17

Interpolate $y(x)$ at $x = 0.5$ and 1.5.

16. Obtain the unique polynomial $p(x)$ of degree 3 or less corresponding to a function $f(x)$ where $f(0) = 1, f'(0) = 2, f(1) = 5, f'(1) = 4$.

Part 3

- **Numerical Integration and Differentiation**
  Introduction, Numerical Differentiation,
  Numerical Integration,
  Trapezoidal Rule, Simpson's $\left(\frac{1}{3}\right)^{rd}$ and $\left(\frac{3}{8}\right)^{th}$ Rule, Boole's Rule,
  Weddle's Rule.

Chapter 5 NUMERICAL INTEGRATION AND DIFFERENTIATION

5.1 INTRODUCTION

Consider a function of a single variable $y = f(x)$. If $f(x)$ is defined as an expression, its derivative or integral may often be determined using the techniques of calculus.

However, when $f(x)$ is a complicated function or when it is given in a tabular form, numerical methods are used.

This section discusses numerical methods for approximating the derivative(s) $f^{(r)}(x)$, $r \geq 1$ of a given function $f(x)$ and for the evaluation of the integral $\int_a^b f(x)\,dx$ where a, b may be finite or infinite.

The accuracy attainable by these methods would depend on the given function and the order of the polynomial used. If the polynomial fitted is exact then the error would be, theoretically, zero. In practice, however, rounding errors will introduce errors in the calculated values.

The error introduced in obtaining derivatives is, in general, much worse than that introduced in determining integrals.

It may be observed that any errors in approximating a function are amplified while taking the derivative whereas they are smoothed out in integration.

Thus numerical differentiations should be avoided if an alternative exists.

5.2 NUMERICAL DIFFERENTIATION

In the case of numerical data, the functional form of $f(x)$ is not known in general. First we have to find an appropriate form of $f(x)$ and then obtain its derivatives. So **"Numerical Differentiation"** is concerned with the method of finding the successive derivatives of a function at a given argument, using the given table of entries corresponding to a set of arguments, equally or unequally spaced. Using the theory of interpolation, a suitable interpolating polynomial can be chosen to represent the function to a good degree of approximation in the given interval of the argument.

For the proper choice of interpolation formula, the criterion is the same as in the case of interpolation problems. In the case of equidistant values of x, if the derivative is to be found at a point near the beginning or the end of the given set of values, Newton's forward or backward difference formula should be used accordingly. Also if the derivative is to be found at a point near the middle of the given set of values, then any one of the central difference formulae should be used. However, if the values of the function are not known at equidistant values of x, Newton's divided difference or Lagrange's formula should be used.

5.3 FORMULAE FOR DERIVATIVES

(1) **Newton's forward difference interpolation formula is**

$$y = y_0 + u\,\Delta y_0 + \frac{u(u-1)}{2!}\Delta^2 y_0 + \frac{u(u-1)(u-2)}{3!}\Delta^3 y_0 + \ldots \quad (1)$$

where $u = \dfrac{x-a}{h}$ (2)

Differentiating eqn. (1) with respect to u, we get

$$\frac{dy}{du} = \Delta y_0 + \frac{2u-1}{2}\Delta^2 y_0 + \frac{3u^2-6u+2}{6}\Delta^3 y_0 + \ldots \quad (3)$$

Differentiating eqn. (2) with respect to x, we get

$$\frac{du}{dx} = \frac{1}{h} \quad (4)$$

We know that

$$\frac{dy}{dx} = \frac{dy}{du}\cdot\frac{du}{dx} = \frac{1}{h}\left[\Delta y_0 + \left(\frac{2u-1}{2}\right)\Delta^2 y_0 + \left(\frac{3u^2-6u+2}{6}\right)\Delta^3 y_0 + \ldots\right] \quad (5)$$

Expression (5) provides the value of $\frac{dy}{dx}$ at any x which is not tabulated.

Formula (5) becomes simple for tabulated values of x, in particular when $x = a$ and $u = 0$

Putting $u = 0$ in (5), we get

$$\left(\frac{dy}{dx}\right)_{x=a} = \frac{1}{h}\left[\Delta y_0 - \frac{1}{2}\Delta^2 y_0 + \frac{1}{3}\Delta^3 y_0 - \frac{1}{4}\Delta^4 y_0 + \frac{1}{5}\Delta^5 y_0 - \ldots\right] \quad (6)$$

Differentiating eqn. (5) with respect to x, we get

$$\frac{d^2y}{dx^2} = \frac{d}{dx}\left(\frac{dy}{dx}\right) = \frac{d}{du}\left(\frac{dy}{dx}\right)\frac{du}{dx}$$

$$= \frac{1}{h}\left[\Delta^2 y_0 + (u-1)\,\Delta^3 y_0 + \left(\frac{6u^2 - 18u + 11}{12}\right)\Delta^4 y_0 + \ldots\right]\frac{1}{h}$$

$$= \frac{1}{h^2}\left[\Delta^2 y_0 + (u-1)\,\Delta^3 y_0 + \left(\frac{6u^2 - 18u + 11}{12}\right)\Delta^4 y_0 + \ldots\right] \quad (7)$$

Putting $u = 0$ in (7), we get

$$\left(\frac{d^2y}{dx^2}\right)_{x=a} = \frac{1}{h^2}\left(\Delta^2 y_0 - \Delta^3 y_0 + \frac{11}{12}\Delta^4 y_0 + \ldots\right) \quad (8)$$

Similarly, we get

$$\left(\frac{d^3y}{dx^3}\right)_{x=a} = \frac{1}{h^3}\left(\Delta^3 y_0 - \frac{3}{2}\Delta^4 y_0 + \ldots\right) \quad (9)$$

and so on.

Formulae for computing higher derivatives may be obtained by successive differentiation.

Aliter: We know that

$$\mathrm{E} = e^{h\mathrm{D}} \Rightarrow 1 + \Delta = e^{h\mathrm{D}}$$

$$\therefore \quad h\mathrm{D} = \log(1 + \Delta) = \Delta - \frac{\Delta^2}{2} + \frac{\Delta^3}{3} - \frac{\Delta^4}{4} + \ldots$$

$$\Rightarrow \qquad D = \frac{1}{h}\left[\Delta - \frac{1}{2}\Delta^2 + \frac{1}{3}\Delta^3 - \frac{1}{4}\Delta^4 + ...\right]$$

Similarly,

$$D^2 = \frac{1}{h^2}\left(\Delta - \frac{1}{2}\Delta^2 + \frac{1}{3}\Delta^3 - \frac{1}{4}\Delta^4 + ...\right)^2 = \frac{1}{h^2}\left(\Delta^2 - \Delta^3 + \frac{11}{12}\Delta^4 - \frac{5}{6}\Delta^5 + ...\right)$$

and $D^3 = \frac{1}{h^3}\left(\Delta^3 - \frac{3}{2}\Delta^4 + ...\right)$

(2) **Newton's backward difference interpolation formula is**

$$y = y_n + u\,\nabla y_n + \frac{u(u+1)}{2!}\nabla^2 y_n + \frac{u(u+1)(u+2)}{3!}\nabla^3 y_n + ... \tag{10}$$

where $u = \frac{x - x_n}{h}$ (11)

Differentiating (10) with respect to, u, we get

$$\frac{dy}{du} = \nabla y_n + \left(\frac{2u+1}{2}\right)\nabla^2 y_n + \left(\frac{3u^2 + 6u + 2}{6}\right)\nabla^3 y_n + ... \tag{12}$$

Differentiating (11) with respect to x, we get

$$\frac{du}{dx} = \frac{1}{h} \tag{13}$$

Now,

$$\frac{dy}{dx} = \frac{dy}{du}\cdot\frac{du}{dx}$$

$$= \frac{1}{h}\left[\nabla y_n + \left(\frac{2u+1}{2}\right)\nabla^2 y_n + \left(\frac{3u^2 + 6u + 2}{6}\right)\nabla^3 y_n + ...\right] \tag{14}$$

Expression (14) provides us the value of $\frac{dy}{dx}$ at any x which is not tabulated.

At $x = x_n$, we have $u = 0$

$\therefore$ Putting $u = 0$ in (14), we get

$$\boxed{\left(\frac{dy}{dx}\right)_{x=x_n} = \frac{1}{h}\left(\nabla y_n + \frac{1}{2}\nabla^2 y_n + \frac{1}{3}\nabla^3 y_n + \frac{1}{4}\nabla^4 y_n + ...\right)} \tag{15}$$

Differentiating (14) with respect to x, we get

$$\frac{d^2y}{dx^2} = \frac{d}{du}\left(\frac{dy}{dx}\right)\frac{du}{dx}$$

$$= \frac{1}{h^2}\left[\nabla^2 y_n + (u+1)\nabla^3 y_n + \left(\frac{6u^2 + 18u + 11}{12}\right)\nabla^4 y_n + \dots\right] \quad (16)$$

Putting $u = 0$ in (16), we get

$$\left(\frac{d^2y}{dx^2}\right)_{x=x_n} = \frac{1}{h^2}\left(\nabla^2 y_n + \nabla^3 y_n + \frac{11}{12}\nabla^4 y_n + \dots\right) \quad (17)$$

Similarly, we get

$$\left(\frac{d^3y}{dx^3}\right)_{x=x_n} = \frac{1}{h^3}\left(\nabla^3 y_n + \frac{3}{2}\nabla^4 y_n + \dots\right) \quad (18)$$

and so on.

Formulae for computing higher derivatives may be obtained by successive differentiation.

Aliter: We know that

$$E^{-1} = 1 - \nabla$$

$$e^{-hD} = 1 - \nabla$$

$$\therefore \quad -hD = \log(1-\nabla) = -\left(\nabla + \frac{1}{2}\nabla^2 + \frac{1}{3}\nabla^3 + \frac{1}{4}\nabla^4 + \dots\right)$$

$$\Rightarrow \quad D = \frac{1}{h}\left(\nabla + \frac{1}{2}\nabla^2 + \frac{1}{3}\nabla^3 + \frac{1}{4}\nabla^4 + \dots\right)$$

Also,

$$D^2 = \frac{1}{h^2}\left(\nabla + \frac{1}{2}\nabla^2 + \frac{1}{3}\nabla^3 + \dots\right)^2$$

$$= \frac{1}{h^2}\left(\nabla^2 + \nabla^3 + \frac{11}{12}\nabla^4 + \dots\right)$$

Similarly, $D^3 = \frac{1}{h^3}\left(\nabla^3 + \frac{3}{2}\nabla^4 + \dots\right)$ and so on.

(3) **Stirling's central difference interpolation formula is**

$$y = y_0 + \frac{u}{1!}\left(\frac{\Delta y_0 + \Delta y_{-1}}{2}\right) + \frac{u^2}{2!}\Delta^2 y_{-1} + \frac{u(u^2-1^2)}{3!}\left(\frac{\Delta^3 y_{-1} + \Delta^3 y_{-2}}{2}\right)$$

$$+ \frac{u^2(u^2-1^2)}{4!}\Delta^4 y_{-2} + \frac{u(u^2-1^2)(u^2-2^2)}{5!}\left(\frac{\Delta^5 y_{-2} + \Delta^5 y_{-3}}{2}\right) + \ldots \tag{19}$$

where $$u = \frac{x-a}{h} \tag{20}$$

Differentiating eqn. (19) with respect to u, we get

$$\frac{dy}{du} = \frac{\Delta y_0 + \Delta y_{-1}}{2} + u\Delta^2 y_{-1} + \left(\frac{3u^2-1}{6}\right)\left(\frac{\Delta^3 y_{-1} + \Delta^3 y_{-2}}{2}\right)$$

$$+ \left(\frac{4u^3-2u}{4!}\right)\Delta^4 y_{-2} + \left(\frac{5u^4-15u^2+4}{5!}\right)\left(\frac{\Delta^5 y_{-2} + \Delta^5 y_{-3}}{2}\right) + \ldots \tag{21}$$

Differentiating (20) with respect to x, we get

$$\frac{du}{dx} = \frac{1}{h} \tag{22}$$

Now,

$$\frac{dy}{dx} = \frac{dy}{du} \cdot \frac{du}{dx}$$

$$= \frac{1}{h}\left[\frac{\Delta y_0 + \Delta y_{-1}}{2} + u\Delta^2 y_{-1} + \left(\frac{3u^2-1}{6}\right)\left(\frac{\Delta^3 y_{-1} + \Delta^3 y_{-2}}{2}\right)\right.$$

$$\left. + \left(\frac{4u^3-2u}{4!}\right)\Delta^4 y_{-2} + \left(\frac{5u^4-15u^2+4}{5!}\right)\left(\frac{\Delta^5 y_{-2} + \Delta^5 y_{-3}}{2}\right) + \ldots\right] \tag{23}$$

Expression (23) provides the value of $\frac{dy}{dx}$ at any x which is not tabulated.

Given $x = a$, we have $u = 0$

$\therefore$ Given $u = 0$ in (23), we get

$$\left(\frac{dy}{dx}\right)_{x=a} = \frac{1}{h}\left[\left(\frac{\Delta y_0 + \Delta y_{-1}}{2}\right) - \frac{1}{6}\left(\frac{\Delta^3 y_{-1} + \Delta^3 y_{-2}}{2}\right) + \frac{1}{30}\left(\frac{\Delta^5 y_{-2} + \Delta^5 y_{-3}}{2}\right) - \ldots\right] \tag{24}$$

Differentiating (23) with respect to x, we get

$$\frac{d^2y}{dx^2} = \frac{d}{du}\left(\frac{dy}{dx}\right)\frac{du}{dx}$$

$$= \frac{1}{h^2}\left[\Delta^2 y_{-1} + u\left(\frac{\Delta^3 y_{-1} + \Delta^3 y_{-2}}{2}\right) + \left(\frac{6u^2 - 1}{12}\right)\Delta^4 y_{-2}\right.$$

$$\left. + \left(\frac{2u^3 - 3u}{12}\right)\left(\frac{\Delta^5 y_{-2} + \Delta^5 y_{-3}}{2}\right) + \ldots\right] \tag{25}$$

Given $u = 0$ in (25), we get

$$\left(\frac{d^2y}{dx^2}\right)_{x=a} = \frac{1}{h^2}\left(\Delta^2 y_{-1} - \frac{1}{12}\Delta^4 y_{-2} + \frac{1}{90}\Delta^6 y_{-3} - \ldots\right) \tag{26}$$

and so on.

Formulae for computing higher derivatives may be obtained by successive differentiation.

(4) **Bessel's central difference interpolation formula is**

$$y = \left(\frac{y_0 + y_1}{2}\right) + \left(u - \frac{1}{2}\right)\Delta y_0 + \frac{u(u-1)}{2!}\left(\frac{\Delta^2 y_{-1} + \Delta^2 y_0}{2}\right)$$

$$+ \frac{u(u-1)\left(u - \frac{1}{2}\right)}{3!}\Delta^3 y_{-1} + \frac{(u+1)\,u(u-1)(u-2)}{4!}\left(\frac{\Delta^4 y_{-2} + \Delta^4 y_{-1}}{2}\right)$$

$$+ \frac{(u+1)\,u(u-1)(u-2)\left(u - \frac{1}{2}\right)}{5!}\Delta^5 y_{-2}$$

$$+ \frac{(u+2)(u+1)\,u(u-1)(u-2)(u-3)}{6!}\left(\frac{\Delta^6 y_{-3} + \Delta^6 y_{-2}}{2}\right) + \ldots \tag{27}$$

$$\text{where} \quad u = \frac{x-a}{h} \tag{28}$$

Differentiating eqn. (27) with respect to u, we get

$$\frac{dy}{du} = \Delta y_0 + \left(\frac{2u-1}{2!}\right)\left(\frac{\Delta^2 y_{-1} + \Delta^2 y_0}{2}\right) + \left(\frac{3u^2 - 3u + \frac{1}{2}}{3!}\right)\Delta^3 y_{-1}$$

$$+ \left(\frac{4u^3 - 6u^2 - 2u + 2}{4!}\right)\left(\frac{\Delta^4 y_{-2} + \Delta^4 y_{-1}}{2}\right) + \left(\frac{5u^4 - 10u^3 + 5u - 1}{5!}\right)\Delta^5 y_{-2}$$

$$+ \left(\frac{6u^5 - 15u^4 - 20u^3 + 45u^2 + 8u - 12}{6!}\right)\left(\frac{\Delta^6 y_{-3} + \Delta^6 y_{-2}}{2}\right) + \ldots \quad (29)$$

Differentiating (28) with respect to x, we get

$$\frac{du}{dx} = \frac{1}{h}$$

Now, $$\frac{dy}{dx} = \frac{dy}{du} \cdot \frac{du}{dx}$$

$$= \frac{1}{h}\left[\Delta y_0 + \left(\frac{2u-1}{2!}\right)\left(\frac{\Delta^2 y_{-1} + \Delta^2 y_0}{2}\right) + \left(\frac{3u^2 - 3u + \frac{1}{2}}{3!}\right)\Delta^3 y_{-1}\right.$$

$$+ \left(\frac{4u^3 - 6u^2 - 2u + 2}{4!}\right)\left(\frac{\Delta^4 y_{-2} + \Delta^4 y_{-1}}{2}\right) + \left(\frac{5u^4 - 10u^3 + 5u - 1}{5!}\right)\Delta^5 y_{-2}$$

$$\left. + \left(\frac{6u^5 - 15u^4 - 20u^3 + 45u^2 + 8u - 12}{6!}\right)\left(\frac{\Delta^6 y_{-3} + \Delta^6 y_{-2}}{2}\right) + \ldots\right] \quad (30)$$

Expression (30) provides us the value of $\frac{dy}{dx}$ at any x which is not tabulated.

Given $x = a$, we have $u = 0$

∴ Given $u = 0$ in (30), we get

$$\left(\frac{dy}{dx}\right)_{x=a} = \frac{1}{h}\left[\Delta y_0 - \frac{1}{2}\left(\frac{\Delta^2 y_{-1} + \Delta^2 y_0}{2}\right) + \frac{1}{12}\Delta^3 y_{-1} + \frac{1}{12}\left(\frac{\Delta^4 y_{-2} + \Delta^4 y_{-1}}{2}\right)\right.$$

$$\left. - \frac{1}{120}\Delta^5 y_{-2} - \frac{1}{60}\left(\frac{\Delta^6 y_{-3} + \Delta^6 y_{-2}}{2}\right) + \ldots\right] \quad (31)$$

Differentiating (30) with respect to x, we get

$$\frac{d^2y}{dx^2} = \frac{d}{dx}\left(\frac{dy}{dx}\right) = \frac{d}{du}\left(\frac{dy}{dx}\right)\frac{du}{dx}$$

$$= \frac{1}{h^2}\left[\left(\frac{\Delta^2 y_{-1} + \Delta^2 y_0}{2}\right) + \left(\frac{2u-1}{2}\right)\Delta^3 y_{-1} + \left(\frac{6u^2 - 6u - 1}{12}\right)\left(\frac{\Delta^4 y_{-2} + \Delta^4 y_{-1}}{2}\right)\right.$$

$$+ \left(\frac{4u^3 - 6u^2 + 1}{24}\right)\Delta^5 y_{-2}$$

$$\left. + \left(\frac{15u^4 - 30u^3 - 30u^2 + 45u + 4}{360}\right)\left(\frac{\Delta^6 y_{-3} + \Delta^6 y_{-2}}{2}\right) + \ldots\right] \quad (32)$$

Given $u = 0$ in (32), we get

$$\left(\frac{d^2y}{dx^2}\right)_{x=a} = \frac{1}{h^2}\left[\left(\frac{\Delta^2 y_{-1} + \Delta^2 y_0}{2}\right) - \frac{1}{2}\Delta^3 y_{-1} - \frac{1}{12}\left(\frac{\Delta^4 y_{-2} + \Delta^4 y_{-1}}{2}\right)\right.$$

$$\left. + \frac{1}{24}\Delta^5 y_{-2} + \frac{1}{90}\left(\frac{\Delta^6 y_{-3} + \Delta^6 y_{-2}}{2}\right) + \ldots\right] \quad (33)$$

and so on.

(5) **For unequally spaced values of the argument**

(*i*) **Newton's divided difference formula is**

$$f(x) = f(x_0) + (x - x_0)\,\Delta f(x_0) + (x - x_0)(x - x_1)\,\Delta^2 f(x_0) + (x - x_0)(x - x_1)$$

$$(x - x_2)\,\Delta^3 f(x_0) + (x - x_0)(x - x_1)(x - x_2)(x - x_3)\,\Delta^4 f(x_0) + \ldots \quad (34)$$

$f'(x)$ is given by

$$f'(x) = \Delta f(x_0) + \{2x - (x_0 + x_1)\}\,\Delta^2 f(x_0) + \{3x^2 - 2x(x_0 + x_1 + x_2)$$

$$+ (x_0x_1 + x_1x_2 + x_2x_0)\}\,\Delta^3 f(x_0) + \ldots \quad (35)$$

(*ii*) **Lagrange's interpolation formula is**

$$f(x) = \frac{(x - x_1)(x - x_2)\ldots(x - x_n)}{(x_0 - x_1)(x_0 - x_2)\ldots(x_0 - x_n)}\,f(x_0)$$

$$+ \frac{(x - x_0)(x - x_2)\ldots(x - x_n)}{(x_1 - x_0)(x_1 - x_2)\ldots(x_1 - x_n)}\,f(x_1) + \ldots \quad (36)$$

$f'(x)$ can be obtained by differentiating $f(x)$ in eqn. (36).

NOTE **1.** *Formula (8) can be extended as*

$$\left(\frac{d^2y}{dx^2}\right)_{x=a} = \frac{1}{h^2}\left(\Delta^2 - \Delta^3 + \frac{11}{12}\Delta^4 - \frac{5}{6}\Delta^5 + \frac{137}{180}\Delta^6 - \frac{7}{10}\Delta^7 + \frac{363}{560}\Delta^8 + \ldots\right) y_0$$

2. *Formula (17) can be extended as*

$$\left(\frac{d^2y}{dx^2}\right)_{x=x_n} = \frac{1}{h^2}\left(\nabla^2 + \nabla^3 + \frac{11}{12}\nabla^4 + \frac{5}{6}\nabla^5 + \frac{137}{180}\nabla^6 + \frac{7}{10}\nabla^7 + \frac{363}{560}\nabla^8 + \ldots\right) y_n.$$

5.4 MAXIMA AND MINIMA OF A TABULATED FUNCTION

Since maxima and minima of $y = f(x)$ can be found by equating $\frac{dy}{dx}$ to zero and solving the equation for the argument x, the same method can be used to determine maxima and minima of tabulated function by differentiating the interpolating polynomial.

For example, if Newton's forward difference formula is used, we have

$$y = y_0 + u\,\Delta y_0 + \frac{u(u-1)}{2!}\Delta^2 y_0 + \frac{u(u-1)(u-2)}{3!}\Delta^3 y_0 + \ldots \quad (37)$$

Differentiating (37) with respect to u, we get

$$\frac{dy}{du} = \Delta y_0 + \frac{2u-1}{2!}\Delta^2 y_0 + \frac{3u^2 - 6u + 2}{3!}\Delta^3 y_0 + \ldots$$

For maxima or minima,

$$\frac{dy}{du} = 0$$

$$\Rightarrow \quad \Delta y_0 + \frac{2u-1}{2!}\Delta^2 y_0 + \frac{3u^2 - 6u + 2}{3!}\Delta^3 y_0 + \ldots = 0 \quad (38)$$

If we terminate L.H.S. series after third differences for convenience, eqn. (38) being a quadratic in u gives two values of u.

Corresponding to these values, $x = a + uh$ will give the corresponding x at which function may be maximum or minimum.

For maximum, $\frac{d^2y}{du^2}$ = (–)ve

For minimum, $\frac{d^2y}{du^2}$ = (+)ve.

EXAMPLES

Example 1. *Find* $\frac{dy}{dx}$ *at x = 0.1 from the following table:*

x:	*0.1*	*0.2*	*0.3*	*0.4*
y:	*0.9975*	*0.9900*	*0.9776*	*0.9604.*

Sol. Take a = 0.1. The difference table is:

x	y	Δy	$\Delta^2 y$	$\Delta^3 y$
0.1	0.9975			
		– 0.0075		
0.2	0.9900		– 0.0049	
		– 0.0124		0.0001
0.3	0.9776		– 0.0048	
		– 0.0172		
0.4	0.9604			

Here $h = 0.1$ and $y_0 = 0.9975$

$$\left[\frac{dy}{dx}\right]_{x=0.1} = \frac{1}{h}\left[\Delta y_0 - \frac{1}{2}\Delta^2 y_0 + \frac{1}{3}\Delta^3 y_0\right]$$

$$= \frac{1}{0.1}\left[-0.0075 - \frac{1}{2}(-0.0049) + \frac{1}{3}(0.0001)\right]$$

$$= -0.050167.$$

Example 2. *The table given below reveals the velocity 'v' of a body during the time 't' specified. Find its acceleration at t = 1.1.*

t:	*1.0*	*1.1*	*1.2*	*1.3*	*1.4*
v:	*43.1*	*47.7*	*52.1*	*56.4*	*60.8.*

Sol. The difference table is:

t	v	Δv	$\Delta^2 v$	$\Delta^3 v$	$\Delta^4 v$
1.0	43.1				
		4.6			
1.1	47.7		– 0.2		
		4.4		0.1	
1.2	52.1		– 0.1		0.1
		4.3		0.2	
1.3	56.4		0.1		
		4.4			
1.4	60.8				

Let $a = 1.1$,

$\therefore$ $v_0 = 47.7$ and $h = 0.1$

Acceleration at $t = 1.1$ is given by

$$\left[\frac{dv}{dt}\right]_{t=1.1} = \frac{1}{h}\left[\Delta v_0 - \frac{1}{2}\Delta^2 v_0 + \frac{1}{3}\Delta^3 v_0\right] = \frac{1}{0.1}\left[4.4 - \frac{1}{2}(-0.1) + \frac{1}{3}(0.2)\right]$$

$$= 45.1667$$

Hence the required acceleration is **45.1667.**

Example 3. *Find f '(1.1) and f "(1.1) from the following table:*

x:	*1.0*	*1.2*	*1.4*	*1.6*	*1.8*	*2.0*
f(x):	*0.0*	*0.1280*	*0.5540*	*1.2960*	*2.4320*	*4.000.*

Sol. Since we are to find $f'(x)$ and $f''(x)$ for non-tabular value of x, we proceed as follows:

Newton's forward difference formula is

$$y = y_0 + u\,\Delta y_0 + \frac{u(u-1)}{2!}\Delta^2 y_0 + \frac{u(u-1)(u-2)}{3!}\Delta^3 y_0 + \frac{u(u-1)(u-2)(u-3)}{4!}\Delta^4 y_0 + \ldots \quad (39)$$

where
$$u = \frac{x-a}{h} \quad (40)$$

Differentiating eqn. (39) with respect to u, we get

$$\frac{dy}{du} = \Delta y_0 + \left(\frac{2u-1}{2}\right)\Delta^2 y_0 + \left(\frac{3u^2-6u+2}{6}\right)\Delta^3 y_0 + \left(\frac{2u^3-9u^2+11u-3}{12}\right)\Delta^4 y_0 + \ldots \quad (41)$$

Differentiating eqn. (40) with respect to x

$$\frac{du}{dx} = \frac{1}{h} \quad (42)$$

$$\therefore \quad \frac{dy}{dx} = \frac{dy}{du}\cdot\frac{du}{dx}$$

$$= \frac{1}{h}\left[\Delta y_0 + \left(\frac{2u-1}{2}\right)\Delta^2 y_0 + \left(\frac{3u^2-6u+2}{6}\right)\Delta^3 y_0 + \left(\frac{2u^3-9u^2+11u-3}{12}\right)\Delta^4 y_0 + \ldots\right] \quad (43)$$

Also, at $x = 1.1$, $u = \frac{1.1-1.0}{0.2} = \frac{1}{2}$ | Here $a = 1.0$ and $h = 0.2$

The forward difference table is as follows:

x	$f(x) = y$	Δy	$\Delta^2 y$	$\Delta^3 y$	$\Delta^4 y$	$\Delta^5 y$
1.0	0.0					
		0.1280				
1.2	0.1280		0.298			
		0.4260		0.018		
1.4	0.5540		0.316		0.06	
		0.7420		0.078		– 0.1
1.6	1.2960		0.394		– 0.04	
		1.1360		0.038		
1.8	2.4320		0.432			
		1.5680				
2.0	4.000					

From eqn. (43),

$$\frac{dy}{dx}=\frac{1}{h}\left[\Delta y_0+\left(\frac{2u-1}{2}\right)\Delta^2 y_0+\left(\frac{3u^2-6u+2}{6}\right)\Delta^3 y_0\right.$$

$$+\left(\frac{2u^3-9u^2+11u-3}{12}\right)\Delta^4 y_0$$

$$\left.+\left(\frac{5u^4-40u^3+105u^2-100u+24}{120}\right)\Delta^5 y_0+\ldots\right] \qquad (44)$$

At $x = 1.1$, we get

$$f'(1.1)=\left(\frac{dy}{dx}\right)_{x=1.1}=\frac{1}{0.2}\left[0.1280+\left\{\frac{2\left(\frac{1}{2}\right)-1}{2}\right\}(0.298)\right.$$

$$+\left\{\frac{3\left(\frac{1}{2}\right)^2-6\left(\frac{1}{2}\right)+2}{6}\right\}(0.018)+\left\{\frac{2\left(\frac{1}{2}\right)^3-9\left(\frac{1}{2}\right)^2+11\left(\frac{1}{2}\right)-3}{12}\right\}(.06)$$

$$\left.+\left\{\frac{5\left(\frac{1}{2}\right)^4-40\left(\frac{1}{2}\right)^3+105\left(\frac{1}{2}\right)^2-100\left(\frac{1}{2}\right)+24}{120}\right\}(-0.1)\right]$$

$$= 0.66724.$$

Differentiating eqn. (44), with respect to x, we get

$$\frac{d^2y}{dx^2}=\frac{d}{du}\left(\frac{dy}{du}\right)\frac{du}{dx}=\frac{1}{h^2}\left[\Delta^2 y_0+(u-1)\,\Delta^3 y_0+\left(\frac{6u^2-18u+11}{12}\right)\Delta^4 y_0\right.$$

$$\left.+\left(\frac{2u^3-12u^2+21u-10}{12}\right)\Delta^5 y_0+\ldots\right]$$

At $x = 1.1$, we get

$$f''(1.1) = \left(\frac{d^2y}{dx^2}\right)_{x=1.1}$$

$$= \frac{1}{(0.2)^2}\left[0.298 + \left(\frac{1}{2} - 1\right)(0.018) + \left\{\frac{6\left(\frac{1}{2}\right)^2 - 18\left(\frac{1}{2}\right) + 11}{12}\right\}(0.06)\right.$$

$$\left. + \left\{\frac{2\left(\frac{1}{2}\right)^3 - 12\left(\frac{1}{2}\right)^2 + 21\left(\frac{1}{2}\right) - 10}{12}\right\}(-0.1)\right]$$

$$= 8.13125.$$

Example 4. *The distance covered by an athlete for the 50 meter race is given in the following table:*

Time (sec):	*0*	*1*	*2*	*3*	*4*	*5*	*6*
Distance (meter):	*0*	*2.5*	*8.5*	*15.5*	*24.5*	*36.5*	*50*

Determine the speed of the athlete at t = 5 sec., correct to two decimals.

Sol. Here we are to find derivative at $t = 5$ which is near the end of the table, hence we shall use the formula obtained from Newton's backward difference formula. The backward difference table is as follows:

t	s	∇s	$\nabla^2 s$	$\nabla^3 s$	$\nabla^4 s$	$\nabla^5 s$	$\nabla^6 s$
0	0						
		2.5					
1	2.5		3.5				
		6		– 2.5			
2	8.5		1		3.5		
		7		1		– 3.5	
3	15.5		2		0		1
		9		1		– 2.5	
4	24.5		3		– 2.5		
		12		– 1.5			
5	36.5		1.5				
		13.5					
6	50						

The speed of the athlete at $t = 5$ sec is given by

$$\left(\frac{ds}{dt}\right)_{t=5} = \frac{1}{h}\left[\nabla s_5 + \frac{1}{2}\nabla^2 s_5 + \frac{1}{3}\nabla^3 s_5 + \frac{1}{4}\nabla^4 s_5 + \frac{1}{5}\nabla^5 s_5\right]$$

$$= \frac{1}{1}\left[12 + \frac{1}{2}(3) + \frac{1}{3}(1) + \frac{1}{4}(0) + \frac{1}{5}(-3.5)\right]$$

$$= 13.1333 \approx 13.13 \text{ metre/sec.}$$

Example 5. *Find* $\frac{dy}{dx}$ *and* $\frac{d^2y}{dx^2}$ *at* $x = 6$, *given that*

x:	*4.5*	*5.0*	*5.5*	*6.0*	*6.5*	*7.0*	*7.5*
y:	*9.69*	*12.90*	*16.71*	*21.18*	*26.37*	*32.34*	*39.15.*

Sol. Here $a = 6.0 \quad \therefore \quad y_0 = 21.18$ and $h = 0.5$

The forward difference table is:

x	y	Δy	$\Delta^2 y$	$\Delta^3 y$	$\Delta^4 y$
4.5	9.69				
		3.21			
5.0	12.9		0.60		
		3.81		0.06	
5.5	16.71		0.66		0
		4.47		0.06	
6.0	21.18		0.72		0
		5.19		0.06	
6.5	26.37		0.78		0
		5.97		0.06	
7.0	32.34		0.84		
		6.81			
7.5	39.15				

We know that

$$\left[\frac{dy}{dx}\right]_{x=6} = \frac{1}{h}\left(\Delta y_0 - \frac{1}{2}\Delta^2 y_0 + \frac{1}{3}\Delta^3 y_0\right)$$

$$= \frac{1}{0.5}\left[5.19 - \frac{1}{2}(0.78) + \frac{1}{3}(0.06)\right] = 9.64$$

and $$\left[\frac{d^2y}{dx^2}\right]_{x=6} = \frac{1}{h^2}\left[\Delta^2 y_0 - \Delta^3 y_0 + \frac{11}{12}\Delta^4 y_0\right]$$

$$= \frac{1}{0.25}\,[0.78 - 0.06] = 4(0.72) = 2.88.$$

Example 6. *From the following table of values of x and y, obtain* $\dfrac{dy}{dx}$ *and* $\dfrac{d^2y}{dx^2}$ *for x = 1.2, 2.2 and 1.6*

x:	*1.0*	*1.2*	*1.4*	*1.6*	*1.8*	*2.0*	*2.2*
y:	*2.7183*	*3.3201*	*4.0552*	*4.9530*	*6.0496*	*7.3891*	*9.0250.*

Sol. The forward difference table is:

x	y	Δy	$\Delta^2 y$	$\Delta^3 y$	$\Delta^4 y$	$\Delta^5 y$	$\Delta^6 y$
1.0	2.7183						
		0.6018					
1.2	3.3201		0.1333				
		0.7351		0.0294			
1.4	4.0552		0.1627		0.0067		
		0.8978		0.0361		0.0013	
1.6	4.9530		0.1988		0.0080		0.0001
		1.0966		0.0441		0.0014	
1.8	6.0496		0.2429		0.0094		
		1.3395		0.0535			
2.0	7.3891		0.2964				
		1.6359					
2.2	9.0250						

(*i*) Here $a = 1.2$

$\therefore \quad y_0 = 3.3201; \quad h = 0.2$

$$\left[\frac{dy}{dx}\right]_{x=1.2} = \frac{1}{0.2}\left[0.7351 - \frac{1}{2}(0.1627) + \frac{1}{3}(0.0361) - \frac{1}{4}(0.008) + \frac{1}{5}(0.0014)\right]$$

$$= 3.3205$$

$$\left[\frac{d^2y}{dx^2}\right]_{x=1.2} = \frac{1}{(0.2)^2}\left[0.1627 - 0.0361 + \frac{11}{12}(0.0080) - \frac{5}{6}(0.0014)\right]$$

$$= 3.318$$

(*ii*) Here $a = 2.2,$

$\therefore$ $y_n = 9.02$ and $h = 0.2$

$$\left[\frac{dy}{dx}\right]_{x=2.2} = \frac{1}{0.2}\left[1.6359 + \frac{1}{2}(0.2964) + \frac{1}{3}(0.0535) + \frac{1}{4}(0.0094) + \frac{1}{5}(0.0014)\right]$$

$$= 9.0228$$

$$\left[\frac{d^2y}{dx^2}\right]_{x=2.2} = \frac{1}{0.04}\left[0.2964 + 0.0535 + \frac{11}{12}(0.0094) + \frac{5}{6}(0.0014)\right]$$

$$= 8.992.$$

(*iii*) Here $a = 1.6$

$\therefore$ $y_0 = 4.9530, y_{-1} = 4.0552$

$y_{-2} = 3.3201, y_{-3} = 2.7183$ and $h = 0.2$

By using Stirling's formula for derivatives, we get

$$\left[\frac{dy}{dx}\right]_{x=1.6} = \frac{1}{0.2}\left[\left(\frac{1.0966 + 0.8978}{2}\right) - \frac{1}{6}\left(\frac{0.0441 + 0.0361}{2}\right) + \frac{1}{30}\left(\frac{0.0014 + 0.0013}{2}\right)\right]$$

$$= 4.9530$$

and $$\left[\frac{d^2y}{dx^2}\right]_{x=1.6} = \frac{1}{0.04}\left[0.1988 - \frac{1}{12}(.0080) + \frac{1}{90}(.0001)\right]$$

$$= 4.9525.$$

Example 7. *Using Bessel's formula, find f '(7.5) from the following table:*

x:	*7.47*	*7.48*	*7.49*	*7.5*	*7.51*	*7.52*	*7.53*
f(x):	*0.193*	*0.195*	*0.198*	*0.201*	*0.203*	*0.206*	*0.208.*

Sol. The difference table is:

x	y	Δy	$\Delta^2 y$	$\Delta^3 y$	$\Delta^4 y$	$\Delta^5 y$	$\Delta^6 y$
7.47	0.193						
		0.002					
7.48	0.195		0.001				
		0.003		– 0.001			
7.49	0.198		0.000		0.000		
		0.003		– 0.001		0.003	
7.50	0.201		– 0.001		0.003		– 0.01
		0.002		0.002		– 0.007	
7.51	0.203		0.001		– 0.004		
		0.003		– 0.002			
7.52	0.206		– 0.001				
		0.002					
7.53	0.208						

Let $a = 7.5,\ h = 0.01$

$$f'(7.5) = \left(\frac{dy}{dx}\right)_{x=7.5} = \frac{1}{0.01}\left[\Delta y_0 - \frac{1}{2}\left(\frac{\Delta^2 y_{-1} + \Delta^2 y_0}{2}\right) + \frac{1}{12}\Delta^3 y_{-1}\right.$$

$$\left. + \frac{1}{12}\left(\frac{\Delta^4 y_{-2} + \Delta^4 y_{-1}}{2}\right) - \frac{1}{120}\Delta^5 y_{-2} - \frac{1}{60}\left(\frac{\Delta^6 y_{-3} + \Delta^6 y_{-2}}{2}\right) + \ldots\right]$$

$$= \frac{1}{0.01}\left[(.002) - \frac{1}{2}\left\{\frac{-.001 + .001}{2}\right\} + \frac{1}{12}(0.002) + \frac{1}{12}\right.$$

$$\left.\left\{\frac{.003 + (-.004)}{2}\right\} - \frac{1}{120}(-0.007) - \frac{1}{60}\left(\frac{-.01}{2}\right)\right]$$

$= 0.226667.$

Example 8. *A rod is rotating in a plane. The following table gives the angle θ (in radians) through which the rod has turned for various values of time t (in seconds)*

t:	*0*	*0.2*	*0.4*	*0.6*	*0.8*	*1.0*	*1.2*
θ:	*0*	*0.12*	*0.49*	*1.12*	*2.02*	*3.20*	*4.67.*

Calculate the angular velocity and angular acceleration of the rod at t = 0.6 sec.

Sol. The forward difference table is:

t	θ	$\Delta\theta$	$\Delta^2\theta$	$\Delta^3\theta$	$\Delta^4\theta$
0	0				
		0.12			
0.2	0.12		0.25		
		0.37		0.01	
0.4	0.49		0.26		0
		0.63		0.01	
0.6	1.12		0.27		0
		0.9		0.01	
0.8	2.02		0.28		0
		1.18		0.01	
1.0	3.20		0.29		
		1.47			
1.2	4.67				

Here $a = 0.6$

$\therefore$ $\theta_0 = 1.12$ and $h = 0.2$

Since the goal is to find derivatives at $t = 0.6$ sec, which is in the middle of the table, use the formula obtained from Stirling's or Bessel's central difference formula.

Choose the formula obtained from Bessel's central difference formula.

Angular velocity at $t = 0.6$ sec is given by

$$\left(\frac{d\theta}{dt}\right)_{t=0.6} = \frac{1}{h}\left[\Delta\theta_0 - \frac{1}{2}\left(\frac{\Delta^2\theta_{-1} + \Delta^2\theta_0}{2}\right) + \frac{1}{12}\Delta^3\theta_{-1}\right]$$

$$= \frac{1}{0.2}\left[0.9 - \frac{1}{2}\left(\frac{0.27 + 0.28}{2}\right) + \frac{1}{12}(0.01)\right]$$

$$= 3.81667 \text{ rad./sec.}$$

Angular acceleration at $t = 0.6$ sec is given by

$$\left(\frac{d^2\theta}{dt^2}\right)_{t=0.6} = \frac{1}{h^2}\left[\left(\frac{\Delta^2\theta_{-1} + \Delta^2\theta_0}{2}\right) - \frac{1}{2}\Delta^3\theta_{-1}\right]$$

$$= \frac{1}{(0.2)^2}\left[\left(\frac{0.27 + 0.28}{2}\right) - \frac{1}{2}(0.01)\right]$$

$$= 6.75 \text{ rad./sec}^2.$$

NOTE *In case we choose the formula obtained from Stirling's formula, at t = 0.6 sec.,*

angular velocity $\left(\frac{d\theta}{dt}\right) = \frac{1}{h}\left[\left(\frac{\Delta\theta_0 + \Delta\theta_{-1}}{2}\right) - \frac{1}{6}\left(\frac{\Delta^3\theta_{-1} + \Delta^3\theta_{-2}}{2}\right)\right]$

$$= \frac{1}{0.2}\left[\left(\frac{.9 + .63}{2}\right) - \frac{1}{6}\left(\frac{.01 + .01}{2}\right)\right]$$

$$= 3.81667 \text{ rad./sec.}$$

and angular acceleration $\left(\frac{d^2\theta}{dt^2}\right) = \frac{1}{h^2}(\Delta^2\theta_{-1}) = \frac{1}{(0.2)^2}(0.27)$

$$= 6.75 \text{ rad./sec}^2.$$

Example 9. *The table below gives the result of an observation. θ is the observed temperature in degrees centigrade of a vessel of cooling water, t is the time in minutes from the beginning of observations:*

t:	1	3	5	7	9
θ:	85.3	74.5	67.0	60.5	54.3

Find the approximate rate of cooling at t = 3 and 3.5.

Sol. The forward difference table is:

t	θ	$\Delta\theta$	$\Delta^2\theta$	$\Delta^3\theta$	$\Delta^4\theta$
1	85.3				
		– 10.8			
3	74.5		3.3		
		– 7.5		– 2.3	
5	67.0		1.0		1.6
		– 6.5		– 0.7	
7	60.5		0.3		
		– 6.2			
9	54.3				

(*i*) When $t = 3$, $\theta_0 = 74.5$

Here $h = 2$

Rate of cooling $= \frac{d\theta}{dt}$

$$\therefore \quad \left(\frac{d\theta}{dt}\right)_{t=3} = \frac{1}{h}\left[\Delta\theta_0 - \frac{1}{2}\Delta^2\theta_0 + \frac{1}{3}\Delta^3\theta_0 - \frac{1}{4}\Delta^4\theta_0\right]$$

$$= \frac{1}{2}\left[-7.5 - \frac{1}{2}(1) + \frac{1}{3}(-0.7)\right]$$

$$= -4.11667°\text{C/min.}$$

(*ii*) $t = 3.5$ is the non-tabular value of t so, we have from Newton's forward difference formula,

$$\frac{dy}{dx} = \frac{1}{h}\left[\Delta y_0 + \left(\frac{2u-1}{2}\right)\Delta^2 y_0 + \left(\frac{3u^2 - 6u + 2}{6}\right)\Delta^3 y_0 + \left(\frac{2u^3 - 9u^2 + 11u - 3}{12}\right)\Delta^4 y_0 + \ldots\right]$$

Here,

$$\frac{d\theta}{dt} = \frac{1}{h}\left[\Delta\theta_0 + \left(\frac{2u-1}{2}\right)\Delta^2\theta_0 + \left(\frac{3u^2 - 6u + 2}{6}\right)\Delta^3\theta_0 + \left(\frac{2u^3 - 9u^2 + 11u - 3}{12}\right)\Delta^4\theta_0 + \ldots\right] \quad (45)$$

At $t = 3.5$, $u = \dfrac{3.5 - 3.0}{2} = \dfrac{0.5}{2} = 0.25$ | Here $a = 3.0$ and $h = 2$

From (45),

$$\left(\frac{d\theta}{dt}\right)_{t=3.5} = \frac{1}{2}\left[-7.5 + \left\{\frac{2(.25) - 1}{2}\right\}(1) + \left\{\frac{3(.25)^2 - 6(.25) + 2}{6}\right\}(-.7)\right]$$

$$= -3.9151°\text{C/min.}$$

Example 10. *Find x for which y is maximum and find this value of y*

x:	*1.2*	*1.3*	*1.4*	*1.5*	*1.6*
y:	*0.9320*	*0.9636*	*0.9855*	*0.9975*	*0.9996.*

Sol. The difference table is as follows:

x	y	Δ	Δ^2	Δ^3	Δ^4
1.2	0.9320				
		0.0316			
1.3	0.9636		– 0.0097		
		0.0219		– 0.0002	
1.4	0.9855		– 0.0099		0.0002
		0.0120		0	
1.5	0.9975		– 0.0099		
		0.0021			
1.6	0.9996				

Let $y_0 = 0.9320$ and $a = 1.2$

By Newton's forward difference formula,

$$y = y_0 + u\,\Delta y_0 + \frac{u(u-1)}{2}\Delta^2 y_0 + \ldots$$

$$= 0.9320 + 0.0316\,u + \frac{u(u-1)}{2}(-\,0.0097) \quad | \text{ Neglecting higher}$$

differences

$$\frac{dy}{du} = 0.0316 + \left(\frac{2u-1}{2}\right)(-\,0.0097)$$

At a maximum, $\frac{dy}{du} = 0$

$$\Rightarrow \quad 0.0316 = \left(u - \frac{1}{2}\right)(0.0097) \quad \Rightarrow \quad u = 3.76$$

$$\therefore \quad x = a + hu = 1.2 + (0.1)(3.76) = 1.576$$

To find $y_{max.}$, we use the backward difference formula,

$$x = x_n + hu$$

$$\Rightarrow \quad 1.576 = 1.6 + (0.1)u \quad \Rightarrow \quad u = -\,0.24$$

$$y(1.576) = y_n + u\,\nabla y_n + \frac{u(u+1)}{2!}\nabla^2 y_n + \frac{u(u+1)(u+2)}{3!}\nabla^3 y_n$$

$$= 0.9996 - (0.24 \times 0.0021) + \frac{(-0.24)(1-0.24)}{2}(-0.0099)$$

$$= 0.9999988 = 0.9999 \text{ nearly}$$

$\therefore$ Maximum $y = 0.9999$ **approximately.**

Example 11. *Assuming Bessel's interpolation formula, prove that*

$$\frac{d}{dx}(y_x) = \Delta y_{x-1/2} - \frac{1}{24}\Delta^3 y_{x-3/2} + \ldots$$

Sol. Bessel's formula is

$$y_x = \left(\frac{y_0 + y_1}{2}\right) + \left(x - \frac{1}{2}\right)\Delta y_0 + \frac{x(x-1)}{2!}\left(\frac{\Delta^2 y_{-1} + \Delta^2 y_0}{2}\right) + \frac{x(x-1)\left(x - \frac{1}{2}\right)}{3!}\Delta^3 y_{-1} + \ldots \quad (46)$$

Replacing x by $x + \frac{1}{2}$, we get

$$y_{x+1/2} = \left(\frac{y_0 + y_1}{2}\right) + x\,\Delta y_0 + \frac{\left(x + \frac{1}{2}\right)\left(x - \frac{1}{2}\right)}{2!}\left(\frac{\Delta^2 y_{-1} + \Delta^2 y_0}{2}\right) + \frac{\left(x + \frac{1}{2}\right)\left(x - \frac{1}{2}\right)x}{3!}\Delta^3 y_{-1} + \ldots \quad (47)$$

Differentiating (47) with respect to x, we get

$$\frac{d}{dx}(y_{x+1/2}) = \Delta y_0 + \frac{2x}{2!}\left(\frac{\Delta^2 y_{-1} + \Delta^2 y_0}{2}\right) + \left(\frac{3x^2 - \frac{1}{4}}{3!}\right)\Delta^3 y_{-1} + \ldots$$

Given $x = 0$, we get

$$\frac{d}{dx}(y_{x+1/2}) = \Delta y_0 - \frac{1}{24}\Delta^3 y_{-1} + \ldots$$

Shifting the origin from $x = 0$ to $x - \frac{1}{2}$, we get

$$\frac{d}{dx}(y_x) = \Delta y_{x-1/2} - \frac{1}{24}\Delta^3 y_{x-3/2} + \ldots$$

Example 12. *Find $f'''(5)$ from the data given below:*

x:	2	4	9	13	16	21	29
$f(x)$:	57	1345	66340	402052	1118209	4287844	21242820

Sol. In this case, the values of argument x are not equally spaced and therefore we shall apply Newton's divided difference formula.

$$f(x) = f(x_0) + (x - x_0) \Delta f(x_0) + (x - x_0)(x - x_1) \Delta^2 f(x_0)$$
$$+ (x - x_0)(x - x_1)(x - x_2) \Delta^3 f(x_0)$$
$$+ (x - x_0)(x - x_1)(x - x_2)(x - x_3) \Delta^4 f(x_0) + \ldots \quad (48)$$

Newton's divided difference table is as follows:

x	$f(x)$	$\Delta f(x)$	$\Delta^2 f(x)$	$\Delta^3 f(x)$	$\Delta^4 f(x)$	$\Delta^5 f(x)$	$\Delta^6 f(x)$
2	57						
		644					
4	1345		1765				
		12999		556			
9	66340		7881		45		
		83928		1186		1	
13	402052		22113		64		0
		238719		2274		1	
16	1118209		49401		89		
		633927		4054			
21	4287844		114265				
		2119372					
29	21242820						

Substituting values in eqn. (48), we get

$$f(x) = 57 + (x - 2)(644) + (x - 2)(x - 4)(1765)$$
$$+ (x - 2)(x - 4)(x - 9)(556)$$
$$+ (x - 2)(x - 4)(x - 9)(x - 13)(45)$$
$$+ (x - 2)(x - 4)(x - 9)(x - 13)(x - 16)(1)$$
$$= 57 + 644(x - 2) + 1765(x^2 - 6x + 8)$$
$$+ 556(x^3 - 15x^2 + 62x - 72)$$
$$+ 45(x^4 - 28x^3 + 257x^2 - 878x + 936)$$
$$+ x^5 - 44x^4 + 705x^3 - 4990x^2 + 14984x - 14976$$

$$f'(x) = 644 + 1765(2x - 6) + 556(3x^2 - 30x + 62)$$
$$+ 45(4x^3 - 84x^2 + 514x - 878)$$
$$+ 5x^4 - 176x^3 + 2115x^2 - 9980x + 14984$$
$$f''(x) = 3530 + 556(6x - 30) + 45(12x^2 - 168x + 514)$$
$$+ 20x^3 - 528x^2 + 4230x - 9980$$
$$f'''(x) = 3336 + 45(24x - 168) + 60x^2 - 1056x + 4230$$
$$= 60x^2 + 24x + 6$$

where $x = 5$,

$$f'''(5) = 60(5)^2 + 24(5) + 6 = 1626$$

Example 13. *Find f '(4) from the following data:*

x:	*0*	*2*	*5*	*1*
f(x):	*0*	*8*	*125*	*1.*

Sol. Though this problem can be solved by Newton's divided difference formula, we are giving here, as an alternative, Lagrange's method. Lagrange's polynomial, in this case, is given by

$$f(x) = \frac{(x-2)(x-5)(x-1)}{(0-2)(0-5)(0-1)}(0) + \frac{(x-0)(x-5)(x-1)}{(2-0)(2-5)(2-1)}(8)$$
$$+ \frac{(x-0)(x-2)(x-1)}{(5-0)(5-2)(5-1)}(125) + \frac{(x-0)(x-2)(x-5)}{(1-0)(1-2)(1-5)}(1)$$
$$= -\frac{4}{3}(x^3 - 6x^2 + 5x) + \frac{25}{12}(x^3 - 3x^2 + 2x) + \frac{1}{4}(x^3 - 7x^2 + 10x)$$
$$= x^3$$
$$\therefore \quad f'(x) = 3x^2$$

when $x = 4$, $f'(4) = 3(4)^2 = 48$

Example 14. *State the three different finite difference approximations to the first derivative $f'(x_0)$ together with the order of their truncation errors.*

Derive the forward difference approximation and its leading error term.

Sol. (*i*) Newton's forward difference approximation is given by

$$f(x) = f_0 + u\,\Delta f_0 + \frac{u(u-1)}{2}\Delta^2 f_0$$

where $u = \dfrac{x - x_0}{h}$ and $E = \dfrac{1}{6}u(u-1)(u-2)h^3 f'''(\xi)$

We have, $$f'(x) = \frac{df}{du} \cdot \frac{du}{dx}$$

$$= \frac{1}{h}\left[\Delta f_0 + \frac{1}{2}(2u - 1)\,\Delta^2 f_0\right]$$

and $$|\,E'(x_0)\,| = |\,E'(u = 0)\,| \leq \frac{h^2}{3} M_3$$

where $$M_3 = \max_{x_0 \leq x \leq x_2} |f'''(x)|$$

(*ii*) Newton's backward difference approximation is given by

$$f(x) = f_2 + u\,\nabla f_2 + \frac{1}{2}\,u(u + 1)\,\nabla^2 f_2$$

where $u = \dfrac{x - x_2}{h}$ and $E = \dfrac{1}{6}\,u\,(u + 1)\,(u + 2)\,h^3 f'''(\xi)$

We have, $$f'(x) = \frac{1}{h}\left[\nabla f_2 + \frac{1}{2}(2u + 1)\,\nabla^2 f_2\right]$$

and $$|\,E'(x_2)\,| = |\,E'(u = 0)\,| \leq \frac{h^2}{3} M_3$$

(*iii*) Central difference approximation is given by

$$f(x) = f_0 + \frac{u}{2}\,(\delta f_{1/2} + \delta f_{-1/2})$$

where $$u = \frac{x - x_0}{h}.$$

We have $$f'(x) = \frac{1}{2h}(\delta f_{1/2} + \delta f_{-1/2})$$

$$= \frac{1}{2h}[(f_1 - f_0) + (f_0 - f_{-1})]$$

$$= \frac{1}{2h}(f_1 - f_{-1})$$

and $$|\,E'(x)\,| \leq \frac{h^2}{6} M_3.$$

ASSIGNMENT 5.1

1. Given that

x:	1.0	1.1	1.2	1.3	1.4	1.5	1.6
y:	7.989	8.403	8.781	9.129	9.451	9.750	10.031

Find $\frac{dy}{dx}$ and $\frac{d^2y}{dx^2}$ at

(*i*) $x = 1.1$ (*ii*) $x = 1.6$.

2. Find first and second derivatives of the function tabulated below at $x = 0.6$

x:	0.4	0.5	0.6	0.7	0.8
y:	1.5836	1.7974	2.0442	2.3275	2.6511.

3. Find $y'(0)$ and $y''(0)$ from the given table:

x:	0	1	2	3	4	5
y:	4	8	15	7	6	2

4. Find $y'(1.5)$ and $y''(1.5)$ from the following table:

x:	1.5	2.0	2.5	3	3.5	4
$f(x)$:	3.375	7	13.625	24	38.875	59.

5. Given the following table of values of x and y:

x:	1	1.05	1.1	1.15	1.2	1.25	1.30
y:	1	1.0247	1.0488	1.0723	1.0954	1.1180	1.1401

Find $\frac{dy}{dx}$ and $\frac{d^2y}{dx^2}$ at

(*i*) $x = 1$ (*ii*) $x = 1.25$ (*iii*) $x = 1.15$.

6. Find $y'(4)$ from the given table:

x:	1	2	4	8	10
y:	0	1	5	21	27.

7. Find the numerical value of $y'(10°)$ for $y = \sin x$ given that:
$\sin 0° = 0.000$, $\sin 10° = 0.1736$,
$\sin 20° = 0.3420$, $\sin 30° = 0.5000$, $\sin 40° = 0.6428$.

8. Find $\frac{d}{dx}(J_0)$ at $x = 0.1$ from the following table:

x:	0.0	0.1	0.2	0.3	0.4
$J_0(x)$:	1	0.9975	0.99	0.9776	0.9604.

9. Find the first and second derivatives for the function tabulated below at the point $x = 3.0$:

x:	3	3.2	3.4	3.6	3.8	4.0
y:	– 14	– 10.032	– 5.296	0.256	6.672	14.

10. (*i*) A slider in a machine moves along a fixed straight rod. Its distance x cm along the rod is given below for various values of the time t seconds. Find the velocity of the slider and its acceleration when $t = 0.3$ second.

t:	0	0.1	0.2	0.3	0.4	0.5	0.6
x:	30.13	31.62	32.87	33.64	33.95	33.81	33.24.

(*ii*) A slider in a machine moves along a fixed straight rod. Its distance x(in cm) along the rod is given at various times t (in secs).

t:	0	0.1	0.2	0.3	0.4	0.5	0.6
x:	30.28	31.43	32.98	33.54	33.97	33.48	32.13

Evaluate $\frac{dx}{dt}$ at $t = .1$ and at $t = .5$.

11. Using Newton's divided difference formula, find $f'(10)$ from the following data:

x:	3	5	11	27	34
$f(x)$:	– 13	23	899	17315	35606

12. From the table below, for what value of x, y is minimum? Also find this value of y

x:	3	4	5	6	7	8
y:	0.205	0.240	0.259	0.262	0.250	0.224.

13. Given the following table of values, find $f'(8)$:

x:	6	7	9	12
$f(x)$:	1.556	1.690	1.908	2.158.

14. Find the minimum value of y from the following table:

x:	0.2	0.3	0.4	0.5	0.6	0.7
y:	0.9182	0.8975	0.8873	0.8862	0.8935	0.9086

15. Prove that

$$\frac{d}{dx}(y_x) = \frac{1}{h}(y_{x+h} - y_{x-h}) - \frac{1}{2h}(y_{x+2h} - y_{x-2h}) + \frac{1}{3h}(y_{x+3h} - y_{x-3h}) - \ldots$$

$$\left[\textbf{Hint: } \text{R.H.S.} = \frac{1}{h}\log\left(\frac{1+E}{1+E^{-1}}\right)y_x = \left(\frac{1}{h}\log E\right)y_x = D(y_x)\right]$$

16. Find $f'(6)$ from the following table:

x:	0	1	3	4	5	7	9
$f(x)$:	150	108	0	– 54	– 100	– 144	– 84

17. Take 10 figure logarithm to base 10 from $x = 300$ to $x = 310$ by unit increments. Calculate the first derivative of $\log_{10} x$ when $x = 310$.

18. Given the following table:

x:	1	1.05	1.1	1.15	1.2	1.25	1.3
$f(x) = \sqrt{x}$:	1	1.0247	1.04881	1.07238	1.09544	1.11803	1.14014

Apply the above results to find $f'(1)$, $f''(1)$ and $f'''(1)$.

19. The following table gives values of pressure P and specific volume V of saturated steam:

P:	105	42.7	25.3	16.7	13
V:	2	4	6	8	10

Find

(a) the rate of change of pressure with respect to volume at V = 2

(b) the rate of change of volume with respect to pressure at P = 105.

20. y is a function of x satisfying the equation $xy'' + ay' + (x - b)y = 0$, where a and b are integers. Find the values of constants a and b if y is given by the following table:

x:	0.8	1	1.2	1.4	1.6	1.8	2	2.2
y:	1.73036	1.95532	2.19756	2.45693	2.73309	3.02549	2.3333	3.65563.

5.5 ERRORS IN NUMERICAL DIFFERENTIATION

In numerical differentiation, the error in the higher order derivatives occurs due to the fact that, although the tabulated function and its approximating polynomial would agree at the set of data points, their slopes at these points may vary considerably. Numerical differentiation is, therefore, an unsatisfactory process and should be used only in rare cases.

The numerical computation of derivatives involves two types of errors: **truncation errors** and **rounding errors.**

The truncation error is caused by replacing the tabulated function by means of an interpolating polynomial.

$$\text{The truncation error in the first derivative} = \frac{1}{6h}\left|\frac{\Delta^3 y_{-2} + \Delta^3 y_{-1}}{2}\right|.$$

$$\text{The truncation error in the second derivative} = \frac{1}{12h^2}\,|\,\Delta^4 y_{-2}\,|.$$

The rounding error is proportional to $\frac{1}{h}$ in the case of the first derivatives, while it is proportional to $\frac{1}{h^2}$ in the case of the second derivatives, and so on.

$$\text{The maximum rounding error in the first derivative} = \frac{3}{2}\frac{\varepsilon}{h}$$

$$\text{The maximum rounding error in the second derivative} = \frac{4\varepsilon}{h^2}$$

where ε is the maximum error in the value of y_i.

Example. *Assuming that the table of values given in Example 6 and the function values are correct to the accuracy given, estimate the errors in* $\frac{dy}{dx}$ *at* $x = 1.6$.

Sol. Since the values are correct to four decimals, it follows that

$$\varepsilon = 0.5 \times 10^{-4}$$

$$\text{Truncation error} = \frac{1}{6h}\left|\frac{\Delta^3 y_{-1} + \Delta^3 y_0}{2}\right| = \frac{1}{1.2}\left(\frac{0.0361 + 0.0441}{2}\right)$$

| See difference table in Example 6

$$= 0.03342$$

$$\text{Rounding error} = \frac{3\varepsilon}{2h} = \frac{3 \times 0.5 \times 10^{-4}}{2 \times 0.2} = 0.00038.$$

5.6 NUMERICAL INTEGRATION

Given a set of tabulated values of the integrand $f(x)$, determining the value of $\int_{x_0}^{x_n} f(x)\, dx$ is called numerical integration. The given interval of integration is subdivided into a large number of subintervals of equal width h and the function tabulated at the points of subdivision is replaced by any one of the interpolating polynomials like Newton-Gregory's, Stirling's, Bessel's over each of the subintervals and the integral is evaluated. There are several formulae for numerical integration which we shall derive in the sequel.

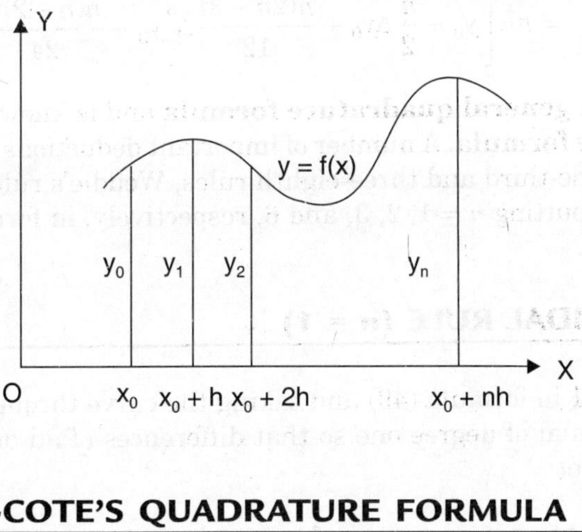

5.7 NEWTON-COTE'S QUADRATURE FORMULA

Let $I = \int_a^b y\, dx$, where y takes the values $y_0, y_1, y_2, \ldots\ldots, y_n$ for $x = x_0, x_1, x_2, \ldots\ldots, x_n$.

Let the interval of integration (a, b) be divided into n equal sub-intervals, each of width $h = \frac{b-a}{n}$ so that

$$x_0 = a, x_1 = x_0 + h, x_2 = x_0 + 2h, ..., x_n = x_0 + nh = b.$$

$$\therefore \qquad I = \int_{x_0}^{x_0 + nh} f(x)\, dx$$

Since any x is given by $x = x_0 + rh$ and $dx = hdr$

$$\therefore \qquad I = h \int_0^n f(x_0 + rh)\, dr$$

$$= h \int_0^n \left[y_0 + r\Delta y_0 + \frac{r(r-1)}{2!}\Delta^2 y_0 + \frac{r(r-1)(r-2)}{3!}\Delta^3 y_0 + ... \right] dr$$

[by Newton's forward interpolation formula]

$$= h \left[ry_0 + \frac{r^2}{2}\Delta y_0 + \frac{1}{2}\left(\frac{r^3}{3} - \frac{r^2}{2}\right)\Delta^2 y_0 + \frac{1}{6}\left(\frac{r^4}{4} - r^3 + r^2\right)\Delta^3 y_0 + ... \right]_0^n$$

$$= nh \left[y_0 + \frac{n}{2}\Delta y_0 + \frac{n(2n-3)}{12}\Delta^2 y_0 + \frac{n(n-2)^2}{24}\Delta^3 y_0 + ... \right] \qquad (49)$$

This is a **general quadrature formula** and is known as **Newton-Cote's quadrature formula.** A number of important deductions *viz.* Trapezoidal rule, Simpson's one-third and three-eighth rules, Weddle's rule can be immediately deduced by putting $n = 1, 2, 3$, and 6, respectively, in formula (49).

5.8 TRAPEZOIDAL RULE (n = 1)

Putting $n = 1$ in formula (49) and taking the curve through (x_0, y_0) and (x_1, y_1) as a polynomial of degree one so that differences of an order higher than one vanish, we get

$$\int_{x_0}^{x_0 + h} f(x)\, dx = h\left(y_0 + \frac{1}{2}\Delta y_0\right) = \frac{h}{2}[2y_0 + (y_1 - y_0)] = \frac{h}{2}(y_0 + y_1)$$

Similarly, for the next sub-interval $(x_0 + h, x_0 + 2h)$, we get

$$\int_{x_0+h}^{x_0+2h} f(x)\,dx = \frac{h}{2}(y_1 + y_2), \ldots\ldots, \int_{x_0+(n-1)h}^{x_0+nh} f(x)\,dx = \frac{h}{2}(y_{n-1} + y_n)$$

Adding the above integrals, we get

$$\boxed{\int_{x_0}^{x_0+nh} f(x)\,dx = \frac{h}{2}\left[(y_0 + y_n) + 2(y_1 + y_2 + \ldots\ldots + y_{n-1})\right]}$$

which is known as **Trapezoidal rule.** By increasing the number of subintervals, thereby making h very small, we can improve the accuracy of the value of the given integral.

5.9 SIMPSON'S ONE-THIRD RULE (n = 2)

Putting $n = 2$ in formula (49) and taking the curve through (x_0, y_0), (x_1, y_1) and (x_2, y_2) as a polynomial of degree two so that differences of order higher than two vanish, we get

$$\int_{x_0}^{x_0+2h} f(x)\,dx = 2h\left[y_0 + \Delta y_0 + \frac{1}{6}\Delta^2 y_0\right]$$

$$= \frac{2h}{6}\left[6y_0 + 6(y_1 - y_0) + (y_2 - 2y_1 + y_0)\right]$$

$$= \frac{h}{3}(y_0 + 4y_1 + y_2)$$

Similarly,

$$\int_{x_0+2h}^{x_0+4h} f(x)\,dx = \frac{h}{3}(y_2 + 4y_3 + y_4), \ \ldots\ldots,$$

$$\int_{x_0+(n-2)h}^{x_0+nh} f(x)\,dx = \frac{h}{3}(y_{n-2} + 4y_{n-1} + y_n)$$

Adding the above integrals, we get

$$\boxed{\begin{aligned}\int_{x_0}^{x_0+nh} f(x)\,dx = \frac{h}{3}\,&[(y_0 + y_n) + 4(y_1 + y_3 + \ldots + y_{n-1}) \\ &+ 2(y_2 + y_4 + \ldots + y_{n-2})]\end{aligned}}$$

which is known as **Simpson's one-third rule.**

While using this formula, the given interval of integration must be divided into an even number of sub-intervals, since we find the area over two sub-intervals at a time.

5.10 SIMPSON'S THREE-EIGHTH RULE (n = 3)

Putting $n = 3$ in formula (49) and taking the curve through (x_0, y_0), (x_1, y_1), (x_2, y_2), and (x_3, y_3) as a polynomial of degree three so that differences of order higher than three vanish, we get

$$\int_{x_0}^{x_0+3h} f(x)\,dx = 3h\left(y_0 + \frac{3}{2}\Delta y_0 + \frac{3}{4}\Delta^2 y_0 + \frac{1}{8}\Delta^3 y_0\right)$$

$$= \frac{3h}{8}\,[8y_0 + 12(y_1 - y_0) + 6(y_2 - 2y_1 + y_0) + (y_3 - 3y_2 + 3y_1 - y_0)]$$

$$= \frac{3h}{8}\,[y_0 + 3y_1 + 3y_2 + y_3]$$

Similarly, $$\int_{x_0+3h}^{x_0+6h} f(x)\,dx = \frac{3h}{8}\,[y_3 + 3y_4 + 3y_5 + y_6], \ldots$$

$$\int_{x_0+(n-3)h}^{x_0+6h} f(x)\,dx = \frac{3h}{8}\,[y_{n-3} + 3y_{n-2} + 3y_{n-1} + y_n]$$

Adding the above integrals, we get

$$\int_{x_0}^{x_0+nh} f(x)\,dx = \frac{3h}{8}\,[(y_0 + y_n) + 3(y_1 + y_2 + y_4 + y_5 + \ldots\ldots + y_{n-2} + y_{n-1}) + 2(y_3 + y_6 + \ldots\ldots + y_{n-3})]$$

which is known as **Simpson's three-eighth rule.**

While using this formula, the given interval of integration must be divided into sub-intervals whose number n is a multiple of 3.

5.11 BOOLE'S RULE

Putting $n = 4$ in formula (49) and neglecting all differences of order higher than four, we get

$$\int_{x_0}^{x_0+4h} f(x)\,dx = h\int_0^4 \left[y_0 + r\Delta y_0 + \frac{r(r-1)}{2!}\Delta^2 y_0 + \frac{r(r-1)(r-2)}{3!}\Delta^3 y_0 \right.$$
$$\left. + \frac{r(r-1)(r-2)(r-3)}{4!}\Delta^4 y_0 \right] dr$$

| By Newton's forward interpolation formula

$$= 4h\left[y_0 + \frac{n}{2}\Delta y_0 + \frac{n(2n-3)}{12}\Delta^2 y_0 + \frac{n(n-2)^2}{24}\Delta^3 y_0 \right.$$
$$\left. + \left(\frac{n^4}{5} - \frac{3n^3}{2} + \frac{11n^2}{3} - 3n\right)\frac{\Delta^4 y_0}{4!} \right]_0^4$$

$$= 4h\left[y_0 + 2\Delta y_0 + \frac{5}{3}\Delta^2 y_0 + \frac{3}{2}\Delta^3 y_0 + \frac{7}{90}\Delta^4 y_0 \right]$$

$$= \frac{2h}{45}(7y_0 + 32y_1 + 12y_2 + 32y_3 + 7y_4)$$

Similarly, $\int_{x_0+4h}^{x_0+8h} f(x)\,dx = \frac{2h}{45}(7y_4 + 32y_5 + 12y_6 + 32y_7 + 7y_8)$ and so on.

Adding all these integrals from x_0 to $x_0 + nh$, where n is a multiple of 4, we get

$$\int_{x_0}^{x_0+nh} f(x)\,dx = \frac{2h}{45}[7y_0 + 32y_1 + 12y_2 + 32y_3 + 14y_4 + 32\,y_5 + 12y_6 + 32y_7 + 14y_8 + \ldots\ldots]$$

This is known as **Boole's rule.**

While applying Boole's rule, the **number of sub-intervals should be taken as a multiple of 4.**

5.12 WEDDLE'S RULE (n = 6)

Putting $n = 6$ in formula (49) and neglecting all differences of order higher than six, we get

$$\int_{x_0}^{x_0+6h} f(x)\,dx = h\int_0^6 \left[y_0 + r\Delta y_0 + \frac{r(r-1)}{2!}\Delta^2 y_0 + \frac{r(r-1)(r-2)}{3!}\Delta^3 y_0 + \frac{r(r-1)(r-2)(r-3)}{4!}\Delta^4 y_0 + \frac{r(r-1)(r-2)(r-3)(r-4)}{5!}\Delta^5 y_0 + \frac{r(r-1)(r-2)(r-3)(r-4)(r-5)}{6!}\Delta^6 y_0 \right] dr$$

$$= h\left[ry_0 + \frac{r^2}{2}\Delta y_0 + \frac{1}{2}\left(\frac{r^3}{3} - \frac{r^2}{2}\right)\Delta^2 y_0 + \frac{1}{6}\left(\frac{r^4}{4} - r^3 + r^2\right)\Delta^3 y_0 + \frac{1}{24}\left(\frac{r^5}{5} - \frac{3r^4}{2} + \frac{11r^3}{3} - 3r^2\right)\Delta^4 y_0 + \frac{1}{120}\left(\frac{r^6}{6} - 2r^5 + \frac{35r^4}{4} - \frac{50r^3}{3} + 12r^2\right)\Delta^5 y_0 + \frac{1}{720}\left(\frac{r^7}{7} - \frac{5r^6}{2} + 17r^5 - \frac{225r^4}{4} + \frac{274r^3}{3} - 60r^2\right)\Delta^6 y_0 \right]_0^6$$

$$= 6h\left[y_0 + 3\Delta y_0 + \frac{9}{2}\Delta^2 y_0 + 4\Delta^3 y_0 + \frac{41}{20}\Delta^4 y_0 + \frac{11}{20}\Delta^5 y_0 + \frac{41}{840}\Delta^6 y_0 \right]$$

$$= \frac{6h}{20}\left[20y_0 + 60\Delta y_0 + 90\Delta^2 y_0 + 80\Delta^3 y_0 + 41\Delta^4 y_0 + 11\Delta^5 y_0 + \frac{41}{42}\Delta^6 y_0 \right]$$

$$= \frac{3h}{10}\,[20y_0 + 60(y_1 - y_0) + 90(y_2 - 2y_1 + y_0) + 80(y_3 - 3y_2 + 3y_1 - y_0) + 41(y_4 - 4y_3 + 6y_2 - 4y_1 + y_0) + 11\,(y_5 - 5y_4 + 10y_3 - 10y_2 + 5y_1 - y_0) + (y_6 - 6y_5 + 15y_4 - 20y_3 + 15y_2 - 6y_1 + y_0)] \qquad \left[\because \frac{41}{42} \simeq 1\right]$$

$$= \frac{3h}{10} [y_0 + 5y_1 + y_2 + 6y_3 + y_4 + 5y_5 + y_6]$$

Similarly,

$$\int_{x_0+6h}^{x_0+12h} f(x)\, dx = \frac{3h}{10} [y_6 + 5y_7 + y_8 + 6y_9 + y_{10} + 5y_{11} + y_{12}]$$

....

....

$$\int_{x_0+(n-6)h}^{x_0+nh} f(x)\, dx = \frac{3h}{10} [y_{n-6} + 5y_{n-5} + y_{n-4} + 6y_{n-3} + y_{n-2} + 5y_{n-1} + y_n]$$

Adding the above integrals, we get

$$\int_{x_0}^{x_0+nh} f(x)\, dx = \frac{3h}{10} [y_0 + 5y_1 + y_2 + 6y_3 + y_4 + 5y_5 + 2y_6 + 5y_7 + y_8 + 6y_9 + y_{10} + 5y_{11} + 2y_{12} + ...]$$

which is known as **Weddle's rule.** Here **n must be a multiple of 6.**

5.13 ALGORITHM OF TRAPEZOIDAL RULE

Step 01. Start of the program.
Step 02. Input Lower limit a
Step 03. Input Upper Limit b
Step 04. Input number of sub intervals n
Step 05. h=(b-a)/n
Step 06. sum=0
Step 07. sum=fun(a)+fun(b)
Step 08. for i=1; i<n; i++
Step 09. sum +=2*fun(a+i)
Step 10. End Loop i
Step 11. result =sum*h/2;
Step 12. Print Output result
Step 13. End of Program
Step 14. Start of Section fun
Step 15. temp = 1/(1+(x*x))
Step 16. Return temp
Step 17. End of Section fun.

5.14 FLOW-CHART FOR TRAPEZOIDAL RULE

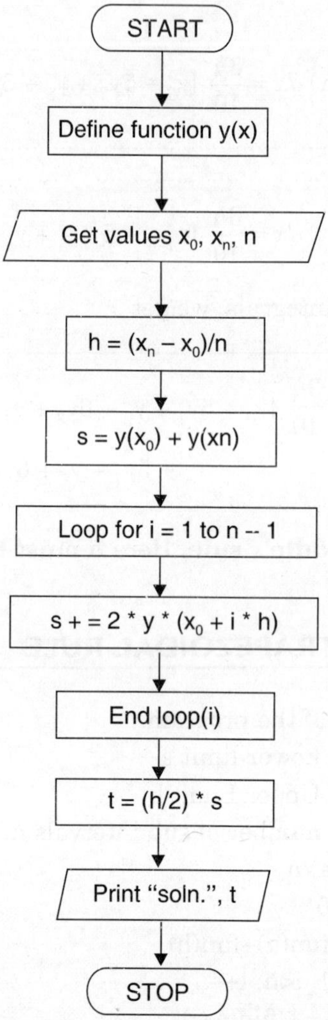

/* **

5.15 PROGRAM TO IMPLEMENT TRAPEZOIDAL METHOD OF NUMERICAL INTEGRATION

** */

```
//... HEADER FILES DECLARATION
# include <stdio.h>
# include <conio.h>
# include <math.h>
# include <process.h>
# include <string.h>

//... Function Prototype Declaration
float fun(float);
//... Main Execution Thread
void main()

{

//... Variable Declaration Field
//... Floating Type
float result=1;
float a,b;
float h,sum;
//... Integer Type

int i,j;
int n;

//... Invoke Clear Screen Function
clrscr();

//... Input Section
//... Input Range

printf("\n\n Enter the range - ");
printf("\n\n Lower Limit a - ");
scanf("%f" ,&a);
```

```
printf("\n\n Upper Limit b - ");
scanf("%f" ,&b);

//... Input Number of subintervals

printf("\n\n Enter number of subintervals - ");
scanf("%d" ,&n);

//... Calculation and Processing Section

h=(b-a)/n;

sum=0;
sum=fun(a)+fun(b);

for(i=1;i<n;i++)
    {
    sum+=2*fun(a+i);
    }
result=sum*h/2;

//... Output Section

printf("n\n\n\n Value of the integral is %6.4f\t",result);

//...Invoke User Watch Halt Function

printf("\n\n\n Press Enter to Exit");
getch();

}

//... Termination of Main Execution Thread
//... Function Body
float fun(float x)
{
float temp;
temp = 1/(1+(x*x));
return temp;
}
//... Termination of Function Body
```

5.16 OUTPUT

```
Enter the range -
Lower Limit a - 0
Upper Limit b - 6
Enter number of subintervals - 6
Value of the integral is 1.4108
Press Enter to Exit
```

5.17 ALGORITHM OF SIMPSON'S 3/8th RULE

Step 01. Start of the program.
Step 02. Input Lower limit a
Step 03. Input Upper limit b
Step 04. Input number of sub itervals n
Step 05. h = (b – a)/n
Step 06. sum = 0
Step 07. sum = fun(a) + fun (b)
Step 08. for i = 1; i < n; i++
Step 09. if i%3=0:
Step 10. sum + = 2*fun(a + i*h)
Step 11. else:
Step 12. sum + = 3*fun(a+(i)*h)
Step 13. End of loop i
Step 14. result = sum*3*h/8
Step 15. Print Output result
Step 16. End of Program
Step 17. Start of Section fun
Step 18. temp = 1/(1+(x*x))
Step 19. Return temp
Step 20. End of section fun

5.18 FLOW-CHART OF SIMPSON'S 3/8th RULE

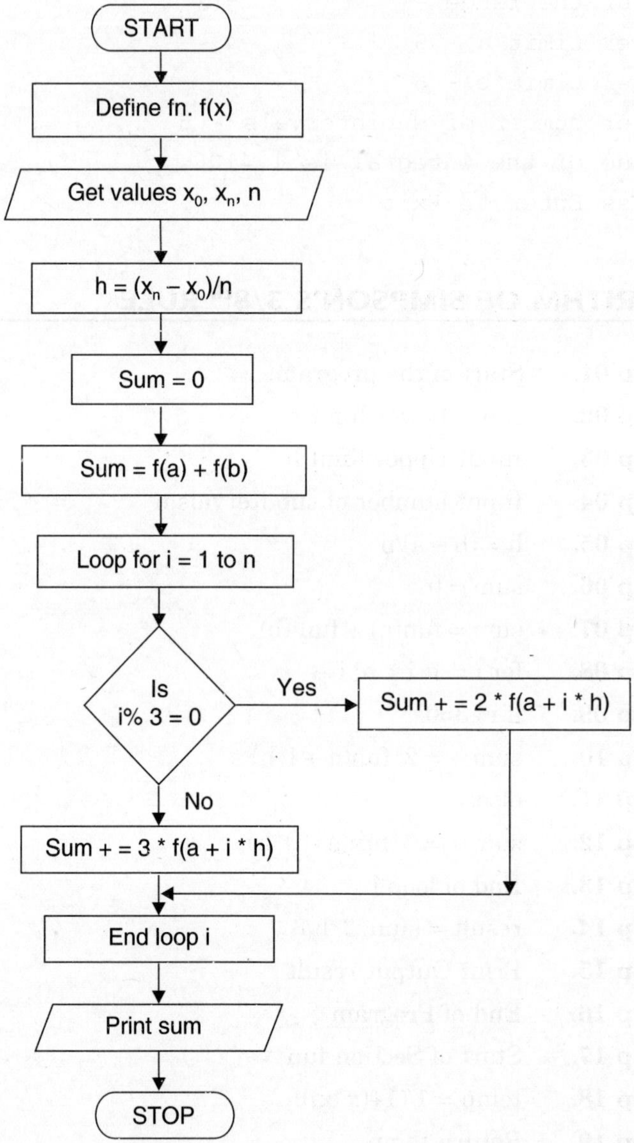

/***

5.19 PROGRAM TO IMPLEMENT SIMPSON'S 3/8th METHOD OF NUMERICAL INTEGRATION

***/

```
//... HEADER FILES DECLARATION
# include <stdio.h>
# include <conio.h>
# include <math.h>
# include <process.h>
# include <string.h>
//... Function Prototype Declaration
float fun(float);
//... Main Execution Thread
void main()
 {
 //... Variable Declaration Field
 //... Floating Type
 float result=1;
 float a,b;
 float h,sum;
 //...Integer Type
 int i,j;
 int n;
 //...Invoke Clear Screen Function
 clrscr();
 //...Input Section
 //...Input Range
 printf("\n\n Enter the range - ");
 printf("\n\n Lower Limit a - ");
 scanf("%f" ,&a);
```

```
printf("\n\n Upper Limit b - ");
scanf("%f" ,&b);

//...Input Number of Subintervals
printf("\n\n Enter number of subintervals - ");
scanf("%d" ,&n);

//...Calculation and Processing Section

h=(b-a)/n;

sum=0;
sum=fun(a)+fun(b);

for(i=1;i<n;i++)
    {
    if(i%3==0)
        {
        sum+=2*fun(a+i*h)
        }
    else
        {
        sum+=3*fun(a+(i)*h);
        }
    }
result=sum*3*h/8;

//... Output Section
printf("\n\n\n\n Value of the integral is %6.4f\t",result);

//... Invoke User Watch Halt Function
printf("\n\n\n Press Enter to Exit");
getch();

}

//... Termination of Main Execution Thread
//... Function Body
```

```
float fun(float x)
{
float temp;
temp=1/(1+(x*x));
return temp;
}
//... Termination of Function Body
```

5.20 OUTPUT

```
Enter the range -
Lower Limit a - 0
Upper Limit b - 6
Enter number of subintervals - 6
Value of the integral is 1.3571
Press Enter to Exit
```

5.21 ALGORITHM OF SIMPSON'S 1/3rd RULE

Step 01. Start of the program.
Step 02. Input Lower limit a
Step 03. Input Upper limit b
Step 04. Input number of subintervals n
Step 05. h=(b–a)/n
Step 06. sum=0
Step 07. sum=fun(a)+4*fun(a+h)+fun(b)
Step 08. for i=3; i<n; i + = 2
Step 09. sum + = 2*fun(a+(i – 1)*h) + 4*fun(a+i*h)
Step 10. End of loop i
Step 11. result=sum*h/3
Step 12. Print Output result
Step 13. End of Program
Step 14. Start of Section fun
Step 15. temp = 1/(1+(x*x))

Step 16. Return temp

Step 17. End of Section fun

5.22 FLOW-CHART OF SIMPSON'S 1/3rd RULE

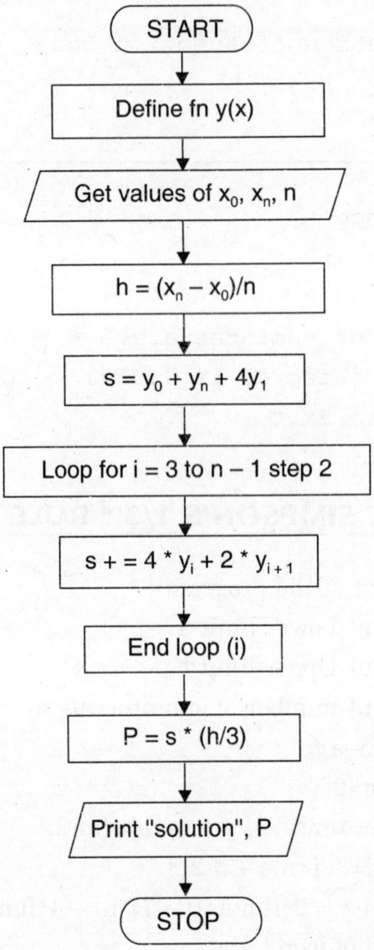

```
/* ***************************************************************
```

5.23 PROGRAM TO IMPLEMENT SIMPSON'S 1/3rd METHOD OF NUMERICAL INTEGRATION

```
*************************************************************** */

//... HEADER FILES DECLARATION

# include <stdio.h>
# include <conio.h>
# include <math.h>
# include <process.h>
# include <string.h>

//... Function Prototype Declaration

float fun(float);

//... Main Execution Thread

void main()
{
//...Variable Declaration Field
//... Floating Type
float result=1;
float a,b;
float h,sum;

//... Integer Type

int i,j;
int n;

//... Invoke Clear Screen Function

clrscr();

//... Input Section

//...Input Range
printf("\n\n Enter the range - ");
```

```
printf("\n\n Lower Limit a - ");
scanf("%f" ,&a);
printf("\n\n Upper Limit b - ");
scanf("%f" ,&b);
//... Input Number of Subintervals
printf("\n\n Enter number of subintervals - ");
scanf("%d",&n);

//... Calculation and Processing Section

h=(b-a)/n;

sum=0;
sum=fun(a)+4*fun(a+h)fun(b);
for(i=3;i<n;i+=2)
    {
    sum+=2*fun(a+(i-1)*h)+4*fun(a+i*h);
    }

result=sum*h/3;

//... Output Section
printf("\n\n\n\n Value of the integral is %6.4f\t",result);

//... Invoke User Watch Halt Function
printf("\n\n\n Press Enter to Exit");
getch();
}

//... Termination of Main Execution Thread

//... Function Body

float fun(float x)
{

float temp;
temp=1/(1+(x*x));
return temp;
}
//... Termination of Function Body
```

5.24 OUTPUT

```
Enter the range -
Lower Limit a - 0
Upper Limit b - 6
Enter number of subintervals - 6
Value of the integral is 1.3662
Press Enter to Exit
```

EXAMPLES

Example 1. *Use Trapezoidal rule to evaluate* $\int_0^1 x^3\, dx$ *considering five sub-intervals.*

Sol. Dividing the interval (0, 1) into 5 equal parts, each of width $h = \frac{1-0}{5}$ = 0.2, the values of $f(x) = x^3$ are given below:

x:	0	0.2	0.4	0.6	0.8	1.0
$f(x)$:	0	0.008	0.064	0.216	0.512	1.000
	y_0	y_1	y_2	y_3	y_4	y_5

By Trapezoidal rule, we have

$$\int_0^1 x^3\, dx = \frac{h}{2}\,[(y_0 + y_5) + 2(y_1 + y_2 + y_3 + y_4)]$$

$$= \frac{0.2}{2}\,[(0 + 1) + 2(0.008 + 0.064 + 0.216 + 0.512)]$$

$$= 0.1 \times 2.6 = 0.26.$$

Example 2. *Evaluate* $\int_0^1 \frac{dx}{1+x^2}$ *using*

(*i*) *Simpson's* $\frac{1}{3}$ *rule taking* $h = \frac{1}{4}$

(*ii*) *Simpson's* $\frac{3}{8}$ *rule taking* $h = \frac{1}{6}$

(*iii*) *Weddle's rule taking* $h = \frac{1}{6}$

Hence compute an approximate value of π *in each case.*

Sol. (*i*) The values of $f(x) = \dfrac{1}{1+x^2}$ at $x = 0, \dfrac{1}{4}, \dfrac{2}{4}, \dfrac{3}{4}$, 1 are given below:

x:	0	$\frac{1}{4}$	$\frac{1}{2}$	$\frac{3}{4}$	1
$f(x)$:	1	$\frac{16}{17}$	0.8	0.64	0.5
	y_0	y_1	y_2	y_3	y_4

By Simpson's $\frac{1}{3}$ rule,

$$\int_0^1 \frac{dx}{1+x^2} = \frac{h}{3} \left[(y_0 + y_4) + 4(y_1 + y_3) + 2y_2\right]$$

$$= \frac{1}{12}\left[(1+0.5) + 4\left\{\frac{16}{17} + .64\right\} + 2(0.8)\right] = 0.785392156$$

Also $$\int_0^1 \frac{dx}{1+x^2} = \left[\tan^{-1} x\right]_0^1 = \tan^{-1} 1 = \frac{\pi}{4}$$

$$\therefore \quad \frac{\pi}{4} \simeq 0.785392156 \quad \Rightarrow \quad \pi \simeq 3.1415686$$

(*ii*) The values of $f(x) = \dfrac{1}{1+x^2}$ at $x = 0, \dfrac{1}{6}, \dfrac{2}{6}, \dfrac{3}{6}, \dfrac{4}{6}, \dfrac{5}{6}$, 1 are given below:

x:	0	$\frac{1}{6}$	$\frac{2}{6}$	$\frac{3}{6}$	$\frac{4}{6}$	$\frac{5}{6}$	1
$f(x)$:	1	$\frac{36}{37}$	$\frac{9}{10}$	$\frac{4}{5}$	$\frac{9}{13}$	$\frac{36}{61}$	$\frac{1}{2}$
	y_0	y_1	y_2	y_3	y_4	y_5	y_6

By Simpson's $\frac{3}{8}$ rule,

$$\int_0^1 \frac{dx}{1+x^2} = \frac{3h}{8} \left[(y_0 + y_6) + 3(y_1 + y_2 + y_4 + y_5) + 2y_3\right]$$

$$= \frac{3\left(\frac{1}{6}\right)}{8}\left[\left(1+\frac{1}{2}\right)+3\left\{\frac{36}{37}+\frac{9}{10}+\frac{9}{13}+\frac{36}{61}\right\}+2\left(\frac{4}{5}\right)\right]$$

$$= 0.785395862$$

Also, $\int_0^1 \frac{dx}{1+x^2} = \frac{\pi}{4}$

$\therefore$ $\frac{\pi}{4} = 0.785395862$

$\Rightarrow$ $\pi = 3.141583$

(*iii*) By Weddle's rule, using the values as in (*ii*),

$$\int_0^1 \frac{dx}{1+x^2} = \frac{3h}{10}(y_0 + 5y_1 + y_2 + 6y_3 + y_4 + 5y_5 + y_6)$$

$$= \frac{3\left(\frac{1}{6}\right)}{10}\left\{1+5\left(\frac{36}{37}\right)+\frac{9}{10}+6\left(\frac{4}{5}\right)+\frac{9}{13}+5\left(\frac{36}{61}\right)+\frac{1}{2}\right\}$$

$$= 0.785399611$$

Since $\int_0^1 \frac{dx}{1+x^2} = \frac{\pi}{4}$

$\therefore$ $\frac{\pi}{4} = 0.785399611$

$\Rightarrow$ $\pi = 3.141598.$

Example 3. *Evaluate*

$$\int_0^6 \frac{dx}{1+x^2} \text{ by using}$$

(*i*) *Simpson's one-third rule*

(*ii*) *Simpson's three-eighth rule*

(*iii*) *Trapezoidal rule*

(*iv*) *Weddle's rule.*

Sol. Divide the interval (0, 6) into six parts each of width $h = 1$.

The values of $f(x) = \dfrac{1}{1+x^2}$ are given below:

x:	0	1	2	3	4	5	6
$f(x)$:	1	0.5	0.2	0.1	$\frac{1}{17}$	$\frac{1}{26}$	$\frac{1}{37}$
	y_0	y_1	y_2	y_3	y_4	y_5	y_6

(*i*) By Simpson's one-third rule,

$$\int_0^6 \frac{dx}{1+x^2} = \frac{h}{3}\,[(y_0 + y_6) + 4(y_1 + y_3 + y_5) + 2(y_2 + y_4)]$$

$$= \frac{1}{3}\left[\left(1+\frac{1}{37}\right) + 4\left(0.5 + 0.1 + \frac{1}{26}\right) + 2\left(0.2 + \frac{1}{17}\right)\right]$$

$$= 1.366173413.$$

(*ii*) By Simpson's three-eighth rule,

$$\int_0^6 \frac{dx}{1+x^2} = \frac{3h}{8}\,[(y_0 + y_6) + 3(y_1 + y_2 + y_4 + y_5) + 2y_3]$$

$$= \frac{3}{8}\left[\left(1+\frac{1}{37}\right) + 3\left(.5 + .2 + \frac{1}{17} + \frac{1}{26}\right) + 2(.1)\right]$$

$$= 1.357080836.$$

(*iii*) By Trapezoidal rule,

$$\int_0^6 \frac{dx}{1+x^2} = \frac{h}{2}\,[(y_0 + y_6) + 2(y_1 + y_2 + y_3 + y_4 + y_5)]$$

$$= \frac{1}{2}\left[\left(1+\frac{1}{37}\right) + 2\left(.5 + .2 + .1 + \frac{1}{17} + \frac{1}{26}\right)\right]$$

$$= 1.410798581.$$

(*iv*) By Weddle's rule,

$$\int_0^6 \frac{dx}{1+x^2} = \frac{3h}{10}\,[y_0 + 5y_1 + y_2 + 6y_3 + y_4 + 5y_5 + y_6]$$

$$= \frac{3}{10}\left[1 + 5(.5) + .2 + 6(.1) + \frac{1}{17} + 5\left(\frac{1}{26}\right) + \frac{1}{37}\right]$$

$$= 1.373447475.$$

Example 4. *The speed, v meters per second, of a car, t seconds after it starts, is shown in the following table:*

t	*0*	*12*	*24*	*36*	*48*	*60*	*72*	*84*	*96*	*108*	*120*
v	*0*	*3.60*	*10.08*	*18.90*	*21.60*	*18.54*	*10.26*	*5.40*	*4.50*	*5.40*	*9.00*

Using Simpson's rule, find the distance travelled by the car in 2 minutes.

Sol. If s meters is the distance covered in t seconds, then

$$\frac{ds}{dt} = v$$

$$\therefore \qquad \Big[s\Big]_{t=0}^{t=120} = \int_0^{120} v\,dt$$

since the number of sub-intervals is **10 (even).** Hence, by using Simpson's $\frac{1}{3}$rd rule,

$$\int_0^{120} v\,dt = \frac{h}{3}\,[(v_0 + v_{10}) + 4(v_1 + v_3 + v_5 + v_7 + v_9) + 2(v_2 + v_4 + v_6 + v_8)]$$

$$= \frac{12}{3}\,[(0 + 9) + 4(3.6 + 18.9 + 18.54 + 5.4 + 5.4)$$
$$+ 2(10.08 + 21.6 + 10.26 + 4.5)]$$

$$= 1236.96 \text{ meters.}$$

Hence, the distance travelled by car in 2 minutes is 1236.96 meters.

Example 5. *Evaluate* $\int_{0.6}^{2} y\,dx$, *where y is given by the following table:*

x:	*0.6*	*0.8*	*1.0*	*1.2*	*1.4*	*1.6*	*1.8*	*2.0*
y:	*1.23*	*1.58*	*2.03*	*4.32*	*6.25*	*8.36*	*10.23*	*12.45.*

Sol. Here the number of subintervals is 7, which is neither even nor a multiple of 3. Also, this number is neither a multiple of 4 nor a multiple of 6, hence using Trapezoidal rule, we get

$$\int_{0.6}^{2} y\,dx = \frac{h}{2}\,[(y_0 + y_7) + 2(y_1 + y_2 + y_3 + y_4 + y_5 + y_6)]$$

$$= \frac{0.2}{2}\,[(1.23 + 12.45) + 2(1.58 + 2.03 + 4.32 + 6.25 + 8.36 + 10.23)]$$

| Here $h = 0.2$

$$= 7.922.$$

Example 6. *Find* $\int_{1}^{11} f(x)\,dx$*, where f(x) is given by the following table, using a suitable integration formula.*

x:	1	2	3	4	5	6	7	8	9	10	11
f(x):	543	512	501	489	453	400	352	310	250	172	95

Sol. Since the number of subintervals is 10 (even) hence we shall use Simpson's $\frac{1}{3}$rd rule.

$$\int_{1}^{11} f(x)\,dx = \frac{h}{3}\,[(y_0 + y_{10}) + 4(y_1 + y_3 + y_5 + y_7 + y_9) + 2(y_2 + y_4 + y_6 + y_8)]$$

$$= \frac{1}{3}\,[(543 + 95) + 4(512 + 489 + 400 + 310 + 172) + 2(501 + 453 + 352 + 250)]$$

$$= \frac{1}{3}\,[638 + 7532 + 3112] = 3760.67.$$

Example 7. *Evaluate* $\int_{0}^{1} \frac{dx}{1+x}$ *by dividing the interval of integration into 8 equal parts. Hence find* $\log_e 2$ *approximately.*

Sol. Since the interval of integration is divided into an even number of subintervals, we shall use Simpson's one-third rule.

Here, $y = \frac{1}{1+x} = f(x)$

$$y_0 = f(0) = \frac{1}{1+0} = 1, \quad y_1 = f\left(\frac{1}{8}\right) = \frac{1}{1+\frac{1}{8}} = \frac{8}{9}, \quad y_2 = f\left(\frac{2}{8}\right) = \frac{4}{5}$$

$$y_3 = f\left(\frac{3}{8}\right) = \frac{8}{11}, \quad y_4 = f\left(\frac{4}{8}\right) = \frac{2}{3}, \quad y_5 = f\left(\frac{5}{8}\right) = \frac{8}{13}$$

$$y_6 = f\left(\frac{6}{8}\right) = \frac{4}{7}, \qquad y_7 = f\left(\frac{7}{8}\right) = \frac{8}{15} \qquad \text{and} \quad y_8 = f(1) = \frac{1}{2}$$

Hence the table of values is

x:	0	$\frac{1}{8}$	$\frac{2}{8}$	$\frac{3}{8}$	$\frac{4}{8}$	$\frac{5}{8}$	$\frac{6}{8}$	$\frac{7}{8}$	1
y:	1	$\frac{8}{9}$	$\frac{4}{5}$	$\frac{8}{11}$	$\frac{2}{3}$	$\frac{8}{13}$	$\frac{4}{7}$	$\frac{8}{15}$	$\frac{1}{2}$
	y_0	y_1	y_2	y_3	y_4	y_5	y_6	y_7	y_8

By Simpson's $\frac{1}{3}$rd rule,

$$\int_0^1 \frac{dx}{1+x} = \frac{h}{3}\,[(y_0 + y_8) + 4(y_1 + y_3 + y_5 + y_7) + 2(y_2 + y_4 + y_6)]$$

$$= \frac{1}{24}\left[\left(1+\frac{1}{2}\right) + 4\left(\frac{8}{9}+\frac{8}{11}+\frac{8}{13}+\frac{8}{15}\right) + 2\left(\frac{4}{5}+\frac{2}{3}+\frac{4}{7}\right)\right]$$

| Here $h = 1/8$

$$= 0.69315453$$

Since, $$\int_0^1 \frac{dx}{1+x} = \Big[\log_e(1+x)\Big]_0^1 = \log_e 2$$

$\therefore$ $\log_e 2 = 0.69315453.$

Example 8. *Find, from the following table, the area bounded by the curve and the x-axis from x = 7.47 to x = 7.52.*

x:	*7.47*	*7.48*	*7.49*	*7.50*	*7.51*	*7.52*
f(x):	*1.93*	*1.95*	*1.98*	*2.01*	*2.03*	*2.06.*

Sol. We know that

$$\text{Area} = \int_{7.47}^{7.52} f(x)\,dx$$

with $h = 0.01$, the trapezoidal rule gives,

$$\text{Area} = \frac{.01}{2}\,[(1.93 + 2.06) + 2(1.95 + 1.98 + 2.01 + 2.03)]$$

$$= 0.09965.$$

Example 9. *Use Simpson's rule for evaluating*

$$\int_{-0.6}^{0.3} f(x)\, dx$$

from the table given below:

x:	– 0.6	– 0.5	– 0.4	– 0.3	– 0.2	– 0.1	0	.1	.2	.3
f(x):	4	2	5	3	– 2	1	6	4	2	8

Sol. Since the number of subintervals is 9(a multiple of 3), we will use Simpson's 3/8th rule here.

$$\therefore \quad \int_{-0.6}^{0.3} f(x)\, dx = \frac{3(.1)}{8} [(4 + 8) + 3\{2 + 5 + (-2) + 1 + 4 + 2\} + 2(3 + 6)]$$

$$= 2.475.$$

Example 10. *Evaluate* $\int_1^2 e^{-\frac{1}{2}x}\, dx$ *using four intervals.*

Sol. The table of values is:

x:	1	1.25	1.5	1.75	2
$y = e^{-x/2}$:	.60653	.53526	.47237	.41686	.36788
	y_0	y_1	y_2	y_3	y_4

Since we have four (even) subintervals here, we will use Simpson's $\frac{1}{3}$rd rule.

$$\therefore \quad \int_1^2 e^{-\frac{1}{2}x}\, dx = \frac{h}{3} [(y_0 + y_4) + 4(y_1 + y_3) + 2y_2]$$

$$= \frac{.25}{3} [(.60653 + .36788) + 4(.53526) + .41686) + 2(.47237)]$$

$$= 0.4773025.$$

Example 11. *Find* $\int_0^6 \frac{e^x}{1+x}\, dx$ *approximately using Simpson's* $\frac{3}{8}$*th rule on integration.*

Sol. Divide the given integral of integration into 6 equal subintervals, the arguments are 0, 1, 2, 3, 4, 5, 6; $h = 1$.

$$f(x) = \frac{e^x}{1+x};\ y_0 = f(0) = 1$$

$$y_1 = f(1) = \frac{e}{2}, \quad y_2 = f(2) = \frac{e^2}{3}, \quad y_3 = f(3) = \frac{e^3}{4},$$

$$y_4 = f(4) = \frac{e^4}{5}, \quad y_5 = f(5) = \frac{e^5}{6}, \quad y_6 = f(6) = \frac{e^6}{7}$$

The table is as below:

x:	0	1	2	3	4	5	6
y:	1	$\frac{e}{2}$	$\frac{e^2}{3}$	$\frac{e^3}{4}$	$\frac{e^4}{5}$	$\frac{e^5}{6}$	$\frac{e^6}{7}$
	y_0	y_1	y_2	y_3	y_4	y_5	y_6

Applying Simpson's three-eighth rule, we have

$$\int_0^6 \frac{e^x}{1+x}\,dx = \frac{3h}{8}\,[(y_0 + y_6) + 3(y_1 + y_2 + y_4 + y_5) + 2y_3]$$

$$= \frac{3}{8}\left[\left(1+\frac{e^6}{7}\right)+3\left(\frac{e}{2}+\frac{e^2}{3}+\frac{e^4}{5}+\frac{e^5}{6}\right)+2\frac{e^3}{4}\right]$$

$$= \frac{3}{8}\,[(1 + 57.6327) + 3(1.3591 + 2.463 + 10.9196 + 24.7355 + 2(5.0214)]$$

$$= 70.1652.$$

NOTE *It is not possible to evaluate* $\int_0^6 \frac{e^x}{1+x}\,dx$ *by using usual calculus method. Numerical integration comes to our rescue in such situations.*

Example 12. *A train is moving at the speed of 30 m/sec. Suddenly brakes are applied. The speed of the train per second after t seconds is given by*

Time (t):	0	5	10	15	20	25	30	35	40	45
Speed (v):	30	24	19	16	13	11	10	8	7	5

Apply Simpson's three-eighth rule to determine the distance moved by the train in 45 seconds.

Sol. If s meters is the distance covered in t seconds, then

$$\frac{ds}{dt} = v \quad \Rightarrow \quad \Big[s\Big]_{t=0}^{t=45} = \int_0^{45} v\,dt$$

Since the number of subintervals is **9 (a multiple of 3)** hence by using Simpson's $\left(\frac{3}{8}\right)^{th}$ rule,

$$\int_0^{45} v\,dt = \frac{3h}{8}\,[(v_0 + v_9) + 3(v_1 + v_2 + v_4 + v_5 + v_7 + v_8) + 2(v_3 + v_6)]$$

$$= \frac{15}{8}\,[(30 + 5) + 3(24 + 19 + 13 + 11 + 8 + 7) + 2(16 + 10)]$$

$$= 624.375 \text{ meters.}$$

Hence the distance moved by the train in 45 seconds is **624.375** meters.

Example 13. *Evaluate* $\int_0^4 \frac{dx}{1+x^2}$ *using Boole's rule taking*

(i) $h = 1$ *(ii)* $h = 0.5$

Compare the results with the actual value and indicate the error in both.

Sol. (*i*) Dividing the given interval into 4 equal subintervals (*i.e.*, $h = 1$), the table is as follows:

x:	0	1	2	3	4
y:	1	$\frac{1}{2}$	$\frac{1}{5}$	$\frac{1}{10}$	$\frac{1}{17}$
	y_0	y_1	y_2	y_3	y_4

using Boole's rule,

$$\int_0^4 y\,dx = \frac{2h}{45}\,[7y_0 + 32y_1 + 12y_2 + 32y_3 + 7y_4]$$

$$= \frac{2(1)}{45}\left[7(1) + 32\left(\frac{1}{2}\right) + 12\left(\frac{1}{5}\right) + 32\left(\frac{1}{10}\right) + 7\left(\frac{1}{17}\right)\right]$$

$$= 1.289412 \text{ (approx.)}$$

$$\therefore \quad \int_0^4 \frac{dx}{1+x^2} = 1.289412.$$

(*ii*) Dividing the given interval into 8 equal subintervals (*i.e.*, $h = 0.5$), the table is as follows:

x:	0	.5	1	1.5	2	2.5	3	3.5	4
y:	1	0.8	0.5	$\frac{4}{13}$	.2	$\frac{4}{29}$	.1	$\frac{4}{53}$	$\frac{1}{17}$
	y_0	y_1	y_2	y_3	y_4	y_5	y_6	y_7	y_8

using Boole's rule,

$$\int_0^4 y\,dx = \frac{2h}{45}[7(y_0) + 32(y_1) + 12(y_2) + 32(y_3) + 7(y_4)$$

$$+ 7(y_4) + 32(y_5) + 12(y_6) + 32(y_7) + 7(y_8)]$$

$$= \frac{1}{45}\left[7(1) + 32(.8) + 12(.5) + 32\left(\frac{4}{13}\right) + 7(.2) + 7(.2)\right.$$

$$\left. + 32\left(\frac{4}{29}\right) + 12(.1) + 32\left(\frac{4}{53}\right) + 7\left(\frac{1}{17}\right)\right]$$

$$= 1.326373$$

$$\therefore \quad \int_0^4 \frac{dx}{1+x^2} = 1.326373$$

But the actual value is

$$\int_0^4 \frac{dx}{1+x^2} = \left(\tan^{-1} x\right)_0^4 = \tan^{-1}(4) = 1.325818$$

$$\text{Error in result I} = \left(\frac{1.325818 - 1.289412}{1.325818}\right) \times 100 = 2.746\%$$

$$\text{Error in result II} = \left(\frac{1.325818 - 1.326373}{1.325818}\right) \times 100 = -0.0419\%.$$

Example 14. *A river is 80 m wide. The depth 'y' of the river at a distance 'x' from one bank is given by the following table:*

x:	0	10	20	30	40	50	60	70	80
y:	0	4	7	9	12	15	14	8	3

Find the approximate area of cross-section of the river using
(i) Boole's rule.

(ii) Simpson's $\frac{1}{3}$rd rule.

Sol. The required area of the cross-section of the river

$$= \int_0^{80} y\,dx$$

Here the number of sub intervals is 8.

(i) By Boole's rule,

$$\int_0^{80} y\,dx = \frac{2h}{45}[7y_0 + 32y_1 + 12y_2 + 32y_3 + 7y_4 + 7y_4 + 32y_5 + 12y_6 + 32y_7 + 7y_8]$$

$$= \frac{2(10)}{45}[7(0) + 32(4) + 12(7) + 32(9) + 7(12) + 7(12) + 32(15) + 12(14) + 32(8) + 7(3)]$$

$$= 708$$

Hence the required area of the cross-section of the river = 708 sq. m.

(ii) By Simpson's $\frac{1}{3}$rd rule

$$\int_0^{80} y\,dx = \frac{h}{3}[(y_0 + y_8) + 4(y_1 + y_3 + y_5 + y_7) + 2(y_2 + y_4 + y_6)]$$

$$= \frac{10}{3}[(0 + 3) + 4(4 + 9 + 15 + 8) + 2(7 + 12 + 14)]$$

$$= 710$$

Hence the required area of the cross-section of the river = 710 sq. m.

Example 15. *Evaluate $\int_{0.2}^{1.4} (\sin x - \log_e x + e^x)\,dx$ approximately using Weddle's rule correct to 4 decimals.*

Sol. Let $f(x) = \sin x - \log x + e^x$. Divide the given interval of integration into 12 equal parts so that the arguments are: 0.2, 0.3, 0.4, 0.5, 0.6, 0.7, 0.8, 0.9, 1.0, 1.1, 1.2, 1.3, 1.4.

The corresponding entries are

$y_0 = f(0.2) = 3.0295,\quad y_1 = f(0.3) = 2.8494,\quad y_2 = f(0.4) = 2.7975,$

$y_3 = f(0.5) = 2.8213,\quad y_4 = f(0.6) = 2.8976,\quad y_5 = f(0.7) = 3.0147$

$y_6 = f(0.8) = 3.1661,\quad y_7 = f(0.9) = 3.3483,\quad y_8 = f(1) = 3.5598,$

$y_9 = f(1.1) = 3.8001,\quad y_{10} = f(1.2) = 4.0698,\quad y_{11} = f(1.3) = 4.3705$

$y_{12} = f(1.4) = 4.7042$

Now, by Weddle's rule,

$$\int_{0.2}^{1.4} f(x)\,dx = \frac{3h}{10}[y_0 + 5y_1 + y_2 + 6y_3 + y_4 + 5y_5 + y_6 + y_6 + 5y_7 + y_8 + 6y_9 + y_{10} + 5y_{11} + y_{12}]$$

$$= \frac{3}{10}(0.1)[3.0295 + 14.2470 + 2.7975 + 16.9278 + 2.8976 + 15.0735 + 3.1661 + 3.1661 + 16.7415 + 3.5598 + 22.8006 + 4.0698 + 21.8525 + 4.7042]$$

$$= (0.03)[135.0335] = 4.051.$$

Example 16. *A solid of revolution is formed by rotating about x-axis, the lines x = 0 and x = 1 and a curve through the points with the following coordinates.*

x:	*0*	*0.25*	*0.5*	*0.75 1*	
y:	*1*	*0.9896*	*0.9589*	*0.9089*	*0.8415*

Estimate the volume of the solid formed using Simpson's rule.

Sol. If V is the volume of the solid formed then we know that

$$V = \pi \int_0^1 y^2\,dx$$

Hence we need the values of y^2 and these are tabulated below correct to four decimal places

x	0	.25	.5	.75	1
y^2	1	.9793	.9195	.8261	.7081

with $h = 0.25$, Simpson's rule gives

$$V = \pi\frac{(0.25)}{3}[(1 + .7081) + 4(.9793 + .8261) + 2(.9195)]$$

$$= 2.8192.$$

Example 17. *A tank is discharging water through an orifice at a depth of x meter below the surface of the water whose area is A m^2. Following are the values of x for the corresponding values of A.*

A:	*1.257*	*1.39*	*1.52*	*1.65*	*1.809*	*1.962*	*2.123*	*2.295*	*2.462*	*2.650*	*2.827*
x:	*1.5*	*1.65*	*1.8*	*1.95*	*2.1*	*2.25*	*2.4*	*2.55*	*2.7*	*2.85*	*3*

Using the formula $(0.018)\ T = \int_{1.5}^{3.0} \frac{A}{\sqrt{x}}\, dx$, *calculate T, the time (in seconds) for the level of the water to drop from 3.0 m to 1.5 m above the orifice.*

Sol. Here $h = 0.15$

The table of values of x and the corresponding values of $\frac{A}{\sqrt{x}}$ is

x	1.5	1.65	1.8	1.95	2.1	2.25	2.4	2.55	2.7	2.85	3
$y = \frac{A}{\sqrt{x}}$	1.025	1.081	1.132	1.182	1.249	1.308	1.375	1.438	1.498	1.571	1.632

Using Simpson's $\frac{1}{3}$rd rule, we get

$$\int_{1.5}^{3} \frac{A}{\sqrt{x}}\, dx = \frac{.15}{3}[(1.025+1.632) + 4(1.081 + 1.182 + 1.308 + 1.438 + 1.571) + 2(1.132 + 1.249 + 1.375 + 1.498)]$$

$$= 1.9743$$

Using the formula

$$(0.018)T = \int_{1.5}^{3} \frac{A}{\sqrt{x}}\, dx$$

We get $\quad 0.018T = 1.9743 \;\Rightarrow\; T = 110$ sec. (approximately).

Example 18. *Using the following table of values, approximate by Simpson's rule, the arc length of the graph* $y = \frac{1}{x}$ *between the points (1, 1) and* $\left(5, \frac{1}{5}\right)$

x:	*1*	*2*	*3*	*4*	*5*
$\sqrt{\frac{1+x^4}{x^4}}$:	*1.414*	*1.031*	*1.007*	*1.002*	*1.001.*

Sol. The given curve is

$$y = \frac{1}{x}$$

$$\therefore \quad \frac{dy}{dx} = -\frac{1}{x^2}$$

$$\therefore \quad \frac{ds}{dx} = \sqrt{1 + \left(\frac{dy}{dx}\right)^2} = \sqrt{1 + \frac{1}{x^4}} = \sqrt{\frac{1 + x^4}{x^4}}$$

$\therefore$ The arc length of the curve between the points (1, 1) and $\left(5, \frac{1}{5}\right)$

$$= \int_1^5 \sqrt{\frac{1 + x^4}{x^4}}\, dx$$

$$= \frac{h}{3}[(1.414 + 1.001) + 4(1.031 + 1.002) + 2(1.007)]$$

$$= \frac{1}{3}(2.415 + 8.132 + 2.014) = 4.187$$

Example 19. *From the following values of y = f(x) in the given range of values of x, find the position of the centroid of the area under the curve and the x-axis*

x:	*0*	$\frac{1}{4}$	$\frac{1}{2}$	$\frac{3}{4}$	*1*
y:	*1*	*4*	*8*	*4*	*1*

Also find

(*i*) *the volume of solid obtained by revolving the above area about x-axis.*

(*ii*) *the moment of inertia of the area about x-axis.*

Sol. Centroid of the plane area under the curve $y = f(x)$ is given by $(\bar{x}, \bar{y})$ where

$$\left.\begin{aligned} \bar{x} &= \frac{\int_0^1 xy\, dx}{\int_0^1 y\, dx} \\ \text{and} \quad \bar{y} &= \frac{\int_0^1 \frac{y}{2} . y\, dx}{\int_0^1 y\, dx} = \frac{\int_0^1 \frac{y^2}{2}\, dx}{\int_0^1 y\, dx} \end{aligned}\right] \quad (50)$$

From the given data, we obtain

x:	0	$\frac{1}{4}$	$\frac{1}{2}$	$\frac{3}{4}$	1
y:	1	4	8	4	1
xy:	0	1	4	3	1
$\frac{y^2}{2}$:	$\frac{1}{2}$	8	32	8	$\frac{1}{2}$

∴ By Simpson's rule,

$$\int_0^1 xy\,dx = \frac{(1/4)}{3}[(0+1)+4(1+3)+2(4)] = \frac{25}{12}$$

$$\int_0^1 \frac{y^2}{2}\,dx = \frac{1}{12}\left[\left(\frac{1}{2}+\frac{1}{2}\right)+4(8+8)+2(32)\right] = \frac{129}{12}$$

$$\int_0^1 y\,dx = \frac{1}{12}[(1+1)+4(4+4)+2(8)] = \frac{50}{12}$$

From (50), $$\bar{x} = \frac{25/12}{50/12} = \frac{1}{2} = 0.5$$

$$\bar{y} = \frac{129/12}{50/12} = \frac{129}{50} = 2.58$$

∴ Centroid is the point (0.5, 2.58).

(*i*) We know that

$$V = \text{Volume} = \pi \int_0^1 y^2\,dx$$

∴ Required volume $= \pi.2 \int_0^1 \frac{y^2}{2}\,dx = 2\pi \times \frac{129}{12} = 67.5442$

(*ii*) We know that moment of inertia of the area about the x-axis is given by

$$\text{M.I.} = \frac{1}{3}\rho \int_a^b y^3\,dx$$

where ρ is the mass per unit area.

Table for y^3 is

x:	0	$\frac{1}{4}$	$\frac{1}{2}$	$\frac{3}{4}$	1
y:	1	4	8	4	1
y^3:	1	64	512	64	1

$$\int_0^1 y^3\, dx = \frac{1}{12}[(1+1) + 4(64+64) + 2(512)] = \frac{769}{6}$$

$$\therefore \qquad \text{Reqd. M.I.} = \frac{1}{3}\rho\left(\frac{769}{6}\right) = \frac{769}{18}\rho = 42.7222\ \rho.$$

Example 20. *A reservoir discharging water through sluices at a depth h below the water surface, has a surface area A for various values of h as given below:*

h (in meters):	*10*	*11*	*12*	*13*	*14*
A (in sq. meters):	*950*	*1070*	*1200*	*1350*	*1530*

If t denotes time in minutes, the rate of fall of the surface is given by

$$\frac{dh}{dt} = -\frac{48}{A}\sqrt{h}$$

Estimate the time taken for the water level to fall from 14 to 10 m above the sluices.

Sol. From $\quad \dfrac{dh}{dt} = -\dfrac{48}{A}\sqrt{h}$, we have

$$dt = -\frac{A}{48}\frac{dh}{\sqrt{h}}$$

Integration yields,

$$t = -\frac{1}{48}\int_{14}^{10}\frac{A}{\sqrt{h}}\,dh = \frac{1}{48}\int_{10}^{14}\frac{A}{\sqrt{h}}\,dh$$

Here, $y = \dfrac{A}{\sqrt{h}}$. The table of values is as follows:

h:	10	11	12	13	14
A:	950	1070	1200	1350	1530
$\frac{A}{\sqrt{h}}$:	300.4164	322.6171	346.4102	374.4226	408.9097

Applying Simpson's $\frac{1}{3}$rd rule, we have

$$\text{time } t = \frac{1}{48} \cdot \frac{1}{3}[(300.4164 + 408.9097) + 4(322.6171 + 374.4226) + 2(346.4102)]$$

$$= 29.0993 \text{ minutes.}$$

ASSIGNMENT 5.2

1. Evaluate $\int_1^2 \frac{1}{x}\, dx$ by Simpson's $\frac{1}{3}$rd rule with four strips and determine the error by direct integration.

2. Evaluate the integral $\int_0^{\pi/2} \sqrt{\cos\theta}\, d\theta$ by dividing the interval into 6 parts.

3. Evaluate $\int_4^{5.2} \log_e x\, dx$ by Simpson's $\frac{3}{8}$th rule. Also write its programme in 'C' language.

4. Evaluate $\int_{30°}^{90°} \log_{10} \sin x\, dx$ by Simpson's $\frac{1}{3}$rd rule by dividing the interval into 6 parts.

5. Evaluate $\int_4^{5.2} \log_e x\, dx$ using

   (*i*) Trapezoidal rule (*ii*) Weddle's rule.

6. Evaluate using Trapezoidal rule

   (*i*) $\int_0^{\pi} t \sin t\, dt$ (*ii*) $\int_{-2}^{2} \frac{t\, dt}{5 + 2t}$

7. Evaluate $\int_3^7 x^2 \log x\, dx$ taking 4 strips.

8. The velocities of a car running on a straight road at intervals of 2 minutes are given below:

Time (in minutes):	0	2	4	6	8	10	12
Velocity (in km/hr):	0	22	30	27	18	7	0

Apply Simpson's rule to find the distance covered by the car.

9. Evaluate $\int_0^1 \cos x\, dx$ using $h = 0.2$.

10. Evaluate $\int_0^4 e^x\, dx$ by Simpson's rule, given that $e = 2.72$, $e^2 = 7.39$, $e^3 = 20.09$, $e^4 = 54.6$ and compare it with the actual value.

11. Find an approximate value of $\log_e 5$ by calculating to 4 decimal places, by Simpson's $\frac{1}{3}$rd rule, $\int_0^5 \frac{dx}{4x+5}$ dividing the range into 10 equal parts.

12. Use Simpson's rule, taking five ordinates, to find an approximate value of $\int_1^2 \sqrt{x - \frac{1}{x}}\, dx$ to 2 decimal places.

13. Evaluate $\int_0^{\pi/2} \sqrt{\sin x}\, dx$ given that

x:	0	$\pi/12$	$\pi/6$	$\pi/4$	$\pi/3$	$5\pi/12$	$\pi/2$
$\sqrt{\sin x}$:	0	0.5087	0.7071	0.8409	0.9306	0.9878	1

14. The velocity of a train which starts from rest is given by the following table, time being reckoned in minutes from the start and speed in kilometers per hour:

Minutes:	0	2	4	6	8	10	12	14	16	18	20
Speed (km/hr):	0	10	18	25	29	32	20	11	5	2	0

Estimate the total distance in 20 minutes. $\left[\textbf{Hint: } \text{Here step-size } h = \frac{2}{60}\right]$

15. A rocket is launched from the ground. Its acceleration is registered during the first 80 seconds and is given in the following table. Using Simpson's $\frac{1}{3}$rd rule, find the velocity of the rocket at $t = 80$ seconds.

t*(sec)*:	0	10	20	30	40	50	60	70	80
f*(cm/sec²)*:	30	31.63	33.34	35.47	37.75	40.33	43.25	46.69	50.67.

16. A curve is drawn to pass through the points given by the following table:

x:	1	1.5	2	2.5	3	3.5	4
y:	2	2.4	2.7	2.8	3	2.6	2.1

Find

(*i*) Center of gravity of the area.

(*ii*) Volume of the solid of revolution.

(*iii*) The area bounded by the curve, the x-axis and lines $x = 1$, $x = 4$.

17. In an experiment, a quantity G was measured as follows:

G(20) = 95.9, G(21) = 96.85, G(22) = 97.77

G(23) = 98.68, G(24) = 99.56, G(25) = 100.41, G(26) = 101.24.

Compute $\int_{20}^{26} G(x)\, dx$ by Simpson's and Weddle's rule, respectively.

18. Using the data of the following table, compute the integral $\int_{0.5}^{1.1} xy\, dx$ by Simpson's rule:

x:	0.5	0.6	0.7	0.8	0.9	1.0	1.1
y:	0.4804	0.5669	0.6490	0.7262	0.7985	0.8658	0.9281

19. Find the value of $\log_e 2$ from $\int_0^1 \frac{x^2}{1+x^3} dx$ using Simpson's $\frac{1}{3}$rd rule by dividing the range of integration into four equal parts. Also find the error.

20. Use Simpson's rule dividing the range into ten equal parts to show that

$$\int_0^1 \frac{\log(1+x^2)}{1+x^2} dx = 0.173$$

21. Find by Weddle's rule the value of the integral

$$I = \int_{0.4}^{1.6} \frac{x}{\sinh x} dx$$

by taking 12 sub-intervals.

22. Evaluate $\int_{0.5}^{0.7} x^{1/2} e^{-x} dx$ approximately by using a suitable formula.

23. (*i*) Compute the integral

$$I = \sqrt{\frac{2}{\pi}} \int_0^1 e^{-(x^2/2)} dx$$

Using Simpson's $\frac{1}{3}$rd rule, taking $h = 0.125$.

(*ii*) Compute the value of I given by

$$I = \int_{0.2}^{1.5} e^{-x^2} dx$$

Using Simpson's $\left(\frac{1}{3}\right)$ rule with four subdivisions.

24. Using Simpson's $\frac{1}{3}$rd rule, Evaluate the integrals:

(*i*) $\int_{1.0}^{1.8} \frac{e^x + e^{-x}}{2} dx$ (taking $h = 0.2$)

(*ii*) $\int_0^{\pi/2} \frac{dx}{\sin^2 x + \frac{1}{4}\cos^2 x}$

25. Evaluate $\int_0^1 \sqrt{\sin x + \cos x}\, dx$ correct to two decimal places using seven ordinates.

26. Use Simpson's three-eighths rule to obtain an approximate value of

$$\int_0^{0.3} (1 - 8x^3)^{1/2}\, dx$$

27. Evaluate $\int_0^{1/2} \frac{dx}{\sqrt{1 - x^2}}$ using Weddle's rule.

28. Evaluate $\int_0^1 \frac{x^2 + 2}{x^2 + 1}\, dx$ using Weddle's rule correct to four places of decimals.

29. Using $\frac{3}{8}$th Simpson's rule,

Evaluate: $\int_0^6 \frac{dx}{1 + x^4}$.

30. Apply Simpson's $\frac{1}{3}$rd rule to evaluate the integral

$$\text{I} = \int_0^1 e^x\, dx \text{ by choosing step size } h = 0.1$$

Show that this step size is sufficient to obtain the result correct to five decimal places.

31. (*i*) Obtain the global truncation error term of trapezoidal method of integration.

(*ii*) Compute the approximate value of the integral

$$l = \int (1 + x + x^2)\, dx$$

Using Simpson's rule by taking interval size h as 1. Write a C program to implement.

32. The function $f(x)$ is known at one point x^* in the interval $[a, b]$. Using this value, $f(x)$ can be expressed as

$$f(x) = p_0(x) + f'\{\xi(x)\}\,(x - x^*) \quad \text{for} \quad x \in (a, b)$$

where $p_0(x)$ is the zeroth-order interpolating polynomial $p_0(x) = f(x^*)$ and $\xi\,(x) \in (a, b)$. Integrate this expression from a to b to derive a quadrature rule with error term. Simplify the error term for the case when $x^* = a$.

5.25 EULER-MACLAURIN'S FORMULA

This formula is based on the expansion of operators. Suppose $\Delta F(x) = f(x)$, then an operator Δ^{-1}, called inverse operator, is defined as

$$F(x) = \Delta^{-1} f(x) \tag{51}$$

Also, $\Delta F(x) = f(x)$ gives

$$F(x_1) - F(x_0) = f(x_0)$$

Similarly,

$$F(x_2) - F(x_1) = f(x_1)$$

$$\vdots \qquad \vdots \qquad \vdots$$

$$F(x_n) - F(x_{n-1}) = f(x_{n-1})$$

On adding,

$$F(x_n) - F(x_0) = \sum_{i=0}^{n-1} f(x_i) \tag{52}$$

where $x_0, x_1, \ldots\ldots, x_n$ are the $(n + 1)$ equidistant values of x with difference h.

From (51),

$$F(x) = (E - 1)^{-1} f(x)$$

$$= (e^{hD} - 1)^{-1} f(x)$$

$$= \left[\left(1 + hD + \frac{h^2D^2}{2!} + \frac{h^3D^3}{3!} + \ldots\ldots\right) - 1\right]^{-1} f(x)$$

$$= \left[hD + \frac{h^2D^2}{2!} + \frac{h^3D^3}{3!} + \ldots\ldots\right]^{-1} f(x)$$

$$= (hD)^{-1}\left[1 + \left(\frac{hD}{2!} + \frac{h^2D^2}{3!} + \ldots\ldots\right)\right]^{-1} f(x)$$

$$= \frac{1}{h} D^{-1}\left[1 - \left(\frac{hD}{2!} + \frac{h^2D^2}{3!} + \ldots\ldots\right)\right.$$

$$\left. + \frac{(-1)(-2)}{2!}\left(\frac{hD}{2!} + \frac{h^2D^2}{3!} + \ldots\ldots\right)^2 + \ldots\ldots\right] f(x)$$

$$= \frac{1}{h} D^{-1}\left[1 - \frac{hD}{2} + \frac{h^2D^2}{12} - \frac{h^4D^4}{720} + \ldots\ldots\right] f(x)$$

$$F(x) = \frac{1}{h}\int f(x)\,dx - \frac{1}{2} f(x) + \frac{h}{12} f'(x) - \frac{h^3}{720} f'''(x) + \ldots\ldots \tag{53}$$

Putting $x = x_n$ and $x = x_0$ in (53) and then subtracting, we get

$$F(x_n) - F(x_0) = \frac{1}{h}\int_{x_0}^{x_n} f(x)\,dx - \frac{1}{2}[f(x_n) - f(x_0)] + \frac{h}{12}[f'(x_n) - f'(x_0)]$$

$$- \frac{h^3}{720}[f'''(x_n) - f'''(x_0)] + \ldots\ldots$$

$$\Rightarrow \quad \sum_{i=0}^{n-1} f(x_i) = \frac{1}{h}\int_{x_0}^{x_n} f(x)\,dx - \frac{1}{2}[f(x_n) - f(x_0)] + \frac{h}{12}[f'(x_n) - f'(x_0)]$$

$$- \frac{h^3}{720}[f'''(x_n) - f'''(x_0)] + \ldots\ldots \quad | \text{ using (52)}$$

$$\Rightarrow \quad \frac{1}{h}\int_{x_0}^{x_n} f(x)\,dx = \sum_{i=0}^{n-1} f(x_i) + \frac{1}{2}[f(x_n) - f(x_0)] - \frac{h}{12}[f'(x_n) - f'(x_0)]$$

$$+ \frac{h^3}{720}[f'''(x_n) - f'''(x_0)] - \ldots\ldots \quad (54)$$

or

$$\int_{x_0}^{x_n} y\,dx = \frac{h}{2}[y_0 + 2y_1 + 2y_2 + \ldots\ldots + y_n]$$

$$- \frac{h^2}{12}(y_n' - y_0') + \frac{h^4}{720}(y_n''' - y_0''') - \ldots\ldots$$

$$= \frac{h}{2}[(y_0 + y_n) + 2(y_1 + y_2 + \ldots\ldots + y_{n-1})]$$

$$- \frac{h^2}{12}(y_n' - y_0') + \frac{h^4}{720}(y_n''' - y_0''') - \ldots\ldots \quad (55)$$

which is called **Euler-Maclaurin's formula.** The first term on the R.H.S. of (55) represents the approximate value of the integral obtained from trapezoidal rule and the other terms denote the successive corrections to this value.

This formula is often used to find the sum of a series of the form

$$y(x_0) + y(x_0 + h) + y(x_0 + 2h) + \ldots\ldots + y(x_0 + nh).$$

5.26 GAUSSIAN QUADRATURE FORMULA

Consider the numerical evaluation of the integral

$$\int_a^b f(x)\,dx \quad (56)$$

So far, we studied some integration formulae which require values of the function at equally spaced points of the interval. Gauss derived a formula which uses the same number of function values but with different spacing and gives better accuracy.

Gauss's formula is expressed in the form

$$\int_{-1}^{1} F(u)\,du = W_1 F(u_1) + W_2 F(u_2) + \ldots\ldots + W_n F(u_n)$$

$$= \sum_{i=1}^{n} W_i F(u_i) \qquad (57)$$

where W_i and u_i are called the weights and abscissae respectively. The formula has an advantage that the abscissae and weights are symmetrical with respect to the middle point of the interval.

In equation (57), there are altogether $2n$ arbitrary parameters and therefore the weights and abscissae can be determined so that the formula is exact when $F(u)$ is a polynomial of degree not exceeding $2n - 1$. Hence, we start with

$$F(u) = C_0 + C_1 u + C_2 u^2 + C_3 u^3 + \ldots\ldots + C_{2n-1} u^{2n-1} \qquad (58)$$

Then from (57),

$$\int_{-1}^{1} F(u)\,du = \int_{-1}^{1} (C_0 + C_1 u + C_2 u^2 + C_3 u^3 + \ldots\ldots + C_{2n-1} u^{2n-1})\,du$$

$$= 2C_0 + \frac{2}{3} C_2 + \frac{2}{5} C_4 + \ldots\ldots \qquad (59)$$

Set $u = u_i$ in (58), we get

$$F(u_i) = C_0 + C_1 u_i + C_2 u_i^2 + C_3 u_i^3 + \ldots\ldots + C_{2n-1} u_i^{2n-1}$$

From (57),

$$\begin{aligned}\int_{-1}^{1} F(u)\,du = {} & W_1 (C_0 + C_1 u_1 + C_2 u_1^2 + \ldots\ldots + C_{2n-1} u_1^{2n-1}) \\ & + W_2 (C_0 + C_1 u_2 + C_2 u_2^2 + \ldots\ldots + C_{2n-1} u_2^{2n-1}) \\ & + W_3 (C_0 + C_1 u_3 + C_2 u_3^2 + \ldots\ldots + C_{2n-1} u_3^{2n-1}) + \ldots\ldots \\ & + W_n (C_0 + C_1 u_n + C_2 u_n^2 + \ldots\ldots + C_{2n-1} u_n^{2n-1})\end{aligned}$$

which can be written as

$$\begin{aligned}\int_{-1}^{1} F(u)\,du = {} & C_0 (W_1 + W_2 + \ldots\ldots + W_n) + C_1(W_1 u_1 + W_2 u_2 \\ & + W_3 u_3 + \ldots\ldots + W_n u_n) + C_2(W_1 u_1^2 + W_2 u_2^2 \\ & + W_3 u_3^2 + \ldots\ldots + W_n u_n^2) + \ldots\ldots \\ & + C_{2n-1}(W_1 u_1^{2n-1} + W_2 u_2^{2n-1} \\ & + W_3 u_3^{2n-1} + \ldots\ldots + W_n u_n^{2n-1})\end{aligned} \qquad (60)$$

Now equations (59) and (60) are identical for all values of C_i and hence comparing the coefficients of C_i, we obtain $2n$ equations

$$\left.\begin{aligned} W_1 + W_2 + W_3 + \ldots\ldots + W_n &= 2 \\ W_1 u_1 + W_2 u_2 + W_3 u_3 + \ldots\ldots + W_n u_n &= 0 \\ W_1 u_1^2 + W_2 u_2^2 + W_3 u_3^2 + \ldots\ldots + W_n u_n^2 &= \frac{2}{3} \\ \vdots \qquad \vdots \qquad \vdots \\ W_1 u_1^{2n-1} + W_2 u_2^{2n-1} + W_3 u_3^{2n-1} + \ldots\ldots + W_n u_n^{2n-1} &= 0 \end{aligned}\right\} \quad (61)$$

in $2n$ unknowns W_i and u_i ($i = 1, 2, \ldots\ldots, n$).

The abscissae u_i and the weights W_i are extensively tabulated for different values of n.

The table up to $n = 5$ is given below:

n	$\pm u_i$	W_i
2	0.57735, 02692	1.0
	0.0	0.88888 88889
3	0.77459 66692	0.55555 55556
4	0.33998 10436	0.65214 51549
	0.86113 63116	0.34785 48451
	0.0	0.56888 88889
5	0.53846 93101	0.47862 86705
	0.90617 98459	0.23692 68851

In general case, the limits of integral in (56) have to be changed to those in (57) by transformation

$$x = \frac{1}{2}\, u\,(b - a) + \frac{1}{2}(a + b).$$

5.27 NUMERICAL EVALUATION OF SINGULAR INTEGRALS

The various numerical integration formulae we have discussed so far are valid if integrand $f(x)$ can be expanded by a polynomial or, alternatively can be expanded in a Taylor's series in the interval $[a, b]$. In a case where function has a singularity, the preceding formulae cannot be applied and special methods will have to be adopted.

5.28 EVALUATION OF PRINCIPAL VALUE INTEGRALS

Consider, $$I(f) = \int_a^b \frac{f(x)}{x-t}\, dx \tag{62}$$

which is singular at $t = x$.

Its Principal value,

$$P(I) = \lim_{\varepsilon \to 0}\left[\int_a^{t-\varepsilon} \frac{f(x)}{x-t}\, dx + \int_{t+\varepsilon}^{b} \frac{f(x)}{x-t}\, dx\right];\ a < t < b \tag{63}$$

$$= I(f) \text{ (for } t < a \text{ or } t > b)$$

Set $x = a + uh$ and $t = a + kh$ in (1), we get

$$P(I) = P\int_0^p \frac{f(a+hu)}{u-k}\, du \tag{64}$$

Replacing $f(a + hu)$ by Newton's forward difference formula at $x = a$ and simplifying, we get

$$I(f) = \sum_{j=0}^{\infty} \frac{\Delta^j f(a)}{j!} C_j \tag{65}$$

where the constants C_j are given by

$$C_j = P\int_0^p \frac{(u)_j}{u-k}\, du \tag{66}$$

In (66), $(u)_0 = 1,\ (u)_1 = u,\ (u)_2 = u\,(u-1)$ etc.

Various approximate formulae can be obtained by truncating the series on R.H.S. of (65).

Eqn. (65) may be written as

$$I_n(f) = \sum_{j=0}^{n} \frac{\Delta^j f(a)}{j!} C_j \tag{67}$$

We obtain rules of orders 1, 2, 3, ... etc. by setting n = 1, 2, 3, ... respectively.

(*i*) **Two point rule** (n = 1): $I_1(f) = \sum_{j=0}^{1} \frac{\Delta^j f(a)}{j!} C_j$

$$= C_0 f(a) + C_1 \Delta f(a)$$

$$= (C_0 - C_1) f(a) + C_1 f(a+h) \tag{68}$$

(*ii*) **Three-point rule** ($n = 2$):

$$I_2(f) = \sum_{j=0}^{2} \frac{\Delta^j f(a)}{j!} C_j = C_0 f(a) + C_1 \Delta f(a) + C_2 \Delta^2 f(a)$$

$$= \left(C_0 - C_1 + \frac{1}{2} C_2\right) f(a) + (C_1 - C_2) f(a+h)$$

$$+ \frac{1}{2} C_2 f(a+2h) \qquad (69)$$

In above relations (68) and (69), values of C_j are given by,

$$C_0 = \log_e \left|\frac{p-k}{k}\right|$$

$$C_1 = p + C_0 k$$

$$C_2 = \frac{1}{2} p^2 + p(k-1) + C_0 k(k-1).$$

EXAMPLES

Example 1. *Apply Euler-Maclaurin formula to evaluate*

$$\frac{1}{51^2} + \frac{1}{53^2} + \frac{1}{55^2} + \ldots\ldots + \frac{1}{99^2}.$$

Sol. Take $\quad y = \frac{1}{x^2}$, $x_0 = 51$, $h = 2$, $n = 24$, we have

$$y' = -\frac{2}{x^3}, \qquad y''' = -\frac{24}{x^5}$$

Then from Euler-Maclaurin's formula,

$$\int_{51}^{99} \frac{dx}{x^2} = \frac{2}{2}\left[\frac{1}{51^2} + \frac{2}{53^2} + \frac{2}{55^2} + \ldots\ldots + \frac{2}{97^2} + \frac{1}{99^2}\right]$$

$$- \frac{(2)^2}{12}\left[\frac{(-2)}{(99)^3} - \frac{(-2)}{(51)^3}\right] + \frac{(2)^4}{720}\left[\frac{(-24)}{(99)^5} - \frac{(-24)}{(51)^5}\right]$$

$$\therefore \quad \frac{1}{51^2} + \frac{2}{53^2} + \frac{2}{55^2} + \ldots\ldots + \frac{2}{97^2} + \frac{1}{99^2}$$

$$= \int_{51}^{99} \frac{dx}{x^2} + \frac{2}{3}\left[\frac{1}{(51)^3} - \frac{1}{(99)^3}\right] - \frac{8}{15}\left[\frac{1}{(51)^5} - \frac{1}{(99)^5}\right] + \ldots\ldots$$

$$\Rightarrow \quad 2\left[\frac{1}{51^2}+\frac{1}{53^2}+\frac{1}{55^2}+......+\frac{1}{99^2}\right]$$

$$= \int_{51}^{99}\frac{dx}{x^2}+\left(\frac{1}{51^2}+\frac{1}{99^2}\right)+\frac{2}{3}\left[\frac{1}{(51)^3}-\frac{1}{(99)^3}\right]$$

$$-\frac{8}{15}\left[\frac{1}{(51)^5}-\frac{1}{(99)^5}\right]+......$$

$$\Rightarrow \quad \frac{1}{(51)^2}+\frac{1}{(53)^2}+\frac{1}{(55)^2}+......+\frac{1}{(99)^2}$$

$$= \frac{1}{2}\int_{51}^{99}\frac{dx}{x^2}+\frac{1}{2}\left[\frac{1}{(51)^2}+\frac{1}{(99)^2}\right]+\frac{1}{3}\left[\frac{1}{(51)^3}-\frac{1}{(99)^3}\right]$$

$$-\frac{4}{15}\left[\frac{1}{(51)^5}-\frac{1}{(99)^5}\right]+......$$

$$= \frac{1}{2}\left(-\frac{1}{x}\right)_{51}^{99}+\frac{1}{2}\left[\frac{1}{(51)^2}+\frac{1}{(99)^2}\right]+\frac{1}{3}\left[\frac{1}{(51)^3}-\frac{1}{(99)^3}\right]$$

$$-\frac{4}{15}\left[\frac{1}{(51)^5}-\frac{1}{(99)^5}\right]+.......$$

$$= 0.00475 + 0.000243 + 0.0000022 + ...$$

$$= 0.00499 \text{ approximately.}$$

Example 2. *Using Euler-Maclaurin's formula, find the value of* $\log_e 2$ *from* $\int_0^1 \frac{dx}{1+x}$.

Sol. Take $\qquad y = \frac{1}{1+x},\ x_0 = 0,\ n = 10,\ h = 0.1,$

we have $\qquad y' = -\frac{1}{(1+x)^2} \quad \text{and} \quad y''' = \frac{-6}{(1+x)^4}$

Then from Euler-Maclaurin's formula, we have

$$\int_0^1 \frac{dx}{1+x} = \frac{0.1}{2}\left[\frac{1}{1+0}+\frac{2}{1+0.1}+\frac{2}{1+0.2}+\frac{2}{1+0.3}+\frac{2}{1+0.4}\right.$$

$$\left.+\frac{2}{1+0.5}+\frac{2}{1+0.6}+\frac{2}{1+0.7}+\frac{2}{1+0.8}+\frac{2}{1+0.9}+\frac{1}{1+1}\right]$$

$$-\frac{(0.1)^2}{12}\left[\frac{(-1)}{(1+1)^2}-\frac{(-1)}{(1+0)^2}\right]+\frac{(0.1)^4}{720}\left[\frac{(-6)}{(1+1)^4}-\frac{(-6)}{(1+0)^4}\right]$$

$$= 0.693773 - 0.000625 + 0.000001 = 0.693149$$

Also, $\displaystyle\int_0^1 \frac{dx}{1+x} = \Big|\log(1+x)\Big|_0^1 = \log 2$

Hence $\log_e 2 = 0.693149.$

Example 3. *Evaluate* $\displaystyle\int_0^{\pi/2} \sin x\, dx$ *using the Euler-Maclaurin formula.*

Sol. $$\int_0^{\pi/2} \sin x\, dx = \frac{h}{2}[y_0 + 2y_1 + 2y_2 + \ldots\ldots + 2y_{n-1} + y_n]$$

$$+\frac{h^2}{12}+\frac{h^4}{720}+\frac{h^6}{30240}+\ldots\ldots$$

To evaluate the integral, let us take $h = \dfrac{\pi}{4}$.

Then we obtain,

$$\int_0^{\pi/2} \sin x\, dx = \frac{\pi}{8}(0+2+0)+\frac{\pi^2}{192}+\frac{\pi^4}{184320}+\ldots\ldots$$

$$= \frac{\pi}{4}+\frac{\pi^2}{192}+\frac{\pi^4}{184320} \text{ (approximately)}$$

$$= 0.785398 + 0.051404 + 0.000528 = 0.837330$$

If we take $h = \dfrac{\pi}{8}$, we get

$$\int_0^{\pi/2} \sin x\, dx = \frac{\pi}{16}[0 + 2(0.382683 + 0.707117 + 0.923879) + 1]$$

$$= 0.987119 + 0.012851 + 0.000033 = 1.000003.$$

Example 4. *Use Euler-Maclaurin's formula to prove that*

$$\sum_{1}^{n} x^2 = \frac{n(n+1)(2n+1)}{6}.$$

Sol. By Euler–Maclaurin's formula,

$$\int_{x_0}^{x_n} y\,dx = \frac{h}{2}[y_0 + 2y_1 + 2y_2 + \text{.........} + 2y_{n-1} + y_n] - \frac{h^2}{12}(y_n' - y_0')$$

$$+ \frac{h^4}{720}(y_n''' - y_0''') - \frac{h^6}{30240}(y_n^{(v)} - y_0^{(v)}) + \text{.....}$$

$$\Rightarrow \quad \frac{1}{2}y_0 + y_1 + y_2 + \text{......} + y_{n-1} + \frac{1}{2}y_n$$

$$= \frac{1}{h}\int_{x_0}^{x_n} y\,dx + \frac{h}{12}(y_n' - y_0') - \frac{h^3}{720}(y_n''' - y_0''')$$

$$+ \frac{h^5}{30240}(y_n^{(v)} - y_0^{(v)}) - \text{.......} \tag{70}$$

Here $y(x) = x^2,\ y'(x) = 2x$ and $h = 1$

$\therefore$ From (70),

$$\text{Sum} = \int_1^n x^2\,dx + \frac{1}{2}(n^2+1) + \frac{1}{12}(2n-2)$$

$$\left|\ \because \quad \frac{1}{2}y_0 = \frac{1}{2},\ \frac{1}{2}y_n = \frac{n^2}{2}\right.$$

$$= \frac{1}{3}(n^3-1) + \frac{1}{2}(n^2+1) + \frac{1}{6}(n-1) = \frac{n(n+1)(2n+1)}{6}.$$

Example 5. *Find* $\int_0^1 x\,dx$ *by Gaussian formula.*

Sol. Let us change the limits as

$$x = \frac{1}{2}u(1-0) + \frac{1}{2}(1+0) = \frac{1}{2}(u+1)$$

This gives,

$$\text{I} = \frac{1}{4}\int_{-1}^{1}(u+1)\,du = \frac{1}{4}\sum_{i=1}^{n} \text{W}_i\ \text{F}(u_i)$$

where $\text{F}(u_i) = u_i + 1$

For simplicity, let $n = 4$ and using the abscissae and weights corresponding to $n = 4$ in the table, we get

$$\text{I} = \frac{1}{4}\,[(-\,0.86114 + 1)\,(0.34785\,) + (-\,0.33998 + 1)\,(0.65214)$$

$$+\,(0.33998 + 1)\,(0.65214) + (0.86114 + 1)\,(0.34785)]$$

$$= 0.49999\,.....$$

where the abscissae and weights have been rounded to 5 decimal places.

Example 6. *Show that the integration formula* $\int_0^h f(x)\,dx = hf\left(\frac{h}{2}\right)$ *is exact for all polynomials of degree less than or equal to 1. Obtain an estimate for the truncation error.*

If $|f''(x)| < 1$ *for all x, then find the step size h so that the truncation error is less than* 10^{-3}.

Sol. If $f(x) = k$ (a constant or zero degree polynomial) then the result is obvious since

$$\int_0^h f(x)\,dx = kh \tag{71}$$

and
$$hf\left(\frac{h}{2}\right) = hk \tag{72}$$

$\therefore$ From (71) and (72),

$$\int_0^h f(x)\,dx = hf\left(\frac{h}{2}\right)$$

If $f(x)$ is a polynomial of degree one then

$$f(x) = ax + b$$

$$\int_0^h f(x)\,dx = \int_0^h (ax + b)\,dx = \frac{ah^2}{2} + bh \tag{73}$$

$$hf\left(\frac{h}{2}\right) = h\left(\frac{ah}{2} + b\right) = \frac{ah^2}{2} + bh \tag{74}$$

From (73) and (74), we have the result.

Now,
$$\int_0^h y\,dx = \int_0^h \left[y_0 + (x - x_0)\,y_0{}' + \frac{(x - x_0)^2}{2}\,y_0{}'' + ...\right] dx$$

$$= hy_0 + \frac{h^2}{2!} y_0' + \frac{h^3}{3!} y_0'' + ... \quad (75)$$

(where $x - x_0 = h$)

Also, $$hf\left(\frac{h}{2}\right) = h\left[y_0 + \frac{h}{2} y_0' + \frac{\left(\frac{h}{2}\right)^2}{2!} y_0'' + ...\right] \quad (76)$$

(75) – (76) gives the truncation error

$$= h^3\left(\frac{1}{6} - \frac{1}{8}\right) y_0'' \text{ (nearly)}$$

Now, $$\left|\frac{h^3}{24} y_0''\right| < \frac{1}{24} h^3$$

$$\Rightarrow \quad \frac{1}{24} h^3 < 10^{-3} \quad \text{or} \quad |h^3| < 24 \times 10^{-3} = 0.024$$

$$\Rightarrow \quad -\sqrt[3]{0.024} < h < \sqrt[3]{0.024}.$$

Example 7. *Find λ such that the quadrature formula* $\int_0^1 \frac{f(x)}{\sqrt{x}} dx \approx Af(0) + Bf(\lambda)$ *+ Cf(1) may be exact for polynomials of degree 3.*

Sol. $$\int_0^1 \frac{f(x)}{\sqrt{x}} dx = Af(0) + Bf(\lambda) + Cf(1)$$

Set $f(x) = 1, x, x^2$ and x^3 in turn,

$$2 = A + B + C \quad (77) \qquad \frac{2}{3} = B\lambda + C \quad (78)$$

$$\frac{2}{5} = B\lambda^2 + C \quad (79) \qquad \frac{2}{7} = B\lambda^3 + C \quad (80)$$

Subtracting (78) from (79), we get

$$B\lambda(\lambda - 1) = -\frac{4}{15}$$

Subtracting (79) from (80), we get

$$B\lambda^2(\lambda \quad 1) = \frac{4}{35}$$

$$\therefore \qquad \lambda = \frac{3}{7}.$$

Example 8. *Determine W_0, W_1 and W_2 as functions of α such that the error R in*

$$\int_{-1}^{1} f(x)\, dx = W_0 f(-\alpha) + W_1 f(0) + W_2 f(\alpha) + R,\ \alpha \neq 0$$

Vanishes when f(x) is an arbitrary polynomial of degree at most 3. Show that the precision is five when $\alpha = \sqrt{\frac{3}{5}}$ and three otherwise.

Compute the error R when $\alpha = \sqrt{\frac{3}{5}}$.

Sol. $\int_{-1}^{1} f(x)\, dx = W_0 f(-\alpha) + W_1 f(0) + W_2 f(\alpha)$ is exact for $f(x) = 1, x, x^2, x^3$.

$$f(x) = 1 \quad \Rightarrow \quad W_0 + W_1 + W_2 = 2$$

$$f(x) = x \quad \Rightarrow \quad W_0 = W_2$$

$$f(x) = x^2 \quad \Rightarrow \quad 2W_0\alpha^2 = \frac{2}{3}$$

$$f(x) = x^3 \quad \Rightarrow \quad W_0 = W_2$$

Solving, we find

$$W_0 = W_2 = \frac{1}{3\alpha^2}, \qquad W_1 = 2\left(1 - \frac{1}{3\alpha^2}\right)$$

Choosing $f(x) = x^4$, we get

$$\frac{2}{5} = 2W_0\alpha^4 = \frac{2}{3}\alpha^2$$

$$\Rightarrow \qquad \alpha = \sqrt{\frac{3}{5}}$$

With this value, $f(x) = x^5$ gives exact value.

$\therefore$ The precision is 5.

If $\qquad \alpha \neq \sqrt{\frac{3}{5}}$ the precision is 3.

With $\qquad \alpha = \sqrt{\frac{3}{5}}$, we have

$$\int_{-1}^{1} f(x)\,dx = \frac{5}{9}\left[f\left(-\sqrt{\frac{3}{5}}\right) + f\left(\sqrt{\frac{3}{5}}\right)\right] + \frac{8}{9} f(0) + \text{R}$$

Hence the error term R is given by

$$\text{R} = \frac{2}{7!} f^{(vi)}(0) + \text{terms involving higher order derivatives}$$

$$= \frac{f^{(vi)}(0)}{2520}.$$

Example 9. *Determine a, b and c such that the formula*

$$\int_0^h f(x)\,dx = h\left\{af(0) + bf\left(\frac{h}{3}\right) + cf(h)\right\}$$

is exact for polynomials of as high order as possible and determine the order of truncation error.

Sol. Making the method exact for polynomials of degree up to 2, we get

For $f(x) = 1$: $\qquad h = h\,(a + b + c) \qquad \Rightarrow \quad a + b + c = 1$

For $f(x) = x$: $\qquad \frac{h^2}{2} = h\left(\frac{bh}{3} + ch\right) \qquad \Rightarrow \quad \frac{b}{3} + c = \frac{1}{2}$

For $f(x) = x^2$: $\qquad \frac{h^3}{3} = h\left(\frac{bh^2}{9} + ch^2\right) \qquad \Rightarrow \quad \frac{b}{9} + c = \frac{1}{3}$

Solving above eqns., we get

$$a = 0,\ b = \frac{3}{4},\ c = \frac{1}{4}$$

Truncation error of the formula $= \frac{c}{3!} f'''(\xi); \qquad 0 < \xi < h$

and $$c = \int_0^h x^3\,dx - h\left(\frac{bh^3}{27} + ch^3\right) = -\frac{h^4}{36}$$

Hence, we have

$$\text{Truncation error} = \frac{h^4}{216} f'''(\xi) = 0\,(h^4).$$

ASSIGNMENT 5.3

1. Using Euler-Maclaurin's formula, evaluate

(i) $\frac{1}{400}+\frac{1}{402}+\frac{1}{404}+\ldots\ldots+\frac{1}{500}$ (ii) $\frac{1}{(201)^2}+\frac{1}{(203)^2}+\frac{1}{(205)^2}+\ldots\ldots+\frac{1}{(299)^2}$.

2. Prove that $\sum_{1}^{n} x^3 = \left\{\frac{n\,(n+1)}{2}\right\}^2$ applying Euler-Maclaurin's formula.

3. Use Euler-Maclaurin's formula to find the value of π from the formula

$$\frac{\pi}{4} = \int_0^1 \frac{dx}{1+x^2}.$$

4. Find the sum of the fourth powers of first n natural numbers by means of Euler-Maclaurin's formula.

OR

Prove that, $\sum_{0}^{n} i^4 = \frac{n^5}{5}+\frac{n^4}{2}+\frac{n^3}{3}+\frac{n}{30}$.

5. Sum the series $\frac{1}{100}+\frac{1}{101}+\frac{1}{102}+\frac{1}{103}+\frac{1}{104}$.

6. Determine α, β, γ and δ such that the relation

$$y'\left(\frac{a+b}{2}\right) = \alpha y\,(a) + \beta y\,(b) + \gamma y''\,(a) + \delta\, y''\,(b)$$

is exact for polynomials of as high degree as possible.

7. Find the values of α_0, α_1, α_2 so that the given rule of differentiation

$$f'(x_0) = \alpha_0 f_0 + \alpha_1 f_1 + \alpha_2 f_2 \quad (x_k = x_0 + kh)$$

is exact for $f \in P_2$.

8. Find the values a, b, c such that the truncation error in the formula

$$\int_{-h}^{h} f(x)\,dx = h\,[af(-h) + bf(0) + af(h) + h^2 c\,\{f'(-h) - f'(h)\}]$$

is minimized.

9. Show that $\sum_{i=1}^{n} i^7 + \sum_{i=1}^{n} i^5 = 2\left(\sum_{i=1}^{n} i^3\right)^2$.

10. Evaluate: $\sum_{m=0}^{\infty} \frac{1}{(10+m)^2}$ by applying Euler-Maclaurin's formula.

Part 4

- **Numerical Solution of Ordinary Differential Equations**
  Picard's Method, Euler's Method, Taylor's Method, Runge-Kutta Methods, Predictor-Corrector Methods, Milne's Method, Adams-Moulton Formula, Stability in the Solution of Ordinary Differential Equations.

Chapter 6

NUMERICAL SOLUTION OF ORDINARY DIFFERENTIAL EQUATIONS

6.1 INTRODUCTION

A physical situation concerned with the rate of change of one quantity with respect to another gives rise to a differential equation.

Consider the first order ordinary differential equation

$$\frac{dy}{dx} = f(x, y) \tag{1}$$

with the initial condition

$$y(x_0) = y_0 \tag{2}$$

Many analytical techniques exist for solving such equations, but these methods can be applied to solve only a selected class of differential equations.

However, a majority of differential equations appearing in physical problems cannot be solved analytically. Thus it becomes imperative to discuss their solution by numerical methods.

In numerical methods, we do not proceed in the hope of finding a relation between variables but we find the numerical values of the dependent variable for certain values of independent variable.

It must be noted that even the differential equations which are solvable by analytical methods can be solved numerically as well.

6.2 INITIAL-VALUE AND BOUNDARY-VALUE PROBLEMS

Problems in which all the conditions are specified at the initial point only are called **initial-value problems**. For example, the problem given by eqns. (1) and (2) is an initial value problem.

Problems involving second and higher order differential equations, in which the conditions at two or more points are specified, are called **boundary-value problems**.

To obtain a unique solution of nth order ordinary differential equation, it is necessary to specify n values of the dependent variable and/or its derivative at specific values of independent variable.

6.3 SINGLE STEP AND MULTI-STEP METHODS

The numerical solutions are obtained step-by-step through a series of equal intervals in the independent variable so that as soon as the solution y has been obtained at $x = x_i$, the next step consists of evaluating y_{i+1} at $x = x_{i+1}$. The methods which require only the numerical value y_i in order to compute the next value y_{i+1} for solving eqn. (1) given above are termed as **single step methods.**

The methods which require not only the numerical value y_i but also at least one of the past values $y_{i-1}, y_{i-2}, ...$ are termed as **multi-step methods.**

6.4 COMPARISON OF SINGLE-STEP AND MULTI-STEP METHODS

The single step method has obvious advantages over the multi-step methods that use several past values $(y_n, y_{n-1}, ..., y_{n-p})$ and that require initial values $(y_1, y_2, ..., y_n)$ that have to be calculated by another method.

The major disadvantage of single-step methods is that they use many more evaluations of the derivative to attain the same degree of accuracy compared with the multi-step methods.

6.5 NUMERICAL METHODS OF SOLUTION OF O.D.E.

In this chapter we will discuss various numerical methods of solving ordinary differential equations.

We know that these methods will yield the solution in one of the two forms:

(*a*) A series for y in terms of powers of x from which the value of y can be obtained by direct substitution.

(*b*) A set of tabulated values of x and y.

Picard's method and Taylor's method belong to class (*a*) while those of Euler's, Runge-Kutta, Adams-Bashforth, Milne's, etc. belong to class (*b*). Methods which belong to class (*b*) are called **step-by-step methods** or **marching methods** because the values of y are computed by short steps ahead for equal intervals of the independent variable.

In Euler's and Runge-Kutta methods, the interval range h should be kept small, hence they can be applied for tabulating y only over a limited range. To get functional values over a wider range, the Adams-Bashforth, Milne, Adams-Moulton, etc. methods may be used since they use finite differences and require starting values, usually obtained by Taylor's series or Runge-Kutta methods.

6.6 PICARD'S METHOD OF SUCCESSIVE APPROXIMATIONS

Picard was a distinguished Professor of Mathematics at the university of Paris, France. He was famous for his research on the Theory of Functions.

Consider the differential equation

$$\frac{dy}{dx} = f(x, y); \quad y(x_0) = y_0 \tag{3}$$

Integrating eqn. (3) between the limits x_0 and x and the corresponding limits y_0 and y, we get

$$\int_{y_0}^{y} dy = \int_{x_0}^{x} f(x, y)\, dx$$

$$\Rightarrow \qquad y - y_0 = \int_{x_0}^{x} f(x, y)\, dx$$

or,

$$y = y_0 + \int_{x_0}^{x} f(x, y)\, dx \tag{4}$$

In equation (4), the unknown function y appears under the integral sign. This type of equation is called integral equation.

This equation can be solved by the method of successive approximations or iterations.

To obtain the first approximation, we replace y by y_0 in the R.H.S. of eqn. (4).

Now, the first approximation is

$$y^{(1)} = y_0 + \int_{x_0}^{x} f(x, y_0)\, dx$$

The integrand is a function of x alone and can be integrated.

For a second approximation, replace y_0 by $y^{(1)}$ in $f(x, y_0)$ which gives

$$y^{(2)} = y_0 + \int_{x_0}^{x} f\{x, y^{(1)}\}\, dx$$

Proceeding in this way, we obtain $y^{(3)}$, $y^{(4)}$, ..., $y^{(n-1)}$ and $y^{(n)}$ where

$$y^{(n)} = y_0 + \int_{x_0}^{x} f\{x, y^{(n-1)}\}\, dx \text{ with } y(x_0) = y_0$$

As a matter of fact, the process is stopped when the two values of y *viz.* $y^{(n-1)}$ and $y^{(n)}$ are the same to the desired degree of accuracy.

Picard's method is of considerable theoretical value. Practically, it is unsatisfactory because of the difficulties which arise in performing the necessary integrations. However, each step gives a better approximation of the required solution than the preceding one.

EXAMPLES

Example 1. *Given the differential eqn.*

$$\frac{dy}{dx} = \frac{x^2}{y^2 + 1}$$

with the initial condition $y = 0$ when $x = 0$. Use Picard's method to obtain y for $x = 0.25$, 0.5 and 1.0 correct to three decimal places.

Sol. (*a*) The given initial value problem is

$$\frac{dy}{dx} = f(x, y) = \frac{x^2}{y^2 + 1}$$

where $y = y_0 = 0$ at $x = x_0 = 0$

We have first approximation,

$$y^{(1)} = y_0 + \int_{x_0}^{x} f(x, y_0)\, dx$$

$$= 0 + \int_0^x \frac{x^2}{0 + 1}\, dx = \frac{1}{3}x^3 \qquad (5)$$

Second approximation,

$$y^{(2)} = y_0 + \int_{x_0}^{x} f\{x, y^{(1)}\}\, dx$$

$$= 0 + \int_0^x \frac{x^2}{\left(\dfrac{x^3}{3}\right)^2 + 1}\, dx$$

$$= \left[\tan^{-1}\frac{x^3}{3}\right]_0^x = \tan^{-1}\frac{x^3}{3}$$

$$= \frac{1}{3}x^3 - \frac{1}{3}\left(\frac{1}{3}x^3\right)^3 + \ldots\ldots$$

$$= \frac{1}{3}x^3 - \frac{1}{81}x^9 + \ldots.. \qquad (6)$$

From (5) and (6), we see that $y^{(1)}$ and $y^{(2)}$ agree to the first term $\frac{x^3}{3}$. To find the range of values of x so that the series with the term $\frac{1}{3}x^3$ alone will give the result correct to three decimal places, we put

$$\frac{1}{81}x^9 \le .0005$$

which gives, $x^9 \le .0405$ or $x \le 0.7$

Hence, $y(.25) = \frac{1}{3}(.25)^3 = .005$

and $y(0.5) = \frac{1}{3}(0.5)^3 = .042$

To find $y(1.0)$, we make use of eqn. (6) which gives,

$$y(1.0) = \frac{1}{3} - \frac{1}{81} = 0.321.$$

Example 2. *Use Picard's method to obtain y for x = 0.2. Given:*

$$\frac{dy}{dx} = x - y \text{ with initial condition } y = 1 \text{ when } x = 0.$$

Sol. Here $f(x, y) = x - y,\ x_0 = 0, y_0 = 1$

We have first approximation,

$$y^{(1)} = y_0 + \int_0^x f(x, y_0)\, dx = 1 + \int_0^x (x - 1)\, dx = 1 - x + \frac{x^2}{2}$$

Second approximation,

$$y^{(2)} = y_0 + \int_0^x f\{x, y^{(1)}\}\, dx = 1 + \int_0^x \{x - y^{(1)}\}\, dx$$

$$= 1 + \int_0^x \left(x - 1 + x - \frac{x^2}{2}\right) dx = 1 - x + x^2 - \frac{x^3}{6}$$

Third approximation,

$$y^{(3)} = y_0 + \int_0^x f\{x, y^{(2)}\}\, dx = 1 + \int_0^x \{x - y^{(2)}\}\, dx$$

$$= 1 + \int_0^x \left(x - 1 + x - x^2 + \frac{x^3}{6} \right) dx$$

$$= 1 - x + x^2 - \frac{x^3}{3} + \frac{x^4}{24}$$

Fourth approximation,

$$y^{(4)} = y_0 + \int_0^x f\{x, y^{(3)}\}\, dx = 1 + \int_0^x \{x - y^{(3)}\}\, dx$$

$$= 1 + \int_0^x \left(x - 1 + x - x^2 + \frac{x^3}{3} - \frac{x^4}{24} \right) dx$$

$$= 1 - x + x^2 - \frac{x^3}{3} + \frac{x^4}{12} - \frac{x^5}{120}$$

Fifth approximation,

$$y^{(5)} = y_0 + \int_0^x f\{x, y^{(4)}\}\, dx = 1 + \int_0^x \{x - y^{(4)}\}\, dx$$

$$= 1 + \int_0^x \left(x - 1 + x - x^2 + \frac{x^3}{3} - \frac{x^4}{12} + \frac{x^5}{120} \right) dx$$

$$= 1 - x + x^2 - \frac{x^3}{3} + \frac{x^4}{12} - \frac{x^5}{60} + \frac{x^6}{720}$$

When $x = 0.2$, we get

$$y^{(1)} = .82, \quad y^{(2)} = .83867, \quad y^{(3)} = .83740$$

$$y^{(4)} = .83746, \quad y^{(5)} = .83746$$

Thus, $y = .837$ when $x = .2$.

Example 3. *Use Picard's method to obtain y for x = 0.1. Given that:*

$$\frac{dy}{dx} = 3x + y^2; \; y = 1 \text{ at } x = 0.$$

Sol. Here $f(x, y) = 3x + y^2,\ x_0 = 0,\ y_0 = 1$

First approximation, $y^{(1)} = y_0 + \int_0^x f(x, y_0)\, dx$

$$= 1 + \int_0^x (3x + 1)\, dx$$

$$= 1 + x + \frac{3}{2} x^2$$

Second approximation, $y^{(2)} = 1 + x + \frac{5}{2}x^2 + \frac{4}{3}x^3 + \frac{3}{4}x^4 + \frac{9}{20}x^5$

Third approximation, $y^{(3)} = 1 + x + \frac{5}{2}x^2 + 2x^3 + \frac{23}{12}x^4 + \frac{25}{12}x^5$

$$+ \frac{68}{45}x^6 + \frac{1157}{1260}x^7 + \frac{17}{32}x^8 + \frac{47}{240}x^9$$

$$+ \frac{27}{400}x^{10} + \frac{81}{4400}x^{11}$$

when $x = 0.1$, we have

$$y^{(1)} = 1.115, \quad y^{(2)} = 1.1264, \quad y^{(3)} = 1.12721$$

Thus, $y = 1.127$ when $x = 0.1$.

Example 4. *If* $\frac{dy}{dx} = \frac{y - x}{y + x}$, *find the value of* y *at* $x = 0.1$ *using Picard's method. Given that* $y(0) = 1$.

Sol. First approximation,

$$y^{(1)} = y_0 + \int_0^x \frac{y_0 - x}{y_0 + x}\, dx = 1 + \int_0^x \left(\frac{1-x}{1+x}\right) dx$$

$$= 1 + \int_0^x \left(\frac{2}{1+x} - 1\right) dx$$

$$= 1 - x + 2 \log (1 + x)$$

Second approximation,

$$y^{(2)} = 1 + x - 2 \int_0^x \frac{x\, dx}{1 + 2\log(1+x)}$$

which is difficult to integrate.

Thus, when, $x = 0.1$, $y^{(1)} = 1 - 0.1 + 2 \log (1.1) = 0.9828$

Here in this example, only I approximation can be obtained and so it gives the approximate value of y for $x = 0.1$.

Example 5. *Solve* $\frac{dy}{dx} = 1 + xy$ *with* $x_0 = 2$, $y_0 = 0$ *using Picard's method of successive approximations.*

Sol. Here,
$$y^{(1)} = y_0 + \int_2^x f(x, y_0)\, dx = 0 + \int_2^x [1 + x(0)]\, dx = x - 2$$

$$y^{(2)} = 0 + \int_2^x \{1 + x(x-2)\}\, dx$$

$$= \left(x - x^2 + \frac{x^3}{3}\right)_2^x = -\frac{2}{3} + x - x^2 + \frac{x^3}{3}$$

And third approximation,

$$y^{(3)} = 0 + \int_2^x \{1 + x\, y^{(2)}\}\, dx$$

$$= -\frac{22}{15} + x - \frac{1}{3}x^2 + \frac{x^3}{3} - \frac{x^4}{4} + \frac{x^5}{15}$$

which is the required solution.

Example 6. *Obtain y when x = 0.1, x = 0.2, given that* $\frac{dy}{dx} = x + y;\ y(0) = 1$. *Check the result with exact value.*

Sol. We have
$$\frac{dy}{dx} = f(x, y) = x + y,\ x_0 = 0,\ y_0 = 1$$

Now first approximation,

$$y^{(1)} = 1 + \int_0^x (1 + x)\, dx = 1 + x + \frac{x^2}{2}$$

Second approximation,

$$y^{(2)} = 1 + \int_0^x \left(x + 1 + x + \frac{x^2}{2}\right) dx = 1 + x + x^2 + \frac{x^3}{6}$$

Third approximation,

$$y^{(3)} = 1 + x + x^2 + \frac{x^3}{3} + \frac{x^4}{24}$$

When $x = .1$, $y^{(1)} = 1.105$

$y^{(2)} = 1.11016$

$y^{(3)} = 1.11033$ (closer appr.)

When $\quad x = .2,$

$$y^{(3)} = 1.2427$$

We can continue further to get the better approximations. Now we shall obtain exact value.

$\frac{dy}{dx} - y = x$ is the given differential equation. General sol. is

$$ye^{-x} = -e^{-x}(1 + x) + c \qquad | \text{ I.F.} = e^{-x}$$

Putting $\quad y = 1, \quad x = 0 \quad$ we obtain, $c = 2$

$\therefore \quad y = -x - 1 + 2e^{x}$

When $\quad x = 0.1, \quad y = 1.11034$

and $\quad x = 0.2, \quad y = 1.24281$

These results reveal that the approximations obtained for $x = 0.1$ is correct to four decimal places while that for $x = 0.2$ is correct to 3 decimal places.

Example 7. *Find the solution of* $\frac{dy}{dx} = 1 + xy$, $y(0) = 1$ *which passes through (0, 1) in the interval (0, 0.5) such that the value of y is correct to three decimal places (use the whole interval as one interval only). Take h = 0.1.*

Sol. The given initial value problem is

$$\frac{dy}{dx} = f(x, y) = 1 + xy; \quad y(0) = 1$$

i.e., $\quad y = y_0 = 1 \quad \text{at} \quad x = x_0 = 0$

Here, $\quad y^{(1)} = 1 + x + \frac{x^2}{2}$

$$y^{(2)} = 1 + x + \frac{x^2}{2} + \frac{x^3}{3} + \frac{x^4}{8}$$

$$y^{(3)} = 1 + x + \frac{x^2}{2} + \frac{x^3}{3} + \frac{x^4}{8} + \frac{x^5}{15} + \frac{x^6}{48}$$

$$y^{(4)} = y^{(3)} + \frac{x^7}{105} + \frac{x^8}{384}$$

when $x = 0$, $\quad y = 1.000$

$x = 0.1, \quad y^{(1)} = 1.105, \quad y^{(2)} = 1.1053 \ldots.$

$\therefore \quad y = 1.105 \qquad$ (correct up to 3 decimals)

$x = 0.2, \quad y^{(1)} = 1.220, \quad y^{(2)} = 1.223 = y^{(3)}$

$\therefore \qquad y = 1.223$ (correct up to 3 decimals)

$x = 0.3, \quad y = 1.355 \quad \text{as} \quad y^{(2)} = 1.355 = y^{(3)}$

$x = 0.4, \quad y = 1.505$ (similarly)

$x = 0.5, \quad y = 1.677 \quad \text{as} \quad y^{(4)} = y^{(3)} = 1.677$

Thus,

x	0	0.1	0.2	0.3	0.4	0.5
y	1.000	1.105	1.223	1.355	1.505	1.677

We have numerically solved the given differential eqn. for x = 0, .1, .2, .3, .4, and .5.

6.7 PICARD'S METHOD FOR SIMULTANEOUS FIRST ORDER DIFFERENTIAL EQUATIONS

Let $\quad \dfrac{dy}{dx} = \phi(x, y, z) \quad \text{and} \quad \dfrac{dz}{dx} = f(x, y, z)$

be the simultaneous differential eqns. with initial conditions $y(x_0) = y_0$; $z(x_0) = z_0$.

Picard's method gives

$$y^{(1)} = y_0 + \int_{x_0}^{x} \phi(x, y_0, z_0)\, dx; \qquad z^{(1)} = z_0 + \int_{x_0}^{x} f(x, y_0, z_0)\, dx$$

$$y^{(2)} = y_0 + \int_{x_0}^{x} \phi\{x, y^{(1)}, z^{(1)}\}\, dx; \qquad z^{(2)} = z_0 + \int_{x_0}^{x} f\{x, y^{(1)}, z^{(1)}\}\, dx$$

and so on as successive approximations.

EXAMPLES

Example 1. *Approximate y and z by using Picard's method for the particular solution of* $\dfrac{dy}{dx} = x + z$, $\dfrac{dz}{dx} = x - y^2$ *given that* $y = 2$, $z = 1$ *when* $x = 0$.

Sol. Let $\qquad \phi(x, y, z) = x + z,\ f(x, y, z) = x - y^2$

Here, $\qquad x_0 = 0,\ y_0 = 2,\ z_0 = 1$

We have, $\qquad \dfrac{dy}{dx} = \phi(x, y, z) \ \Rightarrow\ y = y_0 + \int_{x_0}^{x} \phi(x, y, z)\, dx$

Also, $$\frac{dz}{dx} = f(x, y, z) \Rightarrow z = z_0 + \int_{x_0}^{x} f(x, y, z)\, dx$$

First approximation,

$$y^{(1)} = y_0 + \int_{x_0}^{x} \phi(x, y_0, z_0)\, dx = 2 + \int_0^x (x + z_0)\, dx$$

$$= 2 + \int_0^x (x + 1)\, dx = 2 + x + \frac{x^2}{2}$$

and $$z^{(1)} = z_0 + \int_{x_0}^{x} f(x, y_0, z_0)\, dx = 1 + \int_0^x (x - y_0^2)\, dx$$

$$= 1 + \int_0^x (x - 4)\, dx = 1 - 4x + \frac{x^2}{2}$$

Second approximation,

$$y^{(2)} = y_0 + \int_{x_0}^{x} \phi\{x, y^{(1)}, z^{(1)}\}\, dx$$

$$= 2 + \int_0^x \{x + z^{(1)}\}\, dx$$

$$= 2 + \int_0^x \left(x + 1 - 4x + \frac{x^2}{2}\right) dx$$

$$= 2 + x - \frac{3}{2}x^2 + \frac{x^3}{6}$$

$$z^{(2)} = z_0 + \int_{x_0}^{x} f\{x, y^{(1)}, z^{(1)}\}\, dx$$

$$= 1 + \int_0^x \left[x - \left(2 + x + \frac{x^2}{2}\right)^2\right] dx$$

$$= 1 - 4x - \frac{3}{2}x^2 - x^3 - \frac{x^4}{4} - \frac{x^5}{20}.$$

Example 2. *Solve by Picard's method, the differential equations*

$$\frac{dy}{dx} = z, \quad \frac{dz}{dx} = x^3 (y + z)$$

where $y = 1$, $z = \frac{1}{2}$ *at* $x = 0$. *Obtain the values of y and z from III approximation when* $x = 0.2$ *and* $x = 0.5$.

Sol. Let $\phi(x, y, z) = z, \quad f(x, y, z) = x^3(y + z)$

Here $x_0 = 0, \quad y_0 = 1, \quad z_0 = \frac{1}{2}$

First approximation,

$$y^{(1)} = y_0 + \int_0^x \phi(x, y_0, z_0)\, dx = 1 + \int_0^x z_0\, dx$$

$$= 1 + \frac{1}{2} x$$

$$z^{(1)} = z_0 + \int_0^x f(x, y_0, z_0)\, dx = \frac{1}{2} + \int_0^x x^3 (y_0 + z_0)\, dx$$

$$= \frac{1}{2} + \frac{3}{2} \frac{x^4}{4}.$$

Second approximation,

$$y^{(2)} = 1 + \int_0^x z^{(1)}\, dx = 1 + \int_0^x \left(\frac{1}{2} + \frac{3}{8} x^4 \right) dx$$

$$= 1 + \frac{x}{2} + \frac{3}{40} x^5$$

$$z^{(2)} = \frac{1}{2} + \int_0^x x^3 \{y^{(1)} + z^{(1)}\}\, dx$$

$$= \frac{1}{2} + \int_0^x x^3 \left(\frac{3}{2} + \frac{x}{2} + \frac{3}{8} x^4 \right) dx$$

$$= \frac{1}{2} + \frac{3}{8} x^4 + \frac{x^5}{10} + \frac{3}{64} x^8$$

Third approximation,

$$y^{(3)} = 1 + \int_0^x z^{(2)}\, dx = 1 + \int_0^x \left(\frac{1}{2} + \frac{3x^4}{8} + \frac{x^5}{10} + \frac{3x^8}{64} \right) dx$$

$$= 1 + \frac{x}{2} + \frac{3}{40} x^5 + \frac{x^6}{60} + \frac{3x^9}{576}$$

$$z^{(3)} = \frac{1}{2} + \int_0^x x^3 \{y^{(2)} + z^{(2)}\}\, dx$$

$$= \frac{1}{2} + \int_0^x x^3 \left\{ \frac{3}{2} + \frac{x}{2} + \frac{3}{8} x^4 + \frac{7}{40} x^5 + \frac{3}{64} x^8 \right\} dx$$

$$= \frac{1}{2} + \frac{3}{2} \cdot \frac{x^4}{4} + \frac{1}{2} \cdot \frac{x^5}{5} + \frac{3}{8} \cdot \frac{x^8}{8} + \frac{7}{40} \cdot \frac{x^9}{9} + \frac{3}{64} \cdot \frac{x^{12}}{12}$$

$$= \frac{1}{2} + \frac{3}{8}x^4 + \frac{x^5}{10} + \frac{3}{64}x^8 + \frac{7}{360}x^9 + \frac{3}{768}x^{12}$$

when $x = 0.2$

$$y^{(3)} = 1 + 0.1 + \frac{3}{40}(0.2)^5 + \frac{(0.2)^6}{60} + \frac{3}{576}(0.2)^9$$

$$= 1.100024 \text{ (leaving higher terms)}$$

$$z^{(3)} = \frac{1}{2} + \frac{3}{8}(.2)^4 + \frac{(.2)^5}{10} + \frac{3}{64}(.2)^8 + \frac{7}{360}(.2)^9 + \frac{3}{768}(.2)^{12}$$

$$= .500632 \text{ (leaving higher terms)}$$

when $x = 0.5$

$$y^{(3)} = 1 + \frac{.5}{2} + \frac{3}{40}(.5)^5 + \frac{(.5)^6}{60} + \frac{3}{576}(.5)^9$$

$$= 1.25234375$$

$$z^{(3)} = \frac{1}{2} + \frac{3}{8}(.5)^4 + \frac{(.5)^5}{10} + \frac{3}{64}(.5)^8 + \frac{7}{360}(.5)^9 + \frac{3}{768}(.5)^{12}$$

$$= .5234375.$$

ASSIGNMENT 6.1

1. For the differential equation $\frac{dy}{dx} = x - y^2,\ y(0) = 0$

   Calculate $y(0.2)$ by Picard's method to third approximations and round-off the value at the 4th place of decimals.

2. Find $y(0.2)$ if $\frac{dy}{dx} = \log(x + y)$; $y(0) = 1$. Use Picard's method.

3. Employ Picard's method to obtain the solution of $\frac{dy}{dx} = x^2 + y^2$ for $x = 0.1$ correct to four decimal places, given that $y = 0$ when $x = 0$.

4. Find an approximate value of y when $x = 0.1$ if $\frac{dy}{dx} = x - y^2$ and $y = 1$ at $x = 0$ using Picard's method.

5. Solve numerically $\frac{dy}{dx} = 2x - y,\ y(0) = 0.9$ at $x = 0.4$ by Picard's method with three iterations and compare the result with the exact value.

6. Employ Picard's method to find $y\ (0.2)$ and $y\ (0.4)$ given that $\frac{dy}{dx} = 1 + y^2$ and $y\ (0) = 0$.

7. Explain Picard's method of successive approximation for numerical solution of ordinary differential equations.

8. Approximate y and z by using Picard's method for the solution of simultaneous differential equations

$$\frac{dy}{dx} = 2x + z, \quad \frac{dz}{dx} = 3xy + x^2z$$

with $y = 2$, $z = 0$ at $x = 0$ up to third approximation.

9. Using Picard's method, obtain the solution of $\frac{dy}{dx} = x(1 + x^3y)$, $y\,(0) = 3$

Tabulate the values of $y(0.1)$, $y(0.2)$.

6.8 EULER'S METHOD

Euler's method is the simplest one-step method and has a limited application because of its low accuracy. This method yields solution of an ordinary differential equation in the form of a set of tabulated values.

In this method, we determine the change Δy is y corresponding to small increase in the argument x. Consider the differential equation

$$\frac{dy}{dx} = f(x, y), \quad y(x_0) = y_0 \tag{7}$$

Let $y = g(x)$ be the solution of (7). Let $x_0, x_1, x_2, \ldots\ldots$ be equidistant values of x.

In this method, we use the property that in a small interval, a curve is nearly a straight line. Thus at the point (x_0, y_0), we approximate the curve by the tangent at the point (x_0, y_0).

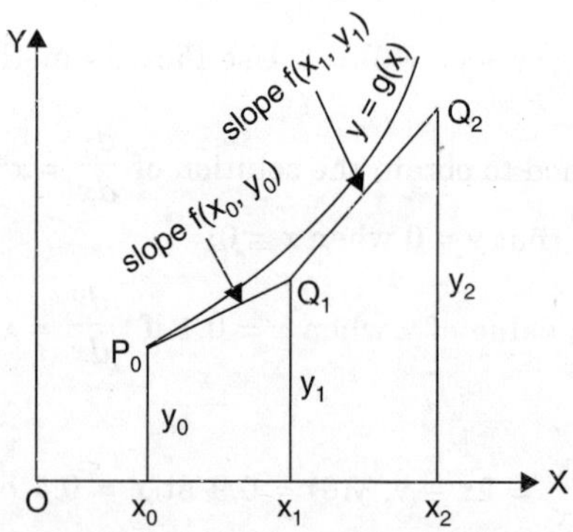

The eqn. of the tangent at $P_0(x_0, y_0)$ is

$$y - y_0 = \left(\frac{dy}{dx}\right)_{P_0} (x - x_0) = f(x_0, y_0)\,(x - x_0)$$

$$\Rightarrow \qquad y = y_0 + (x - x_0)\, f(x_0, y_0) \tag{8}$$

This gives the y-coordinate of any point on the tangent. Since the curve is approximated by the tangent in the interval (x_0, x_1), the value of y on the curve corresponding to $x = x_1$ is given by the above value of y in eqn. (8) approximately.

Putting $x = x_1 (= x_0 + h)$ in eqn. (8), we get

$$y_1 = y_0 + hf(x_0, y_0)$$

Thus Q_1 is (x_1, y_1)

Similarly, approximating the curve in the next interval (x_1, x_2) by a line through $Q_1(x_1, y_1)$ with slope $f(x_1, y_1)$, we get

$$y_2 = y_1 + hf(x_1, y_1)$$

In general, it can be shown that,

$$\boxed{y_{n+1} = y_n + hf(x_n, y_n)}$$

This is called Euler's Formula.

A great disadvantage of this method lies in the fact that if $\frac{dy}{dx}$ changes rapidly over an interval, its value at the beginning of the interval may give a poor approximation as compared to its average value over the interval and thus the value of y calculated from Euler's method may be in much error from its true value. These errors accumulate in the succeeding intervals and the value of y becomes erroneous.

NOTE *In Euler's method, the curve of the actual solution $y = g(x)$ is approximated by a sequence of short lines. The process is very slow. If h is not properly chosen, the curve $P_0Q_1Q_2$ ...... of short lines representing numerical solution deviates significantly from the curve of actual solution.*

To avoid this error, **Euler's modified method** is preferred because in this, we consider the curvature of the actual curve inplace of approximating the curve by sequence of short lines.

6.9 ALGORITHM OF EULER'S METHOD

```
1. Function F(x,y)=(x-y)/(x+y)
2. Input x0,y0,h,xn
3. n=((xn-x0)/h)+1
4. For i=1,n
5. y=y0+h*F(x0,y0)
6. x=x+h
```

```
 7. Print x0,y0
 8. If x<xn then
          x0=x
          y0=y
      ELSE
 9. Next i
10. Stop
```

6.10 FLOW-CHART OF EULER'S METHOD

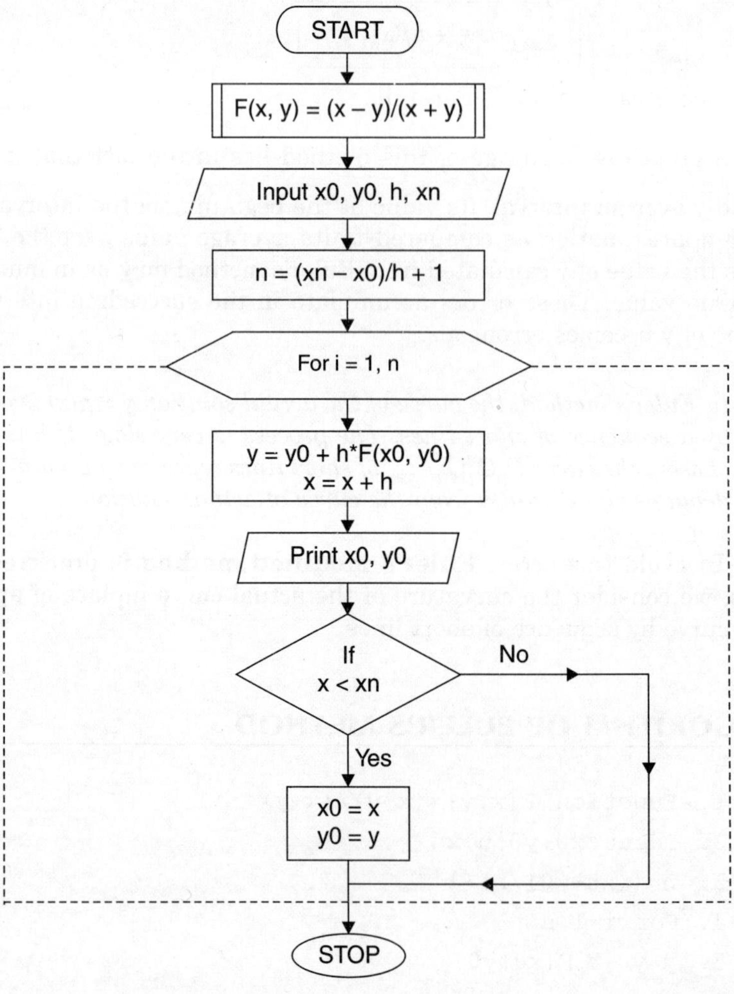

6.11 PROGRAM OF EULER'S METHOD

```
#include<stdio.h>
#define F(x,y)  (x-y)/(x+y)
main ( )
{
int i,n;
float x0,y0,h,xn,x,y;
printf("\n Enter the values: x0,y0,h,xn: \n");
scanf  ("%f%f%f%f",&x0,&y0,&h,&xn);
n=(xn-x0)/h+1;
for  (i=1;i<=n;i++)
 {
 y=y0+h*F(x0,y0);
 x=x0+h;
 printf("\n  X=%f  Y=%f",x0,y0);
   if(x<xn)
   {
   x0=x;
   y0=y;
   }
 }
return;
}
```

6.11.1 Output

```
Enter the values: x0,y0,h,xn:
0 1 0.02 0.1
X=0.000000  Y=1.000000
X=0.020000  Y=0.980000
X=0.040000  Y=0.960800
X=0.060000  Y=0.942399
X=0.080000  Y=0.924793
X=0.100000  Y=0.907978
```

6.11.2 Notations used in the Program

(*i*) $\mathbf{x_0}$ is the initial value of x.

(*ii*) $\mathbf{y_0}$ is the initial value of y.

(*iii*) **h** is the spacing value of x.

(*iv*) $\mathbf{x_n}$ is the last value of x at which value of y is required.

6.12 MODIFIED EULER'S METHOD

The modified Euler's method gives greater improvement in accuracy over the original Euler's method. Here the core idea is that we use a line through (x_0, y_0) whose slope is the average of the slopes at (x_0, y_0) and $(x_1, y_1^{(1)})$ where $y_1^{(1)} = y_0 + hf(x_0, y_0)$. This line approximates the curve in the interval (x_0, x_1).

Geometrically, if L_1 is the tangent at (x_0, y_0), L_2 is a line through $(x_1, y_1^{(1)})$ of slope $f(x_1, y_1^{(1)})$ and $\bar{L}$ is the line through $(x_1, y_1^{(1)})$ but with a slope equal to the average of $f(x_0, y_0)$ and $f(x_1, y_1^{(1)})$ then the line L through (x_0, y_0) and parallel to $\bar{L}$ is used to approximate the curve in the interval (x_0, x_1). Thus the ordinate of the point B will give the value of y_1. Now, the eqn. of the line AL is given by

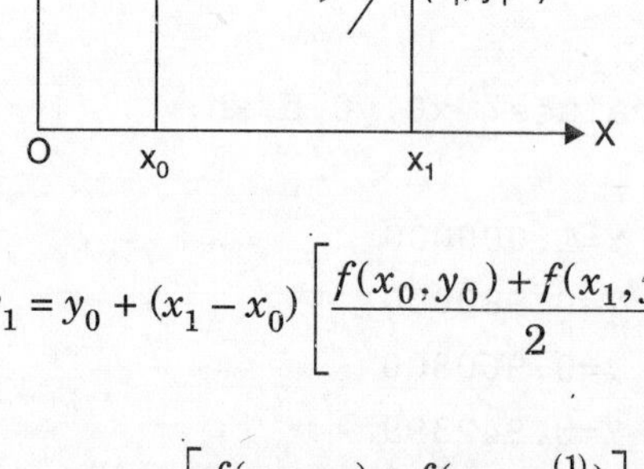

$$y_1 = y_0 + (x_1 - x_0)\left[\frac{f(x_0, y_0) + f(x_1, y_1^{(1)})}{2}\right]$$

$$= y_0 + h\left[\frac{f(x_0, y_0) + f(x_1, y_1^{(1)})}{2}\right]$$

A generalised form of Euler's modified formula is

$$y_1^{(n+1)} = y_0 + \frac{h}{2}\,[f(x_0, y_0) + f(x_1, y_1^{(n)})]\ ;\ n - 0, 1, 2, ...$$

where $y_1^{(n)}$ is the nth approximation to y_1.

The above iteration formula can be started by choosing $y_1^{(1)}$ from Euler's formula

$$y_1^{(1)} = y_0 + hf(x_0, y_0)$$

Since this formula attempts to correct the values of y_{n+1} using the predicted value of y_{n+1} (by Euler's method), it is classified as a one-step predictor-corrector method.

6.13 ALGORITHM OF MODIFIED EULER'S METHOD

```
 1. Function F(x)=(x-y)/(x+y)
 2. Input x(1),y(1),h,xn
 3. yp=y(1)+h*F(x(1),y(1))
 4. itr=(xn-x(1))/h
 5. Print x(1),y(1)
 6. For i=1,itr
 7. x(i+1)=x(i)+h
 8. For n=1,50
 9. yc(n+1)=y(i)+(h/2*(F(x(i),y(i))+F(x(i+1),yp))
10. Print n,yc(n+1)
11. p=yc (n+1)-yp
12. If abs(p)<.0001 then
              goto Step 14
        ELSE
              yp=yc(n+1)
13. Next n
14. y(i+1)=yc(n+1)
15. print x(i+1),yp
16. Next i
17. Stop
```

6.14 FLOW-CHART OF MODIFIED EULER'S METHOD

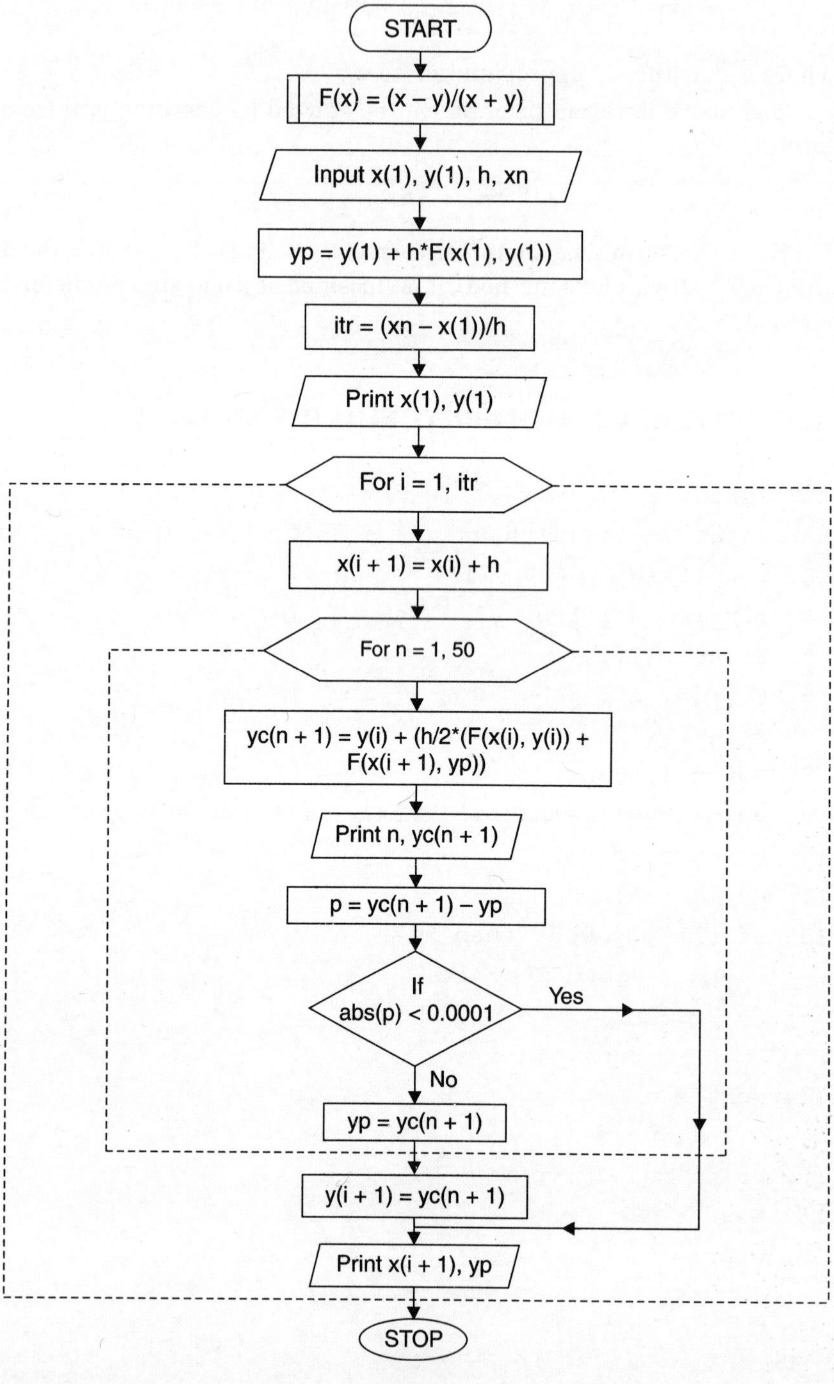

6.15 PROGRAM OF MODIFIED EULER'S METHOD

```
#include<stdio.h>
#include<math.h>
#define F(x,y) (x-y)/(x+y)
main ()
{
int i,n,itr ;
float x[5],y[50],yc[50],h,yp,p,xn;
printf("\n Enter the values: x[1],y[1],h,xn:\n");
scanf("%f%f%f%f",&x[1],&y[1],&h,&xn);
yp=y[1]+h*F(x[1],y[1]);
itr=(xn-x[1])/h;
printf("\n\n X=%f Y=%f\n",x[1],y[1];
for (i=1;i<=itr;i++)
 {
  x[i+1]=x[i]+h;
  for (n=1;n<=50;n++)
      {
yc[n+1]=y[i]+(h/2.0)*(F(x[i],y[i])+F(x[i+1],yp));
printf("\nN=%d Y=%f",n,yc[n+1]);
p=yc[n+1]-yp;
if(fabs (p)<0.0001)
      goto next;
 else
 yp=yc[n+1];
    }
  next:
y[i+1]=yc[n+1];
printf("\n\n X=%f Y=%f\n",x[i+1], yp);
 }
return;
}
```

6.15.1 Output

```
Enter the values: x[1],y[1],h,xn:
0 1 0.02 0.06
          X=0.000000      Y=1.000000
N=1    Y=0.980400
N=2    Y=0.980400
          X=0.020000      Y=0.980400
N=1    Y=0.961584
N=2    Y=0.961598
          X=0.040000      Y=0.961584
N=1    Y=0.943572
N=2    Y=0.943593
          X=0.060000      Y=0.943572
```

6.15.2 Notations used in the Program

(*i*) **x(1)** is an array of the initial value of x.

(*ii*) **y(1)** is an array of the initial value of y.

(*iii*) **h** is the spacing value of x.

(*iv*) $\mathbf{x_n}$ is the last value of x at which value of y is required.

EXAMPLES

Example 1. *Given* $\dfrac{dy}{dx} = \dfrac{y-x}{y+x}$ *with* $y = 1$ *for* $x = 0$. *Find* y *approximately for* $x = 0.1$ *by Euler's method.*

Sol. We have

$$\frac{dy}{dx} = f(x, y) = \frac{y-x}{y+x}\ ;\ x_0 = 0,\ y_0 = 1,\ h = 0.1$$

Hence the approximate value of y at $x = 0.1$ is given by

$$y_1 = y_0 + hf(x_0, y_0) \qquad |\ \text{using } y_{n+1} = y_n + hf(x_n, y_n)$$

$$= 1 + (.1) + \left(\frac{1-0}{1+0}\right) = 1.1$$

Much better accuracy is obtained by breaking up the interval 0 to 0.1 into five steps. The approximate value of y at $x_A = .02$ is given by,

$$y_1 = y_0 + hf(x_0, y_0)$$

$$= 1 + (.02)\left(\frac{1-0}{1+0}\right) = 1.02$$

At $x_B = 0.04$, $\quad y_2 = y_1 + hf(x_1, y_1)$

$$= 1.02 + (.02)\left(\frac{1.02-.02}{1.02+.02}\right) = 1.0392$$

At $x_C = .06$, $\quad y_3 = 1.0392 + (.02)\left(\frac{1.0392-.04}{1.0392+.04}\right) = 1.0577$

At $x_D = .08$, $\quad y_4 = 1.0577 + (.02)\left(\frac{1.0577-.06}{1.0577+.06}\right) = 1.0756$

At $x_E = .1$, $\quad y_5 = 1.0756 + (.02)\left(\frac{1.0756-.08}{1.0756+.08}\right) = 1.0928$

Hence $y = 1.0928$ when $x = 0.1$

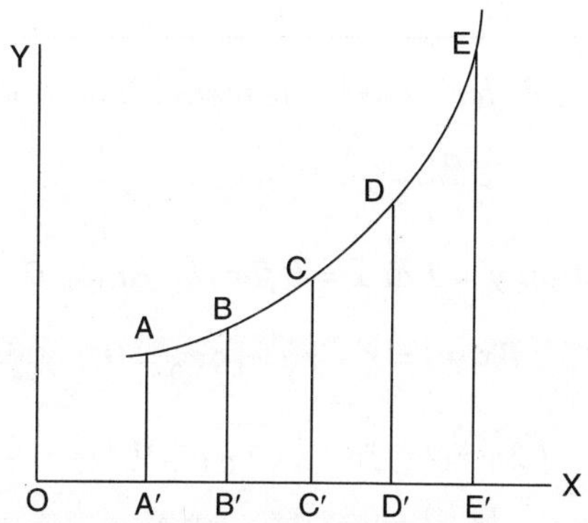

Example 2. *Solve the equation* $\frac{dy}{dx} = 1 - y$ *with the initial condition* $x = 0, y = 0$ *using Euler's algorithm and tabulate the solutions at* $x = 0.1, 0.2, 0.3$.

Sol. Here, $\quad f(x, y) = 1 - y$

Taking $h = 0.1, x_0 = 0, y_0 = 0$, we obtain

$$y_1 = y_0 + hf(x_0, y_0)$$

$$= 0 + (.1)(1 - 0) = .1$$

$\therefore \quad y(0.1) = 0.1$

Again, $y_2 = y_1 + hf(x_1, y_1)$

$= 0.1 + (0.1)(1 - .1)$

$= 0.1 + .09 = .19$

$\therefore \quad y(0.2) = 0.19$

Again, $y_3 = y_2 + hf(x_2, y_2)$

$= .19 + (.1)(1 - .19)$

$= .19 + (.1)(.81) = .271$

$\therefore \quad y(0.3) = .271$

Tabulated values are

x	$y(x)$
0	0
0.1	0.1
0.2	0.19
0.3	0.271

Example 3. *Using Euler's modified method, obtain a solution of the equation*

$$\frac{dy}{dx} = x + |\sqrt{y}| = f(x, y)$$

with initial condition $y = 1$ at $x = 0$ for the range $0 \le x \le 0.6$ in steps of 0.2.

Sol. Here $f(x, y) = x + |\sqrt{y}|$; $x_0 = 0, \quad y_0 = 1, \quad h = .2$

$\therefore \quad f(x_0, y_0) = x_0 + |\sqrt{y_0}| = 0 + 1 = 1$

We have $y_1^{(1)} = y_0 + hf(x_0, y_0)$

$= 1 + (.2) . 1 = 1.2$

$\therefore \quad f(x_1, y_1^{(1)}) = x_1 + |\sqrt{y_1^{(1)}}|$

$= 0.2 + |\sqrt{1.2}| = 1.2954$

The second approximation to y_1 is

$$y_1^{(2)} = y_0 + h\left[\frac{f(x_0, y_0) + f\{x_1, y_1^{(1)}\}}{2}\right]$$

$$= 1 + (0.2)\left(\frac{1 + 1.2954}{2}\right) = 1.2295$$

Again, $f\{x_1, y_1^{(2)}\} = x_1 + |\sqrt{y_1}^{(2)}| = 0.2 + \sqrt{1.2295} = 1.3088$

So, $y_1^{(3)} = y_0 + \frac{h}{2}[f(x_0, y_0) + f\{x_1, y_1^{(2)}\}]$

$= 1 + \frac{0.2}{2}[1 + 1.3088] = 1.2309$

We have $f\{x_1, y_1^{(3)}\} = 0.2 + \sqrt{1.2309} = 1.309$

Then $y_1^{(4)} = 1 + \frac{.2}{2}[1 + 1.309] = 1.2309$

Since, $y_1^{(4)} = y_1^{(3)}$ hence $y_1 = 1.2309$

Now, $y_2^{(1)} = y_1 + hf(x_1, y_1)$

$= 1.2309 + (0.2)[0.2 + \sqrt{1.2309}]$

$= 1.4927$ $\quad | \because \; x_1 = 0.2$

$f\{x_2, y_2^{(1)}\} = x_2 + \sqrt{y_2^{(1)}} = 0.4 + \sqrt{1.4927}$

$= 1.622$ $\quad | \because \; x_2 = 0.4$

Then, $y_2^{(2)} = y_1 + \frac{h}{2}[f(x_1, y_1) + f\{x_2, y_2^{(1)}\}]$

$= 1.2309 + \frac{0.2}{2}[(.2 + \sqrt{1.2309}) + 1.622] = 1.524$

Now, $y_2^{(3)} = y_1 + \frac{h}{2}[f(x_1, y_1) + f\{x_2, y_2^{(2)}\}]$

$= 1.2309 + \frac{0.2}{2}[(.2 + \sqrt{1.2309}) + (.4 + \sqrt{1.524})]$

$= 1.5253$

$y_2^{(4)} = 1.2309 + \frac{0.2}{2}[(.2 + \sqrt{1.2309}) + (.4 + \sqrt{1.5253})]$

Since, $y_2^{(4)} = y_2^{(3)}$ hence $y_2 = 1.5253$

Now, $y_3^{(1)} = y_2 + hf(x_2, y_2)$

$= 1.5253 + (0.2)[.4 + \sqrt{1.5253}] = 1.8523$

$y_3^{(2)} = y_2 + \frac{h}{2}[f(x_2, y_2) + f\{x_3, y_3^{(1)}\}]$

$= 1.5253 + \frac{0.2}{2}[(.4 + \sqrt{1.5253}) + (.6 + \sqrt{1.8523})]$

$= 1.8849$

Similarly, $y_3^{(3)} = 1.8861 = y_3^{(4)}$

Since, $y_3^{(3)} = y_3^{(4)}$

Hence, we take $y_3 = 1.8861.$

Example 4. *Given that* $\frac{dy}{dx} = \log_{10}(x + y)$ *with the initial condition that* $y = 1$ *when* $x = 0$*. Find* y *for* $x = 0.2$ *and* $x = 0.5$ *using Euler's modified formula.*

Sol. Let $x = 0$, $x_1 = 0.2$, $x_2 = .5$ then $y_0 = 1$

y_1 and y_2 are yet to be computed.

Here, $f(x, y) = \log (x + y)$

$\therefore \quad f(x_0, y_0) = \log 1 = 0$

$\therefore \quad y_1^{(1)} = y_0 + hf(x_0, y_0) = 1$

$$f\{x_1, y_1^{(1)}\} = \log \{x_1 + y_1^{(1)}\} = \log (.2 + 1) = \log (1.2)$$

$$\therefore \quad y_1^{(2)} = y_0 + \frac{h}{2} [f(x_0, y_0) + f\{x_1, y_1^{(1)}\}]$$

$$= 1 + \frac{.2}{2} [0 + \log (1.2)] = 1.0079$$

Also, $$y_1^{(3)} = 1 + \frac{.2}{2} [0 + \log (.2 + 1.0079)] = 1.0082$$

$$y_1^{(4)} = 1 + \frac{.2}{2} [0 + \log (.2 + 1.0082)] = 1.0082$$

Since, $y_1^{(4)} = y_1^{(3)}$ hence $y_1 = 1.0082$

To obtain y_2, the value of y at $x = 0.5$, we take,

$$y_2^{(1)} = y_1 + hf(x_1, y_1)$$

$$= 1.0082 + 0.3 \log (.2 + 1.0082)$$

$$= 1.0328 \qquad (\because \ h = .5 - .2 = .3 \text{ here})$$

Now, $$y_2^{(2)} = y_1 + \frac{h}{2} [f(x_1, y_1) + f\{x_2, y_2^{(1)}\}]$$

$$= 1.0082 + \frac{.3}{2} [\log (.2 + 1.0082) + \log (.5 + 1.0328)]$$

$$= 1.0082 + 0.0401 = 1.0483$$

Also, $$y_2^{(3)} = 1.0082 + \frac{.3}{2} [\log (.2 + 1.0082) + \log (.5 + 1.0483)]$$

$$= 1.0082 + .0408 = 1.0490$$

Similarly, $y_2^{(4)} = 1.0490$

Since, $y_2^{(3)} = y_2^{(4)}$ hence, $y_2 = 1.0490$.

Example 5. *Given :* $\frac{dy}{dx} = x - y^2$ *; y(.2) = 0.2, find y(.4) by modified Euler's method correct to 3 decimal places, taking h = 0.2.*

Sol. Here, $f(x, y) = x - y^2$; $x_0 = 0.2$, $y_0 = .02$ and $h = 0.2$

Let $x_1 = 0.4$ then we are to find $y_1 = y(0.4)$

We have $f(x_0, y_0) = x_0 - y_0^2 = 0.2 - (.02)^2 = 0.2 - .0004 = 0.1996$

$$\therefore \quad y_1^{(1)} = y_0 + hf(x_0, y_0) = .02 + (.2)(.1996) = .060$$

$$f\{x_1, y_1^{(1)}\} = x_1 - \{y_1^{(1)}\}^2 = .4 - (.06)^2 = .3964$$

$$\therefore \quad y_1^{(2)} = y_0 + \frac{h}{2}[f(x_0, y_0) + f\{x_1, y_1^{(1)}\}]$$

$$= .02 + \frac{.2}{2}[.1996 + .3964] = .0796 \simeq .080$$

Now, $f\{x_1, y_1^{(2)}\} = x_1 - [y_1^{(2)}]^2 = .4 - (.08)^2 = .3936$

$$\therefore \quad y_1^{(3)} = y_0 + \frac{h}{2}[f(x_0, y_0) + f\{x_1, y_1^{(2)}\}]$$

$$= .02 + \frac{.2}{2}[.1996 + .3936] = .07932 \simeq .079$$

$$f\{x_1, y_1^{(3)}\} = x_1 - [y_1^{(3)}]^2 = .4 - (.079)^2 = .3938$$

$$\therefore \quad y_1^{(4)} = y_0 + \frac{h}{2}[f(x_0, y_0) + f\{x_1, y_1^{(3)}\}]$$

$$= .02 + \frac{.2}{2}[.1996 + .3938] = .0793 \simeq .079$$

Since $y_1^{(3)} = y_1^{(4)}$ hence $y_1 = .079$.

ASSIGNMENT 6.2

1. Find y for $x = 0.2$ and $x = 0.5$ using modified Euler's method, given that

$$\frac{dy}{dx} = \log_e(x + y); \quad y(0) = 1$$

2. Taking $h = .05$, determine the value of y at $x = 0.1$ by Euler's modified method, given that,

$$\frac{dy}{dx} = x^2 + y; \quad y(0) = 1$$

3. Given $\frac{dy}{dx} = x^2 + y$, $y(0) = 1$, find $y(.02)$, $y(.04)$ and $y(.06)$ using Euler's modified method.

4. Apply Euler's method to the initial value problem $\frac{dy}{dx} = x + y$, $y(0) = 0$ at $x = 0$ to $x = 1.0$ taking $h = 0.2$.

5. Use Euler's method with $h = 0.1$ to solve the differential equation $\frac{dy}{dx} = x^2 + y^2$, $y(0) = 1$ in the range $x = 0$ to $x = 0.3$.

6. Solve for y at $x = 1.05$ by Euler's method, the differential equation $\frac{dy}{dx} = 2 - \left(\frac{y}{x}\right)$ where $y = 2$ when $x = 1$. (Take $h = 0.05$).

7. Use Euler's modified method to compute y for $x = .05$ and $.10$. Given that $\frac{dy}{dx} = x + y$ with the initial condition $x_0 = 0$, $y_0 = 1$. Give the correct result up to 4 decimal places.

8. Using Euler's method, compute $y(0.04)$ for the differential eqn. $\frac{dy}{dx} = -y$; $y(0) = 1$. Take $h = 0.01$.

9. Compute $y(0.5)$ for the differential eqn. $\frac{dy}{dx} = y^2 - x^2$ with $y(0) = 1$ using Euler's method.

10. Find $y(2.2)$ using modified Euler's method for $\frac{dy}{dx} = -xy^2$; $y(2) = 1$. Take $h = .1$.

11. Given $\frac{dy}{dx} = x^3 + y, y(0) = 1$. Compute y (0.02) by Euler's method taking $h = 0.01$.

12. Find $y(1)$ by Euler's method from the differential equation $\frac{dy}{dx} = \frac{-y}{1+x}$ when $y(0.3) = 2$. Convert up to four decimal places taking step length $h = 0.1$.

6.16 TAYLOR'S METHOD

Consider the differential equation

$$\left.\begin{array}{l} \dfrac{dy}{dx} = f(x, y) \\ \text{with the initial condition } y(x_0) = y_0. \end{array}\right\} \quad (9)$$

If $y(x)$ is the exact solution of (9) then $y(x)$ can be expanded into a Taylor's series about the point $x = x_0$ as

$$y(x) = y_0 + (x - x_0)\, y_0' + \frac{(x - x_0)^2}{2!}\, y_0'' + \frac{(x - x_0)^3}{3!}\, y_0''' + \ldots\ldots \quad (10)$$

where dashes denote differentiation with respect to x.

Differentiating (9) successively with respect to x, we get

$$y'' = \frac{\partial f}{\partial x} + \frac{\partial f}{\partial y}\frac{dy}{dx} = \frac{\partial f}{\partial x} + f\frac{\partial f}{\partial y} = \left(\frac{\partial}{\partial x} + f\frac{\partial}{\partial y}\right)f \tag{11}$$

$$\therefore \quad y''' = \frac{d}{dx}(y'') = \left(\frac{\partial}{\partial x} + f\frac{\partial}{\partial y}\right)\left(\frac{\partial f}{\partial x} + f\frac{\partial f}{\partial y}\right)$$

$$= \frac{\partial^2 f}{\partial x^2} + \frac{\partial f}{\partial x}\frac{\partial f}{\partial y} + f\frac{\partial^2 f}{\partial x \partial y} + f\frac{\partial^2 f}{\partial y \partial x} + f\left(\frac{\partial f}{\partial y}\right)^2 + f^2\frac{\partial^2 f}{\partial y^2} \tag{12}$$

and so on.

Putting $x = x_0$ and $y = y_0$ in the expressions for $y', y'', y''', \ldots\ldots.$ and substituting them in eqn. (10), we get a power series for $y(x)$ in powers of $x - x_0$.

i.e.,

$$y(x) = y_0 + (x - x_0)y_0' + \frac{(x-x_0)^2}{2!}y_0'' + \frac{(x-x_0)^3}{3!}y_0''' + \ldots\ldots. \tag{13}$$

Putting $x = x_1 (= x_0 + h)$ in (13), we get

$$y_1 = y(x_1) = y_0 + hy_0' + \frac{h^2}{2!}y_0'' + \frac{h^3}{3!}y_0''' + \ldots\ldots. \tag{14}$$

Here $y_0', y_0'', y_0''', \ldots\ldots$ can be found by using (9) and its successive differentiations (11) and (12) at $x = x_0$. The series (14) can be truncated at any stage if h is small.

After obtaining y_1, we can calculate $y_1', y_1'', y_1''', \ldots\ldots$ from (9) at $x_1 = x_0 + h$.

Now, expanding $y(x)$ by Taylor's series about $x = x_1$, we get

$$y_2 = y_1 + hy'_1 + \frac{h^2}{2!}y_1'' + \frac{h^3}{3!}y_1''' + \ldots\ldots.$$

Proceeding, we get

$$y_n = y_{n-1} + hy_{n-1}' + \frac{h^2}{2!}y_{n-1}'' + \frac{h^3}{3!}y_{n-1}''' + \ldots\ldots..$$

Practically, this method is not of much importance because of its need of partial derivatives.

Moreover if we are interested in a better approximation with a small truncation error, the evaluation of higher order derivatives is needed which are complicated in evaluation. Besides its impracticability, it is useful in judging the degree of accuracy of the approximations given by other methods.

We can determine the extent to which any other formula agrees with the Taylor's series expansion. Taylor's method is one of those methods which yield the solution of a differential equation in the form of a power series. This method suffers from a serious disadvantage that h should be small enough so that successive terms in the series diminish quite rapidly.

6.17 TAYLOR'S METHOD FOR SIMULTANEOUS I ORDER DIFFERENTIAL EQUATIONS

Simultaneous differential equations of the type

$$\frac{dy}{dx} = f(x, y, z) \tag{15}$$

and

$$\frac{dz}{dx} = \phi(x, y, z) \tag{16}$$

with initial conditions $y(x_0) = y_0$ and $z(x_0) = z_0$

can be solved by Taylor's method.

If h is the step-size then

$$y_1 = y(x_0 + h) \quad \text{and} \quad z_1 = z(x_0 + h)$$

Taylor's algorithm for (15) and (16) gives

$$y_1 = y_0 + hy_0' + \frac{h^2}{2!} y_0'' + \frac{h^3}{3!} y_0''' + \ldots\ldots \tag{17}$$

and

$$z_1 = z_0 + hz_0' + \frac{h^2}{2!} z_0'' + \frac{h^3}{3!} z_0''' + \ldots\ldots \tag{18}$$

Differentiating (15) and (16) successively, we get y'', y''', ……., z'', z''', …… etc. So the values y_0'', y_0''', …… and z_0'', z_0''', …… can be obtained.

Substituting them in (17) and (18), we get y_1, z_1 for the next step.

$$y_2 = y_1 + hy_1' + \frac{h^2}{2!} y_1'' + \frac{h^3}{3!} y_1''' + \ldots\ldots$$

and

$$z_2 = z_1 + hz_1' + \frac{h^2}{2!} z_1'' + \frac{h^3}{3!} z_1''' + \ldots\ldots.$$

Since y_1 and z_1 are known, y_1', y_1'', y_1''' ……., z_1', z_1'', z_1''', ……. can be calculated. Hence y_2 and z_2 can be obtained. Proceeding in this manner, we get other values of y, step-by-step.

EXAMPLES

Example 1. *Use Taylor's series method to solve*

$$\frac{dy}{dx} = x + y;\ y(1) = 0$$

numerically up to x = 1.2 with h = 0.1. Compare the final result with the value of explicit solution.

Sol. Here, $x_0 = 1, y_0 = 0$

$$y' = x + y \quad i.e., \quad y_0' = x_0 + y_0 = 1$$

$$\Rightarrow \quad y'' = 1 + y' \quad i.e., \quad y_0'' = 1 + y_0' = 2$$

$$\Rightarrow \quad y''' = y'' \quad i.e., \quad y_0''' = y_0'' = 2$$

$$\Rightarrow \quad y^{(iv)} = y''' \quad i.e., \quad y_0^{(iv)} = 2$$

$$\Rightarrow \quad y^{(v)} = y^{(iv)} \quad i.e., \quad y_0^{(v)} = 2$$

By Taylor's series, we have

$$y_1 = y_0 + hy_0' + \frac{h^2}{2!} y_0'' + \frac{h^3}{3!} y_0''' + \frac{h^4}{4!} y_0^{(iv)} + \ldots\ldots$$

$$y(1 + h) = 0 + (0.1)\,1 + \frac{(0.1)^2}{2!}\,2 + \frac{(0.1)^3}{3!}\,2 + \frac{(0.1)^4}{4!}\,2 + \ldots\ldots$$

$$\Rightarrow \quad y(1.1) = 0.1103081 = 0.110 \text{ (app.)}$$

Also, $x_1 = x_0 + h = 1.1$

Again, $y_1' = x_1 + y_1 = 1.1 + 0.11 = 1.21$

$$y_1'' = 1 + y_1' = 1 + 1.21 = 2.21$$

$$y_1''' = y_1'' = 2.21$$

$$y_1^{(iv)} = 2.21$$

$$y_1^{(v)} = 2.21$$

Now, $y(1.1 + h) = y_1 + hy_1' + \frac{h^2}{2!} y_1'' + \frac{h^3}{3!} y_1''' + \ldots\ldots$

$$= 0\,.\,11 + (0.1)\,(1.21) + \frac{(0.1)^2}{2}\,(2.21) + \ldots\ldots$$

$$\Rightarrow \quad y(1.2) = 0.232 \text{ (app.)}$$

The analytical solution of the given differential equation is

$$y = -x - 1 + 2e^{x-1}$$

when $x = 1.2$, we get

$$y = -1.2 - 1 + 2e^{0.2} = 0.242.$$

Example 2. *For the differential eqn.,* $\frac{dy}{dx} = -xy^2$, $y(0) = 2$. *Calculate* $y(0.2)$ *by Taylor's series method retaining four non-zero terms only.*

Sol. Here $x_0 = 0, y_0 = 2$ Also $y' = -xy^2$

Taylor's series for $y(x)$ is given by

$$y(x) = y_0 + xy_0' + \frac{x^2}{2} y_0'' + \frac{x^3}{6} y_0''' + \frac{x^4}{24} y_0^{(iv)}$$

$$+ \frac{x^5}{120} y_0^{(v)} + \ldots\ldots \quad (19)$$

The values of the derivatives $y_0', y_0'', \ldots\ldots$, etc. are obtained as follows:

$$y' = -xy^2 \qquad y_0' = -x_0 y_0^2 = 0$$

$$y'' = -y^2 - 2xyy' \qquad y_0'' = -2^2 - 0 = -4$$

$$y''' = -4yy' - 2xy'^2 - 2xyy'' \qquad y_0''' = 0$$

$$y^{(iv)} = -6y'^2 - 6y'y'' - 6xy'y'' - 2xyy''' \qquad y_0^{(iv)} = 48$$

$$y^{(v)} = -24y'y'' - 8yy''' - 6xy''^2 - 8xy'y''' - 2xyy^{(iv)} \qquad y_0^{(v)} = 0$$

$$y^{(vi)} = -40y'y''' - 30y''^2 - 10\,yy^{(iv)} - 20xy''y''' - 10xy'\,y^{(iv)} - 2xyy^{(v)}. \qquad y_0^{(vi)} = -1440$$

We stop here as we shall get four non-zero terms in the Taylor's series (19).

$$\therefore \quad y(x) = 2 + \frac{x^2}{2}(-4) + \frac{x^4}{24}(48) + \frac{x^6}{720}(-1440) + \ldots\ldots$$

$$= 2 - 2x^2 + 2x^4 - 2x^6 + \ldots\ldots$$

$$\therefore \quad y(0.2) = 2 - 2(0.2)^2 + 2(0.2)^4 - 2\,(0.2)^6 + \ldots\ldots$$

$$= 2 - 0.08 + 0.0032 - 0.000128 = 1.923072$$

$$\simeq 1.9231 \quad \text{correct up to four decimal places.}$$

Example 3. *From the Taylor's series, for* $y(x)$*, find* $y(0.1)$ *correct to four decimal places if* $y(x)$ *satisfies* $\frac{dy}{dx} = x - y^2$ *and* $y(0) = 1$*. Also find* $y(0.2)$*.*

Sol. Here $x_0 = 0$, $y_0 = 1$

$$y' = x - y^2 \qquad y_0' = 0 - 1 = -1$$

$$y'' = 1 - 2yy' \qquad y_0'' = 3$$

$$y''' = -2yy'' - 2y'^2 \qquad y_0''' = -8$$

$$y^{(iv)} = -2yy''' - 6y'y'' \qquad y_0^{(iv)} = 34$$

$$y^{(v)} = -2yy^{(iv)} - 8y'y''' - 6y''^2 \qquad y_0^{(v)} = -186$$

$$\left.\begin{aligned} y^{(vi)} &= -2yy^{(v)} - 10y'y^{(iv)} - 20\,y''y''' \qquad & y_0^{(vi)} &= 1192 \\ y^{(vii)} &= -2yy^{(vi)} - 12y'y^{(v)} - 50\,y''y^{(iv)} - 20\,y'''^2 \qquad & y_0^{(vii)} &= -10996 \end{aligned}\right\} \text{only for } y(0.2)$$

Using these values, Taylor's series becomes

$$y(x) = 1 - x + \frac{3}{2}x^2 - \frac{4}{3}x^3 + \frac{17}{12}x^4 - \frac{31}{20}x^5 + \ldots\ldots \tag{20}$$

Put $x = 0.1$ in (20), we get

$$y(0.1) = 0.91379 \simeq 0.9138 \qquad \text{(upto four decimal places)}$$

To determine $y(0.2)$, we have

$$y(x) = 1 - x + \frac{3}{2}x^2 - \frac{4}{3}x^3 + \frac{17}{12}x^4 - \frac{31}{20}x^5 + \frac{1192}{720}x^6 - \frac{10996}{5040}x^7 + \ldots\ldots\ldots$$

$$= 0.8512 \quad \text{(correct to four decimal places).}$$

Example 4. *Using Taylor's series, find the solution of the differential equation $xy' = x - y$, $y(2) = 2$ at $x = 2.1$ correct to five decimal places.*

Sol. Here $x_0 = 2, y_0 = 2$

Also,
$$y' = 1 - \frac{y}{x} \qquad y_0' = 0$$

$$y'' = -\frac{y'}{x} + \frac{y}{x^2} \qquad y_0'' = -0 + \frac{2}{4} = \frac{1}{2}$$

$$y''' = -\frac{y''}{x} + \frac{2y'}{x^2} - \frac{2y}{x^3} \qquad y_0''' = \frac{-3}{4}$$

$$y^{(iv)} = -\frac{y'''}{x} + \frac{3y''}{x^2} - \frac{6y'}{x^3} + \frac{6y}{x^4} \qquad y_0^{(iv)} = \frac{3}{2} \text{ and so on.}$$

Putting these values in Taylor's series, we get

$$y(2 + h) = 2 + \frac{h^2}{4} - \frac{h^3}{8} + \frac{h^4}{16} + \ldots\ldots.$$

Put $h = 0.1$, we get

$$y\,(2.1) = 2.00238 \text{ (correct to 5 decimal places).}$$

Example 5. *Find y(1) for* $\dfrac{dy}{dx} = 2y + 3e^x$, $y(0) = 0$. *Also check the value.*

Sol. Here $x_0 = 0, y_0 = 0$

$$y'(x) = 2y + 3e^x \qquad y_0' = 3, \qquad y_0'' = 9,$$

$$y''(x) = 2y' + 3e^x \qquad y_0''' = 21, \qquad y_0^{(iv)} = 45$$

$$\vdots \qquad \vdots$$

$$\vdots \qquad \vdots \qquad y_0^{(v)} = 93, \qquad y_0^{(vi)} = 189$$

$$y^{(viii)}(x) = 2y^{(vii)} + 3e^x \qquad y_0^{(vii)} = 381, \qquad y_0^{(viii)} = 765$$

Now, $$y(h) = 3h + \frac{9}{2}h^2 + \frac{7}{2}h^3 + \frac{15}{8}h^4 + \frac{31}{40}h^5 + \frac{21}{80}h^6 + \frac{127}{1680}h^7 + \frac{17}{896}h^8 + \ldots\ldots$$

Put $h = 1$, $y(1) = 14.01$

Exact solution.

$$\frac{dy}{dx} - 2y = 3e^x$$

Solution is $$ye^{-2x} = -3e^{-x} + c$$

$$x = 0, y = 0 \quad \therefore \quad c = 3$$

$$\therefore \quad ye^{-2x} = -3e^{-x} + 3$$

$$\Rightarrow \quad y = 3(e^{2x} - e^x)$$

when $x = 1$,

$$y = 3(e^2 - e) = 14.01 \text{ correct to two decimal places.}$$

Example 6. *Solve the simultaneous equations*

$$y' = 1 + xyz, \quad y\,(0) = 0$$

$$z' = x + y + z, \quad z(0) = 1.$$

Sol. Differentiating the given equations

$$y'' = yz + xy'z + xyz', \qquad y''' = 2y'z + 2yz' + 2xy'z' + xy''z + xyz''$$

$$z'' = 1 + y' + z', \qquad z''' = y'' + z''$$

with $x = 0, y = 0, z = 1$; we get $y' = 1, y'' = 0, y''' = 2$

Also $z' = 1, z'' = 3, z''' = 3$

Hence, $y(x) = x + \dfrac{x^3}{3}$ and $z(x) = 1 + x + \dfrac{3}{2}x^2 + \dfrac{1}{2}x^3.$

ASSIGNMENT 6.3

1. Compute y for $x = 0.1$ and 0.2 correct to four decimal places given: $y' = y - x, y(0) = 2$.
2. Solve by Taylor's method, $y' = x^2 + y^2, y(0) = 1$ compute $y(0.1)$.
3. Solve by Taylor's method: $y' = y - \dfrac{2x}{y}$; $y(0) = 1$. Also compute $y(0.1)$.
4. Using Taylor series method, solve $\dfrac{dy}{dx} = x^2 - y, y(0) = 1$ at $x = 0.1, 0.2, 0.3$ and 0.4. Compare the values with exact solution.
5. Solve $\dfrac{dy}{dx} = x + z, \quad \dfrac{dz}{dx} = x - y^2$ with $y(0) = 2, z(0) = 1$ to get $y(0.1), y(0.2), z(0.1)$ and $z(0.2)$ approximately by Taylor's algorithm.
6. Given the differential equation $\dfrac{dy}{dx} = \dfrac{1}{x^2 + y}$ with $y(4) = 4$

   Obtain $y(4.1)$ and $y(4.2)$ by Taylor's series method.

6.18 RUNGE-KUTTA METHODS

More efficient methods in terms of accuracy were developed by two German Mathematicians **Carl Runge** (1856-1927) and **Wilhelm Kutta** (1867-1944). These methods are well-known as Runge-Kutta methods. They are distinguished by their orders in the sense that they agree with Taylor's series solution up to terms of h^r where r is the order of the method.

These methods do not demand prior computation of higher derivatives of $y(x)$ as in Taylor's method. In place of these derivatives, extra values of the given function $f(x, y)$ are used.

The fourth order Runge-Kutta method is used widely for finding the numerical solutions of linear or non-linear ordinary differential equations.

Runge-Kutta methods are referred to as single step methods. The major disadvantage of Runge-Kutta methods is that they use many more evaluations of the derivative $f(x, y)$ to obtain the same accuracy compared with multi-step methods. A class of methods known as Runge-Kutta methods combines the advantage of high order accuracy with the property of being one step.

6.18.1 First Order Runge-Kutta Method

Consider the differential equation

$$\frac{dy}{dx} = f(x, y); \; y\,(x_0) = y_0 \tag{21}$$

Euler's method gives

$$y_1 = y_0 + hf(x_0, y_0) = y_0 + hy_0' \tag{22}$$

Expanding by Taylor's series, we get

$$y_1 = y(x_0 + h) = y_0 + hy_0' + \frac{h^2}{2!}\, y_0'' + \ldots\ldots \tag{23}$$

Comparing (22) and (23), it follows that Euler's method agrees with Taylor's series solution up to the term in h. Hence *Euler's method is the first order Runge-Kutta method.*

6.18.2 Second Order Runge-Kutta Method

Consider the differential equation

$$y' = f(x, y) \text{ with the initial condition } y(x_0) = y_0$$

Let h be the interval between equidistant values of x then in II order Runge-Kutta method, the first increment in y is computed from the formulae

$$k_1 = hf\,(x_0, y_0)$$

$$k_2 = hf(x_0 + h, y_0 + k_1)$$

$$\Delta y = \tfrac{1}{2}(k_1 + k_2)$$

taken in the given order.

Then, $$x_1 = x_0 + h$$

$$y_1 = y_0 + \Delta y = y_0 + \tfrac{1}{2}\,(k_1 + k_2)$$

In a similar manner, the increment in y for the second interval is computed by means of the formulae,

$$k_1 = hf\,(x_1, y_1)$$

$$k_2 = hf\,(x_1 + h, y_1 + k_1)$$

$$\Delta y = \tfrac{1}{2}(k_1 + k_2)$$

and similarly for the next intervals.

The inherent error in the second order Runge-Kutta method is of order h^3.

6.18.3 Third Order Runge-Kutta Method

This method gives the approximate solution of the initial value problem

$$\frac{dy}{dx} = f(x, y);\ y(x_0) = y_0 \text{ as}$$

$$\left.\begin{aligned} y_1 &= y_0 + \delta y \\ \delta y &= \frac{h}{6}(k_1 + 4k_2 + k_3) \end{aligned}\right\} \quad (24)$$

where

Here,

$$k_1 = f(x_0, y_0)$$

$$k_2 = f\left\{x_0 + \frac{h}{2}, y_0 + \frac{k_1}{2}\right\}$$

$$k_3 = f(x_0 + h, y_0 + k'); \qquad k' = hf(x_0 + h, y_0 + k_1)$$

Formula (24) can be generalized for successive approximations. Expression in (24) agrees with Taylor's series expansion for y_1 up to and including terms in h^3. This method is also known as Runge's method.

6.19 FOURTH ORDER RUNGE-KUTTA METHOD

The fourth order Runge-Kutta Method is one of the most widely used methods and is particularly suitable in cases when the computation of higher derivatives is complicated.

Consider the differential equation $y' = f(x, y)$ with the initial condition $y(x_0) = y_0$. Let h be the interval between equidistant values of x, then the first increment in y is computed from the formulae

$$\left.\begin{aligned} k_1 &= hf(x_0, y_0) \\ k_2 &= hf\left(x_0 + \frac{h}{2}, y_0 + \frac{k_1}{2}\right) \\ k_3 &= hf\left(x_0 + \frac{h}{2}, y_0 + \frac{k_2}{2}\right) \\ k_4 &= hf(x_0 + h, y_0 + k_3) \\ \Delta y &= \frac{1}{6}(k_1 + 2k_2 + 2k_3 + k_4) \end{aligned}\right\} \quad (25)$$

taken in the given order.

Then, $\qquad x_1 = x_0 + h \quad \text{and} \quad y_1 = y_0 + \Delta y$

In a similar manner, the increment in y for the II interval is computed by means of the formulae

$$k_1 = hf(x_1, y_1)$$

$$k_2 = hf\left(x_1 + \frac{h}{2}, y_1 + \frac{k_1}{2}\right)$$

$$k_3 = hf\left(x_1 + \frac{h}{2}, y_1 + \frac{k_2}{2}\right)$$

$$k_4 = hf(x_1 + h, y_1 + k_3)$$

$$\Delta y = \frac{1}{6}(k_1 + 2k_2 + 2k_3 + k_4)$$

and similarly for the next intervals.

This method is also simply termed as *Runge-Kutta's* method.

It is to be noted that the calculations for the first increment are exactly the same as for any other increment. The change in the formula for the different intervals is only in the values of x and y to be substituted. Hence, to obtain Δy for the nth interval, we substitute $x_{n-1}, y_{n-1,}$ in the expressions for k_1, k_2, etc.

The inherent error in the fourth order Runge-Kutta method is of the order h^5.

6.19.1 Algorithm of Runge-Kutta Method

```
 1. Function F(x)=(x-y)/(x+y)
 2. Input x0,y0,h,xn
 3. n=(xn-x0)/h
 4. x=x0
 5. y=y0
 6. For i=0, n
 7. k1=h*F(x,y)
 8. k2=h*F(x+h/2,y+k1/2)
 9. k3=h*F(x+h/2,y+k2/2)
10. k4=h*F(x+h,y+k3)
11. k=(k1+(k2+k3)2+k4)/6
12. Print x,y
13. x=x+h
14. y=y+k
15. Next i
16. Stop
```

6.19.2 Flow-Chart of Runge-Kutta Method

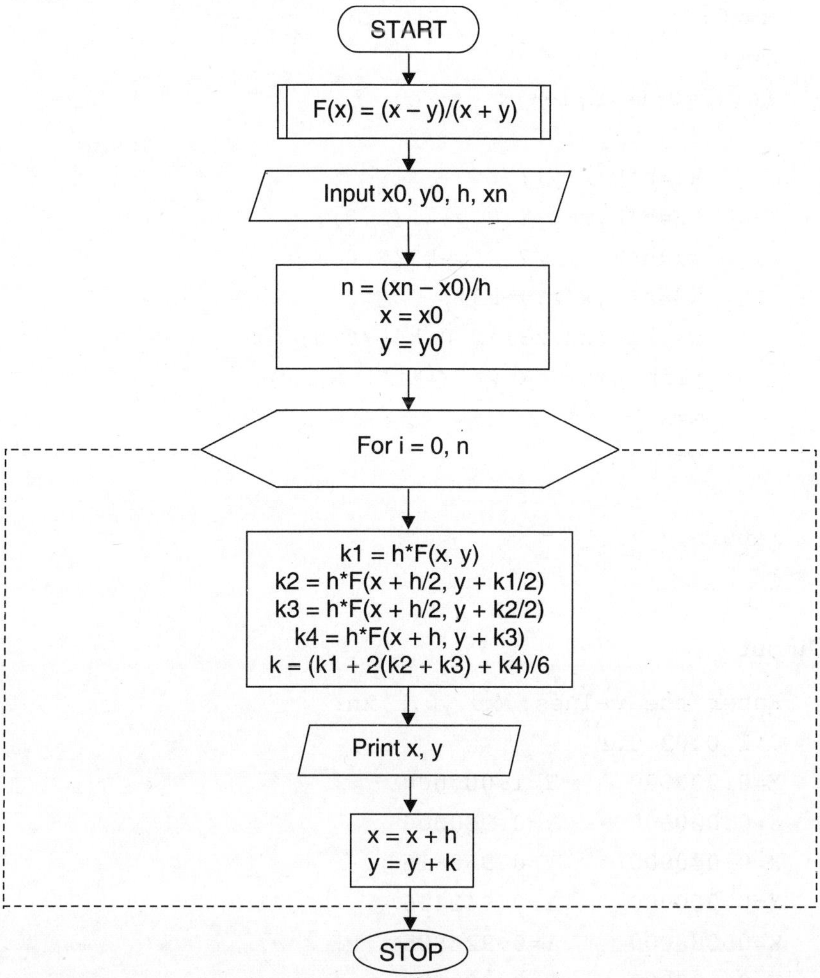

6.19.3 Program of Runge-Kutta Method

```
#include<stdio.h>
#define F(x,y)  (x-y)/(x+y)
main()
{
 int i,n;
 float x0,y0,h,xn,k1,k2,k3,k4,x,y,k;
 printf("\n Enter the values: x0,y0,h,xn:\n");
```

```
scanf("%f%f%f%f", &x0,&y0,&h,&xn);
n=(xn-x0)/h;
x=x0;
y=y0;
for(i=0;i<=n;i++)
    {
    k1=h*F(x,y);
    k2=h*F(x+h/2.0,y+k1/2.0);
    k3=h*F(x+h/2.0,y+k2/2.0);
    k4=h*F(x+h,y+k3);
    k=(k1+(k2+k3)*2.0+k4)/6.0;
    printf("\n X=%f Y=%f", x, y);
    x=x+h;
    y=y+k;
}
return;
}
```

6.19.4 Output

```
Enter the values: x0,y0,h,xn:
0 1 0.02 0.1
X=0.000000    Y=1.000000
X=0.020000    Y=0.980000
X=0.040000    Y=0.960816
X=0.060000    Y=0.942446
X=0.080000    Y=0.924885
X=0.100000    Y=0.908128
```

Notations used in the Program

(*i*) $\mathbf{x_0}$ is the initial value of x.

(*ii*) $\mathbf{y_0}$ is the initial value of y.

(*iii*) **h** is the spacing value of x.

(*iv*) $\mathbf{x_n}$ is the last value of x at which value of y is required.

6.20 RUNGE-KUTTA METHOD FOR SIMULTANEOUS FIRST ORDER EQUATIONS

Consider the simultaneous equations

$$\frac{dy}{dx} = f_1(x, y, z)$$

$$\frac{dz}{dx} = f_2\,(x, y, z)$$

With the initial condition $y(x_0) = y_0$ and $z(x_0) = z_0$. Now, starting from (x_0, y_0, z_0), the increments k and l in y and z are given by the following formulae:

$$k_1 = hf_1(x_0, y_0, z_0); \qquad l_1 = hf_2(x_0, y_0, z_0)$$

$$k_2 = hf_1\left(x_0 + \frac{h}{2}, y_0 + \frac{k_1}{2}, z_0 + \frac{l_1}{2}\right); \qquad l_2 = hf_2\left(x_0 + \frac{h}{2}, y_0 + \frac{k_1}{2}, z_0 + \frac{l_1}{2}\right)$$

$$k_3 = hf_1\left(x_0 + \frac{h}{2}, y_0 + \frac{k_2}{2}, z_0 + \frac{l_2}{2}\right); \qquad l_3 = hf_2\left(x_0 + \frac{h}{2}, y_0 + \frac{k_2}{2}, z_0 + \frac{l_2}{2}\right)$$

$$k_4 = hf_1(x_0 + h, y_0 + k_3\,, z_0 + l_3); \qquad l_4 = hf_2(x_0 + h, y_0 + k_3\,, z_0 + l_3)$$

$$k = \frac{1}{6}(k_1 + 2k_2 + 2k_3 + k_4); \qquad l = \frac{1}{6}(l_1 + 2l_2 + 2l_3 + l_4)$$

Hence $\quad y_1 = y_0 + k, \qquad z_1 = z_0 + l$

To compute y_2, z_2, we simply replace x_0, y_0, z_0 by x_1, y_1, z_1 in the above formulae.

EXAMPLES

Example 1. *Solve the equation* $\frac{dy}{dx} = x + y$ *with initial condition y(0) = 1 by Runge-Kutta rule, from x= 0 to x = 0.4 with h = 0.1.*

Sol. Here $f(x, y) = x + y, h = 0.1, x_0 = 0, y_0 = 1$

We have,

$$k_1 = hf(x_0, y_0) = 0.1\ (0 + 1) = 0.1$$

$$k_2 = hf\left(x_0 + \frac{h}{2},\ y_0 + \frac{k_1}{2}\right) = 0.1\ (0.05 + 1.05) = 0.11$$

$$k_3 = hf\left(x_0 + \frac{h}{2},\ y_0 + \frac{k_2}{2}\right) = 0.1105$$

$$k_4 = hf(x_0 + h,\ \ y_0 + k_3) = 0.12105$$

$$\therefore \qquad \Delta y = \frac{1}{6}(k_1 + 2k_2 + 2k_3 + k_4) = 0.11034$$

Thus, $x_1 = x_0 + h = 0.1$ and $y_1 = y_0 + \Delta y = 1.11034$

Now for the second interval, we have

$$k_1 = hf(x_1, y_1) = 0.1\ (0.1 + 1.11034) = 0.121034$$

$$k_2 = hf\left(x_1 + \frac{h}{2},\ y_1 + \frac{k_1}{2}\right) = 0.13208$$

$$k_3 = hf\left(x_1 + \frac{h}{2},\ y_1 + \frac{k_2}{2}\right) = 0.13263$$

$$k_4 = hf(x_1 + h,\ \ y_1 + k_3) = 0.14429$$

$$\therefore \qquad \Delta y = \frac{1}{6}(k_1 + 2k_2 + 2k_3 + k_4) = 0.132460$$

Hence $x_2 = 0.2$ and $y_2 = y_1 + \Delta y = 1.11034 + 0.13246 = 1.24280$

Similarly, for finding y_3, we have

$$k_1 = hf(x_2, y_2) = 0.14428$$

$$k_2 = 0.15649$$

$$k_3 = 0.15710$$

$$k_4 = 0.16999$$

Repeating the above process

$\therefore \qquad y_3 = 0.13997$

and for $\qquad y_4 = y(0.4)$, we calculate

$$k_1 = 0.16997$$
$$k_2 = 0.18347$$
$$k_3 = 0.18414$$
$$k_4 = 0.19838$$

$\therefore \qquad y_4 = 1.5836$

Example 2. *Given* $\frac{dy}{dx} = y - x,\ y(0) = 2$. *Find y(0.1) and y(0.2) correct to four decimal places (use both II and IV order methods).*

Sol. By II order Method

To find y(0.1)

Here $\qquad y' = f(x, y) = y - x,\ x_0 = 0,\ y_0 = 2$ and $h = 0.1$

Now, $\qquad k_1 = hf(x_0, y_0) = 0.1(2 - 0) = 0.2$

$$k_2 = hf(x_0 + h, y_0 + k_1) = 0.21$$

$\therefore \qquad \Delta y = \frac{1}{2}(k_1 + k_2) = 0.205$

Thus, $\qquad x_1 = x_0 + h = 0.1$ and $y_1 = y_0 + \Delta y = 2.205$

To find y(0.2) we note that,

$$x_1 = 0.1,\ y_1 = 2.205,\ h = 0.1$$

For interval II, we have

$$k_1 = hf(x_1, y_1) = 0.2105$$
$$k_2 = hf(x_1 + h, y_1 + k_1) = 0.22155$$

$\therefore \qquad \Delta y = \frac{1}{2}(k_1 + k_2) = 0.216025$

Thus, $\qquad x_2 = x_1 + h = 0.2$ and $y_2 = y_1 + \Delta y = 2.4210$

Hence $\qquad y(0.1) = 2.205,\quad y(0.2) = 2.421.$

By IV order method- As before

$$k_1 = 0.2,\ k_2 = 0.205,$$
$$k_3 = hf(x_0 + h/2, y_0 + k_{2/2}) = 0.20525$$

and $\qquad k_4 = hf(x_0 + h, y_0 + k_3) = 0.210525$

$\therefore \qquad \Delta y = \frac{1}{6}(k_1 + 2k_2 + 2k_3 + k_4) = 0.2052$

Thus, $\qquad x_1 = x_0 + h = 0 + 0.1 = 0.1$

$$y_1 = y_0 + \Delta y = 2 + 0.2052 = 2.2052$$

Now to determine $y_2 = y(0.2)$, we note that

$$x_1 = x_0 + h = 0.1,\ y_1 = 2.2052,\ h = 0.1$$

For interval II, $k_1 = hf(x_1, y_1) = 0.21052$

$$k_2 = hf\left(x_1 + \frac{h}{2}, y_1 + \frac{k_1}{2}\right) = 0.21605$$

$$k_3 = hf\left(x_1 + h/2, y_1 + \frac{k_2}{2}\right) = 0.216323$$

and $\qquad k_4 = hf(x_1 + h, y_1 + k_3) = 0.221523$

$\therefore \qquad \Delta y = \frac{1}{6}(k_1 + 2k_2 + 2k_3 + k_4) = 0.21613$

Thus, $\qquad x_2 = x_1 + h = 0.1 + 0.1 = 0.2$

and $\qquad y_2 = y_1 + \Delta y = 2.2052 + 0.21613 = 2.4213$

Hence $\qquad y(0.1) = 2.2052, \quad y(0.2) = 2.4213.$

Example 3. *Solve* $\frac{dy}{dx} = yz + x, \quad \frac{dz}{dx} = xz + y;$

given that $y(0) = 1, z(0) = -1$ *for* $y(0.1), z(0.1)$.

Sol. Here, $\qquad f_1(x, y, z) = yz + x$

$$f_2(x, y, z) = xz + y$$

$$h = 0.1, x_0 = 0, y_0 = 1, z_0 = -1$$

$$k_1 = hf_1(x_0, y_0, z_0) = h(y_0 z_0 + x_0) = -0.1$$

$$l_1 = hf_2(x_0, y_0, z_0) = h(x_0 z_0 + y_0) = 0.1$$

$$k_2 = hf_1\left(x_0 + \frac{h}{2}, y_0 + \frac{k_1}{2}, z_0 + \frac{l_1}{2}\right)$$

$$= hf_1(0.05, 0.95, -0.95) = -0.08525$$

$$l_2 = hf_2\left(x_0 + \frac{h}{2}, y_0 + \frac{k_1}{2}, z_0 + \frac{l_1}{2}\right)$$

$$= hf_2(0.05, 0.95, -0.95) = 0.09025$$

$$k_3 = hf_1\left(x_0 + \frac{h}{2}, y_0 + \frac{k_2}{2}, z_0 + \frac{l_2}{2}\right)$$

$$= hf_1(0.05, 0.957375, -0.954875) = -0.0864173$$

$$l_3 = hf_2\left(x_0 + \frac{h}{2}, y_0 + \frac{k_2}{2}, z_0 + \frac{l_2}{2}\right)$$

$$= hf_2(0.05, 0.957375, -0.954875) = -0.0864173$$

$$k_4 = hf_1(x_0 + h, y_0 + k_3, z_0 + l_3) = -0.073048.$$

$$l_4 = hf_2(x_0 + h, y_0 + k_3, z_0 + l_3) = 0.0822679$$

$$k = \frac{1}{6}(k_1 + 2k_2 + 2k_3 + k_4) = -0.0860637$$

$$l = \frac{1}{6}(l_1 + 2l_2 + 2l_3 + l_4) = 0.0907823$$

$$\therefore \quad y_1 = y(0.1) = y_0 + k = 1 - 0.0860637 = 0.9139363$$

$$z_1 = z(0.1) = z_0 + k = -1 + 0.0907823 = -0.9092176$$

ASSIGNMENT 6.4

1. Use the Runge-Kutta Method to approximate y when $x = 0.1$ given that $x = 0$ when $y = 1$ and $\frac{dy}{dx} = x + y$.

2. Apply the Runge-Kutta Fourth Order Method to solve $10\frac{dy}{dx} = x^2 + y^2$; $y(0) = 1$ for $0 < x \le 0.4$ and $h = 0.1$.

3. Use Runge-Kutta Fourth Order Formula to find $y(1.4)$ if $y(1) = 2$ and $\frac{dy}{dx} = xy$. Take $h = 0.2$.

4. Prove that the solution of $y' = y$, $y(0) = 1$ by Second Order Runge-Kutta Method yields

$$y_m = \left(1 + h + \frac{h^2}{2}\right)^m.$$

5. Solve $y' = \frac{1}{x+y}$, $y(0) = 1$ for $x = 0.5$ to $x = 1$ by Runge-Kutta Method ($h = 0.5$).

6. Solve $y' = -xy^2$ and By Runge-Kutta Fourth Order Method, find $y(0.6)$ given that $y = 1.7231$ at $x = 0.4$. Take $h = 0.2$.

7. Use Runge-Kutta Method to find y when $x = 1.2$ in steps of 0.1 given that

$$\frac{dy}{dx} = x^2 + y^2 \quad \text{and} \quad y(1) = 1.5$$

8. Given $y' = x^2 - y$, $y(0) = 1$ find $y(0.1)$, $y(0.2)$ using Runge-Kutta Methods of (*i*) Second Order (*ii*) Fourth Order.

9. Using Runge-Kutta Method of Fourth Order, solve for $y(0.1)$, $y(0.2)$ and $y(0.3)$, given that $y' = xy + y^2$, $y(0) = 1$.

10. Using Runge-Kutta Method, find $y(0.2)$ for the equation

$$\frac{dy}{dx} = \frac{y - x}{y + x}, y(0) = 1. \text{ Take } h = 0.2$$

11. (*i*) Using Runge-Kutta Method, find $y(0.2)$ given that

$$\frac{dy}{dx} = 3x + \frac{1}{2}y, \quad y(0) = 1 \text{ taking } h = 0.1.$$

(*ii*) Use the classical Runge-Kutta Formula of Fourth Order to find the numerical solution at $x = 0.8$ for the differential equation

$$y' = \sqrt{x + y}, y(0.4) = 0.41$$

Assume the step length $h = 0.2$.

12. Solve

$$\frac{dy}{dx} = x + z$$

$$\frac{dz}{dx} = x - y^2$$

for $y(0.1)$, $z(0.1)$ given that $y(0) = 2$, $z(0) = 1$ by Runge-Kutta Method.

13. Use classical Runge-Kutta Method of Fourth Order to find the numerical solution at $x = 1.4$ for $\frac{dy}{dx} = y^2 + x^2$, $y(1) = 0$. Assume step size $h = 0.2$.

14. Explain Runge-Kutta Method with a suitable example. Write a program in C to implement.

15. Write the main steps to be followed in using the Runge-Kutta Method of Fourth Order to solve an ordinary differential equation of the First Order. Hence solve $\frac{dy}{dx} = x^3 + y^3$, $y(0) = 1$ and step length $h = 0.1$ upto three iterations.

16. Given $\frac{dy}{dx} = xy$ with $y(1) = 5$. Using the Fourth Order Runge-Kutta Method, find the solution in the interval (1, 1.5) using step size $h = 0.1$.

17. Using the Runge-Kutta Method of Fourth Order, solve the following differential equation:

$$\frac{dy}{dx} = \frac{y^2 - x^2}{y^2 + x^2} \quad \text{with} \quad y(0) = 1 \quad \text{at } x = 0.2, 0.4.$$

Also write computer program in 'C'

18. Discuss the Fourth Order Runge-Kutta Method for solving differential equations. Give program for the solution of differential equation using Fourth Order Runge-Kutta Method. Use 'C' language.

6.21 PREDICTOR-CORRECTOR METHODS

In Runge-Kutta Methods, we need only the information at (x_i, y_i) to calculate the value of y_{i+1} and no attention is paid to the nature of the solution at the earlier points.

To overcome this defect, Predictor-Corrector Methods are useful. The technique of refining an initially crude predicted estimate of y_i by means of a more accurate corrector formula is called, *Predictor-Corrector Method.*

The modified Euler's Method of solving the initial value problem,

$$y' = f(x, y), y(x_0) = y_0 \tag{26}$$

can be stated as

$$y_1^p = y_0 + hf(x_0, y_0) \tag{27}$$

$$y_1^c = y_0 + \frac{h}{2} [f(x_0, y_0) + f(x_1, y_1^p)] \tag{28}$$

Here we predict the value of y_1 by Euler's Method and use it in (28) to get a corrected or improved value. This is a typical case of Predictor-Corrector Method.

In this section, we will obtain two important Predictor-Corrector Methods, namely, Milne's Simpson Method and Adams-Moulton (or Adams-Bash Fourth) Method. Both of these methods are of IV order and the error is of order h^5. These methods make use of four starting values of y, namely, y_0, y_1, y_2, and y_3. Hence, these methods are also called as *Multi-Step Methods.*

6.22 MILNE'S METHOD

Milne's Method is a simple and reasonably accurate method of solving differential equations numerically. To solve the differential equation $y' = f(x, y)$ by this method, first we get the approximate value of y_{n+1} by predictor formula and then improve this value using a corrector formula. These formula are derived from Newton's Formula.

Newton's Forward Interpolation Formula in terms of y' and u is

$$y' = y_0' + u\Delta y_0' + \frac{u(u-1)}{2}\Delta^2 y_0' + \frac{u(u-1)(u-2)}{6}\Delta^3 y_0' + \frac{u(u-1)(u-2)(u-3)}{24}\Delta^4 y_0' + \ldots\ldots \quad (29)$$

where $u = \dfrac{x - x_0}{h}$ or $x = x_0 + uh$

Now integrating (29) over the interval x_0 to $x_0 + 4h$ (or $u = 0$ to 4), we get

$$\int_{x_0}^{x_0+4h} y'\,dx = h\int_0^4 y'\,du \qquad | \because dx = h\,du$$

or

$$y_4 - y_0 = h\int_0^4 \left[y_0' + u\Delta y_0' + \frac{u(u-1)}{2}\Delta^2 y_0' + \frac{u(u-1)(u-2)}{6}\Delta^3 y_0' + \frac{u(u-1)(u-2)(u-3)}{24}\Delta^4 y_0' + \ldots\ldots \right] du$$

$$= h\left(4y_0' + 8\Delta y_0' + \frac{20}{3}\Delta^2 y_0' + \frac{8}{3}\Delta^3 y_0' + \frac{28}{90}\Delta^4 y_0'\right)$$

| keeping up to IV differences

Here, y_0 and y_4 stand for values of y at $x = x_0$ and $x = x_0 + 4h$ respectively.

Substituting the values of I, II and III differences, we get

$$y_4 - y_0 = h\left(4y_0' + 8(E-1)y_0' + \frac{20}{3}(E-1)^2 y_0' + \frac{8}{3}(E-1)^3 y_0' + \frac{28}{90}\Delta^4 y_0'\right) \quad (30)$$

$$= \frac{4h}{3}(2y_1' - y_2' + 2y_3') + \frac{28}{90}h\Delta^4 y_0'$$

or

$$y_4 = y_0 + \frac{4h}{3}(2y_1' - y_2' + 2y_3') + \frac{28}{90}h\Delta^4 y_0' \quad (31)$$

This is *Milne's Predictor (Extrapolation) formula.*

It is used to predict the value of y_4 when the value of y_0, y_1, y_2, and y_3 are known.

To obtain the corrector formula, we integrate (29) over the interval x_0 to $x_0 + 2h$ (or $u = 0$ to 2) and consequently.

$$y_2 - y_0 = h\left(2y_0' + 2\Delta y_0' + \frac{1}{3}\Delta^2 y_0' - \frac{1}{90}\Delta^4 y_0'\right)$$

Expressing the I, II and III differences in terms of the function value by using D ≡ E – 1,

we obtain,

$$y_2 - y_0 = \frac{h}{3}(y_0' + 4y_1' + y_2') - \frac{h}{90}\,\Delta^4 y_0'$$

$$\Rightarrow \qquad y_2 = y_0 + \frac{h}{3}(y_0' + 4y_1' + y_2') - \frac{h}{90}\,\Delta^4 y_0' \tag{32}$$

This is *Milne's Corrector Formula.*

The value of y_4 obtained from (31) and (32) can be put as

$$y_{n+1} = y_{n-3} + \frac{4h}{3}(2y'_{n-2} - y'_{n-1} + 2y_n') \tag{33}$$

$$y'_{n+1} = y_{n-1} + \frac{h}{3}\,(y'_{n-1} + 4y_n' + y'_{n+1}) \tag{34}$$

It is to be noted that we have considered the differences up to the third order because we fit up a polynomial of degree four.

The terms containing $\Delta^4 y_0'$ are not used explicitly in the formula, but they give the principal parts of the errors in the two values of y_{n+1} as computed from (33) and (34).

We notice that this error in (34) is of opposite sign to that in (33) but it is very small in magnitude.

So we may take, $\quad (y_{n+1})_{\text{exact}} = y_{n+1} + \frac{28}{90}\,h\Delta^4 y'$

and $\quad (y_{n+1})_{\text{exact}} = y^{(1)}{}_{n+1} - \frac{h}{90}\Delta^4 y'$

where y_{n+1} and $y^{(1)}{}_{n+1}$ denote the predicted and first corrected value of y at $x = x_{n+1}$.

Equating these two values, we get

$$y_{n+1} - y^{(1)}{}_{n+1} = -\frac{29}{90}h\Delta^4 y' = 29\,\delta$$

where $\delta = -\frac{h}{90}\,\Delta^4 y'$ denotes the principal part of the error in (34). Thus it gives

$$\delta = \frac{1}{29}\,[y_{n+1} - y^{(1)}{}_{n+1}]$$

Thus we observe that the error in (34) is $\frac{1}{29}$th of the difference between the predicted and corrected values.

6.22.1 Algorithm of Milne's Predictor-Corrector Method

```
 1. Function F(x,y)=x+y
 2. Input xn
 3. For i=0,3
 4. Input x(i),y(i)
 5. Next i
 6. h=x(1)-x(0)
 7. n=(xn-x(0))/h
 8. For i=3,n
 9. x(i+1)=x(i)+h
10. f=F(x(i),y(i))
11. f1=F(x(i-1),y(i-1))
12. f2=F(x(i-2),y(i-2))
13. yp=y(i-3)+4h/3(2f2-f1+2f)
14. yc=y(i-1)+h/3(f1+4f+F(x(i+1),yp))
15. If abs (yp-yc)<0.0005 then
        y(i+1)=yc
        print x(i+1), y(i+1)
    ELSE
        yp=yc
16. Next i
17. Stop
```

6.22.2 Flow-Chart of Milne's Predictor Corrector Method

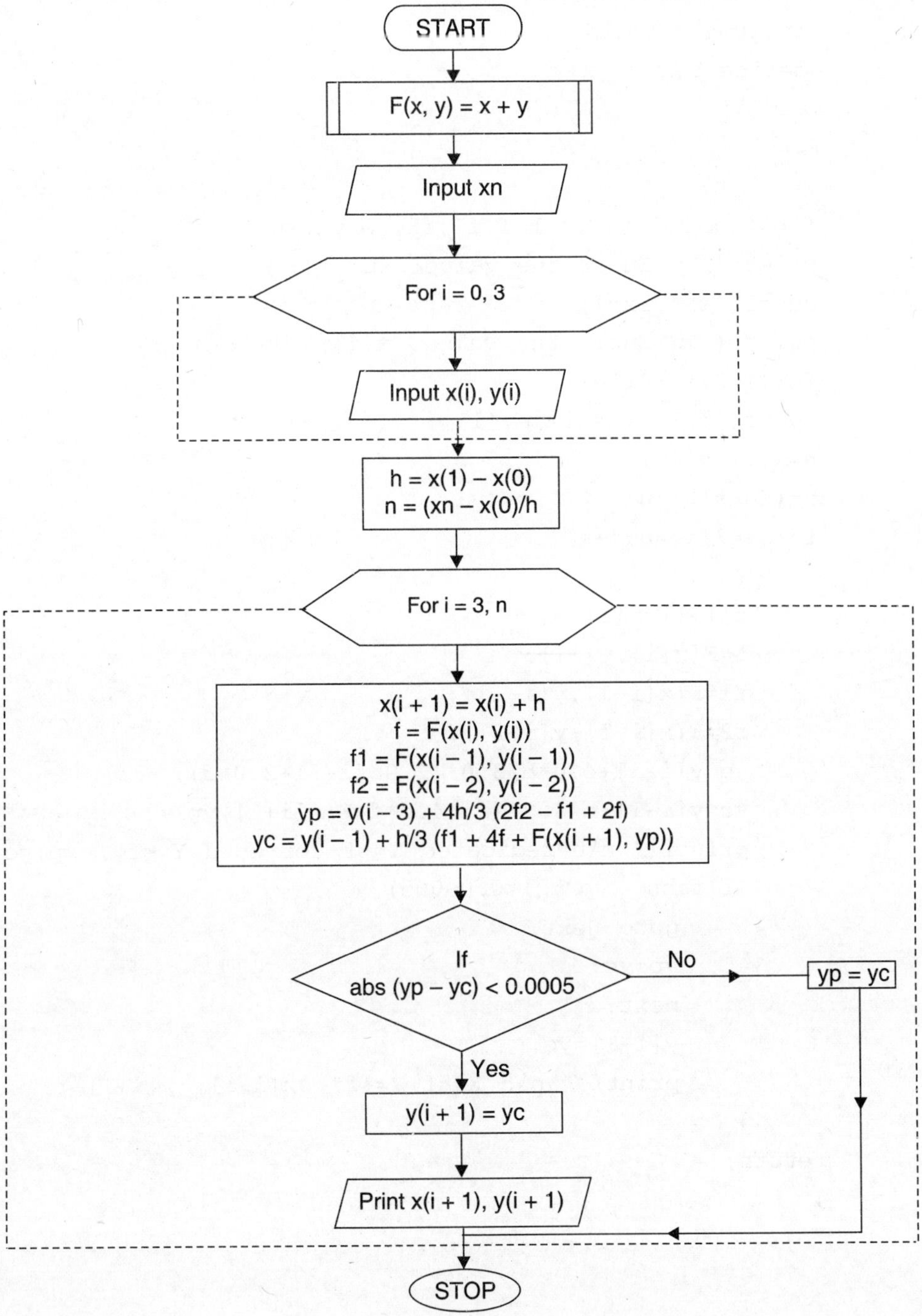

6.22.3 Program of Milne's Method

```
#include<stdio.h>
#include<math.h>
#define F(x,y) x+y
main()
{
 int i,n;
 float  x[20],y[20],h,f,f1,f2,yp,yc,xn;
 printf("\n Enter the value: xn: "};
 scanf{"%f",&xn);
 printf("\n Enter the value: x{i], y[i]:\n"};
 for(i=0;i<=3;i++)
 scanf("%f%f",&x[i],&y[i]);
 h=x[1]-x[0];
 n=(xn-x[0]/h;
 for(i=3;i<=n;i++)
     {
     x[i+1]=x[i]+h;
     f=F[x[i],y[i]);
     f1=F(x[i-1],y[i-1]);
     f2=F(x[i-2],y[i-2]);
     yp=y[i-3]+4.0*h/3.0*(2.0*f2-f1+2.0*f);
     yc=y[i-1]+h/3.0*(f1+4.0*f+F(x[i+1],yp));
     printf("\n\nPredicated Y=%f Correctd Y=%f", yp,yc);
     If(fabs (yp-yc)<0.00005)
          goto next;
          yp=yc;
          next;
          y[i+1]=yc;
          printf("\n\n X=%f Y=%f", x[i+1], y[i+1]);
     }
return;
}
```

6.22.4 Output

```
Enter the value: xn: 1
Entcr thc valuc: x[i], y[i]:
0.0   0.0
0.2   0.02
0.4   0.0906
0.6   0.2214
Predicted Y=0.423147 Corrected Y=0.429650
X=0.800000      Y=0.429650
Predicted Y=0.721307 Corrected Y=0.718820
X=1.000000      Y=0.718820
```

Notations used in the Program

(*i*) $\mathbf{x_n}$ is the last value of x at which value of y is required.

(*ii*) **x(i)** is an array for prior values of x.

(*iii*) **y(i)** is an array for prior values of y.

(*iv*) $\mathbf{y_p}$ is the predicted value of y.

(*v*) $\mathbf{y_c}$ is the corrected value of y.

EXAMPLES

Example 1. *Tabulate by Milne's Method the numerical solution of* $\frac{dy}{dx} = x + y$ *with initial conditions* $x_0 = 0$, $y_0 = 1$ *from* $x = 0.20$ *to* $x = 0.30$.

Sol. To obtain the solution, we find three consecutive values of y and y' corresponding to $x = 0.05$, 0.10 and 0.15, *i.e.*, taking $h = 0.05$

x	y	$y' = dy/dx$
0.00	1	1
0.05	1.0525	1.1025
0.10	1.1103	1.2103
0.15	1.1736	1.3236

(using $y = 2e^x - x - 1$ (35) as explicit solution of given equations)

In general form, Milne's Predictor and Corrector Formulae are

$$y_{n+1} = y_{n-3} + \frac{4h}{3}(2y'_{n-2} - y'_{n-1} + 2y_n') \tag{36}$$

and $$y_{n+1}^{(1)} = y_{n-1} + \frac{h}{3}(y'_{n-1} + 4y_n' + y'_{n+1}) \qquad (37)$$

Put $n = 3$, $h = 0.05$ in (36), we get

$$y_4 = y_0 + \frac{4h}{3}(2y_1' - y_2' + 2y_3')$$

$$= 1 + \frac{4(0.05)}{3}[2.205 - 1.2103 + 2.6472]$$

$$= 1.2428 \text{ (predicted value)}$$

It is corrected by

$$y_4^{(1)} = y_2 + \frac{h}{3}(y_2' + 4y_3' + y_4')$$

$$= 1.1103 + \frac{0.05}{3}[1.2103 + 5.2944 + 1.4428] = 1.2428$$

which is the same as predicted value.

Put $x = 0.20$ and $y = 1.2428$ in $\frac{dy}{dx} = x + y,$

we get $y_4' = 1.4428$

Hence, $y = 1.2428$ when $x = 0.20$ and $y' = 1.4428$

Now, put $n = 4$, $h = 0.05$ in (36), we get

$$y_5 = y_1 + \frac{4h}{3}(2y_2' - y_3' + 2y_4')$$

$$= 1.0525 + \frac{4(0.05)}{3}[2.4206 - 1.3236 + 2.8856]$$

$$= 1.3180$$

which is corrected by

$$y_5^{(1)} = y_3 + \frac{h}{3}(y_3' + 4y_4' + y_5')$$

$$= 1.1736 + \frac{0.05}{3}(1.3236 + 5.7712 + 1.568) = 1.3180$$

which is same as predicted value.

Thus, $y_5 = y_{0.25} = 1.3180$ and $y_5' = 1.5680$

Again putting $n = 5$, $h = 0.05$, we get

$y_6 = 1.3997$ which is corrected by

$$y_6^{(1)} = 1.3997 = y_{0.30}$$

The same as the predicted value.

$$y_6 = 1.3997, y'_6 = 1.6997 \ (y' = x + y)$$

Collecting the results in Tabular form, we get

x	y	$y' = dy/dx$
$x_4 = 0.20$	$y_4 = 1.2428$	$y_4' = 1.4428$
$x_5 = 0.25$	$y_5 = 1.3180$	$y_5' = 1.5680$
$x_6 = 0.30$	$y_6 = 1.3997$	$y_6' = 1.6997$

Example 2. *Find y(2) if y(x) is the solution of* $\frac{dy}{dx} = \frac{1}{2}(x + y)$ *where y(0) = 2,*

$$y(0.5) = 2.636, \ y(1) = 3.595, \ y(1.5) = 4.968$$

Sol. Let $x_0 = 0$, $x_1 = 0.5$, $x_2 = 1$, $x_3 = 1.5$ then we are given y_0, y_1, y_2, y_3 and we require y_4 corresponding to $x_4 = 2$.

By Predictor Formula, we get

$$y_4 = y_0 + \frac{4h}{3}(2y_1' - y_2' + 2y_3') \tag{38}$$

we have, $$y' = \frac{1}{2}(x + y)$$

$\therefore$ $$y_1' = \frac{1}{2}(x_1 + y_1) = 1.568$$

Similarly $$y_2' = 2.2975, \quad y_3' = 3.234$$

$\therefore$ from (38), $$y_4 = 2 + \frac{4(0.5)}{3}[3.136 - 2.2975 + 6.468] = 6.871$$

$\Rightarrow$ $$y_4' = \frac{1}{2}(x_4 + y_4) = 4.4355$$

This is corrected by

$$y_4^{(1)} = y_2 + \frac{h}{3}(y_2' + 4y_3' + y_4')$$

$$= 3.595 + \frac{0.5}{3}[2.2975 + 12.936 + 4.4355] = 6.87317$$

Now, $$(y_4^{(1)})' = \frac{1}{2}[x_4 + y_4^{(1)}] = \frac{1}{2}(2 + 6.87317) = 4.43659$$

Again by the Corrector Formula, we get the second corrected value *i.e.*, $y_{2.00}$.

$$y_4^{(2)} = y_2 + \frac{h}{3} [y_2' + 4y_3' + (y_4^{(1)})']$$

$$= 3.595 + \frac{0.5}{3} [2.2975 + 12.936 + 4.43659] = 6.87335$$

Example 3. *Using Milne's Method, solve $y' = 1 + y^2$ with $y(0) = 0$, $y(0.2) = 0.2027$, $y(0.4) = 0.4228$, $y(0.6) = 0.6841$, obtain $y(0.8)$ and $y(1)$*

Sol. Let $x_0 = 0$, $x_1 = 0.2$, $x_2 = 0.4$, $x_3 = 0.6$. We are given y_0, y_1, y_2, y_3, and we require $y_4 = y(0.8)$ and $y_5 = y(1.0)$. Here $h = 0.2$

We have, $y' = 1 + y^2$

$\therefore$ $y_1' = 1 + y_1^2 = 1 + (0.2027)^2 = 1.0411$

$y_2' = 1 + y_2^2 = 1 + (0.4228)^2 = 1.1788$

$y_3' = 1 + y_3^2 = 1 + (0.6841)^2 = 1.4680$

By Predictor Formula, we get

$$y_4 = y_0 + \frac{4h}{3} (2y_1' - y_2' + 2y_3')$$

$$= 0 + \frac{0.8}{3} [2.0822 - 1.1788 + 2.936] = 1.0238$$

$$y_4' = 1 + y_4^2 = 1 + (1.0238)^2 = 2.0482$$

This is corrected by

$$y_4^{(1)} = y_2 + \frac{h}{3} (y_2' + 4y_3' + y_4')$$

$$= 0.4228 + \frac{0.2}{3} [1.1788 + 5.872 + 2.0482] = 1.0294$$

Now, $[y_4^{(1)}]' = 1 + [y_4^{(1)}]^2 = 1 + (1.0294)^2 = 2.0597$

The second corrected value is,

$$y_4^{(2)} = y_2 + \frac{h}{3} [y_2' + 4y_3' + y_4^{(1)}{}']$$

$$= 0.4228 + \frac{0.2}{3} [1.1788 + 5.872 + 2.0597] = 1.0302$$

Again, $[y_4^{(2)}]' = 1 + [y_4^{(2)}]^2 = 1 + (1.0302)^2 = 2.0613$

Again, $y_4^{(3)} = 1.0303 = y_4^{(4)}$

hence, $y_4 = y(0.8) = 1.0303$

Now, by Predictor Formula, also

$$y_5 = y_1 + \frac{4h}{3}(2y_2' - y_3' + 2y_4')$$

$$= 0.2027 + \frac{0.8}{3}[2.3576 - 1.468 + 4.123] \mid y_4' = 1 + (1.0303)^2$$

$$= 1.5394$$

$$y_5' = 1 + y_5^2 = 3.3698$$

This is corrected by

$$y_5' = y_3 + \frac{h}{3}(y_3' + 4y_4' + y_5')$$

$$= 0.6841 + \frac{0.2}{3}(1.468 + 8.246 + 3.3698) = 1.5564$$

Now, $[y_5^{(1)}]' = 1 + (1.5564)^2 = 3.4224$

The second corrected value is

$$y_5^{(2)} = 1.55999$$

Now, $[y_5^{(2)}]' = 3.4333$

Also, $y_5^{(3)} = 1.5606$

Similarly $y_5^{(4)} = 1.5607 = y_5^{(5)}$

Hence, $y_5 = y(1.0) = 1.5607.$

ASSIGNMENT 6.5

1. Apply Milne's Method to solve the differential equation

$$\frac{dy}{dx} = -xy^2 \text{ at } x = 0.8, \text{ given that}$$

$$y(0) = 2,\ y(0.2) = 1.923,\ y(0.4) = 1.724,\ y(0.6) = 1.471$$

2. Solve $10\frac{dy}{dx} = x^2 + y^2$, $y(0) = 1$ and compute $y(0.4)$ and $y(0.5)$ by Milne's Method given

x:	0.1	0.2	0.3
y:	1.0101	1.0206	1.0317

3. Part of a numerical solution of the differential equation

$$\frac{dy}{dx} = 0.2x + 0.1y$$

is shown in the following table:

x:	0	0.05	0.10	0.15
y:	2	2.0103	2.0212	2.0323

Use Milne's Method to find the next entry in the table.

4. Given $\frac{dy}{dx} = \frac{1}{2}(1 + x^2)\, y^2$ and $y(0) = 1$, $y(0.1) = 1.06$, $y(0.2) = 1.12$, $y(0.3) = 1.21$, evaluate $y(0.4)$ by Milne's Predictor-Corrector Method.

5. The differential equation $\frac{dy}{dx} + \frac{1}{10} y^2 = x$ satisfies the following pairs of values of x and y:

x:	– 0.2	– 0.1	0.0	0.1	0.2
y:	1.04068	1.01513	1	0.99507	1.00013

Compute the values of y when $x = 0.3$ by Milne's Method.

6. Solve the differential equation

$$\frac{dy}{dx} = y - x^2$$

by Milne's Method and compute y at $x = 0.80$ when:

x:	0	0.2	0.4	0.6
y:	1	1.12186	1.46820	1.73790

7. Solve $y' = -y$ with $y(0) = 1$ by the using Milne's Method from $x = 0.5$ to $x = 0.8$ with $h = 0.1$. Given:

x:	0.1	0.2	0.3	0.4
y:	0.9048	0.8188	0.7408	0.6705

8. Given: $\frac{dy}{dx} = 2 - xy^2$ and $y(0) = 1$. Show that by Milne's Method, $y(1) = 1.6505$ taking $h = 0.2$. You may use Picard's Method to obtain the values of $y(0.2)$, $y(0.4)$, $y(0.6)$.

9. Solve the initial value problem $\frac{dy}{dx} = 1 + xy^2$, $y(0) = 1$ for $x = 0.4, 0.5$ by using Milne's Method. It is given that,

x:	0.1	0.2	0.3
y:	1.105	1.223	1.355

10. Derive Milne's Predictor Formula and find the solution of the equation.

$\frac{dy}{dx} = x - y^2$ for $y(0.8)$ and $y(1)$, given the starting values.

x:	0	0.2	0.4	0.6
y:	0	0.02	0.0795	0.1762

11. Given: $y(0) = 2$, $y(0.2) = 2.0933$, $y(0.4) = 2.1755$, $y(0.6) = 2.2493$, find $y(0.8)$ and $y(1.0)$ by solving $\frac{dy}{dx} = \frac{1}{x+y}$ by Milne's Method.

12. Solve numerically

$$\frac{dy}{dx} = 2e^x - y \text{ at } x = 0.4 \text{ and } 0.5 \text{ by Milne's Method given:}$$

x:	0	0.1	0.2	0.3
y:	2	2.010	2.040	2.090

13. Given $\frac{dy}{dx} = -xy$ with $y(0) = 1$. Solve the equation in the interval (0, 1) using step size = 0.5 using Predictor-Corrector Method. Give algorithm of Predictor-Corrector Method.

14. Apply Predictor-Corrector Method on a differential equation

$$\frac{dx}{dt} = f(t, x).$$

Let $$x = x(t)$$

The method is of order IV with step-size h is $x(t + h) = x(t) + \frac{1}{6}(k_1 + 2k_2 + 2k_3 + k_4)$

where,
$$k_1 = h\,f(t, x)$$
$$k_2 = h\,f\left(t + \frac{h}{2}, x + \frac{k_1}{2}\right)$$
$$k_3 = h\,f\left(t + \frac{h}{2}, x + \frac{k_2}{2}\right)$$
$$k_4 = h\,f(t + h, x + k_3)$$

Use this method with $h = 0.1$ to find $x(0.1)$ and $x(0.2)$ where $\frac{dx}{dt} = t - x$ and $x(0) = 0$.

15. Discuss Predictor-Corrector Method for solving differential equation. Illustrate method using figure. Give program of Predictor-Corrector Method in 'C' language.

6.23 ADAMS–MOULTON (OR ADAMS–BASHFORTH) FORMULA

Consider the initial value problem

$$\frac{dy}{dx} = f(x, y) \text{ with } y(x_0) = y_0 \tag{39}$$

We compute $y_{-1} = y(x_0 - h)$, $y_{-2} = y(x_0 - 2h)$, $y_{-3} = y(x_0 - 3h)$,......

Now integrating (39) on both sides with respect to x in $[x_0, x_0 + h]$, we get

$$y_1 = y_0 + \int_{x_0}^{x_0 + h} f(x, y)\, dx \qquad (40)$$

Replacing $f(x, y)$ by Newton's Backward Interpolation Formula, we get

$$y_1 = y_0 + h \int_0^1 \left\{ f_0 + u \nabla f_0 + \frac{u(u+1)}{2} \nabla^2 f_0 + \frac{u(u+1)(u+2)}{6} \nabla^3 f_0 + \dots \right\} du$$

$\because x = x_0 + hu$
$\therefore dx = h\, du$
Limits of u are from 0 to 1

$$= y_0 + h \left(f_0 + \frac{1}{2} \nabla f_0 + \frac{5}{12} \nabla^2 f_0 + \frac{3}{8} \nabla^3 f_0 + \dots \right) \qquad (41)$$

Neglecting the fourth order and higher order differences and using

$\nabla f_0 = f_0 - f_{-1}$

$\nabla^2 f_0 = f_0 - 2f_{-1} + f_{-2}$

$\nabla^3 f_0 = f_0 - 3f_{-1} + 3f_{-2} - f_{-3}$ in (41), we get after simplification,

$$y_1 = y_0 + \frac{h}{24} (55f_0 - 59f_{-1} + 37f_{-2} - 9f_{-3})$$

which is known as ***Adams–Bashforth or Adams–Moulton–Predictor Formula*** and is denoted generally as

$$y^p_{n+1} = y_n + \frac{h}{24} (55f_n - 59f_{n-1} + 37f_{n-2} - 9f_{n-3})$$

or
$$y^p_{n+1} = y_0 + \frac{h}{24} (55y_n' - 59y'_{n-1} + 37y'_{n-2} - 9y'_{n-3})$$

Having found y_1, we find $f_1 = f(x_0 + h, y_1)$

To find *a* better value of y_1, we derive a corrector formula by substituting Newton's Backward Interpolation Formula at f_1 in place of $f(x, y)$ in (40) *i.e.*,

$$y_1 = y_0 + \int_{x_0}^{x_0 + h} \left[f_1 + u \nabla f_1 + \frac{u(u+1)}{2} \nabla^2 f_1 + \frac{u(u+1)(u+2)}{6} \nabla^3 f_1 + \dots \right] dx$$

$$= y_0 + h \int_{-1}^{0} \left[f_1 + u \nabla f_1 + \frac{(u^2 + u)}{2} \nabla^2 f_1 + \left(\frac{u^3 + 3u^2 + 2u}{6} \right) \nabla^3 f_1 + \dots \right] du$$

$\because x = x_1 + hu$
$\therefore dx = h\, du$

$$= y_0 + h\left(f_1 - \frac{1}{2}\nabla f_1 - \frac{1}{12}\nabla^2 f_1 - \frac{1}{24}\nabla^3 f_1 - ...\right) \tag{42}$$

Neglecting the fourth order and higher order differences and using

$\nabla f_1 = f_1 - f_0$, $\nabla^2 f_1 = f_1 - 2f_0 + f_{-1}$, $\nabla^3 f_1 = f_1 - 3f_0 + 3f_{-1} - f_{-2}$ in (42), we get

$$y_1 = y_0 + \frac{h}{24}(9f_1 + 19f_0 - 5f_{-1} + f_{-2})$$

which is known as ***Adams-Bashforth or Adams-Moulton Corrector Formula*** and is denoted generally as

$$y^c_{n+1} = y_n + \frac{h}{24}(9f_{n+1} - 19f_n - 5f_{n-1} + f_{n-2})$$

or $$y^c_{n+1} = y_n + \frac{h}{24}(9y'_{n+1} - 19y_n' - 5y'_{n-1} + y'_{n-2})$$

EXAMPLES

Example 1. *Using Adam's–Moulton–Bashforth Method to find y (1.4) given:*

$$\frac{dy}{dx} = x^2(1+y),\ y(1) = 1,\ y(1.1) = 1.233,\ y(1.2) = 1.548 \text{ and } y(1.3) = 1.979.$$

Sol. Here, $y' = x^2(1+y)$, $h = 0.1$

$x_0 = 1, x_1 = 1.1, x_2 = 1.2, x_3 = 1.3$

$y_0 = 1, y_1 = 1.233, y_2 = 1.548, y_3 = 1.979$

Now, Adams–Bashforth Predictor Formula is

$$y_4^p = y_3 + \frac{h}{24}(55y_3' - 59y_2' + 37y_1' - 9y_0') \tag{43}$$

$y_1' = x_1^2(1+y_1) = 2.70193$

$y_2' = x_2^2(1+y_2) = 3.66912$

$y_3' = x_3^2(1+y_3) = 5.03451$

$\therefore$ from (43),

$$y_4^p = 1.979 + \left(\frac{01}{24}\right)[55(5.03451) - 59(3.66912) + 37(2.70193) - 9(2)]$$

$= 2.5722974$

Now, $(y_4')^p = x_4^2(1+y_4^p) = (1.4)^2(1+2.5722974)$

$= 7.0017029$

Now, the Corrector Formula is

$$y_4^c = y_3 + \frac{h}{24}(9y_4'^p + 19y_3' - 5y_2' + y_1')$$

$$= 1.979 + \left(\frac{0.1}{24}\right)[9(7.0017029) + 19(5.03451)$$

$$- 5(3.66912) + 2.70193]$$

$$= 2.5749473$$

$$\therefore \quad y(0.4) = 2.5749$$

Example 2. *Find y(0.1), y(0.2), y(0.3) from*

$$\frac{dy}{dx} = x^2 - y;\ y(0) = 1$$

by using Taylor's Series Method and hence obtain y(0.4) using Adams–Bashforth Method.

Sol. We have, $y' = x^2 - y,\ y(0) = 1$

By Taylor's Series Method, we have

$$y(0.1) = 0.905125$$

$$y(0.2) = 0.8212352$$

$$y(0.3) = 0.7491509$$

Hence, $x_0 = 0,\ x_1 = 0.1,\ x_2 = 0.2,\ x_3 = 0.3$

$$y_0 = 1,\ y_1 = 0.905125,\ y_2 = 0.8212352,\ y_3 = 0.7491509$$

Also, $y_0' = -1,\ y_1' = -0.895125,\ y_2' = -0.7812352$

and $y_3' = -0.6591509$

Now, Adams–Bashforth Predictor Formula is

$$y_4^p = y_3 + \frac{h}{24}(55y_3' - 59y_2' + 37y_1' - 9y_0')$$

$$= 0.7491509 + \left(\frac{0.1}{24}\right)[55(-0.6591509) - 59(-0.7812352)$$

$$+ 37(-0.895125) - 9(-1)]$$

$$= 0.6896507$$

Now, $y_4'^p = x_4^2 - y_4^p = (0.4)^2 - 0.6896507 = -0.5296507$

The Corrector Formula is

$$y_4^c = y_3 + \frac{h}{24}(9y_4'^p + 19y_3' - 5y_2' + y_1')$$

$$= 0.7491509 + \left(\frac{0.1}{24}\right) [9(-0.5296507)$$

$$+ 19(-0.6591509) - 5(-0.7812352) + (-0.895125)]$$

$$= 0.6896522$$

$$\therefore \quad y(0.4) = 0.6896522$$

ASSIGNMENT 6.6

1. Using Adams–Bashforth Formula, find $y(0.4)$ and $y(0.5)$ if y satisfies the differential equation

$$\frac{dy}{dx} = 3e^x + 2y \text{ with } y(0) = 0.$$

Compute y at $x = 0.1, 0.2, 0.3$ by means of Runge-Kutta Method.

2. Determine $y(0.4)$ given the equation $\frac{dy}{dx} = \frac{1}{2} xy$ using Adams–Moulton Method, given that

$$y(0) = 1, \; y(0.1) = 1.0025, y(0.2) = 1.0101, y(0.3) = 1.0228.$$

3. Using Adams–Bashforth Predictor–Corrector Method, find $y(1.4)$ given that

$$x^2y' + xy = 1; y(1) = 1, y(1.1) = 0.996, y(1.2) = 0.986, y(1.3) = 0.972$$

4. Compute $y(1)$ by Adam's Method given

$$y' = x^2 - y^3, y(0) = 1, y(0.25) = 0.821028, y(0.5)$$
$$= 0.741168, y(0.75) = 0.741043.$$

5. Given $y' = 2y - 1$, $y(0) = 1$. Compute y for $x = 0.1, 0.2, 0.3$ by the IV order Runge-Kutta Method and $y(0.4)$ by Adam's Method.

6.24 STABILITY

A numerical method for solving a mathematical problem is considered *stable* if the sensitivity of the numerical answer to the data is no greater than in the original mathematical problem. Stable problems are also called well-posed problems.

If a problem is not stable, it is called *unstable* or ill-posed.

A problem $f(x, y) = 0$ is said to be stable if the solution y depends in a continuous way on the variable x.

6.25 STABILITY IN THE SOLUTION OF ORDINARY DIFFERENTIAL EQUATIONS

The idea of stability may be defined as

(*i*) A computation is stable if it does not blow up.

(*ii*) Stability is a boundedness of the relative error.

Two types of stability considerations enter in the solution of ordinary differential equations.

(*a*) Inherent stability

(*b*) Numerical stability

Inherent stability is determined by the mathematical formulations of the problem and is dependent on the Eigen values of Jacobean Matrix of the differential equation.

Numerical stability is a function of the error propagation in the numerical method. Three types of errors occur in the application of numerical integration methods:

(*a*) Truncation error (*b*) Round-off error (*c*) Propagation error.

6.26 STABILITY OF I ORDER LINEAR DIFFERENTIAL EQUATION OF FORM $\frac{dy}{dx} = Ay$ WITH INITIAL CONDITION $y(x_0) = y_0$

The solution of this equation is

$$y(x) = y(x_0)\, e^{A(x-x_0)}$$

Let, $$y_n = y(x_n) + \varepsilon_n \text{ at } x_n = x_0 + nh$$

ε_n being the total truncation error.

Let E(A*h*) be the polynomial approximation to e^{-Ah} (for small A*h*). Then the computed result of one step length is

$$y_{n+1} = \text{E}(Ah)\, y_n$$

while the correct solution is

$$y(x_{n+1}) = e^{Ah}\, y(x_n)$$

Thus, $$y_{n+1} - y(x_{n+1}) = \text{E}(Ah)\, y_n - e^{Ah}\, y(x_n)$$

$$= \text{E}(Ah)\, [y(x_n) + \text{E}_n] - e^{Ah}\, y(x_n)$$

$$= [\text{E}(Ah) - e^{Ah}]\, y(x_n) + \text{E}(Ah)\, \varepsilon_n$$

Clearly, the error ε_n will be amplified if $E(Ah) > 1$ which is possible for sufficiently large Ah at $x_{n+k} = x_0 + (n + k) h$. It will have grown by factor $E^k(Ah)$. Thus meaningful results can be obtained only for $E(Ah) < 1$. If $| E(Ah) | < e^{Ah}$ then we say that the method is relatively stable for that value of Ah.

EXAMPLES

Example 1. *How many terms are to be retained if we want to have an accuracy of 10^{-10} in solving $y' = x + y$, $y(0) = 1$, $x \in (0, 1)$ by Taylor's series method?*

Sol. $$y' = x + y$$

$\Rightarrow$ $$y'' = 1 + y', y''' = y'', \ldots, \text{ and so on}$$

$\Rightarrow$ $$y^{(p+1)} = y^{(p)}, p = 2, 3 \ldots$$

$\therefore$ $$y'(0) = 1, y''(0) = 2, \ldots, y^{(p)}(0) = 2$$

Hence, $$y(x) = 1 + x + x^2 + \ldots + \frac{2}{p!} x^p + \ldots$$

In order to obtain results, which will be accurate up to 10^{-10} for $x \le 1$, we have

$$\frac{1}{(p+1)!} < 5 \times 10^{-10}$$

$\Rightarrow$ $$p \approx 15$$

Hence about 15 terms are required to obtain the accuracy of 10^{-10} for solving $\frac{dy}{dx} = x + y$ by Taylor's Series Method when $x \le 1$.

Example 2. *Discuss the stability of Euler's Method for solving the differential equation.*

$$\frac{dy}{dx} = \lambda y$$

Sol. $$\frac{dy}{dx} = \lambda y = f(x, y)$$

True solution is $y(x) = ce^{\lambda x}$ so that

$$y(x_{n+1}) = y(x_n)e^{\lambda h}, h = x_{n+1} - x_n$$

Approximate solution using Euler's Method is

$$y_{n+1} = y_n + h f(x_n, y_n) = y_n + h \lambda y_n$$
$$= (1 + h\lambda) y_n$$

Let $$y_n = y(x_n) + \varepsilon_n$$

where ε_n is the total solution error.

$$\Rightarrow \quad y_{n+1} = y(x_{n+1}) + \varepsilon_{n+1} = (1 + h\lambda)\, y_n$$

$$= (1 + h\lambda)\, [y(x_n) + \varepsilon_n]$$

Therefore,

$$y_{n+1} - y(x_{n+1}) = (1 + \lambda h)\, y(x_n) + (1 + \lambda h)\, \varepsilon_n - y(x_n)\, e^{\lambda h}$$

$$\Rightarrow \quad \varepsilon_{n+1} = (1 + \lambda h - e^{\lambda h})\, y(x_n) + (1 + \lambda h)\, \varepsilon_n$$

The first term on R.H.S. is the total truncation error while the second term is the contribution to the error from the previous step (inherited error).

Hence, we have $E(\lambda h) = 1 + \lambda h$

where $E(\lambda h)$ is a polynomial approximation to $e^{\lambda h}$ for small λh.

Obviously, Euler's Method is absolutely stable if $|\ 1 + \lambda h\ | < 1$ or $-2 < \lambda h < 0$; relatively stable if λh is greater than the solution of $\lambda h = -1 - e^{-\lambda h}$.

Part 5

- **Statistical Computation**

  Frequency Charts, Curve Fitting, Principle of Least Squares, Fitting a Straight Line, Exponential Curves etc., Data Fitting with Cubic Splines, Regression Analysis, Linear Regression, Polynomial Fit: Non-linear Regression, Multiple Linear Regression, Statistical Quality Control.

- **Testing of Hypothesis**

  Population or Universe, Sampling, Parameters of Statistics, Test of Significance, *t*-Test, F-Test, Chi-square (χ^2) Test.

Chapter 7 STATISTICAL COMPUTATION

7.1 THE STATISTICAL METHODS

Statistical methods are devices by which complex and numerical data are so systematically treated as to present a comprehensible and intelligible view of them. In other words, the statistical method is a technique used to obtain, analyze and present numerical data.

7.2 LIMITATION OF STATISTICAL METHODS

There are certain limitations to the Statistics and Statistical Methods.

1. Statistical laws are not exact laws like mathematical or chemical laws. They are derived by taking a majority of cases and are not true for every individual. Thus, the statistical inferences are uncertain.
2. Statistical technique applies only to data reducible to quantitative forms.
3. Statistical technique is the same for the social as for physical sciences.
4. Statistical results might lead to fallacious conclusions if they are quoted short of their context.

7.3 FREQUENCY CHARTS

7.3.1 Variable

A quantity which can vary from one individual to another is called a **variable**. It is also called a **variate.** Wages, barometer readings, rainfall records, heights, and weights are the common examples of variables.

Quantities which can take any numerical value within a certain range are called **continuous variables.** For example, the height of a child at various ages is a continuous variable since, as the child grows from 120 cm to 150 cm, his height assumes all possible values within the limit.

Quantities which are incapable of taking all possible values are called **discontinuous** or **discrete variables.** For example, the number of rooms in a house can take only the integral values such as 2, 3, 4, etc.

7.3.2 Frequency Distributions

The scores of 50 students in mathematics are arranged below according to their roll numbers, the maximum scores being 100.

19, 70, 75, 15, 0, 23, 59, 56, 27, 89, 91, 22, 21, 22, 50, 89, 56, 73, 56, 89, 75, 65, 85, 22, 3, 12, 41, 87, 82, 72, 50, 22, 87, 50, 89, 28, 89, 50, 40, 36, 40, 30, 28, 87, 81, 90, 22, 15, 30, 35.

The data given in the crude form (or raw form) is called **ungrouped data**. If the data is arranged in ascending or descending order of magnitude, it is said to be arranged in an array. Let us now arrange it in the intervals 0–10, 10–20, 20–30, 30–40, 40–50, 50–60, 60–70, 70–80, 80–90, 90–100. This is arranged by a method called the **tally method.**

In this we consider every observation and put it in the suitable class by drawing a vertical line. After every 4 vertical lines, we cross it for the 5th entry and then a little space is left and the next vertical line is drawn.

Scores (Class-interval)	*Number of Students*	*Frequency (f)*	*Cumulative Frequencies*
0—10	||	2	2
10—20	|| ||	4	6
20—30	~~||||~~ ~~||||~~	10	16
30—40	|| ||	4	20
40—50	|||	3	23
50—60	~~||||~~ |||	8	31
60—70	|	1	32
70—80	~~||||~~	5	37
80—90	~~||||~~ ~~||||~~ |	11	48
90—100	||	2	50
Total		$\Sigma f = 50$	

This type of representation is called a **grouped frequency distribution** or simply a **frequency distribution.** The groups are called the **classes** and the boundary ends 0, 10, 20, ... etc. are called **class limits.** In the class limits 10—20, 10 is the **lower limit** and 20 is the **upper limit.** The difference between the upper and lower limits of a class is called its magnitude or **class-interval.** The number of observations falling within a particular class is called its **frequency** or **class frequency.** The frequency of the class 80—90 is 11. The variate value which lies mid-way between the upper and lower limits is called mid-value or mid-point of that class. The mid-points of these are respectively 5, 15, 25, 35, ... The **cumulative frequency** corresponding to a class is the total of all the frequencies up to and including that class. Thus the cumulative frequency of the class 10—20 is 2 + 4, *i.e.,* 6 the cumulative frequency of the class 20—50 is 6 + 10, *i.e.,* 16, and so on.

While preparing the frequency distribution the following points must be remembered:

1. The class-intervals should be of equal width as far as possible A comparison of different distributions is facilitated if the class interval is used for all. The class-interval should be an integer as far as possible.
2. The number of classes should never be fewer than 6 and not more than 30. With a smaller number of classes, the accuracy may be lost, and with a larger number of classes, the computations become tedious.
3. The observation corresponding to the common point of two classes should always be put in the higher class. For example, a number corresponding to the value 30 is to be put up in the class 30—40 and not in 20—30.

The following forms of the above table may also be used:

Cumulative Frequency			
Scores	*Number of Students*	*Scores*	*Number of Students*
Under 10	2	above 90	2
Under 20	6	above 80	13
Under 30	16	above 70	18
Under 40	20	above 60	19
Under 50	23	above 50	27
Under 60	31	above 40	30
Under 70	32	above 30	34
Under 80	37	above 20	44
Under 90	48	above 10	48
Under 100	50	above 0	50

7.4 GRAPHICAL REPRESENTATION OF A FREQUENCY DISTRIBUTION

Representation of frequency distribution by means of a diagram makes the unwieldy data intelligible and conveys to the eye the general run of the observations. The graphs and diagrams have a more lasting effect on the brain. It is always easier to compare data through graphs and diagrams. Forecasting also becomes easier with the help of graphs. Graphs help us in interpolation of values of the variables.

However there are certain disadvantages as well. Graphs do not give measurements of the variables as accurate as those given by tables. The numerical value can be obtained to any number of decimal places in a table, but from graphs it can not be found to 2nd or 3rd places of decimals. Another disadvantage is that it is very difficult to have a proper selection of scale. The facts may be misrepresented by differences in scale.

7.5 TYPES OF GRAPHS AND DIAGRAMS

Generally the following types of graphs are used in representing frequency distributions:

(1) Histograms, (2) Frequency Polygon, (3) Frequency Curve, (4) Cumulative Frequency Curve or the Ogive, (5) Historigrams, (6) Bar Diagrams, (7) Area

Diagrams, (8) Circles or Pie Diagrams, (9) Prisms, (10) Cartograms and Map Diagrams, (11) Pictograms.

7.6 HISTOGRAMS

To draw the histograms of a given grouped frequency distribution, mark off along a horizontal base line all the class-intervals on a suitable scale. With the class-intervals as bases, draw rectangles with the areas proportional to the frequencies of the respective class-intervals. For equal class-intervals, the heights of the rectangles will be proportional to the frequencies. If the class-intervals are not equal, the heights of the rectangles will be proportional to the ratios of the frequencies to the width of the corresponding classes. A diagram with all these rectangles is a **Histogram.**

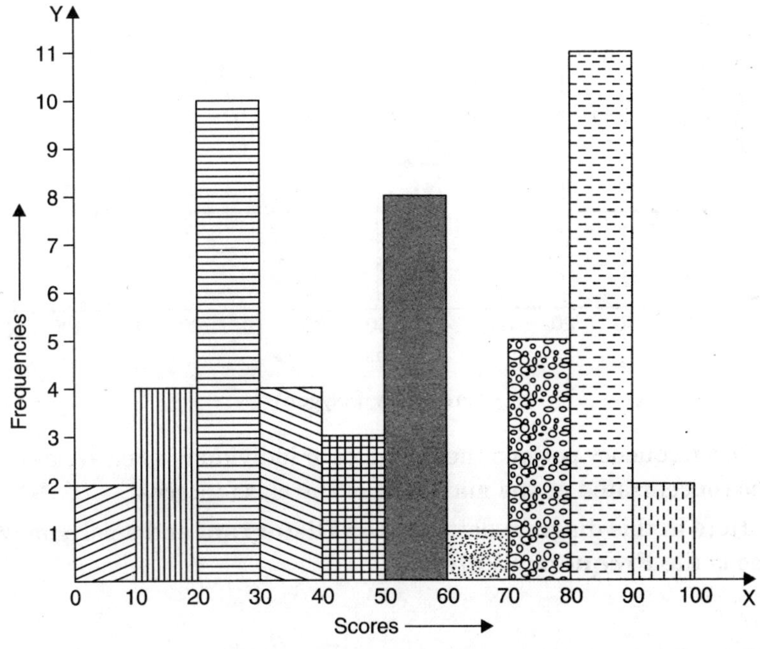

(Histogram for the previous table)

Histograms are also useful when the class-intervals are not of the same width. They are appropriate to cases in which the frequency changes rapidly.

7.7 FREQUENCY POLYGON

If the various points are obtained by plotting the central values of the class intervals as x co-ordinates and the respective frequencies as the y co-ordinates, and these points are joined by straight lines taken in order, they form a polygon called **Frequency Polygon.**

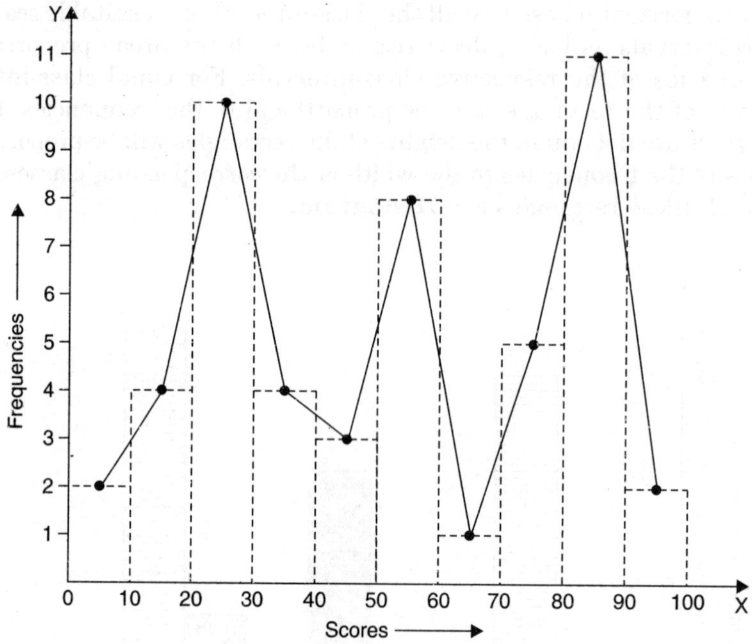

(Frequency Polygon)

In a frequency polygon the variables or individuals of each class are assumed to be concentrated at the mid-point of the class-interval.

Here in this diagram dotted is the **Histogram** and a polygon with lines as sides is the **Frequency Polygon.**

7.8 FREQUENCY CURVE

If through the vertices of a frequency polygon a smooth freehand curve is drawn, we get the **Frequency Curve.** This is done usually when the class-intervals are of small widths.

7.9 CUMULATIVE FREQUENCY CURVE OR THE OGIVE

If from a cumulative frequency table, the upper limits of the class taken as x co-ordinates and the cumulative frequencies as the y co-ordinates and the points are plotted, then these points when joined by a freehand smooth curve give the **Cumulative Frequency Curve or the Ogive.**

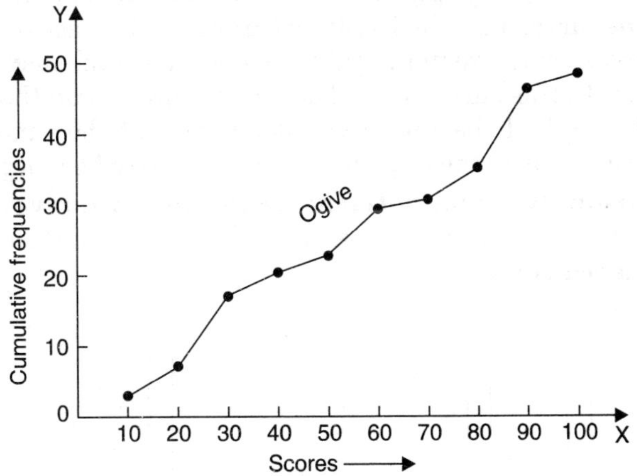

7.10 TYPES OF FREQUENCY CURVES

Following are some important types of frequency curves, generally obtained in the graphical representations of frequency distributions:

1. *Symmetrical curve or bell shaped curve.*
2. *Moderately asymmetrical or skewed curve.*
3. *Extremely asymmetrical or J-shaped curve or reverse J-shaped.*
4. *U-shaped curve.*
5. *A bimodal frequency curve.*
6. *A multimodal frequency curve.*

1. **Symmetrical curve or Bell shaped curve.** If a curve can be folded symmetrically along a vertical line, it is called a symmetrical curve. In this type the class frequencies decrease to zero symmetrically on either side of a central maximum, *i.e.*, the observations equidistant from the central maximum have the same frequency.

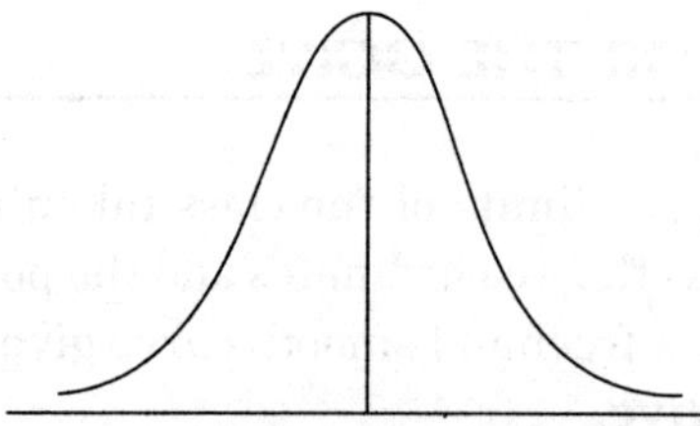

(Bell shaped curve)

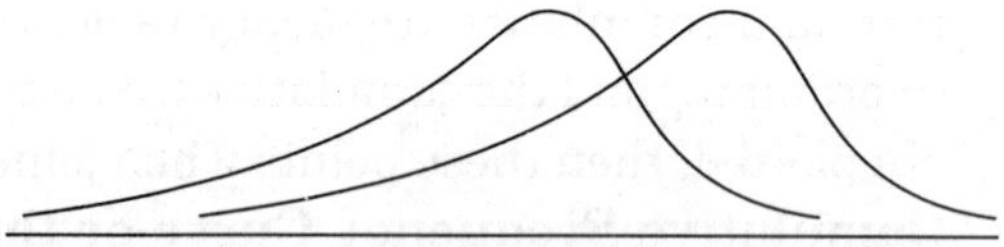

(Skewed curve)

2. **Moderately asymmetrical or skewed curve.** If there is no symmetry in the curve, it is called a **Skew Curve.** In this case the class frequencies decrease with greater rapidity on one side of the maximum than on the other. In this curve one tail is always longer than the other. If the long tail is to the to be a positive side, it is said to be a positive skew curve, if long tail is to the negative side, it is said to be a negative skew curve.
3. **Extremely asymmetrical or J-shaped curve.** When the class frequencies run up to a maximum at one end of the range, they form a J-shaped curve.

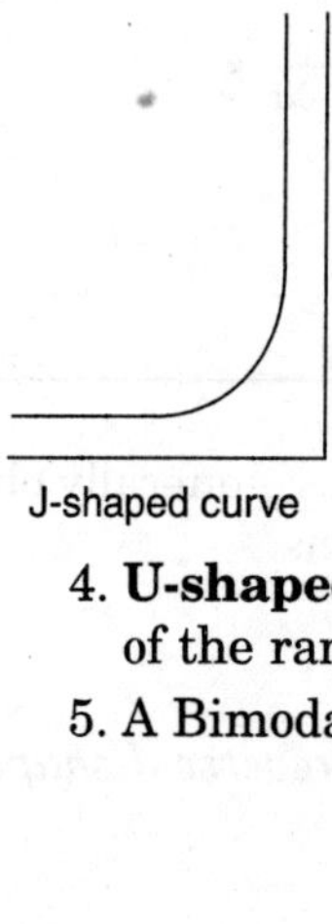

J-shaped curve

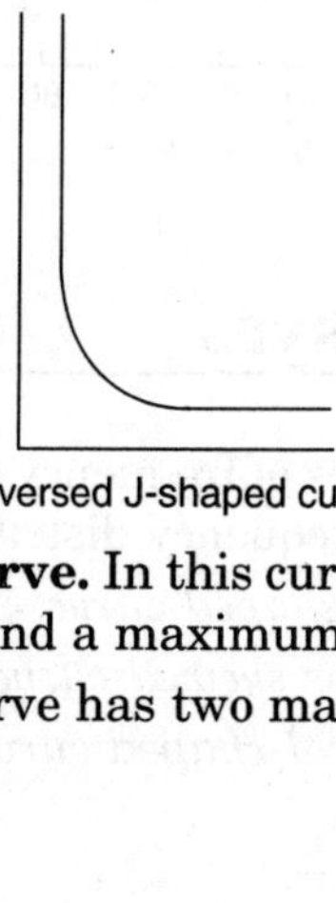

Reversed J-shaped curve

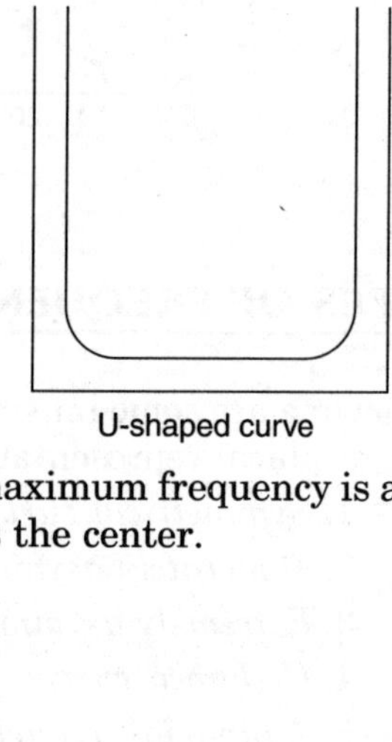

U-shaped curve

4. **U-shaped curve.** In this curve, the maximum frequency is at the ends of the range and a maximum towards the center.
5. A Bimodal curve has two maxima.

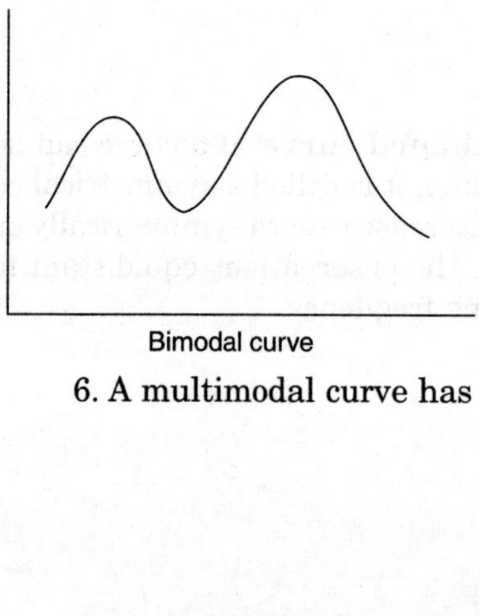

Bimodal curve

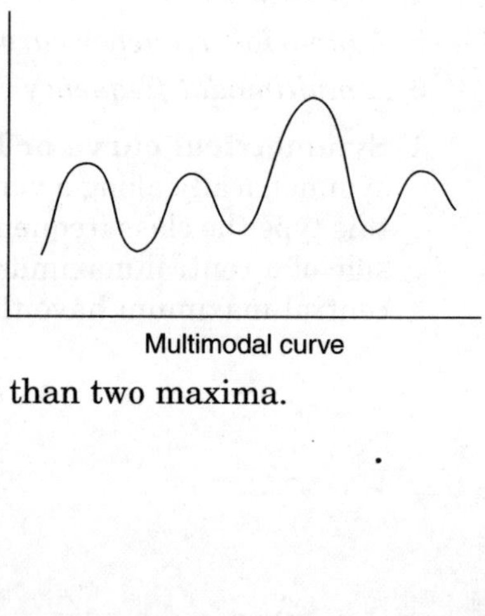

Multimodal curve

6. A multimodal curve has more than two maxima.

7.11 DIAGRAMS

1. **Bar diagrams.** Bar diagrams are used to compare the simple magnitude of different items. In bar diagrams, equal bases on a horizontal or vertical line are selected and rectangles are constructed with the length proportional to the given data. The width of bars is an arbitrary factor. The distance between two bars should be taken at about one-half of the width of a bar.
2. **Area diagrams.** When the difference between two quantities to be compared is large, bars do not show the comparison so clearly. In such cases, squares or circle are used.
3. **Circle or Pie-diagrams.** When circles are drawn to represent an area equivalent to the figures, they are said to form pie-diagrams or circles-diagrams. In case of circles, the square roots of magnitudes are proportional to the radii.

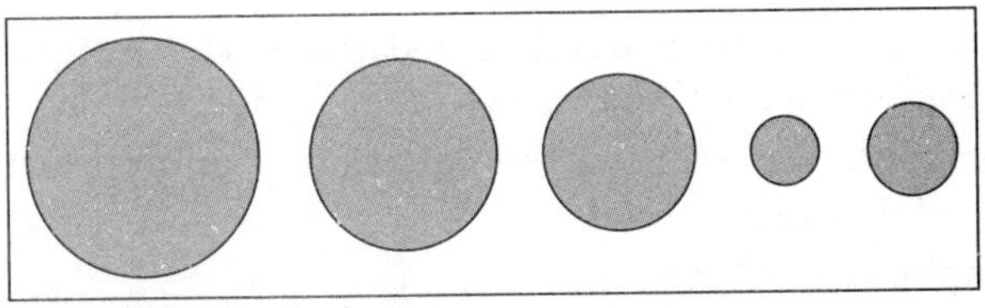

4. **Subdivided Pie-diagram.** Subdivided Pie-diagrams are used when comparison of the component parts is done with another and the total. The total value is equated to 360° and then the angles corresponding to the component parts are calculated.
5. **Prisms and Cubes.** When the ratio between the two quantities to be compared is very great so that even area diagrams are not suitable, the data can be represented by spheres, prisms, or cubes. Cubes are in common use. Cubes are constructed on sides which are taken in the ratio of cube roots of the given quantities.
6. **Cartograms or map diagrams.** Cartograms or map diagrams are most suitable for geographical data. Rainfalls and temperature in different parts of the country are shown with dots or shades in a particular map.
7. **Pictograms.** When numerical data are represented by pictures, they give a more attractive representation. Such pictures are called pictograms.

7.12 CURVE FITTING

Let there be two variables x and y which give us a set of n pairs of numerical values $(x_1, y_1), (x_2, y_2).......(x_n, y_n)$. In order to have an approximate idea about the relationship of these two variables, we plot these n paired points on a graph, thus we get a diagram showing the simultaneous variation in values of both the variables called *scatter or dot diagram.* From scatter diagram, we get only an approximate non-mathematical relation between two variables. *Curve fitting* means an exact relationship between two variables by algebraic equations. In fact, this relationship is the equation of the curve. Therefore, *curve fitting* means to form an equation of the curve from the given data. Curve fitting is considered of immense importance both from the point of view of theoretical and practical statistics.

Theoretically, curve fitting is useful in the study of correlation and regression. Practically, it enables us to represent the relationship between two variables by simple algebraic expressions, for example, polynomials, exponential, or logarithmic functions.

Curve fitting is also used to estimate the values of one variable corresponding to the specified values of the other variable.

The constants occurring in the equation of an approximate curve can be found by the following methods:

(*i*) Graphical method

(*ii*) Method of group averages

(*iii*) Principle of least squares

(*iv*) Method of moments.

Out of the above four methods, we will only discuss and study here *the principle of least squares.*

7.13 PRINCIPLE OF LEAST SQUARES

Principle of least squares provides a unique set of values to the constants and hence suggests a curve of best fit to the given data.

Suppose we have m-paired observations $(x_1, y_1), (x_2, y_2), ..., (x_m, y_m)$ of two variables x and y. It is required to fit a polynomial of degree n of the type

$$y = a + bx + cx^2 + ... + kx^n \tag{1}$$

of these values. We have to determine the constants $a, b, c, ..., k$ such that they represent the curve of best fit of that degree.

In case $m = n$, we get in general a unique set of values satisfying the given system of equations.

But if $m > n$, then we get m equations by putting different values of x and y in equation (1) and we want to find only the values of n constants. Thus there may be no such solution to satisfy all m equations.

Therefore we try to find out those values of $a, b, c, \ldots\ldots, k$ which satisfy all the equations as nearly as possible. We apply the principle of least squares in such cases.

Putting $x_1, x_2, \ldots, x_m$ for x in (1), we get

$$y_1' = a + bx_1 + cx_1^2 + \ldots\ldots + kx_1^n$$
$$y_2' = a + bx_2 + cx_2^2 + \ldots\ldots + kx_2^n$$
$$\vdots \qquad\qquad \vdots$$
$$y_m' = a + bx_m + cx_m^2 + \ldots\ldots + kx_m^n$$

where $y_1', y_2', \ldots\ldots, y_m'$ are the expected values of y for $x = x_1, x_2, \ldots\ldots, x_m$ respectively.

The values $y_1, y_2, \ldots\ldots, y_m$ are called observed values of y corresponding to $x = x_1, x_2, \ldots\ldots, x_m$ respectively.

The expected values are different from the observed values, the difference $y_r - y_r'$ for different values of r are called *residuals.*

Introduce a new quantity U such that

$$U = \Sigma(y_r - y_r')^2 = \Sigma(y_r - a - bx_r - cx_r^2 - \ldots\ldots - kx_r^n)^2$$

The constants $a, b, c, \ldots\ldots, k$ are choosen in such a way that the sum of the squares of the residuals is minimum.

Now the condition for U to be maximum or minimum is $\frac{\partial U}{\partial a} = 0 = \frac{\partial U}{\partial b} = \frac{\partial U}{\partial c}$ $= \ldots\ldots = \frac{\partial U}{\partial k}$. On simplifying these relations, we get

$$\Sigma y = ma + b\Sigma x + \ldots\ldots + k\Sigma x^n$$
$$\Sigma xy = a\Sigma x + b\Sigma x^2 + \ldots\ldots + k\,\Sigma x^{n+1}$$
$$\Sigma x^2 y = a\Sigma x^2 + b\Sigma x^3 + \ldots\ldots + k\,\Sigma x^{n+2}$$
$$\vdots \qquad\qquad \vdots$$
$$\Sigma x^n y = a\Sigma x^n + b\Sigma x^{n+1} + \ldots\ldots + k\,\Sigma x^{2n}$$

These are known as *Normal equations* and can be solved as simultaneous equations to give the values of the constants $a, b, c, \ldots\ldots, k$. These equations are $(n + 1)$ in number.

If we calculate the second order partial derivatives and these values are given, they give a positive value of the function, so U is minimum.

This method does not help us to choose the degree of the curve to be fitted but helps us is finding the values of the constants when the form of the curve has already been chosen.

7.14 FITTING A STRAIGHT LINE

Let (x_i, y_i), $i = 1, 2, ..., n$ be n sets of observations of related data and

$$y = a + bx \tag{2}$$

be the straight line to be fitted. The residual at $x = x_i$ is

$$E_i = y_i - f(x_i) = y_i - a - bx_i$$

Introduce a new quantity U such that

$$U = \sum_{i=1}^{n} E_i^2 = \sum_{i=1}^{n} (y_i - a - bx_i)^2$$

By the principle of Least squares, U is minimum

$$\therefore \quad \frac{\partial U}{\partial a} = 0 \text{ and } \frac{\partial U}{\partial b} = 0$$

$$\therefore \quad 2\sum_{i=1}^{n} (y_i - a - bx_i)(-1) = 0 \quad \text{or} \quad \boxed{\Sigma y = na + b\Sigma x} \tag{3}$$

$$\text{and} \quad 2\sum_{i=1}^{n} (y_i - a - bx_i)(-x_i) = 0 \quad \text{or} \quad \boxed{\Sigma xy = a\Sigma x + b\Sigma x^2} \tag{4}$$

Since x_i, y_i are known, equations (3) and (4) result in a and b. Solving these, the best values for a and b can be known, and hence equation (2).

NOTE *In case of change of origin,*

if n is odd then, $\quad u = \dfrac{x - (\textit{middle term})}{\textit{interval (h)}}$

but if n is even then $\quad u = \dfrac{x - (\textit{mean of two middle terms})}{\frac{1}{2}(\textit{interval})}$.

7.15 ALGORITHM FOR FITTING A STRAIGHT LINE OF THE FORM y = a + bx FOR A GIVEN SET OF DATA POINTS

Step 01. Start of the program.

Step 02. Input no. of terms observ

Step 03. Input the array ax

Step 04. Input the array ay

Step 05. for i=0 to observ

Step 06. sum1+=x[i]

Step 07. sum2+=y[i]

Step 08. xy[i]=x[i]*y[i];

Step 09. sum3+=xy[i]

Step 10. End Loop i

Step 11. for i = 0 to observ

Step 12. x2[i]=x[i]*x[i]

Step 13. sum4+=x2[i]

Step 14. End of Loop i

Step 15. temp1=(sum2*sum4)-(sum3*sum1)

Step 16. a=temp1/((observ *sum4)-(sum1*sum1))

Step 17. b=(sum2-observ*a)/sum1

Step 18. Print output a,b

Step 19. Print "line is: y = a+bx"

Step 20. End of Program

7.16 FLOW-CHART FOR FITTING A STRAIGHT LINE y = a + bx FOR A GIVEN SET OF DATA POINTS

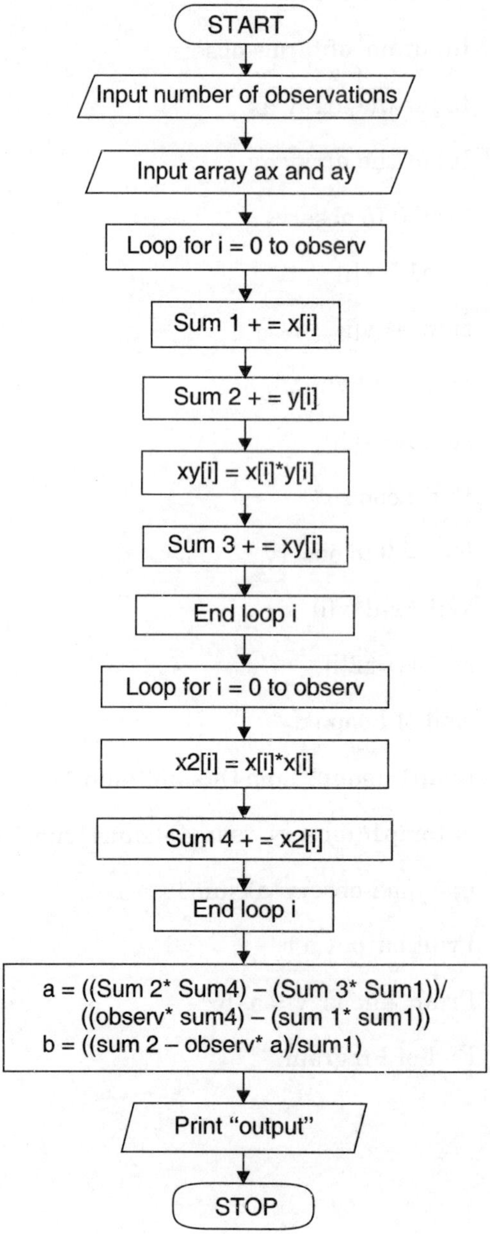

```
/* ******************************************************
```

7.17 PROGRAM TO IMPLEMENT CURVE FITTING TO FIT A STRAIGHT LINE

```
****************************************************** */
    //... HEADER FILE DECLARATION
    # include <stdio.h>
    # include <conio.h>
    # include <math.h>
    //... Main Execution Thread
    void main()
    {
    //... Variable Declaration Field
    //... Integer Type
    int i=0;
    int observ;
    //... Floating Type
    float x[10];
    float y[10];
    float xy[10];
    float x2[10];
    float sum1=0.0;
    float sum2=0.0;
    float sum3=0.0;
    float sum4=0.0;
    //... Double Type
    double a;
    double b;
    //... Invoke Function Clear Screen
    clrscr ();
    //... Input Section
    //... Input Number of Observations
    printf("\n\n Enter the number of observations - ");
    scanf("%d" ,&observ);
```

```
//... Input Sequel For Array X
printf("\n\n\n Enter the values of x - \n");
for (;i<observ;i++)
{
printf("\n\n Enter the Value of x%d: ",i+1);
scanf("%f" ,&x[i]);
sum1 +=x[i];
}
//... Input Sequel For Array Y
printf("\n\n Enter the values of y - \n");
for(i=0;i<observ;i++)
{
printf("\n\n Enter the value of y%d:",i+1);
scanf("%f",&y[i]);
sum2+=y[i];
}
//... Processing and Calculation Section
for(i=0;i<observ;i++)
{
xy[i]=x[i]*y[i];
sum3 +=xy[i];
}
for(i=0;i<observ; i++)
{
x2[i]=x[i]*x[i];
sum4+ =x2[i];
}
a=(sum2*sum4-sum3*sum1)/(observ*sum4-sum1*sum1);
b=(sum2-observ*a)/sum1;
//... Output Section
printf("\n\n\n\n Equation of the STRAIGHT LINE");
printf("of the form y = a + b*x is:");
printf("\n\n\n \t\t\t Y = %.2f + (%.2f) X", a,b);
//... Invoke User Watch Halt Function
```

```
printf("\n\n\n Press Enter to Exit");
getch();
}
//... Termination of Main Execution Thread
```

EXAMPLES

Example 1. *By the method of least squares, find the straight line that best fits the following data:*

x:	*1*	*2*	*3*	*4*	*5*
y:	*14*	*27*	*40*	*55*	*68.*

Sol. Let the straight line of best fit be

$$y = a + bx \tag{5}$$

Normal equations are $\Sigma y = ma + b\Sigma x$ (6)

and $\Sigma xy = a\Sigma x + b\Sigma x^2$ (7)

Here $m = 5$

The table is as below:

x	y	xy	x^2
1	14	14	1
2	27	54	4
3	40	120	9
4	55	220	16
5	68	340	25
$\Sigma x = 15$	$\Sigma y = 204$	$\Sigma xy = 748$	$\Sigma x^2 = 55$

Substituting in (6) and (7), we get

$$204 = 5a + 15b$$

$$748 = 15a + 55b$$

Solving, we get $a = 0$, $b = 13.6$

Hence required straight line is $\boxed{y = 13.6x}$

Example 2. *Fit a straight line to the following data:*

x:	*0*	*1*	*2*	*3*	*4*
y:	*1*	*1.8*	*3.3*	*4.5*	*6.3.*

Sol. Let the straight line obtained from the given data be $y = a + bx$ then the normal equations are

$$\Sigma y = ma + b\,\Sigma x \tag{8}$$

$$\Sigma xy = a\Sigma x + b\Sigma x^2 \tag{9}$$

Here $m = 5$

x	y	xy	x^2
0	1	0	0
1	1.8	1.8	1
2	3.3	6.6	4
3	4.5	13.5	9
4	6.3	25.2	16
$\Sigma x = 10$	$\Sigma y = 16.9$	$\Sigma xy = 47.1$	$\Sigma x^2 = 30$

From (8) and (9), $16.9 = 5a + 10b$

and $47.1 = 10a + 30b$

Solving, we get $a = 0.72, b = 1.33$

$\therefore$ Required line is $\boxed{y = 0.72 + 1.33\,x.}$

Example 3. *Fit a straight line to the following data regarding x as the independent variable:*

x:	*1*	*2*	*3*	*4*	*5*	*6*
y:	*1200*	*900*	*600*	*200*	*110*	*50.*

Sol. Let the equation of the straight line to be fitted be $y = a + bx$

Here $m = 6$

x	y	x^2	xy
1	1200	1	1200
2	900	4	1800
3	600	9	1800
4	200	16	800
5	110	25	550
6	50	36	300
$\Sigma x = 21$	$\Sigma y = 3060$	$\Sigma x^2 = 91$	$\Sigma xy = 6450$

From normal equations, we get

$$3060 = 6a + 21b,\ 6450 = 21a + 91b$$

Solving, we get $a = 1361.97,\ b = -243.42$

$\therefore$ Required line is

$$\boxed{y = 1361.97 - 243.42\,x.}$$

Example 4. *Show that the line of fit to the following data is given by $y = 0.7x + 11.285$:*

x:	0	5	10	15	20	25
y:	12	15	17	22	24	30.

Sol. Since *m* is even,

Let $x_0 = 12.5 \quad h = 5 \quad y_0 = 20$ (say)

Then let, $u = \dfrac{x - 12.5}{2.5}$ and $v = y - 20$

x	y	u	v	uv	u^2
0	12	−5	−8	40	25
5	15	−3	−5	15	9
10	17	−1	−3	3	1
15	22	1	2	2	1
20	24	3	4	12	9
25	30	5	10	50	25
Total		$\Sigma u = 0$	$\Sigma v = 0$	$\Sigma uv = 122$	$\Sigma u^2 = 70$

Normal equations are $0 = 6a$ and $122 = 70b$

$\Rightarrow \quad a = 0,\quad b = 1.743$

Line of fit is $v = 1.743u$

Put $u = \dfrac{x - 12.5}{2.5}$ and $v = y - 20$, we get

$$\boxed{y = 0.7x + 11.285.}$$

Example 5. *Fit a straight line to the following data:*

x:	71	68	73	69	67	65	66	67
y:	69	72	70	70	68	67	68	64.

Sol. Let the equation of the straight line to be fitted be

$$y = a + bx \tag{10}$$

Normal equations are

$$\Sigma y = ma + b\Sigma x \tag{11}$$

and $$\Sigma xy = a\Sigma x + b\Sigma x^2 \tag{12}$$

Here $m = 8$. Table is as below:

x	y	xy	x^2
71	69	4899	5041
68	72	4896	4624
73	70	5110	5329
69	70	4830	4761
67	68	4556	4489
65	67	4355	4225
66	68	4488	4356
67	64	4288	4489
$\Sigma x = 546$	$\Sigma y = 548$	$\Sigma xy = 37422$	$\Sigma x^2 = 37314$

Substituting these values in equations (11) and (12), we get

$$548 = 8a + 546b$$

$$37422 = 546a + 37314b$$

Solving, we get

$$a = 39.5454, \quad b = 0.4242$$

Hence the required line of best fit is

$$\boxed{y = 39.5454 + 0.4242\,x.}$$

Example 6. *Show that the best fitting linear function for the points (x_1, y_1), (x_2, y_2), ..., (x_n, y_n) may be expressed in the form*

$$\begin{vmatrix} x & y & 1 \\ \Sigma x_i & \Sigma y_i & n \\ \Sigma x_i^2 & \Sigma x_i y_i & \Sigma x_i \end{vmatrix} = 0 \qquad (i = 1, 2, ..., n)$$

Show that the line passes through the mean point $(\bar{x}, \bar{y})$.

Sol. Let the best fitting linear function be $y = a + bx$ (13)

Then the normal equations are

$$\Sigma y_i = na + b\Sigma x_i \tag{14}$$

and $$\Sigma x_i y_i = a\Sigma x_i + b\Sigma x_i^2 \tag{15}$$

Equations (13), (14), (15) may be rewritten as

$$bx - y + a = 0$$

$$b\Sigma x_i - \Sigma y_i + na = 0$$

and
$$b\Sigma x_i^2 - \Sigma x_i y_i + a\Sigma x_i = 0$$

Eliminating a and b between these equations

$$\begin{vmatrix} x & y & 1 \\ \Sigma x_i & \Sigma y_i & n \\ \Sigma x_i^2 & \Sigma x_i y_i & \Sigma x_i \end{vmatrix} = 0 \qquad (16)$$

which is the required best fitting linear function for the mean point $(\bar{x}, \bar{y})$,

$$\bar{x} = \frac{1}{n}\Sigma x_i \quad \bar{y} = \frac{1}{n}\Sigma y_i .$$

Clearly, the line (16) passes through point $(\bar{x}, \bar{y})$ as two rows of determinants being equal make it zero.

ASSIGNMENT 7.1

1. Fit a straight line to the given data regarding x as the independent variable:

x	1	2	3	4	6	8
y	2.4	3.1	3.5	4.2	5.0	6.0

2. Find the best values of a and b so that $y = a + bx$ fits the given data:

x	0	1	2	3	4
y	1.0	2.9	4.8	6.7	8.6

3. Fit a straight line approximate to the data:

x	1	2	3	4
y	3	7	13	21

4. A simply supported beam carries a concentrated load P(*lb*) at its mid-point. Corresponding to various values of P, the maximum deflection Y (*in*) is measured. The data are given below. Find a law of the type Y = a + bP

P	100	120	140	160	180	200
Y	0.45	0.55	0.60	0.70	0.80	0.85

5. In the following table y in the weight of potassium bromide which will dissolve in 100 grams of water at temperature x^0. Find a linear law between x and y

$x^0(c)$	0	10	20	30	40	50	60	70
y gm	53.5	59.5	65.2	70.6	75.5	80.2	85.5	90

6. The weight of a calf taken at weekly intervals is given below. Fit a straight line using the method of least squares and calculate the average rate of growth per week.

Age	1	2	3	4	5	6	7	8	9	10
Weight	52.5	58.7	65	70.2	75.4	81.1	87.2	95.5	102.2	108.4

7. Find the least square line for the data points

(– 1, 10), (0, 9), (1, 7), (2, 5), (3, 4), (4, 3), (5, 0) and (6, – 1).

8. Find the least square line $y = a + bx$ for the data:

x_i	– 2	– 1	0	1	2
y_i	1	2	3	3	4

9. If P is the pull required to lift a load W by means of a pulley block, find a linear law of the form $P = mW + c$ connecting P and W, using the data:

P	12	15	21	25
W	50	70	100	120

where P and W are taken in kg-wt.

10. Using the method of least squares, fit a straight line to the following data:

x	1	2	3	4	5
y	2	4	6	8	10

11. Differentiate between interpolating polynomial and least squares polynomial obtained for a set of data.

7.18 FITTING OF AN EXPONENTIAL CURVE $y = ae^{bx}$

Taking logarithms on both sides, we get

$$\log_{10} y = \log_{10} a + bx \log_{10} e$$

i.e., $$\boxed{Y = A + Bx} \qquad (17)$$

where $Y = \log_{10} y$, $A = \log_{10} a$ and $B = b \log_{10} e$

The normal equations for (17) are $\Sigma Y = nA + B\Sigma x$ and $\Sigma xY = A\Sigma x + B\Sigma x^2$

Solving these, we get A and B.

Then $a = \text{antilog } A$ and $b = \dfrac{B}{\log_{10} e}$.

7.19 FITTING OF THE CURVE $y = ax^b$

Taking the logarithm on both sides, we get

$$\log_{10} y = \log_{10} a + b \log_{10} x$$

i.e., $$\boxed{Y = A + bX} \qquad (18)$$

where $Y = \log_{10} y$, $A = \log_{10} a$ and $X = \log_{10} x$.

The normal equations to (18) are $\Sigma Y = nA + b\Sigma X$

and $$\Sigma XY = A\Sigma X + b\Sigma X^2$$

which results A and b on solving and $a = \text{antilog } A$.

7.20 FITTING OF THE CURVE $y = ab^x$

Take the logarithm on both sides,

$$\log y = \log a + x \log b$$

$$\Rightarrow \qquad Y = A + Bx$$

where $Y = \log y$, $A = \log a$, $B = \log b$.

This is a linear equation in Y and x.

For estimating A and B, normal equations are

$$\Sigma Y = nA + B\,\Sigma x$$

and $$\Sigma xY = A\,\Sigma x + B\,\Sigma x^2$$

where n is the number of pairs of values of x and y.

Ultimately, $a = \text{antilog (A)}$ and $b = \text{antilog (B)}$.

7.21 FITTING OF THE CURVE $pv^r = k$

$$pv^r = k \;\Rightarrow\; v = k^{1/r}\,p^{-1/r}$$

Taking logarithm on both sides,

$$\log v = \frac{1}{r}\log k - \frac{1}{r}\log p$$

$$\Rightarrow \qquad \boxed{Y = A + BX}$$

where $Y = \log v$, $A = \frac{1}{r}\log k$, $B = -\frac{1}{r}$ and $X = \log p$

r and k are determined by the above equations. Normal equations are obtained as per that of the straight line.

7.22 FITTING OF THE CURVE OF TYPE $xy = b + ax$

$$xy = b + ax \Rightarrow y = \frac{b}{x} + a$$

$$\Rightarrow \qquad Y = bX + a, \text{ where } X = \frac{1}{x}.$$

Normal equations are $\Sigma Y = na + b\Sigma X$

$$\Sigma XY = a\Sigma X + b\Sigma X^2.$$

7.23 FITTING OF THE CURVE $y = ax^2 + \frac{b}{x}$

Let the n points be $(x_1, y_1), (x_2, y_2), \ldots\ldots, (x_n, y_n)$

Error of estimate for i^{th} point (x_i, y_i) is

$$E_i = \left(y_i - ax_i^2 - \frac{b}{x_i}\right)$$

By principle of Least squares, the values of a and b are such that

$$U = \sum_{i=1}^{n} E_i^2 = \sum_{i=1}^{n} \left(y_i - ax_i^2 - \frac{b}{x_i} \right)^2 \text{ is minimum.}$$

Normal equations are given by

$$\frac{\partial U}{\partial a} = 0$$

$$\Rightarrow \qquad \sum_{i=1}^{n} x_i^2 y_i = a \sum_{i=1}^{n} x_i^4 + b \sum_{i=1}^{n} x_i$$

and

$$\frac{\partial U}{\partial b} = 0$$

$$\Rightarrow \qquad \sum_{i=1}^{n} \frac{y_i}{x_i} = a \sum_{i=1}^{n} x_i + b \sum_{i=1}^{n} \frac{1}{x_i^2}$$

or Dropping the suffix i, normal equations are

$$\Sigma x^2 y = a\,\Sigma x^4 + b\Sigma x$$

and

$$\sum \frac{y}{x} = a\,\Sigma x + b \sum \frac{1}{x^2}.$$

7.24 FITTING OF THE CURVE $y = ax + bx^2$

Error of estimate for i^{th} point (x_i, y_i) is $E_i = (y_i - ax_i - bx_i^2)$

By the principle of Least Squares, the values of a and b are such that

$$U = \sum_{i=1}^{n} E_i^2 = \sum_{i=1}^{n} (y_i - ax_i - bx_i^2)^2 \text{ is minimum.}$$

Normal equations are given by $\frac{\partial U}{\partial a} = 0$

$$\Rightarrow \qquad \sum_{i=1}^{n} x_i y_i = a \sum_{i=1}^{n} x_i^2 + b \sum_{i=1}^{n} x_i^3$$

and

$$\frac{\partial U}{\partial b} = 0$$

$$\Rightarrow \quad \sum_{i=1}^{n} x_i^2 y_i = a \sum_{i=1}^{n} x_i^3 + b \sum_{i=1}^{n} x_i^4$$

or Dropping the suffix i, normal equations are

$$\Sigma xy = a\, \Sigma x^2 + b\Sigma x^3$$

$$\Sigma x^2 y = a\, \Sigma x^3 + b\Sigma x^4.$$

7.25 FITTING OF THE CURVE $y = ax + \frac{b}{x}$

Error of estimate for i^{th} point (x_i, y_i) is

$$E_i = y_i - ax_i - \frac{b}{x_i}$$

By the principle of Least Squares the values of a and b are such that

$$U = \sum_{i=1}^{n} E_i^2 = \sum_{i=1}^{n} \left(y_i - ax_i - \frac{b}{x_i} \right)^2 \text{ is minimum.}$$

Normal equations are given by

$$\frac{\partial U}{\partial a} = 0$$

$$\Rightarrow \quad 2\sum_{i=1}^{n} \left(y_i - ax_i - \frac{b}{x_i} \right)(-x_i) = 0$$

$$\Rightarrow \quad \sum_{i=1}^{n} x_i y_i = a \sum_{i=1}^{n} x_i^2 + nb$$

and

$$\frac{\partial U}{\partial b} = 0$$

$$\Rightarrow \quad 2\sum_{i=1}^{n} \left(y_i - ax_i - \frac{b}{x_i} \right)\left(-\frac{1}{x_i} \right) = 0$$

$$\Rightarrow \quad \sum_{i=1}^{n} \frac{y_i}{x_i} = na + b \sum_{i=1}^{n} \frac{1}{x_i^2}$$

Dropping the suffix i, normal equations are

$$\Sigma xy = a\Sigma x^2 + nb$$

and
$$\sum \frac{y}{x} = na + b\sum \frac{1}{x^2}$$

where n is the number of pairs of values of x and y.

7.26 FITTING OF THE CURVE $y = a + \frac{b}{x} + \frac{c}{x^2}$

Normal equations are

$$\Sigma y = ma + b\sum \frac{1}{x} + c\sum \frac{1}{x^2}$$

$$\sum \frac{y}{x} = a\sum \frac{1}{x} + b\sum \frac{1}{x^2} + c\sum \frac{1}{x^3}$$

$$\sum \frac{y}{x^2} = a\sum \frac{1}{x^2} + b\sum \frac{1}{x^3} + c\sum \frac{1}{x^4}$$

where m is the number of pairs of values of x and y.

7.27 FITTING OF THE CURVE $y = \frac{c_0}{x} + c_1\sqrt{x}$

Error of estimate for i^{th} point (x_i, y_i) is

$$E_i = y_i - \frac{c_0}{x_i} - c_1\sqrt{x_i}$$

By the principle of Least Squares, the values of a and b are such that

$$U = \sum_{i=1}^{n} E_i^2 = \sum_{i=1}^{n} (y_i - \frac{c_0}{x_i} - c_i\sqrt{x_i})^2 \text{ is minimum.}$$

Normal equations are given by

$$\frac{\partial U}{\partial c_0} = 0 \quad \text{and} \quad \frac{\partial U}{\partial c_1} = 0$$

Now,
$$\frac{\partial U}{\partial c_0} = 0$$

$$\Rightarrow \qquad 2\sum_{i=1}^{n}\left(y_i - \frac{c_0}{x_i} - c_1\sqrt{x_i}\right)\left(-\frac{1}{x_i}\right) = 0$$

$$\Rightarrow \qquad \sum_{i=1}^{n}\frac{y_i}{x_i} = c_0\sum_{i=1}^{n}\frac{1}{x_i^{\,2}} + c_1\sum_{i=1}^{n}\frac{1}{\sqrt{x_i}} \qquad (19)$$

Also, $\dfrac{\partial U}{\partial c_1} = 0$

$$\Rightarrow \qquad 2\sum_{i=1}^{n}\left(y_i - \frac{c_0}{x_i} - c_1\sqrt{x_i}\right)(-\sqrt{x_i}) = 0$$

$$\Rightarrow \qquad \sum_{i=1}^{n} y_i\sqrt{x_i} = c_0\sum_{i=1}^{n}\frac{1}{\sqrt{x_i}} + c_1\sum_{i=1}^{n} x_i \qquad (20)$$

Dropping the suffix i, normal equations (19) and (20) become

$$\sum\frac{y}{x} = c_0\sum\frac{1}{x^2} + c_1\sum\frac{1}{\sqrt{x}}$$

and
$$\sum y\sqrt{x} = c_0\sum\frac{1}{\sqrt{x}} + c_1\,\Sigma x.$$

7.28 FITTING OF THE CURVE $2^x = ax^2 + bx + c$

Normal equations are

$$\Sigma\, 2^x x^2 = a\Sigma x^4 + b\Sigma x^3 + c\Sigma x^2$$

$$\Sigma\, 2^x . x = a\Sigma x^3 + b\Sigma x^2 + c\Sigma x$$

and
$$\Sigma\, 2^x = a\Sigma x^2 + b\Sigma x + mc$$

where m is number of points (x_i, y_i)

EXAMPLES

Example 1. *Find the curve of best fit of the type $y = ae^{bx}$ to the following data by the method of Least Squares:*

x:	*1*	*5*	*7*	*9*	*12*
y:	*10*	*15*	*12*	*15*	*21.*

Sol. The curve to be fitted is $y = ae^{bx}$

or $$\text{Y} = \text{A} + \text{B}x,$$

where $\text{Y} = \log_{10} y$, $\text{A} = \log_{10} a$, and $\text{B} = b \log_{10} e$

$\therefore$ The normal equations are $\Sigma\text{Y} = 5\text{A} + \text{B}\Sigma x$

and $$\Sigma x\text{Y} = \text{A}\Sigma x + \text{B}\Sigma x^2$$

x	y	$Y = \log_{10} y$	x^2	xY
1	10	1.0000	1	1
5	15	1.1761	25	5.8805
7	12	1.0792	49	7.5544
9	15	1.1761	81	10.5849
12	21	1.3222	144	15.8664
$\Sigma x = 34$		$\Sigma\text{Y} = 5.7536$	$\Sigma x^2 = 300$	$\Sigma x\text{Y} = 40.8862$

Substituting the values of Σx, etc. calculated by means of above table in the normal equations.

We get $$5.7536 = 5\text{A} + 34\text{B}$$

and $$40.8862 = 34\text{A} + 300\text{B}$$

On solving $\text{A} = 0.9766$; $\text{B} = 0.02561$

$$\therefore \quad a = \text{antilog}_{10} \text{A} = 9.4754; \; b = \frac{\text{B}}{\log_{10} e} = 0.059$$

Hence the required curve is $\boxed{y = 9.4754e^{0.059x}}$.

Example 2. *For the data given below, find the equation to the best fitting exponential curve of the form* $y = ae^{bx}$

x:	*1*	*2*	*3*	*4*	*5*	*6*
y:	*1.6*	*4.5*	*13.8*	*40.2*	*125*	*300.*

Sol. $$y = ae^{bx}$$

Take log, $$\log y = \log a + bx \log e$$

which is of the form $$\text{Y} = \text{A} + \text{B}x$$

where $\text{Y} = \log y$, $\text{A} = \log a$, $\text{B} = b \log e$

x	y	$Y = \log y$	x^2	xY
1	1.6	.2041	1	.2041
2	4.5	.6532	4	1.3064
3	13.8	1.1399	9	3.4197
4	40.2	1.6042	16	6.4168
5	125	2.0969	25	10.4845
6	300	2.4771	36	14.8626
$\Sigma x = 21$		$\Sigma Y = 8.1754$	$\Sigma x^2 = 91$	$\Sigma xY = 36.6941$

Normal equations are

and
$$\left.\begin{aligned}\Sigma Y &= mA + B\Sigma x\\ \Sigma xY &= A\Sigma x + B\Sigma x^2\end{aligned}\right\} \qquad (21)$$

Here $m = 6$

$\therefore$ From (21), $8.1754 = 6A + 21B, \quad 36.6941 = 21A + 91B$

$\Rightarrow$ $A = -0.2534, \quad B = 0.4617$

$\therefore$ $a = \text{antilog } A = \text{antilog } (-.2534)$

$= \text{antilog } (\bar{1}.7466) = 0.5580$

and $b = \dfrac{B}{\log e} = \dfrac{.4617}{.4343} = 1.0631$

Hence required equation is

$$\boxed{y = 0.5580\, e^{1.0631\, x}.}$$

Example 3. *Determine the constants a and b by the Method of Least Squares such that $y = ae^{bx}$ fits the following data:*

x	2	4	6	8	10
y	4.077	11.084	30.128	81.897	222.62

Sol. $y = ae^{bx}$

Taking log on both sides

$$\log y = \log a + bx \log e$$

or $Y = A + BX,$

where $Y = \log y$

$A = \log a$

$$B = b \log_{10} e$$
$$X = x.$$

Normal equations are

$$\Sigma Y = mA + B\Sigma X \tag{22}$$

and
$$\Sigma XY = A\Sigma X + B\Sigma X^2. \tag{23}$$

Here $m = 5$.

Table is as follows:

x	y	X	Y	XY	X^2
2	4.077	2	.61034	1.22068	4
4	11.084	4	1.04469	4.17876	16
6	30.128	6	1.47897	8.87382	36
8	81.897	8	1.91326	15.30608	64
10	222.62	10	2.347564	23.47564	100
		$\Sigma X = 30$	$\Sigma Y = 7.394824$	$\Sigma XY = 53.05498$	$\Sigma X^2 = 220$

Substituting these values in equations (22) and (23), we get

$$7.394824 = 5A + 30B$$

and
$$53.05498 = 30A + 220B.$$

Solving, we get
$$A = 0.1760594$$

and
$$B = 0.2171509$$

$\therefore$
$$a = \text{antilog (A)}$$
$$= \text{antilog } (0.1760594) = 1.49989$$

and
$$b = \frac{B}{\log_{10} e} = \frac{0.2171509}{.4342945} = 0.50001$$

Hence the required equation is

$$\boxed{y = 1.49989\, e^{0.50001x}.}$$

Example 4. *Obtain a relation of the form $y = ab^x$ for the following data by the Method of Least Squares:*

x	2	3	4	5	6
y	8.3	15.4	33.1	65.2	126.4

Sol. The curve to be fitted is $y = ab^x$

or $$Y = A + Bx,$$

where $A = \log_{10} a$, $B = \log_{10} b$ and $Y = \log_{10} y$.

$\therefore$ The normal equations are $\Sigma Y = 5A + B\Sigma x$

and $$\Sigma XY = A\Sigma x + B\Sigma x^2.$$

x	y	$Y = \log_{10} y$	x^2	xY
2	8.3	0.9191	4	1.8382
3	15.4	1.1872	9	3.5616
4	33.1	1.5198	16	6.0792
5	65.2	1.8142	25	9.0710
6	127.4	2.1052	36	12.6312
$\Sigma x = 20$		$\Sigma Y = 7.5455$	$\Sigma x^2 = 90$	$\Sigma xY = 33.1812$

Substituting the values of Σx, etc. from the above table in normal equations, we get

$$7.5455 = 5A + 20B \quad \text{and} \quad 33.1812 = 20A + 90B.$$

On solving $A = 0.31$ and $B = 0.3$

$\therefore$ $$a = \text{antilog } A = 2.04$$

and $$b = \text{antilog } B = 1.995.$$

Hence the required curve is

$$\boxed{y = 2.04(1.995)^x.}$$

Example 5. *By the method of least squares, find the curve $y = ax + bx^2$ that best fits the following data:*

x	1	2	3	4	5
y	1.8	5.1	8.9	14.1	19.8

Sol. Error of estimate for i^{th} point (x_i, y_i) is $E_i = (y_i - ax_i - bx_i^2)$

By the principle of least squares, the values of a and b are such that

$$U = \sum_{i=1}^{5} E_i^2 = \sum_{i=1}^{5} (y_i - ax_i - bx_i^2)^2 \text{ is minimum.}$$

Normal equations are given by

$$\frac{\partial U}{\partial a} = 0$$

$$\Rightarrow \qquad \sum_{i=1}^{5} x_i y_i = a \sum_{i=1}^{5} x_i^2 + b \sum_{i=1}^{5} x_i^3$$

and

$$\frac{\partial U}{\partial b} = 0$$

$$\Rightarrow \qquad \sum_{i=1}^{5} x_i^2 y_i = a \sum_{i=1}^{5} x_i^3 + b \sum_{i=1}^{5} x_i^4$$

Dropping the suffix i, Normal equations are

$$\Sigma xy = a\Sigma x^2 + b\Sigma x^3 \tag{24}$$

and

$$\Sigma x^2 y = a\Sigma x^3 + b\Sigma x^4 \tag{25}$$

Let us form a table as below:

x	y	x^2	x^3	x^4	xy	x^2y
1	1.8	1	1	1	1.8	1.8
2	5.1	4	8	16	10.2	20.4
3	8.9	9	27	81	26.7	80.1
4	14.1	16	64	256	56.4	225.6
5	19.8	25	125	625	99	495
Total		$\Sigma x^2 = 55$	$\Sigma x^3 = 225$	$\Sigma x^4 = 979$	$\Sigma xy = 194.1$	$\Sigma x^2 y = 822.9$

Substituting these values in equations (24) and (25), we get

$$194.1 = 55\,a + 225\,b$$

and

$$822.9 = 225\,a + 979\,b$$

$$\Rightarrow \qquad a = \frac{83.85}{55} \simeq 1.52$$

and

$$b = \frac{317.4}{664} \simeq .49$$

Hence the required parabolic curve is $y = 1.52\,x + 0.49\,x^2$.

Example 6. *Fit the curve $pv^{\gamma} = k$ to the following data:*

p (kg/cm^2)	0.5	1	1.5	2	2.5	3
v (liters)	1620	1000	750	620	520	460

Sol. $$pv^{\gamma} = k$$

$$v = \left(\frac{k}{p}\right)^{1/\gamma} = k^{1/\gamma}\, p^{-1/\gamma}$$

Taking log, $$\log v = \frac{1}{\gamma}\log k - \frac{1}{\gamma}\log p$$

which is of the form $\quad Y = A + BX$

where $\quad Y = \log v,\quad X = \log p,\quad A = \frac{1}{\gamma}\log k \quad$ and $\quad B = -\frac{1}{\gamma}$

p	v	X	Y	XY	X^2
.5	1620	– .30103	3.20952	– .96616	0.09062
1	1000	0	3	0	0
1.5	750	.17609	2.87506	.50627	.03101
2	620	.30103	2.79239	.84059	.09062
2.5	520	.39794	2.716	1.08080	.15836
3	460	.47712	2.66276	1.27046	.22764
Total		$\Sigma X = 1.05115$	$\Sigma Y = 17.25573$	$\Sigma XY = 2.73196$	$\Sigma X^2 = .59825$

Here $m = 6$

Normal equations are

$$17.25573 = 6A + 1.05115\, B$$

and $$2.73196 = 1.05115\, A + 0.59825\, B$$

Solving these, we get

$$A = 2.99911 \quad \text{and} \quad B = -0.70298$$

$\therefore$ $$\gamma = -\frac{1}{B} = \frac{1}{.70298} = 1.42252$$

Again, $$\log k = \gamma A = 4.26629$$

$\therefore$ $$k = \text{antilog}\,(4.26629) = 18462.48$$

Hence the required curve is

$$pv^{1.42252} = 18462.48.$$

Example 7. *Given the following experimental values:*

x:	*0*	*1*	*2*	*3*
y:	*2*	*4*	*10*	*15*

Fit by the method of least squares a parabola of the type $y = a + bx^2$.

Sol. Error of estimate for i^{th} point (x_i, y_i) is $E_i = (y_i - a - bx_i^2)$

By the principle of Least Squares, the values of a, b are such that

$$U = \sum_{i=1}^{4} E_i^2 = \sum_{i=1}^{4} (y_i - a - bx_i^2)^2 \text{ is minimum.}$$

Normal equations are given by

$$\frac{\partial U}{\partial a} = 0 \Rightarrow \Sigma y = ma + b\Sigma x^2 \quad (26)$$

and $$\frac{\partial U}{\partial b} = 0 \quad \Sigma x^2 y = a\Sigma x^2 + b\Sigma x^4 \quad (27)$$

x	y	x^2	x^2y	x^4
0	2	0	0	0
1	4	1	4	1
2	10	4	40	16
3	15	9	135	81
Total	$\Sigma y = 31$	$\Sigma x^2 = 14$	$\Sigma x^2 y = 179$	$\Sigma x^4 = 98$

Here $m = 4$

From (26) and (27), $31 = 4a + 14b$ and $179 = 14a + 98b$

Solving for a and b, we get $a = 2.71$, $b = 1.44$

Hence the required curve is $y = 2.71 + 1.44\, x^2$.

Example 8. *The pressure of the gas corresponding to various volumes V is measured, given by the following data:*

V (cm^3):	*50*	*60*	*70*	*90*	*100*
P (kg cm^{-2}):	*64.7*	*51.3*	*40.5*	*25.9*	*78*

Fit the data to the equation $PV^{\gamma} = C$.

Sol. $PV^{\gamma} = C$

$\Rightarrow$ $P = CV^{-\gamma}$

Take log on both sides,

$$\log P = \log C - \gamma \log V$$

$\Rightarrow$ $Y = A + BX$

where $Y = \log P$, $A = \log C$, $B = -\gamma$, $X = \log V$

Normal equations are

$$\Sigma Y = mA + B\Sigma X$$

and $$\Sigma XY = A\Sigma X + B\Sigma X^2$$

Here $m = 5$

Table is as below:

V	P	$X = \log V$	$Y = \log P$	XY	X^2
50	64.7	1.69897	1.81090	3.07666	2.88650
60	51.3	1.77815	1.71012	3.04085	3.16182
70	40.5	1.84510	1.60746	2.96592	3.40439
90	25.9	1.95424	1.41330	2.76193	3.81905
100	78	2	1.89209	3.78418	4
		$\Sigma X = 9.27646$	$\Sigma Y = 8.43387$	$\Sigma XY = 15.62954$	$\Sigma X^2 = 17.27176$

From Normal equations, we have

$$8.43387 = 5A + 9.27646\,B$$

and $$15.62954 = 9.27646\,A + 17.27176\,B$$

Solving these, we get

$$A = 2.22476,\ \ B = -\,0.28997$$

$\therefore$ $\gamma = -B = 0.28997$

$$C = \text{antilog}\ (A) = \text{antilog}\ (2.22476) = 167.78765$$

Hence the required equation of curve is

$$PV^{0.28997} = 167.78765.$$

Example 9. *Use the Method of Least Squares to fit the curve:* $y = \frac{c_0}{x} + c_1\sqrt{x}$ *to the following table of values:*

x:	*0.1*	*0.2*	*0.4*	*0.5*	*1*	*2*
y:	*21*	*11*	*7*	*6*	*5*	*6.*

Sol. As derived in article 5.16, normal equations to the curve

$$y = \frac{c_0}{x} + c_1\sqrt{x} \text{ are}$$

$$\sum \frac{y}{x} = c_0 \sum \frac{1}{x^2} + c_1 \sum \frac{1}{\sqrt{x}} \quad (28)$$

and

$$\sum y\sqrt{x} = c_0 \sum \frac{1}{\sqrt{x}} + c_1 \sum x \quad (29)$$

The table is as below:

x	y	y/x	$y\sqrt{x}$	$\frac{1}{\sqrt{x}}$	$\frac{1}{x^2}$
0.1	21	210	6.64078	3.16228	100
0.2	11	55	4.91935	2.23607	25
0.4	7	17.5	4.42719	1.58114	6.25
0.5	6	12	4.24264	1.41421	4
1	5	5	5	1	1
2	6	3	8.48528	.70711	0.25
$\Sigma x = 4.2$		$\Sigma(y/x) = 302.5$	$\Sigma y\sqrt{x} = 33.71524$	$\sum \frac{1}{\sqrt{x}} = 10.10081$	$\sum \frac{1}{x^2} = 136.5$

From equations (28) and (29), we have

$$302.5 = 136.5\, c_0 + 10.10081\, c_1$$

and

$$33.71524 = 10.10081\, c_0 + 4.2\, c_1$$

Solving these, we get

$$c_0 = 1.97327 \quad \text{and} \quad c_1 = 3.28182$$

Hence the required equation of curve is

$$y = \frac{1.97327}{x} + 3.28182\sqrt{x}.$$

ASSIGNMENT 7.2

1. Fit an equation of the form $y = ae^{bx}$ to the following data by the method of least squares:

x	1	2	3	4
y	1.65	2.7	4.5	7.35

2. The voltage V across a capacitor at time t seconds is given by the following table. Use the principle of least squares to fit a curve of the form $V = ae^{kt}$ to the data:

t	0	2	4	6	8
V	150	63	28	12	5.6

3. Using the method of least squares, fit the non-linear curve of the form $y = ae^{bx}$ to the following data:

x	0	2	4
y	5.012	10	31.62

4. Fit a curve of the form $y = ax^b$ to the data given below:

x	1	2	3	4	5
y	7.1	27.8	62.1	110	161

5. Fit a curve of the form $y = ab^x$ in least square sense to the data given below:

x	2	3	4	5	6
y	144	172.8	207.4	248.8	298.5

6. Fit an exponential curve of the form $y = ab^x$ to the following data:

x	1	2	3	4	5	6	7	8
y	1	1.2	1.8	2.5	3.6	4.7	6.6	9.1

7. Fit a curve $y = ax^b$ to the following data:

x	1	2	3	4	5	6
y	2.98	4.26	5.21	6.1	6.8	7.5

8. Fit a least square geometric curve $y = ax^b$ to the following data:

x	1	2	3	4	5
y	0.5	2	4.5	8	12.5

9. Derive the least square equations for fitting a curve of the type $y = ax^2 + \frac{b}{x}$ to a set of n points.
Hence fit a curve of this type to the data:

x	1	2	3	4
y	– 1.51	0.99	3.88	7.66

10. Derive the least squares approximations of the type $ax^2 + bx + c$ to the function 2^x at the points $x_i = 0, 1, 2, 3, 4$.

11. A person runs the same race track for 5 consecutive days and is timed as follows:

Day (x)	1	2	3	4	5
Time (y)	15.3	15.1	15	14.5	14

Make a least square fit to the above data using a function $a + \frac{b}{x} + \frac{c}{x^2}$.

12. It is known that the variables x and y hold the relation of the form $y = ax + \frac{b}{x}$.

Fit the curve to the given data:

x	1	2	3	4	5	6	7	8
y	5.43	6.28	8.23	10.32	12.63	14.86	17.27	19.51

13. Fit a curve of the type $xy = ax + b$ to the following data:

x	1	3	5	7	9	10
y	36	29	28	26	24	15

14. Determine the constants of the curve $y = ax + bx^2$ for the following data:

x	0	1	2	3	4
y	2.1	2.4	2.6	2.7	3.4

15. The presssure and volume of a gas are related by the equation $pv^a = b$ where a and b are constants. Fit this equation to the following set of data:

p (kg/cm³)	0.5	1	1.5	2	2.5	3
v (liters)	1.62	1	0.75	0.62	0.52	0.46

7.29 MOST PLAUSIBLE SOLUTION OF A SYSTEM OF LINEAR EQUATIONS

Consider a set of m equations in n variables $x, y, z, \ldots\ldots, t$;

$$\left.\begin{array}{c} a_1x + b_1y + c_1z + \ldots\ldots + k_1t = l_1 \\ a_2x + b_2y + c_2z + \ldots\ldots + k_2t = l_2 \\ \vdots \quad \vdots \quad \vdots \quad \vdots \quad \vdots \quad \vdots \\ a_mx + b_my + c_mz + \ldots\ldots + k_mt = l_m \end{array}\right\} \tag{30}$$

where $a_i, b_i, c_i, \ldots\ldots, k_i, l_i; i = 1, 2, \ldots\ldots, m$ are constants.

In case $m = n$, the system of equation (30) can be solved uniquely by using algebra.

In case $m > n$, we find the values of $x, y, z, \ldots\ldots, t$ which will satisfy the system (30) as nearly as possible using normal equations.

On solving normal equations simultaneously, they give the values of $x, y, z, \ldots\ldots, t$; known as the best or *most plausible values.*

On calculating the second order partial derivatives and substituting values of $x, y, z, \ldots\ldots, t$ so obtained, we will observe that the expression will be positive.

EXAMPLES

Example 1. *Find the most plausible values of x and y from the following equations:*

$$3x + y = 4.95,\ x + y = 3.00,\ 2x - y = 0.5,\ x + 3y = 7.25.$$

Sol. Let $\mathrm{S} = (3x + y - 4.95)^2 + (x + y - 3)^2 + (2x - y - 0.5)^2 + (x + 3y - 7.25)^2 \quad (31)$

Differentiating S partially with respect to x and y separately and equating to zero, we have

$$\frac{\partial \mathrm{S}}{\partial x} = 0 = 2(3x + y - 4.95)(3) + 2(x + y - 3)$$
$$+ 2(2x - y - 0.5)(2) + 2(x + 3y - 7.25)$$

$$\Rightarrow \qquad 30x + 10y = 52.2$$

or $$3x + y = 5.22 \tag{32}$$

and $$\frac{\partial S}{\partial y} = 0 = 2(3x + y - 4.95) + 2(x + y - 3)$$
$$+ 2(2x - y - 0.5)(-1) + 2(x + 3y - 7.25)(3)$$

$$\Rightarrow \qquad 10x + 24y = 58.4$$

or $$x + 2.4y = 5.84 \tag{33}$$

Solving equations (32) and (33), we get

$$x = 1.07871 \quad \text{and} \quad y = 1.98387.$$

Example 2. *Three independent measurements on each of the angles A, B, and C of a triangle are as follows:*

A	*B*	*C*
39.5°	*60.3°*	*80.1°*
39.3°	*63.2°*	*80.3°*
39.6°	*69.1°*	*80.4°*

Obtain the best estimate of the three angles when the sum of the angles is taken to be 180°.

Sol. Let the three measurements of angles A, B, C be $x_1, x_2, x_3; y_1, y_2, y_3$ and z_1, z_2, z_3 respectively. Further suppose the best estimates of the angle A, B, and C to be α, β, γ respectively where $\gamma = 180° - (\alpha + \beta)$

According to Least squares method,

$$S = \sum_{i=1}^{3} (x_i - \alpha)^2 + \sum_{i=1}^{3} (y_i - \beta)^2 + \sum_{i=1}^{3} (z_i - 180 + \alpha + \beta)^2 \tag{34}$$

and $$\frac{\partial S}{\partial \alpha} = 0 = -2\sum_{i=1}^{3} (x_i - \alpha) + 2\sum_{i=1}^{3} (z_i - 180 + \alpha + \beta)$$

$$\frac{\partial S}{\partial \beta} = 0 = -2\sum_{i=1}^{3} (y_i - \beta) + 2\sum_{i=1}^{3} (z_i - 180 + \alpha + \beta)$$

or $$\begin{cases} -\Sigma x + 3\alpha + \Sigma z - 540 + 3\alpha + 3\beta = 0 \\ -\Sigma y + 3\beta + \Sigma z - 540 + 3\alpha + 3\beta = 0 \end{cases}$$

or $$\begin{cases} 6\alpha + 3\beta = 540 + \Sigma x - \Sigma z = 417.6 & (35) \\ 3\alpha + 6\beta = 540 + \Sigma y - \Sigma z = 481.8 & (36) \end{cases}$$

Solving equations (35) and (36), we get

$$\alpha = 39.2667, \beta = 60.6667, \gamma = 80.0666$$

ASSIGNMENT 7.3

1. Find the most plausible values of x and y from the following equations:
$$x + y = 3, x - y = 2, x + 2y = 4, x - 2y = 1$$
2. Find the most plausible values of x and y from the equations:
$$x + y = 3.31, \quad 2x - y = .03, \quad x + 3y = 7.73, \quad 3x + y = 5.47$$
3. Find the most plausible values of x, y, and z from the follwoing equations:
$$x - y + 2z = 3, 3x + 2y - 5z = 5,$$
$$4x + y + 4z = 21, - x + 3y + 3z = 14$$
4. Find the most plausible values of x, y, and z from the following equations:
   (*i*) $x + y = 3.01, 2x - y = 0.03, x + 3y = 7.02$ and $3x + y = 4.97$
   (*ii*) $x + 2y = 4, x = y + 2, x + y - 3 = 0, x - 2y = 1$
   (*iii*) $x + 2.5y = 21, 4x + 1.2y = 42.04, 3.2x - y = 28$ and $1.5x + 6.3y = 40$
   (*iv*) $x - 5y + 4 = 0, 2x - 3y + 5 = 0$
   $x + 2y - 3 = 0, 4x + 3y + 1 = 0$
5. Find the most plausible values of x, y, and z from the following equations:
   (*i*) $3x + 2y - 5z = 13$
   $x - y + 2z = -2$
   $4x + y + 4z = 3$
   $-x + 3y + 3z = 0$
   (*ii*) $x + 2y + z = 1$
   $2x + y + z = 4$
   $-x + y + 2z = 3$
   $4x + 2y - 5z = -7$
   (*iii*) $x - y + 2z = 3, 3x + 2y - 5z = 5$
   $4x + y + 4z = 21, - x + 3y + 3z = 14.$

7.30 CURVE-FITTING BY SUM OF EXPONENTIALS

We are to fit a sum of exponentials of the form

$$y = f(x) = A_1 e^{\lambda_1 x} + A_2 e^{\lambda_2 x} + \ldots\ldots + A_n e^{\lambda_n x} \tag{37}$$

to a set of data points say $(x_1, y_1), (x_2, y_2), \ldots\ldots, (x_n, y_n)$

In equation (37), we assume that n is known and $A_1, A_2, \ldots\ldots, A_n, \lambda_1, \lambda_2, \ldots\ldots, \lambda_n$ are to be determined.

Since equation (37) involves n arbitrary constants,

It can be seen that $f(x)$ satisfies a differential equation of the type

$$\frac{d^n y}{dx^n} + a_1 \frac{d^{n-1} y}{dx^{n-1}} + a_2 \frac{d^{n-2} y}{dx^{n-2}} + \ldots\ldots + a_n y = 0 \tag{38}$$

where coefficients $a_1, a_2, \ldots\ldots, a_n$ are unknown.

According to the Froberg Method, we numerically evaluate the derivatives at the n data points and substitute them in (38) thus obtaining a system of n linear equations for n unknowns $a_1, \ldots\ldots, a_n$ which can be solved thereafter.

Again, since $\lambda_1, \lambda_2, \ldots\ldots, \lambda_n$ are the roots of algebraic equation

$$\lambda^n + a_1\lambda^{n-1} + a_2\lambda^{n-2} + \ldots\ldots + a_n = 0 \tag{39}$$

which, when solved, enables us to compute $A_1, A_2, \ldots\ldots, A_n$ from equation (37) by the method of least squares.

An obvious disadvantage of the method is the numerical evaluation of the derivatives whose accuracy deteriorates with their increasing order, leading to unreliable results.

In 1974, Moore described a computational technique which leads to more reliable results.

We demonstrate the method for the case $n = 2$.

Let the function to be fitted to a given data be of the form

$$y = A_1 e^{\lambda_1 x} + A_2 e^{\lambda_2 x} \tag{40}$$

which satisfies a differential equation of the form

$$\frac{d^2 y}{dx^2} = a_1 \frac{dy}{dx} + a_2 y \tag{41}$$

where the constants a_1 and a_2 have to be determined.

Assuming that a is the initial value of x, we obtain by integrating (41) from a to x, the following equation

$$y'(x) - y'(a) = a_1 y(x) - a_1 y(a) + a_2 \int_a^x y(x)\, dx \tag{42}$$

where $y'(x)$ denotes $\frac{dy}{dx}$.

Integrating (42) again from a to x, we get

$$y(x) - y(a) - y'(a)(x - a) = a_1 \int_a^x y(x)\, dx - a_1(x - a)\, y(a)$$

$$+ a_2 \int_a^x \int_a^x y(x)\, dx\, dx \tag{43}$$

using the formula,

$$\int_a^x \ldots\ldots \int_a^x f(x)\,dx \ldots\ldots dx = \frac{1}{(n-1)!}\int_a^x (x-t)^{n-1} f(t)\,dt \tag{44}$$

equation (43) simplifies to,

$$y(x) - y(a) - (x-a)\,y'(a) = a_1 \int_a^x y(x)\,dx - a_1(x-a)\,y(a) + a_2 \int_a^x (x-t)\,y(t)\,dt \tag{45}$$

In order to use equation (45) to set up a linear system for a_1 and a_2, $y'(a)$ should be eliminated.

To do this, we choose two data points x_1 and x_2 such that

$$a - x_1 = x_2 - a$$

then from (45),

$$y(x_1) - y(a) - (x_1 - a)\,y'(a)$$

$$= a_1 \int_a^{x_1} y(x)\,dx - a_1(x_1 - a)\,y(a) + a_2 \int_a^{x_1} (x_1 - t)\,y(t)\,dt$$

$$y(x_2) - y(a) - (x_2 - a)\,y'(a)$$

$$= a_1 \int_a^{x_2} y(x)\,dx - a_1(x_2 - a)\,y(a) + a_2 \int_a^{x_2} (x_2 - t)\,y(t)\,dt$$

Adding the above equations and simplifying, we get

$$y(x_1) + y(x_2) - 2y(a) = a_1 \left[\int_a^{x_1} y(x)\,dx + \int_a^{x_2} y(x)\,dx\right]$$

$$+ a_2 \left[\int_a^{x_1} (x_1 - t)\,y(t)\,dt + \int_a^{x_2} (x_2 - t)\,y(t)\,dt\right] \tag{46}$$

we find integrals using Simpson's rule and equation (46) can be used to set up a linear system of equations for a_1 and a_2, then we obtain λ_1 and λ_2 from the characteristic equation

$$\lambda^2 = a_1\lambda + a_2 \tag{47}$$

Finally, A_1 and A_2 can be obtained by the Method of Least Squares.

Example. *Fit a function of the form*

$$y = A_1 e^{\lambda_1 x} + A_2 e^{\lambda_2 x}$$

to the data given by

x:	*1.0*	*1.1*	*1.2*	*1.3*	*1.4*	*1.5*	*1.6*	*1.7*	*1.8*
y:	*1.54*	*1.67*	*1.81*	*1.97*	*2.15*	*2.35*	*2.58*	*2.83*	*3.11.*

Sol. Choose $x_1 = 1,\quad x_2 = 1.4,\quad a = 1.2$

so that, $a - x_1 = x_2 - a$ then,

$$y(x_1) + y(x_2) - 2y(a) = a_1\left[\int_a^{x_1} y(x)\,dx + \int_a^{x_2} y(x)\,dx\right] + a_2\left[\int_a^{x_1} (x_1 - t)\,y(t)\,dt + \int_a^{x_2} (x_2 - t)\,y(t)\,dt\right]$$

$$\Rightarrow \quad 1.54 + 2.15 - 3.62 = a_1\left[-\int_1^{1.2} y(x)\,dx + \int_{1.2}^{1.4} y(x)\,dx\right] + a_2\left[-\int_1^{1.2}(1 - t)\,y(t)\,dt + \int_{1.2}^{1.4} (1.4 - t)\,y(t)\,dt\right] \quad (48)$$

Evaluation of $\int_1^{1.2} y(x)\,dx$

The table of values is

x:	1	1.1	1.2
$y(x)$:	1.54	1.67	1.81

By Simpson's $\frac{1}{3}$rd rule,

$$\int_1^{1.2} y(x)\,dx = \frac{0.1}{3}\,[(1.54 + 1.81) + 4(1.67)] = 0.33433$$

Evaluation of $\int_{1.2}^{1.4} y(x)\,dx$

The table of values is

x:	1.2	1.3	1.4
$y(x)$:	1.81	1.97	2.15

By Simpson's $\frac{1}{3}$rd rule,

$$\int_{1.2}^{1.4} y(x)\,dx = \frac{0.1}{3}\,[(1.81 + 2.15) + 4(1.97)] = 0.39466$$

Evaluation of $\int_1^{1.2} (1-t)\, y(t)\, dt$

The table of values is

t:	1	1.1	1.2
$y(t)$:	1.54	1.67	1.81
$(1-t)\,y(t)$:	0	– 0.167	– 0.362

By Simpson's $\frac{1}{3}$rd rule,

$$\int_1^{1.2} (1-t)\, y(t)\, dt = \frac{0.1}{3}[0 - .362 + 4(-.167)] = -.03433$$

Evaluation of $\int_{1.2}^{1.4} (1.4-t)\, y(t)\, dt$

The table of values is

t:	1.2	1.3	1.4
$(1.4-t)$:	.2	.1	0
$y(t)$:	1.81	1.97	2.15
$(1.4-t)\,y(t)$:	.362	.197	0

By Simpson's $\frac{1}{3}$rd rule,

$$\int_{1.2}^{1.4} (1.4-t)\, y(t)\, dt = \frac{0.1}{3}[(0.362 + 0) + 4(.197)] = 0.03833$$

Substituting values of above obtained integrals in equation (48), we get

$$0.07 = a_1[-0.33433 + 0.39466] + a_2[0.03433 + 0.03833]$$

$$0.07 = 0.06033\, a_1 + 0.07266\, a_2$$

$$\Rightarrow \quad 1.8099\, a_1 + 2.1798\, a_2 = 2.10$$

or $$1.81\, a_1 + 2.18\, a_2 = 2.10 \quad (49)$$

Again, letting $x_1 = 1.4$, $a = 1.6$ and $x_2 = 1.8$

so that $a - x_1 = x_2 - a$ then,

$$y(x_1) + y(x_2) - 2y(a) = a_1\left[\int_a^{x_1} y(x)\, dx + \int_a^{x_2} y(x)\, dx\right]$$

$$+ a_2\left[\int_a^{x_1} (x_1 - t)\, y(t)\, dt + \int_a^{x_2} (x_2 - t)\, y(t)\, dt\right]$$

$$\Rightarrow \quad 2.15 + 3.11 - 5.16 = a_1\left[-\int_{1.4}^{1.6} y(x)\,dx + \int_{1.6}^{1.8} y(x)\,dx\right]$$

$$+ a_2\left[-\int_{1.4}^{1.6} (1.4 - t)\,y(t)\,dt + \int_{1.6}^{1.8} (1.8 - t)\,y(t)\,dt\right]$$

Evaluating all of the above integrals by Simpson's $\frac{1}{3}$rd rule and substituting, we obtain

$$2.88\,a_1 + 3.104\,a_2 = 3.00 \qquad (50)$$

Solving (49) and (50), we get

$$a_1 = 0.03204,\ a_2 = 0.9364$$

Characteristic equation is

$$\lambda^2 = a_1\lambda + a_2$$

$$\Rightarrow \quad \lambda^2 - 0.03204\lambda - 0.9364 = 0$$

$$\Rightarrow \quad \lambda_1 = 0.988 \approx 0.99$$

and $\quad \lambda_2 = -\,0.96$

Now the curve to be fitted is

$$y = A_1e^{0.99x} + A_2e^{-0.96x} \qquad (51)$$

Residual $\quad E_i = y_i - A_1e^{0.99x_i} - A_2e^{-0.96x_i}$

Consider $\quad U = \sum_{i=1}^{n} E_i^{\,2} = \sum_{i=1}^{n} (y_i - A_1e^{0.99x_i} - A_2e^{-0.96x_i})^2$

By the Method of Least Squares, values of A_1 and A_2 are chosen such that U is the minimum.

For U to be minimum,

$$\frac{\partial U}{\partial A_1} = 0 \quad \text{and} \quad \frac{\partial U}{\partial A_2} = 0$$

Now, $\quad \frac{\partial U}{\partial A_1} = 0 \quad \Rightarrow \quad 2\sum (y - A_1e^{.99x} - A_2e^{-.96x})(-\,e^{.99x}) = 0$

$$\Rightarrow \quad \boxed{\sum ye^{.99x} = A_1e^{1.98x} + A_2\sum e^{.03x}} \qquad (52)$$

and $\frac{\partial U}{\partial A_2} = 0 \quad \Rightarrow \quad 2\sum (y - A_1 e^{.99x} - A_2 e^{-.96x})(-e^{-.96x}) = 0$

$$\Rightarrow \boxed{\sum ye^{-.96x} = A_1 \sum e^{.03x} + A_2 \sum e^{-1.92x}} \quad (53)$$

Solving normal equations (52) and (53) using values of x and y given in the table, we get

$$A_1 = 0.499 \quad \text{and} \quad A_2 = 0.491$$

Hence the required function is

$$y = 0.499\, e^{0.99x} + 0.491\, e^{-0.96x}.$$

7.31 SPLINE INTERPOLATION

When computers were not available, the draftsman used a device to draw a smooth curve through a given set of points such that the slope and curvature were also continuous along the curve, *i.e.*, $f(x)$, $f'(x)$, and $f''(x)$ were continuous on the curve. Such a device was called a **spline** and plotting of the curve was called **spline fitting.**

The given interval $[a, b]$ is subdivided into n subintervals $[x_0, x_1]$, $[x_1, x_2]$,......, $[x_{n-1}, x_n]$ where $a = x_0 < x_1 < x_2 < ..... < x_n = b$. The nodes (knots) $x_1, x_2, ..., x_{n-1}$ are called internal nodes.

7.32 SPLINE FUNCTION

A spline function of degree n with knots (nodes) x_i, $i = 0, 1, ..., n$ is a function $F(x)$ satisfying the properties

(*i*) $F(x_i) = f(x_i)$; $i = 0, 1, ..., n$.

(*ii*) on each subinterval $[x_{i-1}, x_i]$, $1 \le i \le n$, $F(x)$ is a polynomial in x of degree at most n.

(*iii*) $F(x)$ and its first $(n - 1)$ derivatives are continuous on $[a, b]$

(*iv*) $F(x)$ is a polynomial of degree one for $x < a$ and $x > b$.

7.33 CUBIC SPLINE INTERPOLATION

A cubic spline satisfies the following properties:

(*i*) $F(x_i) = f_i$, $i = 0, 1, ..., n$

(*ii*) On each subinterval $[x_{i-1}, x_i]$, $1 \le i \le n$, $F(x)$ is a third degree polynomial.

(*iii*) $F(x)$, $F'(x)$ and $F''(x)$ are continuous on $[a, b]$.

Since $F(x)$ is piecewise cubic, polynomial $F''(x)$ is a linear function of x in the interval $x_{i-1} \le x \le x_i$ and hence can be written as

$$F''(x) = \frac{x_i - x}{x_i - x_{i-1}} F''(x_{i-1}) + \frac{x - x_{i-1}}{x_i - x_{i-1}} F''(x_i) \tag{54}$$

For equally spaced intervals,

$$x_i - x_{i-1} = h; \ 1 \le i \le n$$

From (54), $$F''(x) = \frac{1}{h} [(x_i - x) F''(x_{i-1}) + (x - x_{i-1}) F''(x_i)] \tag{55}$$

Integrating equation (55) twice, we get

$$F(x) = \frac{1}{h}\left[\frac{(x_i - x)^3}{6} F''(x_{i-1}) + \frac{(x - x_{i-1})^3}{6} F''(x_i)\right] + c_1(x_i - x) + c_2(x - x_{i-1}) \tag{56}$$

where c_1 and c_2 are arbitrary constants which are to be determined by conditions

$$F(x_i) = f_i; \ i = 0, 1, 2, ..., n$$

Then, $$f_i = \frac{1}{h}\left[\frac{h^3}{6} F''(x_i)\right] + c_2 h$$

$$\Rightarrow \quad c_2 = \frac{f_i}{h} - \frac{h}{6} F''(x_i) \tag{57}$$

and $$f_{i-1} = \frac{1}{h}\left[\frac{h^3}{6} F''(x_{i-1})\right] + c_1 h$$

$$\Rightarrow \quad c_1 = \frac{f_{i-1}}{h} - \frac{h}{6} F''(x_{i-1}) \tag{58}$$

Putting the values of c_1 and c_2 in equation (56), we get

$$F(x) = \frac{1}{h}\left[\frac{(x_i - x)^3}{6} F''(x_{i-1}) + \frac{(x - x_{i-1})^3}{6} F''(x_i) + (x_i - x)\left\{f_{i-1} - \frac{h^2}{6} F''(x_{i-1})\right\} + (x - x_{i-1})\left\{f_i - \frac{h^2}{6} F''(x_i)\right\}\right] \tag{59}$$

Denoting $F''(x_i) = M_i$, we have

$$F(x) = \frac{1}{6h}[(x_i - x)^3 M_{i-1} + (x - x_{i-1})^3 M_i + (x_i - x)\{6f_{i-1} - h^2 M_{i-1}\} + (x - x_{i-1})\{6f_i - h^2 M_i\}] \quad (60)$$

Now, $$F'(x) = \frac{1}{6h}[-3(x_i - x)^2 M_{i-1} + 3(x - x_{i-1})^2 M_i + 6(f_i - f_{i-1}) + h^2M_{i-1} - h^2M_i] \quad (61)$$

Now, we require that the derivative $F'(x)$ be continuous at $x = x_i \pm \varepsilon$ as $\varepsilon \to 0$

Therefore,

(*i*) $$F'(x_{i-1} + 0) = \frac{1}{6h}[-3h^2M_{i-1} + h^2M_{i-1} - h^2M_i + 6(f_i - f_{i-1})]$$

$$= \frac{1}{6h}[-h^2M_i - 2h^2M_{i-1} + 6(f_i - f_{i-1})] \quad (62)$$

Again in the interval $[x_{i-2}, x_{i-1}]$,

$$F'(x) = \frac{1}{6h}[-3(x_{i-1} - x)^2 M_{i-2} + 3(x - x_{i-2})^2 M_{i-1} + 6(f_{i-1} - f_{i-2}) + h^2M_{i-2} - h^2M_{i-1}] \quad (63)$$

(*ii*) From (63),

$$F'(x_{i-1} - 0) = \frac{1}{6h}[3h^2M_{i-1} + 6f_{i-1} - 6f_{i-2} + h^2M_{i-2} - h^2M_{i-1}]$$

$$= \frac{1}{6h}[2h^2M_{i-1} + h^2M_{i-2} + 6f_{i-1} - 6f_{i-2}] \quad (64)$$

As $F'(x)$ is continuous at x_{i-1},

$$\therefore \quad F'(x_{i-1} - 0) = F'(x_{i-1} + 0)$$

$$\therefore \quad 2h^2M_{i-1} + h^2M_{i-2} + 6f_{i-1} - 6f_{i-2} = -h^2M_i - 2h^2M_{i-1} + 6f_i - 6f_{i-1}$$

or $$h^2(M_i + 4M_{i-1} + M_{i-2}) = 6(f_i - 2f_{i-1} + f_{i-2})$$

For the interval $[x_{i-1}, x_i]$,

we have $$h^2[M_{i+1} + 4M_i + M_{i-1}] = 6(f_{i+1} - 2f_i + f_{i-1}) \quad (65)$$

where $i = 1, 2, \ldots\ldots, n$

This gives a system of $(n - 1)$ linear equations with $(n + 1)$ unknowns $M_0, M_1, ..., M_n$.

Two additional conditions may be taken in one of the following forms:

(*i*) $\mathbf{M_0 = M_n = 0}$ **(Natural spline)**

(*ii*) $\mathbf{M_0 = M_n, M_1 = M_{n+1}, f_0 = f_n, f_1 = f_{n+1}, h_1 = h_{n+1}}$

A spline satisfying the above conditions is called a **periodic spline.**

(*iii*) For a **non-periodic spline,** we use the conditions

$$F'(a) = f'(a) = f_0' \text{ and } F'(b) = f'(b) = f_n'$$

Splines usually provide a better approximation of the behavior of functions that have abrupt local changes. Further, splines perform better than higher order polynomial approximations.

7.34 STEPS TO OBTAIN CUBIC SPLINE FOR GIVEN DATA

Step 1. For interval (x_{i-1}, x_i), write cubic spline as

$$F(x) = \frac{1}{6h} [(x_i - x)^3 M_{i-1} + (x - x_{i-1})^3 M_i + (x_i - x) \{6f_{i-1} - h^2M_{i-1}\} + (x - x_{i-1})\{6f_i - h^2M_i\}]$$

Step 2. If not given, choose $M_0 = 0 = M_3$ (for the interval $0 \le x \le 3$)

Step 3. For $i = 1, 2, ..., n$, choose values of M_1 and M_2 such that

$$h^2[M_{i+1} + 4M_i + M_{i-1}] = 6[f_{i+1} - 2f_i + f_{i-1}]$$

exists for two sub intervals $0 \le x \le 1$ and $1 \le x \le 2$ respectively, where h is the interval of differencing.

Step 4. Find $F(x)$ for different sub-intervals and tabulate at last.

EXAMPLES

Example 1. *Obtain the cubic spline for the following data:*

x:	*0*	*1*	*2*	*3*
y:	*2*	*– 6*	*– 8*	*2.*

Sol. For the interval (x_{i-1}, x_i), the cubic spline is

$$F(x) = \frac{1}{6h} [(x_i - x)^3 M_{i-1} + (x - x_{i-1})^3 M_i + (x_i - x) \{6f_{i-1} - h^2M_{i-1}\} + (x - x_{i-1}) \{6f_i - h^2M_i\}]$$

With $M_0 = M_3 = 0$ and for $i = 1, 2, \ldots\ldots, n$; we also have

$$h^2[M_{i-1} + 4\,M_i + M_{i+1}] = 6\,[f_{i+1} - 2f_i + f_{i-1}]$$

Here $h = 1$

$\therefore$ $$M_0 + 4M_1 + M_2 = 6(f_2 - 2f_1 + f_0) \quad | \text{ For } 0 \le x \le 1$$

and $$M_1 + 4M_2 + M_3 = 6(f_3 - 2f_2 + f_1) \quad | \text{ For } 1 \le x \le 2$$

Here, $$M_2 + 4M_1 + M_0 = 6[-8 - 2(-6) + 2] = 36$$

and $$M_3 + 4M_2 + M_1 = 6\,[2 - 2\,(-8) + (-6) = 72$$

Putting $M_0 = M_3 = 0$, we get

$$M_2 + 4M_1 = 36$$

$$4M_2 + M_1 = 72$$

Solving, we get $M_1 = 4.8,\ M_2 = 16.8$

Hence for $0 \le x \le 1$,

$$F(x) = \frac{1}{6}\,[(1 - x)^3\,M_0 + (x - 0)^3\,M_1 + (1 - x)\,(6f_0 - M_0) + (x - 0)\,(6f_1 - M_1)]$$

$$= \frac{1}{6}\,[x^3(4.8) + (1 - x)\,(12) + x\,(-36 - 4.8)]$$

$$= 0.8x^3 - 8.8x + 2$$

For $1 \le x \le 2$,

$$F(x) = \frac{1}{6}\,[(2 - x)^3\,M_1 + (x - 1)^3\,M_2 + (2 - x)\,\{6f_1 - M_1\} + (x - 1)\,\{6f_2 - M_2\}]$$

$$= \frac{1}{6}\,[(2 - x)^3\,(4.8) + (x - 1)^3\,(16.8) + (2 - x)\,\{-36 - 4.8\} + (x - 1)\,\{-48 - 16.8\}]$$

$$= 2x^3 - 3.6x^2 - 5.2x + 0.8$$

For $2 \le x \le 3$,

$$F(x) = \frac{1}{6}\,[(3 - x)^3\,M_2 + (x - 2)^3\,M_3 + (3 - x)\,\{6f_2 - h^2M_2\} + (x - 2)\,\{6f_3 - h^2M_3\}]$$

$$= \frac{1}{6}\,[(3 - x)^3\,(16.8) + (3 - x)\,\{-48 - 16.8\} + (x - 2)\,(12)]$$

| using $M_3 = 0$

$$\Rightarrow \quad F(x) = \frac{1}{6}\,[(27 - x^3 - 27x + 9x^2)\,(16.8) - 64.8\,(3 - x) + 12x - 24]$$

$$= \frac{1}{6}\,[-\,16.8x^3 + 151.2x^2 - 376.8x + 235.2]$$

$$= -\,2.8x^3 + 25.2x^2 - 62.8x + 39.2$$

Therefore, cubic splines in different intervals are tabulated as below:

Interval	*Cubic spline*
[0, 1]	$0.8x^3 - 8.8x + 2$
[1, 2]	$2x^3 - 3.6x^2 - 5.2x + 0.8$
[2, 3]	$-\,2.8x^3 + 25.2x^2 - 62.8x + 39.2.$

Example 2. *Obtain the cubic spline for every subinterval from the given data:*

x:	*0*	*1*	*2*	*3*
f(x):	*1*	*2*	*33*	*244*

with the end conditions $M_0 = M_3 = 0$. *Hence find an estimate of* $f(2.5)$.

Sol. For the interval (x_{i-1}, x_i), the cubic spline is

$$F(x) = \frac{1}{6h}\,[(x_i - x)^3\,M_{i-1} + (x - x_{i-1})^3\,M_i + (x_i - x)\,\{6f_{i-1} - h^2M_{i-1}\}$$

$$+ (x - x_{i-1})\,\{6f_i - h^2M_i\}] \qquad (66)$$

For $i = 1, 2, \ldots\ldots, n$, we have

$$h^2\,[M_{i-1} + 4M_i + M_{i+1}] = 6[f_{i+1} - 2f_i + f_{i-1}] \qquad (67)$$

and

$$M_0 = M_3 = 0 \qquad (68)$$

Here $h = 1$

$\therefore$ From (67), For $0 \le x \le 1$,

$$M_0 + 4M_1 + M_2 = 6(f_2 - 2f_1 + f_0) \qquad (69)$$

and for $1 \le x \le 2$,

$$M_1 + 4M_2 + M_3 = 6(f_3 - 2f_2 + f_1) \qquad (70)$$

From (69), we get

$$M_0 + 4M_1 + M_2 = 6[33 - 4 + 1] = 180 \qquad (71)$$

and

$$M_1 + 4M_2 + M_3 = 6[244 - 66 + 2] = 1080 \qquad (72)$$

Using (68), equations (71) and (72) reduce to

$$4M_1 + M_2 = 180$$

and

$$M_1 + 4M_2 = 1080$$

Solving, we get

$$M_1 = -24 \text{ and } M_2 = 276 \tag{73}$$

Hence **for 0 ≤ x ≤ 1,**

$$F(x) = \frac{1}{6}[(1-x)^3 M_0 + (x-0)^3 M_1 + (1-x)\{6f_0 - M_0\}$$

$$+ (x-0)\{6f_1 - M_1\}] \quad | \because h = 1$$

$$= \frac{1}{6}[x^3(-24) + (1-x)\{6\} + x(12+24)]$$

$$= \frac{1}{6}[-24x^3 + 6 - 6x + 36x] = -4x^3 + 5x + 1$$

For $1 \le x \le 2$,

$$F(x) = \frac{1}{6}[(2-x)^3 M_1 + (x-1)^3 M_2 + (2-x)\{6f_1 - M_1\}$$

$$+ (x-1)\{6f_2 - M_2\}]$$

$$= \frac{1}{6}[(2-x)^3(-24) + (x-1)^3(276) + (2-x)(12+24)$$

$$+ (x-1)\{198 - 276\}]$$

$$= \frac{1}{6}[(2-x)^3(-24) + 276(x-1)^3 + 36(2-x) - 78(x-1)]$$

$$= 50x^3 - 162x^2 + 167x - 53$$

For $2 \le x \le 3$,

$$F(x) = \frac{1}{6}[(3-x)^3 M_2 + (x-2)^3 M_3 + (3-x)(6f_2 - M_2)$$

$$+ (x-2)(6f_3 - M_3)]$$

$$= \frac{1}{6}[(3-x)^3(276) + (x-2)^3(0) + (3-x)(198-276)$$

$$+ (x-2)\{(6 \times 244) - 0\}]$$

$$= \frac{1}{6}[(27 - x^3 - 27x + 9x^2)(276) + (3-x)(-78) + 1464(x-2)]$$

$$= -46x^3 + 414x^2 - 985x + 715$$

Therefore, the cubic splines in different intervals are tabulated as below:

Interval	*Cubic Spline*
[0, 1]	$-4x^3 + 5x + 1$
[1, 2]	$50x^3 - 162x^2 + 167x - 53$
[2, 3]	$-46x^3 + 414x^2 - 985x + 715$

An estimate at $x = 2.5$ is

$$f(2.5) = -46\,(2.5)^3 + 414(2.5)^2 - 985\,(2.5) + 715 = 121.25.$$

7.35 APPROXIMATIONS

The problem of approximating a function is an important problem in numerical analysis due to its wide application in the development of software for digital computers. The functions commonly used for approximating given functions are polynomials, trigonometric functions, exponential functions, and rational functions. However, from an application point of view, the polynomial functions are mostly used.

7.36 LEGENDRE AND CHEBYSHEV POLYNOMIALS

In the theory of approximation of functions, we often use the well known orthogonal polynomials, Legendre and Chebyshev polynomials, as the coordinate functions while applying the method of least squares.

Chebyshev polynomials are also used in the economization of power series.

7.37 LEGENDRE POLYNOMIALS

$P_n(x)$ is a Legendre polynomial in x of degree n and satisfies the Legendre differential equation

$$(1 - x^2)\frac{d^2y}{dx^2} - 2x\frac{dy}{dx} + n\,(n+1)\,y = 0$$

we have $$P_n(-x) = (-1)^n\,P_n(x).$$

From this, we conclude that $P_n(x)$ is an even function of x if n is even and an odd function of x if n is odd.

Legendre polynomials satisfy the recurrence relation

$$(n+1)\,P_{n+1}(x) = (2n+1)\,xP_n(x) - nP_{n-1}(x)$$

$$P_0(x) = 1,\ P_1(x) = x$$

we have

$$P_n(x) = \frac{1.3.5\ldots\ldots(2n-1)}{n\,!}\left[x^n - \frac{n(n-1)}{2(2n-1)}x^{n-2} + \frac{n(n-1)(n-2)(n-3)}{2.4.(2n-1)(2n-3)}x^{n-4} - \ldots\ldots\right]$$

In particular,

$$P_2(x) = \frac{3x^2 - 1}{2}, \qquad P_3(x) = \frac{5x^3 - 3x}{2}$$

$$P_4(x) = \frac{35x^4 - 30x^2 + 3}{8}, \qquad P_5(x) = \frac{63x^5 - 70x^3 + 15x}{8}$$

Legendre polynomials $P_n(x)$ are orthogonal on the interval $[-1, 1]$ with respect to the weight function $W(x) = 1$

We have

$$\int_{-1}^{1} P_m(x)\, P_n(x)\, dx = \begin{Bmatrix} 0, & \text{if } m \neq n \\ \dfrac{2}{2n+1}, & \text{if } m \neq n \end{Bmatrix}$$

7.38 CHEBYSHEV POLYNOMIALS

The Chebyshev polynomial of first kind of degree n over the interval $[-1, 1]$ is denoted by $T_n(x)$ and is defined by the relation

$$T_n(x) = \cos(n \cos^{-1} x) = \cos n\theta$$

where $\theta = \cos^{-1} x$ or $x = \cos\theta$

we have, $T_0(x) = 1$ and $T_1(x) = x$

The Chebyshev polynomial of second kind of degree n over the interval $[-1, 1]$ is denoted by $U_n(x)$ and is defined by the relation

$$U_n(x) = \sin(n \cos^{-1} x) = \sin n\theta$$

where $\theta = \cos^{-1} x$ or $x = \cos\theta$

NOTE

1. *Chebyshev's polynomials are also known as Tchebichef or Tchebicheff or Tchebysheff.*
2. *Sometimes the Chebyshev polynomial of the second kind is defined by*

$$U_n(x) = \frac{\sin\{(n+1)\cos^{-1} x\}}{\sqrt{1-x^2}} = \frac{U_{n+1}(x)}{\sqrt{1-x^2}}.$$

7.39 SPECIAL VALUES OF CHEBYSHEV POLYNOMIALS

$T_0(x) = \cos 0 = 1$

$T_1(x) = \cos(\cos^{-1} x) = x$

$T_2(x) = \cos(2\cos^{-1} x) = 2\cos^2(\cos^{-1} x) - 1 = 2x^2 - 1$

$T_3(x) = \cos(3\cos^{-1} x) = 4\cos^3(\cos^{-1} x) - 3\cos(\cos^{-1} x) = 4x^3 - 3x$

$T_4(x) = \cos(4\cos^{-1} x) = 2\cos^2(2\cos^{-1} x) - 1$

$= 2(2x^2 - 1)^2 - 1 = 8x^4 - 8x^2 + 1$

$T_5(x) = \cos(5\cos^{-1} x) = \cos(3\cos^{-1} x)\cos(2\cos^{-1} x)$

$- \sin(3\cos^{-1} x)\sin(2\cos^{-1} x)$

$= 16x^5 - 20x^3 + 5x$

Similarly, $T_6(x) = 32x^6 - 48x^4 + 18x^2 - 1$ and so on.

7.40 ORTHOGONAL PROPERTIES

To prove:

(1) $$\int_{-1}^{1} \frac{T_n(x)\,T_m(x)}{\sqrt{1-x^2}}\,dx = \begin{cases} 0; & \text{if } m \neq n \\ \pi/2; & \text{if } m = n \neq 0 \\ \pi; & \text{if } m = n = 0 \end{cases}$$

(2) $$\int_{-1}^{1} \frac{U_n(x)\,U_m(x)}{\sqrt{1-x^2}}\,dx = \begin{cases} 0; & \text{if } m \neq n \\ \pi/2; & \text{if } m = n \neq 0 \\ 0; & \text{if } m = n = 0 \end{cases}.$$

7.41 RECURRENCE RELATIONS

1. $T_{n+1}(x) - 2x\,T_n(x) + T_{n-1}(x) = 0.$
2. $(1 - x^2)\,T_n'(x) = -nxT_n(x) + n\,T_{n-1}(x).$
3. $U_{n+1}(x) - 2x\,U_n(x) + U_{n-1}(x) = 0.$
4. $(1 - x^2)\,U_n'(x) = -nx\,U_n(x) + nU_{n-1}(x).$

7.42 ALITER TO FIND CHEBYSHEV POLYNOMIALS

The recurrence relation

$$T_{n+1}(x) = 2x\, T_n(x) - T_{n-1}(x) \tag{74}$$

Can also be used to compute all $T_n(x)$ successively since we know $T_0(x)$ and $T_1(x)$.

$$T_0(x) = 1, \quad T_1(x) = x$$

Given $n = 1$ in (74), we have

$$T_2(x) = 2xT_1(x) - T_0(x) = 2x^2 - 1$$

Given $n = 2$ in (74), we get

$$T_3(x) = 2x\, T_2(x) - T_1(x) = 2x\,(2x^2 - 1) - x = 4x^3 - 3x$$

Given $n = 3$ in (74), we get

$$T_4(x) = 2x\, T_3(x) - T_2(x) = 2x\,(4x^3 - 3x) - (2x^2 - 1)$$

$$= 8x^4 - 6x^2 - 2x^2 + 1 = 8x^4 - 8x^2 + 1$$

Given $n = 4$ in (74), we get

$$T_5(x) = 2x\, T_4(x) - T_3(x) = 2x\,(8x^4 - 8x^2 + 1) - (4x^3 - 3x)$$

$$= 16x^5 - 20x^3 + 5x$$

Similarly, $T_6(x) = 2x\, T_5(x) - T_4(x)$

$$= 2x\,(16x^5 - 20x^3 + 5x) - (8x^4 - 8x^2 + 1)$$

$$= 32x^6 - 48x^4 + 18x^2 - 1.$$

7.43 EXPRESSION OF POWERS OF X INTERMS OF CHEBYSHEV POLYNOMIALS

$$1 = T_0(x)$$

$$x = T_1(x)$$

$$x^2 = \frac{1}{2}\,[T_0(x) + T_2(x)]$$

$$x^3 = \frac{1}{4}\,[3\, T_1(x) + T_3(x)]$$

$$x^4 = \frac{1}{8}\,[3\, T_0(x) + 4T_2(x) + T_4(x)]$$

$$x^5 = \frac{1}{16} [10\,T_1(x) + 5T_3(x) + T_5(x)]$$

$$x^6 = \frac{1}{32} [10\,T_0(x) + 15T_2(x) + 6T_4(x) + T_6(x)]$$

and so on.

The above expressions will be useful in the economization of power series.

7.44 PROPERTIES OF CHEBYSHEV POLYNOMIALS

(*i*) $T_n(x)$ is a polynomial of degree n. We have $T_n(-x) = (-1)^n\, T_n(x)$ so that $T_n(x)$ is an even function of x if n is even and it is an odd function of x if n is odd.

(*ii*) $T_n(x)$ has n simple zeros.

$$x_k = \cos\left(\frac{2k-1}{2n}\pi\right),\ k = 1, 2, \ldots\ldots, n \text{ on the interval } [-1, 1]$$

(*iii*) $T_n(x)$ assumes extreme values at $(n + 1)$ points $x_k = \cos\frac{k\pi}{n}$, $k = 0, 1, 2, \ldots\ldots, n$ and the extreme value at x_k is $(-1)^k$.

(*iv*) $|\,T_n(x)\,| \le 1,\ x \in [-1, 1]$

(*v*) $T_n(x)$ are orthogonal on the interval $[-1, 1]$ with respect to the weight function

$$W(x) = \frac{1}{\sqrt{1-x^2}}$$

(*vi*) If $p_n(x)$ is any monic polynomial of degree n and $\tilde{T}_n(x) = \frac{T_n(x)}{2^{n-1}}$ is the monic Chebyshev polynomial, then

$$\max_{-1 \le x \le 1} |\tilde{T}_n(x)| \le \max_{-1 \le x \le 1} |p_n(x)|.$$

7.45 CHEBYSHEV POLYNOMIAL APPROXIMATION

Let $f(x)$ be a continuous function defined on the interval $[-1, 1]$ and let $c_0 + c_1 x + c_2 x^2 + \ldots\ldots + c_n x^n$ be the required minimax (or uniform) polynomial approximation for $f(x)$.

Suppose $f(x) = \frac{a_0}{2} + \sum_{i=1}^{\infty} a_i \, T_i(x)$ is the Chebyshev series expansion for $f(x)$.

Then the truncated series or the partial sum

$$P_n(x) = \frac{a_0}{2} + \sum_{i=1}^{n} a_i \, T_i(x) \qquad (75)$$

is very nearly the solution to the problem

$$\max_{-1 \le x \le 1} \left| f(x) - \sum_{i=0}^{n} c_i \, x^i \right| = \min_{-1 \le x \le 1} \left| f(x) - \sum_{i=0}^{n} c_i \, x^i \right|$$

i.e., the partial sum (75) is nearly the best uniform approximation to $f(x)$.

Reason. Suppose we write

$$f(x) = \frac{a_0}{2} + a_1 T_1(x) + a_2 T_2(x) + \ldots\ldots + a_n T_n(x) + a_{n+1} T_{n+1}(x) + \text{remainder} \qquad (76)$$

Neglecting the remainder, we obtain from (76),

$$f(x) - \left[\frac{a_0}{2} + \sum_{i=1}^{n} a_i T_i(x) \right] = a_{n+1} T_{n+1}(x) \qquad (77)$$

Since $T_{n+1}(x)$ has $n + 2$ equal maxima and minima which alternate in sign, therefore by Chebyshev equioscillation theorem, the polynomial (75) of degree n is the best uniform approximation to $f(x)$.

7.46 LANCZOS ECONOMIZATION OF POWER SERIES FOR A GENERAL FUNCTION

First we express the given function $f(x)$ as a power series in x in the form

$$f(x) = \sum_{i=0}^{\infty} a_i x^i, \; -1 \le x \le 1 \qquad (78)$$

Then we change each power of x in (78) in terms of Chebyshev polynomials and we obtain

$$f(x) = \sum_{i=0}^{\infty} c_i T_i(x) \qquad (79)$$

as the Chebyshev series expansion for $f(x)$ on [– 1, 1]. It has been found that for a large number of functions $f(x)$, the series (79) converges more rapidly than the power series given by eqn. (78). If we truncate series (79) at $T_n(x)$, then the partial sum

$$P_n(x) = \sum_{i=0}^{n} c_i T_i(x) \tag{80}$$

is a good uniform approximation to $f(x)$ in the sense

$$\max_{-1 \le x \le 1} | f(x) - P_n(x) | \le | c_{n+1} | + | c_{n+2} | + \ldots\ldots \le \varepsilon \quad \text{(say)}$$

For a given ε, it is possible to find the number of terms that should be retained in eqn. (80). This process is known as **Lanczos Economization.** Replacing each $T_i(x)$ in eqn. (80) by its polynomial form and rearranging the terms, we get the required economized polynomial approximation for $f(x)$.

EXAMPLES

Example 1. *Prove that*

$$\sqrt{1 - x^2}\; T_n(x) = U_{n+1}(x) - x\, U_n(x).$$

Sol. If $x = \cos\theta$, we get

$$T_n(\cos\theta) = \cos n\theta$$

and $$U_n(\cos\theta) = \sin n\theta$$

Then we are to prove,

$$\sin\theta \cos n\theta = \sin(n+1)\theta - \cos\theta \sin n\theta$$

Now, $$\text{R.H.S.} = \sin n\theta \cos\theta + \cos n\theta \sin\theta - \cos\theta \sin n\theta$$

$$= \sin\theta \cos n\theta = \text{L.H.S.}$$

Example 2. *Find the best lower order approximation to the cubic* $2x^3 + 3x^2$.

Sol. We know that

$$x^3 = \frac{1}{4}[3T_1(x) + T_3(x)]$$

$$2x^3 + 3x^2 = 2\left[\frac{1}{4}\{3T_1(x) + T_3(x)\}\right] + 3x^2$$

$$= \frac{3}{2}T_1(x) + \frac{1}{2}T_3(x) + 3x^2 = 3x^2 + \frac{3}{2}x + \frac{1}{2}T_3(x)$$

$$[\because \quad T_1(x) = x]$$

Since $|T_3(x)| \le 1, -1 \le x \le 1$ therefore, the polynomial $3x^2 + \frac{3}{2}x$ is the required lower order approximation to the given cubic with a max. error $\pm \frac{1}{2}$ in range $[-1, 1]$.

Example 3. *Express* $2T_0(x) - \frac{1}{4}T_2(x) + \frac{1}{8}T_4(x)$ *as polynomials in x.*

Sol. $2T_0(x) - \frac{1}{4}T_2(x) + \frac{1}{8}T_4(x)$

$$= 2(1) - \frac{1}{4}(2x^2 - 1) + \frac{1}{8}(8x^4 - 8x^2 + 1)$$

$$= 2 - \frac{1}{2}x^2 + \frac{1}{4} + x^4 - x^2 + \frac{1}{8}$$

$$= x^4 - \frac{3}{4}x^2 + \frac{19}{8}.$$

Example 4. *Express* $1 - x^2 + 2x^4$ *as sum of Chebyshev polynomials.*

Sol.
$$1 - x^2 + 2x^4 = 1 - x^2 + 2\left[\frac{1}{8}\{3T_0(x) + 4T_2(x) + T_4(x)\}\right]$$

$$= 1 - x^2 + \frac{3}{4}T_0(x) + T_2(x) + \frac{1}{4}T_4(x)$$

$$= 1 - \frac{1}{2}[T_0(x) + T_2(x)] + \frac{3}{4}T_0(x) + T_2(x) + \frac{1}{4}T_4(x)$$

$$= T_0(x) - \frac{1}{2}T_0(x) - \frac{1}{2}T_2(x) + \frac{3}{4}T_0(x) + T_2(x) + \frac{1}{4}T_4(x)$$

$$= \frac{5}{4}T_0(x) + \frac{1}{2}T_2(x) + \frac{1}{4}T_4(x).$$

Example 5. *Economize the power series:* $\sin x \approx x - \frac{x^3}{6} + \frac{x^5}{120} - \frac{x^7}{5040} + \ldots\ldots$ *to three significant digit accuracy.*

Sol. The truncated series is

$$\sin x \approx x - \frac{x^3}{6} + \frac{x^5}{120} \tag{81}$$

which is obtained by truncating the last term since $\frac{1}{5040} = 0.000198$ will produce a change in the fourth decimal place only.

Converting the powers of x in (81) into Chebyshev polynomials, we get

$$\sin x \approx T_1(x) - \frac{1}{6}\left[\frac{1}{4}\{3T_1(x) + T_3(x)\}\right] + \frac{1}{120}\left[\frac{1}{16}\{10T_1(x) + 5T_3(x) + T_5(x)\}\right]$$

$$\approx T_1(x) - \frac{1}{24}[3T_1(x) + T_3(x)] + \frac{1}{120 \times 16}[10T_1(x) + 5T_3(x) + T_5(x)]$$

$$\approx \frac{169}{192}T_1(x) - \frac{5}{128}T_3(x) + \frac{1}{1920}T_5(x)$$

Truncated series is

$$\sin x \approx \frac{169}{192}T_1(x) - \frac{5}{128}T_3(x)$$

which is obtained by truncating the last term since $\frac{1}{1920} = 0.00052$ will produce a change in the fourth decimal place only.

Economized series is

$$\sin x \approx \frac{169}{192}x - \frac{5}{128}(4x^3 - 3x)$$

$$= \frac{383}{384}x - \frac{5}{32}x^3 = 0.9974x - 0.1526x^3$$

which gives sin x to three significant digit accuracy.

Example 6. *Using the Chebyshev polynomials, obtain the least squares approximation of second degree for $f(x) = x^4$ on $[-1, 1]$.*

Sol. Let $\quad f(x) \approx P(x) = C_0T_0(x) + C_1T_1(x) + C_2T_2(x)$

We have

$$U(C_0, C_1, C_2) = \int_{-1}^{1} \frac{1}{\sqrt{1-x^2}}(x^4 - C_0T_0 - C_1T_1 - C_2T_2)^2\, dx$$

which is to be minimum.

Normal equations are given by

$$\frac{\partial U}{\partial C_0} = 0 \Rightarrow \int_{-1}^{1}(x^4 - C_0T_0 - C_1T_1 - C_2T_2)\frac{T_0}{\sqrt{1-x^2}}\, dx = 0$$

$$\frac{\partial U}{\partial C_1} = 0 \Rightarrow \int_{-1}^{1} (x^4 - C_0T_0 - C_1T_1 - C_2T_2)\frac{T_1}{\sqrt{1-x^2}}\,dx = 0$$

and
$$\frac{\partial U}{\partial C_2} = 0 \Rightarrow \int_{-1}^{1} (x^4 - C_0T_0 - C_1T_1 - C_2T_2)\frac{T_2}{\sqrt{1-x^2}}\,dx = 0$$

We find that

$$C_0 = \frac{1}{\pi}\int_{-1}^{1} \frac{x^4 T_0}{\sqrt{1-x^2}}\,dx = \frac{3}{8}$$

$$C_1 = \frac{2}{\pi}\int_{-1}^{1} \frac{x^4 T_1}{\sqrt{1-x^2}}\,dx = 0$$

$$C_2 = \frac{2}{\pi}\int_{-1}^{1} \frac{x^4 T_2}{\sqrt{1-x^2}}\,dx = \frac{1}{2}$$

Hence the required approximation is $f(x) = \frac{3}{8}T_0 + \frac{1}{2}T_2$.

Example 7. *Find a uniform polynomial approximation of degree four or less to e^x on [– 1, 1] using Lanczos economization with a tolerance of $\varepsilon = 0.02$.*

Sol. We have

$$f(x) = e^x = 1 + x + \frac{x^2}{2} + \frac{x^3}{6} + \frac{x^4}{24} + \frac{x^5}{120} + \ldots\ldots$$

Since $\frac{1}{120} = 0.008\ldots\ldots$, therefore

$$e^x = 1 + x + \frac{x^2}{2} + \frac{x^3}{6} + \frac{x^4}{24} \qquad (82)$$

with a tolerance of $\varepsilon = 0.02$.

Changing each power of x in (82) in terms of Chebyshev polynomials, we get

$$e^x = T_0 + T_1 + \frac{1}{4}(T_0 + T_2) + \frac{1}{24}(3T_1 + T_3) + \frac{1}{192}(3T_0 + 4T_2 + T_4)$$

$$= \frac{81}{64}T_0 + \frac{9}{8}T_1 + \frac{13}{48}T_2 + \frac{1}{24}T_3 + \frac{1}{192}T_4 \qquad (83)$$

We have $\dfrac{1}{192} = 0.005 \ldots\ldots$

$\therefore$ The magnitude of last term on R.H.S. of (83) is less than 0.02.

Hence the required economized polynomial approximation for e^x is given by

$$e^x = \frac{81}{64}T_0 + \frac{9}{8}T_1 + \frac{13}{48}T_2 + \frac{1}{24}T_3$$

or
$$e^x = \frac{x^3}{6} + \frac{13}{24}x^2 + x + \frac{191}{192}.$$

Example 8. *The function f is defined by*

$$f(x) = \frac{1}{x}\int_0^x \frac{1-e^{-t^2}}{t^2}\,dt$$

Approximate f by a polynomial $P(x) = a + bx + cx^2$ such that

$$\max_{|x| \le 1} |f(x) - P(x)| \le 5 \times 10^{-3}.$$

Sol. The given function

$$f(x) = \frac{1}{x}\int_0^x \left(1 - \frac{t^2}{2} + \frac{t^4}{6} - \frac{t^6}{24} + \frac{t^8}{120} - \frac{t^{10}}{720} + \ldots\ldots\right) dt$$

$$= 1 - \frac{x^2}{6} + \frac{x^4}{30} - \frac{x^6}{168} + \frac{x^8}{1080} - \frac{x^{10}}{7920} + \ldots\ldots \quad (84)$$

The tolerable error is $5 \times 10^{-3} \approx 0.005$.

Truncating the series (84) at x^8, we get

$$P(x) = 1 - \frac{x^2}{6} + \frac{x^4}{30} - \frac{x^6}{168} + \frac{x^8}{1080}$$

$$= T_0 - \frac{1}{12}(T_2 + T_0) + \frac{1}{240}(T_4 + 4T_2 + 3T_0)$$

$$- \frac{1}{5376}(T_6 + 6T_4 + 15T_2 + 10T_0)$$

$$+ \frac{1}{138240}(T_8 + 8T_6 + 28T_4 + 56T_2 + 35T_0)$$

$$= 0.92755973\ T_0 - 0.06905175\ T_2 + 0.003253\ T_4 - 0.000128\ T_6 + 0.000007\ T_8 \quad (85)$$

Truncating R.H.S. of (85) at T_2, we obtain the required polynomial

$$P(x) = 0.92755973\ T_0 - 0.06905175\ T_2$$
$$= 0.99661148 - 0.13810350x^2$$
$$= 0.9966 - 0.1381x^2$$

The maximum absolute error in the neglected terms is obviously less than the tolerable error.

ASSIGNMENT 7.4

1. Express $1 + x - x^2 + x^3$ as sum of Chebyshev polynomials.
2. Prove that $x^2 = \frac{1}{2}[T_0(x) + T_2(x)]$
3. Express $T_0(x) + 2T_1(x) + T_2(x)$ as polynomials in x.
4. Obtain the best lower degree approximation to the cubic $x^3 + 2x^2$.
5. Explain how to fit a function of the form

$$y = A_1 e^{\lambda_1 x} + A_2 e^{\lambda_2 x}$$

to the given data.

6. Obtain $y(1.5)$ from the following data using cubic spline.

x:	1	2	3
y:	– 8	– 1	18

7. Economize the series

$$f(x) = 1 - \frac{x}{2} - \frac{x^2}{8} - \frac{x^3}{16}$$

8. Economize the series $\sinh x = x + \frac{x^3}{6} + \frac{x^5}{120} + \frac{x^7}{5040}$ on the interval [– 1, 1] allowing for a tolerance of 0.0005.
9. Economize the series $\cos x = 1 - \frac{x^2}{2} + \frac{x^4}{24} - \frac{x^6}{720}$.
10. Obtain the cubic spline approximation valid in [3, 4], for the function given in the tabular form

x:	1	2	3	4
$f(x)$:	3	10	29	65

under the natural spline conditions:

$$M(1) = 0 = M(4)$$

11. Obtain the cubic spline fit for the data

x:	0	1	2	3
$f(x)$:	1	4	10	8

under the end conditions $f''(0) = 0 = f''(3)$ and valid in the interval [1, 2].

Hence obtain the estimate of $f(1.5)$.

12. Fit the following four points by the cubic splines:

x:	1	2	3	4
y:	1	5	11	8

Use the end conditions $y''(1) = 0 = y''(4)$. Hence compute $y(1.5)$.

13. Find the natural cubic spline that fits the data

x:	1	2	3	4
$f(x)$:	0	1	0	0

14. Find whether the following functions are splines or not?

$$(i)\ f(x) = \left.\begin{matrix} -x^2 - 2x^3, & -1 \le x \le 0 \\ -x^2 + 2x^3, & 0 \le x \le 1 \end{matrix}\right\}$$

$$(ii)\ f(x) = \left.\begin{matrix} -x^2 - 2x^3, & -1 \le x \le 0 \\ x^2 + 2x^3, & 0 \le x \le 1 \end{matrix}\right\}$$

[**Hint:** Check the continuity of $f(x)$, $f'(x)$ and $f''(x)$ at $x = 0$]

15. Find the values of α and β such that the function

$$f(x) = \begin{Bmatrix} x^2 - \alpha x + 1, 1 \le x \le 2 \\ 3x - \beta, 2 \le x \le 3 \end{Bmatrix}$$

is a quadratic spline. [**Hint:** For $f(x)$ to be continuous at $x = 2$, $5 - 2\alpha = 6 - \beta$ and For $f'(x)$ to be continuous at $x = 2$, $4 - \alpha = 3$]

16. We are given the following values of a function of the variable t:

t:	0.1	0.2	0.3	0.4
f:	0.76	0.58	0.44	0.35

Obtain a least squares fit of the form

$$f = ae^{-3t} + be^{-2t}.$$

17. Evaluate

$$I = \int_0^1 \frac{1}{1+x}\,dx \text{ using the cubic spline method.}$$

18. Explain approximation of function by Taylor series by taking suitable example.

7.47 REGRESSION ANALYSIS

The term 'regression' was first used by Sir Francis Galton (1822–1911), a British biometrician in connection with the height of parents and their offspring. He found that the offspring of tall or short parents tend to regress to the average height. In other words, though tall fathers do tend to have tall sons, the average height of tall fathers is more than the average height of their sons and the average height of short fathers is less than the average height of their sons.

The term 'regression' stands for some sort of functional relationship between two or more related variables. The only fundamental difference, if any, between problems of curve-fitting and regression is that in regression, any of the variables may be considered as independent or dependent while in curve-fitting, one variable cannot be dependent.

Regression measures the nature and extent of correlation. Regression is the estimation or prediction of unknown values of one variable from known values of another variable.

7.48 CURVE OF REGRESSION AND REGRESSION EQUATION

If two variates x and y are correlated, *i.e.,* there exists an association or relationship between them, then the scatter diagram will be more or less concentrated round a curve. This curve is called the *curve of regression* and the relationship is said to be expressed by means of *curvilinear regression.*

The mathematical equation of the regression curve is called regression equation.

7.49 LINEAR REGRESSION

When the points of the scatter diagram concentrate round a straight line, the regression is called linear and this straight line is known as the line of regression.

The regression will be called non-linear if there exists a relationship other than a straight line between the variables under consideration.

7.50 LINES OF REGRESSION

A line of regression is the straight line which gives the best fit in the least square sense to the given frequency.

In case of n pairs (x_i, y_i); $i = 1, 2, ..., n$ from a bivariate data, we have no reason or justification to assume y as a dependent variable and x as an independent variable. Either of the two may be estimated for the given values of the other. Thus, if we wish to estimate y for given values of x, we shall have the regression equation of the form $y = a + bx$, called the regression line of y on x. If we wish to estimate x for given values of y, we shall have the regression line of the form $x = A + By$, called the regression line of x on y.

Thus it implies, in general, *we always have two lines of regression.*

If the line of regression is so chosen that the sum of the squares of deviation parallel to the axis of y is minimized [*See Figure (a)*], it is called *the line of regression of y on x* and it gives *the best estimate of y for any given value of x.*

If the line of regression is so chosen that the sum of the squares of deviations parallel to the axis of x is minimized [*See Figure (b)*], it is called *the line of regression of x on y* and it gives *the best estimate of x for any given value of y.*

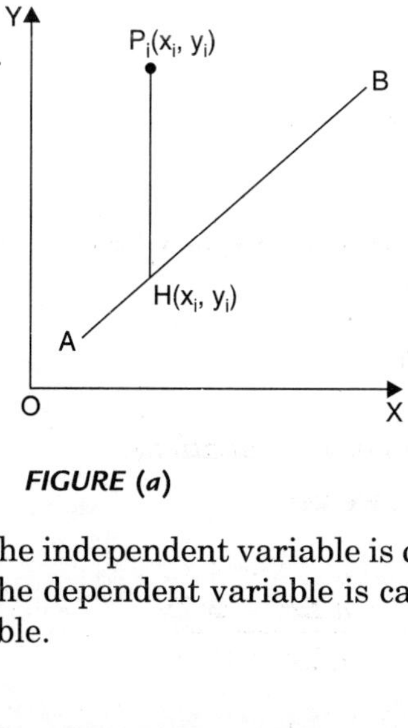

FIGURE (a)

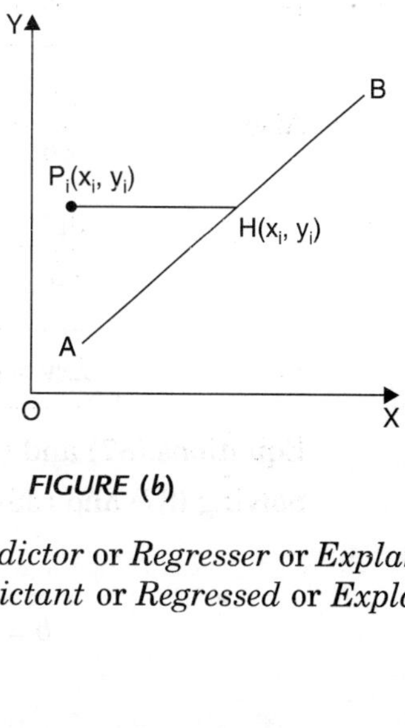

FIGURE (b)

The independent variable is called the *predictor* or *Regresser* or *Explanator* and the dependent variable is called the *predictant* or *Regressed* or *Explained* variable.

7.51 DERIVATION OF LINES OF REGRESSION

7.51.1 Line of Regression of y on x

To obtain the line of regression of y on x, we shall assume y as dependent variable and x as independent variable.

Let $y = a + bx$ be the equation of regression line of y on x.

The residual for i^{th} point is $E_i = y_i - a - bx_i$.

Introduce a new quantity U such that

$$U = \sum_{i=1}^{n} E_i^2 = \sum_{i=1}^{n} (y_i - a - bx_i)^2 \quad (86)$$

According to the *principle of Least squares*, the constants a and b are chosen in such a way that the sum of the squares of residuals is minimum.

Now, the condition for U to be maximum or minimum is

$$\frac{\partial U}{\partial a} = 0 \quad \text{and} \quad \frac{\partial U}{\partial b} = 0$$

From (86), $$\frac{\partial U}{\partial a} = 2\sum_{i=1}^{n} (y_i - a - bx_i)(-1)$$

$$\frac{\partial U}{\partial a} = 0 \text{ gives } 2\sum_{i=1}^{n} (y_i - a - bx_i)(-1) = 0$$

$$\Rightarrow \quad \boxed{\Sigma y = na + b\,\Sigma x} \tag{87}$$

Also, $$\frac{\partial U}{\partial b} = 2\sum_{i=1}^{n} (y_i - a - bx_i)(-x_i)$$

$$\frac{\partial U}{\partial b} = 0 \text{ gives } 2\sum_{i=1}^{n} (y_i - a - bx_i)(-x_i) = 0$$

$$\Rightarrow \quad \boxed{\Sigma xy = a\,\Sigma x + b\,\Sigma x^2} \tag{88}$$

Equations (87) and (88) are called *normal equations.*

Solving (87) and (88) for 'a' and 'b', we get

$$b = \frac{\Sigma xy - \frac{1}{n}\Sigma x\,\Sigma y}{\Sigma x^2 - \frac{1}{n}(\Sigma x)^2} = \frac{n\,\Sigma xy - \Sigma x\,\Sigma y}{n\,\Sigma x^2 - (\Sigma x)^2} \tag{89}$$

and $$a = \frac{\Sigma y}{n} - b\frac{\Sigma x}{n} = \bar{y} - b\bar{x} \tag{90}$$

Eqn. (90) gives $\bar{y} = a + b\bar{x}$

Hence $y = a + bx$ line passes through point $(\bar{x}, \bar{y})$.

Putting $a = \bar{y} - b\bar{x}$ in equation of line $y = a + bx$, we get

$$\boxed{y - \bar{y} = b(x - \bar{x})} \tag{91}$$

Equation (91) is called regression line of y on x. 'b' is called the regression coefficient of y on x and is usually denoted by b_{yx}.

Hence eqn. (91) can be rewritten as

$$y - \bar{y} = b_{yx}(x - \bar{x})$$

where $\bar{x}$ and $\bar{y}$ are mean values while

$$b_{yx} = \frac{n\,\Sigma xy - \Sigma x\,\Sigma y}{n\,\Sigma x^2 - (\Sigma x)^2}$$

In equation (88), shifting the origin to $(\bar{x}, \bar{y})$, we get

$$\Sigma(x - \bar{x})(y - \bar{y}) = a\,\Sigma(x - \bar{x}) + b(x - \bar{x})^2$$

$$\Rightarrow \qquad nr\,\sigma_x\sigma_y = a(0) + bn\sigma_x^2$$

$$\because \quad \Sigma(x - \bar{x}) = 0, \quad \frac{1}{n}\Sigma(x - \bar{x})^2 = \sigma_x^2 \quad \text{and} \quad \frac{\Sigma(x - \bar{x})(y - \bar{y})}{n\sigma_x\sigma_y} = r$$

$$\Rightarrow \qquad b = r\,\frac{\sigma_y}{\sigma_x}$$

Hence regression coefficient b_{yx} can also be defined as

$$\boxed{b_{yx} = r\,\frac{\sigma_y}{\sigma_x}}$$

where r is the coefficient of correlation, σ_x and σ_y are the standard deviations of x and y series respectively.

7.51.2 Line of Regression of x on y

Proceeding in the same way as 7.16.1, we can derive the regression line of x on y as

$$\boxed{x - \bar{x} = b_{xy}(y - \bar{y})}$$

where b_{xy} is the regression coefficient of x on y and is given by

$$\boxed{b_{xy} = \frac{n\,\Sigma xy - \Sigma x\,\Sigma y}{n\,\Sigma y^2 - (\Sigma y)^2}}$$

or

$$\boxed{b_{xy} = r\,\frac{\sigma_x}{\sigma_y}}$$

where the terms have their usual meanings.

NOTE *If r = 0, the two lines of regression become $y = \bar{y}$ and $x = \bar{x}$ which are two straight lines parallel to x and y axes respectively and passing through their means $\bar{y}$ and $\bar{x}$. They are mutually perpendicular. If r = ± 1, the two lines of regression will coincide.*

7.52 USE OF REGRESSION ANALYSIS

(*i*) In the field of Business, this tool of statistical analysis is widely used. Businessmen are interested in predicting future production, consumption, investment, prices, profits and sales etc.

(*ii*) In the field of economic planning and sociological studies, projections of population, birth rates, death rates and other similar variables are of great use.

7.53 COMPARISON OF CORRELATION AND REGRESSION ANALYSIS

Both the correlation and regression analysis helps us in studying the relationship between two variables yet they differ in their approach and objectives.

(*i*) Correlation studies are meant for studying the covariation of the two variables. They tell us whether the variables under study move in the same direction or in reverse directions. The degree of their covariation is also reflected in the correlation co-efficient but the correlation study does not provide the nature of relationship. It does not tell us about the relative movement in the variables and we cannot predict the value of one variable corresponding to the value of other variable. This is possible through regression analysis.

(*ii*) Regression presumes one variable as a cause and the other as its effect. The independent variable is supposed to be affecting the dependent variable and as such we can estimate the values of the dependent variable by projecting the relationship between them. However, correlation between two series is not necessarily a cause-effect relationship.

(*iii*) Coefficient of correlation cannot exceed unity but one of the regression coefficients can have a value higher than unity but the product of two regression coefficients can never exceed unity.

7.54 PROPERTIES OF REGRESSION CO-EFFICIENTS

Property I. Correlation co-efficient is the geometric mean between the regression co-efficients.

Proof. The co-efficients of regression are $\dfrac{r\sigma_y}{\sigma_x}$ and $\dfrac{r\sigma_x}{\sigma_y}$.

Geometric mean between them $= \sqrt{\dfrac{r\sigma_y}{\sigma_x} \times \dfrac{r\sigma_x}{\sigma_y}} = \sqrt{r^2} = r =$ co-efficient of correlation.

Property II. If one of the regression co-efficients is greater than unity, the other must be less than unity.

Proof. The two regression co-efficients are $b_{yx} = \dfrac{r\sigma_y}{\sigma_x}$ and $b_{xy} = \dfrac{r\sigma_x}{\sigma_y}$.

Let $\quad b_{yx} > 1$, then $\dfrac{1}{b_{yx}} < 1 \qquad (92)$

Since $\quad b_{yx} \cdot b_{xy} = r^2 \leq 1 \qquad (\because \; -1 \leq r \leq 1)$

$\therefore \quad b_{xy} \leq \dfrac{1}{b_{yx}} < 1. \qquad$ | using (92)

Similarly, if $\quad b_{xy} > 1$, then $b_{yx} < 1$.

Property III. Arithmetic mean of regression co-efficients is greater than the correlation co-efficient.

Proof. We have to prove that

$$\frac{b_{yx} + b_{xy}}{2} > r$$

or $\quad r\dfrac{\sigma_y}{\sigma_x} + r\dfrac{\sigma_x}{\sigma_y} > 2r$

or $\quad \sigma_x^2 + \sigma_y^2 > 2\sigma_x\sigma_y$

or $\quad (\sigma_x - \sigma_y)^2 > 0$ which is true.

Property IV. Regression co-efficients are independent of the origin but not of scale.

Proof. Let $u = \dfrac{x-a}{h}, v = \dfrac{y-b}{k}$, where a, b, h and k are constants

$$b_{yx} = \frac{r\sigma_y}{\sigma_x} = r \cdot \frac{k\sigma_v}{h\sigma_u} = \frac{k}{h}\left(\frac{r\sigma_v}{\sigma_u}\right) = \frac{k}{h} b_{vu}$$

Similarly, $$b_{xy} = \frac{h}{k} b_{uv}.$$

Thus, b_{yx} and b_{xy} are both independent of a and b but not of h and k.

Property V. The correlation co-efficient and the two regression co-efficients have same sign.

Proof. Regression co-efficient of y on $x = b_{yx} = r \dfrac{\sigma_y}{\sigma_x}$

Regression co-efficient of x on $y = b_{xy} = r \dfrac{\sigma_x}{\sigma_y}$

Since σ_x and σ_y are both positive; b_{yx}, b_{xy} and r have same sign.

7.55 ANGLE BETWEEN TWO LINES OF REGRESSION

If θ is the acute angle between the two regression lines in the case of two variables x and y, show that

$$\tan \theta = \frac{1-r^2}{r} \cdot \frac{\sigma_x \sigma_y}{\sigma_x^2 + \sigma_y^2}, \qquad \textit{where } r, \sigma_x, \sigma_y \textit{ have their usual meanings.}$$

Explain the significance of the formula when r = 0 and r = ± 1.

Proof. Equations to the lines of regression of y on x and x on y are

$$y - \bar{y} = \frac{r\sigma_y}{\sigma_x}(x - \bar{x}) \qquad \text{and} \qquad x - \bar{x} = \frac{r\sigma_x}{\sigma_y}(y - \bar{y})$$

Their slopes are $$m_1 = \frac{r\sigma_y}{\sigma_x} \qquad \text{and} \qquad m_2 = \frac{\sigma_y}{r\sigma_x}.$$

$$\therefore \qquad \tan \theta = \pm \frac{m_2 - m_1}{1 + m_2 m_1} = \pm \frac{\dfrac{\sigma_y}{r\sigma_x} - \dfrac{r\sigma_y}{\sigma_x}}{1 + \dfrac{\sigma_y^2}{\sigma_x^2}}$$

$$= \pm \frac{1-r^2}{r} \cdot \frac{\sigma_y}{\sigma_x} \cdot \frac{\sigma_x^2}{\sigma_x^2 + \sigma_y^2} = \pm \frac{1-r^2}{r} \cdot \frac{\sigma_x \sigma_y}{\sigma_x^2 + \sigma_y^2}$$

Since $r^2 \leq 1$ and σ_x, σ_y are positive.

$\therefore$ +ve sign gives the acute angle between the lines.

Hence $\tan\theta = \frac{1-r^2}{r} \cdot \frac{\sigma_x\sigma_y}{\sigma_x^2+\sigma_y^2}$

when $r = 0$, $\theta = \frac{\pi}{2}$ $\therefore$ The two lines of regression are perpendicular to each other.

Hence the estimated value of y is the same for all values of x and vice-versa.

When $r = \pm 1$, $\tan\theta = 0$ so that $\theta = 0$ or π

Hence the lines of regression coincide and there is perfect correlation between the two variates x and y.

7.56 ALGORITHM FOR LINEAR REGRESSION

```
1. Read n
2. sum x ← 0
3. sum xsq ← 0
4. sum y ← 0
5. sum xy ← 0
6. for i = 1 to n do
7. Read x,y
8. sum x ← sum x + x
9. sum xsq ← sum xsq + x²
10. sum y ← sum y + y
11. sum xy ← sum xy + x × y
    end for
12. denom ← n × sum x sq - sum x × sum x
13. a ← (sum y × sum x sq - sum x × sum xy)/denom
14. b ← (n × sum xy - sum x × sum y)/denom
15. Write b,a
16. Stop
```

7.57 PROGRAM TO IMPLEMENT LEAST SQUARE FIT OF A REGRESSION LINE OF Y ON X

```
#include<stdio.h>
#include<conio.h>
#include<math.h>
void main()
{
int data,i;
float x[10],y[10],xy[10],x2[10],z;
float sum1=0.0,sum2=0.0,sum3=0.0,sum4=0.0;
clrscr();
printf("Enter the number of data points:");
scanf("%d",&data);
printf("Enter the value of x: \n");
for(i=0;i<data;i++)
{
     printf("Value of x%d:",i+1);
     scanf("%f",&x[i]);
}
printf{"\nEnter the value of f(x):\n"};
for(i=0;i<data;i++)
{
     printf("Value of f(x%d):",i+1);
     scanf("%f",&y[i]);
}
for(i=0;i<data;i++)
}
     xy[i]=x[i]*y[i];
     x2[i]=x[i]*x[i];
     sum1 +=xy[i];
     sum2 +=x2[i];
     sum3 +=x[i];
     sum4 +=y[i];
}
```

```
sum3 =sum3/2;
sum4 =sum4/2;
//printf("%.2f %.2f %.2f", %.2f" sum1,sum2,sum3,sum4);
sum1=(sum1/sum2);
z=(sum1*sum3)-sum4;
printf("\n\nThe REGRESSION LINE OF Y on X is:\n");
printf("\t\t\t y=%.2f *x - (%.2f)",sum1,z);
getch(1);
}
```

7.58 PROGRAM TO IMPLEMENT LEAST SQUARE FIT OF A REGRESSION LINE OF X ON Y

```
#include<stdio.h>
#include<conio.h>
#include<math.h>
void main()
{
int data,i;
float x[10],y[10],xy[10],y2[10],z;
float sumx=0.0,sumy=0.0,sumxy=0.0,sumy2=0.0;
clrscr();
printf("Enter the number of data points: ");
scanf("%d",&data);
printf("Enter the value of x: \n");
for(i=0;i<data;i++)
{
    printf("Value of x%d: ",i+1);
    scanf("%f",&x[i]);
}
printf("\nEnter the value of f(x): \n");
for(i=0;i<data; i++)
{
    printf("Value of f(x%d):", i+1);
    scanf("%f",&y[i]);
}
```

```
for(i=0;i<data;i++)
{
      xy[i]=x[i]*y[i];
      y2[i]=y[i]*y[i];
      sumxy +=xy[i];
      sumy2 +=y2[i];
      sumx +=x[i];
      sumy +=y[i];
}
sumx =sumx/2;
sumy =sumy/2;
sumxy=(sumxy/sumy2);
z=(sumxy*sumy)-sumx;
printf("\n\nThe REGRESSION LINE OF X on Y is:\n");
printf("\t\t\t x = %.2f *y - (%.2f)",sumxy, z);
getch();
}
```

EXAMPLES

Example 1. *If the regression coefficients are 0.8 and 0.2, what would be the value of coefficient of correlation?*

Sol. We know that,

$$r^2 = b_{yx} \,.\, b_{xy} = 0.8 \times 0.2 = 0.16$$

Since r has the same sign as both the regression coefficients b_{yx} and b_{xy}

Hence $\quad r = \sqrt{0.16} = 0.4.$

Example 2. *Calculate linear regression coefficients from the following:*

x	→	1	2	3	4	5	6	7	8
y	→	3	7	10	12	14	17	20	24

Sol. Linear regression coefficients are given by

$$b_{yx} = \frac{n\,\Sigma xy - \Sigma x\,\Sigma y}{n\,\Sigma x^2 - (\Sigma x)^2}$$

and
$$b_{xy} = \frac{n\,\Sigma xy - \Sigma x\,\Sigma y}{n\,\Sigma y^2 - (\Sigma y)^2}$$

Let us prepare the following table:

x	y	x^2	y^2	xy
1	3	1	9	3
2	7	4	49	14
3	10	9	100	30
4	12	16	144	48
5	14	25	196	70
6	17	36	289	102
7	20	49	400	140
8	24	64	576	192
$\Sigma x = 36$	$\Sigma y = 107$	$\Sigma x^2 = 204$	$\Sigma y^2 = 1763$	$\Sigma xy = 599$

Here $n = 8$

$$\therefore \quad b_{yx} = \frac{(8 \times 599) - (36 \times 107)}{(8 \times 204) - (36)^2} = \frac{4792 - 3852}{1632 - 1296} = \frac{940}{336} = 2.7976$$

and $$b_{xy} = \frac{(8 \times 599) - (36 \times 107)}{(8 \times 1763) - (107)^2} = \frac{940}{2655} = 0.3540$$

Example 3. *The following table gives age (x) in years of cars and annual maintenance cost (y) in hundred rupees:*

x:	*1*	*3*	*5*	*7*	*9*
y:	*15*	*18*	*21*	*23*	*22*

Estimate the maintenance cost for a 4 year old car after finding the regression equation.

Sol.

x	y	xy	x^2
1	15	15	1
3	18	54	9
5	21	105	25
7	23	161	49
9	22	198	81
$\Sigma x = 25$	$\Sigma y = 99$	$\Sigma xy = 533$	$\Sigma x^2 = 165$

Here, $n = 5$

$$\bar{x} = \frac{\Sigma x}{n} = \frac{25}{5} = 5$$

$$\bar{y} = \frac{\Sigma y}{n} = \frac{99}{5} = 19.8$$

$$\therefore \quad b_{yx} = \frac{n\,\Sigma xy - \Sigma x\,\Sigma y}{n\,\Sigma x^2 - (\Sigma x)^2} = \frac{(5 \times 533) - (25 \times 99)}{(5 \times 165) - (25)^2} = 0.95$$

Regression line of y on x is given by

$$y - \bar{y} = b_{yx}(x - \bar{x})$$

$$\Rightarrow \quad y - 19.8 = 0.95(x - 5)$$

$$\Rightarrow \quad y = 0.95x + 15.05$$

When $x = 4$ years, $y = (0.95 \times 4) + 15.05$

$= 18.85$ hundred rupees = Rs. 1885.

Example 4. *In a partially destroyed laboratory record of an analysis of a correlation data, the following results only are eligible:*

Variance of x = 9

Regression equations: 8x – 10y + 66 = 0, 40x – 18y = 214.

What were (a) the mean values of x and y (b) the standard deviation of y and the co-efficient of correlation between x and y.

Sol. (*a*) **Since both lines of regression pass through the point** $(\bar{x}, \bar{y})$ therefore, we have

$$8\bar{x} - 10\bar{y} + 66 = 0 \tag{93}$$

$$40\bar{x} - 18\bar{y} - 214 = 0 \tag{94}$$

Multiplying (93) by 5, $40\bar{x} - 50\bar{y} + 330 = 0$ (95)

Subtracting (95) from (94), $32\bar{y} - 544 = 0$

$$\therefore \quad \bar{y} = 17$$

$\therefore$ From (93), $8\bar{x} - 170 + 66 = 0$

or $8\bar{x} = 104 \quad \therefore \quad \bar{x} = 13$

Hence $\bar{x} = 13, \quad \bar{y} = 17$

(*b*) Variance of $x = \sigma_x^2 = 9$ (given)

$$\therefore \quad \sigma_x = 3$$

The equations of lines of regression can be written as

$$y = .8x + 6.6 \quad \text{and} \quad x = .45y + 5.35$$

$\therefore$ The regression co-efficient of y on x is $\dfrac{r\sigma_y}{\sigma_x} = .8$ (96)

The regression co-efficient of x on y is $\dfrac{r\sigma_x}{\sigma_y} = .45$ (97)

Multiplying (96) and (97), $r^2 = .8 \times .45 = .36$ $\quad \therefore \quad r = 0.6$

(+ve sign with square root is taken because regression co-efficients are +ve).

From (96), $\qquad \sigma_y = \dfrac{.8\sigma_x}{r} = \dfrac{.8 \times 3}{0.6} = 4.$

Example 5. *The regression lines of y on x and x on y are respectively $y = ax + b$, $x = cy + d$. Show that*

$$\frac{\sigma_y}{\sigma_x} = \sqrt{\frac{a}{c}},\ \bar{x} = \frac{bc + d}{1 - ac} \quad \textit{and} \quad \bar{y} = \frac{ad + b}{1 - ac}.$$

Sol. The regression line of y on x is

$$y = ax + b \tag{98}$$

$\therefore \qquad b_{yx} = a$

The regression line of x on y is

$$x = cy + d \tag{99}$$

$\therefore \qquad b_{xy} = c$

We know that, $\qquad b_{yx} = r\,\dfrac{\sigma_y}{\sigma_x}$ (100)

and $\qquad b_{xy} = r\,\dfrac{\sigma_x}{\sigma_y}$ (101)

Dividing eqn. (100) by (101), we get

$$\frac{b_{yx}}{b_{xy}} = \frac{{\sigma_y}^2}{{\sigma_x}^2} \Rightarrow \frac{a}{c} = \frac{{\sigma_y}^2}{{\sigma_x}^2} \Rightarrow \frac{\sigma_y}{\sigma_x} = \sqrt{\frac{a}{c}}$$

Since both the regression lines pass through the point $(\bar{x}, \bar{y})$ therefore,

$$\bar{y} = a\bar{x} + b \text{ and } \bar{x} = c\bar{y} + d$$

$$\Rightarrow \qquad a\bar{x} - \bar{y} = -b \tag{102}$$

$$\bar{x} - c\bar{y} = d \tag{103}$$

Multiplying equation (103) by a and then subtracting from (102), we get

$$(ac - 1)\ \bar{y} = -ad - b \quad \Rightarrow \quad \bar{y} = \frac{ad + b}{1 - ac}$$

Similarly, we get $\bar{x} = \dfrac{bc + d}{1 - ac}$.

Example 6. *For two random variables, x and y with the same mean, the two regression equations are*

$$y = ax + b \quad \textit{and} \quad x = \alpha y + \beta$$

Show that $\dfrac{b}{\beta} = \dfrac{1 - a}{1 - \alpha}$.

Find also the common mean.

Sol. Here, $b_{yx} = a,\ b_{xy} = \alpha$

Let the common mean be m, then regression lines are

$$y - m = a\ (x - m)$$

$$\Rightarrow \quad y = ax + m\ (1 - a) \quad (104)$$

and

$$x - m = \alpha(y - m)$$

$$\Rightarrow \quad x = \alpha y + m\ (1 - \alpha) \quad (105)$$

Comparing (104) and (105) with the given equations.

$$b = m\ (1 - a),\ \beta = m\ (1 - \alpha)$$

$$\therefore \quad \frac{b}{\beta} = \frac{1 - a}{1 - \alpha}$$

Again $m = \dfrac{b}{1 - a} = \dfrac{\beta}{1 - \alpha}$

Since regression lines pass through $(\bar{x}, \bar{y})$

$$\therefore \quad \bar{x} = \alpha \bar{y} + \beta$$

and $\bar{y} = a\bar{x} + b$ will hold.

$$\Rightarrow \quad m = am + b$$

$$m = \alpha m + \beta$$

$$\Rightarrow \quad am + b = \alpha m + \beta$$

$$\Rightarrow \quad m = \frac{\beta - b}{a - \alpha}.$$

Example 7. *Obtain the line of regression of y on x for the data given below:*

x:	*1.53*	*1.78*	*2.60*	*2.95*	*3.42*
y:	*33.50*	*36.30*	*40.00*	*45.80*	*53.50.*

Sol. The line of regression of y on x is given by

$$y - \bar{y} = b_{yx}(x - \bar{x}) \qquad (106)$$

where b_{yx} is the coefficient of regression given by

$$b_{yx} = \frac{n\,\Sigma xy - \Sigma x\,\Sigma y}{n\,\Sigma x^2 - (\Sigma x)^2}$$

Now we form the table as,

x	y	x^2	xy
1.53	33.50	2.3409	51.255
1.78	36.30	2.1684	64.614
2.60	40.00	6.76	104
2.95	45.80	8.7025	135.11
3.42	53.50	11.6964	182.97
$\Sigma x = 12.28$	$\Sigma y = 209.1$	$\Sigma x^2 = 32.6682$	$\Sigma xy = 537.949$

Here, $n = 5$

$$b_{yx} = \frac{(5 \times 537.949) - (12.28 \times 209.1)}{(5 \times 32.6682) - (12.28)^2} = \frac{121.997}{12.543} = 9.726$$

Also, mean $\bar{x} = \dfrac{\Sigma x}{n} = \dfrac{12.28}{5} = 2.456$

and $\bar{y} = \dfrac{\Sigma y}{n} = \dfrac{209.1}{5} = 41.82$

$\therefore$ From (106), we get

$$y - 41.82 = 9.726(x - 2.456) = 9.726x - 23.887$$

$$y = 17.932 + 9.726x$$

which is the required line of regression of y on x.

Example 8. *For 10 observations on price (x) and supply (y), the following data were obtained (in appropriate units):*

$$\Sigma x = 130, \quad \Sigma y = 220, \quad \Sigma x^2 = 2288, \quad \Sigma y^2 = 5506 \text{ and } \Sigma xy = 3467$$

Obtain the two lines of regression and estimate the supply when the price is 16 units.

Sol. Here, $n = 10,\ \bar{x} = \frac{\Sigma x}{n} = 13$ and $\bar{y} = \frac{\Sigma y}{n} = 22$

Regression coefficient of y on x is

$$b_{yx} = \frac{n\ \Sigma xy - \Sigma x\ \Sigma y}{n\ \Sigma x^2 - (\Sigma x)^2} = \frac{(10 \times 3467) - (130 \times 220)}{(10 \times 2288) - (130)^2}$$

$$= \frac{34670 - 28600}{22880 - 16900} = \frac{6070}{5980} = 1.015$$

$\therefore$ Regression line of y on x is

$$y - \bar{y} = b_{yx}(x - \bar{x})$$

$$y - 22 = 1.015(x - 13)$$

$$\Rightarrow \qquad y = 1.015x + 8.805$$

Regression coefficient of x on y is

$$b_{xy} = \frac{n\ \Sigma xy - \Sigma x\ \Sigma y}{n\ \Sigma y^2 - (\Sigma y)^2}$$

$$= \frac{(10 \times 3467) - (130 \times 220)}{(10 \times 5506) - (220)^2} = \frac{6070}{6660} = 0.9114$$

Regression line of x on y is

$$x - \bar{x} = b_{xy}(y - \bar{y})$$

$$x - 13 = 0.9114(y - 22)$$

$$x = 0.9114y - 7.0508$$

Since we are to estimate supply (y) when price (x) is given therefore we are to use regression line of y on x here.

When $x = 16$ units,

$$y = 1.015(16) + 8.805 = 25.045 \text{ units.}$$

Example 9. *The following results were obtained from records of age (x) and systolic blood pressure (y) of a group of 10 men:*

	x	y
Mean	*53*	*142*
Variance	*130*	*165*

and $\Sigma(x - \bar{x})(y - \bar{y}) = 1220$

Find the approximate regression equation and use it to estimate the blood pressure of a man whose age is 45.

Sol. Given:

Mean	$\bar{x} = 53$
Mean	$\bar{y} = 142$
Variance	$\sigma_x^2 = 130$
Variance	$\sigma_y^2 = 165$
Number of men,	$n = 10$

$$\Sigma(x - \bar{x})(y - \bar{y}) = 1220$$

$\therefore$ Coefficient of correlation,

$$r = \frac{\Sigma(x-\bar{x})(y-\bar{y})}{n\sigma_x\sigma_y} = \frac{1220}{10\sqrt{130 \times 165}} = \frac{122}{146.458} = 0.83.$$

Since we are to estimate blood pressure (y) of a 45 years old man, we will find regression line of y on x.

Regression coefficient $b_{yx} = r\,\dfrac{\sigma_y}{\sigma_x} = 0.83 \times \sqrt{\dfrac{165}{130}} = 0.935.$

Regression line of y on x is given by

$$y - \bar{y} = b_{yx}(x - \bar{x})$$

$$\Rightarrow \quad y - 142 = 0.935(x - 53) = 0.935x - 49.555$$

$$\Rightarrow \quad y = 0.935x + 92.445$$

when $x = 45$,

$$y = (0.935 \times 45) + 92.445 = 134.52.$$

Hence the required blood pressure = 134.52.

Example 10. *The following results were obtained from scores in Applied Mechanics and Engineering Mathematics in an examination:*

	Applied Mechanics (x)	*Engineering Mathematics (y)*
Mean	*47.5*	*39.5*
Standard Deviation	*16.8*	*10.8*

r = 0.95.

Find both the regression equations. Also estimate the value of y for x = 30.

Sol. $\bar{x} = 47.5, \quad \bar{y} = 39.5$

$\sigma_x = 16.8, \quad \sigma_y = 10.8 \quad$ and $\quad$ ^ 95

Regression coefficients are

$$b_{yx} = r\frac{\sigma_y}{\sigma_x} = 0.95 \times \frac{10.8}{16.8} = 0.6107$$

and $$b_{xy} = r\frac{\sigma_x}{\sigma_y} = 0.95 \times \frac{16.8}{10.8} = 1.477.$$

Regression line of y on x is

$$y - \bar{y} = b_{yx}(x - \bar{x})$$

$\Rightarrow$ $$y - 39.5 = 0.6107\,(x - 47.5) = 0.6107x - 29.008$$

$$y = 0.6107x + 10.49 \quad (107)$$

Regression line of x on y is

$$x - \bar{x} = b_{xy}\,(y - \bar{y})$$

$\Rightarrow$ $$x - 47.5 = 1.477\,(y - 39.5)$$

$\Rightarrow$ $$x - 47.5 = 1.477y - 58.3415$$

$$x = 1.477y - 10.8415$$

Putting $x = 30$ in equation (107), we get

$$y = (0.6107)(30) + 10.49 = 18.321 + 10.49 = 28.81.$$

Example 11. *From the following data. Find the most likely value of y when $x = 24$:*

	y	x
Mean	*985.8*	*18.1*
S.D.	*36.4*	*2.0*

$r = 0.58.$

Sol. Given: $\bar{y} = 985.8$, $\bar{x} = 18.1$, $\sigma_y = 36.4$, $\sigma_x = 2$, $r = 0.58$

Regression coefficient,

$$b_{yx} = r\frac{\sigma_y}{\sigma_x} = (0.58)\frac{36.4}{2} = 10.556.$$

Regression line of y on x is

$$y - \bar{y} = b_{yx}(x - \bar{x})$$

$\Rightarrow$ $$y - 985.8 = 10.556(x - 18.1)$$

$$y - 985.8 = 10.556x - 191.06$$

$$\Rightarrow \qquad y = 10.556x + 794.73$$

when $x = 24$,

$$y = (10.556 \times 24) + 794.73$$

$$y = 1048 \text{ (approximately)}.$$

Example 12. *The equations of two regression lines, obtained in a correlation analysis of 60 observations are:*

$$5x = 6y + 24 \text{ and } 1000y = 768x - 3608.$$

What is the correlation coefficient? Show that the ratio of coefficient of variability of x to that of y is $\frac{5}{24}$. *What is the ratio of variances of x and y?*

Sol. Regression line of x on y is

$$5x = 6y + 24$$

$$x = \frac{6}{5}y + \frac{24}{5}$$

$$\therefore \qquad b_{xy} = \frac{6}{5} \qquad (108)$$

Regression line of y on x is

$$1000y = 768x - 3608$$

$$y = 0.768x - 3.608$$

$$\therefore \qquad b_{yx} = 0.768 \qquad (109)$$

From (108), $$r\frac{\sigma_x}{\sigma_y} = \frac{6}{5} \qquad (110)$$

From (109), $$r\frac{\sigma_y}{\sigma_x} = 0.768 \qquad (111)$$

Multiplying equations (110) and (111), we get

$$r^2 = 0.9216 \Rightarrow r = 0.96 \qquad (112)$$

Dividing (111) by (110), we get

$$\frac{{\sigma_x}^2}{{\sigma_y}^2} = \frac{6}{5 \times 0.768} = 1.5625.$$

Taking the square root, we get

$$\frac{\sigma_x}{\sigma_y} = 1.25 = \frac{5}{4} \qquad (113)$$

Since the regression lines pass through the point $(\bar{x}, \bar{y})$, we have

$$5\bar{x} = 6\bar{y} + 24$$

$$1000\bar{y} = 768\bar{x} - 3608.$$

Solving the above equations for $\bar{x}$ and $\bar{y}$, we get

$$\bar{x} = 6, \ \bar{y} = 1.$$

Coefficient of variability of $x = \dfrac{\sigma_x}{\bar{x}}$,

Coefficient of variability of $y = \dfrac{\sigma_y}{\bar{y}}$.

$\therefore$ Required ratio $= \dfrac{\sigma_x}{\bar{x}} \times \dfrac{\bar{y}}{\sigma_y} = \dfrac{\bar{y}}{\bar{x}}\left(\dfrac{\sigma_x}{\sigma_y}\right) = \dfrac{1}{6} \times \dfrac{5}{4} = \dfrac{5}{24}$. | using (113)

Example 13. *The following data regarding the heights (y) and weights (x) of 100 college students are given:*

$\Sigma x = 15000,\ \Sigma x^2 = 2272500,\ \Sigma y = 6800,\ \Sigma y^2 = 463025$ *and* $\Sigma xy = 1022250.$

Find the equation of the regression line of height on weight.

Sol.

$$\bar{x} = \frac{\Sigma x}{n} = \frac{15000}{100} = 150$$

$$\bar{y} = \frac{\Sigma y}{n} = \frac{6800}{100} = 68$$

Regression coefficient of y on x,

$$b_{yx} = \frac{n\,\Sigma xy - \Sigma x\,\Sigma y}{n\,\Sigma x^2 - (\Sigma x)^2} = \frac{(100 \times 1022250) - (15000 \times 6800)}{(100 \times 2272500) - (15000)^2}$$

$$= \frac{102225000 - 102000000}{227250000 - 225000000}$$

$$= \frac{225000}{2250000} = 0.1$$

Regression line of height (y) on weight (x) is given by

$$y - \bar{y} = b_{yx}(x - \bar{x})$$

$$\Rightarrow \quad y - 68 = 0.1(x - 150)$$

$$\Rightarrow \quad y = 0.1x - 15 + 68$$

$$\Rightarrow \quad y = 0.1x + 53.$$

Example 14. *Find the coefficient of correlation when the two regression equations are*

$$X = -\,0.2Y + 4.2$$

$$Y = -\,0.8X + 8.4.$$

Sol. We have the regression lines

$$X = -\,0.2\text{Y} + 4.2 \qquad (114)$$

$$Y = -\,0.8\text{X} + 8.4. \qquad (115)$$

Let us assume that eqn. (114) is the regression line of X on Y and eqn. (115) is the regression line of Y on X then,

Regression coefficient of X on Y is

$$b_{\text{XY}} = -\,0.2$$

Regression coefficient of Y on X is

$$b_{\text{YX}} = -\,0.8$$

Since b_{XY} and b_{YX} are of the same sign and $b_{\text{XY}}b_{\text{YX}} = 0.16\ (< 1)$ hence our assumption is correct.

We know that

$$b_{\text{XY}}\, b_{\text{YX}} = r^2 \qquad |\ \text{where } r \text{ is the correlation coefficient}$$

$$\Rightarrow \qquad (-\,0.2)(-\,0.8) = r^2$$

$$\Rightarrow \qquad r^2 = 0.16$$

$$\Rightarrow \qquad r = -\,0.4. \qquad |\ \text{Since } r,\ \sigma_x \text{ and } \sigma_y \text{ have the same sign}$$

Example 15. *A panel of two judges, A and B, graded seven TV serial performances by awarding scores independently as shown in the following table:*

Performance	1	2	3	4	5	6	7
Scores by A	46	42	44	40	43	41	45
Scores by B	40	38	36	35	39	37	41

The eighth TV performance, which judge B could not attend, was awarded 37 scores by judge A. If judge B had also been present, how many scores would be expected to have been awarded by him to the eighth TV performance?

Use regression analysis to answer this question.

Sol. Let the scores awarded by judge A be denoted by x and the scores awarded by judge B be denoted by y.

Here, $n = 7$; $\bar{x} = \frac{\Sigma x}{n} = \frac{46 + 42 + 44 + 40 + 43 + 41 + 45}{7} = 43$

$$\bar{y} = \frac{\Sigma y}{n} = \frac{40 + 38 + 36 + 35 + 39 + 37 + 41}{7} = 38$$

Let us form the table as

x	y	xy	x^2
46	40	1840	2116
42	38	1596	1764
44	36	1584	1936
40	35	1400	1600
43	39	1677	1849
41	37	1517	1681
45	41	1845	2025
$\Sigma x = 301$	$\Sigma y = 266$	$\Sigma xy = 11459$	$\Sigma x^2 = 12971$

Regression coefficient,

$$b_{yx} = \frac{n\,\Sigma xy - \Sigma x\,\Sigma y}{n\,\Sigma x^2 - (\Sigma x)^2} = \frac{(7 \times 11459) - (301 \times 266)}{(7 \times 12971) - (301)^2}$$

$$= \frac{80213 - 80066}{90797 - 90601} = \frac{147}{196} = 0.75$$

Regression line of y on x is given by

$$y - \bar{y} = b_{yx}(x - \bar{x})$$

$$y - 38 = 0.75(x - 43)$$

$$\Rightarrow \quad y = 0.75x + 5.75$$

when $x = 37$,

$$y = 0.75(37) + 5.75 = 33.5 \text{ marks}$$

Hence, if judge B had also been present, 33.5 scores would be expected to have been awarded to the eighth T.V. performance.

ASSIGNMENT 7.5

1. Find the regression line of y on x from the following data:

x:	1	2	3	4	5
y:	2	5	3	8	7

2. In a study between the amount of rainfall and the quantity of air pollution removed the following data were collected:

Daily rainfall: (in .01 cm)	4.3	4.5	5.9	5.6	6.1	5.2	3.8	2.1
Pollution removed: (mg/m³)	12.6	12.1	11.6	11.8	11.4	11.8	13.2	14.1

Find the regression line of y on x.

3. If F is the pull required to lift a load W by means of a pulley block, fit a linear law of the form $F = mW + c$ connecting F and W, using the data

W:	50	70	100	120
F:	12	15	21	25

where F and W are in kg wt. Compute F when W = 150 kg wt.

4. The two regression equations of the variables x and y are $x = 19.13 - 0.87\, y$ and $y = 11.64 - 0.50\, x$. Find (*i*) mean of x's (*ii*) mean of y's and (*iii*) correlation coefficient between x and y.

5. Two random variables have the regression lines with equations $3x + 2y = 26$ and $6x + y = 31$. Find the mean values and the correlation coefficient between x and y.

6. In a partially destroyed laboratory data, only the equations giving the two lines of regression of y on x and x on y are available and are respectively

$$7x - 16y + 9 = 0$$

$$5y - 4x - 3 = 0$$

Calculate the coefficient of correlation, $\bar{x}$ and $\bar{y}$.

7. A simply supported beam carries a concentrated load P (kg) at its mid-point. The following table gives maximum deflection y (cm) corresponding to various values of P:

P:	100	120	140	160	180	200
y:	0.45	0.55	0.60	0.70	0.80	0.85

Find a law of the form $y = a + bP$.

Also find the value of maximum deflection when P = 150 kg.

8. If $a_1x + b_1y + c_1 = 0$ and $a_2x + b_2y + c_2 = 0$ are the equations of the regression lines of y on x and x on y respectively, prove that

$$a_1b_2 \le a_2b_1$$

given that the constants a_1, a_2, b_1, b_2 are either all positive or all negative.

9. The regression equations calculated from a given set of observations for two random variables are

$$x = -\,0.4y + 6.4 \quad \text{and} \quad y = -\,0.6x + 4.6$$

Calculate (*i*) $\bar{x}$ (*ii*) $\bar{y}$ (*iii*) r.

10. The following regression equations were obtained from a correlation table:

$$y = 0.516x + 33.73$$

$$x = 0.512y + 32.52$$

Find the value of (*i*) r (*ii*) $\bar{x}$ (*iii*) $\bar{y}$.

11. Find the regression line of y on x for the following data:

x:	1	3	4	6	8	9	11	14
y:	1	2	4	4	5	7	8	9.

12. Given N = 50, Mean of y = 44

Variance of x is $\frac{9}{16}$ of the variance of y.

Regression equation of x on y is $3y - 5x = -180$

Find (*i*) Mean of x (*ii*) Coefficient of correlation between x and y.

13. For an army personnel of strength 25, the regression of weight of kidneys (y) on weight of heart (x), both measured in ounces is

$$y - 0.399x - 6.934 = 0$$

and the regression of weight of heart on weight of kidney is $x - 1.212y + 2.461 = 0$. Find the correlation coefficient between x and y and their mean values. Can you find out the standard deviation of x and y as well?

14. A panel of judges A and B graded 7 debators and independently awarded the following scores:

Debator:	1	2	3	4	5	6	7
Scores *by A*:	40	34	28	30	44	38	31
Scores *by B*:	32	39	26	30	38	34	28

An eighth debator was awarded 36 scores by judge A while judge B was not present. If judge B were also present, how many scores would you expect him to award to the eighth debator assuming that the same degree of relationship exists in their judgement.

15. The following results were obtained in the analysis of data on yield of dry bark in ounces (y) and age in years (x) of 200 cinchona plants:

	x	y
Average:	9.2	16.5
Standard deviation:	2.1	4.2

Correlation coefficient = 0.84

Construct the two lines of regression and estimate the yield of dry bark of a plant of age 8 years.

16. Given that $x = 4y + 5$ and $y = kx + 4$ are the lines of regression of x on y and y on x respectively. Show that $0 \le 4k \le 1$.

If $k = \frac{1}{16}$, find $\bar{x}$, $\bar{y}$ and coefficient of correlation between x and y.

17. The means of a bivariate frequency distribution are at (3, 4) and $r = 0.4$. The line of regression of y on x is parallel to the line $y = x$. Find the two lines of regression and estimate value of x when $y = 1$.

18. Assuming that we conduct an experiment with 8 fields planted with corn, four fields having no nitrogen fertilizer and four fields having 80 kgs of nitrogen fertilizer. The resulting corn yields are shown in table in bushels per acre:

Field:	1	2	3	4	5	6	7	8
Nitrogen (kgs) x:	0	0	0	0	80	80	80	80
Corn yield y: (acre)	120	360	60	180	1280	1120	1120	760

(*a*) Compute a linear regression equation of y on x.

(*b*) Predict corn yield for a field treated with 60 kgs of fertilizer.

19. Find both the lines of regression of following data:

x:	5.60	5.65	5.70	5.81	5.85
y:	5.80	5.70	5.80	5.79	6.01

20. Obtain regression line of x on y for the given data:

x:	1	2	3	4	5	6
y:	5.0	8.1	10.6	13.1	16.2	20.0

7.59 POLYNOMIAL FIT: NON-LINEAR REGRESSION

Let
$$y = a + bx + cx^2$$
be a second degree parabolic curve of regression of y on x to be fitted for the data (x_i, y_i), $i = 1, 2, \ldots\ldots, n$.

Residual at $x = x_i$ is
$$E_i = y_i - f(x_i) = y_i - a - bx_i - cx_i^2$$

Now, let
$$U = \sum_{i=1}^{n} E_i^2 = \sum_{i=1}^{n} (y_i - a - bx_i - cx_i^2)^2$$

By principle of Least squares, U should be minimum for the best values of a, b and c.

For this,
$$\frac{\partial U}{\partial a} = 0, \frac{\partial U}{\partial b} = 0 \text{ and } \frac{\partial U}{\partial c} = 0$$

$$\frac{\partial U}{\partial a} = 0 \Rightarrow 2\sum_{i=1}^{n} (y_i - a - bx_i - cx_i^2)(-1) = 0$$

$$\Rightarrow \boxed{\Sigma y = na + b\Sigma x + c\Sigma x^2} \quad (116)$$

$$\frac{\partial U}{\partial b} = 0 \quad \Rightarrow \quad 2\sum_{i=1}^{n} (y_i - a - bx_i - cx_i^2)(-x_i) = 0$$

$$\Rightarrow \quad \boxed{\Sigma xy = a\Sigma x + b\Sigma x^2 + c\Sigma x^3} \qquad (117)$$

$$\frac{\partial U}{\partial c} = 0 \quad \Rightarrow \quad 2\sum_{i=1}^{n} (y_i - a - bx_i - cx_i^2)(-x_i^2) = 0$$

$$\Rightarrow \quad \boxed{\Sigma x^2 y = a\Sigma x^2 + b\Sigma x^3 + c\Sigma x^4} \qquad (118)$$

Equations (116), (117) and (118) are the normal equations for fitting a second degree parabolic curve of regression of y on x. Here n is the number of pairs of values of x and y.

EXAMPLES

Example 1. (*a*) *Fit a second degree parabola to the following data:*

x:	*0.0*	*1.0*	*2.0*
y:	*1.0*	*6.0*	*17.0*

(*b*) *Fit a second degree curve of regression of y on x to the following data:*

x:	*1.0*	*2.0*	*3.0*	*4.0*
y:	*6.0*	*11.0*	*18.0*	*27*

(*c*) *Fit a second degree parabola in the following data:*

x:	*0.0*	*1.0*	*2.0*	*3.0*	*4.0*
y:	*1.0*	*4.0*	*10.0*	*17.0*	*30.0*

Sol. The equation of second degree parabola is given by

$$y = a + bx + cx^2 \qquad (119)$$

Normal equations are

$$\Sigma y = ma + b\Sigma x + c\Sigma x^2 \qquad (120)$$

$$\Sigma xy = a\Sigma x + b\Sigma x^2 + c\Sigma x^3 \qquad (121)$$

and

$$\Sigma x^2 y = a\Sigma x^2 + b\Sigma x^3 + c\Sigma x^4 \qquad (122)$$

(a) Here $m = 3$

The table is as follows:

x	y	x^2	x^3	x^4	xy	x^2y
0	1	0	0	0	0	0
1	6	1	1	1	6	6
2	17	4	8	16	34	68
Total	24	5	9	17	40	74

Substituting in eqns. (120), (121) and (122), we get

$$24 = 3a + 3b + 5c \tag{123}$$

$$40 = 3a + 5b + 9c \tag{124}$$

$$74 = 5a + 9b + 17c \tag{125}$$

Solving eqns. (123), (124) and (125), we get

$$a = 1, b = 2, c = 3$$

Hence the required second degree parabola is

$$y = 1 + 2x + 3x^2$$

(b) Here $m = 4$

The table is as follows:

x	y	x^2	x^3	x^4	xy	x^2y
1	6	1	1	1	6	6
2	11	4	8	16	22	44
3	18	9	27	81	54	162
4	27	16	64	256	108	432
$\Sigma x = 10$	$\Sigma y = 62$	$\Sigma x^2 = 30$	$\Sigma x^3 = 100$	$\Sigma x^4 = 354$	$\Sigma xy = 190$	$\Sigma x^2y = 644$

Substituting values in eqns. (120), (121) and (122), we get

$$62 = 4a + 10b + 30c \tag{126}$$

$$190 = 10a + 30b + 100c \tag{127}$$

$$644 = 30a + 100b + 354c \tag{128}$$

Solving equations (126), (127) and (128), we get

$$a = 3, b = 2, c = 1$$

Hence the required second degree parabola is

$$y = 3 + 2x + x^2$$

(c) Here $m = 5$

The table is as follows:

x	y	x^2	x^3	x^4	xy	x^2y
0.0	1.0	0	0	0	0	0
1.0	4.0	1	1	1	4	4
2.0	10.0	4	8	16	20	40
3.0	17.0	9	27	81	51	153
4.0	30.0	16	64	256	120	480
$\Sigma x = 10$	$\Sigma y = 62$	$\Sigma x^2 = 30$	$\Sigma x^3 = 100$	$\Sigma x^4 = 354$	$\Sigma xy = 195$	$\Sigma x^2y = 677$

Substituting values in eqns. (120), (121) and (122), we get

$$62 = 5a + 10b + 30c \tag{129}$$

$$195 = 10a + 30b + 100c \tag{130}$$

$$677 = 30a + 100b + 354c \tag{131}$$

Solving eqns. (129), (130) and (131), we get

$$a = 1.2, b = 1.1 \text{ and } c = 1.5$$

Hence the required second degree parabola is

$$y = 1.2 + 1.1x + 1.5x^2$$

Example 2. *Fit a parabola $y = ax^2 + bx + c$ in least square sense to the data*

x:	*10*	*12*	*15*	*23*	*20*
y:	*14*	*17*	*23*	*25*	*21.*

Sol. The normal equations to the curve are

and
$$\left.\begin{aligned} \Sigma y &= a\Sigma x^2 + b\Sigma x + 5c \\ \Sigma xy &= a\Sigma x^3 + b\Sigma x^2 + c\Sigma x \\ \Sigma x^2 y &= a\Sigma x^4 + b\Sigma x^3 + c\Sigma x^2 \end{aligned}\right\} \tag{132}$$

The values of Σx, Σx^2,...... etc., are calculated by means of the following table:

x	y	x^2	x^3	x^4	xy	x^2y
10	14	100	1000	10000	140	1400
12	17	144	1728	20736	204	2448
15	23	225	3375	50625	345	5175
23	25	529	12167	279841	575	13225
20	21	400	8000	160000	420	8400
$\Sigma x = 80$	$\Sigma y = 100$	$\Sigma x^2 = 1398$	$\Sigma x^3 = 26270$	$\Sigma x^4 = 521202$	$\Sigma xy = 1684$	$\Sigma x^2y = 30648$

Substituting the obtained values from the table in normal equation (132), we have

$$100 = 1398a + 80b + 5c$$

$$1684 = 26270a + 1398b + 80c$$

$$30648 = 521202a + 26270b + 1398c$$

On solving, $a = -0.07,\ b = 3.03,\ c = -8.89$

$\therefore$ The required equation is

$$y = -0.07x^2 + 3.03x - 8.89.$$

Example 3. *Fit a parabolic curve of regression of y on x to the following data:*

x:	*1.0*	*1.5*	*2.0*	*2.5*	*3.0*	*3.5*	*4.0*
y:	*1.1*	*1.3*	*1.6*	*2.0*	*2.7*	*3.4*	*4.1*

Sol. Here $m = 7$ (odd)

Let $u = \dfrac{x - 2.5}{0.5} = 2x - 5$ and $v = y$

The results in tabular form are:

x	y	u	v	u^2	uv	u^2v	u^3	u^4
1.0	1.1	– 3	1.1	9	– 3.3	9.9	– 27	81
1.5	1.3	– 2	1.3	4	– 2.6	5.2	– 8	16
2.0	1.6	– 1	1.6	1	– 1.6	1.6	– 1	1
2.5	2.0	0	2.0	0	0	0	0	0
3.0	2.7	1	2.7	1	2.7	2.7	1	1
3.5	3.4	2	3.4	4	6.8	13.6	8	16
4.0	4.1	3	4.1	9	12.3	36.9	27	81
Total		0	16.2	28	14.3	69.9	0	196

Let the curve to be fitted be $v = a + bu + cu^2$ so that the normal equations are

$$\Sigma v = 7a + b\Sigma u + c\Sigma u^2$$

$$\Sigma uv = a\Sigma u + b\Sigma u^2 + c\Sigma u^3$$

and $$\Sigma u^2 v = a\Sigma u^2 + b\Sigma u^3 + c\Sigma u^4$$

$\Rightarrow$ $$16.2 = 7a + 28c, \quad 14.3 = 28b, \quad 69.9 = 28a + 196c$$

Solving, we get $a = 2.07, \quad b = 0.511, \quad c = 0.061$

Hence the curve of fit is

$$v = 2.07 + 0.511u + 0.061u^2$$

$\Rightarrow$ $$y = 2.07 + 0.511\,(2x - 5) + 0.061\,(2x - 5)^2$$

$$= 1.04 - 0.193x + 0.243x^2.$$

Example 4. *Fit a second degree parabola to the following data by the Least Squares Method:*

x:	*1929*	*1930*	*1931*	*1932*	*1933*	*1934*	*1935*	*1936*	*1937*
y:	*352*	*356*	*357*	*358*	*360*	*361*	*361*	*360*	*359.*

Sol. Here $m = g$ (odd)

$\therefore$ Let $x_0 = 1933, \quad h = 1, \quad y_0 = 357$

then $$u = \frac{x - 1933}{1} = x - 1933$$

$$v = y - 357$$

and the equation $y = a + bx + cx^2$ is transformed to

$$v = a' + b'u + c'u^2$$

x	u	y	v	uv	u^2	u^2v	u^3	u^4
1929	– 4	352	– 5	20	16	– 80	– 64	256
1930	– 3	356	– 1	3	9	– 9	– 27	81
1931	– 2	357	0	0	4	0	– 8	16
1932	– 1	358	1	– 1	1	1	– 1	1
1933	0	360	3	0	0	0	0	0
1934	1	361	4	4	1	4	1	1
1935	2	361	4	8	4	16	8	16
1936	3	360	3	9	9	27	27	81
1937	4	359	2	8	16	32	64	256
Total	$\Sigma u = 0$		$\Sigma v = 11$	$\Sigma uv = 51$	$\Sigma u^2 = 60$	$\Sigma u^2v = -9$	$\Sigma u^3 = 0$	$\Sigma u^4 = 708$

Putting the above values in normal equations, we get

$$11 = 9a' + 60c', \quad 51 = 60b', \quad -9 = 60a' + 708c'$$

$$\Rightarrow \quad a' = 3, \quad b' = 0.85, \quad c' = -0.27.$$

Fitted parabola in u and v is given by

$$v = 3 + 0.85\, u - 0.27\, u^2$$

Putting $\quad u = x - 1933 \quad$ and $\quad v = y - 357$

$$y - 357 = 3 + 0.85\,(x - 1933) - .27\,(x - 1933)^2$$

$$\Rightarrow \quad y = -0.27x^2 + 1044.67x - 1010135.08$$

which is the required equation.

Example 5. *Fit a second degree parabola to the following data by Least Squares Method:*

x:	*1*	*2*	*3*	*4*	*5*
y:	*1090*	*1220*	*1390*	*1625*	*1915*

Sol. Here $\quad m = 5$ (odd)

Let $\quad u = x - 3, \quad v = y - 1220$

x	y	u	v	u^2	u^2v	uv	u^3	u^4
1	1090	−2	−130	4	−520	260	−8	16
2	1220	−1	0	1	0	0	−1	1
3	1390	0	170	0	0	0	0	0
4	1625	1	405	1	405	405	1	1
5	1915	2	695	4	2780	1390	8	16
Total		$\Sigma u = 0$	$\Sigma v = 1140$	$\Sigma u^2 = 10$	$\Sigma u^2v = 2665$	$\Sigma uv = 2055$	$\Sigma u^3 = 0$	$\Sigma u^4 = 34$

Putting these values in normal equations, we get

$$1140 = 5a' + 10c', \quad 2055 = 10b', \quad 2655 = 10a' + 34c'$$

$$\Rightarrow \quad a' = 173, \quad b' = 205.5, \quad c' = 27.5$$

$$\therefore \quad v = 173 + 205.5u + 27.5u^2 \qquad (133)$$

Put $\quad u = x - 3 \quad$ and $\quad v = y - 1220$

From (133), $\quad y - 1220 = 173 + 205.5\,(x - 3) + 27.5\,(x - 3)^2$

$$\Rightarrow \quad y = 27.5x^2 + 40.5x + 1024.$$

Example 6. *Fit a second degree parabola to the following data taking y as dependent variable:*

x	1	2	3	4	5	6	7	8	9
y	2	6	7	8	10	11	11	10	9

Sol. Normal equations to fit a second degree parabola of the form

$$y = a + bx + cx^2 \text{ are}$$

and

$$\left.\begin{aligned} \Sigma y &= ma + b\Sigma x + c\Sigma x^2 \\ \Sigma xy &= a\Sigma x + b\Sigma x^2 + c\Sigma x^3 \\ \Sigma x^2 y &= a\Sigma x^2 + b\Sigma x^3 + c\Sigma x^4 \end{aligned}\right\} \quad (134)$$

Here, $m = 9$

x	y	x^2	x^3	x^4	xy	x^2y
1	2	1	1	1	2	2
2	6	4	8	16	12	24
3	7	9	27	81	21	63
4	8	16	64	256	32	128
5	10	25	125	625	50	250
6	11	36	216	1296	66	396
7	11	49	343	2401	77	539
8	10	64	512	4096	80	640
9	9	81	729	6561	81	729
$\Sigma x = 45$	$\Sigma y = 74$	$\Sigma x^2 = 285$	$\Sigma x^3 = 2025$	$\Sigma x^4 = 15333$	$\Sigma xy = 421$	$\Sigma x^2y = 2771$

Putting in (134), we get

$$74 = 9a + 45b + 285c$$

$$421 = 45a + 285b + 2025c$$

$$2771 = 285a + 2025b + 15333c$$

Solving the above equations, we get

$$a = -1, \quad b = 3.55, \quad c = -0.27$$

Hence the required equation of second degree parabola is

$$y = -1 + 3.55x - 0.27x^2.$$

Example 7. *Employ the method of least squares to fit a parabola $y = a + bx + cx^2$ in the following data:*

$$(x, y): (-1, 2), (0, 0), (0, 1), (1, 2)$$

Sol. Normal equations to the parabola $y = a + bx + cx^2$ are

$$\Sigma y = ma + b\Sigma x + c\Sigma x^2 \tag{135}$$

$$\Sigma xy = a\Sigma x + b\Sigma x^2 + c\Sigma x^3 \tag{136}$$

and
$$\Sigma x^2 y = a\Sigma x^2 + b\Sigma x^3 + c\Sigma x^4 \tag{137}$$

Here $m = 4$

The table is as follows:

x	y	x^2	x^3	x^4	xy	x^2y
– 1	2	1	– 1	1	– 2	2
0	0	0	0	0	0	0
0	1	0	0	0	0	0
1	2	1	1	1	2	2
$\Sigma x = 0$	$\Sigma y = 5$	$\Sigma x^2 = 2$	$\Sigma x^3 = 0$	$\Sigma x^4 = 2$	$\Sigma xy = 0$	$\Sigma x^2y = 4$

Substituting these values in equations (135), (136) and (137); we get

$$5 = 4a + 2c \tag{138}$$

$$0 = 2b \tag{139}$$

and
$$4 = 2a + 2c \tag{140}$$

Solving (138), (139) and (140), we get

$$a = 0.5, b = 0 \text{ and } c = 1.5$$

Hence the required second degree parabola is

$$y = 0.5 + 1.5x^2$$

7.59.1 Algorithm of Second Degree Parabolic Curve Fitting

```
1. Input n
2. For i=0,3
3. For j=0,4
4. u(i,j)=0
5. Next j
6. Next i
7. u(0,0)=n
8. For i=0,n
9. Input x,y
```

```
10. x2=x*x
11. u(0,1)+=x
12. u(0,2)+=x2
13. u(1,2)+=x*x2
14. u(2,2)+=x2*x2
15. u(0,3)+=y
16. u(1,3)+=x*y
17. u(2,3)+=x2*y
18. Next i
19. u(1,1)=u(0,2)
20. u(2,1)=u(1,2)
21. u(1,0)=u(0,1)
22. u(2,0)=u(1,1)
23. For j=0,3
24. For i=0,3
25. If i!=j then
            goto step 26
        ELSE
            goto step 24
26. y=u(i,j)/u(j,j)
27. For k=0,4
28. u(i,k)-=u(j,k)*p
29. Next k
30. Next i
31. Next j
32. a=u(0,3)/u(0,0)
33. b=u(1,3)/u(1,1)
34. c=u(2,3)/u(2,2)
35. Print a,b,c
36. Stop
```

7.59.2 Flow-Chart of Second Degree Parabolic Curve Fitting

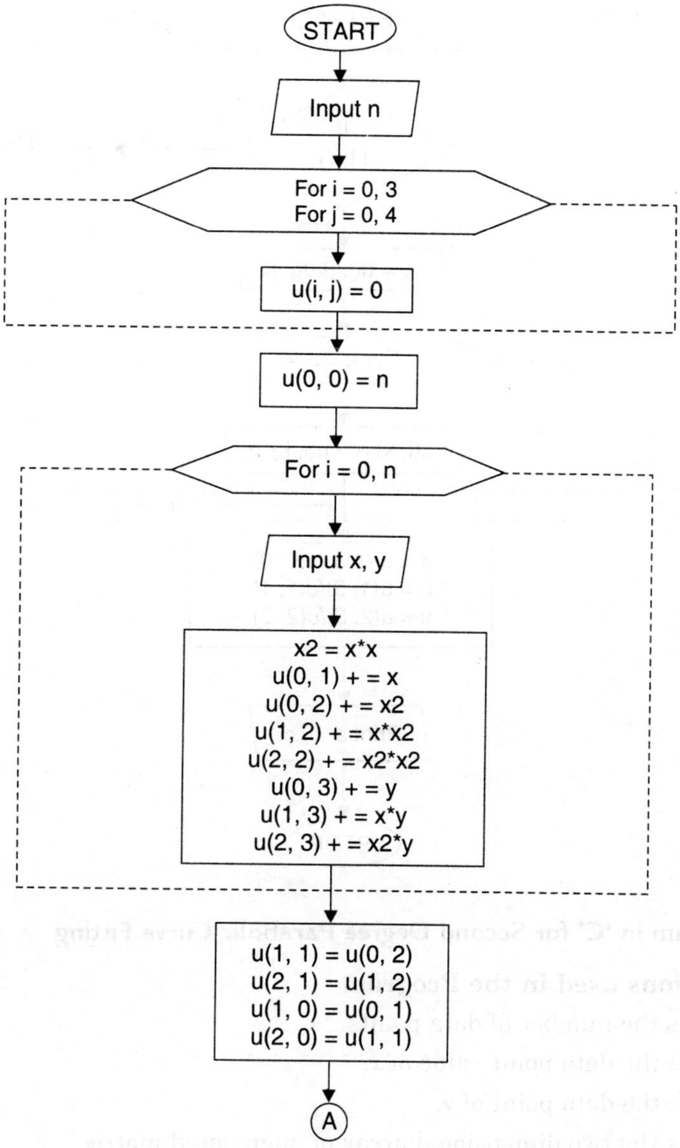

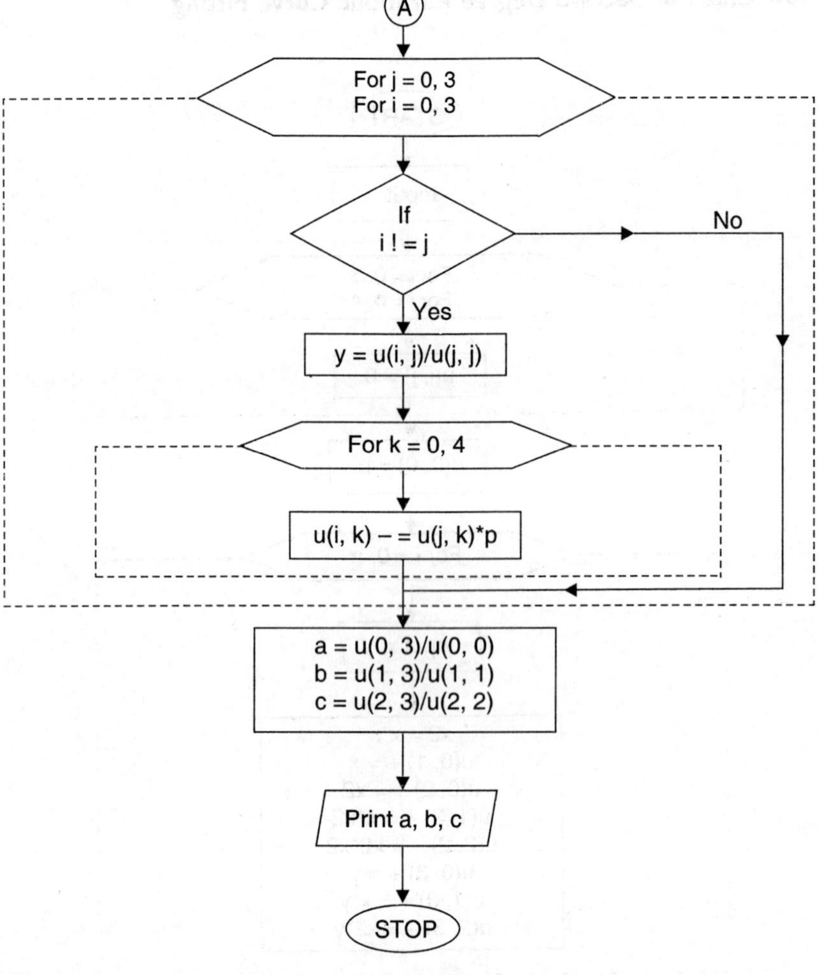

7.59.3 Program in 'C' for Second Degree Parabolic Curve Fitting

Notations used in the Program

(*i*) **n** is the number of data points.

(*ii*) **x** is the data point value of x.

(*iii*) **y** is the data point of y.

(*iv*) **u** is the two dimensional array of augmented matrix.

```
#include<stdio.h>
main()
{
int i,j,k,n;
```

```
float u[3][4], x,y,x2,p,a,b,c;
printf("\nEnter the value of data set n:");
scanf("%d",&n);
for(i=0; i<3; i++)
for(j=0; j<4; j++)
u[i][j]=0;
u[0][0]=n;
printf("\nEnter the value of x & y:\n");
for(i=0; i<n; i++)
 {
 scanf("%f%f", &x, &y);
 x2=x*x;
 u[0][1]+=x;
 u[0][2]+=x2;
 u[1][2]+=x*x2;
 u[2][2]+=x2*x2;
 u[0][3]+=y;
 u[1][3]+=x*y;
 u[2][3]+=x2*y;
    }
u[1][1]=u[0][2];
u[2][1]=u[1][2];
u[1][0]=u[0][1];
u[2][0]=u[1][1];
/* Finding the value of a,b,c */
for (j=0;j<3;j++)
for (i=0;i<3;i++)
 if(i!=j)
    {
     p=u[i][j]/u[j][j];
     for(k=0;k;k++)
     u[i][k]-=u[j][k]*p;
    }
a=u[0][3]/u[0][0];
b=u[1][3]/u[1][1];
```

```
c=u[2][3]/u[2][2];
printf("\na=%f b=%f  c=%f ", a,b,c);
printf("\n\nEquation of parabola is: y=a+bx+cx^2 \n");
printf("\ny=%f+(%f)x+(%f)x^2",a,b,c);
return;
}
```

7.59.4 Output

```
Enter the value of data set n: 5
Enter the value of x & y:
1 10.9
2 12.2
3 13.9
4 16.3
5 19.2
a=10.239998 b=0.398574 c=0.278571
Equation of parabola is: y = a+bx+cx^2
y=10.239998+(0.398574)x+(0.278571)x^2
```

7.60 MULTIPLE LINEAR REGRESSION

Now we proceed to discuss the case where the dependent variable is a function of two or more linear or non-linear independent variables. Consider such a linear function as

$$y = a + bx + cz$$

The sum of the squares of residual is

$$U = \sum_{i=1}^{n} (y_i - a - bx_i - cz_i)^2$$

Differentiating U partially with respect to a, b, c; we get

$$\frac{\partial U}{\partial a} = 0 \Rightarrow 2\sum_{i=1}^{n} (y_i - a - bx_i - cz_i)(-1) = 0$$

$$\frac{\partial U}{\partial b} = 0 \Rightarrow 2\sum_{i=1}^{n} (y_i - a - bx_i - cz_i)(-x_i) = 0$$

and $$\frac{\partial U}{\partial c} = 0 \Rightarrow 2\sum_{i=1}^{n} (y_i - a - bx_i - cz_i)(-z_i) = 0$$

which on simplification and omitting the suffix i, yields.

$$\Sigma y = ma + b\Sigma x + c\Sigma z$$
$$\Sigma xy = a\Sigma x + b\Sigma x^2 + c\Sigma xz$$
$$\Sigma yz = a\Sigma z + b\Sigma xz + c\Sigma z^2$$

Solving the above three equations, we get values of a, b and c. Consequently, we get the linear function $y = a + bx + cz$ called **regression plane.**

Example. *Obtain a regression plane by using multiple linear regression to fit the data given below:*

x:	*1*	*2*	*3*	*4*
z:	*0*	*1*	*2*	*3*
y:	*12*	*18*	*24*	*30*

Sol. Let $y = a + bx + cz$ be the required regression plane where a, b, c are the constants to be determined by following equations:

$$\Sigma y = ma + b\Sigma x + c\Sigma z$$
$$\Sigma yx = a\Sigma x + b\Sigma x^2 + c\Sigma zx$$
and $$\Sigma yz = a\Sigma z + b\Sigma zx + c\Sigma z^2$$

Here $m = 4$

x	z	y	x^2	z^2	yx	zx	yz
1	0	12	1	0	12	0	0
2	1	18	4	1	36	2	18
3	2	24	9	4	72	6	48
4	3	30	16	9	120	12	90
$\Sigma x = 10$	$\Sigma z = 6$	$\Sigma y = 84$	$\Sigma x^2 = 30$	$\Sigma z^2 = 14$	$\Sigma yx = 240$	$\Sigma zx = 20$	$\Sigma yz = 156$

Substitution yields, $84 = 4a + 10b + 6c$

$$240 = 10a + 30b + 20c$$
and $$156 = 6a + 20b + 14c$$

Solving, we get $a = 10, b = 2, c = 4$

Hence the required regression plane is

$$y = 10 + 2x + 4z.$$

ASSIGNMENT 7.6

1. Fit a second degree parabola to the following data taking x as the independent variable:

x:	0	1	2	3	4
y:	1	5	10	22	38

2. Fit a second degree parabola to the following data by Least Squares Method:

x:	0	1	2	3	4
y:	1	1.8	1.3	2.5	6.3

3. The profit of a certain company in X^{th} year of its life are given by:

x:	1	2	3	4	5
y:	1250	1400	1650	1950	2300

Taking $u = x - 3$ and $v = \dfrac{y - 1650}{50}$, show that the parabola of second degree of v on u is $v + 0.086 = 5.3\,u + 0.643u^2$ and deduce that the parabola of second degree of y on x is

$$y = 1144 + 72x + 32.15x^2.$$

4. The following table gives the results of the measurements of train resistances, V is the velocity in miles per hour, R is the resistance in pounds per ton:

V:	20	40	60	80	100	120
R:	5.5	9.1	14.9	22.8	33.3	46

If R is related to V by the relation $R = a + bV + cV^2$; find a, b and c by using the Method of Least Squares.

5. Determine the constants a, b, and c by the Method of Least Squares such that $y = ax^2 + bx + c$ fits the following data:

x:	2	4	6	8	10
y:	4.01	11.08	30.12	81.89	222.62

7.61 STATISTICAL QUALITY CONTROL

A quality control system performs inspection, testing and analysis to ensure that the quality of the products produced is as per the laid down quality standards. It is called **"Statistical Quality Control"** when statistical techniques are employed to control, improve and maintain quality or to solve quality problems. Building an information system to satisfy the concept of prevention and control and improving upon product quality requires statistical thinking.

Statistical quality control (S.Q.C.) is systematic as compared to guess-work of haphazard process inspection and the mathematical statistical approach neutralizes personal bias and uncovers poor judgement. S.Q.C. consists of three general activities:

(1) Systematic collection and graphic recording of accurate data

(2) Analyzing the data

(3) Practical engineering or management action if the information obtained indicates significant deviations from the specified limits.

Modern techniques of statistical quality control and acceptance sampling have an important part to play in the improvement of quality, enhancement of productivity, creation of consumer confidence, and development of industrial economy of the country.

The following statistical tools are generally used for the above purposes:

(*i*) **Frequency distribution.** Frequency distribution is a tabulation of the number of times a given quality characteristic occurs within the samples. Graphic representation of frequency distribution will show:

(*a*) Average quality

(*b*) Spread of quality

(*c*) Comparison with specific requirements

(*d*) Process capability.

(*ii*) **Control chart.** Control chart is a graphical representation of quality characteristics, which indicates whether the process is under control or not.

(*iii*) **Acceptance sampling.** Acceptance sampling is the process of evaluating a portion of the product/material in a lot for the purpose of accepting or rejecting the lot on the basis of conforming to a quality specification.

It reduces the time and cost of inspection and exerts more effective pressure on quality improvement than it is possible by 100% inspection.

It is used when assurance is desired for the quality of materials/products either produced or received.

(*iv*) **Analysis of data.** Analysis of data includes analysis of tolerances, correlation, analysis of variance, analysis for engineering design, problem solving technique to eliminate cause to troubles. Statistical methods can be used in arriving at proper specification limits of product, in designing the product, in purchase of raw-material, semi-finished and finished products, manufacturing processes, inspection, packaging, sales, and also after sales service.

7.62 ADVANTAGES OF STATISTICAL QUALITY CONTROL

1. **Efficiency.** The use of statistical quality control ensures rapid and efficient inspection at a minimum cost. It eliminates the need of 100% inspection of finished products because the acceptance sampling in statistial quality control exerts more effective pressure for quality improvement.
2. **Reduction of scrap.** Statistial quality control uncovers the cause of excessive variability in manufactured products forecasting trouble before rejections occur and reducing the amount of spoiled work.
3. **Easy detection of faults.** In statistical quality control, after plotting the control charts ($\overline{X}$, R, P, C, U) etc., when the points fall above the upper control limits or below the lower control limit, an indication of deterioration in quality is given. Necessary corrective action may then be taken immediately.
4. **Adherence to specifications.** So long as a statistical quality control continues, specifications can be accurately predicted for the future by which it is possible to assess whether the production processes are capable of producing the products with the given set of specifications.
5. **Increases output and reduces wasted machine and man hours.**
6. **Efficient utilization of personnel, machines and materials** results in higher productivity.
7. **Creates quality awareness in employees.** However, it should be noted that statistical quality control is not a panacea for assuring product quality.
8. **Provides a common language** that may be used by designers, production personnel, and inspectors in arriving at a rational solution of mutual problems.
9. **Points out when and where 100% inspection, sorting or screening is required.**
10. **Eliminates bottlenecks** in the process of manufacturing.

It simply furnishes 'perspective facts' upon which intelligent management and engineering action can be based. Without such action, the method is ineffective.

Even the application of standard procedures is very dangerous without adequate study of the process.

7.63 REASONS FOR VARIATIONS IN THE QUALITY OF A PRODUCT

Two extremely similar things are rarely obtained in nature. This fact holds good for production processes as well. No production process is good enough to produce all items or products exactly alike. The variations are due to two main reasons:

(*i*) **Chance or random causes.** Variations due to chance causes are inevitable in any process or product. They are difficult to trace and to control even under the best conditions of production.

These variations may be due to some inherent characteristic of the process or machine which functions at random.

If the variations are due to chance factors alone, the observations will follow a "normal curve." The knowledge of the behaviour of chance variation is the foundation on which control chart analysis rests. The conditions which produce these variations are accordingly said to be **"under control."** On the other hand, if the variations in the data do not conform to a pattern that might reasonably be produced by chance causes, then in this case, conditions producing the variations are said to be **"out of control"** as it may be concluded that one or more assignable causes are at work.

(*ii*) **Assignable causes.** The variations due to assignable causes possess greater magnitude as compared to those due to chance causes and can be easily traced or detected. The power of the shewhart control chart lies in its ability to separate out these assignable causes of quality variations, for example, in length thickness, weight, or diameter of a component.

The variations due to assignable causes may be because of following factors:

(*i*) Differences among machines
(*ii*) Differences among workers
(*iii*) Differences among materials
(*iv*) Differences in each of these factors over time
(*v*) Differences in their relationship to one another.

These variations may also be caused due to change in working conditions, mistake on the part of the operator, etc.

7.64 TECHNIQUES OF STATISTICAL QUALITY CONTROL

To control the quality characteristics of the product, there are two main techniques:

1. **Process Control.** Process control is a process of monitoring and measuring variability in the performance of a process or a machine through the

interpretation of statistical techniques and it is employed to manage in-process quality. This technique ensures the production of requisite standard product and makes use of control charts.

2. **Product control.** This technique is concerned with the inspection of already produced goods to ascertain whether they are fit to be dispatched or not. To achieve the objectives, product control makes use of sampling inspection plans.

7.65 CONTROL CHART

A control chart is a graphical representation of the collected information. It detects the variation in processing and warns if there is any departure from the specified tolerance limits. In other words, control charts is a device which specifies the state of statistical control or is a device for attaining quality control or is a device to judge whether the statistical control has been attained.

The control limits on the chart are so placed as to disclose the presence or absence of the assignable causes of quality variation which makes the diagnosis possible and brings substantial improvements in product quality and reduction of spoilage and rework.

Moreover, by identifying chance variations, the control chart tells when to leave the process alone and thus prevents unnecessarily frequent adjustments that tend to increase the variability of the process rather than to decrease it.

There are many types of control charts designed for different control situations. Most commonly used control charts are:

(*i*) **Control charts for variables.** These are useful to measure quality characteristics and to control fully automatic process. It includes $\overline{X}$ and R-charts and charts for $\overline{X}$ and σ.

(*ii*) **Control charts for attributes.** These include P-chart for fraction defective. A fraction defective control chart discloses erratic fluctuations in the quality of inspection which may result in improvement in inspection practice and inspection standards.

It also includes C-chart for number of defects per unit.

7.66 OBJECTIVES OF CONTROL CHARTS

Control charts are based on statistical techniques.

1. $\overline{X}$ and R or $\overline{X}$ and σ charts are used in combination for control process. $\overline{X}$-chart shows the variation in the averages of samples. It is the most

commonly used variables chart. R-chart shows the uniformity or consistency of the process, *i.e.*, it shows the variations in the ranges of samples. It is a chart for measure of spread. σ-chart shows the variation of process.

2. To determine whether a given process can meet the existing specifications without a fundamental change in the production line or to tell whether the process is in control and if so, at what dispersion.
3. To secure information to be used in establishing or changing production procedures.
4. To secure information when it is necessary to widen the tolerances.
5. To provide a basis for current decisions or acceptance or rejection of manufactured or purchased product.
6. To secure information to be used in establishing or changing inspection procedure or acceptance procedure or both.

7.67 CONSTRUCTION OF CONTROL CHARTS FOR VARIABLES

First of all, a random sample of size n is taken during a manufacturing process over a period of time and quality measurements $x_1, x_2, \ldots\ldots, x_n$ are noted

Sample mean $$\bar{x} = \frac{x_1 + x_2 + \ldots\ldots + x_n}{n} = \frac{1}{n}\sum_{i=1}^{n} x_i$$

Sample range $R = x_{max.} - x_{min.}$

If the process is found stable, k consecutive samples are selected and for each sample, $\bar{x}$ and R are calculated. Then we find $\bar{\bar{x}}$ and $\bar{R}$ as

$$\bar{\bar{x}} = \frac{\bar{x}_1 + \bar{x}_2 + \ldots\ldots + \bar{x}_k}{k} = \frac{1}{k}\sum_{i=1}^{k} \bar{x}_i$$

and $$\bar{R} = \frac{R_1 + R_2 + \ldots\ldots + R_k}{k} = \frac{1}{k}\sum_{i=1}^{k} R_i$$

For $\bar{X}$-chart

$$\text{Central line} = \begin{cases} \bar{\bar{x}}, \text{ when tolerance limits are not given} \\ \mu, \text{ when tolerance limits are given} \end{cases}$$

where $$\mu = \frac{1}{2}[\text{LCL} + \text{UCL}]$$

LCL is lower control limit and UCL is upper control limit

Now, LCL (for $\bar{X}$-chart) $= \bar{\bar{x}} - A_2\bar{R}$ and UCL (for $\bar{X}$-chart) $= \bar{\bar{x}} + A_2\bar{R}$ are set.

A_2 depends on sample size n and can be found from the following table:

Sample size (n)	2	3	4	5	6	7	8	9	10	11	12	13	14	15	16	17	18	19	20
A_2	1.88	1.02	0.73	0.58	0.48	0.42	0.37	0.34	0.31	0.29	0.27	0.25	0.24	0.22	0.21	0.20	0.19	0.19	0.18

For R-chart Central line (CL) = $\overline{R}$

Now, LCL (for R-chart) = $D_3\overline{R}$ UCL (for R-chart) = $D_4\overline{R}$ are set.

where D_3 and D_4 depend on sample size and are found from the following table:

Sample size (n)	D_3	D_4	d_2
2	0	3.27	1.13
3	0	2.57	1.69
4	0	2.28	2.06
5	0	2.11	2.33
6	0	2.00	2.53
7	0.08	1.92	2.70
8	0.14	1.86	2.85
9	0.18	1.82	2.97
10	0.22	1.78	3.08
11	0.26	1.74	3.17
12	0.28	1.72	3.26
13	0.31	1.69	3.34
14	0.33	1.67	3.41
15	0.35	1.65	3.47
16	0.36	1.64	3.53
17	0.38	1.62	3.59
18	0.39	1.61	3.64
19	0.40	1.60	3.69
20	0.41	1.59	3.74

To compute upper and lower process tolerance limits for the values of x, we have

$$\text{LTL} = \overline{\overline{x}} - \frac{3\overline{R}}{d_2} \qquad \text{UTL} = \overline{\overline{x}} + \frac{3\overline{R}}{d_2}$$

where d_2 is found from the above table.

Moreover, The process capability is given by $6\sigma = 6\dfrac{\overline{R}}{d_2}$ where σ is standard deviation.

While plotting the $\overline{X}$-chart the central line on the $\overline{X}$ chart should be drawn as a solid horizontal line at $\overline{X}$. The upper and lower control limits for $\overline{X}$ chart should be drawn as dotted horizontal lines at the computed values.

Similarly, for R-chart, the central line should be drawn as a solid horizontal line at $\overline{R}$. The upper control limit should be drawn as dotted horizontal line at the computed value of UCL_R. If the subgroup size is 7 or more, the lower control limit should be drawn as dotted horizontal line at LCL_R. However, if the subgroup size is ≤ 6, the lower control limit for R is zero.

Plot the averages of subgroups in $\overline{X}$-chart, in the order collected and ranges in R-chart which should be below the $\overline{X}$-chart so that the subgroups correspond to one-another in both the charts. Points outside the control limits are indicated with cross ($\times$) on $\overline{X}$-chart and the points outside the limits on R chart by a circle ($\odot$).

7.68 CONTROL CHARTS FOR ATTRIBUTES

The following control charts will be discussed here

(*i*) P chart (*ii*) *np* chart

(*iii*) C chart (*iv*) *u* chart.

As an alternative to $\overline{X}$ and R chart and as a substitute when characteristic is measured only by attribute, a control chart based on fraction defective p is used, called P-chart.

$$p = \frac{\text{Number of defective articles found in any inspection}}{\text{Total number of articles actually inspected}}.$$

(*i*) **Control limits (3σ limits) on P-chart.** We know that for binomial distribution, the mean value of total number of defectives in a sample n is np and standard deviation is $\sqrt{npq}$ or $\sqrt{np(1-p)}$.

∴ Mean value of fraction defective is p and standard deviation

$$\sigma_p = \frac{1}{n}\sqrt{np(1-p)} = \sqrt{\frac{p(1-p)}{n}}$$

∴ $$\text{CL} = p$$

The upper and lower limits for P-chart are,

$$\text{UCL}_P = p + 3\sigma_p = p + 3\sqrt{\frac{p(1-p)}{n}}$$

and $$\text{LCL}_P = p - 3\sigma_p = p - 3\sqrt{\frac{p(1-p)}{n}}.$$

Due to the lower inspection and maintenance costs of P-charts, they usually have a greater area of economical applications.

(*ii*) **Control limits for np chart.** Whenever subgroup size is variable, P-chart is used but if it is constant, the chart for actual number of defectives called *np* chart is used.

$$\text{CL} = n\overline{p} \quad \text{where} \quad \overline{p} = \frac{\Sigma np}{\Sigma n}$$

$$\text{UCL}_{np} = n\overline{p} + 3\sigma_{np} = n\overline{p} + 3\sqrt{n\overline{p}\,(1-\overline{p})} \qquad (\text{where } \sigma_{np} = n\sigma_p)$$

and $$\text{LCL}_{np} = n\overline{p} - 3\sqrt{n\overline{p}\,(1-\overline{p})}.$$

NOTE *In case of $\overline{X}$ and R chart, it may not be necessary to draw lines connecting the points which represent the successive subgroups. But incase of P-chart, a line connecting the points is usually helpful in interpretation of the chart. Such a line assists in the interpretation of trends.*

(*iii*) **Control limits for C chart**

(*a*) **Difference between a defect and defective**

An item is called defective if it fails to conform to the specifications in any of the characteristics. Each characteristic that does not meet the specifications is a defect. An item is defective if it contains atleast one defect. The *np* chart applies to the number of defectives in subgroups of constant size while C chart applies to the number of defects in a subgroup of constant size.

(*b*) **Basis for control limits on C chart**

Control limits on C chart are based on **Poisson distribution.** Hence two conditions must be satisfied. The first condition specifies that the area of opportunity for occurrence of defects should be fairly constant from period to period. Second condition specifies that opportunities for defects are large while the chances of a defect occurring in any one spot are small.

(*c*) **Calculation of control limits on C chart**

Standard deviation

$$\sigma_c = \sqrt{\text{C}}$$

Thus 3σ limits on a C chart are

$$\text{UCL}_c = \overline{\text{C}} + 3\sqrt{\overline{\text{C}}} \text{ and } \text{LCL}_c = \overline{\text{C}} - 3\sqrt{\overline{\text{C}}}$$

and central line CL = $\overline{C}$

where $$\overline{C} = \frac{\text{Number of defects in all samples}}{\text{Total number of samples}}.$$

(*iv*) **u chart.** When the subgroup size varies from sample to sample, it is necessary to use *u* charts. The control limits on *u* chart will however vary. If *c* is total number of defects found in any sample and *n* is number of inspection units in a sample,

$$\overline{u} = \frac{C}{n} = \frac{\text{Number of defects in a sample}}{\text{Number of units in a sample}}$$

The larger the number of units in a sample, the narrower the limits. Formulae for control limits on *u* chart are:

$$UCL_u = \overline{u} + 3\sqrt{\frac{\overline{u}}{n}}\,;\ LCL_u = \overline{u} - 3\sqrt{\frac{\overline{u}}{n}} \text{ and central line CL} = \overline{u}.$$

EXAMPLES

Example 1. *The following are the mean lengths and ranges of lengths of a finished product from 10 samples each of size 5. The specification limits for length are 200 ± 5 cm. Construct $\overline{X}$ and R-chart and examine whether the process is under control and state your recommendations.*

Sample number	*1*	*2*	*3*	*4*	*5*	*6*	*7*	*8*	*9*	*10*
Mean ($\overline{X}$)	*201*	*198*	*202*	*200*	*203*	*204*	*199*	*196*	*199*	*201*
Range (R)	*5*	*0*	*7*	*3*	*3*	*7*	*2*	*8*	*5*	*6*

Assume for $n = 5$, $A_2 = 0.58$, $D_4 = 2.11$ *and* $D_3 = 0$.

Sol. (*i*) **Control limits for $\overline{X}$ chart:**

Central limit CL = 200 | ∵ Tolerance / specification limits are given ∴ $\mu = 200$

$$UCL_{\overline{x}} = \overline{\overline{x}} + A_2\overline{R} = \mu + A_2\overline{R}$$

$$LCL_{\overline{x}} = \overline{\overline{x}} - A_2\overline{R} = \mu - A_2\overline{R}$$

where $$\overline{R} = \frac{R_1 + R_2 + \ldots\ldots + R_{10}}{10} = \frac{46}{10} = 4.6$$

Then, $$UCL_{\overline{X}} = 200 + (0.58 \times 4.6) = 202.668$$

$$LCL_{\overline{X}} = 200 - (0.58 \times 4.6) = 197.332.$$

(*ii*) **Control limits for R chart.**

Central limit $\quad CL = \overline{R} = 4.6$

$$UCL_R = D_4\overline{R} = 2.11 \times 4.6 = 9.706$$

$$LCL_R = D_3\overline{R} = 0 \times 4.6 = 0$$

The $\overline{X}$ and R-charts are drawn below:

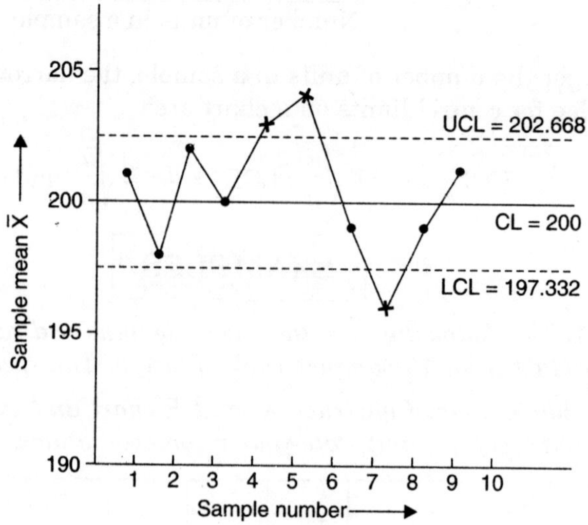

X-Chart

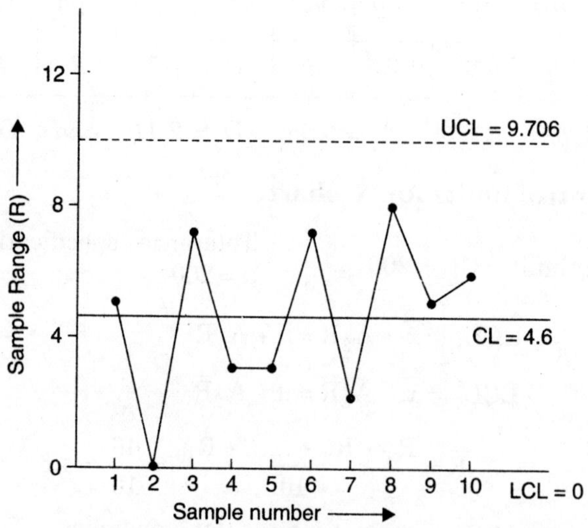

R-Chart

It is noted that all points lie within the control limits on the R chart. Hence the process variability is under control. But in X-chart, points corresponding to sample number 5, 6, and 8 lie outside the control limits. Therefore the **process is not in statistical control.** The process should be halted and it is recommended to check for any assignable causes. Fluctuation will remain until these causes, if found, are removed.

Example 2. *A drilling machine bores holes with a mean diameter of 0.5230 cm and a standard deviation of 0.0032 cm. Calculate the 2-sigma and 3-sigma upper and lower control limits for means of sample of 4.*

Sol. Mean diameter $\bar{\bar{x}} = 0.5230$ cm

S.D. $\sigma = 0.0032$ cm

$n = 4$

(*i*) 2-sigma limits are as follows:

$$CL = \bar{\bar{x}} = 0.5230 \text{ cm}$$

$$UCL = \bar{\bar{x}} + 2\frac{\sigma}{\sqrt{n}} = 0.5230 + 2 \times \frac{0.0032}{\sqrt{4}} = 0.5262 \text{ cm}$$

$$LCL = \bar{\bar{x}} - 2\frac{\sigma}{\sqrt{n}} = 0.5230 - 2 \times \frac{0.0032}{\sqrt{4}} = 0.5198 \text{ cm.}$$

(*ii*) 3-sigma limits are as follows:

$$CL = \bar{\bar{x}} = 0.5230 \text{ cm}$$

$$UCL = \bar{\bar{x}} + 3\frac{\sigma}{\sqrt{n}} = 0.5230 + 3 \times \frac{0.0032}{\sqrt{4}} = 0.5278 \text{ cm}$$

$$LCL = \bar{\bar{x}} - 3\frac{\sigma}{\sqrt{n}} = 0.5230 - 3 \times \frac{0.0032}{\sqrt{4}} = 0.5182 \text{ cm.}$$

Example 3. *In a blade manufacturing factory, 1000 blades are examined daily. Draw the np chart for the following table and examine whether the process is under control?*

Date:	*1*	*2*	*3*	*4*	*5*	*6*	*7*	*8*	*9*	*10*	*11*	*12*	*13*	*14*	*15*
Number of defective blades:	*9*	*10*	*12*	*8*	*7*	*15*	*10*	*12*	*10*	*8*	*7*	*13*	*14*	*15*	*16*

Sol. Here, $n = 1000$

Σnp = total number of defectives = 166

Σn = total number inspected = 1000 × 15

$$\therefore \quad \bar{p} = \frac{\Sigma np}{\Sigma n} = \frac{166}{1000 \times 15} = 0.011$$

$\therefore \quad n\bar{p} = 1000 \times 0.011 = 11$

Control limits are CL = $n\bar{p}$ = 11

$$\text{UCL}_{np} = n\bar{p} + 3\sqrt{n\bar{p}(1-\bar{p})} = 11 + 3\sqrt{11(1-0.011)} = 20.894$$

$$\text{LCL}_{np} = n\bar{p} - 3\sqrt{n\bar{p}(1-\bar{p})} = 11 - 3\sqrt{11(1-0.011)} = 1.106$$

The *np* chart is drawn in the figure. Since all the points lie within the control limits, the process is under control.

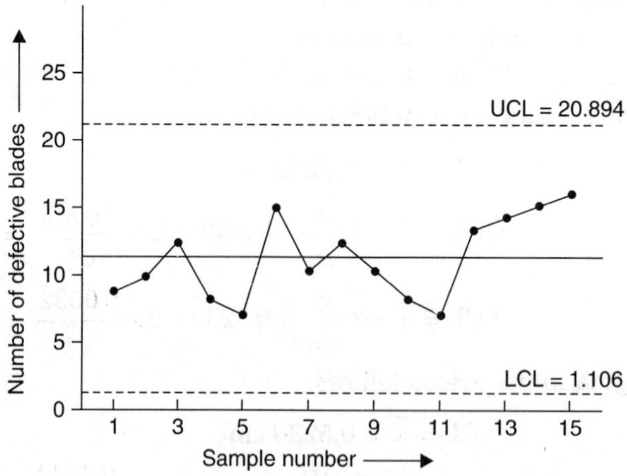

(*np*-chart)

Example 4. *In a manufacturing process, the number of defectives found in the inspection of 20 lots of 100 samples is given below:*

Lot number	*Number of defectives*	*Lot number*	*Number of defectives*
1	5	*11*	7
2	4	*12*	6
3	3	*13*	3
4	5	*14*	5
5	4	*15*	4
6	6	*16*	2
7	9	*17*	8
8	15	*18*	7
9	11	*19*	6
10	6	*20*	4

(i) Determine the control limits of p-chart and state whether the process is in control.

(ii) Determine the new value of mean fraction defective if some points are out of control. Compute the corresponding control limits and state whether the process is still in control or not.

(iii) Determine the sample size when a quality limit not worse than 9% is desirable and a 10% bad product will not be permitted more than three times in thousand.

Sol. *(i)* $\bar{p} = \dfrac{\text{Total number of defectives}}{\text{Total number of items inspected}} = \dfrac{120}{20 \times 100} = 0.06$

$$\text{UCL}_P = \bar{p} + 3\sqrt{\frac{\bar{p}(1-\bar{p})}{n}} = 0.06 + 3\sqrt{\frac{0.06\,(1-0.06)}{100}} = 0.13095$$

$$\text{LCL}_P = \bar{p} - 3\sqrt{\frac{\bar{p}(1-\bar{p})}{n}} = 0.06 - 3\sqrt{\frac{0.06\,(1-0.06)}{100}} = -\,0.01095$$

Since the fraction defective cannot be (–) ve

$$\therefore \quad \text{LCL}_P = 0$$

After observing the values of defectives in the given example, it is clear that only 8th lot having fraction defective $\dfrac{15}{100} = 0.15$ will go above UCL_P.

(ii) After eliminating the 8th lot,

$$\text{Revised value of } \bar{p} = \frac{120 - 15}{100 \times 19} = 0.056$$

Revised control limits will be

$$\text{UCL}_P = 0.056 + 3\sqrt{\frac{0.056\,(1-0.056)}{100}} = 0.125$$

$$\text{LCL}_P = 0.056 - 3\sqrt{\frac{0.056\,(1-0.056)}{100}} = -\,0.013 \textit{ i.e., } \text{zero.}$$

It is clear that all the points are within control limits.

$$\therefore \quad \text{Revised quality level } \bar{p} = 0.056$$

(iii) Since a probability that a defective more than a 9% defective quality will not be permitted, is more than 3 times in a thousand (0.3%) in corresponding 3σ limits:

$$\therefore \quad \bar{p} + 3p = 0.09$$

$$0.056 + 3\sqrt{\frac{0.056\,(1-0.056)}{n}} = 0.09 \Rightarrow \sqrt{\frac{0.056 \times 0.944}{n}} = \frac{0.034}{3}$$

Squaring,
$$\frac{0.056 \times 0.944}{n} = \left(\frac{0.034}{3}\right)^2 = (0.01133)^2$$

$$n = \frac{0.056 \times 0.944}{0.01133 \times 0.01133} = 333.$$

Example 5. *A control chart for defects per unit u uses probability limits corresponding to probabilities of 0.975 and 0.025. The central line on the control chart is at $\bar{u}$ = 2.0. The limits vary with the value of n. Determine the correct position of these upper and lower control limits when n = 5. (Assume σ = 1.96)*

Sol.
$$UCL_u = \bar{u} + \sigma\sqrt{\frac{\bar{u}}{n}} = 2 + 1.96\sqrt{\frac{2}{5}} = 3.239$$

$$LCL_u = 2 - 1.96\sqrt{\frac{2}{5}} = 0.761.$$

Example 6. *Determine the control limits for $\overline{X}$ and R charts if $\Sigma\overline{X}$ = 357.50, ΣR = 9.90, number of subgroups = 20. It is given that A_2 = 0.18, D_3 = 0.41, D_4 = 1.59 and d_2 = 3.736. Also find the process capability.*

Sol.
$$\overline{X} = \frac{\Sigma\overline{X}}{N} = \frac{357.50}{20} = 17.875$$

$$\overline{R} = \frac{\Sigma R}{N} = \frac{9.90}{20} = 0.495$$

$$UCL_{\overline{X}} = \overline{\overline{X}} + A_2\overline{R} = 17.875 + (0.18 \times 0.495) = 17.9641$$

$$LCL_{\overline{X}} = \overline{\overline{X}} - A_2\overline{R} = 17.875 - (0.18 \times 0.495) = 17.7859$$

$$UCL_R = D_4\overline{R} = 1.59 \times 0.495 = 0.78705$$

$$LCL_R = D_3\overline{R} = 0.41 \times 0.495 = 0.20295$$

$$\sigma = \frac{\overline{R}}{d_2} = \frac{0.495}{3.735} = 0.13253$$

∴ Process capability = 6σ = 6 × 0.13253 = 0.79518.

Example 7. *If the average fraction defective of a large sample of a product is 0.1537, Calculate the control limits given that sub-group size is 2000.*

Sol. Average fraction defective

$$\bar{p} = 0.1537$$

Sub-group size is 2000

$\therefore \qquad n = 2000$

Central line $\quad CL = n\bar{p} = 2000 \times 0.1537 = 307.4$

$$UCL_{np} = n\bar{p} + 3\sigma_{np} = n\bar{p} + 3\sqrt{n\bar{p}(1-\bar{p})}$$

$$= 307.4 + 3\sqrt{307.4\,(1-0.1537)} = 307.4 + 48.38774204$$

$$= 355.787742$$

and

$$LCL_{np} = n\bar{p} - 3\sqrt{n\bar{p}\,(1-\bar{p})} = 307.4 - 48.38774204$$

$$= 259.012258$$

ASSIGNMENT 7.7

1. A company manufactures screws to a nominal diameter 0.500 ± 0.030 cm. Five samples were taken randomly from the manufactured lots and 3 measurements were taken on each sample at different lengths. Following are the readings:

Sample number	*Measurement per sample x(in cm)*		
	1	*2*	*3*
1	0.488	0.489	0.505
2	0.494	0.495	0.499
3	0.498	0.515	0.487
4	0.492	0.509	0.514
5	0.490	0.508	0.499

Calculate the control limits of $\overline{X}$ and R charts. Draw $\overline{X}$ and R charts and examine whether the process is in statistical control?
[Take $A_2 = 1.02$, $D_4 = 2.57$, $D_3 = 0$ for $n = 3$]

2. The average percentage of defectives in 27 samples of size 1500 each was found to be 13.7%. Construct P-chart for this situation. Explain how the control chart can be used to control quality.

[**Hint:** $\bar{p} = 0.137$]

3. The number of customer complaints received daily by an organization is given below:

Day:	1	2	3	4	5	6	7	8	9	10	11	12	13	14	15
Complaints:	2	3	0	1	9	2	0	0	4	2	0	7	0	2	4

Does it mean that the number of complaints is under statistical control? Establish a control scheme for the future.

4. It was found that when a manufacturing process is under control, the average number of defectives per sample batch of 10 is 1.2. What limits would you set in a quality control chart based on the examination of defectives in sample batches of 10?

   [**Hint:** $\overline{p} = 0.12, n\overline{p} = 1.2$]

5. The following data shows the value of sample mean $\overline{X}$ and range R for 10 samples of size 5 each. Calculate the values for central line and control limits for $\overline{X}$-chart and R chart and determine whether the process is under control.

Sample number:	1	2	3	4	5	6	7	8	9	10
Mean $\overline{X}$:	11.2	11.8	10.8	11.6	11	9.6	10.4	9.6	10.6	10
Range R:	7	4	8	5	7	4	8	4	7	9

   Assume for $n = 5$, $A_2 = 0.577$, $D_3 = 0$ and $D_4 = 2.115$.

6. What are statistical quality control techniques? Discuss the objectives and advantages of statistical quality control.

7. The following table shows the number of missing rivets observed at the time of inspection of 12 aircrafts. Find the control limits for the number of defects chart and comment on the state of control.

Air craft number:	1	2	3	4	5	6	7	8	9	10	11	12
Number of missing rivets:	7	15	13	18	10	14	13	10	20	11	22	15

Chapter 8 TESTING OF HYPOTHESIS

8.1 POPULATION OR UNIVERSE

An aggregate of objects (animate or inanimate) under study is called **population or universe.** It is thus a collection of individuals or of their attributes (qualities) or of results of operations which can be numerically specified.

A universe containing a finite number of individuals or members is called a **finite inverse.** For example, the universe of the weights of students in a particular class.

A universe with infinite number of members is known as an **infinite universe.** For example, the universe of pressures at various points in the atmosphere.

In some cases, we may be even ignorant whether or not a particular universe is infinite, for example, the universe of stars.

The universe of concrete objects is an **existent universe.** The collection of all possible ways in which a specified event can happen is called a **hypothetical universe.** The universe of heads and tails obtained by tossing a coin an infinite number of times (provided that it does not wear out) is a hypothetical one.

8.2 SAMPLING

The statistician is often confronted with the problem of discussing a universe of which he cannot examine every member, *i.e.*, of which complete enumeration is impracticable. For example, if we want to have an idea of the average per capita income of the people of a country, enumeration of every earning individual in the country is a very difficult task. Naturally, the question arises: What can be said about a universe of which we can examine only a limited number of members? This question is the origin of the **Theory of Sampling.**

A finite subset of a universe is called a **sample.** A sample is thus a small portion of the universe. The number of individuals in a sample is called the **sample size.** The process of selecting a sample from a universe is called **sampling.**

The theory of sampling is a study of relationship existing between a population and samples drawn from the population. The fundamental object of sampling is to get as much information as possible of the whole universe by examining only a part of it. An attempt is thus made through sampling to give the maximum information about the parent universe with the minimum effort.

Sampling is quite often used in our day-to-day practical life. For example, in a shop we assess the quality of sugar, rice, or any other commodity by taking only a handful of it from the bag and then decide whether to purchase it or not. A housewife normally tests the cooked products to find if they are properly cooked and contain the proper quantity of salt or sugar, by taking a spoonful of it.

8.3 PARAMETERS OF STATISTICS

The statistical constants of the population such as mean, the variance, etc. are known as the parameters. The statistical concepts of the sample from the members of the sample to estimate the parameters of the population from which the sample has been drawn is known as *statistic*.

Population mean and variance are denoted by μ and σ^2, while those of the samples are given by $\overline{x}$, s^2.

8.4 STANDARD ERROR

The standard deviation of the sampling distribution of a statistic is known as the **standard error (S.E.).** It plays an important role in the theory of large samples and it forms a basis of the testing of hypothesis. If t is any statistic, for large sample.

$$z = \frac{t - E(t)}{S.E(t)}$$ is normally distributed with mean 0 and variance unity.

For large sample, the standard errors of some of the well known statistic are listed below:

n—sample size; σ^2—population variance; s^2—sample variance; p—population proportion ; $Q = 1 - p$; n_1, n_2—are sizes of two independent random samples.

Number	*Statistic*	*Standard error*
1.	$\bar{x}$	$\sigma/\sqrt{n}$
2.	s	$\sqrt{\sigma^2/2n}$
3.	Difference of two sample means $\bar{x}_1 - \bar{x}_2$	$\sqrt{\frac{\sigma_1^2}{n_1} + \frac{\sigma_2^2}{n_2}}$
4.	Difference of two sample standard deviation $s_1 - s_2$	$\sqrt{\frac{\sigma_1^2}{2n_1} + \frac{\sigma_2^2}{2n_2}}$
5.	Difference of two sample proportions $p_1 - p_2$	$\sqrt{\frac{P_1Q_1}{n_1} + \frac{P_2Q_2}{n_2}}$
6.	Observed sample proportion p	$\sqrt{PQ/n}$

8.5 TEST OF SIGNIFICANCE

An important aspect of the sampling theory is to study the test of significance which will enable us to decide, on the basis of the results of the sample, whether

(*i*) *the deviation between the observed sample statistic and the hypothetical parameter value or*

(*ii*) *the deviation between two sample statistics is significant or might be attributed due to chance or the fluctuations of the sampling.*

For applying the tests of significance, we first set up a hypothesis which is a definite statement about the population parameter called **Null hypothesis** denoted by H_0.

Any hypothesis which is complementary to the null hypothesis ($\mathbf{H_0}$) is called an **Alternative hypothesis** denoted by $\mathbf{H_1}$.

For example, if we want to test the null hypothesis that the population has a specified mean μ_0, then we have

$$\mathbf{H_0}: \mu = \mu_0$$

Alternative hypothesis will be

(*i*) $H_1: \mu \neq \mu_0$ ($\mu > \mu_0$ *or* $\mu < \mu_0$) (two tailed alternative hypothesis).

(*ii*) $H_1: \mu > \mu_0$ (right tailed alternative hypothesis (*or*) single tailed).

(*iii*) $H_1: \mu < \mu_0$ (left tailed alternative hypothesis (*or*) single tailed).

Hence alternative hypothesis helps to know whether the test is two tailed test or one tailed test.

8.6 CRITICAL REGION

A region corresponding to a statistic t, in the sample space S which amounts to rejection of the null hypothesis H_0 is called as **critical region** or **region of rejection.** The region of the sample space S which amounts to the acceptance of H_0 is called *acceptance region*.

8.7 LEVEL OF SIGNIFICANCE

The probability of the value of the variate falling in the critical region is known as level of significance. The probability α that a random value of the statistic t belongs to the critical region is known as the **level of significance.**

$$P(t \in \omega \mid H_0) = \alpha$$

i.e., the level of significance is the size of the type I error or the maximum producer's risk.

8.8 ERRORS IN SAMPLING

The main aim of the sampling theory is to draw a valid conclusion about the population parameters on the basis of the sample results. In doing this we may commit the following two types of errors:

Type I Error. When H_0 is true, we may reject it.

$$P(\text{Reject } H_0 \text{ when it is true}) = P(\text{Reject } H_0/H_0) = \alpha$$

α is called the size of the type I error also referred to as **producer's risk.**

Type II Error. When H_0 is wrong we may accept it P(Accept H_0 when it is wrong) = P(Accept H_0/H_1) = β . β is called the size of the type II error, also referred to as **consumer's risk.**

NOTE *The values of the test statistic which separates the critical region and acceptance region are called the **critical values** or **significant values.** This value is dependent on (i) the level of significance used and (ii) the alternative hypothesis, whether it is one-tailed or two-tailed.*

For larger samples corresponding to the statistic t, the variable $z = \dfrac{t - E(t)}{S.E(t)}$ is normally distributed with mean 0 and variance 1. The value of z given above under the null hypothesis is known as **test statistic.**

The critical value of z_α of the test statistic at level of significance α for a two-tailed test is given by

$$p(|z| > z_\alpha) = \alpha \qquad (1)$$

i.e., z_α is the value of z so that the total area of the critical region on both tails is α. Since the normal curve is symmetrical, from equation (1), we get

$$p(z > z_\alpha) + p(z < -z_\alpha) = \alpha;\ i.e.,\ 2p(z > z_\alpha) = \alpha;\ p(z > z_\alpha) = \alpha/2$$

i.e., the area of each tail is $\alpha/2$.

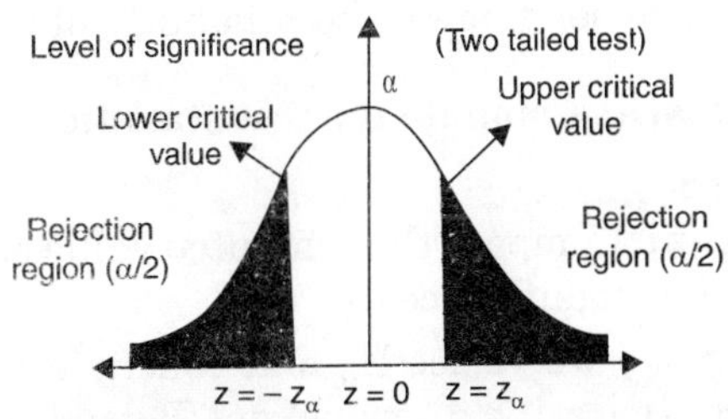

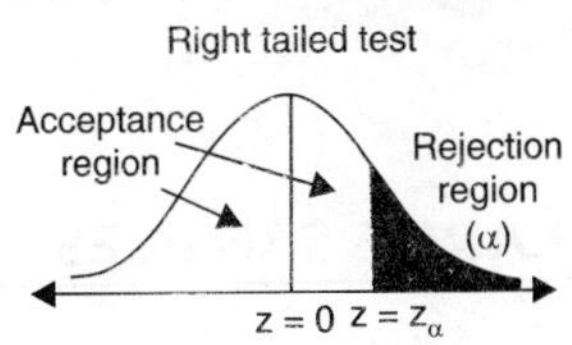

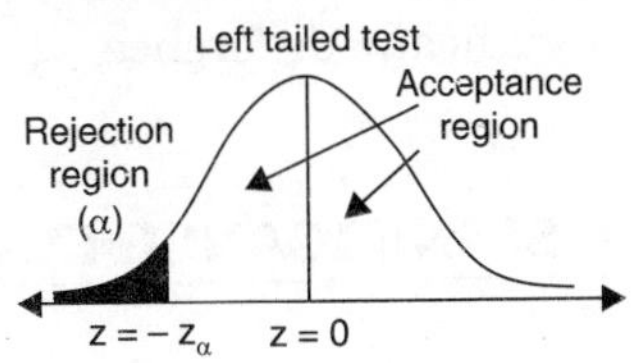

The critical value z_α is that value such that the area to the right of z_α is $\alpha/2$ and the area to the left of $-z_\alpha$ is $\alpha/2$.

In the case of the one-tailed test,

$$p(z > z_\alpha) = \alpha \text{ if it is right-tailed; } p(z < -z_\alpha) = \alpha \text{ if it is left-tailed.}$$

The critical value of z for a single-tailed test (right or left) at level of significance α is same as the critical value of z for two-tailed test at level of significance 2α.

Using the equation, also using the normal tables, the critical value of z at different levels of significance (α) for both single tailed and two tailed test are calculated and listed below. The equations are

$$p(|z| > z_\alpha) = \alpha; \ p(z > z_\alpha) = \alpha; \ p(z < -z_\alpha) = \alpha$$

	Level of significance		
	1% (0.01)	5% (0.05)	10% (0.1)
Two tailed test	$\lvert z_\alpha \rvert = 2.58$	$\lvert z \rvert = 1.966$	$\lvert z \rvert = 0.645$
Right tailed	$z_\alpha = 2.33$	$z_\alpha = 1.645$	$z_\alpha = 1.28$
Left tailed	$z_\alpha = -2.33$	$z_\alpha = -1.645$	$z_\alpha = -1.28$

8.9 STEPS IN TESTING OF STATISTICAL HYPOTHESIS

Step 1. Null hypothesis. Set up H_0 in clear terms.

Step 2. Alternative hypothesis. Set up H_1, so that we could decide whether we should use one tailed test or two tailed test.

Step 3. Level of significance. Select the appropriate level of significance in advance depending on the reliability of the estimates.

Step 4. Test statistic. Compute the test statistic $z = \dfrac{t - E(t)}{S.E(t)}$ under the null hypothesis.

Step 5. Conclusion. Compare the computed value of z with the critical value z_α at level of significance (α).

If $|z| > z_\alpha$, we reject H_0 and conclude that there is significant difference. If $|z| < z_\alpha$, we accept H_0 and conclude that there is no significant difference.

8.10 TEST OF SIGNIFICANCE FOR LARGE SAMPLES

If the sample size $n > 30$, the sample is taken as large sample. For such sample we apply normal test, as Binomial, Poisson, chi square, etc. are closely approximated by normal distributions assuming the population as normal.

Under large sample test, the following are the important tests to test the significance:

1. *Testing of significance for single proportion.*
2. *Testing of significance for difference of proportions.*

3. *Testing of significance for single mean.*
4. *Testing of significance for difference of means.*
5. *Testing of significance for difference of standard deviations.*

8.10.1 Testing of Significance for Single Proportion

This test is used to find the significant difference between proportion of the sample and the population. Let X be the number of successes in n independent trials with constant probability P of success for each trial.

$$E(X) = nP;\ V(X) = nPQ;\ Q = 1 - P = \text{Probability of failure.}$$

Let $\quad p = X/n$ called the observed proportion of success.

$$E(p) = E(X/n) = \frac{1}{n}E(x) = \frac{np}{n} = p;\ E(p) = p$$

$$V(p) = V(X/n) = \frac{1}{n^2}V(X) = \frac{1(PQ)}{n} = PQ/n$$

$$S.E.(p) = \sqrt{\frac{PQ}{n}};\ z = \frac{p - E(p)}{S.E.(p)} = \frac{p - p}{\sqrt{PQ/n}} \sim N(0, 1)$$

This z is called test statistic which is used to test the significant difference of sample and population proportion.

NOTE

1. *The probable limit for the observed proportion of successes are* $p \pm z_\alpha\sqrt{PQ/n}$, *where* z_α *is the significant value at level of significance* α.

2. *If* p *is not known, the limits for the proportion in the population are* $p \pm z_\alpha\sqrt{pq/n}$, $q = 1 - p$.

3. *If* α *is not given, we can take safely* 3σ *limits.*

Hence, the confidence limits for observed proportion p are $p \pm 3\sqrt{\frac{PQ}{n}}$.

The confidence limits for the population proportion p are $p \pm \sqrt{\frac{pq}{n}}$.

EXAMPLES

Example 1. *A coin was tossed 400 times and the head turned up 216 times. Test the hypothesis that the coin is unbiased.*

Sol. H_0: The coin is unbiased *i.e.,* P = 0.5.

H_1: The coin is not unbiased (biased); P ≠ 0.5

Here $n = 400$; X = Number of success = 216

$$p = \text{proportion of success in the sample } \frac{X}{n} = \frac{216}{400} = 0.54.$$

Population proportion = 0.5 = P; Q = 1 – P = 1 – 0.5 = 0.5.

Under H_0, test statistic $z = \dfrac{p - P}{\sqrt{PQ/n}}$

$$| z | = \left| \frac{0.54 - 0.5}{\sqrt{\dfrac{0.5 \times 0.5}{400}}} \right| = 1.6$$

we use a two-tailed test.

Conclusion. Since $| z | = 1.6 < 1.96$

i.e., $| z | < z_\alpha$, z_α is the significant value of z at 5% level of significance.

i.e., the coin is unbiased is P = 0.5.

Example 2. *A manufacturer claims that only 4% of his products supplied by him are defective. A random sample of 600 products contained 36 defectives. Test the claim of the manufacturer.*

Sol. (*i*) P = observed proportion of success.

i.e., P = proportion of defective in the sample $= \dfrac{36}{600} = 0.06$

p = proportion of defectives in the population = 0.04

H_0: $p = 0.04$ is true.

i.e., the claim of the manufacturer is accepted.

H_1: (*i*) $P \neq 0.04$ (two tailed test)

(*ii*) If we want to reject, only if $p > 0.04$ then (right tailed).

$$\text{Under } H_0,\ z = \frac{p - P}{\sqrt{PQ/n}} = \frac{0.06 - 0.04}{\sqrt{\dfrac{0.04 \times 0.96}{600}}} = 2.5.$$

Conclusion. Since $| z | = 2.5 > 1.96$, we reject the hypothesis H_0 at 5% level of significance two tailed.

If H_1 is taken as $p > 0.04$ we apply right tailed test.

$| z | = 2.5 > 1.645$ (z_α) we reject the null hypothesis here also.

In both cases, manufacturer's claim is not acceptable.

Example 3. *A machine is producing bolts a certain fraction of which are defective. A random sample of 400 is taken from a large batch and is found to contain 30 defective bolts. Does this indicate that the proportion of defectives is larger than that claimed by the manufacturer if the manufacturer claims that only 5% of his product are defective? Find 95% confidence limits of the proportion of defective bolts in batch.*

Sol. Null hypothesis H_0: The manufacturer claim is accepted *i.e.,*

$$P = \frac{5}{100} = 0.05$$

$$Q = 1 - P = 1 - 0.05 = 0.95$$

Alternative hypothesis. $p > 0.05$ (Right tailed test).

$$p = \text{observed proportion of sample} = \frac{30}{400} = 0.075$$

Under H_0, the test statistic

$$z = \frac{p - P}{\sqrt{PQ/n}} \quad \therefore \quad z = \frac{0.075 - 0.05}{\sqrt{\frac{0.05 \times 0.95}{400}}} = 2.2941.$$

Conclusion. The tabulated value of z at 5% level of significance for the right-tailed test is

$z_\alpha = 1.645$. Since $| z | = 2.2941 > 1.645$,

H_0 is rejected at 5% level of significance. *i.e.,* the proportion of defective is larger than the manufacturer claim.

To find 95% confidence limits of the proportion.

It is given by $p \pm z_\alpha \sqrt{PQ/n}$

$$0.05 \pm 1.96 \sqrt{\frac{0.05 \times 0.95}{400}} = 0.05 \pm 0.02135 = 0.07136, 0.02865$$

Hence 95% confidence limits for the proportion of defective bolts are (0.07136, 0.02865).

Example 4. *A bag contains defective articles, the exact number of which is not known. A sample of 100 from the bag gives 10 defective articles. Find the limits for the proportion of defective articles in the bag.*

Sol. Here p = proportion of defective articles $= \frac{10}{100} = 0.1$;

$$q = 1 - p = 1 - 0.1 = 0.9$$

Since the confidence limit is not given, we assume it is 95%. $\therefore$ level of significance is 5% $z_\alpha = 1.96$.

Also the proportion of population P is not given. To get the confidence limit, we use P and it is given by

$$P \pm z_\alpha \sqrt{pq/n} = 0.1 \pm 1.96 \sqrt{\frac{0.1 \times 0.9}{100}}$$

$$= 0.1 \pm 0.0588 = 0.1588,\ 0.0412.$$

Hence 95% confidence limits for defective articles in the bag are (0.1588, 0.0412).

ASSIGNMENT 8.1

1. A sample of 600 persons selected at random from a large city shows that the percentage of males in the sample is 53. It is believed that the ratio of males to the total population in the city is 0.5. Test whether the belief is confirmed by the observation.
2. In a city a sample of 1000 people was taken and 540 of them are vegetarian and the rest are non-vegetarian. Can we say that both habits of eating (vegetarian or non-vegetarian) are equally popular in the city at (*i*) 1% level of significance (*ii*) 5% level of significance?
3. 325 men out of 600 men chosen from a big city were found to be smokers. Does this information support the conclusion that the majority of men in the city are smokers?
4. A random sample of 500 bolts was taken from a large consignment and 65 were found to be defective. Find the percentage of defective bolts in the consignment.
5. In a hospital 475 female and 525 male babies were born in a week. Do these figures confirm the hypothesis that males and females are born in equal number?
6. 400 apples are taken at random from a large basket and 40 are found to be bad. Estimate the proportion of bad apples in the basket and assign limits within which the percentage most probably lies.

8.10.2 Testing of Significance for Difference of Proportions

Consider two samples X_1 and X_2 of sizes n_1 and n_2, respectively, taken from two different populations. Test the significance of the difference between the sample proportion p_1 and p_2. The test statistic under the null hypothesis H_0, that there is no significant difference between the two sample proportion, we have

$$z = \frac{p_1 - p_2}{\sqrt{PQ\left(\frac{1}{n_1} + \frac{1}{n_2}\right)}}, \quad \text{where } P = \frac{n_1 p_1 + n_2 p_2}{n_1 + n_2}$$

and $\quad Q = 1 - P.$

EXAMPLES

Example 1. *Before an increase in excise duty on tea, 800 people out of a sample of 1000 persons were found to be tea drinkers. After an increase in the duty, 800 persons were known to be tea drinkers in a sample of 1200 people. Do you think that there has been a significant decrease in the consumption of tea after the increase in the excise duty?*

Sol. Here $n_1 = 800, n_2 = 1200$

$$p_1 = \frac{X_1}{n_1} = \frac{800}{1000} = \frac{4}{5};\ p_2 = \frac{X_2}{n_2} = \frac{800}{1200} = \frac{2}{3}$$

$$P = \frac{p_1n_1 + p_2n_2}{n_1 + n_2} = \frac{X_1 + X_2}{n_1 + n_2} = \frac{800 + 800}{1000 + 1200} = \frac{8}{11};\ Q = \frac{3}{11}$$

Null hypothesis H_0: $p_1 = p_2$, *i.e.*, there is no significant difference in the consumption of tea before and after increase of excise duty.

H_1: $p_1 > p_2$ (right-tailed test)

The test statistic

$$z = \frac{p_1 - p_2}{\sqrt{PQ\left(\frac{1}{n_1} + \frac{1}{n_2}\right)}} = \frac{0.8 - 0.6666}{\sqrt{\frac{8}{11} \times \frac{3}{11}\left(\frac{1}{1000} + \frac{1}{1200}\right)}} = 6.842.$$

Conclusion. Since the calculated value of $| z | > 1.645$ also $| z | > 2.33$, both the significant values of z at 5% and 1% level of significance. Hence H_0 is rejected, *i.e.,* there is a significant decrease in the consumption of tea due to increase in excise duty.

Example 2. *A machine produced 16 defective articles in a batch of 500. After overhauling it produced 3 defectives in a batch of 100. Has the machine improved?*

Sol. $p_1 = \frac{16}{500} = 0.032;\ n_1 = 500 \qquad p_2 = \frac{3}{100} = 0.03;\ n_2 = 100$

Null hypothesis H_0: The machine has not improved due to overhauling, $p_1 = p_2$.

H_1: $p_1 > p_2$ (right-tailed)

$$\therefore \quad P = \frac{p_1n_1 + p_2n_2}{n_1 + n_2} = \frac{19}{600} \cong 0.032$$

Under H_0, the test statistic

$$z = \frac{p_1 - p_2}{\sqrt{PQ\left(\frac{1}{n_1} + \frac{1}{n_2}\right)}} = \frac{0.032 - 0.03}{\sqrt{(0.032)(0.968)\left(\frac{1}{500} + \frac{1}{100}\right)}} = 0.104.$$

Conclusion. The calculated value of $| z | < 1.645$, the significant value of z at 5% level of significance, H_0 is accepted, *i.e.*, the machine has not improved due to overhauling.

Example 3. *In two large populations, there are 30% and 25%, respectively, of fair haired people. Is this difference likely to be hidden in samples of 1200 and 900, respectively, from the two populations.*

Sol. p_1 = proportion of fair haired people in the first population = 30% = 0.3; p_2 = 25% = 0.25; $Q_1 = 0.7$; $Q_2 = 0.75$.

H_0: Sample proportions are equal, *i.e.*, the difference in population proportions is likely to be hidden in sampling.

$H_1: p_1 \neq p_2$

$$z = \frac{P_1 - P_2}{\sqrt{\frac{P_1Q_1}{n_1} + \frac{P_2Q_2}{n_2}}} = \frac{0.3 - 0.25}{\sqrt{\frac{0.3 \times 0.7}{1200} + \frac{0.25 \times 0.75}{900}}} = 2.5376.$$

Conclusion. Since $| z | > 1.96$, the significant value of z at 5% level of significance, H_0 is rejected. However $| z | < 2.58$, the significant value of z at 1% level of significance, H_0 is accepted. At 5% level, these samples will reveal the difference in the population proportions.

Example 4. *500 articles from a factory are examined and found to be 2% defective. 800 similar articles from a second factory are found to have only 1.5% defective. Can it reasonably be concluded that the product of the first factory are inferior to those of second?*

Sol. $n_1 = 500$, $n_2 = 800$

p_1 = proportion of defective from first factory = 2% = 0.02

p_2 = proportion of defective from second factory = 1.5% = 0.015

H_0: There is no significant difference between the two products, *i.e.*, the products do not differ in quality.

$H_1: p_1 < p_2$ (one tailed test)

Under H_0, $z = \dfrac{p_1 - p_2}{\sqrt{PQ\left(\frac{1}{n_1} + \frac{1}{n_2}\right)}}$

$$P = \frac{n_1 p_1 + n_2 p_2}{n_1 + n_2} = \frac{0.02(500) + (0.015)(800)}{500 + 800} = 0.01692;$$

$$Q = 1 - P = 0.9830$$

$$z = \frac{0.02 - 0.015}{\sqrt{0.01692 \times 0.983\left(\frac{1}{500} + \frac{1}{800}\right)}} = 0.68$$

Conclusion. As $| z | < 1.645$, the significant value of z at 5% level of significance, H_0 is accepted *i.e.,* the products do not differ in quality.

ASSIGNMENT 8.2

1. A random sample of 400 men and 600 women were asked whether they would like to have a school near their residence. 200 men and 325 women were in favor of the proposal. Test the hypothesis that the proportion of men and women in favor of the proposal are the same at 5% level of significance.
2. In a town A, there were 956 births, of which 52.5% were males while in towns A and B combined, this proportion in total of 1406 births was 0.496. Is there any significant difference in the proportion of male births in the two towns?
3. In a referendum submitted to the student body at a university, 850 men and 560 women voted. 500 men and 320 women voted yes. Does this indicate a significant difference of opinion between men and women on this matter at 1% level?
4. A manufacturing firm claims that its brand A product outsells its brand B product by 8%. If it is found that 42 out of a sample of 200 persons prefer brand A and 18 out of another sample of 100 persons prefer brand B. Test whether the 8% difference is a valid claim.

8.10.3 Testing of Significance for Single Mean

To test whether the difference between sample mean and population mean is significant or not.

Let $X_1, X_2, ..., X_n$ be a random sample of size n from a large population $X_1, X_2, ..., X_N$ of size N with mean μ and variance σ^2. $\therefore$ the standard error of mean of a random sample of size n from a population with variance σ^2 is $\sigma/\sqrt{n}$.

To test whether the given sample of size n has been drawn from a population with mean μ, *i.e.* to test whether the difference between the sample mean and the population mean is significant. Under the null hypothesis, there is no difference between the sample mean and population mean.

The test statistic is $z = \dfrac{\bar{x} - \mu}{\sigma/\sqrt{n}}$, where σ is the standard deviation of the population.

If σ is not known, we use the test statistic $z = \frac{\overline{X} - \mu}{s/\sqrt{n}}$, where s is the standard deviation of the sample.

NOTE *If the level of significance is a and z_α is the critical value*

$$- z_\alpha < | z | = \left| \frac{\overline{x} - \mu}{\sigma/\sqrt{n}} \right| < z_\alpha$$

The limits of the population mean μ are given by

$$\overline{x} - z_\alpha \frac{\sigma}{\sqrt{n}} < \mu < \overline{x} + z_\alpha \frac{\sigma}{\sqrt{n}}.$$

At 5% level of significance, 95% confidence limits are

$$\overline{x} - 1.96 \frac{\sigma}{\sqrt{n}} < \mu < \overline{x} + 1.96 \frac{\sigma}{\sqrt{n}}$$

At 1% level of significance, 99% confidence limits are

$$\overline{x} - 2.58 \frac{\sigma}{\sqrt{n}} < \mu < \overline{x} + 2.58 \frac{\sigma}{\sqrt{n}}.$$

These limits are called confidence limits or fiducial limits.

EXAMPLES

Example 1. *A normal population has a mean of 6.8 and standard deviation of 1.5. A sample of 400 members gave a mean of 6.75. Is the difference significant?*

Sol. H_0: There is no significant difference between $\overline{x}$ and μ.

H_1: There is significant difference between $\overline{x}$ and μ.

Given $\mu = 6.8$, $\sigma = 1.5$, $\overline{x} = 6.75$ and $n = 400$

$$| z | = \left| \frac{\overline{x} - \mu}{\sigma/\sqrt{n}} \right| = \left| \frac{6.75 - 6.8}{1.5/\sqrt{900}} \right| = | - 0.67 | = 0.67$$

Conclusion. As the calculated value of $| z | < z_\alpha = 1.96$ at 5% level of significance, H_0 is accepted, *i.e.*, there is no significant difference between $\overline{x}$ and μ.

Example 2. *A random sample of 900 members has a mean 3.4 cms. Can it be reasonably regarded as a sample from a large population of mean 3.2 cms and standard deviation 2.3 cms?*

Sol. Here $n = 900$, $\overline{x} = 3.4$, $\mu = 3.2$, $\sigma = 2.3$

H_0: Assume that the sample is drawn from a large population with mean 3.2 and standard deviation = 2.3

H_1: $\mu \neq 3.25$ (Apply two-tailed test)

$$\text{Under } H_0;\ z = \frac{\bar{x} - \mu}{\sigma/\sqrt{n}} = \frac{3.4 - 3.2}{2.3/\sqrt{900}} = 0.261.$$

Conclusion. As the calculated value of $|z| = 0.261 < 1.96$, the significant value of z at 5% level of significance, H_0 is accepted, *i.e.*, the sample is drawn from the population with mean 3.2 and standard deviation = 2.3.

Example 3. *The mean weight obtained from a random sample of size 100 is 64 gms. The standard deviation of the weight distribution of the population is 3 gms. Test the statement that the mean weight of the population is 67 gms at 5% level of significance. Also set up 99% confidence limits of the mean weight of the population.*

Sol. Here $n = 100$, $\mu = 67$, $\bar{x} = 64$, $\sigma = 3$

H_0: There is no significant difference between sample and population mean.

i.e., $\mu = 67$, the sample is drawn from the population with $\mu = 67$.

H_1: $\mu \neq 67$ (Two-tailed test).

$$\text{Under } H_0,\ z = \frac{\bar{x} - \mu}{\sigma/\sqrt{n}} = \frac{64 - 67}{3/\sqrt{100}} = -10 \quad \therefore \quad |z| = 10.$$

Conclusion. Since the calculated value of $|z| > 1.96$, the significant value of z at 5% level of significance, H_0 is rejected, *i.e.*, the sample is not drawn from the population with mean 67.

To find 99% confidence limits, given by

$$\bar{x} \pm 2.58\, \sigma/\sqrt{n} = 64 \pm 2.58(3/\sqrt{100}) = 64.774,\ 63.226.$$

Example 4. *The average score in mathematics of a sample of 100 students was 51 with a standard deviation of 6 points. Could this have been a random sample from a population with average scores 50?*

Sol. Here $n = 100$, $\bar{x} = 51$, $s = 6$, $\mu = 50$; σ is unknown.

H_0: The sample is drawn from a population with mean 50, $\mu = 50$

H_1: $\mu \neq 50$

$$\text{Under } H_0,\ z = \frac{\bar{x} - \mu}{s/\sqrt{n}} = \frac{51 - 50}{6/\sqrt{100}} = \frac{10}{6} = 1.6666.$$

Conclusion. Since $|z| = 1.666 < 1.96$, z_α the significant value of z at 5% level of significance, H_0 is accepted, *i.e.*, the sample is drawn from the population with mean 50.

ASSIGNMENT 8.3

1. A sample of 1000 students from a university was taken and their average weight was found to be 112 pounds with a standard deviation of 20 pounds. Could the mean weight of students in the population be 120 pounds?
2. A sample of 400 male students is found to have a mean height of 160 cms. Can it be reasonably regarded as a sample from a large population with mean height 162.5 cms and standard deviation 4.5 cms?
3. A random sample of 200 measurements from a large population gave a mean value of 50 and a standard deviation of 9. Determine 95% confidence interval for the mean of population.
4. The guaranteed average life of certain type of bulbs is 1000 hours with a standard deviation of 125 hours. It is decided to sample the output so as to ensure that 90% of the bulbs do not fall short of the guaranteed average by more than 2.5%. What must be the minimum size of the sample?
5. The heights of college students in a city are normally distributed with standard deviation 6 cms. A sample of 1000 students has mean height 158 cms. Test the hypothesis that the mean height of college students in the city is 160 cms.

8.10.4 Test of Significance for Difference of Means of Two Large Samples

Let $\bar{x}_1$ be the mean of a sample of size n_1 from a population with mean μ_1, and variance σ_1^2. Let $\bar{x}_2$ be the mean of an independent sample of size n_2 from another population with mean μ_2 and variance σ_2^2. The test statistic is given by $z = \dfrac{\bar{x}_1 - \bar{x}_2}{\sqrt{\dfrac{\sigma_1^2}{n_1} + \dfrac{\sigma_2^2}{n_2}}}$.

Under the null hypothesis that the samples are drawn from the same population where $\sigma_1 = \sigma_2 = \sigma$, *i.e.*, $\mu_1 = \mu_2$ the test statistic is given by

$$z = \frac{\bar{x}_1 - \bar{x}_2}{\sigma\sqrt{\dfrac{1}{n_1} + \dfrac{1}{n_2}}}.$$

NOTE **1.** *If σ_1, σ_2 are not known and $\sigma_1 \neq \sigma_2$ the test statistic in this case is*

$$z = \frac{\bar{x}_1 - \bar{x}_2}{\sqrt{\dfrac{s_1^2 + s_2^2}{n_1 + n_2}}}.$$

2. *If σ is not known and $\sigma_1 = \sigma_2$. We use* $\sigma^2 = \dfrac{n_1 s_1^2 + n_2 s_2^2}{n_1 + n_2}$ *to calculate* σ;

$$z = \frac{\bar{x}_1 - \bar{x}_2}{\sqrt{\dfrac{n_1 s_1^2 + n_2 s_2^2}{n_1 + n_2}\left(\dfrac{1}{n_1} + \dfrac{1}{n_2}\right)}}.$$

EXAMPLES

Example 1. *The average income of persons was 210 with a standard deviation of 10 in a sample of 100 people. For another sample of 150 people, the average income was 220 with a standard deviation of 12. The standard deviation of incomes of the people of the city was 11. Test whether there is any significant difference between the average incomes of the localities.*

Sol. Here $n_1 = 100$, $n_2 = 150$, $\bar{x}_1 = 210$, $\bar{x}_2 = 220$, $s_1 = 10$, $s_2 = 12$.

Null hypothesis. The difference is not significant, *i.e.*, there is no difference between the incomes of the localities.

$$H_0: \bar{x}_1 = \bar{x}_2, \quad H_1: \bar{x}_1 \neq \bar{x}_2$$

Under H_0, $$z = \frac{\bar{x}_1 - \bar{x}_2}{\sqrt{\dfrac{s_1^2}{n_1} + \dfrac{s_2^2}{n_2}}} = \frac{210 - 220}{\sqrt{\dfrac{10^2}{100} + \dfrac{12^2}{150}}} = -7.1428 \quad \therefore \quad |z| = 7.1428.$$

Conclusion. As the calculated value of $|z| > 1.96$, the significant value of z at 5% level of significance, H_0 is rejected *i.e.*, there is significant difference between the average incomes of the localities.

Example 2. *Intelligence tests were given to two groups of boys and girls.*

	Mean	*Standard deviation*	*Size*
Girls	*75*	*8*	*60*
Boys	*73*	*10*	*100*

Examine if the difference between mean scores is significant.

Sol. Null hypothesis H_0: There is no significant difference between mean scores, *i.e.*, $\bar{x}_1 = \bar{x}_2$.

$$H_1: \bar{x}_1 \neq \bar{x}_2$$

Under the null hypothesis $$z = \frac{\bar{x}_1 - \bar{x}_2}{\sqrt{\dfrac{s_1^2}{n_1} + \dfrac{s_2^2}{n_2}}} = \frac{75 - 73}{\sqrt{\dfrac{8^2}{60} + \dfrac{10^2}{100}}} = 1.3912.$$

Conclusion. As the calculated value of $| z | < 1.96$, the significant value of z at 5% level of significance, H_0 is accepted *i.e.*, there is no significant difference between mean scores.

ASSIGNMENT 8.4

1. Intelligence tests on two groups of boys and girls gave the following results. Examine if the difference is significant.

	Mean	*Standard Deviation*	*Size*
Girls	70	10	70
Boys	75	11	100

2. Two random samples of 1000 and 2000 farms gave an average yield of 2000 kg and 2050 kg, respectively. The variance of wheat farms in the country may be taken as 100 kg. Examine whether the two samples differ significantly in yield.
3. A sample of heights of 6400 soldiers has a mean of 67.85 inches and a standard deviation of 2.56 inches. While another sample of heights of 1600 sailors has a mean of 68.55 inches with standard deviation of 2.52 inches. Do the data indicate that sailors are, on the average, taller than soldiers?
4. In a survey of buying habits, 400 women shoppers are chosen at random in supermarket A. Their average weekly food expenditure is 250 with a standard deviation of 40. For 500 women shoppers chosen at supermarket B, the average weekly food expenditure is 220 with a standard deviation of 45. Test at 1% level of significance whether the average food expenditures of the two groups are equal.
5. A random sample of 200 measurements from a large population gave a mean value of 50 and standard deviation of 9. Determine the 95% confidence interval for the mean of the population.
6. The means of two large samples of 1000 and 2000 members are 168.75 cms and 170 cms, respectively. Can the samples be regarded as drawn from the same population of standard deviation 6.25 cms?

8.10.5 Test of Significance for the Difference of Standard Deviations

If s_1 and s_2 are the standard deviations of two independent samples, then under the null hypothesis H_0: $\sigma_1 = \sigma_2$, *i.e.*, the sample standard deviations don't differ significantly, the statistic

$$z = \frac{s_1 - s_2}{\sqrt{\frac{\sigma_1^2}{2n_1} + \frac{\sigma_2^2}{2n_2}}},$$ where σ_1 and σ_2 are population standard deviations.

When population standard deviations are not known, then $z = \frac{s_1 - s_2}{\sqrt{\frac{s_1^2}{2n_1} + \frac{s_2^2}{2n_2}}}$.

EXAMPLE

Example. *Random samples drawn from two countries gave the following data relating to the heights of adult males:*

	Country A	*Country B*
Mean height (in inches)	*67.42*	*67.25*
Standard deviation	*2.58*	*2.50*
Number in samples	*1000*	*1200*

(*i*) *Is the difference between the means significant?*

(*ii*) *Is the difference between the standard deviations significant?*

Sol. Given: $n_1 = 1000$, $n_2 = 1200$, $\bar{x}_1 = 67.42$; $\bar{x}_2 = 67.25$, $s_1 = 2.58$, $s_2 = 2.50$

Since the samples size are large we can take $\sigma_1 = s_1 = 2.58$; $\sigma_2 = s_2 = 2.50$.

(*i*) **Null hypothesis:** $H_0 = \mu_1 = \mu_2$ *i.e.*, sample means do not differ significantly.

Alternative hypothesis: H_1: $\mu_1 \neq \mu_2$ (two tailed test)

$$z = \frac{\bar{x}_1 - \bar{x}_2}{\sqrt{\frac{s_1^2}{n_1} + \frac{s_2^2}{n_2}}} = \frac{67.42 - 67.25}{\sqrt{\frac{(2.58)^2}{1000} + \frac{(2.50)^2}{1200}}} = 1.56.$$

Since $|z| < 1.96$ we accept the null hypothesis at 5% level of significance.

(*ii*) We set up the null hypothesis.

H_0: $\sigma_1 = \sigma_2$ *i.e.*, the sample standard deviations do not differ significantly.

Alternative hypothesis: $H_1 = \sigma_1 \neq \sigma_2$ (two tailed)

∴ The test statistic is given by

$$z = \frac{s_1 - s_2}{\sqrt{\frac{\sigma_1^2}{2n_1} + \frac{\sigma_2^2}{2n_2}}} = \frac{s_1 - s_2}{\sqrt{\frac{s_1^2}{2n_1} + \frac{s_2^2}{2n_2}}}$$

($\because$ $\sigma_1 = s_1$, $\sigma_2 = s_2$ for large samples)

$$= \frac{2.58 - 2.50}{\sqrt{\frac{(2.58)^2}{2 \times 1000} \times \frac{(2.50)^2}{2 \times 1200}}} = \frac{0.08}{\sqrt{\frac{6.6564}{2000} + \frac{6.25}{2400}}} = 1.0387.$$

Since $| z | < 1.96$ we accept the null hypothesis at 5% level of significance.

ASSIGNMENT 8.5

1. The mean yield of two sets of plots and their variability are as given. Examine
   (*i*) whether the difference in the mean yield of the two sets of plots is significant.
   (*ii*) whether the difference in the variability in yields is significant.

Set of 40 plots	*Set of 60 plots*	
Mean yield per plot	1258 lb	1243 lb
Standard deviation per plot	34	28

2. The yield of wheat in a random sample of 1000 farms in a certain area has a standard deviation of 192 kg. Another random sample of 1000 farms gives a standard deviation of 224 kg. Are the standard deviation significantly different ?

8.11 TEST OF SIGNIFICANCE OF SMALL SAMPLES

When the size of the sample is less than 30, then the sample is called small sample. For such sample it will not be possible for us to assume that the random sampling distribution of a statistic is approximately normal and the values given by the sample data are sufficiently close to the population values and can be used in their place for the calculation of the standard error of the estimate.

t-TEST

8.12 STUDENT'S t-DISTRIBUTION

This t-distribution is used when sample size is ≤ 30 and the population standard deviation is unknown.

t-statistic is defined as $t = \dfrac{\bar{x} - \mu}{s/\sqrt{n}} \sim t(n - 1\ d.f)$ d.f–degrees of freedom

where $$s = \sqrt{\frac{\Sigma(X - \overline{X})^2}{n - 1}}.$$

8.12.1 The t-Table

The t-table given at the end is the probability integral of t-distribution. The t-distribution has different values for each degrees of freedom and when the degrees of freedom are infinitely large, the t-distribution is equivalent to normal distribution and the probabilities shown in the normal distribution tables are applicable.

8.12.2 Applications of t-Distribution

Some of the applications of t-distribution are given below:

1. *To test if the sample mean* $(\overline{X})$ *differs significantly from the hypothetical value* μ *of the population mean.*
2. *To test the significance between two sample means.*
3. *To test the significance of observed partial and multiple correlation coefficients.*

8.12.3 Critical Value of t

The critical value or significant value of t at level of significance α degrees of freedom γ for two tailed test is given by

$$P[\,|\,t\,|\, > t_\gamma(\alpha)] = \alpha$$

$$P[\,|\,t\,|\, \leq t_\gamma(\alpha)] = 1 - \alpha$$

The significant value of t at level of significance α for a single tailed test can be determined from those of two-tailed test by referring to the values at 2α.

8.13 TEST I: t-TEST OF SIGNIFICANCE OF THE MEAN OF A RANDOM SAMPLE

To test whether the mean of a sample drawn from a normal population deviates significantly from a stated value when variance of the population is unknown.

H_0: There is no significant difference between the sample mean $\bar{x}$ and the population mean μ, *i.e.*, we use the statistic

$$t = \frac{\overline{X} - \mu}{s/\sqrt{n}} \qquad \text{where } \overline{X} \text{ is mean of the sample.}$$

$$s^2 = \frac{1}{n-1} \sum_{i=1}^{n} (X_i - \overline{X})^2 \text{ with degrees of freedom } (n - 1).$$

At a given level of significance α_1 and degrees of freedom $(n - 1)$. We refer to t-table t_α (two-tailed or one-tailed). If calculated t value is such that $|t| < t_\alpha$ the null hypothesis is accepted. $|t| > t_\alpha$, H_0 is rejected.

8.13.1 Fiducial Limits of Population Mean

If t_α is the table of t at level of significance α at $(n - 1)$ degrees of freedom.

$$\left| \frac{\overline{X} - \mu}{s/\sqrt{n}} \right| < t_\alpha \text{ for acceptance of } H_0.$$

$$\bar{x} - t_\alpha\, s/\sqrt{n} < \mu < \bar{x} + t_\alpha\, s/\sqrt{n}$$

95% confidence limits (level of significance 5%) are $\overline{X} \pm t_{0.05} s/\sqrt{n}$.

99% confidence limits (level of significance 1%) are $\overline{X} \pm t_{0.01} s/\sqrt{n}$.

NOTE *Instead of calculating s, we calculate S for the sample.*

Since $$s^2 = \frac{1}{n-1} \sum_{i=1}^{n} (X_i - \overline{X})^2$$

$\therefore$ $$S^2 = \frac{1}{n} \sum_{i=1}^{n} (X_i - \overline{X})^2. \qquad \mid \because (n-1)s^2 = nS^2$$

EXAMPLES

Example 1. *A random sample of size 16 has 53 as mean. The sum of squares of the derivation from mean is 135. Can this sample be regarded as taken from the population having 56 as mean? Obtain 95% and 99% confidence limits of the mean of the population.*

Sol. H_0: There is no significant difference between the sample mean and hypothetical population mean.

$$H_0: \mu = 56; \quad H_1: \mu \neq 56 \quad \text{(Two-tailed test)}$$

$$t: \frac{\overline{X} - \mu}{s/\sqrt{n}} \sim t(n-1 \text{ difference})$$

Given: $\overline{X} = 53, \mu = 56, n = 16, \Sigma(X - \overline{X})^2 = 135$

$$s = \sqrt{\frac{\Sigma(X-\overline{X})^2}{n-1}} = \sqrt{\frac{135}{15}} = 3; \; t = \frac{53-56}{3/\sqrt{16}} = -4$$

$$|t| = 4 \,.\, d.fv. = 16 - 1 = 15.$$

Conclusion. $t_{0.05} = 1.753$.

Since $|t| = 4 > t_{0.05} = 1.753$, the calculated value of t is more than the table value. The hypothesis is rejected. Hence, the sample mean has not come from a population having 56 as mean.

95% confidence limits of the population mean

$$= \overline{X} \pm \frac{s}{\sqrt{n}} t_{0.05} = 53 \pm \frac{3}{\sqrt{16}} (1.725) = 51.706; 54.293$$

99% confidence limits of the population mean

$$= \overline{X} \pm \frac{s}{\sqrt{n}} t_{0.01,} = 53 \pm \frac{3}{\sqrt{16}} (2.602) = 51.048; 54.951.$$

Example 2. *The lifetime of electric bulbs for a random sample of 10 from a large consignment gave the following data:*

Item	*1*	*2*	*3*	*4*	*5*	*6*	*7*	*8*	*9*	*10*
Life in '000' hrs.	*4.2*	*4.6*	*3.9*	*4.1*	*5.2*	*3.8*	*3.9*	*4.3*	*4.4*	*5.6*

Can we accept the hypothesis that the average lifetime of a bulb is 4000 hrs?

Sol. H_0: There is no significant difference in the sample mean and population mean. *i.e.,* $\mu = 4000$ hrs.

Applying the t-test: $t = \dfrac{\overline{X} - \mu}{s/\sqrt{n}} \sim t(10 - 1 \text{ difference})$

X	4.2	4.6	3.9	4.1	5.2	3.8	3.9	4.3	4.4	5.6
$X - \overline{X}$	– 0.2	0.2	– 0.5	– 0.3	0.8	– 0.6	– 0.5	– 0.1	0	1.2
$(X - \overline{X})^2$	0.04	0.04	0.25	0.09	0.64	0.36	0.25	0.01	0	1.44

$$\overline{X} = \frac{\Sigma X}{n} = \frac{44}{10} = 4.4 \qquad \Sigma(X - \overline{X})^2 = 3.12$$

$$s = \sqrt{\frac{\Sigma(X - \overline{X})^2}{n-1}} = \sqrt{\frac{3.12}{9}} = 0.589; \; t = \frac{4.4 - 4}{\frac{0.589}{\sqrt{10}}} = 2.123$$

For $\gamma = 9$, $t_{0.05} = 2.26$.

Conclusion. Since the calculated value of t is less than table $t_{0.05}$. $\therefore$ The hypothesis μ = 4000 hrs is accepted, *i.e.*, the average lifetime of bulbs could be 4000 hrs.

Example 3. *A sample of 20 items has mean 42 units and standard deviation 5 units. Test the hypothesis that it is a random sample from a normal population with mean 45 units.*

Sol. H_0: There is no significant difference between the sample mean and the population mean. *i.e.*, μ = 45 units

H_1: $\mu \neq 45$ (Two tailed test)

Given: $n = 20$, $\overline{X} = 42$, $S = 5$; $\gamma = 19$ difference

$$s^2 = \frac{n}{n-1} S^2 = \left[\frac{20}{20-1}\right](5)^2 = 26.31 \qquad \therefore s = 5.129$$

Applying t-test $\quad t = \dfrac{\overline{X} - \mu}{s/\sqrt{n}} = \dfrac{42 - 45}{5.129/\sqrt{20}} = -2.615; \; |\, t \,| = 2.615$

The tabulated value of t at 5% level for 19 d.f. is $t_{0.05} = 2.09$.

Conclusion. Since $|\, t \,| > t_{0.05}$, the hypothesis H_0 is rejected, *i.e.*, there is significant difference between the sample mean and population mean. *i.e.*, the sample could not have come from this population.

Example 4. *The 9 items of a sample have the following values 45, 47, 50, 52, 48, 47, 49, 53, 51. Does the mean of these values differ significantly from the assumed mean 47.5?*

Sol. $H_0: \mu = 47.5$

i.e., there is no significant difference between the sample and population mean.

$H_1: \mu \neq 47.5$ (two tailed test); Given: $n = 9$, $\mu = 47.5$

X	45	47	50	52	48	47	49	53	51
$X - \bar{X}$	– 4.1	– 2.1	0.9	2.9	– 1.1	– 2.1	– 0.1	3.9	1.9
$(X - \bar{X})^2$	16.81	4.41	0.81	8.41	1.21	4.41	0.01	15.21	3.61

$$\bar{X} = \frac{\Sigma x}{n} = \frac{442}{9} = 49.11;\ \Sigma(X - \bar{X})^2 = 54.89;\ s^2 = \frac{\Sigma(X - \bar{X})^2}{(n-1)} = 6.86$$

$$\therefore \qquad s = 2.619$$

Applying t-test
$$t = \frac{\bar{X} - \mu}{s/\sqrt{n}} = \frac{49.1 - 47.5}{2.619/\sqrt{8}} = \frac{(1.6)\sqrt{8}}{2.619} = 1.7279$$

$$t_{0.05} = 2.31 \text{ for } \gamma = 8.$$

Conclusion. Since $|\ t\ | < t_{0.05}$, the hypothesis is accepted *i.e.,* there is no significant difference between their mean.

ASSIGNMENT 8.6

1. Ten individuals are chosen at random from a normal population of students and their scores found to be 63, 63, 66, 67, 68, 69, 70, 70, 71, 71. In the light of these data discuss the suggestion that mean score of the population of students is 66.
2. The following values gives the lengths of 12 samples of Egyptian cotton taken from a consignment: 48, 46, 49, 46, 52, 45, 43, 47, 47, 46, 45, 50. Test if the mean length of the consignment can be taken as 46.
3. A sample of 18 items has a mean 24 units and standard deviation 3 units. Test the hypothesis that it is a random sample from a normal population with mean 27 units.
4. A filling machine is expected to fill 5 kg of powder into bags. A sample of 10 bags gave the following weights: 4.7, 4.9, 5.0, 5.1, 5.4, 5.2, 4.6, 5.1, 4.6, and 4.7. Test whether the machine is working properly.

8.14 TEST II: t-TEST FOR DIFFERENCE OF MEANS OF TWO SMALL SAMPLES (FROM A NORMAL POPULATION)

This test is used to test whether the two samples $x_1, x_2, \ldots\ldots, x_{n_1}, y_1, y_2, \ldots\ldots, y_{n_2}$ of sizes n_1, n_2 have been drawn from two normal populations with mean μ_1

and μ_2 respectively, under the assumption that the population variance are equal. ($\sigma_1 = \sigma_2 = \sigma$).

H_0: The samples have been drawn from the normal population with means μ_1 and μ_2, *i.e.*, H_0: $\mu_1 \neq \mu_2$.

Let $\overline{X}$, $\overline{Y}$ be their means of the two samples.

Under this H_0 the test of statistic t is given by

$$t = \frac{(\overline{X} - \overline{Y})}{s\sqrt{\frac{1}{n_1} + \frac{1}{n_2}}} \sim t(n_1 + n_2 - 2 \text{ difference})$$

NOTE **1.** *If the two sample's standard deviations s_1, s_2 are given, then we have*

$$s^2 = \frac{n_1 s_1^{\,2} + n_2 s_2^{\,2}}{n_1 + n_2 - 2}.$$

2. *If $n_1 = n_2 = n$, $t = \dfrac{\overline{X} - \overline{Y}}{\sqrt{\dfrac{s_1^{\,2} + s_2^{\,2}}{n - 1}}}$ can be used as a test statistic.*

3. *If the pairs of values are in some way associated (correlated) we can't use the test statistic as given in Note 2. In this case, we find the differences of the associated pairs of values and apply for single mean i.e., $t = \dfrac{\overline{X} - \mu}{s/\sqrt{n}}$ with degrees of freedom n – 1.*

The test statistic is

$$t = \frac{\overline{d}}{s/\sqrt{n}}$$

or $$t = \frac{\overline{d}}{s/\sqrt{n-1}},$$ where $\overline{d}$ is the mean of paired difference.

i.e., $d_i = x_i - y_i$

$\overline{d_i} = \overline{X} - \overline{Y}$, where (x_i, y_i) are the paired data $i = 1, 2, ..., n$.

EXAMPLES

Example 1. *Two samples of sodium vapor bulbs were tested for length of life and the following results were obtained:*

	Size	*Sample mean*	*Sample S.D.*
Type I	8	*1234 hrs*	*36 hrs*
Type II	7	*1036 hrs*	*40 hrs*

Is the difference in the means significant to generalize that Type I is superior to Type II regarding length of life?

Sol. $H_0: \mu_1 = \mu_2$ *i.e.,* two types of bulbs have same lifetime.

$H_1: \mu_1 > \mu_2$ *i.e.,* type I is superior to Type II.

$$s^2 = \frac{n_1 s_1^2 + n_2 s_2^2}{n_1 + n_2 - 2} = \frac{8(36)^2 + 7(40)^2}{8+7-2} = 1659.076$$

$$\therefore \quad s = 40.7317$$

The t-statistic
$$t = \frac{\overline{X}_1 - \overline{X}_2}{s\sqrt{\frac{1}{n_1} + \frac{1}{n_2}}} = \frac{1234 - 1036}{40.7317\sqrt{\frac{1}{8} + \frac{1}{7}}}$$

$$= 18.1480 \sim t(n_1 + n_2 - 2 \text{ difference})$$

$t_{0.05}$ at difference 13 is 1.77 (one tailed test).

Conclusion. Since calculated $| t | > t_{0.05}$, H_0 is rejected, *i.e.* H_1 is accepted.

$\therefore$ Type I is definitely superior to Type II.

where $\overline{X} = \sum_{i=1}^{n_1} \frac{X_i}{n_i}$, $\overline{Y} = \sum_{j=1}^{n_2} \frac{Y_j}{n_2}$; $s^2 = \frac{1}{n_1 + n_2 - 2}[\Sigma(X_i - \overline{X})^2 + (Y_j - \overline{Y})^2]$

is an unbiased estimate of the population variance σ^2.

t follows t-distribution with $n_1 + n_2 - 2$ degrees of freedom.

Example 2. *Samples of sizes 10 and 14 were taken from two normal populations with standard deviation 3.5 and 5.2. The sample means were found to be 20.3 and 18.6. Test whether the means of the two populations are the same at 5% level.*

Sol. $H_0: \mu_1 = \mu_2$ *i.e.,* the means of the two populations are the same.

$H_1 : \mu_1 \neq \mu_2$.

Given $\overline{X} = 20.3, \overline{X}_2 = 18.6; n_1 = 10, n_2 = 14, s_1 = 3.5, s_2 = 5.2$

$$s^2 = \frac{n_1 s_1^2 + n_2 s_2^2}{n_1 + n_2 - 2} = \frac{10(3.5)^2 + 14(5.2)^2}{10 + 14 - 2} = 22.775 \quad \therefore \quad s = 4.772$$

$$t = \frac{\overline{X}_1 - \overline{X}_2}{s\sqrt{\frac{1}{n_1} + \frac{1}{n_2}}} = \frac{20.3 - 18.6}{\left(\sqrt{\frac{1}{10} + \frac{1}{14}}\right) 4.772} = 0.8604$$

The value of t at 5% level for 22 difference is $t_{0.05} = 2.0739$.

Conclusion. Since $| t | = 0.8604 < t_{0.05}$ the hypothesis is accepted, *i.e.*, there is no significant difference between their means.

Example 3. *The height of 6 randomly chosen sailors in inches is 63, 65, 68, 69, 71, and 72. Those of 9 randomly chosen soldiers are 61, 62, 65, 66, 69, 70, 71, 72, and 73. Test whether the sailors are, on average, taller than soldiers.*

Sol. Let X_1 and X_2 be the two samples denoting the heights of sailors and soldiers.

Given the sample size $n_1 = 6$, $n_2 = 9$, $H_0: \mu_1 = \mu_2$,

i.e., the means of both populations are the same.

$H_1: \mu_1 > \mu_2$ (one tailed test)

Calculation of two sample means:

X_1	63	65	68	69	71	72
$X_1 - \overline{X}_1$	– 5	– 3	0	1	3	4
$(X_1 - \overline{X}_1)^2$	25	9	0	1	9	16

$$\overline{X}_1 = \frac{\Sigma X_1}{n_1} = 68; \ \Sigma(X_1 - \overline{X}_1)^2 = 60$$

X_2	61	62	65	66	69	70	71	72	73
$X_2 - \overline{X}_2$	– 6.66	– 5.66	– 2.66	1.66	1.34	2.34	3.34	4.34	5.34
$(X_2 - \overline{X}_2)^2$	44.36	32.035	7.0756	2.7556	1.7956	5.4756	11.1556	18.8356	28.5156

$$\overline{X}_2 = \frac{\Sigma X_2}{n_2} = 67.66; \ \Sigma(X_2 - \overline{X}_2)^2 = 152.0002$$

$$s^2 = \frac{1}{n_1 + n_2 - 2}[\Sigma(X_1 - \overline{X}_1)^2 + \Sigma(X_2 - \overline{X}_2)^2]$$

$$= \frac{1}{6+9-2}[60 + 152.0002] = 16.3077 \quad \therefore \quad s = 4.038$$

Under H_0, $t = \dfrac{\overline{X}_1 - \overline{X}_2}{s\sqrt{\dfrac{1}{n_1} + \dfrac{1}{n_2}}} = \dfrac{68 - 67.666}{4.0382\sqrt{\dfrac{1}{6} + \dfrac{1}{9}}}$

$$= 0.3031 \sim t(n_1 + n_2 - 2 \text{ difference})$$

The value of t at 10% level of significance ($\because$ the test is one-tailed) for 13 difference is 1.77.

Conclusion. Since $| t | = 0.3031 < t_{0.05} = 1.77$, the hypothesis H_0 is accepted.

There is no significan difference between their average.

The sailors are not, on average, taller than the soldiers.

Example 4. *A certain stimulus administered to each of 12 patients resulted in the following increase in blood pressure: 5, 2, 8, – 1, 3, 0, – 2, 1, 5, 0, 4, 6. Can it be concluded that the stimulus will in general be accompanied by an increase in blood pressure?*

Sol. To test whether the mean increase in blood pressure of all patients to whom the stimulus is administered will be positive, we have to assume that this population is normal with mean μ and standard deviation σ which are unknown.

H_0: $\mu = 0$; H_1: $\mu_1 > 0$

The test statistic under H_0

$$t = \frac{\overline{d}}{s/\sqrt{n-1}} \sim t(n - 1 \text{ degrees of freedom})$$

$$\overline{d} = \frac{5+2+8+(-1)+3+0+6+(-2)+1+5+0+4}{12} = 2.583$$

$$s^2 = \frac{\Sigma d^2}{n} - \overline{d}^2 = \frac{1}{12}[5^2 + 2^2 + 8^2 + (-1)^2 + 3^2 + 0^2 + 6^2 + (-2)^2 + 1^2 + 5^2 + 0^2 + 4^2] - (2.583)^2$$

$$= 8.744 \quad \therefore \quad s = 2.9571$$

$$t = \frac{\overline{d}}{s/\sqrt{n-1}} = \frac{2.583}{2.9571/\sqrt{12-1}} = \frac{2.583\sqrt{11}}{2.9571}$$

$$= 2.897 \sim t(n - 1 \text{ difference})$$

Conclusion. The tabulated value of $t_{0.05}$ at 11 difference is 2.2.

$\because \quad |t| > t_{0.05}$, H_0 is rejected.

i.e., the stimulus does not increase the blood pressure. The stimulus in general will be accompanied by an increase in blood pressure.

Example 5. *Memory capacity of 9 students was tested before and after a course of meditation for a month. State whether the course was effective or not from the data below (in same units):*

Before	*10*	*15*	*9*	*3*	*7*	*12*	*16*	*17*	*4*
After	*12*	*17*	*8*	*5*	*6*	*11*	*18*	*20*	*3*

Sol. Since the data are correlated and concerned with the same set of students we use paired t-test.

H_0: Training was not effective $\mu_1 = \mu_2$

H_1: $\mu_1 \neq \mu_2$ (Two-tailed test).

Before training (X)	*After training (Y)*	$d = X - Y$	d^2
10	12	− 2	4
15	17	− 2	4
9	8	1	1
3	5	− 2	4
7	6	1	1
12	11	1	1
16	18	− 2	4
17	20	− 3	9
4	3	1	1
		$\Sigma d = -7$	$\Sigma d^2 = 29$

$$\bar{d} = \frac{\Sigma d}{n} = \frac{-7}{9} = -0.7778;\ s^2 = \frac{\Sigma d^2}{n} - (\bar{d})^2 = \frac{29}{9} - (-0.7778)^2 = 2.617$$

$$t = \frac{\bar{d}}{s/\sqrt{n-1}} = \frac{-0.7778}{\sqrt{2.6172/\sqrt{8}}} = \frac{-0.7778 \times \sqrt{8}}{1.6177} = -1.359$$

The tabulated value of $t_{0.05}$ at 8 difference is 2.31.

Conclusion. Since $|t| = 1.359 < t_{0.05}$, H_0 is accepted, training was not effective in improving performance.

Example 6. *The following figures refer to observations in live independent samples:*

Sample I	25	30	28	34	24	20	13	32	22	38
Sample II	40	34	22	20	31	40	30	23	36	17

Analyse whether the samples have been drawn from the populations of equal means.

Sol. H_0: The two samples have been drawn from the population of equal means, *i.e.*, there is no significant difference between their means

i.e., $\mu_1 = \mu_2$

H_1: $\mu_1 \neq \mu_2$ (Two tailed test)

Given n_1 = Sample I size = 10 ; n_2 = Sample II size = 10

To calculate the two sample mean and sum of squares of deviation from mean. Let X_1 be the Sample I and X_2 be the Sample II.

X_1	25	30	28	34	24	20	13	32	22	38
$X_1 - \overline{X}_1$	– 1.6	3.4	1.4	7.4	– 2.6	– 6.6	– 13.6	5.4	4.6	11.4
$(X_1 - \overline{X}_1)^2$	2.56	11.56	1.96	54.76	6.76	43.56	184.96	29.16	21.16	129.96
X_2	40	34	22	20	31	40	30	23	36	17
$X_2 - \overline{X}_2$	10.7	4.7	– 7.3	– 9.3	1.7	10.7	0.7	– 6.3	6.7	– 12.3
$(X_2 - \overline{X}_2)^2$	114.49	22.09	53.29	86.49	2.89	114.49	0.49	39.67	44.89	151.29

$$\overline{X}_1 = \sum_{i=1}^{10} \frac{X_1}{n_1} = 26.6 \qquad \overline{X}_2 = \sum_{i=1}^{10} \frac{X_2}{n_2} = \frac{293}{10} = 29.3$$

$$\Sigma(X_1 - \overline{X}_1)^2 = 486.4 \qquad \Sigma(X_2 - \overline{X}_2)^2 = 630.08$$

$$s^2 = \frac{1}{n_1 + n_2 - 2}[\Sigma(X_1 - \overline{X}_1)^2 + \Sigma(X_2 - \overline{X}_2)^2]$$

$$= \frac{1}{10 + 10 - 2}[486.4 + 630.08] = 62.026$$

$$\therefore \quad s = 7.875$$

Under H_0 the test statistic is given by

$$t = \frac{\overline{X}_1 - \overline{X}_2}{s\sqrt{\frac{1}{n_1} + \frac{1}{n_2}}} = \frac{26.6 - 29.3}{7.875\sqrt{\frac{1}{10} + \frac{1}{10}}} = -\,0.7666 \sim t(n_1 + n_2 - 2 \text{ difference})$$

$| t | = 0.7666.$

Conclusion. The tabulated value of t at 5% level of significance for 18 difference is 2.1. Since the calculated value $| t | = 0.7666 < t_{0.05}$, H_0 is accepted. There is no significant difference between their means.

The two samples have been drawn from the populations of equal means.

ASSIGNMENT 8.7

1. The mean life of 10 electric motors was found to be 1450 hrs with a standard deviation of 423 hrs. A second sample of 17 motors chosen from a different batch showed a mean life of 1280 hrs with a standard deviation of 398 hrs. Is there a significant difference between means of the two samples ?
2. The scores obtained by a group of 9 regular course students and another group of 11 part time course students in a test are given below:

Regular:	56	62	63	54	60	51	67	69	58		
Part time:	62	70	71	62	60	56	75	64	72	68	66

Examine whether the scores obtained by regular students and part time students differ significantly at 5% and 1% level of significance.

3. A group of 10 boys fed on diet A and another group of 8 boys fed on a different diet B recorded the following increase in weight (kgs):

Diet A:	5	6	8	1	12	4	3	9	6	10
Diet B:	2	3	6	8	10	1	2	8		

Does it show the superiority of diet A over the diet B?

4. Two independent samples of sizes 7 and 9 have the following values:

Sample A:	10	12	10	13	14	11	10		
Sample B:	10	13	15	12	10	14	11	12	11

Test whether the difference between the means is significant.

5. To compare the prices of a certain product in two cities, 10 shops were visited at random in each city. The price was noted below:

City 1:	61	63	56	63	56	63	59	56	44	61
City 2:	55	54	47	59	51	61	57	54	64	58

Test whether the average prices can be said to be the same in two cities.

6. The average number of articles produced by two machines per day are 200 and 250 with standard deviation 20 and 25 respectively on the basis of records of 25 days production. Are both machines equally efficient at 5% level of significance?

8.15 SNEDECOR'S VARIANCE RATIO TEST OR F-TEST

In testing the significance of the difference of two means of two samples, we assumed that the two samples came from the same population or populations with equal variance. The object of the F-test is to discover whether two independent estimates of population variance differ significantly or whether the two samples may be regarded as drawn from the normal populations having the same variance. Hence before applying the t-test for the significance of the difference of two means, we have to test for the equality of population variance by using the F-test.

Let n_1 and n_2 be the sizes of two samples with variance s_1^2 and s_2^2. The estimate of the population variance based on these samples is $s_1^2 = \frac{n_1 s_1^2}{n_1 - 1}$ and $s_2^2 = \frac{n_2 s_2^2}{n_2 - 1}$. The degrees of freedom of these estimates are $\nu_1 = n_1 - 1$, $\nu_2 = n_2 - 1$.

To test whether these estimates, s_1^2 and s_2^2, are significantly different or if the samples may be regarded as drawn from the same population or from two populations with same variance σ^2, we set-up the null hypothesis

$$H_0: \sigma_1^2 = \sigma_2^2 = \sigma^2,$$

i.e., the independent estimates of the common population do not differ significantly.

To carry out the test of significance of the difference of the variances we calculate the test statistic $F = \frac{s_1^2}{s_2^2}$, the Numerator is greater than the Denominator, *i.e.*, $s_1^2 > s_2^2$.

Conclusion. If the calculated value of F exceeds $F_{0.05}$ for $(n_1 - 1), (n_2 - 1)$ degrees of freedom given in the table, we conclude that the ratio is significant at 5% level.

We conclude that the sample could have come from two normal population with same variance.

The assumptions on which the F-test is based are:

1. *The populations for each sample must be normally distributed.*
2. *The samples must be random and independent.*

3. *The ratio of σ_1^2 to σ_2^2 should be equal to 1 or greater than 1. That is why we take the larger variance in the Numerator of the ratio.*

Applications. *F-test is used to test*

(*i*) *whether two independent samples have been drawn from the normal populations with the same variance σ^2.*

(*ii*) *Whether the two independent estimates of the population variance are homogeneous or not.*

EXAMPLES

Example 1. *Two random samples drawn from 2 normal populations are as follows:*

A	17	27	18	25	27	29	13	17
B	16	16	20	27	26	25	21	

Test whether the samples are drawn from the same normal population.

Sol. To test if two independent samples have been drawn from the same population we have to test (*i*) equality of the means by applying the *t*-test and (*ii*) equality of population variance by applying F-test.

Since the *t*-test assumes that the sample variances are equal, we shall first apply the F-test.

F-test. 1. Null hypothesis H_0: $\sigma_1^2 = \sigma_2^2$ *i.e.*, the population variance do not differ significantly.

Alternative hypothesis. $H_1: \sigma_1^2 \neq \sigma_2^2$

Test statistic: $F = \dfrac{s_1^2}{s_2^2}$, (if $s_1^2 > s_2^2$)

Computations for s_1^2 and s_2^2

X_1	$X_1 - \overline{X}_1$	$(X_1 - \overline{X}_1)^2$	X_2	$X_2 - \overline{X}_2$	$(X_2 - \overline{X}_2)^2$
17	– 4.625	21.39	16	– 2.714	7.365
27	5.735	28.89	16	– 2.714	7.365
18	– 3.625	13.14	20	1.286	1.653
25	3.375	11.39	27	8.286	68.657
27	5.735	28.89	26	7.286	53.085
29	7.735	54.39	25	6.286	39.513
13	– 8.625	74.39	21	2.286	5.226
17	– 4.625	21.39			

$$\overline{X}_1 = 21.625;\ n_1 = 8;\ \Sigma(X_1 - \overline{X}_1)^2 = 253.87$$

$$\overline{X}_2 = 18.714;\ n_2 = 7;\ \Sigma(X_2 - \overline{X}_2)^2 = 182.859$$

$$s_1^2 = \frac{\Sigma(X_1 - \overline{X}_1)^2}{n_1 - 1} = \frac{253.87}{7} = 36.267;$$

$$s_2^2 = \frac{\Sigma(X_2 - \overline{X}_2)^2}{n_2 - 1} = \frac{182.859}{6} = 30.47$$

$$F = \frac{s_1^2}{s_2^2} = \frac{36.267}{30.47} = 1.190.$$

Conclusion. The table value of F for $\nu_1 = 7$ and $\nu_2 = 6$ degrees of freedom at 5% level is 4.21. The calculated value of F is less than the tabulated value of F. $\therefore$ H_0 is accepted. Hence we conclude that the variability in two populations is same.

t-test: Null hypothesis. H_0: $\mu_1 = \mu_2$ *i.e.,* the population means are equal.

Alternative hypothesis. H_1: $\mu_1 \neq \mu_2$

Test of statistic

$$s^2 = \frac{\Sigma(X_1 - \overline{X}_1)^2 + \Sigma(X_2 - \overline{X}_2)^2}{n_1 + n_2 - 2} = \frac{253.87 + 182.859}{8 + 7 - 2} = 33.594$$

$$\therefore \quad s = 5.796$$

$$t = \frac{\overline{X}_1 - \overline{X}_2}{s\sqrt{\frac{1}{n_1} + \frac{1}{n_2}}} = \frac{21.625 - 18.714}{5.796\sqrt{\frac{1}{8} + \frac{1}{7}}} = 0.9704 \sim t(n_1 + n_2 - 2) \text{ difference}$$

Conclusion. The tabulated value of t at 5% level of significance for 13 difference is 2.16.

The calculated value of t is less than the tabulated value. H_0 is accepted, *i.e.,* there is no significant difference between the population mean. *i.e.,* $\mu_1 = \mu_2$. $\therefore$ We conclude that the two samples have been drawn from the same normal population.

Example 2. *Two independent sample of sizes 7 and 6 had the following values:*

Sample A	28	30	32	33	31	29	34
Sample B	29	30	30	24	27	28	

Examine whether the samples have been drawn from normal populations having the same variance.

Sol. H_0: The variance are equal. *i.e.*, $\sigma_1^2 = \sigma_2^2$
i.e., the samples have been drawn from normal populations with same variance.

$$H_1: \sigma_1^2 \neq \sigma_2^2$$

Under null hypothesis, the test statistic $F = \dfrac{s_1^2}{s_2^2} (s_1^2 > s_2^2)$

Computations for s_1^2 and s_2^2

X_1	$X_1 - \overline{X}_1$	$(X_1 - \overline{X}_1)^2$	X_2	$X_2 - \overline{X}_2$	$(X_2 - \overline{X}_2)^2$
28	– 3	9	29	1	1
30	– 1	1	30	2	4
32	1	1	30	2	4
33	2	4	24	– 4	16
31	0	0	27	– 1	1
29	– 2	4	28	0	0
34	3	9			
		28			26

$$\overline{X}_1 = 31, \quad n_1 = 7; \quad \Sigma(X_1 - \overline{X}_1)^2 = 28$$

$$\overline{X}_2 = 28, \quad n_2 = 6; \quad \Sigma(X_2 - \overline{X}_2)^2 = 26$$

$$s_1^2 = \frac{\Sigma(X_1 - \overline{X}_1)^2}{n_1 - 1} = \frac{28}{6} = 4.666; \quad s_2^2 = \frac{\Sigma(X_2 - \overline{X}_2)^2}{n_2 - 1} = \frac{26}{5} = 5.2$$

$$F = \frac{s_2^2}{s_1^2} = \frac{5.2}{4.666} = 1.1158. \qquad (\because \; s_2^2 > s_1^2)$$

Conclusion. The tabulated value of F at $v_1 = 6 - 1$ and $v_2 = 7 - 1$ difference for 5% level of significance is 4.39. Since the tabulated value of F is less than the calculated value, H_0 is accepted, *i.e.*, there is no significant difference between the variance. The samples have been drawn from the normal population with same variance.

Example 3. *The two random samples reveal the following data:*

Sample number	*Size*	*Mean*	*Variance*
I	*16*	*440*	*40*
II	*25*	*460*	*42*

Test whether the samples come from the same normal population.

Sol. A normal population has two parameters namely the mean μ and the variance σ^2. To test whether the two independent samples have been drawn from the same normal population, we have to test

(*i*) the equality of means (*ii*) the equality of variance.

Since the *t*-test assumes that the sample variance are equal, we first apply F-test.

F-test: Null hypothesis. $\sigma_1^2 = \sigma_2^2$

The population variance do not differ significantly.

Alternative hypothesis. $\sigma_1^2 \neq \sigma_2^2$

Under the null hypothesis the test statistic is given by $F = \frac{s_1^2}{s_2^2}, (s_1^2 > s_2^2)$

Given: $n_1 = 16, n_2 = 25; s_1^2 = 40, s_2^2 = 42$

$$\therefore \quad F = \frac{s_1^2}{s_2^2} = \frac{\frac{n_1 s_1^2}{n_1 - 1}}{\frac{n_2 s_2^2}{n_2 - 1}} = \frac{16 \times 40}{15} \times \frac{24}{25 \times 42} = 0.9752.$$

Conclusion. The calculated value of F is 0.9752. The tabulated value of F at 16 – 1, 25 – 1 difference for 5% level of significance is 2.11.

Since the calculated value is less than that of the tabulated value, H_0 is accepted, the population variance are equal.

t-test: Null hypothesis. $H_0: \mu_1 = \mu_2$ *i.e.*, the population means are equal.

Alternative hypothesis. $H_1: \mu_1 \neq \mu_2$

Given: $n_1 = 16, n_2 = 25, \overline{X}_1 = 440, \overline{X}_2 = 460$

$$s^2 = \frac{n_1 s_1^2 + n_2 s_2^2}{n_1 + n_2 - 2} = \frac{16 \times 40 + 25 \times 42}{16 + 25 - 2} = 43.333$$

$$\therefore \quad s = 6.582$$

$$t = \frac{\overline{X}_1 - \overline{X}_2}{s\sqrt{\frac{1}{n_1} + \frac{1}{n_2}}} = \frac{440 - 460}{6.582\sqrt{\frac{1}{16} + \frac{1}{25}}}$$

$$= -9.490 \text{ for } (n_1 + n_2 - 2) \text{ difference}$$

Conclusion. The calculated value of $| t |$ is 9.490. The tabulated value of *t* at 39 difference for 5% level of significance is 1.96.

Since the calculated value is greater than the tabulated value, H_0 is rejected, *i.e.*, there is significant difference between means. *i.e.*, $\mu_1 \neq \mu_2$.

Since there is significant difference between means, and no significant difference between variance, we conclude that the samples do not come from the same normal population.

ASSIGNMENT 8.8

1. From the following two sample values, find out whether they have come from the same population:

Sample 1	17	27	18	25	27	29	27	23	17
Sample 2	16	16	20	16	20	17	15	21	

2. The daily wages in Rupees of skilled workers in two cities are as follows:

	Size of sample of workers	*Standard deviation of wages in the sample*
City A	16	25
City B	13	32

3. The standard deviation calculated from two random samples of sizes 9 and 13 are 2.1 and 1.8 respectively. Can the samples be regarded as drawn from normal populations with the same standard deviation?
4. Two independent samples of size 8 and 9 had the following values of the variables:

Sample I	20	30	23	25	21	22	23	24	
Sample II	30	31	32	34	35	29	28	27	26

Do the estimates of the population variance differ significantly?

8.16 CHI-SQUARE (χ^2) TEST

When a coin is tossed 200 times, the theoretical considerations lead us to expect 100 heads and 100 tails. But in practice, these results are rarely achieved. The quantity χ^2 (a Greek letter, pronounced as chi-square) describes the magnitude of discrepancy between theory and observation. If $\chi = 0$, the observed and expected frequencies completely coincide. The greater the discrepancy between the observed and expected frequencies, the greater is the value of χ^2. Thus χ^2 **affords a measure of the correspondence between theory and observation.**

If O_i ($i = 1, 2, ..., n$) is a set of observed (experimental) frequencies and E_i ($i = 1, 2, ..., n$) is the corresponding set of expected (theoretical or hypothetical) frequencies, then, χ^2 **is defined as**

$$\chi^2 = \sum_{i=1}^{n} \left[\frac{(O_i - E_i)^2}{E_i} \right]$$

where $\Sigma O_i = \Sigma E_i = N$ (total frequency) and degrees of freedom (difference) $= (n - 1)$.

NOTE *(i) If $\chi^2 = 0$, the observed and theoretical frequencies agree exactly.*

(ii) If $\chi^2 > 0$ they do not agree exactly.

8.16.1 Degrees of Freedom

While comparing the calculated value of χ^2 with the table value, we have to determine the degrees of freedom.

If we have to choose any four numbers whose sum is 50, we can exercise our independent choice for any three numbers only, the fourth being 50 minus the total of the three numbers selected. Thus, though we were to choose any four numbers, our choice was reduced to three because of one condition imposed. There was only one restraint on our freedom and our degrees of freedom were $4 - 1 = 3$. If two restrictions are imposed, our freedom to choose will be further curtailed and degrees of freedom will be $4 - 2 = 2$.

In general, the number of degrees of freedom is the total number of observations less the number of independent constraints imposed on the observations. Degrees of freedom (difference) are usually denoted by ν (the letter 'nu' of the Greek alphabet).

Thus, $\nu = n - k$, where k is the number of independent constraints in a set of data of n observations.

NOTE *(i) For a $p \times q$ contingency table (p columns and q rows), $\nu = (p - 1)(q - 1)$*

(ii) In the case of a contingency table, the expected frequency of any class

$$= \frac{\text{Total of rows in which it occurs} \times \text{Total of columns in which it occurs}}{\text{Total number of observations}}$$

8.16.2 Applications

χ^2 test is one of the simplest and the most general test known. It is applicable to a very large number of problems in practice which can be summed up under the following heads:

(*i*) as a test of goodness of fit.

(*ii*) as a test of independence of attributes.

(*iii*) as a test of homogeneity of independent estimates of the population variance.

(*iv*) as a test of the hypothetical value of the population variance s^2.

(*v*) as a list to the homogeneity of independent estimates of the population correlation coefficient.

8.16.3 Conditions for Applying χ^2 Test

Following are the conditions which should be satisfied before χ^2 test can be applied:

(*a*) N, the total number of frequencies should be large. It is difficult to say what constitutes largeness, but as an arbitrary figure, we may say that **N should be atleast 50,** however small the number of cells.

(*b*) No theoretical cell-frequency should be small. Here again, it is difficult to say what constitutes smallness, but 5 should be regarded as the very minimum and **10 is better.** If small theoretical frequencies occur (*i.e.*, < 10), the difficulty is overcome by grouping two or more classes together before calculating (O – E). **It is important to remember that the number of degrees of freedom is determined with the number of classes after regrouping.**

(*c*) The constraints on the cell frequencies, if any, should be linear.

NOTE *If any one of the theoretical frequency is less than 5, then we apply a corrected given by F Yates, which is usually known as 'Yates correction for continuity', we add 0.5 to the cell frequency which is less than 5 and adjust the remaining cell frequency suitably so that the marginal total is not changed.*

8.17 THE χ^2 DISTRIBUTION

For large sample sizes, the sampling distribution of χ^2 can be closely approximated by a continuous curve known as the chi-square distribution. The probability function of χ^2 distribution is given by

$$f(\chi^2) = c(\chi^2)^{(\nu/2-1)}\, e^{-x^2/2}$$

where e = 2.71828, ν = number of degrees of freedom; c = a constant depending only on ν.

Symbolically, the degrees of freedom are denoted by the symbol ν or by difference and are obtained by the rule $\nu = n - k$, where k refers to the number of independent constraints.

In general, when we fit a binomial distribution the number of degrees of freedom is one less than the number of classes; when we fit a Poisson distribution the degrees of freedom are 2 less than the number of classes, because we use the total frequency and the arithmetic mean to get the parameter of the Poisson distribution. When we fit a normal curve the number of degrees of freedom are 3 less than the number of classes, because in this fitting we use the total frequency, mean and standard deviation.

If the data is given in a series of "n" numbers then degrees of freedom

$= n - 1.$

In the case of Binomial distribution difference $= n - 1$

In the case of Poisson distribution difference $= n - 2$

In the case of Normal distribution difference $= n - 3.$

8.18 χ^2 TEST AS A TEST OF GOODNESS OF FIT

χ^2 test enables us to ascertain how well the theoretical distributions such as Binomial, Poisson or Normal etc. fit empirical distributions, *i.e.*, distributions obtained from sample data. If the **calculated value of χ^2 is less than the table value** at a specified level (generally 5%) of significance, the **fit is considered to be good,** *i.e.*, the divergence between actual and expected frequencies is attributed to fluctuations of simple sampling. If the calculated value of χ^2 is greater than the table value, the fit is considered to be poor.

EXAMPLES

Example 1. *The following table gives the number of accidents that took place in an industry during various days of the week. Test if accidents are uniformly distributed over the week.*

Day	*Mon*	*Tue*	*Wed*	*Thu*	*Fri*	*Sat*
Number of accidents	*14*	*18*	*12*	*11*	*15*	*14*

Sol. Null hypothesis H_0: The accidents are uniformly distributed over the week.

Under this H_0, the expected frequencies of the accidents on each of these days $= \frac{84}{6} = 14$

Observed frequency O_i	14	18	12	11	15	14
Expected frequency E_i	14	14	14	14	14	14
$(O_i - E_i)^2$	0	16	4	9	1	0

$$\chi^2 = \frac{\Sigma(O_i - E_i)^2}{E_i} = \frac{30}{14} = 2.1428.$$

Conclusion. Table value of χ^2 at 5% level for (6 – 1 = 5 d.f.) is 11.09.

Since the calculated value of χ^2 is less than the tabulated value, H_0 is accepted, the accidents are uniformly distributed over the week.

Example 2. *A die is thrown 270 times and the results of these throws are given below*:

Number appeared on the die	*1*	*2*	*3*	*4*	*5*	*6*
Frequency	*40*	*32*	*29*	*59*	*57*	*59*

Test whether the die is biased or not.

Sol. Null hypothesis H_0: Die is unbiased.

Under this H_0, the expected frequencies for each digit is $\frac{276}{6} = 46$.

To find the value of χ^2

O_i	40	32	29	59	57	59
E_i	46	46	46	46	46	46
$(O_i - E_i)^2$	36	196	289	169	121	169

$$\chi^2 = \frac{\Sigma(O_i - E_i)^2}{E_i} = \frac{980}{46} = 21.30.$$

Conclusion. Tabulated value of χ^2 at 5% level of significance for (6 – 1 = 5) d.f. is 11.09. Since the calculated value of χ^2 = 21.30 > 11.07 the tabulated value, H_0 is rejected.

i.e., die is not unbiased or die is biased.

Example 3. *The following table shows the distribution of digits in numbers chosen at random from a telephone directory:*

Digits	*0*	*1*	*2*	*3*	*4*	*5*	*6*	*7*	*8*	*9*
Frequency	*1026*	*1107*	*997*	*966*	*1075*	*933*	*1107*	*972*	*964*	*853*

Test whether the digits may be taken to occur equally frequently in the directory.

Sol. Null hypothesis H_0: The digits taken in the directory occur equally frequently.

i.e., there is no significant difference between the observed and expected frequency.

Under H_0, the expected frequency is given by $= \dfrac{10{,}000}{10} = 1000$

To find the value of χ^2

O_i	1026	1107	997	996	1075	1107	933	972	964	853
E_i	1000	1000	1000	1000	1000	1000	1107	1000	1000	1000
$(O_i - E_i)^2$	676	11449	9	1156	5625	11449	4489	784	1296	21609

$$\chi^2 = \frac{\Sigma(O_i - E_i)^2}{E_i} = \frac{58542}{1000} = 58.542.$$

Conclusion. The tabulated value of χ^2 at 5% level of significance for 9 difference is 16.919. Since the calculated value of χ^2 is greater than the tabulated value, H_0 is rejected.

There is significant difference between the observed and theoretical frequency.

The digits taken in the directory do not occur equally frequently.

Example 4. *Records taken of the number of male and female births in 800 families having four children are as follows:*

Number of male births	*0*	*1*	*2*	*3*	*4*
Number of female births	*4*	*3*	*2*	*1*	*0*
Number of families	*32*	*178*	*290*	*236*	*94*

Test whether the data are consistent with the hypothesis that the Binomial law holds and the chance of male birth is equal to that of female birth, namely $p = q = 1/2$.

Sol. H_0: The data are consistent with the hypothesis of equal probability for male and female births, *i.e.*, $p = q = 1/2$.

We use Binomial distribution to calculate theoretical frequency given by:

$$N(r) = N \times P(X = r)$$

where N is the total frequency. N(r) is the number of families with r male children:

$$P(X = r) = {}^nC_r p^r q^{n-r}$$

where p and q are probability of male and female births, n is the number of children.

$$N(0) = \text{Number of families with 0 male children} = 800 \times {}^4C_0 \left(\frac{1}{2}\right)^4$$

$$= 800 \times 1 \times \frac{1}{2^4} = 50$$

$$N(1) = 800 \times {}^4C_1 \left(\frac{1}{2}\right)^1 \left(\frac{1}{2}\right)^3 = 200; \; N(2) = 800 \times {}^4C_2 \left(\frac{1}{2}\right)^2 \left(\frac{1}{2}\right)^2$$

$$= 300$$

$$N(3) = 800 \times {}^4C_3 \left(\frac{1}{2}\right)^1 \left(\frac{1}{2}\right)^3 = 200; \; N(4) = 800 \times {}^4C_4 \left(\frac{1}{2}\right)^0 \left(\frac{1}{2}\right)^4$$

$$= 50$$

Observed frequency O_i	32	178	290	236	94
Expected frequency E_i	50	200	300	200	50
$(O_i - E_i)^2$	324	484	100	1296	1936
$\frac{(O_i - E_i)^2}{E_i}$	6.48	2.42	0.333	6.48	38.72

$$\chi^2 = \frac{\Sigma(O_i - E_i)^2}{E_i} = 54.433.$$

Conclusion. Table value of χ^2 at 5% level of significance for 5 – 1 = 4 difference is 9.49.

Since the calculated value of χ^2 is greater than the tabulated value, H_0 is rejected.

The data are not consistent with the hypothesis that the Binomial law holds and that the chance of a male birth is not equal to that of a female birth.

NOTE *Since the fitting is Binomial, the degrees of freedom*

$$\nu = n - 1 \text{ i.e., } \nu = 5 - 1 = 4.$$

Example 5. *Verify whether Poisson distribution can be assumed from the data given below:*

Number of defects	*0*	*1*	*2*	*3*	*4*	*5*
Frequency	*6*	*13*	*13*	*8*	*4*	*3*

Sol. H_0: Poisson fit is a good fit to the data.

Mean of the given distribution $= \dfrac{\Sigma f_i x_i}{\Sigma f_i} = \dfrac{94}{47} = 2$

To fit a Poisson distribution we require m. Parameter $m = \bar{x} = 2$.

By Poisson distribution the frequency of r success is

$$N(r) = N \times e^{-m} \cdot \frac{m^r}{r!}, \text{ N is the total frequency.}$$

$$N(0) = 47 \times e^{-2} \cdot \frac{(2)^0}{0!} = 6.36 \approx 6; \; N(1) = 47 \times e^{-2} \cdot \frac{(2)^1}{1!} = 12.72 \approx 13$$

$$N(2) = 47 \times e^{-2} \cdot \frac{(2)^2}{2!} = 12.72 \approx 13; \; N(3) = 47 \times e^{-2} \cdot \frac{(2)^3}{3!} = 8.48 \approx 9$$

$$N(4) = 47 \times e^{-2} \cdot \frac{(2)^4}{4!} = 4.24 \approx 4; \; N(5) = 47 \times e^{-2} \cdot \frac{(2)^5}{5!} = 1.696 \approx 2.$$

X	0	1	2	3	4	5
O_i	6	13	13	8	4	3
E_i	6.36	12.72	12.72	8.48	4.24	1.696
$\dfrac{(O_i - E_i)^2}{E_i}$	0.2037	0.00616	0.00616	0.02716	0.0135	1.0026

$$\chi^2 = \frac{\Sigma(O_i - E_i)^2}{E_i} = 1.2864.$$

Conclusion. The calculated value of χ^2 is 1.2864. Tabulated value of χ^2 at 5% level of significance for $\gamma = 6 - 2 = 4$ d.f. is 9.49. Since the calculated value of χ^2 is less than that of tabulated value. H_0 is accepted *i.e.,* Poisson distribution provides a good fit to the data.

Example 6. *The theory predicts the proportion of beans in the four groups, G_1, G_2, G_3, G_4 should be in the ratio 9: 3: 3: 1. In an experiment with 1600 beans the numbers in the four groups were 882, 313, 287 and 118. Does the experimental result support the theory.*

Sol. H_0: The experimental result support the theory. *i.e.,* there is no significant difference between the observed and theoretical frequency under H_0, the theoretical frequency can be calculated as follows:

$$E(G_1) = \frac{1600 \times 9}{16} = 900; \; E(G_2) = \frac{1600 \times 3}{16} = 300;$$

$$E(G_3) = \frac{1600 \times 3}{16} = 300; \; E(G_4) = \frac{1600 \times 1}{16} = 100$$

To calculate the value of χ^2.

Observed frequency O_i	882	313	287	118
Expected frequency E_i	900	300	300	100
$\frac{(O_i - E_i)^2}{E_i}$	0.36	0.5633	0.5633	3.24

$$\chi^2 = \frac{\Sigma(O_i - E_i)^2}{E_i} = 4.7266.$$

Conclusion. The table value of χ^2 at 5% level of significance for 3 difference is 7.815. Since the calculated value of χ^2 is less than that of the tabulated value. Hence H_0 is accepted and the experimental results support the theory.

ASSIGNMENT 8.9

1. The following table gives the frequency of occupance of the digits 0, 1, ..., 9 in the last place in four logarithm of numbers 10–99. Examine if there is any peculiarity.

Digits:	0	1	2	3	4	5	6	7	8	9
Frequency:	6	16	15	10	12	12	3	2	9	5

2. The sales in a supermarket during a week are given below. Test the hypothesis that the sales do not depend on the day of the week, using a significant level of 0.05.

Days:	Mon	Tues	Wed	Thurs	Fri	Sat
Sales:	65	54	60	56	71	84

3. A survey of 320 families with 5 children each revealed the following information:

Number of boys:	5	4	3	2	1	0
Number of girls:	0	1	2	3	4	5
Number of families:	14	56	110	88	40	12

Is this result consistent with the hypothesis that male and female births are equally probable?

4. 4 coins were tossed at a time and this operation is repeated 160 times. It is found that 4 heads occur 6 times, 3 heads occur 43 times, 2 heads occur 69 times, one head occurs 34 times. Discuss whether the coin may be regarded as unbiased?

5. Fit a Poisson distribution to the following data and best the goodness of fit:

x:	0	1	2	3	4
f:	109	65	22	3	1

6. In the accounting department of bank, 100 accounts are selected at random and estimated for errors. The following results were obtained:

Number of errors:	0	1	2	3	4	5	6
Number of accounts:	35	40	19	2	0	2	2

Does this information verify that the errors are distributed according to the Poisson probability law?

7. In a sample analysis of examination results of 500 students, it was found that 180 students failed, 170 secured a third class, 90 secured a second class and the rest, a first class. Do these figures support the general belief that the above categories are in the ratio 4:3:2:1, respectively?

8. What is χ^2–test?

A die is thrown 90 times with the following results:

Face:	1	2	3	4	5	6	Total
Frequency:	10	12	16	14	18	20	90

Use χ^2-test to test whether these data are consistent with the hypothesis that die is unbiased.

Given $\chi^2_{0.05} = 11.07$ for 5 degrees of freedom.

9. A survey of 320 families with 5 children shows the following distribution:

Number of boys & girls:	5 boys & 0 girl	4 boys & 1 girl	3 boys & 2 girls	2 boys & 3 girls	1 boy & 4 girls	0 boy & 5 girls	Total
Number of families:	18	56	110	88	40	8	320

Given that values of χ^2 for 5 degrees of freedom are 11.1 and 15.1 at 0.05 and 0.01 significance level respectively, test the hypothesis that male and female births are equally probable.

8.19 χ^2 TEST AS A TEST OF INDEPENDENCE

With the help of χ^2 test, we can find whether or not two attributes are associated. We take the null hypothesis that there is no association between the attributes under study, *i.e.*, **we assume that the two attributes are independent. If the calculated value of χ^2 is less than the table value** at a specified level (generally 5%) of significance, the hypothesis holds good, *i.e.*, **the attributes are independent** and do not bear any association. On the other hand, if the calculated value of χ^2 is greater than the table value at a specified level of significance, we say that the results of the experiment do not support the hypothesis. In other words, the attributes are associated. Thus a very useful application of χ^2 test is to investigate the relationship between trials or attributes which can be classified into two or more categories.

The sample data set out into two-way table, called **contingency table.**

Let us consider two attributes A and B divided into r classes A_1, A_2, A_3, ..., A_r, and B divided into s classes B_1, B_2, B_3, ..., B_s. If (A_i), (B_j) represents the number of persons possessing the attributes A_i, B_j respectively, (i = 1, 2, ..., r, j = 1, 2, ..., s) and $(A_i B_j)$ represent the number of persons possessing attributes A_i and B_j. Also we have $\sum_{i=1}^{r} A_i = \sum_{j=1}^{s} B_j$ = N where N is the total frequency. The contingency table for $r \times s$ is given below:

B \ A	A_1	A_2	A_3	...A_r	*Total*
B_1	(A_1B_1)	(A_2B_1)	(A_3B_1)	......(A_rB_1)	B_1
B_2	(A_1B_2)	(A_2B_2)	(A_3B_2)	......(A_rB_2)	B_2
B_3	(A_1B_3)	(A_2B_3)	(A_3B_3)	......(A_rB_3)	B_3
......	......	......	......	......	......
......	......	......	......	......	......
B_s	(A_1B_s)	(A_2B_s)	(A_3B_s)	......(A_rB_s)	(B_s)
Total	(A_1)	(A_2)	(A_3)	......(A_r)	N

H_0: Both the attributes are independent. *i.e.*, A and B are independent under the null hypothesis, we calculate the expected frequency as follows:

$P(A_i)$ = Probability that a person possesses the attribute

$$A_i = \frac{(A_i)}{N} \quad i = 1, 2, ..., r$$

$P(B_j)$ = Probability that a person possesses the attribute $B_j = \dfrac{(B_j)}{N}$

$P(A_iB_j)$ = Probability that a person possesses both attributes A_i and B_j

$$= \frac{(A_iB_j)}{N}$$

If $(A_iB_j)_0$ is the expected number of persons possessing both the attributes A_i and B_j

$$(A_iB_j)_0 = NP(A_iB_j) = NP(A_i)(B_j)$$

$$= N\frac{(A_i)}{N}\frac{(B_j)}{N} = \frac{(A_i)(B_j)}{N} \qquad (\because \text{ A and B are independent})$$

Hence $$\chi^2 = \sum_{i=1}^{r}\sum_{j=1}^{s}\left[\frac{[(A_iB_j) - (A_iB_j)_0]^2}{(A_iB_j)_0}\right]$$

which is distributed as a χ^2 variate with $(r-1)(s-1)$ degrees of freedom.

NOTE

1. *For a 2 × 2 contingency table where the frequencies are* $\frac{a/b}{c/d}$, χ^2 *can be calculated from independent frequencies as*

$$\chi^2 = \frac{(a+b+c+d)(ad-bc)^2}{(a+b)(c+d)(b+d)(a+c)}.$$

2. *If the contingency table is not 2 × 2, then the formula for calculating* χ^2 *as given in Note 1, can't be used. Hence, we have another formula for calculating the expected frequency* $(A_iB_j)_0 = \frac{(A_i)(B_j)}{N}$ *i.e., expected frequency in each cell is* $= \frac{\text{Product of column total and row total}}{\text{whole total}}$.

3. *If* $\frac{a|b}{c|d}$ *is the 2 × 2 contingency table with two attributes,* $Q = \frac{ad-bc}{ad+bc}$ *is called the coefficient of association. If the attributes are independent then* $\frac{a}{b} = \frac{c}{d}$.

4. ***Yates's Correction.*** *In a 2 × 2 table, if the frequencies of a cell is small, we make Yates's correction to make* χ^2 *continuous.*

Decrease by $\frac{1}{2}$ *those cell frequencies which are greater than expected frequencies, and increase by* $\frac{1}{2}$ *those which are less than expectation. This will not affect the marginal columns. This correction is known as Yates's correction to continuity.*

$$\text{After Yates's correction } \chi^2 = \frac{N\left(bc - ad - \frac{1}{2}N\right)^2}{(a+c)(b+d)(c+d)(a+b)} \quad \text{when } ad - bc < 0$$

$$\chi^2 = \frac{N\left(ad - bc - \frac{1}{2}N\right)^2}{(a+c)(b+d)(c+d)(a+b)} \quad \text{when} \quad ad - bc > 0.$$

EXAMPLES

Example 1. *What are the expected frequencies of 2 × 2 contingency tables given below:*

(*i*)

a	*b*
c	*d*

(*ii*)

2	10
6	6

Sol. Observed frequencies → Expected frequencies

(*i*) Observed frequencies

a	*b*	*a* + *b*
c	*d*	*c* + *d*
a + *c*	*b* + *d*	*a* + *b* + *c* + *d* = N

Expected frequencies

$\frac{(a+c)(a+b)}{a+b+c+d}$	$\frac{(b+d)(a+b)}{a+b+c+d}$
$\frac{(a+c)(c+d)}{a+b+c+d}$	$\frac{(b+d)(c+d)}{a+b+c+d}$

(*ii*) Observed frequencies

2	10	12
6	6	12
8	16	24

Expected frequencies

$\frac{8 \times 12}{24} = 4$	$\frac{16 \times 12}{24} = 8$
$\frac{8 \times 12}{24} = 4$	$\frac{16 \times 12}{24} = 8$

Example 2. *From the following table regarding the color of eyes of father and son test if the color of son's eye is associated with that of the father.*

		Eye color of son	
		Light	*Not light*
Eye color of father	*Light*	*471*	*51*
	Not light	*148*	*230*

Sol. Null hypothesis H_0: The color of son's eye is not associated with that of the father, *i.e.*, they are independent.

Under H_0, we calculate the expected frequency in each cell as

$$= \frac{\text{Product of column total and row total}}{\text{Whole total}}$$

Expected frequencies are:

Eye color of son / *Eye color of father*	*Light*	*Not light*	*Total*
Light	$\frac{619 \times 522}{900} = 359.02$	$\frac{289 \times 522}{900} = 167.62$	522
Not light	$\frac{619 \times 378}{900} = 259.98$	$\frac{289 \times 378}{900} = 121.38$	378
Total	619	289	900

$$\chi^2 = \frac{(471-359.02)^2}{359.02} + \frac{(51-167.62)^2}{167.62} + \frac{(148-259.98)^2}{259.98} + \frac{(230-121.38)^2}{121.38}$$

$= 261.498.$

Conclusion. Tabulated value of χ^2 at 5% level for 1 difference is 3.841.

Since the calculated value of $\chi^2 >$ tabulated value of χ^2, H_0 is rejected. They are dependent, *i.e.*, the color of son's eye is associated with that of the father.

Example 3. *The following table gives the number of good and bad parts produced by each of the three shifts in a factory:*

	Good parts	*Bad parts*	*Total*
Day shift	*960*	*40*	*1000*
Evening shift	*940*	*50*	*990*
Night shift	*950*	*45*	*995*
Total	*2850*	*135*	*2985*

Test whether or not the production of bad parts is independent of the shift on which they were produced.

Sol. Null hypothesis H_0: The production of bad parts is independent of the shift on which they were produced.

The two attributes, production and shifts are independent.

Under H_0, $$\chi^2 = \sum_{i=1}^{2} \sum_{j=1}^{3} \left[\frac{[(A_iB_j)_0 - (A_iB_j)]^2}{(A_iB_j)_0} \right]$$

Calculation of expected frequencies

Let A and B be the two attributes namely production and shifts. A is divided into two classes A_1, A_2 and B is divided into three classes B_1, B_2, B_3.

$$(A_1B_1)_0 = \frac{(A_1)(B_2)}{N} = \frac{(2850) \times (1000)}{2985} = 954.77;$$

$$(A_1B_2)_0 = \frac{(A_1)(B_2)}{N} = \frac{(2850) \times (990)}{2985} = 945.226$$

$$(A_1B_3)_0 = \frac{(A_1)(B_3)}{N} = \frac{(2850) \times (995)}{2985} = 950;$$

$$(A_2B_1)_0 = \frac{(A_2)(B_1)}{N} = \frac{(135) \times (1000)}{2985} = 45.27$$

$$(A_2B_2)_0 = \frac{(A_2)(B_2)}{N} = \frac{(135) \times (990)}{2985} = 44.773;$$

$$(A_2B_3)_0 = \frac{(A_2)(B_3)}{N} = \frac{(135) \times (995)}{2985} = 45.$$

To calculate the value of χ^2

Class	O_i	E_i	$(O_i - E_i)^2$	$(O_i - E_i)^2/E_i$
(A_1B_1)	960	954.77	27.3529	0.02864
(A_1B_2)	940	945.226	27.3110	0.02889
(A_1B_3)	950	950	0	0
(A_2B_1)	40	45.27	27.7729	0.61349
(A_2B_2)	50	44.773	27.3215	0.61022
(A_2B_3)	45	45	0	0
				1.28126

Conclusion. The tabulated value of χ^2 at 5% level of significance for 2 degrees of freedom $(r - 1)(s - 1)$ is 5.991. Since the calculated value of χ^2 is less than the tabulated value, we accept H_0, *i.e.*, the production of bad parts is independent of the shift on which they were produced.

ASSIGNMENT 8.10

1. In a locality 100 persons were randomly selected and asked about their educational achievements. The results are given below:

Education				
		Middle	*High school*	*College*
Sex	Male	10	15	25
	Female	25	10	15

Based on this information can you say the education depends on sex.

2. The following data is collected on two characters:

	Smokers	*Non smokers*
Literate	83	57
Illiterate	45	68

Based on this information can you say that there is no relation between habit of smoking and literacy.

3. In an experiment on the immunisation of goats from anthrax, the following results were obtained. Derive your inferences on the efficiency of the vaccine.

	Died anthrax	*Survived*
Inoculated with vaccine	2	10
Not inoculated	6	6

TABLE 1: Significant values t_v (α) of t-distribution (Two Tail Areas)
$[|t| > t_v(\alpha)] = \alpha$

difference	*Probability (Level of significance)*					
(ν)	*0.50*	*0.10*	*0.05*	*0.02*	*0.01*	*0.001*
1	1.00	6.31	12.71	31.82	63.66	636.62
2	0.82	0.92	4.30	6.97	6.93	31.60
3	0.77	2.32	3.18	4.54	5.84	12.94
4	0.74	2.13	2.78	3.75	4.60	8.61
5	0.73	2.02	2.57	3.37	4.03	6.86
6	0.72	1.94	2.45	3.14	3.71	5.96
7	0.71	1.90	2.37	3.00	3.50	5.41
8	0.71	1.80	2.31	2.90	3.36	5.04
9	0.70	1.83	2.26	2.82	3.25	4.78
10	0.70	1.81	2.23	2.76	3.17	4.59
11	0.70	1.80	2.20	2.72	3.11	4.44
12	0.70	1.78	2.18	2.68	3.06	4.32
13	0.69	1.77	2.16	2.65	3.01	4.22
14	0.69	1.76	2.15	2.62	2.98	4.14
15	0.69	1.75	2.13	2.60	2.95	4.07
16	0.69	1.75	2.12	2.58	2.92	4.02
17	0.69	1.74	2.11	2.57	2.90	3.97
18	0.69	1.73	2.10	2.55	2.88	3.92
19	0.69	1.73	2.09	2.54	2.86	3.88
20	0.69	1.73	2.09	2.53	2.85	3.85
21	0.69	1.72	2.08	2.52	2.83	3.83
22	0.69	1.72	2.07	2.51	2.82	3.79
23	0.69	1.71	2.07	2.50	2.81	3.77
24	0.69	1.71	2.06	2.49	2.80	3.75
25	0.68	1.71	2.06	2.49	2.79	3.73
26	0.68	1.71	2.06	2.48	2.78	3.71
27	0.68	1.70	2.05	2.47	2.77	3.69
28	0.68	1.70	2.05	2.47	2.76	3.67
29	0.68	1.70	2.05	2.46	2.76	3.66
30	0.68	1.70	2.04	2.46	2.75	3.65
∞	0.67	1.65	1.96	2.33	2.58	3.29

TABLE 2: F-Distribution

Values of F for F-Distributions with 0.05 of the Area in The Right Tall

	Degrees of freedom for numerator																		
	1	*2*	*3*	*4*	*5*	*6*	*7*	*8*	*9*	*10*	*12*	*15*	*20*	*24*	*20*	*40*	*60*	*120*	*∞*
1	161	200	216	225	230	234	237	239	241	242	244	246	248	249	250	251	252	253	254
2	18.5	19.0	19.2	19.2	19.3	19.3	19.4	19.4	19.4	19.4	19.4	19.4	19.4	19.5	19.5	19.5	19.5	19.5	19.5
3	10.1	9.55	9.28	9.12	9.01	9.94	8.89	8.85	8.81	8.79	8.74	8.70	8.66	8.64	8.62	8.59	8.57	8.55	8.53
4	7.71	6.94	6.59	6.39	6.26	6.16	6.09	6.04	6.00	5.96	5.91	5.86	5.80	5.77	5.75	5.72	5.69	6.66	5.63
5	6.61	5.79	5.41	5.19	5.05	4.95	4.88	4.82	4.77	4.74	4.68	4.62	4.56	4.53	4.50	4.46	4.43	4.40	4.37
6	5.99	5.14	4.76	4.53	4.39	4.28	4.21	4.15	4.10	4.06	4.00	3.94	3.87	3.84	3.81	3.77	3.74	3.70	3.67
7	5.59	4.74	4.35	4.12	3.97	3.87	3.79	3.73	3.68	3.64	3.57	3.51	3.44	3.41	3.38	3.34	3.30	3.27	3.23
8	5.32	4.46	4.07	3.84	3.69	3.58	3.50	3.44	3.39	3.35	3.28	3.22	3.15	3.12	3.08	3.04	3.01	2.97	2.93
9	5.12	4.26	3.86	3.63	3.48	3.37	3.29	3.23	3.18	3.14	3.07	3.01	2.94	2.90	2.86	2.83	2.79	2.75	2.71
10	4.96	4.10	3.71	3.48	3.33	3.22	3.14	3.07	3.02	2.98	2.91	2.85	2.77	2.74	2.70	2.66	2.62	2.58	2.54
11	4.84	3.98	3.59	3.36	3.20	3.09	3.01	2.95	2.90	2.85	2.79	2.72	2.65	2.61	2.57	2.53	2.49	2.45	2.40
12	4.75	3.89	3.49	3.26	3.11	3.00	2.91	2.85	2.80	2.75	2.69	2.62	2.54	2.51	2.47	2.43	2.38	2.34	2.30
13	4.67	3.81	3.41	3.18	3.03	2.92	2.83	2.77	2.71	2.67	2.60	2.53	2.46	2.42	2.38	2.34	2.30	2.25	2.21
14	4.60	3.74	3.34	3.11	3.96	2.85	2.76	2.70	2.65	2.60	2.53	2.46	2.39	2.35	2.31	2.27	2.22	2.18	2.13
15	4.54	3.68	3.29	3.06	3.90	2.79	2.71	2.64	2.59	2.54	2.48	2.40	2.33	2.29	2.25	2.20	2.16	2.11	2.07
16	4.49	3.63	3.24	3.01	2.85	2.74	2.66	2.59	2.54	2.49	2.42	2.35	2.28	2.24	2.19	2.15	2.11	2.06	2.01
17	4.45	3.59	3.20	2.96	2.81	2.70	2.61	2.55	2.49	2.45	2.38	2.31	2.23	2.19	2.15	2.10	2.06	2.01	1.96
18	4.41	3.55	3.16	2.93	2.77	2.66	2.58	2.51	2.46	2.41	2.34	2.27	2.19	2.15	2.11	2.06	2.02	1.97	1.92

19	4.38	3.52	3.13	2.90	2.74	2.63	2.54	2.48	2.42	2.38	2.31	2.23	2.16	2.11	2.07	2.03	1.98	1.93	1.88
20	4.35	3.49	3.10	2.87	2.17	2.60	2.51	2.45	2.39	2.35	2.28	2.20	2.12	2.08	2.04	1.99	1.95	1.90	1.84
21	4.32	3.47	3.07	2.84	2.68	2.57	2.49	2.42	2.37	2.32	2.25	2.18	2.10	2.05	2.01	1.96	1.92	1.87	1.81
22	4.30	3.44	3.05	2.82	2.66	2.55	2.46	2.40	2.34	2.30	2.23	2.15	2.07	2.03	1.98	1.94	1.89	1.84	1.78
23	4.28	3.42	3.03	2.80	2.64	2.53	2.44	2.37	2.32	2.27	2.20	2.13	2.05	2.01	1.96	1.91	1.86	1.81	1.76
24	4.26	3.40	3.01	2.78	2.62	2.51	2.42	2.36	2.30	2.25	2.18	2.11	2.03	1.98	1.94	1.98	1.84	1.79	1.73
25	4.24	3.39	2.99	2.76	2.60	2.94	2.40	2.34	2.28	2.24	2.16	2.29	2.01	1.96	1.92	1.87	1.82	1.77	1.71
30	4.17	3.32	2.92	2.69	2.53	2.42	2.33	2.27	2.21	2.16	2.09	2.01	1.93	1.89	1.84	1.79	1.74	1.64	1.62
40	4.08	3.23	2.84	2.61	2.45	2.34	2.25	2.18	2.12	2.08	2.00	1.92	1.84	1.79	1.74	1.69	1.64	1.58	1.51
60	4.00	3.15	2.76	2.53	2.37	2.25	2.17	2.10	2.04	1.99	1.92	1.84	1.75	1.70	1.65	1.59	1.53	1.47	1.39
120	3.92	3.07	2.68	2.45	2.29	2.18	2.09	2.02	1.96	1.91	1.83	1.75	1.66	1.61	1.55	1.50	1.43	1.35	1.25
∞	3.84	3.00	2.60	2.37	2.21	2.10	2.01	1.94	1.88	1.83	1.75	1.67	1.57	1.52	1.46	1.39	1.32	1.22	1.00

TABLE 3: CHI-SQUARE DISTRIBUTION

Significant Values χ^2 (α) of Chi-Square Distribution Right Tail Areas for Given Probability α, $P = P_r (\chi^2 > \chi^2 (\alpha)) = \alpha$ And ν Degrees of Freedom (difference)

Degrees of freedom (ν)	*Probability (Level of significance)*						
	0 = .99	*0.95*	*0.50*	*0.10*	*0.05*	*0.02*	*0.01*
1	.000157	.00393	.455	2.706	3.841	5.214	6.635
2	.0201	.103	1.386	4.605	5.991	7.824	9.210
3	.115	.352	2.366	6.251	7.815	9.837	11.341
4	.297	.711	3.357	7.779	9.488	11.668	13.277
5	.554	1.145	4.351	9.236	11.070	13.388	15.086
6	.872	2.635	5.348	10.645	12.592	15.033	16.812
7	.1.239	2.167	6.346	12.017	14.067	16.622	18.475
8	3.646	2.733	7.344	13.362	15.507	18.168	20.090
9	2.088	3.325	8.343	14.684	16.919	19.679	21.669
10	2.558	3.940	9.340	15.987	18.307	21.161	23.209
11	3.053	4.575	10.341	17.275	19.675	22.618	24.725
12	3.571	5.226	11.340	18.549	21.026	24.054	26.217
13	4.107	5.892	12.340	19.812	22.362	25.472	27.688
14	4.660	6.571	13.339	21.064	23.685	26.873	29.141
15	4.229	7.261	14.339	22.307	24.996	28.259	30.578
16	5.812	7.962	15.338	23.542	26.296	29.633	32.000
17	6.408	8.672	15.338	24.769	27.587	30.995	33.409
18	7.015	9.390	17.338	25.989	28.869	32.346	34.805
19	7.633	10.117	18.338	27.204	30.144	33.687	36.191
20	8.260	10.851	19.337	28.412	31.410	35.020	37.566
21	8.897	11.591	20.337	29.615	32.671	36.343	38.932
22	9.542	12.338	21.337	30.813	33.924	37.659	40.289
23	10.196	13.091	22.337	32.007	35.172	38.968	41.638
24	10.856	13.848	23.337	32.196	36.415	40.270	42.980
25	11.524	14.611	24.337	34.382	37.65	41.566	44.314
26	12.198	15.379	25.336	35.363	38.885	41.856	45.642
27	12.879	16.151	26.336	36.741	40.113	41.140	46.963
28	13.565	16.928	27.336	37.916	41.337	45.419	48.278
29	14.256	17.708	28.336	39.087	42.557	46.693	49.588
30	14.933	18.493	29.336	40.256	43.773	47.962	50.892

NOTE *For degrees of freedom (ν) greater than 30, the quantity $\sqrt{2\chi^2} - \sqrt{2\nu - 1}$ may be used as a normal variate with unit variance.*

Part 6 APPENDICES

APPENDIX A
ANSWERS TO SELECTED EXERCISES

ASSIGNMENT 1.1

5. printf ("the given value is %f", 22.23);

7. $x = 10.0$

$$\text{Sum} = 1 + \frac{1}{2} + \frac{1}{3} + \frac{1}{4} + \frac{1}{5} + \frac{1}{6} + \frac{1}{7} + \frac{1}{8} + \frac{1}{9}.$$

19. 3

ASSIGNMENT 2.1

1. 3.264, 35.47, 4986000, 0.7004, 0.0003222, 1.658, 30.06, 0.8594, 3.142.

3. 0.0005

5. 48.21, 2.37, 52.28, 2.38, 2.38, 81.26

7. (*i*) 0.004, 0.0015772 (*ii*) 0.006, 0.0023659

9. (34.5588, 35.9694)

ASSIGNMENT 2.2

3. 0.00355, 0.0089

5. 12

7. $q = 3.43636$, $e_r = 0.020857$

ASSIGNMENT 2.3

1. .4485 E 8

7. .1010 E 1, .1012 E 1; correct value = .1012034 E 1

9. (*i*) $x = -$ .3217 E 2, $y =$ .1666 E 2; yes

(*ii*) $x = -$ .2352 E 2, $y =$ .1250 E 2.

11. $.168 \times 10^3$.

ASSIGNMENT 3.1

1. (*i*)

x:	-4	-3	-2	-1	0	1	2	3	4
$f(x)$:	1.0625	.125	$-.75$	-1.5	-2	-2	-1	2	9

Roots lie in $(-3, -2)$ and $(2, 3)$.

(*ii*) 1.7281 in interval (1, 2).

3. 0.111

5. 2.02875625

7. 4.712389

9. 2.374

11. .56714333

13. (*i*) $-$ 2.1048 (*ii*) 2.621 (*iii*) .682 (*iv*) .657, 1.834

15. .322

17. 0.39188

19. 2.94282

21. (*i*) $(-3, -2)$ (*ii*) Root lies in the interval $(-2.5, -2.25)$

ASSIGNMENT 3.2

1. 0.0912

3. (*i*) 2.9353 (*ii*) $-$ .420365 (*iii*) 1.83928

(*iv*) $-$ .682327803 (*v*) 2.690647448 (*vi*) 2.594313016

5. 5.4772

7. 0.10260

ASSIGNMENT 3.3

1. 2.942821 **3.** 1.875

7. (*i*) 1.860, .2541 (*ii*) 1.69562 (*iii*) 1.2134 (*iv*) 2.7473

13. – 1.25115 and 0.55000

ASSIGNMENT 3.4

3. 0.5177573637

ASSIGNMENT 3.5

1. $x^2 - 2.40402 + 3.0927$ **3.** $x^2 + 1.94184x + 1.95685$

ASSIGNMENT 3.6

1. (*i*) 1.324 (*ii*) 1.839286755

3. (*i*) 2.279 (*ii*) 3.20056 (*iii*) .76759

ASSIGNMENT 3.7

1. 5.12487, 1.63668, 0.23845

ASSIGNMENT 3.8

1. (*i*) 2.7698 (*ii*) 2.231 (*iii*) 3.107

ASSIGNMENT 3.9

1. 1.856

3. (*i*) 2.094568 (*ii*) 2.279

5. (*i*) 0.511 (*ii*) 0.657 (*iii*) 2.908 (*iv*) – 2.533 (*v*) 1.171 (*vi*) .739 (*vii*) 1.896 (*viii*) 1.756 (*ix*) 4.4934

9. 4.9324 **11.** 1.442

13. (*a*) 5.099 (*b*) 5.384 (*c*) 5.916

15. $p = \frac{5}{9}, q = \frac{5}{9}, r = -\frac{1}{9}$; Third order

17. Roots lie in (0, 1) and (1, 2); 0.100336, 1.679631

19. 0.298 **21.** – 0.5081

ASSIGNMENT 3.10

1. (*iii*) Newton-Raphson method since it deals with multiple roots as well.

ASSIGNMENT 3.11

1. (*i*) 2, 1, 1 (*ii*) 2.556, 2.861, 0.8203 (*iii*) 1.3247, – .6624 ± .5622i

ASSIGNMENT 3.12

1. .56704980

3. 1, 0, 1.0, 0.5, .66666, .75000, .666666, .666666, .69230769

ASSIGNMENT 4.1

1. 239, 371 **9.** (*i*) $3x^2 - 3x + 1$ (*ii*) $6x$

ASSIGNMENT 4.2

1. 16.1, 2^x is not a polynomial **3.** 0.4147

5. 27, 125

ASSIGNMENT 4.3

1. 244

ASSIGNMENT 4.4

1. 15.6993 nautical miles
3. 43.704
5. 0.23589625
7. 51
9. (*a*) 27 (*b*) 27
11. 0.1205

ASSIGNMENT 4.5

1. 0.3057
3. 15.47996
5. 421.875
7. 0.783172
9. 219
11. 6.36, 11.02

ASSIGNMENT 4.6

1. 19.407426
3. 2290.0017
5. .046

ASSIGNMENT 4.7

1. 22898
3. 1.2662
5. 0.70696

ASSIGNMENT 4.8

1. 0.9391002
3. 0.19573
5. 0.32495

ASSIGNMENT 4.9

1. 0.496798
3. 7957.1407
5. 1.904082
7. 3250.875

ASSIGNMENT 4.10

1. 3.3756

3. 4913, 5052, 5185, 5315

5. 3250.875

7. 14.620947

9. 19523.5, 215914

11. 3.7084096, 3.7325079, 3.7563005, 3.7797956

13. 1.904082

15. 6.7531

ASSIGNMENT 4.11

1. 37.8, 73; 2^x is not a polynomial

3. (*i*) 100.99999 (*ii*) 25

5. 0.64942084

7. 1294.8437

9. $x^4 - 3x^3 + 5x^2 - 6$

11. 12.45

13. 53

17. 2.4786

19. $x^5 - 9x^4 + 18x^3 - x^2 + 9x - 18$

ASSIGNMENT 4.12

1. 810

3. 521

5. 328

7. $(x-1)^3 + 2(x-1)^2 + 4(x-1) + 11$

9. $\dfrac{1}{2(x-1)} + \dfrac{1}{x-2} - \dfrac{1}{2(x+1)}$

11. 2.49136

13. 10.

ASSIGNMENT 4.13

1. $f(x) = 2x^4 - x^2 + x + 1, \dfrac{11}{8}, \dfrac{3}{8}.$

3. $\dfrac{1}{2}(5x^3 - 3x^5).$

5. 0.86742375.

7. $(1 + 3x)(1 - x)^2 + (2 - x)ex^2$; 1.644; 1.859.

9. 1.02470.

11. 0.993252.

13. (*i*) $29.556\,x^3 - 85.793\,x^2 + 97.696\,x - 34.07$; 19.19125.

(*ii*) Same polynomial as in (*i*).

15. (*i*) $0.0068\,x^5 + 0.002\,x^4 - 0.1671\,x^3 - 0.0002\,x^2 + x$; 0.6816.

(*ii*) $x^3 - 6x^2 - 5x + 4$; 0.125, – 13.625.

ASSIGNMENT 5.1

1. 3.946, – 3.545, 2.727, – 1.703 **3.** – 27.9, 117.67

5. (*i*) 0.5005, – 0.2732 (*ii*) 0.4473, – 0.1583 (*iii*) 0.4662, – 0.2043

7. 0.9848 **9.** 18, 18

11. 232.869 **13.** 0.10848

17. 0.0018 **19.** (*a*) – 52.4 (*b*) – 0.01908.

ASSIGNMENT 5.2

1. 0.69325; 0.0001 **3.** 1.8278

5. (*i*) 1.82765512 (*ii*) 1.82784789 **7.** 177.483

9. 0.83865 **11.** 1.61

13. 1.1615 **15.** 30.87 m/sec

17. (*i*) 591.85333 (*ii*) 591.855 **19.** 0.693255; 0.0001078

21. 1.0101996 **23.** (*i*) 0.6827 (*ii*) 0.658596

25. 1.14 **27.** 0.52359895

29. 1.019286497.

ASSIGNMENT 5.3

1. (*i*) 0.01138 (*ii*) 0.00083 **3.** 3.1428

5. 0.0490291.

ASSIGNMENT 6.1

1. .019984, .0200 **3.** 0.0214

5. 0.7432, 0.7439 **9.** $y(0.1) = 3.005$, $y(0.2) = 3.020$.

ASSIGNMENT 6.2

1. $y(0.2) = 1.0199$, $y(0.5) = 1.1223$

3. $y(.02) = 1.0202$, $y(.04) = 1.0408$, $y(.06) = 1.0619$

5. $y(.1) = 1.222$, $y(.2) = 1.375$, $y(.3) = 1.573$

7. 1.0526, 1.1104 **9.** 1.76393

11. $y(.01) = 1.01$, $y(.02) = 1.0201$.

ASSIGNMENT 6.3

1. 2.2052, 2.4214

3. $y(x) = 1 + x - \frac{x^2}{2} + \frac{x^3}{2} - \frac{5}{8}x^4$; 1.0954

5. $y(0.1) = 2.0845$, $z(0.1) = 0.5867$
$y(0.2) = 2.1366338$, $z(0.2) = 0.1549693$.

ASSIGNMENT 6.4

1. 1.11034

3. $y(1.2) = 2.4921$, $y(1.4) = 3.2320$

5. $y(0.5) = 1.375$, $y(1.0) = 1.6030$

7. $y(1.1) = 1.8955$, $y(1.2) = 2.5041$.

9. $y(0.1) = 1.1168873$, $y(0.2) = 1.2773914$, $y(0.3) = 1.50412$

11. (*i*) 1.1749, (*ii*) $y(0.6) = 0.61035$, $y(0.8) = 0.84899$

13. $y(1.2) = 0.246326$, $y(1.4) = 0.622751489$

15. $y(0.1) = 1.118057$, $y(0.2) = 1.291457$, $y(0.3) = 1.584057$

17. $y(0.2) = 1.195999$, $y(0.4) = 1.375269$.

ASSIGNMENT 6.5

1. $y_4^{(3)} = y(0.8) = 1.218$

3. 2.0444

5. $y(0.3) = 1.0150$

7. $y(0.5) = 1.3571$, $y(1) = 1.5837$, $y(1.5) = 1.7555$, $y(2) = 1.8957$

9. $y(0.4) = 1.538$, $y(0.5) = 1.751$

11. $y(0.8) = 2.3164$, $y(1.0) = 2.3780$

13. $y(0.1) = 0.60475$.

ASSIGNMENT 6.6

1. $y(0.4) = 2.2089$, $y(0.5) = 3.20798$

3. $y(1.4) = 0.9996$

5. 1.1107, 1.2459, 1.4111, 1.61287.

ASSIGNMENT 7.1

1. $y = 2.4333 + 0.4x$

3. $y = -4 + 6x$

5. $y = 54.35 + 0.5184x°$

7. $y = -1.6071429x + 8.6428571$

9. $P = 2.2759 + 0.1879 W$

ASSIGNMENT 7.2

1. $y = e^{0.5x}$

3. $y = 4.642\, e^{0.46x}$

5. $y = 99.86\,(1.2)^x$

7. $y = 2.978\, x^{0.5143}$

9. $y = 0.509x^2 - \frac{2.04}{x}$

11. $y = 13.0065 + \frac{6.7512}{x} - \frac{4.4738}{x^2}$

13. $xy = 16.18x + 40.78$

15. $pv^{1.42} = 0.99.$

ASSIGNMENT 7.3

1. $x = 2.5, \quad y = 0.7$

3. $x = 2.47, y = 3.55, \quad z = 1.92$

5. (*i*) $x = 1.54, \; y = 1.27, \; z = -1.08$

(*ii*) $x = 1.16, \; y = -.76, \; z = 2.8$

(*iii*) $x = 6.9, \; y = 3.6, \; z = 4.14.$

ASSIGNMENT 7.4

1. $\frac{1}{2} T_0(x) + \frac{7}{4} T_1(x) - \frac{1}{2} T_2(x) + \frac{1}{4} T_3(x)$

3. $2x + 2x^2$

7. $\frac{15}{16} - \frac{1}{2} x$

9. $\frac{191}{192} - \frac{1}{2} x^2$

11. $M_1 = 8, M_2 = -14$

$F(x) = \frac{-11x^3 + 45x^2 - 40x + 18}{3}; \quad F(1.5) = 7.375$

13. $M_1 = -\frac{18}{5}, \quad M_2 = \frac{12}{5}$

For $1 \le x \le 2, \quad F(x) = \frac{-3x^3 + 9x^2 - x - 5}{5}$

For $2 \le x \le 3, \quad F(x) = \frac{5x^3 - 39x^2 + 95x - 69}{5}$

For $3 \le x \le 4, \quad F(x) = \frac{-2x^3 + 24x^2 - 94x + 120}{5}$

15. $\alpha = 1, \beta = 3$

17. For $0 \le x \le \frac{1}{3}, \quad F(x) = 0.63x^3 - 0.82x + 1$

For $\frac{1}{3} \le x \le \frac{2}{3}, \quad F(x) = -0.45x^3 + 1.08x^2 - 1.18x + 1.0$

For $\frac{2}{3} \le x \le 1, \quad F(x) = -0.18x^3 + 0.54x^2 - 0.8x + 0.96$

$$I = 0.695$$

ASSIGNMENT 7.5

1. $y = 1.3x + 1.1$

3. $F = 0.18793W + 2.27595; \quad F = 30.4654$ kg wt.

5. $\bar{x} = 4, \bar{y} = 7, r = -0.5$

7. $y = 0.04765 + 0.004071\,P; y = 0.6583$ cm

9. $\bar{x} = 6, \bar{y} = 1, r = -0.48989$ **11.** $7x - 11y + 6 = 0$

13. $r = 0.70, \bar{x} = 11.5086, \bar{y} = 11.5261$, no

15. $y = 1.68x + 1.044, x = 0.42y + 2.27; y = 14.484$

17. $y = x + 1; x = 0.16y + 2.36; x = 2.52$

19. Regression line of y on x: $y = 0.74306\,x + 1.56821$

Regression line of x on y: $x = 0.63602\,y + 2.0204$.

ASSIGNMENT 7.6

1. $y - 1.43 + 0.24x + 2.21x^2$

5. $a = 5.358035714, \quad b = -38.89492857, \quad c = 67.56.$

ASSIGNMENT 7.7

1. $CL_{\overline{X}} = 0.4988$, $UCL_{\overline{X}} = 0.5172$, $LCL_{\overline{X}} = 0.4804$, $CL_R = 0.018$, $UCL_R = 0.0463$, $LCL_R = 0$. The process is in control.

3. $CL_C = 2.4$, $UCL_C = 7.05$, $LCL_C = 0$, the process is not under control

5. $CL_{\overline{X}} = 10.66$, $UCL_{\overline{X}} = 14.295$, $LCL_{\overline{X}} = 7.025$, $CL_R = 0.3$, $UCL_R = 13.32$, $LCL_R = 0$; The process is under control

7. $UCL_C = 25.23$, $LCL_C = 2.77$. The process is in control.

ASSIGNMENT 8.1

1. H_0 rejected at 5% level

3. H_0 rejected at 5% level

5. H_0 accepted at 5% level.

ASSIGNMENT 8.2

1. H_0: Accepted

3. H_0: Accepted.

ASSIGNMENT 8.3

1. H_0 is rejected

3. 48.8 and 51.2

5. H_0 rejected both at 1% to 5% level of significance.

ASSIGNMENT 8.4

1. Significant difference

3. Highly significant

5. 48.75, 51.25.

ASSIGNMENT 8.5

1. z = 2.315, Difference significant at 5% level; z = 1.31, Difference not significant at 5% level.

ASSIGNMENT 8.6

1. accepted

3. rejected.

ASSIGNMENT 8.7

1. accepted

3. accepted

5. accepted.

ASSIGNMENT 8.8

1. rejected

3. accepted.

ASSIGNMENT 8.9

1. no

3. accepted

5. Poisson law fits the data

7. yes.

9. Accepted at 1% level of significance and rejected at 5% level of significance.

ASSIGNMENT 8.10

1. No

3. Not effective.

APPENDIX B
SAMPLE EXAMINATION

1. Attempt any **FOUR** parts of the following:

(*a*) Define the term 'absolute error'. Given that

$$a = 10.00 \pm 0.05, \quad b = 0.0356 \pm 0.0002$$
$$c = 15300 \pm 100, \quad d = 62000 \pm 500$$

Find the maximum value of the absolute error in

(*i*) $a + b + c + d$ (*ii*) $a + 5c - d$ (*iii*) d^3

(*b*) Use the series

$$\log_e \left(\frac{1+x}{1-x}\right) = 2\left(x + \frac{x^3}{3} + \frac{x^5}{5} + \ldots\ldots\right)$$

to compute the value of $\log_e (1.2)$ correct to seven decimal places and find the number of terms retained.

(*c*) Explain underflow and overflow conditions of error with suitable examples in floating point's addition and subtraction.

(*d*) Explain the Bisection method to calculate the roots of an equation. Write an algorithm and implement it in 'C'.

(*e*) Using the method of false position, find the root of equation $x^6 - x^4 - x^3 - 1 = 0$ up to four decimal places.

(*f*) Determine p, q, and r so that the order of the iterative method

$$x_{n+1} = px_n + \frac{qa}{x_n^2} + \frac{ra^2}{x_n^5}$$

for $a^{1/3}$ becomes as high as possible.

2. Attempt any **FOUR** parts of the following:

(*a*) Prove that the nth differences of a polynomial of nth degree are constant and all higher order differences are zero when the values of the independent variable are at equal interval.

(*b*) Find the missing terms in the following table:

x	1	2	3	4	5	6	7	8
$f(x)$	1	8	?	64	?	216	343	512

(*c*) Find the number of students from the following data who secured scores not more than 45:

Scores range	30–40	40–50	50–60	60–70	70–80
Number of students	35	48	70	40	22

(*d*) State and prove Stirling's formula.

(*e*) By means of Lagrange's formula, prove that

$$y_1 = y_3 - 0.3\,(y_5 - y_{-3}) + 0.2\,(y_{-3} - y_{-5})$$

(*f*) Prove that the nth divided differences of a polynomial of nth degree are constant.

3. Attempt any **TWO** parts of the following:

(*a*) y is a function of x satisfying the equation $xy'' + ay' + (x - b)\,y = 0$ where a and b are integers. Find the values of constants a and b if y is given by the following table:

x	0.8	1	1.2	1.4	1.6	1.8	2	2.2
y	1.73036	1.95532	2.19756	2.45693	2.73309	3.02549	2.3333	3.65563

(*b*) Find, from the following table, the area bounded by the curve and the x-axis from $x = 7.47$ to $x = 7.52$.

x	7.47	7.48	7.49	7.50	7.51	7.52
$f(x)$	1.93	1.95	1.98	2.01	2.03	2.06

(*c*) Derive Simpson's $\left(\frac{1}{3}\right)^{rd}$ rule from Newton-Cote's quadrature formula. Give its algorithm and write a program in 'C' to implement.

4. Attempt any **TWO** parts of the following:

(*a*) Obtain y for $x = 0.25, 0.5$ and 1.0 correct to three decimal places using Picard's method, given the differential equation

$$\frac{dy}{dx} = \frac{x^2}{y^2 + 1}$$

with the initial condition $y = 0$ when $x = 0$.

(*b*) Use Runge-Kutta method to approximate y when $x = 1.4$ given that $y = 2$ at $x = 1$ and $\frac{dy}{dx} = xy$ taking $h = 0.2$.

(*c*) Explain Predictor-Corrector methods. Write the algorithm of Milne's Predictor-corrector method and also give a code in 'C' to implement.

5. Attempt any **FOUR** parts of the following:

(*a*) Write a short note on Frequency charts.

(*b*) Find the least square line for the data points:

$(-1, 10), (0, 9), (1, 7), (2, 5), (3, 4), (4, 3), (5, 0)$ and $(6, -1)$.

(*c*) Find the most plausible values of x and y from the following equations:

$$3x + y = 4.95,\ x + y = 3.00,\ 2x - y = 0.5,\ x + 3y = 7.25.$$

(*d*) Prove that the regression coefficients are independent of the origin but not of scale.

(*e*) The average percentage of defectives in 27 samples of size 1500 each was found to be 13.7%. Construct p-chart for this situation. Explain how the control chart can be used to control quality.

(*f*) Fit a curve of the type $xy = ax + b$ to the following data:

x	1	3	5	7	9	10
y	36	29	28	26	24	15

APPENDIX C
ABOUT THE CD-ROM

- Included on the CD-ROM are simulations, figures from the text, third party software, and other files related to topics in numerical methods and statistics.
- See the "README" files for any specific information/system requirements related to each file folder, but most files will run on Windows 2000 or higher and Linux.

INDEX

A

Absolute error, 37
Acceptance sampling, 655
Adams-Moulton (or Adams-Bashforth) formula, 537
Adams-Moulton corrector formula, 539
Adams-Moulton predictor formula, 538
Advantages of statistical quality control, 656
Advantages/Features of 'C' language, 7
Algebraic and transcendental equations, 77
Algorithm for linear regression, 621
Algorithm of Euler's method, 493
Algorithm of Milne's predictor-corrector method, 528
Algorithm of modified Euler's method, 497
Algorithm of Runge-Kutta method, 516
Algorithm of second degree parabolic curve fitting, 647
Algorithm of Simpson's 1/3rd rule, 437
Algorithm of Simpson's 3/8th rule, 433
Algorithm of trapezoidal rule, 429
Algorithmic errors, 31
Alternative hypothesis, 673
Analysis of data, 655
Angle between two lines of regression, 620
Applications of t-distribution, 691
Approximations, 601
Area diagrams, 555
Argument, 202
Arrays, 18
Assembler, 6
Assumptions for interpolation, 200
Asymptotic error constant, 80
Averaging operator μ, 205

B

Backward difference operator, 203
Backward differences, 203

Bell shaped curve, 553
Bessel's interpolation formula, 312
Bisection (or Bolzano) method, 77
Boole's rule, 426

C

'C' constants, 8
"C instructions", 10
"C" variables, 9
χ^2 test as a test of goodness of fit, 711
χ^2 test as a test of independence, 718
Carl Runge, 513
Cartograms, 555
Central difference operator, 204
Central differences, 204
Chebyshev formula of third order, 175
Chebyshev polynomial approximation, 605
Chi-square (χ^2) test, 708
Class frequency, 549
Comparison of correlation and regression analysis, 618
Comparison of iterative methods, 189
Computational errors, 31
Conditions for applying χ^2 test, 710
Confidence limits or fiducial limits, 684
Continuous variables, 548
Control chart, 655, 658
Control charts for attributes, 661
Convergence of a sequence, 81
Convergence of iteration method, 96
Convergence of regula-falsi method, 130
Critical region, 674
Critical value of t, 691
Cubic spline interpolation, 594
Cumulative frequency, 549
Cumulative frequency curve or the ogive, 553
Curve fitting, 556
Curve of regression, 614
Curve-Fitting by sum of exponentials, 588

D

Debugging, 80
Decision making instructions in "C", 14
Degrees of freedom, 709
Detection of errors by use of difference tables, 234
Differences of a polynomial, 207
Discrete variables, 548
Divided differences, 361

E

Error formula, 42
Error in a series approximation, 56
Error in Lagrange's interpolation formula, 357
Errors in numerical computations, 43
Errors in numerical differentiation, 422
Errors in polynomial interpolation, 200
Errors in sampling, 674
Escape sequences, 12
Euler-Maclaurin's Formula, 461
Euler's formula, 493
Euler's method, 492
Euler's modified method, 493
Evaluation of principal value integrals, 466
Expression of rational function as a sum of partial fractions, 359
Extrapolation, 199

F

Factorial notation, 225
Fibonacci numbers, 27

Finite differences, 202
Finite inverse, 671
First order Runge-Kutta method, 514
Floating point representation of numbers, 61
Flow-chart for trapezoidal rule, 430
Flow-chart of Euler's method, 494
Flow-chart of Milne's predictor-corrector method, 529
Flow-chart of modified Euler's method, 498
Flow-chart of Runge-Kutta method, 517
Flow-chart of second degree parabolic curve fitting, 649
Flow-chart of Simpson's 1/3rd rule, 438
Flow-chart of Simpson's 3/8th rule, 434
Forward difference operator, 202
Forward differences, 202
Fourth order Runge-Kutta method, 515
Frequency charts, 548
Frequency curve, 552
Frequency distributions, 548, 655
Frequency polygon, 552
Fundamental operator, 205

G

Gauss's backward difference formula, 289
Gauss's forward difference formula, 278
Gaussian quadrature formula, 463
Graeffe's root-squaring method, 190
Grouped frequency distribution, 549

H

Hermite's interpolating polynomial, 381
Hermite's interpolation formula, 381, 382
Horner's method, 156
Hypothetical universe, 671

I

Initial-value and boundary-value problems, 480
Interpolating polynomial, 200
Interpolation by unevenly spaced points, 338
Inverse interpolation, 360
Inverse problems, 46
Iteration method, 94

J

J-shaped curve, 554

L

Lagrange's interpolation formula, 339
Lanczos economization of power series, 606
Laplace-Everett's formula, 327
Legendre and chebyshev polynomials, 601
Lin-bairstow's method, 135
Linear regression, 614
Lines of regression, 614
Loop control structure, 17
Lower limit, 549

M

Machine computation, 71
Machine epsilon, 34
Maclaurin's expansion, 61
Marching methods, 481
Mathematical preliminaries, 60
Maxima and minima of a tabulated function, 402

Mean value theorem for derivatives, 61
Merits and demerits of Lagrange's formula, 365
Method for complex root, 135
Method of false position, 113
Method of linear interpolation, 113
Method of separation of symbols, 234
Methods for multiple roots, 182
Milne's corrector formula, 527
Milne's method, 525
Milne's predictor (extrapolation) formula, 526
Modified Euler's method, 496
Muller's method, 141

N

Natural spline, 597
Newton-Cote's quadrature formula, 423
Newton-Raphson method, 158
Newton-Raphson's extended formula, 175
Newton's divided difference interpolation formula, 363
Newton's Gregory backward interpolation formula, 262
Newton's Gregory forward interpolation formula, 243
Newton's iterative formulae, 163
Non-periodic spline, 597
Normalized floating point, 62
np chart, 662
Numerical evaluation of singular integrals, 465
Numerical solution of ordinary differential equations, 479

O

One-step predictor-corrector method, 497
Order of convergence, 80
Orthogonal properties, 603
Osculating interpolation formula, 381

P

P chart, 661
Periodic spline, 597
Picard, 481
Picard's method of successive approximations, 481
Predictor-corrector methods, 525
Principle of least squares, 556
Prisms and cubes, 555
Procedual errors or numerical errors, 35
Program to implement trapezoidal method, 431
Program to implement simpson's 3/8th method, 435
Program in 'C' for second degree parabolic curve fitting, 650
Program of Euler's method, 495
Program of Milne's method, 530
Program of modified Euler's method, 499
Program of Runge-Kutta method, 517
Program to implement least square fit of a regression, 622, 623
Program to implement Simpson's 1/3rd method, 439
Program writing, 80
Properties of chebyshev polynomials, 605
Properties of divided differences, 362
Properties of regression co-efficients, 619

Q

Quotient-difference method, 152

R

Ramanujan's method, 195
Region of rejection, 674
Regression analysis, 614
Regression equation, 614
Regression plane, 653
Regula-Falsi method, 113
Residuals, 557
Rolle's theorem, 60
Runge-Kutta methods, 513

S

Scatter or dot diagram, 556
Secant method, 132
Second order formula, 161
Second order Runge-Kutta method, 514
Significant values χ^2 (α) of Chi-square distribution, 727
Significant values t_v (α) of t-distribution, 724
Simpson's one-third rule, 425
Simplson's three-eighth rule, 426
Snedecor's variance ratio test or F-test, 703
Special values of Chebyshev polynomials, 603
Spline function, 594
Spline interpolation, 594
Stability in the solution of ordinary differential equations, 542
Statistical quality control, 654
Stirling's formula, 301
Student's t-distribution, 691
Successive approximation method, 94

T

t-statistic, 691
Taylor's method, 506
Taylor's series for a function of one variable, 61
Taylor's series for a function of two variables, 61
Test of significance, 673
Test of significance for large samples, 676
Test of significance of small samples, 690
Test statistic, 675
Testing of hypothesis, 671
The χ^2 distribution, 710
The t-table, 691
Third order Runge-Kutta method, 515
Trapezoidal rule, 424
Two point rule, 466
Type I error, 674
Type II error, 675
Types of frequency curves, 553

U

u-chart, 661
U-shaped curve, 554
Use of regression analysis, 618

V

Values of F for F-distributions, 725

W

Weddle's rule, 427
Wilhelm Kutta, 513

Y

Yates's correction, 719